D0876073

REALMS OF MEMORY

European Perspectives

REALMS

COLUMBIA UNIVERSITY PRESS   NEW YORK

Rethinking the French Past

OF MEMORY

VOLUME I: CONFLICTS AND DIVISIONS

Under the Direction of Pierre Nora

ENGLISH-LANGUAGE EDITION EDITED AND WITH A FOREWORD BY LAWRENCE D. KRITZMAN

Translated by Arthur Goldhammer

To honor Clifford E. Rybolt, Jr. and Mary Grace Rickert Rybolt, friends of France, Edwin W. Rickert has made a gift to the Press toward the costs of publishing this book.

Columbia University Press wishes to express its appreciation for assistance given by the government of France through Le Ministère de la Culture in the preparation of the translation.

Columbia University Press

Publishers since 1893

New York   Chichester, West Sussex

Copyright (c) 1996 Columbia University Press

Les Lieux de Mémoire (c) Editions Gallimard, 1992

Library of Congress Cataloging-in-Publication Data

Les Lieux de mémoire. English

    Realms of memory: rethinking the French past / under the
direction of Pierre Nora ; English language edition edited and with
a foreword by Lawrence D. Kritzman ; translated by Arthur Goldhammer

      p. cm. — (European perspectives)

    Revised and abridged translation of the original work in French.

    Includes bibliographical references and index.

    Contents: v. 1. Conflicts and divisions.

    ISBN 0-231-08404-8 (alk. paper)

    1. France—Civilization—Philosophy. 2. Memory. 3. Symbolism.
4. National characteristics, French. 5. Nationalism—France.
1. Nora, Pierre. 11. Kritzman, Lawrence D. 111. Title.
1v. Series.

    DC33.L6513 1996

    944—dc20   95-49349

                                            CIP

Casebound editions of Columbia University Press books are printed on permanent and durable acid-free paper.

Designed by Linda Secondari

Printed in the United States of America

c 10 9 8 7 6 5 4 3 2 1

EUROPEAN PERSPECTIVES

A Series in Social Thought and Cultural Criticism
Lawrence D. Kritzman, Editor

European Perspectives presents English translations of books by leading European thinkers. With both classic and outstanding contemporary works, the series aims to shape the major intellectual controversies of our day and to facilitate the tasks of historical understanding.

Julia Kristeva, *Strangers to Ourselves*
Theodor W. Adorno, *Notes to Literature*, vols. 1 and 2
Richard Wolin, editor, *The Heidegger Controversy*
Antonio Gramsci, *Prison Notebooks*, vol. 1
Jacques LeGoff, *History and Memory*
Alain Finkielkraut, *Remembering in Vain: The Klaus Barbie Trial and Crimes Against Humanity*
Julia Kristeva, *Nations Without Nationalism*
Pierre Bourdieu, *The Field of Cultural Production*
Pierre Vidal-Naquet, *Assassins of Memory: Essays on the Denial of the Holocaust*
Hugo Ball, *Critique of the German Intelligentsia*
Gilles Deleuze and Félix Guattari, *What Is Philosophy?*
Karl Heinz Bohrer, *Suddenness: On the Moment of Aesthetic Appearance*
Alain Finkielkraut, *The Defeat of the Mind*
Elisabeth Badinter, *XY: On Masculine Identity*
Gilles Deleuze, *Negotiations, 1972–1990*
Pierre Vidal-Naquet, *The Jews: History, Memory, and the Present*

CONTENTS

In Remembrance of Things French

Pierre Nora's *Realms of Memory* (1984–1992) is one of the great French intellectual achievements of the Mitterrand era. Nora and his colleagues from a variety of academic disciplines—history, literary studies, political science, sociology—seek to locate the "memory places" of French national identity as they have been constructed since the middle ages. This history of memory is realized through the imaginary representations and historical realities that occupy the symbolic sites that form French social and cultural identity. Memory, which also includes forgetting, should not be taken literally. It is to be understood in its "sacred context" as the variety of forms through which cultural communities imagine themselves in diverse representational modes. In this sense, as a critical category "memory" distinguishes itself from history, which is regarded as an intellectual practice more deeply rooted in the evidence derived from the study of empirical reality. The recollection of the French past as it emerges from this work is the result of a cataloging of the memory places produced over time which depict the "imaginary communities" binding national memory.[1]

Nora's *magnum opus* represents the symptomology of a certain form of cultural melancholia as well as the sign of an attempt to construct a symbolic encyclopedia that attests to the values and belief systems of the French nation. Conceived as a history of France through memory, Nora's work not only demonstrates how memory binds communities together and creates social identities but also dramatizes how one's consciousness of the past is symptomatic of the disappearance of certain living traditions.

Nora's idea of the nation is drawn from the concept of the memory place, a term he gleans from Frances Yates's *The Art of Memory* and Maurice Halbwachs' *The*

Collective Memory.[2] Drawing on rhetorical tradition that dates back to Cicero and Quintilian, *Realms of memory* functions as an inventory of *loci memoriae*. Nora's conception of memory is broad: he uses it to discuss geographical place or *locus* (Reims, Paris, the prehistoric caves of Lascaux), historical figures (Joan of Arc), monuments and buildings (Versailles and the Eiffel Tower), literary and artistic objects (Descartes' *Discourse on Method* and Proust's *Remembrance of Things Past)*, emblems, commemorations, and symbols (the French flag, the "Marseillaise") all of which are the result of an imaginary process that codifies and represents the historical consciousness of "quintessential France." If memory places are symbolic in nature it is because they signify the context and totemic meaning from which collective identity emerges.

Nora's "symbolic typology" presents both ideas and the material realities that structure France's national identity. Yet memory as Nora conceives of it does not constitute a monolithic entity. Beyond the repertoire of monuments, institutions, events and commemorative dates, *Realms of Memory* also evokes the conflictual spaces and symbolic divisions within France that reconfigure its relationship with the past: the *ancien régime* and the Revolution, French and foreigners, Right and Left, and Paris-Province. As the general title of the last three volumes of the French edition indicates (the plural *Les France*), the idea of France has never been a totalized concept since its sense of identity is plural and unsettled. Indeed, a "realm of memory" is a polyreferential entity that can draw on a multiplicity of cultural myths that are appropriated for different ideological or political purposes. For example, in his insightful essay on Joan of Arc (which appears in volume 3) Michel Winock dramatizes this phenomenon by demonstrating how that historical figure emerged as a political emblem simultaneously functioning for the mythology of both the left and the right alike. For xenophobic groups such as the paramilitary fascist leagues of the 1930s or the acerbic neo-nationalism of Jean Marie Le Pen, Joan of Arc represents a totemic figure capable of symbolically forestalling foreign incursions into the homeland whereas for the left she incarnates courage in doing battle against the corruption of the Church.

The idea of France as it emerges from these volumes is one that is, at times, self-contradictory and that threatens the realization of its universalistic pretensions. The organic idea of the nation or the French "super-ego" that Nora refers to in the first volumes of the French-language edition seem to operate most potently at historical moments when those Hegelian heroes—Louis XIV, Napoleon, de Gaulle—reify the very possibility of movement and change. What remains, those temporal expanses situated between the privileged moments perceived as periods of historical greatness, is but the peripatetic and destabilizing movement of time.

In articulating the concept of memory Nora's work represents a rethinking of certain key ideas found in Maurice Halbwachs's theory of collective memory. To be

sure, Halbwachs's sociological conceptualization of memory is diametrically opposite to that of the philosopher Henri Bergson who thought of memory as a purely
subjective phenomenon. On the contrary, Halbwachs displaces memory from the
individual realm to domain of the "social frames" (what he terms the *cadres sociaux*)
of collective experience. In essence, the act of remembering is always related to the
repository of images and ideals that constitute the social relations of which we partake. Places of memory are therefore determined by the mix of individuals that constitute the social group to which they relate.

If Nora speculates on the idea of collective memory he does so in order to delineate the metamorphoses that French memory has undergone in recent times. By
reflecting on the phenomenon of the nation as republic Nora demonstrates how
Republican France was constructed as a series of principles meant to defend a singular moral imperative functioning in the name of a social totality. For example, the
memory of the "Declaration of the Rights of Man" evoked a past through which
the very idea of the Republic could be created and commemorated; it gave the social
community a narrative through which it could continue to forge its identity.
However more recently, in the shadow of the infelicitous historical events experienced during this past half-century—the Vichy collaboration, torture in Algeria—
the universalistic principles underlying republican memory and the humanism associated with it had come undone. France had now left itself open to an agonistic
encounter that would be played out in the postwar period between Gaullism and
Communism in an attempt to take hold of the republican tradition and derive from
it renewed national myths. Memory would now take shape in divided and competing spheres of political influence; it would make the republican values of cohesion
associated with the universal principles of Enlightenment thought no longer capable of creating true consensus. In this context the memorial process activates a
renewed sense of national self-consciousness by dividing the "unitary framework"
of collective memory into smaller configurations or identities resulting in the politicization of memory.

Nora's collection presents a series of highly innovative essays that signal a new
approach to the writing of national history. This new historiography distances itself
from the chronological and teleological theoretical presuppositions of its predecessors. History conceived either in terms of the definable causes and effects of
Comtean positivism or the artificial determinism of the Annales school is viewed as
no longer critically acceptable.

To be sure, the ostensible target of Nora's new historiography is the nineteenth
century historian Ernest Lavisse, who in his eighteen-volume history of France,
conjoined scientific and affective concerns in order to produce a positivist history.
Lavisse is regarded as the historian most responsible for drawing historical interpretations from archival data; the archive was the place where memory was stored

and from which history could be materialized in written form. Ironically the discursive manifestation of archival memory for all the scientific pretensions it espoused was filtered through a romantic consciousness whose *modus operandi* was to sustain political myths. Furthermore, archival memory limited the parameters of the true memorialist enterprise since it put constraints on what constituted cultural memorabilia and the many *loci*—museums, monuments, public spaces—from which representations could possibly emerge.

One might argue that Nora's concept of historiography constitutes a history of the present in as much as many of the essays in *Realms of Memory* focus on the discontinuous thread of the past remembered. Nora contends that even if references to memory are ever present in the contemporary world it is paradoxically because we are currently living in a historical society where memory functions as a mere historical trace that can exist only as a simulation of the past. "*Lieux de mémoire* exist because there are no longer any *milieux de mémoire*, settings in which memory is a real part of everyday experience" (p. 1). If premodern societies reenact memory through traditions and rituals where present and past exist simultaneously in a kind of atemporal space in which act and meaning coalesce, then the historical world of the present is one that represents historical consciousness as disembodied memories. The creation of "realms of memory" is the result of modern society's inability to live within real memory; the consecration of a "realm of memory" takes place because real environments of memory have disappeared. The projection of a "realm of memory" is therefore the sign of memory's disappearance and society's need to represent what ostensibly no longer exists.

The most striking aspect of this theoretical practice stems from the manner in which temporality is conceived. In modern societies the past is experienced as "historical" since it is no longer authentically lived. The present mode of historical perception is derived from an imaginative form of consciousness based more on myths than on facts. Our knowledge of the past is less a question of our empirical grip on the past than on our apprehension of the past as we represent it through the lens of the present. Accordingly, Nora and his contributors engage in an archaeological quest through which they are able to retrospectively "uncover" traditions and delineate the manner in which they took shape.

To be sure, many of the contemporary notions concerning France in its prerevolutionary origins stem from nineteenth-century constructions of the French past where, for example, Michelet credits Joan of Arc with the birth of the nation. The medieval cathedral, as we think of it today, can be seen as a monument belonging less to Christian tradition than to the secularized domain of the national *patrimoine* or cultural heritage; the imaginary representations of the past derive from a hermeneutic practice that reinterprets them in terms of the social exigencies of the present in order to uncover other traditions. Accordingly, the cathedral is constructed *a posteriori* as a "memory place" associated with the creative energy achieved through the secularized collective activity of the masons; from this perspective the re-presentation of this cultural activity as a nonreligious endeavor is used as the narrative frame for the reinterpretation of the collective memory of the French Middle Ages and as a celebration of the newer traditions of Third Republic France. Secular values transformed the cathedral into the locus of contemporary conceptualizations of the past. Or perhaps more recently, we are shown through the example of the Eiffel Tower in Henri Loyette's essay (volume 3) how the corrosive force of time strips away the ideological roots of that monument (its function as a symbol of revolutionary modernism) and thereby transforms that "realm of memory" into its contemporary incarnation as part of the "poetry of Paris."

The "realms of memory" explored in the essays in these three volumes produce a multiplicity of interpretations that give new meaning to history through what might be termed a form of genealogical revisionism. If a "realm of memory" is to exist it must have a capacity for metamorphosis: the recycling of knowledge through associations and new symbolic representations. In becoming a synonym for national identity, a "realm of memory" enables successive generations to mediate their cultural myths by inculcating them with their desires.

Ironically, Nora's new reading of history uncovers the symptomology of a certain French *fin de siècle* melancholia. As Nora points out the French Revolution and the traditions associated with it functioned as the determining element in the construction of national identity through references to narratives of the past. The social order of the modern nation-state, rooted in the secularized traditions of the Republic, could be legitimized in a collective identity whose consciousness was based on a teleological view of the nation as pedagogical authority in the representation of its values. From this perspective, memory overdetermines history in its quest to be universal and create a patriotic synthesis. The consubstantiality between memory and history that coalesced in what Nora terms the "memory nation" has broken down in our own *fin de siècle* where the former "centralizing Jacobinism" of national culture can no longer unify. Furthermore, national memory, as Nora and his colleagues now conceive of it, can be found in the institutions of the *ancien régime* and the collective heritage of the monumental and physical landscape as they now partake of France's memorial legacy.

But for now, what remains of the idea of nationhood is engendered by a nostalgic reflection, articulated through the disjunctive remembrance of things past. In a way, one might argue that the quest for memory in the contemporary world is nothing more than an attempt to master the perceived loss of one's history. It is also, as Nora so brilliantly teaches us, an attempt to read the signs of culture in places, objects, and images that are marked by vestiges of the past, and remembered in the vicissitudes of contemporary consciousness. When all is said and done the idea of

France that emerges from these volumes is based more on the imaginary constructions of memory than on the encyclopedic compilation of empirical data.

Nora's remembrance of things French ultimately suggests a new critical model through which the history of memory may be written. What appears to be a book about memory and French national identity becomes a study with critical dimensions that might at first not be obvious. Although Nora consistently draws our attention to the specificity of the French context, the reader will nevertheless find in these pages the ways in which a nation can rediscover its identity by rearranging the logic constituting its "realms of memory." Each nation has its official memories and myths; just as the French have fashioned their history according to the so-called universal values of the French Revolution, Americans have anchored their own in the idealistic dream of "liberty and justice for all." By focusing on how the disappearance of certain memorialist practices in France enabled historians to uncover the patterns of other traditions, Nora suggests how the rewriting of the history of memory can forge new paradigms of cultural identity. The reader will find in the essays that make up *Realms of Memory* an exhilarating intellectual project whose exemplarity lies in its power to translate the vicissitudes of national self-consciousness and the disjunctions between the original meanings attached to memory sites and the heuristic processes currently used to describe them. In this "era of commemoration," Nora and his colleagues enable us to see how the history of memory functions as a mirror of the changing role of cultural politics and how national commemoration in the age of global politics has given way to the heterogeneous and divided character of contemporary remembrance. Always insightful, always nuanced, always sensitive to epistemological shifts over time, *Realms of Memory* will remain a landmark in cultural criticism and historiography for years to come.

Lawrence D. Kritzman
Dartmouth College
May 1996

From *Lieux de mémoire* to *Realms of Memory*

Pierre Nora

These three volumes of *Realms of Memory* are, in the strongest possible sense, a translation of the seven volumes published in French under the title *Les Lieux de mémoire*. They offer what Rabelais would call the *substantifique moelle*, the very marrow of the work, and are the concentrated, condensed product of a lengthy intellectual and publishing venture that developed over a period of almost a decade, from 1984 to 1992. This venture was collective as well as individual: collective, because it involved nearly 120 contributors, most of them French, to whom I owe a very real debt of gratitude, for without the effort and talent of each and every one of them this work would be of little interest; and personal, because the project as a whole—its overall conception and detailed structure, revised at various stages along the way—was a solitary work, which evolved as it progressed.

The point of departure, the original idea, which I first tried out on my seminar at the Ecole des Hautes Etudes en Sciences Sociales in Paris, was to study national feeling not in the traditional thematic or chronological manner but instead by analyzing the places in which the collective heritage of France was crystallized, the principal *lieux*, in all senses of the word, in which collective memory was rooted, in order to create a vast topology of French symbolism. Though not really a neologism, the term did not exist in French when I first used it.[1] It met with remarkable success, however, to the point where it was included in the 1993 edition of the *Grand Dictionnaire Robert de la langue française*. I took it from ancient and medieval rhetoric as described by Frances Yates in her admirable book, *The Art of Memory* (1966), which recounts an important tradition of mnemonic techniques. The classical art of memory was based on a systematic inventory of *loci memoriae*, or "memory places." In French, the association of the words *lieu* and *mémoire* proved to have profound connotations—historical, intellectual emotional, and largely unconscious (the effect was something like that of the English word "roots"). These connotations arise in part from the specific role that memory played in the construction of the French idea of the nation and in part from recent changes in the attitude of the French toward their national past. The goal of this book is to shed light on that specific role and to illustrate those changes in attitude—in short, to elaborate and make sense of the very term *lieu de mémoire.*

From the first I envisioned a work in three parts: *La République, La Nation,* and *Les France* (although the last remained rather vague in my mind). The intention was to move from the simple to the complex, from content to form, from what was most easily dated to what was most difficult to pin down, from the most local to the most general, from the most recent to the most ancient, from the most political to the most carnal, from the most unitary to the most diverse, from the most evident to the most problematic. But if the English-speaking reader is to understand the scope and ambition of a project of which these three volumes can be seen as both a culmination and a synopsis, I must take a moment to explain the slow process by which that project came into being. For the work is in no sense linear; each of its three segments has, like the stages of a rocket, its own internal logic and dynamic.

La République (1984) required only one volume, but *La Nation* (1986) took three. For the study of the Republic, it proved sufficient to look at a selection of sites and illustrative examples mainly from the founding years of the Third Republic. But "the nation," whose conceptual underpinnings were not as thoroughly explored as one might expect, called for a more systematic, sweeping, and carefully structured investigation.

The first volume of *La Nation* deals with what might be called the *immaterial* aspects of memory: the long-term "legacy" of the monarchy as embodied in *lieux* such as the anointment ritual of Rheims; the key works that enabled "historiography" to revamp the very foundations of historical memory; and, finally, the way in which scholars and painters organized the "landscape" of France. The second volume deals with the *material,* namely, "the territory" of France, its borders, and its symbolic representation as a hexagon; "the state," with its monumental or symbolic instruments, like Versailles; and "the patrimony," or legacy of historical monuments and sites, together with the men who did most to preserve it, such as Prosper Mérimée and Eugène Viollet-le-Duc. The third volume is concerned with the *ideal,* namely, the two fundamental ideas upon which the nation was built: "glory," both military and civilian, and "words," France being a country in which the relation between language and literature on the one hand and political power, the state, and the national idea on the other hand has always been close. Here, for instance, one finds "Verdun" alongside "La Coupole" (the familiar term for the Académie

Française), and "The Louvre," that residence of kings that became a temple of the arts, alongside "Classic Textbooks."

After the publication of the three-volume edition of *La Nation* in 1986, the project came to a temporary halt. Following a lengthy period in which the country's leading historians seemed to have rejected the nation as a framework for doing history, numerous signs pointed to a return to a more nation-centered history. A number of "Histories of France" suddenly appeared. Indeed, Fernand Braudel himself, the leading light of the *Annales* movement, seemed to move in this direction with his *Identité de la France* (1986). To be sure, *Les Lieux de mémoire* began with a different premise and reflected a radically different point of view. Yet if, initially, it had seemed possible to define the idea of a *lieu de mémoire* and demonstrate its fruitfulness by bringing together, for example, such subjects as "monuments to the dead" and the widely read children's text entitled *La Tour de la France par deux enfants*, I felt that in order to go on, to treat such often-studied yet inevitable subjects as Joan of Arc, the court, or the Eiffel Tower as *lieux de mémoire*, it would be necessary to take a more theoretical approach. It was no longer enough simply to select objects; instead those objects would have to be *constructed*: in each case one would have to look beyond the historical reality to discover the symbolic reality and recover the memory that it sustained.

In fact, planning *Les France* forced me to move from a relatively narrow to a relatively broad concept of *lieu de mémoire*. The narrow approach had consisted in taking actual memorials such as the Pantheon and showing how these were actually closely related to such seemingly different objects as museums, commemorations, emblems, and mottoes; as well as to even more remote objects, including institutions such as the Académie Francaise, realities such as borders, regions such as Alsace and the Vendée, and men such as François Guizot, who was responsible for creating so many of the instruments by means of which memories are perpetuated; and, in addition, to more abstract notions such as that of a dynasty, which did so much to preserve the memory of the high and mighty. Now, this broader conception, which emerged only with the third part of the series, entitled *Les France*, involved a systematic analysis and dismantling of the most typical forms of French national symbolism and mythology, of the most expressive and revealing elements of "Frenchness." If the expression *lieu de mémoire* must have an official definition, it should be this: a *lieu de mémoire* is any significant entity, whether material or non-material in nature, which by dint of human will or the work of time has become a symbolic element of the memorial heritage of any community (in this case, the French community). The narrow concept had emphasized the *site*: the goal was to exhume significant sites, to identify the most obvious and crucial centers of national memory, and then to reveal the existence of invisible bonds tying them all together. As revealing and sweeping as this approach was, however, it tended to create the impression that *lieux de mémoire* constituted a simple objective category. The broader conception required by the planning of *Les France* placed the accent instead on *memory*, on the discovery and exploration of latent or hidden aspects of national memory and its whole spectrum of sources, regardless of their nature. This simple change of method, this natural extension of the original notion of a *lieu de mémoire*, in fact gave rise to a far more ambitious project: a history of France through memory.

This was of course a far more difficult project, but also a tempting one. Whatever "France" may be, neither science nor conscience can today show it to be the culmination of a single, unitary pattern of development or even the product of a variety of clearly identifiable deterministic processes. If, instead, it were possible to show that France is an entirely symbolic reality, then those deterministic processes could be seen for what they are: namely, inexhaustible, hence justifying the plural of the title, *Les France*. Such a symbolic unity would justify the disconcerting approach of studying the subject in terms of independent symbolic entities and would clearly reveal the unifying logic. What began as an empirical, experimental, almost playful attempt to track down *lieux de mémoire* would thus open up infinitely more exciting new vistas: a notion improvised for the needs of the moment would then become a category in terms of which contemporary history could be made intelligible, or perhaps even more than a category, a "concept"—a thing quite rare in history. This might help to institute a symbolic history better suited than traditional history to the civic as well as intellectual needs of our time. The French case, which is particularly apt for an exercise of this kind, would then serve to demonstrate a new approach to national history that might prove useful in other national contexts. It was this prospect that impelled me to go back to work and solicit sixty-six additional essays, constituting three thick new volumes of a thousand pages each. These new volumes were conceived to follow the natural articulations of memory itself, which the historian can only approach by way of its divisions, its real or imaginary continuities, and its symbolic fixations. *Les France* (1992) can thus be seen as the culmination of the whole enterprise, its most complete achievement, its most vital and expressive component. That is why I chose its overall architecture as the framework and foundation for putting together this American edition.

The problem of reducing the seven volumes of the French edition to three volumes for the English-language version imposed a number of difficult choices, which I discussed at length with the American publisher. Sacrifices were inevitable. But we were determined to come up with a well-designed, well-balanced structure, one that makes sense rhetorically and that, far from watering down the original conception of the work, fully embodies its method, principal results, and theoretical reach. Since each stage of the French edition reconsidered, expanded on, and deepened the work of the preceding stages, it seemed natural to use the final stage of the

French edition as the basis for a work that would be just as intellectually coherent and perhaps somewhat less dense than the French version.

The first of these English volumes, *Conflicts and Divisions*, is concerned with the major political, religious, and geo-historical divisions that give French memory its structure. The second, *Traditions*, is entirely devoted to roots. It begins by exploring the oldest social models whose legacy remains active today: the peasant model with "the land," the Christian model with "the cathedral," and the monarchical model with "the court." It continues with an in-depth analysis of a series of key books, which in themselves contain a portrait of French identity. And it concludes with several "very French" specialties, things that foreign and French observers alike agree are distinctively French. Finally, the third volume, *Symbols*, begins by bringing together the most official of France's national emblems: the tricolor flag, the *Marseillaise*, Bastille Day. It proceeds to survey a number of important places from Lascaux to the Eiffel Tower where the heart of France can truly be said to beat. And it concludes with some of the most typical incarnations of the image of France, such as the republican motto, emblematic figures like Joan of Arc and René Descartes, and the "genius" of the French language.

In strictly quantitative terms, these *Realms of Memory* represent a third of the *Lieux de mémoire*.[2] But these volumes are in no sense "selected excerpts." The overall plan has been modified in significant ways. The French text is a complex construction, which I have jokingly compared at times to a giant Erector set, at other times to a labyrinth or cathedral: it is itself a monument that has become, in its way, a *lieu de mémoire*. The English-language version is a microcosm. It offers a simplified, purified structure, but one that is quite representative of the spirit and style of the original edifice. It is ordered differently, but it accomplishes the same mission.

Realms of Memory is thus, in its own distinctive way, an attempt to subvert as well as to exemplify and magnify that traditional genre known as the "history of France." The archetype of that genre, its canonical and to this day unsurpassed model, is the twenty-seven volume *Histoire de France* by Ernest Lavisse, a powerful attempt—at the beginning of the twentieth century when the Third Republic was at its height—to reknit the garment of history rent by the French Revolution and create one seamless, synthetic nation: France and the Republic. The originality of *Realms of Memory* consists in the effort to decompose that unity, to dismantle its chronological and teleological continuity, and to scrutinize under the historian's microscope the very building blocks out of which traditional representations of France were constructed. Of course those building blocks came in many varieties, so that the range of possible topics is infinite, and exhaustiveness is by definition impossible.

The success of the enterprise depends entirely on the eloquence of the ensemble and on the skill with which the task is executed. The goal is to pass French identity through a prism, to relate the symbolic whole to its symbolic fragments. It is one thing to describe the prehistoric paintings on the walls of Lascaux and quite another to analyze, using the speech delivered by the President of the Republic on the fiftieth anniversary of the cave's discovery, how archaeology provided France with a memory extending back in time well beyond "our ancestors the Gauls." It is one thing to recount the history of the Tour de France bicycle race since 1903, to revisit its great moments, its heroes, its reporters, and its gradual commercialization, and quite another to use the race to show how that "democratic horse," the bicycle, by retracing, intially, the route once followed by apprentice craftsmen as they toured France to acquire the skills of their trades, enabled ordinary people to learn the country's geography, to discover its plains and coasts, in the very year that the learned geographer and historian Paul Vidal de La Blache described France's geographical diversity in his celebrated *Tableau de la géographie de la France*, which served as an introduction to Lavisse's *Histoire de France*. It is one thing to analyze the work of Marcel Proust, the man widely acknowledged to be "the greatest writer of the twentieth century," and even to enumerate the many *lieux de mémoire* that appear in his text, from the *petite madeleine* to the uneven paving stones in the courtyard of the Guermantes to the steeples of Martinville; it is quite another to study, as is done here for the first time, how a writer who stood at first outside the dominant currents of French literature—a homosexual, a Jew, and a social butterfly whose literary talents were underestimated by André Gide and André Breton, André Malraux and Jean-Paul Sartre—came to occupy the zenith of the literary firmament. And so it is with all the subjects treated in these volumes.

Readers are of course free to group these subjects as they will, as one might group the cards in a hand of poker. One can proceed chronologically, for example, to reveal a strong, centralizing continuity in the creation of which the nineteenth century played a preponderant role, but beyond which we can make out several sedimentary layers corresponding to the key stages of nation-building, none of which has dropped out of memory or lost its symbolic effectiveness: we go from a "royal memory" of the feudal age to a "state memory" of the absolutist monarchy to a "national memory" of the immediate post-Revolutionary period, and from there to a "citizen memory" of the republican schools and finally to the "patrimonial memory" of our age. Or one can group the subjects thematically to reveal how this type of symbolic history, which points up the links between the material base of social existence and the most elaborate productions of culture and thought, allows specialists in such diverse fields as art history, literary history, political history, the history of law, historical demography, and economic history to work together. In each case the goal is the same: to restore the original strangeness of the subject, to show how each element reflects the whole and is involved in the entire national identity. It also allows us to explore radically new subjects, which no linear thematic or chronological history of France would have any reason to take into account, such as the soldier Chauvin. Everybody is familiar with the term "chauvinism," which has found its way into many languages other than French. Some may know that the word comes from the name of Nicolas Chauvin, a veteran of the wars of the Revolution and Empire, who allegedly returned home to his native La Rochelle covered with wounds and medals, "to live out his days among his people," to borrow a celebrated line of Du Bellay's. But in fact Chauvin never existed. He was a myth forged by the caricaturists and *chansonniers*, or songsters, of the Restoration and July Monarchy, a "remake" of the peasant-soldier of Roman Antiquity and Rousseauist ideology whose ghost has returned countless times in such diverse forms as the "unknown soldier," the heroic peasant soldier of Pétainist ideology, and various figments of rural Catholic nationalism. When juxtaposed with the inevitable article on Verdun, however, a detailed analysis of this myth takes us deep into the heart of French identity and reveals a distinctive feature of the French tradition.

Such juxtapositions and short-circuits, which distinguish this work from other works of history, may trouble or even shock some readers. The approach taken here may seem to deny that a national dynamic of any kind exists, be it spiritual or material, nationalistic, patriotic, or revolutionary. To set an ironic, almost caricatural symbol such as the Gallic cock alongside the palace of Versailles or the battle of Verdun, to treat the French taste for gastronomy in the same analytic terms as Joan of Arc or General de Gaulle, to focus the same kind of attention on the Bicentennial of the French Revolution as on the Revolution itself, is to blur the distinctions between the greatest and most brilliant accomplishments of French history and tradition and the humblest instruments for fabricating that history and that tradition, and to do so runs the risk of appearing to diminish those accomplishments. Therein, however, lies the very principle of this project, whose ambition is to think about the nation without nationalism and about France without any universalistic *a priori*; whose inspiration is almost ethnographic; and whose method therefore consists in shedding light on the construction of representations, the formation of historical objects over time. It incorporates a dimension of analysis familiar to Americans but by its very nature long foreign to the spirit of French history: the historiographic dimension.

*

Adopting a historiographical approach is not intended to sidestep the many difficulties—political, scientific, moral, and civic—that a synthetic approach or unitary narrative would present in the France of today; it is an approach dictated, I feel, by current tendencies in history and historiography.

Ever since history, and particularly national history, first emerged as a scientific discipline, advances in the field have depended on methodological revisions. Such revisions require historians to distinguish clearly between what contemporaries believe they have experienced or are experiencing and what critical evaluation can reveal about this common fund of beliefs and traditions. To make such distinctions is to mark a discontinuity in the discipline. Moreover, every important advance in the field of history has been associated with a major historical upheaval, as a result of which historians have been led to explore new sources, methods, and interests. Thus France's traumatic defeat at the hands of the Prussians in 1870 and subsequent rivalry with Germany led French historians to develop a new categorical imperative, not to say a civic and national duty: to test the whole received national tradition against the archival evidence. This led to a sharp, clear distinction between narrative sources, which were viewed as suspect, and archival sources, which were seen as proof positive. For the "methodical" or "positivist" school of historians, this was a *critical* discontinuity. Then World War I, followed by the Crash of 1929—the year in which the celebrated *Annales* were founded—revealed the importance of economic trends and statistics, particularly demographic statistics, and this new emphasis led to the discovery of a *structural* discontinuity. Historians saw an opposition between individual and collective consciousness of historical experience and the undeniable consequences of long-term deterministic processes, of medium-to-long range historical cycles that affect how groups of people live, love, and die. A clear expression of this kind of structural discontinuity can be seen in Braudel's famous *durées*, which taught us that the apparent homogeneity of historical time is largely illusory. As this historical process continued, the impact of decolonization and economic "takeoff" made us aware, intimately as well as scientifically, of how alienated we can be from ourselves in space as well as time, and this "inner distance" became even more familiar as a result of the growing influence of psychoanalysis in the same period. Call this third discontinuity *ethnological*. It gave rise to the history of "mentalities" and to a new interest in marginal social groups, to the "colonized" within our own societies: workers, women, Jews, provincials, and so on. It also led to historical study of apparently atemporal topics, such as the body, climate, myths, and festivals, as well as of seemingly trivial subjects, such as cooking, hygiene, and smells. Meanwhile, along with the rise of the media, it provoked a surge of interest in public opinion, images, and "events"—new themes that Jacques Le Goff and I tried to survey in a three-volume work entitled *Faire de l'histoire*.[3]

The discontinuity that we are experiencing today can be seen as yet another of history's continual self-revisions, an expansion and deepening of the mechanism of discontinuity but with one important difference: this time the entire French historical tradition has been set aside and subjected to a fundamental rethinking. We have entered the age of *historiographical* discontinuity. This latest discontinuity is at once more diffuse and more radical than those that have gone before. More diffuse, because it reflects the convergence of a number of phenomena that are themselves complex and far-reaching: the political and national impact of de Gaulle's disappearance, the consequences of the demise of the revolutionary idea, and the aftereffects of economic crisis. But also more radical, because these three phenomena converged in the middle seventies to form a new constellation that profoundly alters our relationship to the past and to traditional forms of French national sentiment.[4]

The new importance of memory and the search for the *lieux* that embody it, the return to our collective heritage and focus on the country's shattered identities, are inscribed in this new constellation. This transition from one type of national consciousness to another, this shift from one model of the nation to another, is what underlies this project and gives it meaning.

A nation that was long agricultural, providentialist, universalist, imperialist, and state-centered has passed away, and in its place has emerged a nation conscious of its diminished power, reshaped by European integration and internal "regionalization," redefined by the fading of the national-revolutionary equation of 1789, and, finally, tested by an influx of immigrants not easily adaptable to the traditional norms of "Frenchness." At the same time, however, France has been revitalized and its attachment to its national roots has been transformed. That attachment is no longer based solely on history: it now includes a deep consciousness of its threatened countryside, lost traditions, wrecked ways of life—its very "identity." France has rediscovered its heritage.

This polyphonic study of *lieux de mémoire* is intended to be a response to this new historical turning point. It derives from a type of history that is at once highly traditional and yet quite new. Highly traditional because it does not assume any particular methodology and concentrates on subjects with which everyone is familiar. In some ways the work might seem to be a throwback to the era of positivist history or beyond, because it calls for an almost literary treatment. But at the same time it is quite new, because the history of memory is history that has become critical through and through, and not just of its own tools: history has entered its epistemological age.

There are, to put it strongly, three types of national history. The first type was the creation of Michelet: his goal was to integrate all the material and spiritual facts in an organic whole, a living entity, to present France "as a soul and a person." Here, post-Revolutionary romanticism achieved its culmination. The second type of national history is typified by the work of Lavisse: his goal was to test the entire national tradition against the documents in the archives. Lavisse's work stands as a monument to the age of republican positivism. The third type of national history was created by Braudel, who unfortunately died before his work was complete: His goal was to use the results of the social sciences to characterize the various stages and levels of *durée*; to integrate the geography of Vidal de La Blache into history; to extrapolate from economic cycles; and to make Marxist concepts less rigid and adapt them to the French climate. This is the fruit of the *Annales*.

These three types of national history are now joined by a fourth, exemplified by the present attempt to write a history in multiple voices. The central point, the goal is to reinterpret the history of France in symbolic terms, to define France as a reality that is entirely symbolic, and thus to reject any definition that would reduce it to phenomena of another order. Adopting such a view opens the way to a new kind of history: a history less interested in causes than in effects; less interested in actions remembered or even commemorated than in the traces left by those actions and in the interaction of those commemorations; less interested in events themselves than in the construction of events over time, in the disappearance and reemergence of their significations; less interested in "what actually happened" than in its perpetual reuse and misuse, its influence on successive presents; less interested in traditions than in the way in which traditions are constituted and passed on. In short, a history that is neither a resurrection nor a reconstitution nor a reconstruction nor even a representation but, in the strongest possible sense, a "rememoration"—a history that is interested in memory not as remembrance but as the overall structure of the past within the present: history of the second degree.

I am not unaware of how ambitious this project is. But experience has shown that only such a history, at once scholarly and accessible to the broader public, is capable of responding to the needs of the moment, of reconciling, in France and perhaps elsewhere as well, the requirements of science with the demands of conscience.

This English-language edition could not have existed without the enthusiasm, competence, and devoted work of those to whom I have the pleasure of expressing my profound gratitude.

I am indebted above all to Lawrence D. Kritzman. Every meeting we had to discuss the project was highly agreeable and deeply fruitful. His advice was of great help in the difficult task of selecting texts. His initiative was indispensable in making the project a reality: his persuasive ardor gained the support of John Moore, the President and Director of Columbia University Press, to whom I offer my deepest thanks for his wilingness to embark on such a complex venture.

Jennifer Crewe, the Press's Publisher for the Humanities, guided the project from start to finish. Without her vast professional experience and patient, tolerant understanding, this difficult enterprise would never have reached its happy conclusion.

And nothing would have been possible without Arthur Goldhammer, his exemplary talent for translation, his intimate and instinctive understanding of the project, backed by knowledge of every subject, his intelligent and sensitive suggestions, and, above all, his unflagging energy, which earned my admiration and gratitude, and my friendship.

REALMS OF MEMORY

General Introduction: Between Memory and History

Pierre Nora

The End of Memory-History

Acceleration of history: the metaphor needs to be unpacked. Things tumble with increasing rapidity into an irretrievable past. They vanish from sight, or so it is generally believed. The equilibrium between the present and the past is disrupted. What was left of experience, still lived in the warmth of tradition, in the silence of custom, in the repetition of the ancestral, has been swept away by a surge of deeply historical sensibility. Our consciousness is shaped by a sense that everything is over and done with, that something long since begun is now complete. Memory is constantly on our lips because it no longer exists.

Our curiosity about the places in which memory is crystallized, in which it finds refuge, is associated with this specific moment in French history, a turning point in which a sense of rupture with the past is inextricably bound up with a sense that a rift has occurred in memory. But that rift has stirred memory sufficiently to raise the question of its embodiment: there are sites, *lieux de mémoire*, in which a residual sense of continuity remains. *Lieux de mémoire* exist because there are no longer any *milieux de mémoire*, settings in which memory is a real part of everyday experience.

Think, for example, of the irrevocable breach marked by the disappearance of peasant culture, that quintessential repository of collective memory whose vogue as an object of historical study coincided with the heyday of industrial expansion. This collapse of a central component of our memory is only one example among many, however. Globalization, democratization, and the advent of mass culture and the media have turned the world upside down. Among the new nations, independence has swept into history societies only recently roused from their ethnological slumbers by the rape of colonization. At the same time a sort of internal decolonization has had a similar effect on ethnic minorities, families, and subcultures that until recently had amassed abundant reserves of memory but little in the way of history. Societies based on memory are no more: the institutions that once transmitted values from generation to generation—churches, schools, families, governments— have ceased to function as they once did. And ideologies based on memory have ceased to function as well, ideologies that once smoothed the transition from past to future or indicated what the future should retain from the past, whether in the name of reaction, progress, or even revolution. More than that, our very perception of history has, with much help from the media, expanded enormously, so that memory, once the legacy of what people knew intimately, has been supplanted by the thin film of current events.

The "acceleration of history" thus brings us face to face with the enormous distance that separates real memory—the kind of inviolate social memory that primitive and archaic societies embodied, and whose secret died with them—from history, which is how modern societies organize a past they are condemned to forget because they are driven by change; the distance between an integrated memory, all-powerful, sweeping, un–self-conscious, and inherently present-minded—a memory without a past that eternally recycles a heritage, relegating ancestral yesterdays to the undifferentiated time of heroes, inceptions, and myth—and our form of memory, which is nothing but history, a matter of sifting and sorting. This distance has steadily increased since modern man accorded himself the right, the capacity, and even the duty to change. It has now reached the breaking point.

This uprooting of memory, its eradication by the conquering force of history, has had the effect of a revelation, as if an ancient bond of identity had been broken, calling into question something once taken for granted: the close fit between history and memory. French and English suffer from an often-remarked deficiency: there is only one word to denote both lived history and the intellectual operation that makes it intelligible (German, on the other hand, distinguishes between *Geschichte* and *Historie*). Here we see the profound truth of this linguistic deficiency: the changes in our lives are of the same nature as the changes in the way we represent our lives. If we still dwelled among our memories, there would be no need to consecrate sites embodying them. *Lieux de mémoire* would not exist, because memory would not have been swept away by history. Every one of our acts, down to the most quotidian, would be experienced, in an intimate identification of act and meaning, as a religious repetition of sempiternal practice. With the appearance of "the trace," of distance and mediation, however, we leave the realm of true memory and enter that of history. Think of the Jews faithfully observing their traditional ritual: as the "people of memory," history was no concern of theirs until exposure to the modern world obliged them to discover a need for historians.

Memory and history, far from being synonymous, are thus in many respects opposed. Memory is life, always embodied in living societies and as such in permanent evolution, subject to the dialectic of remembering and forgetting, unconscious of the distortions to which it is subject, vulnerable in various ways to appropriation and manipulation, and capable of lying dormant for long periods only to be suddenly reawakened. History, on the other hand, is the reconstruction, always problematic and incomplete, of what is no longer. Memory is always a phenomenon of the present, a bond tying us to the eternal present; history is a representation of the past. Memory, being a phenomenon of emotion and magic, accommodates only those facts that suit it. It thrives on vague, telescoping reminiscences, on hazy general impressions or specific symbolic details. It is vulnerable to transferences, screen memories, censorings, and projections of all kinds. History, being an intellectual, nonreligious activity, calls for analysis and critical discourse. Memory situates remembrance in a sacred context. History ferrets it out; it turns whatever it touches into prose. Memory wells up from groups that it welds together, which is to say, as Maurice Halbwachs observed, that there are as many memories as there are groups, that memory is by nature multiple yet specific; collective and plural yet individual. By contrast, history belongs to everyone and to no one and therefore has a universal vocation. Memory is rooted in the concrete: in space, gesture, image, and object. History dwells exclusively on temporal continuities, on changes in things and in the relations among things. Memory is an absolute, while history is always relative.

At the heart of history is a criticism destructive of spontaneous memory. Memory is always suspect in the eyes of history, whose true mission is to demolish it, to repress it. History divests the lived past of its legitimacy. What looms on the horizon of every historical society, at the limit of a completely historicized world, is presumably a final, definitive disenchantment. The thrust of history, the ambition of the historian, is not to exalt what actually happened but to annihilate it. A generalized critical history would no doubt preserve some museums, medallions, and monuments as materials necessary for its own work but would drain them of what makes them, for us, *lieux de mémoire*. Ultimately, a society living wholly under the sign of history would not need to attach its memory to specific sites any more than traditional societies do.

Perhaps the most tangible sign of the split between history and memory has been the emergence of a history of history, the awakening (quite recent in France) of a historiographical consciousness. History, especially the history of France's development as a nation, has been our most powerful collective tradition, our *milieu de mémoire* par excellence. From the chroniclers of the Middle Ages to modern historians of "total" history, France's entire historical tradition has developed as a disciplined exercise of the mnemonic faculty, an instinctive delving into memory in order to reconstruct the past seamlessly and in its entirety. Surely none of the great French historians since Froissart has felt that he was representing only a part of the national memory. Commynes had no notion that he was recording only dynastic memories, or La Popelinière only "French" memories, or Bossuet only memories of the "most Christian monarchy," or Voltaire only memories of the progress of the human race, or Michelet only memories of "the people," or Lavisse only memories of the nation. On the contrary, each of these historians was convinced that his task was to correct his predecessors by making memory more factual, comprehensive, and useful as an explanation of the past. The scientific arsenal with which history has equipped itself over the past century has done nothing but reinforce this view of history as a critical method whose purpose is to establish true memory. Every major revision of historical method has been intended to broaden the base of collective memory.

In a country like France, the history of history cannot be innocent, because it lays bare the subversion from within of memory-history by critical history. All history is by nature critical, and all historians denounce the supposedly fraudulent mythologies of their predecessors. But when history begins to write its own history, a fundamental change takes place. Historiography begins when history sets itself the task of uncovering that in itself which is not history, of showing itself to be the victim of memory and seeking to free itself from memory's grip. In countries where history has not assumed the same didactic role in forming the national consciousness, the history of history need not burden itself with such polemical content. For example, in the United States, a country of plural memories and diverse traditions, historiographical reflection has long been part of the discipline. Different interpretations of the American Revolution or the Civil War may involve high stakes but do not threaten to undermine the American tradition because, in a sense, there is no such thing, or, if there is, it is not primarily a historical construct. In France, by contrast, historiography is iconoclastic and irreverent. It seizes on the most clearly defined objects in the tradition—a key battle such as Bouvines or a standard textbook like the *petit Lavisse*—in order to take them apart, to show how they function and how they came to be. In so doing, historiography sows doubt; it runs the blade of a knife between the heartwood of memory and the bark of history. When we study the historiography of the French Revolution, when we reconstruct its myths and interpretations, we indicate that we no longer identify fully with its heritage. When we question a tradition, however venerable, we separate ourselves from it to a degree. Nor is the history of history concerned solely with the most sacred elements of the national tradition. History in general has begun to question its own conceptual and material resources, its production processes and social means of distribution, its origins and tradition; it has thus entered the historiographic age, consummating its divorce from memory—which in turn has become a possible object of history.

At one time, the Third Republic seemed to draw together and crystallize, through history and around the concept of "the nation," one tradition of French memory, a tradition that runs, if we set the chronological limits broadly, from Augustin Thierry's *Lettres sur l'histoire de France* (1827) to Charles Seignobos's *Histoire sincère de la nation française* (1933). Throughout this period, history, memory, and the nation enjoyed an unusually intimate communion, a symbiotic complementarity at every level—scientific and pedagogical, theoretical and practical. The nationalistic definition of the present cried out for justification through a highlighting of the past. Yet that present had been made tenuous by the trauma of the Revolution, which forced a wholesale reevaluation of the monarchical past; and it was made still more tenuous by the defeat of 1870, which made it even more urgent for France—which had lost out to German science and pedagogy even more than to the German army—to develop its own archival scholarship and scholarly institutions for the transmission of memory. Historians, speaking half as soldiers, half as priests, bore the burden of responsibility on behalf of the nation. Their tone is remarkable: witness, for instance, Gabriel Monod's editorial in the first issue of the *Revue historique* (1876), in which he saw no reason not to look forward "henceforth to painstaking, methodical, collaborative scientific investigation" leading in a "discreet, confident manner to the grandeur of the fatherland as well as the human race." This text and a hundred others like it make one wonder how the idea that positivist history was not cumulative ever gained credibility. Indeed, in the teleological perspective of the nation, the political, the military, the biographical, and the diplomatic were all pillars of continuity. The defeat at Agincourt, the dagger of Ravaillac, the Day of Dupes, and the secret clauses of the Treaty of Westphalia were all included in a scrupulous accounting. Erudition of the most assiduous kind defined the reserve of capital that constituted the nation by adding a detail here, taking away another there. This "memorial space" possessed a powerful unity: from France's roots in Greek and Roman antiquity to her colonial empire under the Third Republic the distance was no greater than that between the high-level scholarship that annexed new conquests to the national heritage and the textbooks that imposed the new dogma. History was holy because the nation was holy. The nation became the vehicle that allowed French memory to remain standing on its sanctified foundation.

Why did this synthesis break down? Because its sacred character was undermined in the crisis of the 1930s, when the state was divorced from the nation and eventually the old couple was supplanted by a new one: state and society. At the same time, and for the same reasons, history, which had become a tradition of memory, was transformed into social self-understanding. In France, this transformation was particularly remarkable. The new social history was able to shed light on many kinds of memory and even to transform itself into a laboratory for investigating past mentalities. But when it shed its identification with the nation, it lost its subjective force as well as its pedagogical mission, the transmission of values, as the current educational crisis attests. The nation is no longer the unifying framework that defines the collective consciousness. The definition of the nation ceased to be an issue, and peace, prosperity, and France's diminished status as a world power did the rest. Once society had supplanted the nation, legitimation by the past, hence by history, gave way to legitimation by the future. The past was something one could only study and venerate, and the nation something one could only serve, but the future is something for which the groundwork has to be laid. Thus the three terms—nation, history, memory—regained their autonomy: the nation ceased to be a cause and became a given; history became a social science; and memory became a purely private phenomenon. The memory-nation was thus the last incarnation of memory-history.

The study of *lieux de mémoire* thus lies at the intersection of two developments that define its importance and significance. One of these is purely historiographical: French historians have begun to reflect on history as a practice. The other is historical: the end of a tradition of memory. Places, *lieux de mémoire,* become important even as the vast fund of memories among which we used to live on terms of intimacy has been depleted, only to be replaced by a reconstructed history. Historical work has achieved an unprecedented depth, while at the same time the legacy of the past has been consolidated. Critical discourse obeys an internal dynamic: the old political and intellectual framework that once shaped historical research is in disarray. It is still too substantial to ignore entirely yet too flimsy to be of much use; only its most powerful symbols have any life left in them. Taken together, these two developments, one historical, the other historiographical, force us to reexamine both the basic tools of historical research and the basic symbols that define our memory: the archives and the tricolor; libraries and festivals; dictionaries and the Pantheon; museums and the Arc de Triomphe; the *Dictionnaire Larousse* and the Wall of the Fédérés (where defenders of the Paris Commune were massacred by the French Army in 1871).

Lieux de mémoire are fundamentally vestiges, the ultimate embodiments of a commemorative consciousness that survives in a history which, having renounced memory, cries out for it. The notion has emerged because society has banished ritual. It is a notion produced, defined, established, constructed, decreed, and maintained by the artifice and desire of a society fundamentally absorbed by its own transformation and renewal. By its very nature that society values the new over the old, youth over old age, the future over the past. Museums, archives, cemeteries, collections, festivals, anniversaries, treaties, depositions, monuments, sanctuaries, private associations—these are relics of another era, illusions of eternity. That is what makes these pious undertakings seem like exercises in nostalgia, sad and life-less. They are the rituals of a ritual-less society; fleeting incursions of the sacred into a disenchanted world; vestiges of parochial loyalties in a society that is busily effacing all parochialisms; de facto differentiations in a society that levels on princi-ple; signs of recognition and group affiliation in a society that tends to recognize only individuals, assumed to be equal if not identical.

Lieux de mémoire arise out of a sense that there is no such thing as spontaneous memory, hence that we must create archives, mark anniversaries, organize celebra-tions, pronounce eulogies, and authenticate documents because such things no longer happen as a matter of course. When certain minorities create protected enclaves as preserves of memory to be jealously safeguarded, they reveal what is true of all *lieux de mémoire:* that without commemorative vigilance, history would soon sweep them away. These bastions buttress our identities, but if what they defended were not threatened, there would be no need for them. If the remem-brances they protect were truly living presences in our lives, they would be useless. Conversely, if history did not seize upon memories in order to distort and transform them, to mold them or turn them to stone, they would not turn into *lieux de mémoire,* which emerge in two stages: moments of history are plucked out of the flow of his-tory, then returned to it—no longer quite alive but not yet entirely dead, like shells left on the shore when the sea of living memory has receded.

Take, for example, "La Marseillaise" (France's national anthem) or the monu-ments to the dead of World War I found in most French villages. In 1790, the Fourteenth of July (Bastille Day) both was and was not already a *lieu de mémoire.* When Bastille Day was made a national holiday in 1880, it became an official *lieu de mémoire,* but the republican spirit, then very much alive, made it something more than that: a genuine return to the source. But what does it mean today? The loss of our national memory as a living presence forces us to look at it with eyes that are neither naive nor indifferent. The memory we see tears at us, yet it is no longer entirely ours: what was once sacred rapidly ceased to be so, and for the time being we have no further use for the sacred. We feel a visceral attachment to that which made us what we are, yet at the same time we feel historically estranged from this legacy, which we must now coolly assess. These *lieux* have washed up from a sea of memory in which we no longer dwell: they are partly official and institutional, partly affective and sentimental. We all recognize them without feeling any sense of unanimity about them. The old symbols no longer arouse militant conviction or passionate participation, but the life has not entirely gone out of them. The memo-rial has swung over into the historical. A world that once contained our ancestors has become a world in which our relation to what made us is merely contingent. Totemic history has become critical history: it is the age of *lieux de mémoire.* We no longer celebrate the nation, but we study the nation's celebrations.

Memory Grasped by History

What we call memory today is therefore not memory but already history. The so-called rekindling of memory is actually its final flicker as it is consumed by history's flames. The need for memory is a need for history.

Of course, it is impossible to do without the word, but when we use it, we should be aware of the difference between true memory, which today subsists only in gestures and habits, unspoken craft traditions, intimate physical knowledge, ingrained reminiscences, and spontaneous reflexes, and memory transformed by its passage through history, which is practically the opposite: willful and deliberate, experienced as a duty rather than as spontaneous; psychological, individual and subjective, rather than social, collective, and all-embracing. How did the transition from the first, immediate form of memory to the second, indirect form take place? The best way to find out is to look at the outcome of this recent metamorphosis.

Modern memory is first of all archival. It relies entirely on the specificity of the trace, the materiality of the vestige, the concreteness of the recording, the visibility of the image. The process that began with writing has reached its culmination in high-fidelity recording. The less memory is experienced from within, the greater its need for external props and tangible reminders of that which no longer exists except *qua* memory—hence the obsession with the archive that marks an age and in which we attempt to preserve not only all of the past but all of the present as well. The fear that everything is on the verge of disappearing, coupled with anxiety about the precise significance of the present and uncertainty about the future, invests even the humblest testimony, the most modest vestige, with the dignity of being potentially memorable. Have we not often enough deplored the loss or destruction of what might have enabled us to know those who came before us, and so wish to avoid a similar reproach from those who will come after? Remembering has become a matter of meticulously minute reconstruction. Memory has begun to keep records: delegating the responsibility for remembering to the archive, it deposits its signs as the snake deposits its shed skin. In the past, collectors, scholars, and monks devoted their lives to amassing documents on the fringes of a society that was oblivious of them and of a history that was written without their aid. Later, memory-history seized on this treasure trove and used it as the basis of its work, disseminating the fruits of its labors through a myriad of social institutions tailored to the purpose. Now that historians have abandoned the cult of the document, society as a whole has acquired the religion of preservation and archivalization. What we call memory is in fact a gigantic and breathtaking effort to store the material vestiges of what we cannot possibly remember, thereby amassing an unfathomable collection of things that we might someday need to recall. Leibniz's "paper memory" has become an institution in its own right, comprising museums, libraries, depositories, documentation centers, and databases. Specialists estimate that the number of documents stored in public archives alone has multiplied a thousandfold in just a few decades. No previous epoch ever stocked archives at such a prodigious rate: modern society spews out greater volumes of paper than ever before, and we now possess unprecedented means for reproducing and preserving documents, but more than that, we feel a superstitious respect and veneration for the trace. As traditional memory has vanished, we have felt called upon to accumulate fragments, reports, documents, images, and speeches—any tangible sign of what was—as if this expanding dossier might some day be subpoenaed as evidence before who knows what tribunal of history. The trace negates the sacred but retains its aura. We cannot know in advance what should be remembered, hence we refrain from destroying anything and put everything in archives instead. The realm of the memorable has expanded without reason: we suffer from hypertrophy of memory, which is inextricably intertwined with our sense of memory's loss and concomitant institutionalization. Old-fashioned professional archivists, who used to be accused of suffering from a mania to preserve, have switched roles in a curious way with those who produce the materials that now fill our archives. Today's archivists are trained by private firms and government bureaucracies, which insist that everything be preserved, whereas the older archivists knew that controlled destruction was the trick of the trade.

In just a few years, then, memory embodied in material form has expanded prodigiously; it has also been copied, decentralized, and democratized. In the old days, there were three main sources of archives: the great families, the church, and the state. Nowadays who does not feel called upon to record his reminiscences or write his memoirs? Everyone has gotten into the act: not just people whose role in history was minor at best, but also the relatives of such people and their doctors and lawyers and anyone else who happened to be standing about. The less extraordinary the testimony, the more aptly it is taken to illustrate the average mentality.

The imperative of the age is not only to keep everything, to preserve every sign (even when we are not quite sure what it is we are remembering), but also to fill archives. The French social security archives can serve as an object lesson: they contain an unimaginable mass of documents, some two hundred linear miles of paper all told. If explored with the aid of a computer, these documents might well provide a compendium of French society, a *summa* of the normal and the pathological in matters ranging from diets to lifestyles, all classified by region and occupation. But just to preserve let alone exploit this massive material requires drastic, unfeasible choices. Archive as much as you like: something will always be left out. Or, to take another revealing case, consider the recent proliferation of oral histories in France. Across the country there are now more than three hundred teams employed in collecting what Philippe Joutard has called "the voices that come to us from the past." Well and good. But think for a moment: these are not ordinary archives. It takes thirty-six hours of work to produce just one hour of tape, and the recordings make sense only if listened to in their entirety; they cannot be sampled. Under these conditions one has to ask what possible purpose they might serve. Whose will to remember do they ultimately reflect, that of the interviewer or that of the interviewee? The sheer mass of material changes the significance and status of the archive. It is no longer a more or less intentional record of actual memory but a deliberate and calculated compilation of a vanished memory. It adds a secondary or prosthetic memory to actual experience, which is often altered by the very fact of being recorded (witness the effect of live news broadcasts on the events being covered). The indiscriminate filling of archives is a troublesome by-product of the new consciousness, the clearest expression yet of the "terroristic" effect of historicized memory.

Historicized memory comes to us from without. Because it is no longer a social practice, we internalize it as an individual constraint. The transition from memory to history requires every social group to redefine its identity by dredging up its past. The resulting obligation to remember makes every man his own historian. Thus the historical imperative has reached well beyond the limited circle of professional historians. Those who used to be left out of the official histories are not the only ones obsessed with recovering their buried pasts. Practically every organized social group, and not just the intellectual or educated, has followed the lead of the ethnic minorities in seeking their own roots and identities. There is hardly a family today in which some member has not sought to reconstruct the hidden ancestral past as fully as possible. The proliferation of genealogical research is a striking recent phenomenon: the annual report of the Archives Nationales for 1982 reports that 43 percent of those engaged in archival work were doing genealogical research (whereas 38 percent were doing academic work of some kind). Another striking fact is that the most significant histories of biology, physics, medicine, and music have been written not by professional historians but by biologists, physicists, physicians, and musicians. Educators themselves have assumed responsibility for the history of education from "phys ed" to the teaching of philosophy. As the established intellectual disciplines have come under attack, each has sought to justify itself by delving into its origins. Sociology has gone in search of its founding fathers, while anthropology has explored its past from sixteenth-century chroniclers to colonial administrators. Even literary criticism has attempted to trace the origins of its categories and traditions. As for history, the positivist approach, long since abandoned by professional historians, has discovered a new-found popularity as a result of this urgently felt need to resurrect the past. The demise of memory-history has multiplied the number of private memories demanding their own individual histories.

The commandment of the hour is thus "Thou shalt remember." It is the self that remembers, and what it remembers is itself, hence the historical transformation of memory has led to a preoccupation with individual psychology. The two phenomena are closely related—so closely that one can hardly refrain from pointing out that they coincide exactly in time. At the end of the last century, when rural society collapsed and age-old social equilibria were disrupted, memory became a central issue in philosophical thinking with Bergson, in psychological thinking with Freud, and in autobiographical literature with Proust. The disintegration of the traditional French image of memory as something rooted in the soil and the sudden emergence of memory as something central to individual identity were like two sides of a single coin, as well as the beginning of a process that has today reached an explosive stage. We owe to Freud and Proust those two intimate yet universal *lieux de mémoire,* the primal scene and the celebrated *petite madeleine.* This transformation of memory marks a decisive shift from the historical to the psychological, from the social to the individual, from the concrete message to its subjective representation, from repetition to remembrance. Memory became a private affair. As a result of this psychologization, the self now stands in a new relation to memory and the past.

Ultimately, memory constrains the behavior of individuals, and individuals alone. By defining the relation to the past, it shapes the future. The atomization of memory (as collective memory is transformed into private memory) imposes a duty to remember on each individual. This "law of remembrance" has great coercive force: for the individual, the discovery of roots, of "belonging" to some group, becomes the source of identity, its true and hidden meaning. Belonging, in turn, becomes a total commitment. When memory ceases to be omnipresent, it ceases to be present at all unless some isolated individual decides to assume responsibility for it. The less collective the experience of memory is, the greater the need for individuals to bear the burden, as if an inner voice were needed to tell each Corsican "You must be Corsican" and each Breton "You must be Breton." The force of this phenomenon is perhaps most evident among nonpracticing Jews, many of whom have felt a need in recent years to explore memories of the Jewish past. In the Jewish tradition, whose history *is* its memory, to be Jewish is to remember being Jewish. If truly internalized, such a memory inexorably asserts its claim over a person's whole being. What kind of memory is this? In a sense, it is memory of memory itself. The psychologization of memory makes each individual feel that his or her salvation ultimately depends on discharging a debt that can never be repaid.

Thus far we have explored two types of memory: archival memory and memory as an individual duty. To complete this portrait of the modern metamorphosis of memory we must add a third type: alienated memory. When we try to puzzle out our relation to the past by studying significant historical works, we discover that our historical knowledge is not at all like memory: instead of placing us in a continuous relation with the past, it creates a sense of discontinuity. Of course for the memory-history of an earlier time, the past was not yet over: it could be revived by an effort of remembrance. In a sense, the present itself was seen as a retrieved, updated past, its presentness conjured away by being grafted onto and rooted in what went before. True, in order for a sense of "pastness" to exist, a thin wedge had to inserted between yesterday and today, opening up a "before" and an "after." This distance was not seen as implying a radical difference, however; it was rather a gap, a hiatus, and as such called for a restoration of continuity. The two great themes of history in the modern era, progress and decadence, both reflect this cult of continuity, this certainty of knowing to whom and to what we are indebted for being what we are. From this came the important notion of "origins," that secularized version of myth which gave a French society in the process of nationalist secularization its idea of and need for the sacred. The grander France's origins were, the more they magnified the grandeur of the French. Through the past we venerated ourselves.

This connection has been severed. Just as the future—once a visible, predictable, manipulable, well-marked extension of the present—has come to seem invisible, so have we gone from the idea of a visible past to one of an invisible past; from a firmly rooted past to a past that we experience as a radical break in continuity; from a history that we believed lay in the continuity of some sort of memory to a memory that we think of as projected onto the discontinuity of history. We no longer speak of "origins" but rather of "inceptions." Given to us as radically other, the past is a world from which we are fundamentally cut off. We discover the truth about our memory when we discover how alienated from it we are.

It is a mistake, however, to think that our sense of discontinuity is somehow vague or ambiguous, a gap in the night. Paradoxically, distance requires rapprochement to counteract its effects and give it emotional resonance. Never have we longed more for the feel of mud on our boots, for the terror that the devil inspired in the year 1000, or for the stench of an eighteenth-century city. But such hallucinatory re-creations of the past are conceivable only in terms of discontinuity. The whole dynamic of our relation to the past is shaped by the subtle interplay between the inaccessible and the nonexistent. If the old ideal was to resurrect the past, the new ideal is to create a representation of it. Resurrection, no matter how complete, implied a careful manipulation of light and shadow to create an illusion of perspective with an eye to present purposes. Now that we no longer have a single explanatory principle, we find ourselves in a fragmented universe. At the same time, nothing is too humble, improbable, or inaccessible to aspire to the dignity of historical mystery. We used to know whose children we were; now we are the children of no one and everyone. Since the past can now be constructed out of virtually anything, and no one knows what tomorrow's past will hold, our anxious uncertainty turns everything into a "trace," a potential piece of evidence, a taint of history with which we contaminate the innocence of everything we touch. When we look at the past, we take violent possession of what we know is no longer ours. Since we no longer know what we are looking for, we have had to narrow our focus. Broad, panoramic views are no longer admissible; we eschew fragments as well as frescoes. Instead, we spotlight selected elements of the past, concentrating on "representative samples." Our memory is intensely retinal, powerfully televisual. The much-touted "return of the narrative" in recent historical writing has to be linked to the ubiquity of visual images and film in contemporary culture—even if this new narrative is very different from traditional narrative, which was episodic and self-contained. Our scrupulous respect for archival documents (which we examine for ourselves, with our own eyes) and our new-found interest in oral history (in which we quote participants directly and listen to the sound of their own voices) are surely linked to the way in which live news broadcasts have accustomed us to a certain immediacy. We study the everyday life of the past because we want to return to a slower-paced, more savory existence, and we read biographies of ordinary people as if to say that the "masses" can never be understood simply by, as it were, measuring their mass. And from countless "microhistories" we take shards of the past and try to glue them together, in the hope that the history we reconstruct might seem more like the history we experience. One might try to sum all this up by coining a term like "mirror-memory," but the problem is that mirrors reflect only identical copies of ourselves, whereas what we seek in history is difference—and, through difference, a sudden revelation of our elusive identity. We seek not our origins but a way of figuring out what we are from what we are no longer.

Strangely, this alchemy of essences has helped to make the practice of history—which the relentless drive toward the future might have been thought to have rendered otiose—the repository of the secrets of the present. Indeed, this magical transformation has been accomplished not so much by history as by the historian. Consider the historian's strange fate. Once upon a time his role was simple, his place in society clearly defined: he was the spokesman for the past and the guide who pointed the way to the future. As such, his individual personality was less important than the service he rendered: scholarship was to be worn lightly, to serve only as a bridge, an all but imperceptible link between the physical mass of the documentation and its inscription in memory—whose absence, one might say, produced an obsession with objectivity. With the disintegration of memory-history, however, a new kind of historian has emerged, a historian prepared, unlike his predecessors, to avow his close, intimate, and personal ties to his subject. Indeed, he is ready to proclaim the closeness of his relationship to the past, to deepen it, to treat it not as an obstacle to understanding but as a tool. His work is entirely dependent on his subjectivity, creativity, and capacity to re-create. He performs a metabolic function, taking something lifeless and meaningless and investing it with life and meaning.

Imagine a society wholly preoccupied with the here and now: it would be incapable of producing historians. Living entirely for the future, it would content itself mechanical devices for recording and cataloging the present while indefinitely poning the task of understanding itself to a later day. Our society is quite different: it has changed so radically that it has lost its memory and become obsessed with understanding itself historically. This accounts for the increasingly central role of the historian: he prevents history from being *merely* history.

Thus we compensate for our alienated perspective by trying to view the past in close-up and artificial hyper-reality. And as our perception of the past changes, we discover reasons to look again at traditional subjects that once seemed to hold no further interest, the commonplaces, as it were, of our national memory. We find ourselves back on the doorstep of the house we grew up in: the old homestead is uninhabited and all but unrecognizable. The old family heirlooms are still there, but we see them in a new light. The old workshop is still where it used to be, but the work to be done is different. We recognize familiar rooms, but what are we to use them for? Historiography has entered the epistemological age; the era of identity is over. History has confiscated memory. And so the historian can no longer be a "memory man." Instead, he has become, in his very being, a *lieu de mémoire*.

Realms of Memory: Another History

Lieux de mémoire are complex things. At once natural and artificial, simple and ambiguous, concrete and abstract, they are *lieux*—places, sites, causes—in three senses: material, symbolic, and functional. An archive is a purely material site that becomes a *lieu de mémoire* only if imagination invests it with a symbolic aura. A textbook, will, or veterans' group is a purely functional object that becomes a *lieu de mémoire* only when it becomes part of a ritual. The observance of a commemorative minute of silence, which might seem to be a strictly symbolic act, disrupts time, thus concentrating memory. These three aspects of embodied memory—the material, the symbolic, and the functional—always coexist. What *lieu de mémoire* could be more abstract than the notion of a historical generation? A generation is material in a demographic sense; functional by hypothesis, since memories are crystallized in generations and passed on from one to another; and symbolic by definition, since the term "generation" implies that the experience of a small number of people can be used to characterize a much larger number who did not participate in its central event or events.

Lieux de mémoire are created by the interaction between memory and history, an interaction resulting in a mutual overdetermination. A will to remember must be present initially. Without this criterion, the definition would be so broad as to encompass almost any object worthy of remembrance. Think back to the good old rules of historical criticism: historians at one time distinguished carefully between "direct sources" (such as laws and works of art, things intentionally produced by a society in full knowledge that they would be reproduced) and "indirect sources" (testimony unwittingly left behind for historians to use as they see fit). Without an intent to remember, *lieux de mémoire* would be *lieux d'histoire*.

Yet if history—time and change—did not intervene, we would be dealing not with *lieux de mémoire* but with simple memorials. The *lieux* of which I speak are hybrid places, mutants in a sense, compounded of life and death, of the temporal and the eternal. They are like Möbius strips, endless rounds of the collective and the individual, the prosaic and the sacred, the immutable and the fleeting. For although it is true that the fundamental purpose of a *lieu de mémoire* is to stop time, to inhibit forgetting, to fix a state of things, to immortalize death, and to materialize the immaterial (just as gold, they say, is the memory of money)—all in order to capture the maximum possible meaning with the fewest possible signs—it is also clear that *lieux de mémoire* thrive only because of their capacity for change, their ability to resurrect old meanings and generate new ones along with new and unforeseeable connections (that is what makes them exciting).

Consider two very different examples. First, the new calendar adopted for a time during the French Revolution: this revolutionary calendar is a *lieu de mémoire* if ever there was one, since, being a calendar, it was intended to be a framework for memory, and, being revolutionary, it offered a new system of names and symbols intended, as its principal author ambitiously claimed, "to open a new book to history" and, as another sponsor suggested, "to make the French feel at home again." In so doing, the calendar was also supposed to stop the clock of history at the moment of the Revolution: the future's days, months, years, and centuries would forever call to mind images of the revolutionary epic. Surely that alone would be enough to qualify the revolutionary calendar as a *lieu de mémoire!* But what further establishes its claim in our eyes is its failure to fill the role foreseen for it by its authors. If the revolutionary calendar had truly become our calendar, it would be as familiar as the Gregorian calendar, hence no longer a *lieu de mémoire*. It would have melted into the landscape of memory, and its only purpose would be to fix the dates of other conceivable *lieux de mémoires*. What makes the case even more interesting, however, is the fact that the failure of the revolutionary calendar was not complete. Certain events remain forever attached to the names of its months: Vendémiaire, Thermidor, Brumaire. Thus the *lieu de mémoire* is a distorting mirror, twisting its own themes in ways that define its significance. Such intricate convolution is part of the definition of the *lieu de mémoire*.

For our second example, consider the well-known children's book entitled *La Tour de la France par deux enfants,* another incontrovertible *lieu de mémoire,* for like the *petit Lavisse* it shaped the memory of millions of French boys and girls. When schoolchildren throughout France studied it, the minister of public instruction could take out his pocket watch at 8:05 A.M. on a certain day of the year and confidently declare, "All our children are just now crossing the Alps." Moreover, the *Tour* was a compendium of what every child should know about France, a story about identity and a journey of initiation. But the story is more complicated than it first appears: a careful reading shows that when the *Tour* was published in 1877, it already portrayed a France that no longer existed. On May 16 of that year, the Third Republic finally consolidated its hold on power, but the book derived its seductive appeal from a subtle enchantment with the past. As is so often the case with children's books, the *Tour* owed its initial success to its appeal to grown-ups and their memories. And later? Thirty-five years after the work's first publication, it still reigned supreme among French children's texts, but it was read for its nostalgic appeal, as evidenced by the fact that the first edition sold better than later, revised ones. Subsequently the book dropped out of favor and continued to be used only in remote rural areas. Slipping out of collective memory, it entered first historical memory and then pedagogical memory. In 1977, when the Breton writer Pierre-Jakez Hélias's provincial autobiography *Le Cheval d'orgueil* became a million-seller as Giscard d'Estaing's industrialized France, then in the throes of economic crisis, rediscovered its oral tradition and peasant roots, a new edition of the *Tour* was published and the book once again entered the collective memory—albeit a different collective memory this time, and of course without any guarantee that it would not be forgotten yet again. So here we have a prime candidate for a *lieu de mémoire*. But does it qualify as such because of the book's original intention or because of its role in subsequent cycles of national memory? Clearly both: all *lieux de mémoire* are, to borrow from the language of heraldry, objects *en abîme,* which is to say, objects containing representations of themselves (hence implying an infinite regress).

Indeed, this dual identity of *lieux de mémoire* allows us to delimit, classify, and categorize different types. Certain broad categories of the genre stand out: anything having to do with the cult of the dead, the national heritage, or the presence of the past can be considered a *lieu de mémoire*. But certain objects that do not fit the strict definition have to be included, while others that seem to fit have to be ruled out. For example, some important prehistoric, geographical, and archaeological sites must be considered *lieux de mémoire* despite the absence of any intent to remember, because that absence is compensated for by the work of time and science and by man's dreams and memories, which constitute an overwhelming brief in favor of inclusion. Not every border marker has the same claim to be considered a *lieu de mémoire* as the Rhine, say, or the "Finistère," that "Land's End" at the tip of Brittany that is celebrated in the pages of Michelet. Any constitution or diplomatic treaty is a *lieu de mémoire,* but the Constitution of 1793 has a different status from the Constitution of 1791 owing to the fundamental importance of the Declaration of the Rights of Man, and the treaty of Nijmegen has a different status from, say, the division of the Carolingian Empire at Verdun in 843 or the Yalta Conference of 1944, to take examples from early and late European history.

Memory dictates and history writes. Both history books and historical events deserve special attention: both are implements that memory uses to inscribe itself on the historical record. Hence they stake out the boundaries of our domain. Is not every great work of history—even the genre of history itself—a *lieu de mémoire?* And is not every great event—indeed the very notion of event—by definition a *lieu de mémoire?* These two questions call for detailed answers.

Only certain works of history are *lieux de mémoire,* namely, those that reshape memory in some fundamental way or that epitomize a revision of memory for pedagogical purposes. Relatively few works have managed to give new historical memories firm roots in French soil. In the thirteenth century the *Grandes Chroniques de France* condensed dynastic memory and established a model for historical work for centuries thereafter. In the sixteenth century, during the Wars of Religion, the school of "perfect history," as it was called, destroyed the myth of the monarchy's Trojan origins and resurrected the Gauls: Étienne Pasquier's *Recherches de la France* may serve as an emblem of this school, as evidenced by the very modernity of its title (which indicated a preference for "research" over chronicle and "France" over dynasties). The historiography of the late Restoration introduced the modern concept of history: Augustin Thierry's *Lettres sur l'histoire de France,* whose serial publication began in 1820, was first on the scene. The various fragments of Thierry's were collected and published as a bound volume in 1827, within a few months of the publication of the *Précis d'histoire moderne,* the first book by an illustrious newcomer, Jules Michelet, and Guizot's first lectures on "the history of civilization in Europe and in France." Finally, positivist national history began with a manifesto in the *Revue historique* (1876) and culminated in Lavisse's monumental twenty-seven volume *Histoire de France.*

Memoirs, too, can be *lieux de mémoire* (as the word suggests). Chateaubriand's *Mémoires d'outre-tombe,* Stendhal's *Vie de Henry Brulard,* and Henri Amiel's *Journal intime* belong to the genre not because they are bigger and better than other memoirs but because, beyond simply exercising memory, they also interrogate it. The same can be said of statesmen's memoirs. From Sully to de Gaulle, from Richelieu's *Testament* to the *Mémorial de Sainte-Hélène* and the *Journal* of Poincaré, the genre exhibits certain constant and specific features despite variations in the quality of individual texts. The memoir writer must be aware of other memoirs. He must be a man of the pen as well as a man of action. He must find a way to identify his individual story with a more general story. And he must somehow make his personal rationale consonant with public rationality. Taken together, these characteristics of the genre compel us to think of its exemplars as *lieux de mémoire.*

As for "great events," only two types are pertinent here and not in any sense on account of their greatness. To begin with, there are events that may have seemed relatively minor and gone almost unnoticed at the time but upon which posterity has conferred the grandeur of a new beginning or the solemnity of an inaugural break with the past. And then there are events (which may not be events at all, in the sense that nothing concrete needs to happen) that are immediately invested with symbolic significance and treated, even as they are unfolding, as if they were being commemorated in advance. In recent years the media have treated us to countless abortive attempts to create events of this second type. As an example of the first type, one can take, say, the election of Hugh Capet, in itself an unremarkable incident but one that has taken on enormous weight owing to ten centuries of subsequent history ending on the scaffold. As examples of the second type, consider the German surrender in World War I (which took place in a railway car near Rethondes), the handshake between Hitler and Pétain at Montoire (sealing Franco-German collaboration in World War II), or de Gaulle's march down the Champs-Élysées at the Liberation. Call events of the first type foundational and events of the second type spectacular. In neither case is the event itself what counts. The notion of *lieu de mémoire* would cease to have any specific meaning if we included "events." Indeed, it is the exclusion of the event *qua* event that defines the *lieu de mémoire*. Memory fastens upon sites, whereas history fastens upon events.

There is, however, no reason why we cannot imagine a variety of possible arrangements or classifications of objects within the category of *lieux de mémoire*. Some such objects are part of everyday experience: cemeteries, museums, commemorations. Others are products of reflection, such as the concept of a historical generation, which was mentioned earlier, or the lineage, or the "region" as an object of memory, or certain "divisions" in the way the French perceive their national territory (Paris-provinces, for example, or north-south), or of the notion that the French landscape is a "painting" that comes to mind if one thinks of Corot or of Cézanne's paintings of the Montagne Sainte-Victoire. Emphasizing the physical aspect of the *lieu* would reveal another broad spectrum. Some *lieux de mémoire* are portable, and their importance cannot be overlooked, because the people of memory, the Jews, offer a prime example of one in the Torah. Other *lieux* are topographical: what matters is their specific location, their rootedness. Examples include tourist sites generally, as well as the Bibliothèque Nationale (in what used to be the residence of Cardinal Mazarin) and the Archives Nationales (in what used to be the residence of the Prince de Soubise). Some sites are monumental, not to be confused with others that are architectural. Statues and monuments to the dead, for example, derive their significance from their very existence. Although location is by no means unimportant with such monuments, they could be placed elsewhere without altering their meaning. Structures that develop over time are different: their meaning stems from the complex relationship of their component parts, so that they become mirrors of a society or a period, like the cathedral of Chartres or the palace of Versailles.

If, instead of the physical aspect, we were to emphasize the functional dimension, a different picture would emerge. Some *lieux de mémoire*, like veterans' organizations, are clearly intended to preserve an incommunicable experience and are doomed to vanish with those who shared that experience. Others, equally ephemeral, are designed to serve a pedagogical purpose: textbooks, dictionaries, and the last wills and testaments and ledger-journals that heads of household once used to convey their wishes and admonitions to their descendants.

And finally, if we were to emphasize the symbolic element, we might want to distinguish between "dominant" *lieux de mémoire* and "dominated" ones. Dominant sites are spectacles, celebrations of triumph. They are imposing as well as generally imposed from above by the government or some official organization, and typically cold and solemn, like official ceremonies. One doesn't visit such places; one is summoned to them. Dominated sites are places of refuge, sanctuaries of instinctive devotion and hushed pilgrimages, where the living heart of memory still beats. Among dominant sites we may include the Sacré-Coeur Church in Paris (commemorating the end of the Commune), the official funeral of Paul Valéry, and the funeral ceremony for de Gaulle at Notre Dame; among dominated sites, the popular pilgrimage to Lourdes, the funeral of Jean-Paul Sartre, and de Gaulle's burial site at Colombey.

These classifications could be refined *ad infinitum*. One could contrast public sites with private ones; pure sites, whose only function is commemorative (such as funeral eulogies, the war memorial at Douaumont, and the Wall of the Fédérés), and composite ones, whose commemorative dimension is but one of many symbolic meanings (such as the national flag, festival itineraries, pilgrimages, and so on). This preliminary typology should not be construed as being either rigorous or comprehensive or as limiting possibility in any way: all that matters is that it can be done. It shows that an invisible thread links ostensibly unrelated objects. It suggests that bringing the Père-Lachaise cemetery and the Statistique Générale de la France together within the covers of one book is not quite as provocative a gesture as, say, the surrealist conjunction of an umbrella with a steam iron. All of these different identities belong to a complex network, an unconscious organization of collective memory that it is up to us to bring to consciousness. The *lieux de mémoire* constitute our moment in the history of France.

What sets the kind of history we are attempting here apart from all other kinds of history, ancient or modern, is one simple but decisive element. Every previous historical or scientific approach to memory (whether concerned with national memory or social "mentalities") dealt with *realia*, with things in themselves, in their immediate reality. Unlike historical objects, *lieux de mémoire* have no referents in reality; or, rather, they are their own referents—pure signs. This is not to say that they are without content, physical presence, or history—on the contrary. But what makes them *lieux de mémoire* is precisely that which allows them to escape from history. The *lieu* is a *templum:* something singled out within the continuum of the profane (whether in space, time, or both), a circle within which everything counts, everything is symbolic, everything is significant. In this sense, the *lieu de mémoire* has a dual nature: it is a hermetic excrescence upon the world, defined by its identity and summed up by its name but at the same time open to an infinite variety of possible other meanings.

Hence the history of *lieux de mémoire* could not be more banal or more extraordinary. The topics are obvious, the material is standard, the sources are readily available, and the methods could not be less sophisticated. Such a history gives the appearance of reverting to long-outdated models. But nothing could be further from the truth. The only way to approach the subject is to delve into empirical detail, but what one seeks in this way cannot be expressed in terms of traditional historical categories. Reflecting on *lieux de mémoire* transforms historical criticism into critical history—history critical of more than just its own methods. It brings history back to life, giving it a second level of existence. The new history is a purely transferential history, and as in the art of war, everything is in the execution, a matter of tact in the historian's tenuous relation to his new object and of finding the right depth of immersion in the subject. Ultimately, it is a history that depends on its ability to avail itself of a tenuous, intangible, almost ineffable bond: what remains of our inexpugnable, intimate attachment to those faded symbols of the past. It is the revival of history as it was practiced by Michelet, which inevitably calls to mind the mourning for lost love so well described by Proust: that moment when the obsessive grip of passion finally loosens, in which the real sadness is that one can no longer suffer from that for which one has already suffered so much. The head takes over from the heart, and one is left with only reasons where once there was sublime unreason.

Of course to invoke the name of Proust is to make a very literary reference. Is this cause for regret, or should I try to justify it? The answer, once again, is linked to our current historical situation. Memory has known only two forms of legitimacy: historical and literary. These have run on parallel tracks but until now have always remained separate. Lately the boundary between the two has blurred. Out of the virtually simultaneous demise of memory-history and memory-fiction has come a new type of history, which owes its prestige and legitimacy to a new type of relation to the past—and to a different past. History has become our substitute for imagination. Recent years have seen a revival of the historical novel, a vogue for personal memoirs, a revitalization of historical drama, and the rise of oral history. What can account for all these things if not that they are somehow stand-ins for faltering fiction? Our interest in the *lieux de mémoire* in which our depleted fund of collective memory is rooted, concentrated, and expressed stems from this new sensibility. History offers profundity to an epoch devoid of it, true stories to an epoch devoid of real novels. Memory has been promoted to the center of history: thus do we mourn the loss of literature.

Conflicts and Divisions

Pierre Nora

From the standpoint of memory, France is not diversity but division. The insistence on diversity, at once problematic and providential, corresponded to an era of state-centered national synthesis, in which endless invocations of unity reflected an imperious need, more insistently felt in France than in many other countries, to overcome powerful heterogeneous and contradictory forces through a vast effort of central organization. Republican France, one and indivisible—the France not only of Michelet and Vidal de La Blache but also of Charles de Gaulle and Fernand Bruadel—had its own "memory-history," full of sound and fury, a colorful history in which an infinite diversity of locales, peoples, and languages was merely the visible, perceptible face of a tenacious effort to achieve unity through the temporal construction of politics and history. Unity and diversity: this antithetical yet complementary pair has come apart before our eyes, and with it a comprehensive perception of France has lost its usefulness and relevance.

When the Third Republican synthesis evaporated, a new kind of intelligibility began to emerge, one whose overall organic unity depended not on historical unity and territorial harmony achieved through conquest but rather on a feeling of identity sustained by an enduring sense of its own divisions, of the powerful polarities out of which it was built: these included not only political polarities but also religious and geo-historical ones. The three parts of this volume reflect these three themes.

Let us take political polarities first. As numerous as the conflicts, battles, divisions, and vicissitudes of French political history are, the political myths on which our idea of France is based stem from a relatively limited number of fundamental oppositions, each reflecting and reinforcing the others. It would have made no sense to choose some of these rather than others. All had to be taken into account not only as they unfolded in time but also as sources of specific conceptual instruments in terms of which they rationalized their own existence. First, there was the fundamental division of the Revolution, which became the source of a series of religious, political, social, and national oppositions with powerful, perpetually regenerated connotations. On top of this, the twentieth century superimposed three further divisions, each associated with a specific historical moment; taken together, these new divisions altered the old national-revolutionary equation. France being a country in which immigration was an older, more continuous phenomenon than in any of its neighbors, there was first of all the basic antinomy resulting from the periodic influx of large numbers of foreigners, who, owing to the country's basic ideological principles and social realities, were at once welcomed and rejected. Then there was Vichy, born of defeat and occupation: division was implicit in the very name, which suggested a resurgence of the whole counterrevolutionary past. And finally there was the great moment of hegemonic partition of the national memory reflected in the bipolar opposition between Gaullists and Communists.

Nevertheless, this series of archetypal divisions would be of merely descriptive interest were it not for the fact that the intrinsically conflictual nature of French history (which made it, for Marx, the very model of national history in general) is reflected in both the beginning and end of the saga: in the country's myth of origin (the prehistory of the French model, so to speak) and in the "democratic age," the keystone of the model as well as the source of a retrospective interpretation of the whole of French history. In fact, from the sixteenth century on, the French myth of origin rested on the duality of Franks and Gauls; revivals of this myth—in the eighteenth century with Boulainvilliers and again, in contradictory fashion, in the nineteenth century with Augustin Thierry and François Guizot—established the idea that the history of France is a story of eternal conflict between victors and vanquished; this idea became firmly rooted in the subsoil of the national imagination. Meanwhile, another duality, the opposition between right and left, became the structural underpinning of all political "space" in contemporary France, providing politics with both its driving dynamic and its interpretive framework. What is striking is not merely the similarity between these two dualities but the fact that in both cases the original polarization reflects both what is most distinctive about France and most exemplary, most specific and most universal, since the class struggle originated in the struggle between the races, and the right-left division, which grew out of the first revolutionary assembly, became a fundamental feature of democratic political structures everywhere. These two examples show just how fruitful symbolic history can be.

The same mechanism is at work with religious minorities. Many countries have more substantial Jewish populations than France, yet no other country has linked its revolutionary identity to Jewish emancipation, and to an assimilationist version of that emancipation, in such a way as to give such dramatic prominence to the national debate about discrimination against Jews from the Dreyfus Affair to the anti-Jewish statute of 1940 under Pétain. All European countries were affected to one degree or another by the Reformation, and several endured religious wars, but none other than France made this religious conflict a permanent part of its identity or treated it as a symbol of tolerance and persecution to the same degree. And no other country had to contend with the phenomenon of Jansenism, a dissident movement within Catholicism that perpetuated the doctrinal struggles of the sixteenth century.

The same principle of division, coupled with the same types of conflict and tension, has also presided over the construction, perception, and representation of space and time in France. But unlike the divisions underlying the political and religious imagination, divisions of this third type come in many varieties. Some of the most significant ones are treated in this volume. What could be more important than divisions decreed by nature, especially that between the north and the south of France? And which divisions have been more crucial than those in terms of which the French learned to perceive and master their vaunted diversity, beginning with the persistent opposition between Paris and the provinces? Finally, what chronological division is more significant than the notion of a historical generation, which—in all countries but especially in France, from the romantic era to May '68—has had the power to infuse the natural replacement of the old by the young with mobilizing energy?

Many people feel that the resurrection of these symbols of division is fueling a crisis in a France that has begun to question its identity and ceased to recognize itself. By studying the logic of the historical construction and development of such symbols we hope to arrive at a more adequate understanding. We shall see what no longer works and on what basis renewal is possible. The signs and markers may be partially obscured, yet we can still make out the unbroken path, the permanence of an identity even now in the throes of fundamental change.

PART I

BETWEEN MEMORY AND HISTORY

FIGURE 1.0 *Vercingetorix*, from Nodier, Taylor, and Cailleux, *Voyages pittoresques dans l'ancienne France;*
lithograph by Engelmann after Lacroix, 1829.

CHAPTER I

Franks and Gauls[1]

Krzysztof Pomian

> Problems of the time. The *bloc* system beloved by politicians (Clemenceau said, "The Revolution is a *bloc*") and detested by historians; historians have a duty to break down monoliths or, as the paleontologists say, to "stratify" them.
>
> —*Camille Jullian*

The heroic memory of the ancient Gauls is often recalled by monuments such as the *Vercingétorix* in Clermont or the *Gaul* on the Pont d'Iéna in Paris; by street names, Alésia, Gergovie, and Vercingétorix being among the most common; and by signs. One Paris restaurant calls itself simply Nos Ancêtres les Gaulois. With *Astérix* the Gauls have triumphed even in the world of comic books. And there is no shortage of paperback editions of books dealing with them, from Caesar's *Gallic Wars* to Camille Jullian's *Vercingétorix*, Albert Grenier's *Les Gaulois,* and Paul-Marie Duval's *Dieux de la Gaule,* among many others. Anyone who wants to learn more about them can easily find enough to satisfy his or her initial curiosity in any bookstore. More demanding readers can turn to libraries, where they will find, counting journal articles, tens of thousands of titles on every conceivable aspect of the subject.

Nor are printed texts the end of it. Archaeological excavation sites, some famous and visited by large numbers of tourists, others more modest and of purely local importance, offer a glimpse of vestiges of the Gauls and the Gallo-Romans: their *oppida,* their cities, their *villae.* Meanwhile, archaeological museums contain row upon row of statues of their gods and exhibits of their tools, utensils, weapons, coins, art works, and everyday objects; and fine art museums exhibit paintings, statues, engravings, and drawings that show how they were imagined in the nineteenth and the early part of the twentieth century. To top it all off, there is a whole apparatus of special exhibitions, tourist information signs, guidebooks, catalogues, folders, maps, plaster casts, photographs, and postcards—a whole literature in itself, with its own iconography. All of this is supposed to help visitors know what to look for and teach them how to study the remains of the past with an objective eye while instilling a deep and lasting interest in the subject, but at the same time it inculcates certain beliefs, including a belief in the Gallic origins of the French, along with certain values, primarily patriotism.

All these facts are duly established. But taken together, as we have just done, they create the impression that French national memory reserves an exceptionally large place for the Gauls. Experience, though, does not bear this out. Only a small percentage of the total number of monuments, street names, and signs in France allude to them. The same can be said of books, even if we include comics and paperbacks. Gallic sites and Gallic objects in museums account for only a small portion of the archaeological remains and artifacts on display in France, a country in which countless populations have left traces ranging from prehistoric cave paintings to paleolithic sites to obsolete nineteenth-century factories. Yet the French attach more importance to the Gauls than to the other peoples that formerly inhabited the territory of France, including even the Franks. This is a distinctive feature of French historical memory, just as the importance attached to the ancient Germanic tribes is a distinctive feature of German memory and the importance ascribed to Rome is a distinctive feature of Italian memory.

To judge by publications aimed at the general public, the privileged status that the Gauls enjoy today stems from a composite of three images. (The relative importance of each image by itself cannot be ascertained.) The first of these is an image of splendor, of Celtic gold or of the treasures of Celtic princes, the general public making no distinction between the prehistoric Celts and the Gauls.[2] The second image is one of powerful esoteric knowledge supposedly possessed by the Druids, who allegedly transmitted that knowledge from generation to generation in secret nocturnal ceremonies. Certain contemporary adepts of the occult claim to be the inheritors of this tradition.[3] The third image is that of "nos ancêtres les Gaulois." Some years ago, the history and manifestations of this third image were discussed at a major gathering of scholars, who emphasized its mythical character.[4] Nevertheless, it still has its champions, who are quick to deplore what they see as an unjust discrediting of an important truth.[5] "Our ancestors the Gauls" are generally depicted as valiant warriors, usually either in triumph or on the point of death but almost never without helmet and sword—especially when they enter an enemy temple and find awaiting them beautiful captives, naked and with fear in their eyes. In contemporary representations of the Gauls we thus find, strangely enough, the three functions that according to Georges Dumézil structure the ideology of the Indo-Europeans: sacred royalty in its dual aspect, luminous and somber, Mithraic and Varunian; warriors, with their victories and miseries; and fertility, which has ensured the continuity of the race down to the present day and which cries out to be associated with the symbol of the cock and *gauloiserie* (salacious storytelling).[6] Too facile to be taken altogether seriously, such an analysis does not, in my view, yield a satisfactory account of the Gallic presence in French national memory, but the possibility deserved to be mentioned.

In Ideological Battle: Vichy

But for the use of the "Celtic cross" by a small sectarian group on the extreme right and rare mentions in official speeches, the Gauls are today all but absent from the French political scene. This has been true, however, only since the end of the war; less than fifty years separates us, in fact, from the last major effort to dragoon them into service. On August 30, 1942, the Légion, a veterans' organization created by Vichy that later became Joseph Darnand's Milice (militia, Vichy's paramilitary ideological police—TRANS.), celebrated its second anniversary in great pomp beneath symbols of "la Terre de France" and national unity. Preparations had begun the week before in metropolitan France and even earlier in the colonies. Local Légion leaders in every commune had solemnly dug up shovelfuls of the local soil to be sent in a sealed bag to Gergovie, where on August 30 all the bags containing their samples of French earth—*les Terres* of France (the capital letter being *de rigueur* in this period)—were to be deposited in a marble cenotaph and sealed up by Marshal Pétain in person.[7] And that is exactly what happened.

Sealed up in the cenotaph along with the samples of French soil was a document from the pen of René Giscard d'Estaing, transcribed onto illuminated parchment. It drew several parallels between the most ancient past and the most recent present: it had been two years since the founding of the "Légion française des combattants et des volontaires de la Révolution nationale" and twenty centuries since the awakening of national sentiment in Gaul; succeeding Vercingetorix, the leader of the Arverni, was Marshal Philippe Pétain, leader of *l'État français;* alongside the monument to Vercingetorix erected in 1901 there was the crypt built to hold French soil "collected in the metropolis and in the colonies, from all the places upon which the spirit of France has breathed and in which is preserved the memory of those who have created its greatness."[8] At Gergovie, in other words, the Vichy regime set itself up as both the guardian of national territorial integrity and the heir to all of France's past, including, though not without considerable hesitation, the Third Republic.[9] At the same time, however, it portrayed itself as the force responsible for the rebirth of France: as General Campet put it, France "was born the day our forefathers came together and agreed to submit to the discipline of a single leader."[10] That founding event had occurred at Gergovie, and Vichy was now assuming the leadership first conferred there.

The ceremony at Gergovie, which Maurice Schumann rightly blasted as "comedy or sacrilege,"[11] appears to have marked the end of the Vichy regime's attempts to mobilize the Gallic ancestors on behalf of the "national revolution." Those attempts had begun in September 1940 with the adoption of the *francisque gallique,* the two-headed Gallic axe, as the symbol of "French unity under the orders of its commander" and a mark of support for the marshal. The *francisque,* according to its creator, combined the star-studded baton of the marshal of France with the "two-headed weapon carried by the Gauls and their leader Vercingetorix in the era of the first ordeal from which our country was to emerge."[12] This formulation portrays Pétain as virtually a reincarnation of Vercingétorix, and it was to be used again at Gergovie.

Vichy propaganda co-opted the Gauls for its own purposes in two ways. First, the regime paid homage to the Gauls' heroic struggle against Caesar's legions: that is why Vichy chose the *francisque* as its symbol and Gergovie as a place of commemoration. Having thus flattered the nation's sense of honor, however, the government insisted forcefully on the Gauls' realism, which led them, once the battle was lost, to acknowledge Rome's superiority. Gaul "accepted its defeat: Julius Caesar brought the Roman peace; vanquished and victors reached an understanding and from this great clash was born the Gallo-Roman civilization that made us what we are. After two millennia we find ourselves in the same position as our forefathers the Gauls, and we hope with all our hearts that, from the accord between victors and vanquished, there will at last be born the European peace which alone can save the world."[13]

Later in this article I will examine the roots of the idea that the Gauls had no choice but to accept defeat and submit to Rome and, furthermore, that this defeat gave birth to Gallo-Roman civilization and thus "made us what we are." For now it is enough to note that this idea had already been used, between 1870 and 1914, to suggest that irreducible differences would always divide Gallo-Roman France from Germanic Germany, and between 1914 and 1918 to bestow a spiritual dimension on the war by casting it as a clash between civilization and a barbarism that hid behind a mask of *Kultur.*[14] The attempt by Vichy to root itself in the Gallic past thus borrowed what was originally an anti-German theme and used it to justify collaboration with the Nazis in the name of a new European civilization of the future.

All this appears to have occupied only a minor, even a marginal, place in Vichy propaganda. Nevertheless, the reflex of turning to the Gauls to lend credibility to the claim that the regime was creating and representing French unity is significant. In so doing, Vichy was in fact repeating a traditional pattern that can be traced back to the Second Empire and that became a part of republican ritual after that empire fell: the invocation of an alleged community of ancestors, identified in this instance with the Gauls, has the effect of presenting the French as people of a common blood, members of a single family and thus different from peoples unable to claim such ancestry. To be sure, the official discourse of the Third Republic imputed a significance that was more cultural than biological, more spiritual than racial, to the Gallic past. The racial theme was never far from consciousness, however, and the politicians and pamphleteers of the extreme right really acknowledged no other basis of national unity.[15]

Who is French? What is the nature of French national identity, and where does it reside? According to the laws and customs of the Republic, in order to be French it suffices to be a French citizen imbued with French culture or, rather, with the French spirit, which is the bearer of French identity. According to the extreme right, by contrast, one is French only if one has French blood, for blood, along with soil, is the substrate of the national identity. Republican ideology distinguishes the French from the Germans but also from the English, the Italians, and all other nations. The extreme right obviously accepts those distinctions, but its primary interest is to establish a visible boundary between the "true French," those who are French by blood, and those who pass themselves off as French without really being French because they have in their veins something that is usually, though not always, supposed to manifest itself in external appearance: the shape of the nose, the color of the skin, the curliness of the hair. In this and many other respects, the supposedly unifying discourse of Vichy actually drew its inspiration directly from the ideas of the extreme right, and its exclusionary policies were accompanied by violent attacks on, and the murder or execution of, many categories of French citizens.

Yet Vichy's exploitation of the Gallic theme, inspired by the extreme right, was only the most recent battle in a conflict that dates back to the beginning of the eighteenth century: a conflict over ancestry. Were the ancestors of the French the Franks or the Gauls or both? It was also a conflict about France: When did France begin? With the arrival of the Franks or of the Gauls? If the former, did the Franks come in the wake of a bloody conquest to feast on the spoils, or was their settlement a peaceful one followed by a fusion of the two peoples? And last but not least, it was a conflict over the belief on the part of some Frenchmen that they were more French than others, a belief justified by the claim that their ancestors were the true founders of the nation and supposedly the source of rights to which other French people could advance no legitimate claim. This last conflict at first took the form of a clash of orders: the nobility versus the third estate. Later it took the form of class struggle: the aristocracy versus the bourgeoisie. Like the idea of a nation, therefore, the ideas of social class and class struggle also figure in the controversy surrounding "nos ancêtres les Gaulois."

The Gallic reference thus stands at the intersection of the various polemics and conflicts through which French national integration was achieved. That integration was vertical, ultimately according equal rights to all French nationals and French nationality to all citizens of the Republic (provided that they assimilated French culture). It was also horizontal, establishing a clear boundary between French and non-French. In the long Franco-French and Franco-foreign war over national identity and memory, the Gallic reference played a much larger role than one might guess from the frequency of its explicit invocations.

Now it was able to play this role only because there were good reasons for people to believe that the Gauls (unlike their predecessors as the designated ancestral people, the Trojans) were not a figment of the imagination; they had indeed left on French soil traces that enabled one to assert with a probability approaching certainty that they had lived there, built there, cultivated the earth, buried their dead, prayed to their gods, and fought with their enemies. All of this took place, moreover, not in mythical time immemorial but in an era to which dates could be assigned. The conflict over the Gauls is therefore intimately bound up with the results of research into their past, research that provided the contending parties to the conflict with their arguments, while in turn the conflict conferred on the findings and discoveries of the scholars a significance that was not merely intellectual but quite often political or even cultural. It is this interaction between historical research and ideological conflict that will be the primary focus of our attention here.

Images and Relics

The total mass of texts, images, and relics that refer in one way or another to the Gauls can be thought of as comprising a number of distinct strata, each deposited in a different era. Comic books discovered the Gauls in the late 1940s, but success came only with *Astérix* some ten years later. That success has continued right up to the present, and it has brought the rest of French history into comic books along with it.[16] This most recent stratum lies atop earlier layers of Gallic imagery. Leaving aside a few paintings that were ahead of their time, the most ancient stratum began to form in the late 1820s, when a *Vercingétorix* by Lacroix appeared in the volume on Auvergne in Nodier, Taylor, and Cailleux's *Voyages pittoresques*.[17] The first edition of Henri Martin's *Histoire de France* included two engravings: *Les Druides recueillant le gui sacré* (Druids gathering the sacred mistletoe) and *Vercingétorix devant le tribunal de César* (Vercingetorix before Caesar's tribunal).[18] Throughout the century these themes were recycled by illustrators of books on the Gauls, among them *La Fondation de Marseille, Brenn qui met son sabre dans la balance,* and *La Bataille du Rhône*.[19] Painters soon followed. At the Salon of 1831 it was possible to see an *Episode de la révolte des Gaulois contre les Romains au IIIe siècle,* and in the 1830s Delacroix thought of painting the capture of Rome by the Gauls but never actually executed the work.[20] Paintings depicting the Gauls, and especially Vercingetorix, proliferated in the 1850s (think of Chassériau's *La Défense des Gaules*) and even more after 1870: Luminais all but made the subject his specialty, while many other painters sought inspiration from France's ancient past.[21] Sculpture developed along similar lines.[22] Overall, the period 1870–1914 seems to have produced more works on the Gauls than all other eras of French art combined. What is more, curio dealers sold thousands of engravings representing subjects identical to those treated in these book illustrations, along with plaster casts of Gallic artifacts unearthed by archaeological excavations and postcards representing Gallic themes. Between 1906 and 1914 more than a hundred different postcards were available from vendors at Alesia alone.[23]

Images of the Gauls thus appeared first in connection with texts. They freed themselves from the written word in the second half of the nineteenth century, as though by then it was assumed that everyone knew the history of Gaul and its heroes. Today, images are once again found in conjunction with texts, but not as illustrations: an illustration depends on a text that can do without its support, whereas in comic books the text is inseparable from and subordinate to the image, without which the words are often meaningless. As representations of the Gauls evolved, these images, once considered a minor genre, were accepted into the pantheon of high culture, receiving state patronage and being celebrated in salons and fine art museums. Then, after going into eclipse for a time, they reemerged in youth culture, which for a long time remained outside of official culture, until it received the aesthetic sanction of the pop art movement in the United States and the political backing of the left-wing intelligentsia in France.

Note that the period in which images of the Gauls were accompanied by at most minimal texts (titles of paintings, inscriptions on monuments) was also the period when those images were a part of the official high culture. Here is evidence that spectators were so imbued with Gallic themes that a mere evocation of those themes was sufficient to make a painted scene or sculpted figure immediately intelligible. This ceased to be the case after World War I. Among official institutions, only the educational system has continued right up to the present day to teach, through its textbooks, that the Gauls became first Gallo-Romans and ultimately Frenchmen.[24] Comic books—to the delight of their readers—accordingly allude primarily to what is taught in school or rather to what students remember of what they have been taught in school.

Along with these changes in the status of Gallic imagery came changes in content and style. In the nineteenth century the most widespread and symptomatic images depicted if not historical characters then at least historical scenes, generally scenes of pathos, whose content was attested by documents and rendered with concern for archaeological exactitude, using the resources of an elevated artistic style. Today, images of the Gauls generally portray fictional characters taking part in comical adventures set against a background that is in many cases anachronistic if not utterly fantastic, and the representation is irreverent if not downright satirical. Within the space of a century the character of Gallic imagery has gone from the epic to the burlesque.[25] *Astérix* adopts the same attitude toward the Gallic tradition as *La Belle Hélène* does toward the classic tradition.

Let us turn now from the most recent stratum (itself divided into several layers), which involves representations of the Gauls by people who thought of themselves as their descendants or who played on such beliefs, to what appears to be the most ancient stratum, consisting of relics left by the Gauls themselves: ruins and artifacts *in situ* as well as objects displayed in archaeological museums. Note that I call this the stratum that *appears* to be the most ancient: that is because, while the material objects themselves come to us from the time of the Gauls, it is only recently that those objects have acquired the status of relics. For centuries before, the vestiges of the Gauls, along with those of other ancient peoples, were treated as refuse, buried in the earth, forgotten, and likely to be misinterpreted if encountered by chance. Until quite recently, for instance, old Roman paths were thought to be the work of Queen Brunhilde, who had become a figure of legend.[26]

A new interest in ancient monuments began to emerge in the sixteenth century. It is true, of course, that the antiquarians and history buffs of the time were primarily interested in Roman, Greek, and Egyptian artifacts. Nevertheless, they did not turn up their noses at objects deemed apt for illustrating the local or national past or even at mere curiosities that seemed strikingly strange or enigmatic. Some spectacular discoveries showed people where to look. In 1653, for example, Childeric's tomb was located in Tournai. Now Childeric, of course, was not a Gaul, but the riches found in his tomb aroused the interest of antiquarians in sepulchers.[27] In 1685 the ossuary of Cocherel was uncovered, although its description was not published until much later, at which time it was interpreted as a "Gallic sepulcher."[28] In 1711, in the course of repairs to Notre-Dame in Paris, the altar of the boatmen of the Seine was discovered along with its inscriptions, its Ésus tree, and its bull with three cranes.[29] The (allegedly) Gallic objects went on display in antiquarian shops. Montfaucon, himself a collector, reproduced some of them in his *Antiquité expliquée*.[30] Occasionally a more methodical excavation was attempted: Nicolas-Joseph Foucault, the intendant of Normandy, ordered one such at Valogne in 1691.[31] In the eighteenth century Président de Robien (of the *parlement* of Rennes) was certainly not the only magistrate to order excavations on his own estates.[32] Also worth mentioning are the excavations at Gergovie in 1755, begun at the behest of the Société Littéraire of Clermont,[33] and on Mont Auxois in 1784, which may have been initiated by the Estates General of Burgundy.[34]

The year 1759 marks an important date in the constitution of a corpus of Gallic and Gallo-Roman artifacts, for it was then that Caylus included Gallic antiquities along with Egyptian, Etruscan, Greek, and Roman ones in the third volume of his *Recueil*. It is not out of the question that the idea was suggested to him by Maffei's work on the antiquities of Gaul.[35] In any case, it was in the volume in which he discussed certain of Maffei's opinions that Caylus published his list of Gallic antiquities. He ascribed no artistic value to them: "I have commissioned engravings of the

FIGURE 1.1   Henri Motte, *Cutting Mistletoe;* Salon of 1901.

works of the Aborigenes, the first Etruscans, and the Sards, whose merit may in some ways be inferior to that of the Gauls. I should therefore be entitled to record the ancient productions of my country, even if they were in worse taste and conveyed no notion of divinity, as evidence of a great precision and breadth of mind."[36] On this point Caylus never changed his mind: "What have I said, and what can be said, about the Gauls?" he asked in the conclusion of the final volume to be published during his lifetime. "Fighting was all they knew. True, one does glimpse a few crude artifacts acquired through trade with Greece. But after having fought bravely, they seem, so far as the arts are concerned, greatly inferior to those who defeated them by force of arms." [37]

Caylus's interest in the Gauls was thus motivated exclusively by patriotism: "I think that I can boast of having provided more details on the antiquity of the Gauls than anyone else. I have done my country this small service."[38] Most of the monuments of Roman Gaul that he reproduced reflected his taste and that of his correspondents. He never passed up any opportunity, however, to present any monument that seemed "patently" Gallic.[39] He called for the publication of an *Antique Gaul,*[40] praised Pelloutier's *History of the Celts,* kept abreast of research on northern antiquities, and criticized Dom Martin for attributing an Etruscan monument to the Druids.[41] He devoted three plates to Gergovie, summarized the debate over its location, and reported the results of the excavations that had been carried out there.[42] He reproduced certain "Gallic medals" while dismissing them as mere curiosities, "because they cannot teach us about history and it is impossible to make any conjecture concerning the time and place of their fabrication."[43] In this they were no different from other Gallic artifacts, all of them being "in general very difficult to explain" and still more difficult to date.[44] Last but not least, he took an interest in the raised stone of Poitiers and other megalithic monuments.

Strange as it may seem, megalithic monuments in general did not begin to attract attention until the second half of the sixteenth century.[45] It was not until a century later, moreover, that people began to approach them with archaeological interest. The earliest known excavation was at Cocherel, an attempt to discover what was hidden beneath a hill on which two stones had been implanted. For Montfaucon, as we saw a moment ago, this was a "Gallic sepulcher," and stones found in various other locations were also identified as Gallic artifacts, namely, weapons.[46] As for the raised stone at Poitiers, Caylus said that "it is probable that works of this type and nature are from the time of the Gauls and that their construction must have predated the wars with Caesar by several centuries." He prudently assumed that the stone in question must be a tomb of some kind.[47]

He took a different position, however, in regard to the megaliths of Brittany, which were brought to his attention by La Sauvagère and Président de Robien, who sent him his father's maps and drawings.[48] While disagreeing with Deslandes, who

FIGURE 1.2   Gallic coins; Caylus, *Recueil d'antiquités* (1752–1767).

FIGURE 1.3   Evariste Luminais, *Gallic Lookouts*.

saw the rows of stones at Carnac as "a consequence of revolutions occurring in the surface of the earth," and with La Sauvagère, who saw them as vestiges of old Roman camps, Caylus refused to attribute them to the ancient Gauls. The Gauls, he argued, would have raised such structures "at several places on the continent," but "none has ever been found except in provinces located on the seacoast or in any case not far away." Furthermore, what was known of the customs and religion of the Gauls did not justify imputing to them the "kind of superstition" that the megaliths seemed to indicate. After noting "the absolute silence that even tradition has maintained concerning a custom so often repeated," Caylus concluded that "one can infer from this an even more remote antiquity, memory of which had been lost in Roman times."[49]

Caylus truly inaugurated Gallic archaeology. Various anthologies, some of which claim to be continuations of Caylus's own,[50] extend his contribution by adding information about new discoveries and the results of recent excavations. Not only did the Revolution not halt such research, but it actually stimulated new interest by promoting the nation's antiquities, especially those of the Gauls. I shall have more to say about this period later on, but for now it will suffice to note the publication by Legrand d'Aussy of an important report on French burial sites, a report which unwittingly provided archaeological justification for the extravagances of Celtomania. The purpose of this epoch-making report was scientifically irreproachable: to classify burial places from the ancient past down to the Renaissance and to establish a typology and (for the older sites) a relative chronology, while drawing whatever historical lessons were available from the sites and urging the government to organize excavations both in Paris and in the *départements*.[51]

Legrand therefore took an obvious interest in "Gallic tombs," which, contrary to Caylus, he identified as megalithic monuments. He was the first to distinguish clearly among the various types of such monuments and to give them names, nearly all of which subsequently entered into common parlance. He introduced the word *menhir*, for example, in these terms: "I am told that in low Breton these crude obelisks are called *ar-men-ir*. I accept the expression all the more readily because, in addition to allowing me to avoid circumlocution, it has the advantage of belonging to France and of conveying to the mind a precise meaning in a word whose pronunciation is not unduly disagreeable."[52] From Deslandes he borrowed the word *lécavène*, which has not survived. And he launched the word *dolmen* (he spelled it *dolmine*): "M. Coret, in discussing tables of a sort that I am about to describe and which can be seen at Lockmariaker, says that in low Breton they are known as *dolmin*. Once again I shall avail myself of this expression, which, like the two previous ones, is necessary to my exposition. In a subject that is totally new, and for which as a consequence no terminology exists, I have been forced to create one for myself. And while I have every right to coin new words, I prefer to adopt already existing ones, especially when, as with words borrowed from low Breton, they offer the hope of representing the old Gaulish nomenclature. I shall therefore take up the word *dolmine* and use it to refer to the tables I am about to describe."[53]

Legrand devoted a section of his report to each type of megalithic monument and another to burial mounds, which, he said, "are to France today what the pyramids are to Egypt."[54] One step at a time, his work thus created an object that did not previously exist, and in so doing he changed the very perception of the landscape. He was fully conscious of the innovative nature of his work: "Who would believe that objects standing in the open in plain view and massive enough to attract and hold the eye are nevertheless as unknown as if they did not exist? During the sixteenth and much of the seventeenth centuries, all but a few scholars in France were interested only in Roman antiquities. They valued, and were receptive to, only what was Roman. It was only after Montfaucon and Caylus, having undertaken to treat antiquities generally, were obliged to concern themselves with those of the Gauls that people seemed to recognize the extent to which we ought to be interested in everything related to the primitive history of our forefathers."[55] The monuments they left behind consequently became both objects of science and subjects of general curiosity: "In order to make the various types of Gallic tombs interesting, it was necessary to consider both their moral and scientific aspects. The fruit of a belief in a very strange afterlife, they represent religious views and mores whose description was useful yet entirely neglected."[56] As a result, "we know nothing, absolutely nothing, about the monuments that lie at the core of our archaeology, of the primitive history of our nation, our country, and our arts."[57]

Legrand's appeal did not go unheeded. The Académie Celtique, founded in Paris in 1804, set itself the following goals: "1. To pursue research on the Celtic language and to produce etymologies for all its derivative tongues, especially French. 2. To describe, explain, and have engravings made of the ancient monuments of the Gauls."[58] Usually only the first of these goals is emphasized, and scholars have called attention to the etymological mania evident in the writings of some of the academy's founders. As a result, there is a tendency to forget that this flamboyant Celtism did not enjoy unanimous support,[59] and that differences over linguistic excesses and other "extravagances of the imagination" led the members of the academy to change its name in 1813 to the Société des Antiquaires de France, which became a model for the antiquary societies that began to proliferate in the provinces after 1824.[60] The change affected not only the organization's name but the very focus of its activities. Initially the academy had simultaneously pursued work on linguistics, monuments, and ethnography.[61] After 1813 archaeology—not only medieval and Gallo-Roman but also Gallic archaeology—became its exclusive preoccupation.

Gallic archaeology was based on an axiom set forth by Henri Martin at the beginning of his *Histoire de France* though accepted much earlier: "The first men to populate the west of Europe, in a period well before any historical tradition, were the Gauls, who are our true ancestors because their blood predominates in the successive mixture of diverse races that has shaped the modern French."[62] Megalithic monuments as well as objects in stone and bone unearthed by excavation were attributed to the Celts, who were identified with the Gauls.[63] These vestiges became the seeds around which crystallized patriotic-mythological dreams and fanciful reconstructions of religious cults, which took information gleaned from Caesar, Strabo, Pliny, and others and ascribed it to the world of menhirs and dolmens. The very extravagance of Cambry's book on Celtic monuments is illustrative of this approach.[64]

Other interpretations were admittedly more sober.[65] Nevertheless, the Celtic and Gallic attributions, as well as the chronological representations on which they were based, were completely erroneous. Yet it is by no means the case that research on megalithic monuments yielded only trivial or negative results. It led in fact to a major discovery, a discovery so great that it was foreseen by no one. Having set out in search of the Celts, archaeologists instead found human fossils. Gallic archaeology turned out to be prehistoric archaeology. The title of Boucher de Perthes's pioneering book, *Antiquités celtiques et antédiluviennes,* bears the trace of the transition from one to the other. Since that transition went hand in hand with an increase in the estimate of the length of time man had inhabited this earth, it was necessary to give up the idea that the Celts, either by themselves or together with the Ligurians and the Iberians, were the earliest inhabitants of Gaul.[66] It was also necessary to revise the attribution of the dolmens and menhirs.

In 1861 the Académie des Inscriptions offered a prize for the best essay on the topic of Celtic monuments. In the conclusion of the winning entry, Alexandre Bertrand set forth a series of "hypotheses to be combated" on the subject: "General hypotheses: 1. that menhirs, dolmens, tumuli, and cromlechs are monuments erected by the Celts; 2. that these monuments were once found throughout Gaul, unevenly distributed to be sure but nearly everywhere. The reason why they are no longer found everywhere is that they were destroyed. Specific hypotheses: 1. that the menhirs are idols; 2. that the menhirs are commemorative stones at gravesites; 3. that the menhirs are altars; 4. that rocking stones (*pierres branlantes*) are of Druidic origin; 5. that hollowed-out stones were used for sacrificial purposes; 6. that dolmens were altars for the sacrifice of human victims."[67] Naturally these assertions met with opposition and resistance. But in 1867 the International Congress on Prehistoric Anthropology and Archaeology officially introduced the term "megalithic" to refer to monuments previously attributed to the Celts and Druids.[68] Traces of the earlier attribution persist, however: if Obélix is "a menhir deliveryman by trade," it is because of Legrand d'Aussy.

Promoting a Museum of National Antiquities

As Gallic archaeology progressed over the course of the nineteenth century, its adepts urged the authorities, with growing insistence, to create a Museum of National Antiquities. Once again, Legrand d'Aussy was in the forefront. His paper on burial sites included a "Proposal for the French Museum of Monuments" in which, after remarking on the institution's value and importance, he lamented the fact that the museum contained only monuments of the most recent period, which in his periodization was called the "age of mausoleums." Indeed, the period prior to the arrival of the Franks seems to have been represented in Alexandre Lenoir's museum only by the altar of the Parisian boatmen (*nautes*).[69] The Gauls before the Roman conquest were missing, to Legrand's dismay: "I want menhirs, *lécavènes*, dolmens, rows of dolmens, colonnades. Let us try to create in Paris a savage décor, the first of its type to be seen there. Let us heighten its effects and strengthen its impression by making it accurate in every detail, that is, by composing authentic tombs, to be selected from among the finest examples that neighboring *départements* have to offer and transported to the museum grounds, where they will be arranged as scrupulously as they once were." As for monuments that might prove too costly to transport, "they may be duplicated here as accurately as possible," along with "tumulary hills" that unfortunately could not be moved. "Then [Lenoir's museum] will truly be entitled to call itself the *museum of French monuments*, for only then will its collection be complete back to most remote periods of the past: no type of monument will be lacking. What other museum in Europe will offer such an unusual, stimulating, and novel spectacle?"[70]

Legrand's proposal, along with his excavation plans, was taken up by another collector of Gallic and Gallo-Roman artifacts, Grivaud de la Vincelle, in conjunction with others interested in the subject. The goals of the project changed, however, even as the associated terminology became increasingly precise. Grivaud called for "the establishment of a truly national museum, that is, a museum composed solely of ancient monuments found in France." This would differ from Lenoir's museum in that, rather than give pride of place to works of art and the Middle Ages, it would make room for every available vestige of France's most remote past:

If there were a place in the capital especially designed to receive every ancient monument discovered in France, that collection would, with a modicum of care and at very little expense, grow daily in extent and richness. Since each object would be classified along with the date and place of its discovery, scholars engaged in research on ancient Gaul would find among the exhibits evidence to support their conjectures. They would find material for interesting dissertations and would certainly revive throughout the country the taste for antiquity, which today is almost extinct. One could excavate, with the certainty of finding an abundant harvest, the Châtelet plateau, two-thirds of which has not been touched; the *Mons Seleucus,* whose ancient soil has barely been scratched; and many other places where once stood establishments of considerable size, whose invaluable vestiges remain hidden in the earth from which they would be wrested to become, in the French Museum, irrefutable evidence of the ancient splendor of France.[71]

In the same year, 1807, Quatremère de Quincy, who first became interested in the Palais des Thermes (baths) in Year II of the Republic, called for the creation of a Gallo-Roman museum. Ten years later, the political climate had changed and the government had issued a decree closing the Museum of French Monuments, in the wake of which Grivaud renewed his earlier proposal; Quatremère wrote a review of his book on his collection and claimed to have initiated the call for a Gallo-Roman museum, whose first promoters were in fact Maffei and Caylus.[72] Like them, Quatremère proposed a museum of ancient sculpture either produced in or imported into France. He cared as little for Celtic monuments as for those of the Middle Ages. In 1819 his plan came close to realization. Taking advantage of the Duc d'Angoulême's visit to the Palais des Thermes, he secured a promise of funds for the preservation of the edifice and had himself appointed curator of the future Gallo-Roman museum. In 1820, however, after the fall of the Decazes government, work on the project was halted.[73]

The idea of a national museum did not resurface until after the July Revolution. In 1831 the city of Paris bought the Baths. The vogue was now for the Middle Ages, however, and writers, artists, and people of fashion were flocking to the Du Sommerard collection on display in the Hôtel de Cluny. It will come as no surprise, then, that among the numerous proposals floated at the time for a museum of national monuments, the public favored that of Albert Lenoir, whose central idea was to link the two adjoining buildings at the site, one ancient, the other medieval, so as to offer the public a "complete chronology" and in order "to display the monuments of our history in a series of architectural spaces contemporary with the major epochs that bequeathed them to us."

Lenoir proposed that the exhibits of Roman monuments, which were naturally to be housed in the Baths, be preceded by an exhibit of "Druidic monuments," to be collected in a "Gallic court" with entry by way of bridges constructed "in the manner of dolmens, that is, with an enormous stone spanning the ditch." Furthermore, "the Druidic fragments that Paris possesses, steles of local interest that were unearthed in the excavations at Notre-Dame in 1711, along with those found at Saint-Landry in 1829, should provide ample matter for the Gallic exhibit that is to lead up to the Roman one. These could be augmented with the Venus of Quinipily and the statue of Vercingetorix, a celebrated general, discovered this past century in Auvergne, which is probably stored in some obscure place from which it is to be hoped it may be retrieved."[74]

The rest of the story is well known. In 1843 the National Assembly and Senate approved the allocation of funds to purchase the Du Sommerard collection. François Arago, who sponsored the bill in the Assembly, did not fail to allude to his memories of the Museum of French Monuments or to invoke patriotism in his plea on behalf of the new museum: "Gentlemen, we find in various institutions around Paris Greek collections, Roman collections, Egyptian collections. Not even the savages of Oceania have been neglected. It is high time that we gave some thought to our ancestors. Let us see to it that the capital of France also includes a French historical museum."[75] His call was heeded. The Musée de Cluny, which was dedicated on March 17, 1844, in general reflected Lenoir's proposal, except that the Gallic exhibit was omitted. The lion's share of the space went to the Middle Ages.[76] Although the museum proved quite popular, it therefore failed to satisfy those who had hoped to see the establishment of a museum of French antiquities—a group whose numbers were growing.

By the 1820s excavations were being organized virtually everywhere in France by local organizations, private individuals, and government bodies. The artifacts they unearthed went into private collections or were displayed in one of the archaeological museums that many provincial cities established.[77] The Gauls, introduced into literature by Chateaubriand at the turn of the century and featured in a number of operas devoted to *Velléda* as well as in Bellini's *Norma* and Gounod's cantata *Gallia*,[78] also figured in a growing number of historical works after 1830. One gauge of the growing public interest in the nation's ancient past is the number of editions through which some of these works went, and I have already mentioned the increased attention paid to the Gauls by painters and sculptors after 1850. Another measure of the intensity of this interest is the number of works devoted to the location of Alesia (as well as the degree of passion invested in them). Was it Alise-Sainte-Reine in Burgundy or the new contender that entered the race in 1855, Alaise in Franche-Comté? Besançon versus Semur-en-Auxois. Quicherat alone contributed nearly twenty times to this debate, challenging most of the leading lights of French archaeology. The polemic raged for several years with the participation of some fifty authors who hurled political allusions and insults back and forth, drawing the attention of the press and general public.[79]

In 1861, Henri Martin, one of the most stalwart champions of the Gallic cause, summed up his impressions of a visit to the Celtic gallery of the British Museum in terms that echo the sentiments of Arago's speech: "The sight of such a fine national collection in a country devoid of centralization inevitably turns the thoughts of a

French archaeologist to the Louvre, whose cosmopolitan galleries are open to antiquities from all over the world except those of our forefathers, while our institutions of higher learning offer classes in all languages, even Javanese and Manchu, of which we strongly approve, yet not one chair in Celtic."[80] The end of this state of affairs was imminent. Napoleon III, who in 1858, at the height of the battle over Alesia, created a Commission on the Topography of the Gauls, decided in 1860 to pursue plans for a *History of Julius Caesar*. In 1861 he therefore requested that Ludwig Lindenschmidt, director of the museum of Mainz (founded in 1852), provide him with reproductions of Germanic and Roman arms.[81] It was in these circumstances, apparently, that Legrand d'Aussy's old idea, updated to meet the needs of the moment, finally began to move toward accomplishment.

On November 8, 1862, a decree was issued establishing the château of Saint-Germain-en-Laye as "a museum of Celtic and Gallo-Roman antiquities subsidiary to the Museum of Antiques," that is, the Louvre. The new institution was to be called the Gallo-Roman Museum, later changed to the Museum of National Antiquities, the name that it still bears today. The museum was dedicated on May 12, 1867, its holdings enriched by the acquisition of the Boucher de Perthes collections (which Cluny had rejected in 1858) and by donations from Napoleon III, whose name appears on the donors' list twenty-five times and whose gifts included mainly Gallic and Gallo-Roman artifacts.[82] Initially traces of the institution's association with the history of Caesar project were quite apparent, so much so that visitors were astonished to "see a French museum of national archaeology start off with monuments located in Italy celebrating a Roman emperor's victories over the Dacians."[83] Under the Third Republic the Saint-Germain museum accentuated both its scientific and its patriotic character, symbolized by a change of name: the "temporary Hall of Caesar and the Conquest" became the "Hall of Alesia."[84] In 1881, Gaston Boissier had this to say at the conclusion of one visit: "It can be said that the Museum of National Antiquities exists and that anyone who tours the fifteen or twenty halls it contains will be making a quick but comprehensive survey of our ancient history from the most remote past to the beginning of the Middle Ages."[85]

Over the past hundred years archaeological museums in France have to one degree or another undergone changes and reorganizations that have ultimately affected the ways in which visitors perceive the exhibits and therefore the image of the past they take away with them. Today, in contrast to a hundred years ago, objects are no longer restored and displayed in such a way as to efface their history and create the illusion of a direct confrontation between the spectator and a past ostensibly brought back to life in ways envisioned by Guizot, Michelet, and Viollet-le-Duc. Nowadays the emphasis is rather on the historical distance that separates us from the past whose vestiges we admire: the restored portions of artifacts are clearly indicated, objects are displayed as found *in situ,* and their laboratory treatment is described. Furthermore, the manner of display is different from what it was a century ago. New interpretations determine the arrangement of artifacts as well as the accompanying commentary and thus the significance attached to each object.

These new interpretations are in part the result of recent finds, such as the discovery of a princely burial site at Vix in 1953, as well as modern dating techniques (especially the use of carbon 14), pollen studies, and metallurgical, chemical, physical, and other analyses. Advances in Celtic and Indo-European linguistics have also been important, from Zeuss's *Grammatica celtica* (1853) and the work of Arbois de Jubainville to Vendryes, Benveniste, and beyond; the same can be said of the innovative work on beliefs, myths, and religions done primarily by Georges Dumézil and his followers. In short, the oldest representations of the Gauls, in the form of surviving artifacts once treated as worthless junk, embody all later representations, in that their significance and in some cases even their physical appearance bear the earmarks of countless discoveries, techniques, and theories from the time of Montfaucon and Caylus to the archaeologists of today.

From Caesar to Louis XIV

The number of ancient texts that instruct us about Gaul prior to the mid-fifth century of the Common Era is impressive. According to Paul-Marie Duval, who has established the most comprehensive bibliography, "by the year 460 some 350 works by single authors, anonymous authors, or several hands yield some mention of Gaul proper or its inhabitants and in some cases a good deal more. More than 190 of these are in Latin, the others in Greek; roughly 275 are in the pagan tradition, while 75 are of Christian inspiration."[86] These texts did not all play the same historical role. Some were exhumed only recently, whereas others have been known and used for a long time. But one and only one has never been forgotten. Only one work has, ever since it first appeared, been read, quoted, copied, translated, printed and reprinted, paraphrased, glossed, and discussed: Julius Caesar's *Commentaries on the Gallic Wars*.

There are numerous manuscripts of the work: 33 in the Vatican Library, 25 in the Bibliothèque Nationale, 17 in Florence.[87] Printed editions appeared in rapid succession: 10 in the fifteenth century, 39 in the sixteenth century, 20 in the seventeenth century, 22 in the eighteenth century, and 214 in the nineteenth century if one includes both separate publications and editions of the complete works and counts reprint editions.[88] There are also numerous French translations, which are especially significant since scholars know Latin, so that the existence of vernacular versions demonstrates that the work was being read by a broad audience. The first translated edition dates from the beginning of the thirteenth century; it formed the second part of the *Fait des Romains,* a compilation of several ancient works that enjoyed an enormous success.[89] Of the next two translations, both from the final decades of the fifteenth century, one, by Robert Gaguin, was also widely read.[90] Then came the printed editions: 10 in the fifteenth and sixteenth centuries, 19 in the seventeenth century, 9 in the eighteenth century, and 61 in the nineteenth century.[91] Finally, to round out the picture, I should also mention the many biographies of Caesar, commentaries on his work, and discussions of its details. In 1880 there were some 70 of these, 55 of which had been published in the previous thirty years, and these figures are surely far from complete.[92]

There is little mention of Gauls and Romans in French oral traditions, and it is highly probable, moreover, that what mentions there are derive from books.[93] The name "Gaul" was preserved first of all by the Church. Throughout the Middle Ages it used the word *Gallia* to refer to the territory under the jurisdiction of the primate of Lyons, whereas the names *Francia* and *regnum Francorum* were applied to the profane entity. The word *Gallia*, which many writers used as a geographic term, also took on political significance in the twelfth century, when it appeared in expressions such as *regnum Galliae* for the kingdom of France or when the kings of France were characterized as kings of the geographic territory known in French as *les Gaules* and in Latin as *Galliae* (e.g., *Lodoycus rex Galliarum*) or of the Gallic people (e.g., *Philippus rex Gallorum*).[94]

More than the name was at issue, however. For sixteen centuries, from the time of the Roman conquest to the French elite's discovery that the Gauls were their ancestors, it was solely thanks to a few ancient authors, Caesar first and foremost among them, that memory was kept alive of the people who had once inhabited the various parts of Gaul, of various episodes in their history, of their customs, institutions, and beliefs, and of the deeds and actions of their most illustrious figures. Caesar conquered Gaul with implacable brutality and cruelty, but to it he also erected a monument *aere perennius*. It would have been disastrous if the works of the various ancient authors who had written of Gaul and the Gauls had disappeared in the fifth century, yet if Caesar's work had survived, the bulk of our knowledge would have remained intact. If one had to single out one place—one formative place—where the memory of things Gallic was and is still preserved, it would surely be that diaspora of individual places constituting all the extant volumes of *The Gallic Wars*.

As readers of ancient writers and above all of Caesar, the chroniclers of the Middle Ages included what they had learned about Gaul and its inhabitants in their works. For example, Héri, a Benedictine from Auxerre, embellished his poem on the life of Saint Germanus with a reference to Caesar, Gaul, and the siege of Alesia, which he clearly identified with Alise in Auxois. His opinion on the subject was borrowed by the monks of the nearby abbey at Flavigny, who had also read Caesar, and inscribed in their martyrology.[95] This is a good example of the use in local and sacred history of knowledge derived from the ancients. An example of the use of such knowledge in national and profane history can be found in Aimoin de Fleury's preface to his *Historia Francorum*. Using the testimony of Pliny, Caesar, Sallust, and Orosius, he compares Gaul to Germania and points out that the Gauls captured Rome and sowed fear in Italy.[96] This preface served as the inspiration for the *Grandes Chroniques de France*: "But since we mention the two provinces of Gaul, which now is called France, it is well that we pause here for a description of Gaul as given by Julius Caesar, who in ten years achieved its conquest, and with which Pliny and many other philosophers are in agreement."[97]

Implicit in Aimoin and explicit in the *Grandes Chroniques*, the idea that what had been called Gaul now bore the name of France seems to have been quite widespread from the twelfth century on:

> France aveit nun Galle a cel jur.
> Si n'i aveit rei ne seinnur.
> Romain en demainne l'aveient
> [France in those days went by the name Gaul.
> It had neither king nor lord.
> The Roman had it in his dominion]

we read in the *Roman de Brut* by Wace (1155). Similar formulations can be found elsewhere, and the same opinion is expressed in *Li Fait des Romains*, whose wide circulation has already been mentioned.[98] In short, from at least the twelfth century on, men of learning generally agreed that France was the successor to Gaul. Nevertheless, this did not prevent chroniclers and historians from following Aimoin and the *Grandes Chroniques* in suggesting that the French were the descendants not of the Gauls but of the Franks; they did so by beginning their histories of France with the earliest Frankish kings and relegating Gaul from the main body of the text to the introduction or preface. This also made it possible to explain how, why, and under what circumstances Gaul had changed its name, while at the same time assuring the French of a privileged place in universal history.

France owed its place in universal history to the notion that the French, being Franks, were in reality Trojans and therefore younger brothers of the Romans. From the seventh century on this idea was echoed not only by French historians, naturally enough, but also by Germans, Spaniards, Italians, Belgians, Poles, and Scandinavians. Only a few Englishmen remained skeptical of these Frankish claims, and they ascribed Trojan roots to either the inhabitants of Britannia or its ruling dynasty.[99] This virtually unanimous European opinion began to break down in the fifteenth century, when Italian humanists began to argue that peoples descended from barbarian tribes could not possibly have Trojan origins, unlike the Romans and their legitimate heirs, the inhabitants of Italy.[100] This "Italianization" of the Trojans (did not Antenor die in Padua?) had its counterpart in other

FIGURE 1.4   Julius Caesar, *Commentaires;* French translation (1482).

European nations in the form of a search for a glorious past that was purely national, a search that was facilitated by the revival and circulation of long forgotten or little known texts: Livy, for example, was rediscovered in the fourteenth century, along with Tacitus' *Germania* and various Latin and Greek geographers, especially Strabo. Of a total of thirty-four manuscripts by Strabo, twenty date from the fifteenth century, which also saw five editions of the Latin translation of his works. An edition of the original Greek text did not appear until 1516.[101]

What began to change was thus the very framework of the secular universal history that gave meaning to the various ethnic and national histories. Henceforth, what distinguished the "historical peoples"—those whose feats had implications for all mankind—was not so much Trojan ancestry as ancientness, especially when attested by the allegedly most ancient authors, and military exploits, especially against the Romans. Thus the modern Germans drew glory from their Germanic ancestors, the Spanish from the Iberians, the Poles from the Sarmatians, and the Swedes from the Goths (despite their unenviable reputation elsewhere). The promotion of Gaul and the Gauls, which, along with that of Brennus,[102] played an increasing role in the history of France from the fourteenth century on (as did the promotion of Arminius in Germany and of various legendary conquerors of the Romans elsewhere), was part of this European movement and accelerated with it after 1450. "By 1480 a Frenchmen most definitely had Gallic ancestors he did not have in 1400."[103] To be sure, these new ancestors were not yet in a position to replace the Trojans, to whom the French felt attached by long habit and who, throughout the sixteenth century, coexisted with the Gauls, resisting repeated attempts to purge them from the history of France. But in the end the Trojans lost this war too: by the seventeenth century it was no more than a memory.[104]

Universal history also had its sacred component, however. This was vastly more important than the profane component, because Genesis provided the ultimate answer to the question of national origins in the genealogy of Noah's descendants and the story of the diaspora following the failed attempt to build the tower

FIGURE 1.5   Remus presents his daughter to Francus with the city of Reims in the background; sixteenth-century tapestry, studio of Beauvais.

of Babel. The Trojans had held a place in this genealogy for more than a thousand years: they were descendants of Japhet. The ancestors that the European nations chose for themselves in the fifteenth century—Germans, Sarmatians, Gauls— therefore had to legitimate themselves by producing their own genealogies going all the way back to Japhet as originator of the line, the father of all Europeans. The chain not only had to be traced back generation after generation, it also had to be authenticated by authority adequate to ensure its acceptance. Annius of Viterbo resolved both of these problems by a stroke of genius that ensured his work an audience throughout Europe. He claimed to be publishing for the first time texts of very ancient historians, among them Manetho and Berosus, writers who had been widely quoted and highly respected in antiquity but whose works had disappeared. On its face there was nothing impossible about this claim. The texts Annius published, especially those of Berosus, contained genealogies showing how the various peoples of Europe had descended from Japhet. In connection with the Gauls, for example, the pseudo-Berosus gave a list containing the names of their first twenty-five kings.[105] It did not take long for Annius to be labeled a forger, but the controversy over the authenticity of the texts he published lasted for nearly two centuries.[106]

In French culture, the sixteenth century was the great century of the Gauls. Books dealing with the subject clearly enjoyed the favor of the public. Between 1509 and 1599 there were (not counting the works of Caesar) more than sixty editions of authentic or apocryphal ancient works pertaining to the history of Gaul, as well as a large number of other texts at least partly devoted to the subject.[107] Berosus was published many times both with and without the comments of his self-styled editor, and his list of Gallic kings was included by Jean Lemaire de Belges in his influential book, *Les Illustrations de la Gaule et les singularitez de Troye*, whose very title is evidence of the coexistence of the two ethnogenetic legends. These kings became sufficiently well known for a canon of Beauvais cathedral, about 1530, to commission five tapestries depicting, respectively, Samothes, the first king of the Gauls with the Celtic Jupiter; Hercules of Libya, the tenth king of the Gauls and the founder of Alesia; Galathes, the son of Hercules and eleventh king of the Gauls with Lugdus, the founder of Lyons; Belgius, the fourteenth king of the Gauls, with Jasius and Paris, the founder of Paris; and, finally, Francus and Remus, the twenty-third and twenty-fifth kings of the Gauls.[108]

The Gauls' introduction into the history of France raised an immediate problem: their relation to the Franks. As long as the Franks were identified with the Trojans, the problem could be solved by invoking mythical genealogies.[109] But when that identification ceased to be taken for granted, things became more complicated. What had to be avoided at all cost was any suggestion that the French monarchy had originated with an invasion and conquest. For philosophical as much as political reasons there always had to be unity at the beginning. Two types of solutions were worked out. François Hotman identified the Franks with the Germans, who had always been allies of the Gauls in their struggle with Rome and who came to Gaul as liberators: the two united peoples formed a nation and elected their first king.[110] For Hotman, in other words, ethnic difference became blurred within a single political community. Bodin proposed a different solution, which was popularized by Claude Fauchet and others. He held that "the Franks mixed easily and united with the Gauls because they sprang from the same origins and shared similar customs."[111] In other words, the Franks were Gauls who had migrated across the Rhine. What began as one community subsequently divided, but in the end the divided segments reunited to form a single nation. There is no doubt that in speaking of Gauls and Franks Hotman was also thinking of Catholics and Protestants; he says as much himself in his preface. All indications are that Fauchet shared this view, along with other historians close to the so-called *politiques*.[112]

Between the end of the Wars of Religion and the French Revolution, the idea of tracing the ancestry of the Gauls back to Noah continued to hold a certain attraction. A book by Father Pezron, who was by no means the only person to cling to such notions in seventeenth- and eighteenth-century Europe, is a good example of how intellectual interests and methods, some of which dated as far back as the early Middle Ages, coexisted with more recent developments, such as occasional ethnographic objectivity, an interest in the language spoken by ordinary people, and a desire to study modern languages in a comparative light.[113] These survivals of older methods persisted much longer in the study of European prehistory than in other historical disciplines. The biblical-etymological speculations of Father Pezron are not so far removed from the techniques employed in seemingly more modern histories of the Gauls and Celts, which include investigations of their beliefs, manners, and customs. These later efforts took ancient texts as authorities rather than as sources to be studied with a critical eye. Influenced, wittingly or unwittingly, by the book of Genesis, they were hamstrung by biblical chronology, as well as steeped in historically minded patriotism. Hence they were doomed in advance to revive old myths and create new ones, as can be seen in the work of Dom Jacques Martin[114] and, later, Simon Pelloutier.[115] Despite criticism by Leibniz and Fréret, the Franks could thus still be seen as Gauls who had returned to their homeland.[116] Even relatively narrow and more scholarly works were often shaped by legend. The only exceptions were the historical geographies of Adrien de Valois in the seventeenth century and d'Anville in the eighteenth century,[117] along with Caylus's archaeology, which was mentioned previously.

Franks versus Gauls

To be completely comprehensive, we should also include research by local scholars, references in the *Encyclopédie,* and literary allusions: even so, the harvest remains quite meager. Between the end of the Wars of Religion and the French Revolution, the Gauls elicited only moderate interest.[118] Of marginal importance in the history of France, which truly began only with the Franks, they did not arouse great passions. Toward the end of Louis XIV's reign, however, relations between the two groups began to be redefined, and this eventually led to a new view of the history of France in its entirety and, in particular, to a new approach to the Gallic period. It is impossible here to delve into the political, ideological, and social context of this turning point, whose effects were soon felt in the debate over the French constitution.[119] Over the course of the next century there would be further profound effects on historical research and the overall presentation of French history: rather than view the history of France in the traditional terms of unity and harmony interrupted only by accidents, people began to see the country as the site of an age-old antagonism, a confrontation between the descendants of the Gauls and the heirs of the Franks. In this connection it will suffice to recall the principal views of the Comte de Boulainvilliers, who was the first to envision the national past in this new way.[120]

According to Boulainvilliers, French history began with the conquest of Gaul by the Franks. The territory was divided up, and the Gauls were subjected to rule by new masters. At the time of the conquest, moreover, the Franks were not subjects of any king. All were noble, and they lived in an aristocratic regime under an elective kingship, with no obligation to the monarch other than military service.[121] Accordingly, the Gauls were subjugated not by a king but by landed nobles: "This truth is so certain that in the usage of the Monarchy, the Third Estate was constituted only after it was emancipated by the Lords. It sought the protection of the Kings and claimed to be immediately subject to the monarch. In this undertaking it was supported in contravention of the obvious rights of the Owners of land and of the fundamental law of the Government."[122]

From the time of Clovis on, kings had tried to strip the Franks of their liberties and privileges by relying, if necessary, on the Gauls and helping them in their struggle against their masters. Had Clovis lived longer, he might have succeeded in reducing the Franks to servitude.[123] This finally did happen during the reign of Pepin, but Charlemagne restored harmony between the king and the Franks: "This great Prince saw that despotic and arbitrary government, of the kind that his grandfather Charles Martel had hoped to establish, was absolutely contrary to the genius of the Nation and its certain and evident rights and therefore that it could not last, and he consequently decided to give the French the justice due them by reestablishing the ancient form of government."[124]

It was Charlemagne who consecrated feudal rights and introduced fiefs "without doing undue violence to the laws."[125] He also revived the role of the national assemblies as supreme tribunals and authorities with the power to make all decisions concerning taxation, war, armed forces, and alliances and to settle differences between lay and ecclesiastical lords. These assemblies consisted exclusively of the clergy and nobility, because "the French, after conquering the Gauls during the reign of Clovis I, established their government entirely apart from the subject Nation, which, remaining in a state between Roman servitude and a kind of liberty, was always regarded by the Conquerors as destined to labor and to the cultivation of the land and not to share the honors of sovereign administration."[126]

For Boulainvilliers, the central axis of French history from Charlemagne to his own day was the erosion of feudal rights and, as a necessary consequence, of the rights of peerage, that is, a degradation of the nobility, one of the causes of which was "the policy of the Capetian family," together with a rise of the third estate, which consisted of emancipated serfs abetted by the same Capetians.[127] In the end the Franks lost and the Gauls won. Against this it might be objected that nothing is left of the Gauls in this formulation other than the name, which is used, moreover, to refer not to the inhabitants of independent Gaul but to the Gallo-Romans, indeed as a synonym for their enslavement. True enough, but this truth only scratches the surface. In the first place, "Gaul" was not just any name: it was the name of a people that for two centuries had enjoyed the reputation (either directly or by way of the Franks) of being the ancestor of the French nation. For Boulainvilliers, however, only a part of the French nation descended from the Gauls, namely, the commoners. The nobility, therefore, was in his view like a foreign body. To be sure, he acknowledged that mixed marriages and other factors had resulted in a situation where, "by the accession of Hugh Capet, the two peoples had become fused in shared rights and a single national body."[128] Nevertheless, he saw the rights of conquest as the cornerstone of noble privileges, which he presented as a perpetuation of the original antagonism between Franks and Gauls. Thus a direct link was established between the history of the Gauls, ancestors of the third estate, and the history of the government of France: the monarchy, legislative assemblies, municipal rights and feudal rights.

This became flagrant from the moment Abbé Dubos published his methodical refutation of Boulainvilliers's idea of French history. Boulainvilliers was wrong because in the fifth century there were no Gauls in Gaul; they had all "metamorphosed" into Romans.[129] The Franks, moreover, were by no means savages encountering civilization for the first time: they had for centuries been trading and forming alliances with Rome, and many of them had served Rome. Indeed, they were "the most civilized of the barbarian nations."[130] Thus there was no "Frankish conquest," except of the territory held by Syagrius, but rather voluntary submission[131] of Romans to Frankish kings. Furthermore, this submission was ratified by the Empire, which conferred power and legitimacy upon those kings and, pursuant to valid legal forms, ceded to them rights over Gaul.[132] That is why Frankish settlement initially had such negligible effects: "The general idea that one should have of the state of the Gauls under Clovis and throughout the reign of his sons and grandsons is that it was, at first glance, much the same as it had been under Honorius and Valentinian III." Of course barbarians now filled offices that had previously been closed to them, and a foreign prince was pretorian prefect. "As for the rest, the face of the country was the same. Bishops governed their dioceses with the same authority they had before the Franks became rulers of the Gauls. All Romans continued to live under Roman law. In every city the officers were the same as before. The same taxes were levied. The same shows were staged. In short, manners and customs were the same as when people were obedient to the sovereigns of Rome."[133]

Dubos did not stop at contrasting the image of a violent and bloody conquest with that of a peaceful settlement, however. He challenged the whole range of Boulainvilliers's contentions concerning the Franks' regime before and after their arrival in Gaul. He insisted that the Frankish monarchy had always been hereditary, and rejected the notion that the nobles had elected the king.[134] He showed that the Franks paid taxes under the sons of Clovis[135] and that the Merovingian kings wielded absolute authority over their subjects.[136] He maintained that some Franks had been slaves while others were free and that the free men formed a single order,[137] and he denied both that the only profession of free men was that of arms and that in Gaul after the arrival of the Franks only the Franks bore arms: Romans were also soldiers.[138] All this evidence provided further support for Dubos's central argument: that the Franks did not subjugate the Romans, who rather became subjects of the French monarchy. In so doing, the Romans retained the right to hold any employment; entered into marriages with the Franks, who quickly and adeptly mastered Latin; maintained the division of the population into three orders; and retained ownership of their land.[139]

Dubos thus refuted Boulainvilliers's identification of the nobility with the Franks and of the third estate with the Gauls. According to him, free Franks joined an already existing nobility without overturning the social structure that predated their arrival in Roman Gaul. Along with Roman law (and municipal law in particular), that social structure survived the arrival of the Franks. Furthermore, feudal rights did not originate in this period and could not therefore have been consecrated under Charlemagne. A much later development, these so-called rights were in fact a vast usurpation: the lords entrusted by the prince with the administration of territories within his power seized the opportunity afforded by a weakening of the monarchy to claim rights that legally belonged to the king alone. In so doing, they arbitrarily rewrote the laws for their own benefit and stripped the people of their freedom. "The old tribunals suffered the same fate as the old laws. Our usurpers arrogated to themselves the right to administer justice or else entrusted it to officers whom they nominated and removed as they saw fit. Finally, they asserted the right to levy both personal and real taxes at will. It was then that Gaul truly became a conquered land."[140]

Conflict therefore did not figure in Dubos's account as an effect of conquest. It emerged, rather, as a result of the institution of feudalism by a tyrannical and arbitrary nobility working to the detriment of both monarchy and people. In Dubos's eyes, moreover, this conflict was a social conflict devoid of ethnic coloration, because the two nations had merged and become one. They had begun to speak a common derivative of Latin, to dress in the same fashion, and to live under one law.[141] Nevertheless, the conflict between them had dangerous implications for France. "Not even experience could teach the inhabitants of Gaul to overcome those of their vices most inimical to the perpetuation of society, especially their natural flightiness and their haste to resort to arms and violence, which has so often caused them to fight when no real issue was at stake. These vices, which opened the gates of Gaul to the Romans and later delivered the country into the hands of the Barbarians, will always cause grave harm so long as the peoples of Gaul do not live under a sovereign with authority sufficient both to prevent them from destroying one another and to force them to live happily in the most beautiful country in Europe."[142]

The idea, introduced into French history by Boulainvilliers, of an enduring antagonism between the heirs of the Franks and the descendants of the Gauls was not laid to rest by Dubos's arguments. Dubos's reputation suffered from Montesquieu's criticism.[143] It suffered further from his insistence on the need for unity when the climate was one of conflict between nobility and third estate. Boulainvilliers's way of looking at things made it possible to think about this conflict in both historical-legal and political-polemical terms, the two modes being at times distinguished but frequently combined. In the historical-legal mode, writers from Boulainvilliers himself to Montesquieu, Mably, and Montlosier constructed "systems" that proposed solutions, presumably compatible with the alleged underlying factors, of such problems as the relation between the monarchy and representative institutions, the role of the *parlements*, and the legitimacy or illegitimacy of noble privileges.[144] In the political-polemical mode, the Gauls became symbols of the third estate and the Franks of the nobility. Writers speaking in the name of the third estate could thus identify that group with the nation as a whole and ask, as Sieyès did, why it did not dispatch "to the forests of Franconia all those families that cling to the absurd pretension of having sprung from a race of conquerors and of having inherited the rights of conquest? The Nation, thus purged, will be able to take consolation in being reduced to the belief that it consists solely of descendants of the Gauls and the Romans." The exclusionary principle in politics, which Boulainvilliers employed against the *noblesse de robe* and the third estate, was thus turned back against the nobility.[145] The idea of an enduring antagonism born of the Frankish conquest would thus serve throughout the Revolution to justify the exclusion of the nobility. From now on, a person could be French only if his or her ancestors were Gauls.[146]

Amédée Thierry and His Contemporaries

Writers primarily interested in the Gauls or the Celts generally stayed out of the controversy begun by Boulainvilliers. Prior to the Revolution, Pelloutier had nothing to say about it. Nor did La Tour d'Auvergne Corret later on, although he was careful to include the bards, the Druids, Ossian, the Breton peasants whose dress had remained unchanged for twenty centuries, and etymologies tracing words from various languages back to their roots in the "Celto-Breton of Armorica." As for relations between the Gauls and the Franks, the most plausible hypothesis, in his view, was that the Franks were the progeny of "one of the many colonies that Sigovese established in Germany." If so, he argued, "the Franks, in driving the Romans out of Gaul, were merely reclaiming their ancestors' ancient heritage, returning to their country of origin."[147] We thus come full circle back to the sixteenth century.

Jean Picot's book took a very different line. Picot, who prided himself on not giving in to the "credulity of ancient historians" and who took Gibbon as his model of critical scholarship, tried to eliminate traditional "fables" from his work.[148] He was interested not just in historical events but also in the climate and soil of Gaul and in what the country produced as well as in the physical and moral characteristics of the Gauls along with their diet, clothing, education, marriage and funeral customs, techniques of hunting and making war, government, religion, population, and wealth. As the titles of his treatises indicate, he did statistics as well as history. If La Tour d'Auvergne's book corresponds to the pre-romantic sensibility, Picot's was close to that of the *idéologues*.[149] He presents relations between the Gauls and the Franks in an imperial spirit, emphasizing the reconciliation of two formerly warring peoples. To be sure, the Gauls "were obliged to adopt some of the laws of the Franks, but their own influence was far greater than one might think. The advantages of number and enlightenment made themselves felt. These gave the conquered people a glorious ascendancy. The Franks unwittingly adopted most of their manners and customs. Before long, having truly become Gauls, they preserved virtually none of the qualities of the Franks who had once inhabited Germania, other than the name and the conquests."[150]

Perceptible in the Charter of 1814, this spirit of reconciliation was attacked by the ultras at the beginning of the Restoration—as evidenced, in our domain, by Montlosier's book[151]—and subsided rapidly after 1820. The liberal response was not long in coming. It consisted in a reaffirmation of the centrality, in the France of the present as well as of the past, of the conflict between the heirs of the Franks and the descendants of the Gauls. After invoking Boulainvilliers, Montlosier, and other "noble writers," Augustin Thierry affirmed "this somber and terrible truth: there are two enemy camps on the soil of France." Against the nobility, associated with "Chlodowig's Sicambrians," he insisted on his own ancestry: "We are the sons of the men of the third estate; the third estate emerged from the communes, and the communes were the asylum of the serfs; the serfs were the people vanquished in the conquest."[152] Meanwhile, Guizot proudly asserted "that since the beginning of our monarchy France has been troubled by a struggle between two peoples, and the revolution was simply the triumph of the new victors over the former masters of power and of the land." The two peoples in question were "Franks and Gauls, lords and peasants, nobles and commoners."[153]

It took just a few years for Guizot and Augustin Thierry to discover that this idea, if generalized, could render historical progress intelligible, both in France since the arrival of the Franks and in England since the Norman Conquest. Both Guizot and Thierry assumed that history has a direction: it moves from barbarism toward an ever more perfect civilization. In the political realm it tends to replace chaos with order, force with justice, arbitrariness with law, servitude with liberty, private will with public power. Both men saw the driving force behind this ascendant movement in the conflict between "social conditions" or "classes," each embodying its own way of exercising power and its own principle of legitimacy. There were in their view five such conditions or classes: royalty, clergy, nobility, bourgeoisie, and peasantry. Thus Guizot and Thierry introduced a major innovation in the study of the political life of the past: the idea that a nation, as subject and object of history, is not a unified, homogeneous entity personified by its king and court but a composite of various groups in conflict, whose antagonistic coexistence is a source of progress.[154]

Guizot and Thierry did not agree on every point. The latter, inclined to view all social conflict in the light of the Greek struggle for independence, emphasized the ethnic dimension, whereas Guizot stressed the "class struggle."[155] Still, both writers were interested in how nations, which by nature incorporated conflict, were formed out of groups differentiated primarily by ethnic characteristics. Conquest easily found its place in such a conceptual framework. It resulted in domination based on force alone, arbitrary domination for the benefit of private interests: such was the original form of aristocratic rule. Revolution also found its place: through it, a once subordinate class came to occupy a dominant position, with a concomitant change in the form of government and principle of legitimacy. It thus became possible, as Guizot showed in his lectures, to propose a synthetic overview of French and European history from the fall of the Roman Empire to the French Revolution. One could identify the true actors in this historical drama as well as grasp, beyond events themselves, the hidden mechanism that caused them to occur.[156]

In 1828, Amédée Thierry, Augustin's brother, published the *Histoire des Gaulois*, which between then and 1877 went through ten editions (one of which, the 1857, was reprinted four times), despite criticism by archaeologists in the 1860s.[157] Thierry's description of Gallic life found its way into the school curriculum. It was repeated by every writer on the subject, and there were a good many of them, most notably Henri Martin and Théophile Lavallée, whose books were widely disseminated.[158] Most of our graphical images of the Gauls, whether in painting or sculpture, with their horned or winged helmets crowned by tall, bushy plumes and their four-sided, multicolored shields, seem to have come from Thierry as well: "A wrought metal breastplate in the Greek or Roman style, or a coat of mail of Gallic invention; an enormous saber hanging by iron or copper chains beside the right thigh; sometimes a shoulder-harness gleaming with gold, silver, and coral, along with a gold necklace, bracelets, and rings encircling the arm and middle finger; breeches and cape in bright diamond patterns or magnificently embroidered; and, last but not least, a long reddish mustache: so we may imagine the military accoutrement of the Arvernian, Aeduan, or Biturigan noble of the second century B.C."[159]

For the nineteenth century, Amédée Thierry's book thus served as a reference book on the earliest periods of French history, and it so happens that the historical account it gives was based on the ideas of Augustin Thierry and Guizot. In transalpine and cisalpine Gaul, in Thrace, in Asia Minor, the Gauls abandoned the nomadic life in favor of a sedentary one. Thereupon they found themselves exposed to the influence of Greek civilization, which softened them and corrupted the purity of their way of life[160] but at the same time led them to renounce such savage customs as drinking from human skulls at banquets "honoring the conqueror and the victory of the nation." Thierry tells us that "such brutal and ferocious customs long held sway throughout Gaul. Civilization in its gradual advance slowly but surely did away with them. By the beginning of the second century, they were confined to the fiercest tribes of the north and west, where Posidonius found them flourishing still.... By the middle of the first century no trace of such barbarism remained anywhere in Gaul."[161]

In transalpine Gaul, to which the influence of Greek civilization was transmitted via Marseilles, the Gauls experienced two major political revolutions. Initially they lived under the rule of priests. This theocracy[162] was abolished by the tribal chieftains, who arrogated to themselves the political power they took from the Druids. But "if the aristocratic revolution benefitted Gaul, it was because it sowed the seeds of another, more salutary revolution. As cities grew in number and size, they created a unique people in an excellent position to understand and covet independence. And the people did in fact covet independence, and, encouraged by dissension among the leaders of the aristocracy, succeeded gradually in conquering it. A new principle and new forms of government were born inside city walls: popular election replaced the ancient privilege of heredity."[163] This was so in all the cities of the region, although "the constitutions that emerged from the popular revolution" varied according "to particular and local circumstances." The movement began in the east and south, where people were most susceptible to the influence of Greek civilization. "By the middle of the first century, it had already made itself felt throughout Gaul."[164] This account of the social history of the Gauls is obviously in many ways analogous to the history of the Middle Ages as it was presented in the time of Amédée Thierry, with the War of Investitures and the emancipation of the communes as central episodes.

Following this account, then, the Romans came to Gaul at a time when the center of gravity was in the process of shifting from rural villages to cities beginning to develop their own distinctive civilization.[165] To what extent were the inhabitants of this Gaul the ancestors of the French? In genealogical terms, "nineteen-twentieths" of the latter were descended from the former.[166] But for Amédée Thierry, the bond between the two peoples was far stronger. He defined it in terms of belonging to a single "race," a word that for him meant a temperament, a psychic character, a "moral type." To be sure, it was but a short step from the moral to the somatic, as is evident from a pamphlet on the "physiological characteristics of the human races" that was inspired by Thierry's book.[167] But Thierry himself was interested only in the "moral type," whose "salient traits," the defining characteristics of the "Gallic family," he summarized as follows: "A personal gallantry without equal among the ancient peoples. A frank, impetuous spirit open to all impressions, eminently intelligent; but also an extreme fickleness, a lack of constancy, a marked repugnance for the ideas of discipline and order that are so powerful among the Germanic races, a great deal of ostentation, and, last but not least, a perpetual disunity born of excessive vanity."[168] For Amédée Thierry it was the apparent permanence of these traits

FIGURE 1.6   *Gaul Invaded: The Franks;* illustrations by Raffin for Devinat and Toursel, *Histoire de France.*

1. Un chef, Clovis. — Où est le chef? *Sur bouclier ou pavois, c'est Clovis.* — Qui le porte? *Quatre guerriers francs, d'autres l'acclament, dire pourquoi.* — Armes des guerriers? *Angon ou lance à crochet, francisque, bouclier.* — Vêtements? *Toile, peaux.* — Visage? *Cheveux, moustaches.* — *Vont par bandes, deviendront maîtres de la Gaule.*

2. Les Francs pillards. — Où sont entrés les Francs? *Riche villa.* — Que font-ils? *Meurtre, pillage.* — Qu'emportent-ils? *Coffrets, belles étoffes, vases précieux.* — Que vont-ils en faire? *Partage.* — La Gaule n'éta t donc pas défendue? *Mal défendue, longue paix, peu de soldats, proie facile. La Gaule, pillée, ruinée, malheureuse.*

3. Les Francs cruels. — Que fait l'homme à cheval? *Regarde hutte en flammes.* — Pourquoi des soldats poussent-ils la porte? *Gens enfermés qu'ils empêchent de sortir.* — C'était Chramne, fils révolté du roi Clotaire. Son père le faisait brûler vif avec sa femme et ses enfants. — Que pensez-vous de ce roi franc? *Barbare, sans pitié.*

4. Le roi Dagobert. — *Cent ans après Clovis, Dagobert dans son palais; à ses côtés, évêque.* — Les habits du roi? *Comme anciens chefs romains; en outre, couronne.* — Geste? Pourquo ? *Un trône d'or.* — Saint Eloi avait reçu de l'or pour faire un trône; très habile et très honnête, il en avait fait deux; devint ministre de Dagobert.

that established a sort of psychological continuity between the Gauls and the French: the former were the ancestors of the latter in the sense that the Gauls bequeathed to the French their inner constitution, which in turn caused the French to feel a natural sense of solidarity with and sympathy for the Gauls.

Furthermore, Amédée Thierry recounted the Roman conquest from the point of view of the Gauls. He emphasized the unfortunate effects of Massalian policy, which culminated in an alliance between Rome and the Aedui, whom the Romans henceforth treated as friends and allies. "Thus were uttered for the first time in the history of the Gallic nations the words *allies, friends, brothers* of the Roman people, words of discord and ruin, fatal powers that would, for an entire century, isolate, sow conflict among, and weaken those nations, ultimately to reunite them all, without exception, in a common servitude."[169] This indignant and patriotic tone is particularly noticeable in the passages devoted to Vercingetorix, whose party is characterized as the "national party" and whose army was a "national army" serving the "national cause," the "cause of liberty."[170] As for Vercingetorix himself, this was the first time that he was portrayed in so clear and unambiguous a fashion as the defender of "Gaul's independence," the incontrovertible hero of the struggle against the Roman invaders, whose words in sending the cavalry to bring help to Alesia resounded "as the distress cry of the fatherland itself."[171] Had he not been alone in his struggle, he would have won. "If Comm the Atrebate, Virdumar, and Eporedorix had backed Vergesilaun's stubborn efforts; if the outer line toward the plain had been attacked as boldly as Vercingetorix attacked the inner line, Gaul would have been saved, and the name Caesar, which came to stand for danger to the peace and freedom of all nations, would have gone down in history alongside the names Crassus and Varus for the comfort of peoples and the everlasting terror of [would-be] conquerors."[172]

Thus there can be no doubt about Amédée Thierry's judgment of the Roman conquest. One problem remains, however, because Caesar, in conquering Gaul, brought not only Roman domination but also Roman civilization, which Thierry acknowledges to have been superior to that of the Gauls. The patriotic point of view thus conflicted with the philosophical. Which are we to choose, or, if no choice is to be made, how are we to reconcile the two? Guizot did not hesitate for a moment. In a remark worthy of Hegel, he indicated his preference for civilization: "When the imperial administration prevailed in Gaul, however bitter and legitimate the resentments and regrets of patriots may have been, it was surely more enlightened, more impartial, more preoccupied with general views and truly public interests than the former national governments had been."[173] As we have seen, Amédée Thierry preferred the patriotic point of view. But once the Gauls are defeated, he emphasizes the efforts by Caesar and his successors to win them over, along with "the taste for study in the upper classes and for agriculture in the people," which,

"encouraged by the government, absorbed the anxious energy of the Gallic character and miraculously eased the transition to the institutions of the conquest."[174]
While he sympathetically described every manifestation of Gallic resistance, he
nevertheless did not condemn the Gauls for participating in the cultural and political life of Rome. For him, Roman civilization, while not a value superior to national
independence, apparently compensated for its loss. For Gaul, caught between the
Romans and the Germans,[175] it was certainly better then a relapse into barbarism.

The Gauls Between the Romans and the Germans

The eighty years that elapsed between Amédée Thierry's *Histoire des Gaulois* and
Camille Jullian's *Histoire de la Gaule* witnessed an explosion of interest in the Gallic
and Gallo-Roman periods, several symptoms of which we have already mentioned.
There was, in particular, a rapid increase in knowledge. A rough estimate of that
increase can be made by comparing the three volumes of Thierry's work with the
four of Jullian's, paying attention not only to the relative lengths (Jullian's is
approximately three times as long) but also to the number of references to source
documents, maps, inscriptions, coins, and sculpted monuments (at least ten times as
many in Jullian as in Thierry). There is nothing surprising about this. Archaeology
was flourishing: the discipline had had its own journal since 1844, and Jules
Quicherat had been teaching it at the École des Chartes since 1847.[176] Many excavations were under way, most notably on Mount Beuvray (Bibracte) under the direction of Bulliot and de Déchelette[177] and at Alesia, initially from 1861 to 1865 under
the patronage of Napoleon III and, after 1906, at the behest of the Société des
Sciences Historiques et Naturelles of Semur.[178] Important works appeared in rapid
succession, including the *Dictionnaire archéologique de la Gaule* (1875–1878), produced by a committee appointed by Napoleon III in 1858, and Joseph Déchelette's
textbook, which is still in use today.[179]

Other "sciences ancillary to history" were by no means left behind: historical
geography produced the summa of Desjardins,[180] epigraphy contributed the volumes devoted to Gaul in the *Corpus Inscriptionum Latinarum* (after 1888), numis-
matics offered the work of Blanchet,[181] Espérandieu catalogued sculpted monuments,[182] and Henri Gaidoz's founding, in 1870, of the *Revue celtique* provided a
forum for reporting on the latest work in philology and linguistics.[183] Most of the
material thus made accessible referred to the period of Roman domination, but there
was also much more work than before that shed a new light on independent Gaul.

Even the situation in higher education was changing, at long last rendering
superfluous Henri Martin's bitter comments (quoted earlier) on France's neglect of
her ancient past. In a single year, 1882, Alexandre Bertrand began teaching courses
on French archaeology at the École du Louvre, and Héron de Villefosse did the

same at the École Pratique des Hautes Études, where he devoted most of his teaching on Roman epigraphy and antiquities to Gaul, while Arbois de Jubainville was elected to the chair of Celtic literature at the Collège de France.[184] In December 1905, Camille Jullian delivered an inaugural lecture for the chair in history and national antiquities at the Collège de France, in which he made a fervent appeal for cooperation between historians and archaeologists, for parallel study of texts and stones, documents and monuments: "A true national history must be constantly in touch with the soil that nourished men and the stones they erected upon it. To speak of the past without studying that soil and those stones is nothing less than to sever our history from its roots."[185]

During the eight decades in question, the Gallic and Gallo-Roman periods occupied an increasing portion of works treating the history of France in its entirety: from fifty-odd pages in Michelet (1834) to a hundred in Henri Martin's first edition (1833) to more than three hundred in the third edition (1844) and the fourth (1855), to a thick volume by Gustave Bloch (1911) in Lavisse's *Histoire*. Yet while everyone agreed that it was absolutely essential to include Gaul in any history of France, several issues remained controversial. Was there a genuine connection between Gaul and France? If so, what was its nature? And finally, what was the state of Gaul on the eve of the Roman conquest, and what were the effects of that conquest and of the Germanic invasions? The old problem of the Franks' relation to the Gauls and Gallo-Romans had survived, even if it was stated differently now from the way it had been a century before, and along with it subsisted the old division between "Germanists" and "Romanists."

Sismondi appears to have been the person who went the farthest in denying that there was any link between the history of France and the history of Gaul. "Two nations whose characters are dissimilar and whose institutions are absolutely different, the Gallic and the French, successively occupied the beautiful country that extends from the Alps and the Rhine to the Pyrenees and the two seas. The history of one is independent of that of the other; each is complete unto itself." To be sure, many French people were descendants of Gauls, and the "race" had not been completely made over. But the history of the Gauls did not merge seamlessly into the history of the French. The two were separated by "an interval of four centuries...during which the Gauls were merely a province of the Roman Empire, without a national spirit or government of their own, without a will or a life." Accordingly, the "true origin of the French people" was the final invasion of the barbarians on December 31, 406.[186]

This was the view against which, without saying so, Amédée Thierry was reacting. It represented an extreme position in a debate whose other extreme was defended by Henri Martin. I have already quoted the sentence with which Martin began the history he published in 1833. Eleven years later the opinion expressed there had evolved to this: "The people who first populated the center and west of Europe were the Gauls, our true ancestors; for their blood is by far the predominant element in the successive mixture of various peoples that formed our nation, and their spirit is still in us. Their virtues and their vices, preserved in the heart of the French people, along with the essential traits of their physical type, recognizable beneath the degeneration induced by a change of mores and a mingling of populations, still attest to that ancient origin."[187] For Martin, in other words, the French were still effectively Gauls, physically as well as morally. Politically, however, they were not Gauls, because the French were a nation, whereas the Gauls, having been a nation once, became captives of the Roman Empire. It was therefore necessary for the German barbarians to come and liberate them, thereby reviving the martial character and virtues of a people gone soft: the Germans were needed in order to "provide at last the mortar that would bind together the building blocks of French nationality."[188] It remains to be seen how Martin reconciled his view that the mingling of populations (associated with Thierry's idea of racial continuity) had been a source of degeneration with his belief in the progressive character of the French nation.

He surely took that belief from Michelet,[189] whose work also influenced other historians and archaeologists who studied Gaul, including Jules Quicherat, perhaps Fustel de Coulanges, and certainly Camille Jullian.[190] Michelet, though an adversary of the "tyrant" he saw in the Thierry brothers' "exclusive, systematic perpetuity-of-race viewpoint,"[191] was unwilling to go to the other extreme of assuming a radical discontinuity between Gaul and France. The French, he argued, were "mixed Celts,"[192] descendants not only of the Gauls but also of the Greeks, Romans, and Germans. All of these races, which had successively occupied the territory of Gaul, multiplying there and superimposing their distinctive contributions, were simply "elements," "living components," without which the French nation could not have become what it was yet which by themselves were incapable of constituting France. Before the nation could come into being, these elements had to be subjected to "internal processing," or self-transformation. "The process or series of changes that our fatherland underwent in the course of transforming itself—that is the subject of the history of France."[193]

For Michelet, then, there was continuity in the history of France, for the French nation was present virtually from the first, internalizing and assimilating what came to it from outside and building its own body from what it took in. But there was also discontinuity, for in so doing France revealed its latent potential, transformed itself, and changed its identity yet remained the same, just as an acorn changes its identity yet remains the same when it becomes an oak, to borrow a Hegelian—and quintessentially Gallic—metaphor used by Michelet himself.[194] In the beginning were the Celts, with their clannish spirit, their "warrior's resistance to discipline," their disunity and self-regard—in short, their "barbarian and bellicose chaos," which the

Druids and "men of the oaks" never managed to master.[195] In order to rescue Gaul from "the ebb and flow of barbarism," some outside element was needed, and this came first from Greece, later from Rome.[196] It was Rome that brought organization, administration, and urban life to Gallic soil. If, moreover, the Celtic element survived in the French language and therefore also "in customs as well as language, in action as well as thought,"[197] it did so only within the framework of Roman organization, whose power proved such that even as "the barbarians seemed on the verge of destroying it, they would be subjected to its force in spite of themselves. Like it or not, they would have to dwell beneath invincible vaults that they could not shake. Vanquishers though they were, they would nevertheless bow their heads and accept the law of defeated Rome." Among the fundamental tenets of that law, which Rome had implanted in French soil, was the "idea of equality under one monarch, so contrary to the aristocratic principle of Germania." Taken up by the Church, preserved in popular traditions, revived by Charlemagne and Saint Louis, this idea would slowly but surely lead to the "abolition of the aristocracy, to equality, to the equity of Modern Times."[198]

The Roman conquest established order and unity in Gaul. This order and this unity were "external," to be sure, "and material," capable of subduing "the obstinate discord of heterogeneous elements" only by force,[199] yet their effects left a lasting stamp on French institutions, just as Celtic traditions left a lasting stamp on French individuals. In other words, Michelet disputed Amédée Thierry's contention that the Gauls were a nation before the Roman conquest. On this point Fustel de Coulanges sided with Michelet: "The Gauls were not a nation; they were no more unified politically than they were racially. They did not possess a system of public institutions and practices capable of forging them into a single body. They were roughly sixty tribes not united by any federal bond, higher authority, or even a clear idea of a common fatherland. The only kind of patriotism they were capable of knowing was love of the tiny state of which each of them formed a part."[200]

The Gallic heritage, Fustel argued, remained visible in the pattern of land use in France, in territorial divisions, in the location of urban centers, and in the persistence of local allegiances: "Three-quarters of our French cities are former Gallic cities. Until fairly recently, moreover, these *civitates* retained their ancient boundaries. The *pagi* or *pays* [rural regions] still exist, and the memories and affections of rural people remain firmly attached to them. Neither the Romans nor the Germans nor feudalism destroyed these living units, whose very names have come down to us through the ages."[201] In the age of the Gauls, however, these local loyalties created divisions and conflicts between and within tribes, and these were the primary source of the disorder responsible for the weakness of Gaul and its inability to resist first the Cimbri and, later, Ariovistus. To resist an invasion, Fustel insists, individual courage is not enough. Nations are defended only by the strength of their public institutions and social discipline.[202] Although he was speaking of Gaul before the Roman conquest, he was thinking of post-1871 France, where he believed dissension and conflict were present dangers.

Clearly these patriotic and philosophical views were very different from, not to say incompatible with, those of Amédée Thierry discussed above. In this area, Michelet followed Guizot, although Michelet believed even more strongly that the progress of civilization coincided with the formation of the French nation, which led to the position that the Roman conquest was both an ordeal and a blessing: violent and cruel, it was nevertheless necessary for civilization to progress to the next higher phase, resuming its steady march toward history's ultimate goal, France, the embodiment of the universal. In contrast to Amédée Thierry, for whom an independent Gaul was almost an end in itself, Michelet saw it exclusively as a stage in the development of France. He accordingly absolved the Roman conquest in the name of reason, even though his heart remained Celtic. And he treated Roman Gaul the same way: once Gaul, along with the rest of the Empire, fell into decadence, the invasions became necessary so that the barbarians might regenerate the country with new blood, albeit at great cost in devastation, brutality, and a temporary regression of civilization.

Wary of romantic myths and visions, historians born around 1830 had good reason, concerning Gaul and other matters, to trust more in archaeology than in poetry and to repudiate their elders' fascination with the barbarians.[203] The defeat of 1871 further accentuated this tendency to regard the Roman conquest as qualitatively different from the German invasions. Thus, according to Fustel, the Romans, by bringing order and discipline, literally saved Gaul from a relapse into barbarism, which would have been the consequence of rule by Ariovistus and his allies. The Romans made Gaul into a "substantial and solid body" and enabled its inhabitants to gain access to civilization and in that sense to become Romans without relinquishing their Gallic identity. The inhabitants of Gaul were intelligent enough to take advantage of this opportunity. Therefore "one should not say that the Romans civilized Gaul, cultivated it, turned forest into farmland, drained the swamps, built roads, and erected temples and schools. Rather, one should say that under Roman rule, and thanks to the peace and security it secured, the Gauls became farmers, built roads, toiled, and, as a result of that toil, came to know wealth and luxury. Guided by the Roman spirit and by laudable imitation of what was best, they erected temples and schools."[204]

Unlike the Roman conquest, the Germanic invasions, as Fustel saw them, were spread out over several centuries and took various forms involving "slow infiltration, one at a time, by individuals and small groups." They did not immediately transform the country or establish anything new.[205] In advancing this view Fustel was close to Dubos and still closer to Guizot, who argued that "the invasions were essentially limited, local, sporadic events." But Guizot took up one of

Montesquieu's themes with his assertion that "the Germans brought us the spirit of liberty,"[206] an idea that Fustel rejected. In his view, the Germans as such brought nothing at all: not new blood or a new language or a new religion or private law or novel institutions. The Germanic invasion had the effects that an invasion by any people would have had. It disrupted the normal functioning of society and influenced its evolution, but "it did not result in the supplanting, on Gallic soil, of the

FIGURE 1.7   The statue of Vercingetorix rides in an automobile; cover of the illustrated supplement to *Le Petit Journal* (December 22, 1901).

Gallo-Roman character and spirit by a Germanic character and spirit."[207] Thus Fustel saw the Germanic invasions as a side episode, an important one, to be sure, but comparable to others, whereas the Roman conquest, which brought about a synthesis of the Roman spirit with the Gallic spirit, was a unique act, nothing less than the founding act of the history of France, the effects of which would continue to be felt in the modern era.

This view of the matter never enjoyed unanimous support. Opposition came not only from "Germanists" but also from the fact that independent Gaul could always claim some champions, who felt that the Roman conquest had violently imposed foreign rule.[208] Between 1871 and 1914, however, this position appears to have been in the minority. It was expressed in writings intended for the general public and especially during festivities honoring Vercingetorix where subtleties would have been out of place, but it appears to have been missing from academic historiography. Academic writers were rather inclined to argue that the Roman victory over the champions of Gallic independence was not only a lesser evil, as Amédée Thierry implied, but actually a boon for Gaul and hence that there was no reason to grieve over it: "When I see everything that we owe to Rome,...when I realize that the language I speak is virtually its language...[and] that I have taken from Rome so many feelings and ideas along with a particular cast of mind and way of judging things, qualities of which I am proud as well as defects to which I am as attached as I am to my qualities, and that, in short, I am almost as much a Roman as I am a Gaul, I confess...that it is impossible for me to feel annoyed with Caesar and that the defeat of our forefathers seems to me not something to be greatly deplored."[209]

FIGURE 1.8   Gallic warrior's costume; Paris, Musée de l'Armée.

These words of Gaston Boissier's were echoed five years later by the judgment of Camille Jullian: "Gaul had no alternative but to choose between two dominations. By ridding it of Germans, even at the price of its liberty, Rome rescued it from barbarism and may have saved its race and its historical existence."[210] It should therefore come as no surprise that in 1915, *Pro Alesia,* the "journal of the Alise excavations and of questions concerning Alesia," which, though it strove to maintain a tone of scientific neutrality, was also the journal of the cult of Vercingetorix, which flourished in what Salomon Reinach called the "holy shrine of Gaul,"[211] changed its orientation and became a "Gallo-Roman journal." Here is the crucial passage in the editorial justifying this decision: "At stake in the struggle between Vercingetorix and Caesar was the very future of Gaul. Had victory bestowed its favors on the Gauls, Gaul might have remained, as Germania did after the Varus disaster, outside the Roman Empire for several more centuries. The defeat of Vercingetorix was poignant and painful, but its consequences were incalculable. Out of it Roman Gaul was born."[212] Less than a century earlier, Amédée Thierry, steeped in patriotic principles, had also pondered the consequences that might have ensued had the Gauls won: the tribes of Gaul, he believed, would have lived in freedom. Patriotic principles were still at work now, but hatred of Germany had intervened to produce the belief that the effects of a Gallic victory would have been uniformly negative, so that one now rejoiced in the fact that such a victory had not taken place and bestowed equal admiration on Vercingetorix, the soul and conscience of Gaul, and Caesar, who had forged its body and its strength.

Camille Jullian and His *History of Gaul*

Published between 1907 and 1926, Camille Jullian's *Histoire de la Gaule* was the realization of an ambition that its author had conceived in 1873, when as a student in his next-to-last year of high school, he received Amédée Thierry's *Histoire des Gaulois* as a prize, read it, and resolved to rewrite that history in his own way.[213] He therefore made his book a compendium of all the research, all the thinking, and all the controversies concerning Gaul and its inhabitants not just since the publication of Thierry's book but since they first entered the historical arena. Jullian's prodigious erudition, reflected in his notes, gives the impression that he had read, scrutinized, and carefully weighed every line written on his subject in antiquity, the Middle Ages, and modern times. It would be impossible in the space available to do justice to a summa which, taken as a whole, remains unsurpassed even today, even though certain points must of course be rejected, corrected, or revised in light of more recent work.[214] I shall therefore confine my remarks to a discussion of Jullian's positions on some of the controversial issues discussed above.

Before turning to that task, however, I must mention how strikingly original the *Histoire de la Gaule* was compared with the historical literature of its day. Jullian was in fact the first French historian to challenge, both in his statements of intention and in his practice, the dogma that history is based on the interpretation of texts (which he took to mean texts *alone*). Jullian wrote history based on the evidence of earth and stone as well. Immediately impressed by Vidal de La Blache's *Tableau de la France*, to which he devoted courses in 1905–1906 and 1906–1907,[215] Jullian began his great book with a sort of tableau of Gaul: a description of its structure, of its situation in the ancient world, and of the nature and aspect of its terrain. Similar chapters, imbued with the Vidalian spirit, can also be found in other volumes.[216]

Jullian's history was thus associated with geography. It was also connected with archaeology and above all with prehistory, within limits defined by the available documentation. Priority was given to written sources: texts, inscriptions, and legends on coins. But Jullian also derived whatever information he could from figurative monuments and everyday objects such as tools, artifacts, and weapons.[217] Last but not least, Jullian raised sociological questions (and here one senses the influence of Fustel): he was interested in tribes and clans, in political institutions and social organization, in the family and the nation. In short, his history aimed at reconstructing the past in all areas to which the sources granted access. "For history," he wrote, "is a portrait or narrative of what human actions produce. Everything that emanates from man, from his will, his intelligence, and his sentiments, is within the

FIGURE 1.9 Monument to the dead; Boën, Loire.

FIGURE 1.10   Monument to the dead; Barbizon, Seine-et-Marne.

historian's domain.... Hence any monument, whatever its nature and no matter how small, everything that man planned in his mind and shaped with his hand, everything that he set down on the soil of France, ought to find a place in a chapter of our national history. And from the moment the mark of man's thought and man's hand first appears on a piece of flint, the historian has the duty to intervene. Arrows, dolmens, and painted caves are as much his business as the Acropolis, Notre-Dame of Paris, or the Maison Carrée."[218]

The *Histoire de la Gaule* was the realization of this program. But it was also (and in this respect by no means exceptional) the work of a patriot and, indirectly, of an ideological and political conjuncture. Such factors cannot be neglected, especially when it comes to subjects as delicate and controversial as the state of Gaul before the Roman conquest and the effects of that conquest. On both of these matters Jullian staked out new ground. The central axis of the history of Gaul during the half-millennium between the arrival of the Celts and that of Caesar was, he argued, the formation of the Gallic nation, which led it to adopt a political organization. The Gauls, he argued, had the idea of a common fatherland and referred to themselves by a single name. If they were divided into tribes, those tribes were linked by language and commercial exchanges, by alliances and relations of domination, and by "a community of traditions, institutions, teachings, and hopes" that were kept alive in "periodic gatherings around gods, priests, and common sanctuaries."[219] All the elements of a "national fraternity" were therefore present. The destiny imposed on Gaul by the configuration of its terrain and the dreams of its inhabitants was to form "a single empire, similar to those that had come into being in the vast natural regions of the oriental world."[220] Jullian did not neglect the forces that worked against this unifying tendency. He analyzed them at length in geographic and political terms.[221] Nevertheless, he claimed to have shown that the Arverni were ideally placed to undertake the unification of Gaul. His analysis thus provided an explanation for the emergence of the "Arverni Empire" during Hannibal's wars in the late third century B.C. During the next century "the Arverni acquired most of Celtic and Belgian Gaul." Of course this was not a "compact state with homogeneous parts obedient to a very powerful sovereign." The bonds that tied the various Gallic tribes to it "were necessarily diverse and variable."[222] The "Arverni Empire" nevertheless represented the first historical incarnation of Gallic unity, as well as incorporating "the seeds of a fruitful entente and progressive fusion."[223]

All this was destroyed by the Romans sixty years before Caesar. It was destroyed in the first place by arms, when the legions that came to defend Marseilles defeated the Arverni king Bituit, thereby reducing part of Gaul to a colony and eventually a province of Rome. And it was destroyed thereafter by Roman policy, which favored the municipal nobility by abolishing kingship among the Arverni, thus undermining their domination of Gaul. Rome also served its own interests by awarding favorable treatment to certain tribes, allowing anarchy to smolder: "In this way, through favors still more pernicious than violence, Rome completed the destruction of Gaul's unity."[224] The decline of Gallic civilization and the "moral poverty" of Gaul by the time of Caesar's arrival were thus the fruit of the Romans' own efforts, as was the Gauls' inability to defend themselves first against the Cimbri and the Teutons and later against Ariovistus' Germans—an inability that the Romans invoked to justify their conquest.[225]

Unlike Amédée Thierry, Jullian denied that a Gallic nation existed on the eve of Caesar's arrival, and what Thierry characterized as a "popular revolution" Jullian saw as nothing more than a Roman machination. Unlike Michelet and Fustel, however, he argued that the anarchy that Gaul exhibited at the time was not a result of the Gallic character but a recent development due to deleterious influence from the outside. His view of the Roman conquest and his judgment of its evolution and effects point up what he regarded as essential in the history of independent Gaul, namely, its incomplete development as a nation. It was the Romans' violent interruption of Gaul's national development that marked the beginning of the conquest. In fact, it was more than the beginning: after the defeat of Bituit and the creation of a Roman province, the conquest was already half completed.[226] Caesar had only to carry it through to its conclusion. In order to do so, however, he had to contend with what was left of national sentiment among the Gauls, a national sentiment fed by memories of lost unity. The cooperation of the Gallic tribes and the choice of Vercingetorix as supreme commander were possible only thanks to that residual national sentiment and the memories that sustained it. "In this crisis, which would decide its future, Gaul reverted to the old forms of its national life, and, as in the previous century, it was the king of the Arverni who put himself forward as its champion before the Roman people."[227]

To Jullian the facts of the matter were thus clear: Vercingetorix represented both the memory and the dream of a "free, united, and powerful" Gallic fatherland,[228] and in the confrontation with Caesar he alone deserves sympathy and admiration. Jullian makes this point unambiguously: "Between Caesar and [Vercingetorix] I have no hesitation: [Vercingetorix] was the true hero."[229] He says this without anxiety at the thought that his hero might actually have won, for he now repudiated, as we have just seen, his old argument that the Romans had saved Gaul from Germanic barbarism. Jullian avoids hypotheticals, but he probably believed that if Vercingetorix had won, a "free, united, and powerful" Gaul would have been in a position to defend itself against all its enemies. In short, in narrating this episode in the history of Gaul, Jullian plainly and unequivocally championed the Gallic cause. In his view no mitigating circumstance lessened the crime of the Romans, not even the superiority of their civilization, and Caesar embodied two kinds of oppression, of the Romans themselves and of the peoples he conquered in their name, as was symbolized by the deaths, three months apart, of Cato and Vercingetorix.[230] In later volumes on Gallo-Roman civilization Jullian would stress the positive aspects of Rome's effort in Gaul, but he became more critical in dealing with the Late Empire. In the general conclusion, he insisted on the harm that the Roman Conquest did to Gaul:[231] "If Domitian and Caesar had not come, a great nation would have completed its formation on the ground, where it would have cut a noble figure." Starting from a fascination with Rome and its civilization, so evident in *Gallia,* Jullian ultimately came, in the *Histoire de la Gaule,* to regard the national interest of the Gauls as the only valid criterion. It would take a more detailed analysis to gauge the relative importance of the various factors contributing to this change of attitude: objective data (one generally speaks of Augustan Rome differently from the empire in decline), the evolution of Jullian's own opinions, and changes in the ideological and political climate in which he wrote, owing first and foremost to the First World War.

From a Genealogical Issue to an Object of Memory

The *Histoire de la Gaule* marked the end of an era. From the 1920s the Gauls were no longer a fixture of the common culture, widely represented in art, literature, and publications aimed at the general public. Even archaeology gave up on them: the Bibracte excavations, halted after Déchelette's departure in 1907, would not be resumed until 1984, and *Pro Alesia* ceased publication in 1932, although Toutain bucked the tide to continue exploration of the site. Politicians also turned their backs on the Gauls, except for an occasional mention, usually by orators of the far right, and of course Vichy's abortive attempt to bring them back into the limelight. Only the schools kept the faith. The Gauls thus apparently went into eclipse until Astérix and his friends revived interest in them. But the kind of interest they now attract seems profoundly different from the kind of interest they aroused in the past: the great issues of national identity, which were central to almost every work on the subject from the sixteenth century up to and including the writings of Camille Jullian, are no longer framed in terms of France's relation to Gaul. The Gauls are irrelevant. It is the very notion of national identity that has changed in essential ways since the beginning of the twentieth century.

At that time people believed that national identity was based on a hereditary national character that was assumed to be connected with certain equally hereditary physical peculiarities. In other words, national identity was based on "race," in both its psychological and physical senses. Questions of national identity were therefore posed in terms of kinship relations between nations and hence also of heredity. They concerned the length of time that a particular people had been settled on the land it now occupied—a land that was supposed to have contributed to shaping its collective consciousness and behavior. They also concerned the place that each people's ancestors had occupied in the history of Europe and of the world and the rights that that place was supposed to justify. To be sure, nationalist ideology, which invokes (sometimes implicitly) blood and soil, still rears its head from time to time in the form of outbursts of racism and xenophobia. It has nevertheless become marginal. National identity is today held to be based on cultural continuity, where culture is understood as both a semiotic and a material fact, whose continuity is ensured by the transmission of works of the past understood in the broadest possible sense, together with the models and examples they contain, and combined with the knowledge necessary to understand, preserve, and reproduce them and add to their repertoire. Hence the problems that national identity raises are nowadays stated in terms not of genealogy but of memory.

One result of this is that our attitude toward "our ancestors the Gauls" has become rather ironical. Another is that, while we are no longer interested in a supposed kinship between the inhabitants of pre-Roman Gaul and the French population today, we are interested in how these alleged Gallic origins are reflected in our national traditions. What effects did the Gallic past have, and what role did it play? This has led to looking at the Gauls themselves in new ways. Some current archaeological investigations are focused on their sanctuaries and rituals, while others attempt to assess the importance in their lives of hunting and husbandry, of war and weaponry, of trade, of metalworking, and of agriculture. Still other scholars are working to understand the Gauls' sense of space and social organization. All this work is aimed at demystifying the Gauls and restoring them to their rightful place in the history of France, which is a religious and cultural as well as a social and economic history.[232] The "return of the Gauls" that has apparently been going on for some time now[233] is thus very different from earlier returns. This time it is not so much the Gauls themselves who are coming back as it is France's Gallic memory, which is becoming a subject of historical and intellectual investigation. My purpose in the pages that remain is to understand the nature and function of that memory.

France's Gallic memory is a memory of long duration. Having been in continuous existence since Caesar's publication of the *Gallic Wars*, it is the longest-lived of France's historical memories. None of the predecessors of the Gauls left evidence sufficient to enable us to pierce their anonymity. For some fifteen centuries, the *Gallic Wars* and a few works of lesser importance were all there was to preserve the memory of the Gauls and assure them of a place in history. In the sixteenth century, narratives concerning the Gauls proliferated, incorporating various ancient testimony along with modern fables. Research on Gallic relics began tentatively in the seventeenth century and was carried on more systematically in the eighteenth century. The nineteenth century began to portray them in images, to set them to music and on the stage, to write about them in poems and novels. These constitute the principal stages in the evolution of France's memory of the Gauls. Each later stage superimposed itself on its predecessors and exerted a retroactive influence: owing to historical criticism and archaeology, our reading of Caesar is different from what it would have been a century ago, just as the visual images of that time differ from images of the Gauls that we are nowadays prepared to accept as accurate.[234]

Envisioned over five centuries, the history of France's Gallic memory is first of all the history of the growth in the number of texts and objects supposed to embody that memory. This is so despite the elimination of texts and objects that failed to withstand ever more rigorous standards of critical scrutiny. It is also the history of a qualitative diversification of the whole body of texts and objects dealing with the Gauls, a history of successive classifications and distinct hierarchizations. This, meanwhile, went hand in hand with an increasing specialization of those in charge of preserving and studying those texts and objects. It is, furthermore, the history of an ever wider diffusion of historical knowledge and legends concerning the Gauls, all of it brought within reach of the entire population through compulsory schooling and inexpensive books. Last but not least, it is the history of the changing function and status of the Gallic theme within French national memory.

Careful scrutiny shows that these changes did not come about in a uniform way. One can identify four periods during which interest in the Gauls was particularly intense, and these periods stand out from stretches of relative indifference: they are the end of the fifteenth and beginning of the sixteenth century; the second half of the sixteenth century; the end of the eighteenth and beginning of the nineteenth century; and the eight decades from the late 1820s to 1914, with two brief periods of particular intensity whose effects were cumulative, the first around mid-century, the second after 1870. Now, each of these periods corresponds to a particularly grave moment in French history: the end of the struggle between the Armagnacs and the Burgundians, which coincided with and helped to fuel the Anglo-French war; the Wars of Religion, which were coupled with war with Spain; the final years of the Revolution and the Empire, during which conflict between proponents of the Old and New Regimes continued unabated, while France was at war with all of Europe; the social struggles of 1848 and the Commune and the two wars with Germany. Only the last thirty years, symbolized by Astérix, appear not to fit the pattern, which is probably related to the fact that the Gallic theme is now dealt with at one remove, in either a burlesque or a reflective mode.

It is by examining these periods one after another that we have been able to perceive the changes in the function and status of the Gallic theme. At the outset it figured in a myth of ethnic origin that was at first associated with and later supplanted the Trojan myth; in this form it played a unifying role. The Franks and the Gauls were considered to be two branches of a single family, and the Franks' entry into Gaul was portrayed as a homecoming. Within this broad family the king of France occupied the place of the father and the nobles occupied the place of elder brothers, whose superiority, immediately perceived as natural, needed no justification. As French society transformed itself from a society of orders into a society of classes (the very word *class* first came into use at the end of the seventeenth century), the legitimacy of noble privileges became a subject of controversy. There were only two ways to legitimate such privileges: as recompense for services rendered to the monarchy or as prizes won in open combat in the remote past and passed down through the generations.

The attempt to justify noble privileges as the spoils of conquest by identifying nobles with Franks and commoners with Gauls altered the function of the Gallic theme: a unifying myth based on ethnic origins gradually gave way to an ideology that articulated and justified social conflict. Despite efforts to restore the original function of the Gallic theme, the pitting of Gauls against Franks, of the vanquished against their vanquishers, served, from the beginning of the eighteenth century to the end of the Second Empire and beyond, as a way of thinking about the confrontation within French society between the nobility and the Third Estate, the aristocracy and the bourgeoisie. "It was born with class antagonism and grew as class antagonism grew."[235]

The Gauls were not pitted solely against the Franks, however. They were also involved in struggle with the Romans on the one hand and the Germans on the other. This was how they were seen first by antiquarians, readers of ancient texts, and collectors of ancient objects, and later by archaeologists, who turned the national past into an object of science, and historians, who increasingly relied on the results of archaeological research. Unlike the "class" conflict between the Gauls and the Franks, the triangular struggle among Gauls, Romans, and Germans set nation against nation. In the eighteenth century, however, no clear distinction was made between the two. It was only after the Revolution that a definitive line would be drawn: the Franks and the Gauls were two groups within a single nation, whereas the Gauls confronted the Romans (or the Germans) as two distinct, enemy societies. After the middle of the nineteenth century, and especially after 1870, the antagonism between Gauls and Germans became the dominant theme, a change accompanied by yet another change in its status and function.

The status of the Gallic theme changed because now it was supposed to be the role of historical science to prove that these two nations had always been hostile to each other. Its function changed because from the mid-nineteenth century until 1914 the idea of everlasting Gallo-German hostility served to unify France in the face of a threat from outside. Thus the Gallic theme was restored to its original role, except that now its function was to unify not a monarchy but a nation. To be sure, the national bond was reduced by some to a matter of "race"—a dangerously ambiguous term at first that later became sinisterly unambiguous—or "blood," which opened the door to all kinds of abuses. In particular, some French men and women were excluded from the nation on the pretext that they were French only in appearance and not in essence, that essence being defined of course by "race" or "blood."

More recently, however, a broad consensus has held that nationality and culture are inseparable. Indeed, it was the identification of national bonds with cultural community that would emerge victorious from World War II.

Enlisted initially in the class struggle and later in the struggle between nations, the Gauls served in every war in which Frenchmen confronted other Frenchmen or foreign enemies. Now, however, they are free to become what they are: from mythological self-mockery to object of research, a unique and central *lieu de mémoire* of the nation France.

FIGURE 1.11 Late nineteenth century advertisement for "Gallic Elixir."

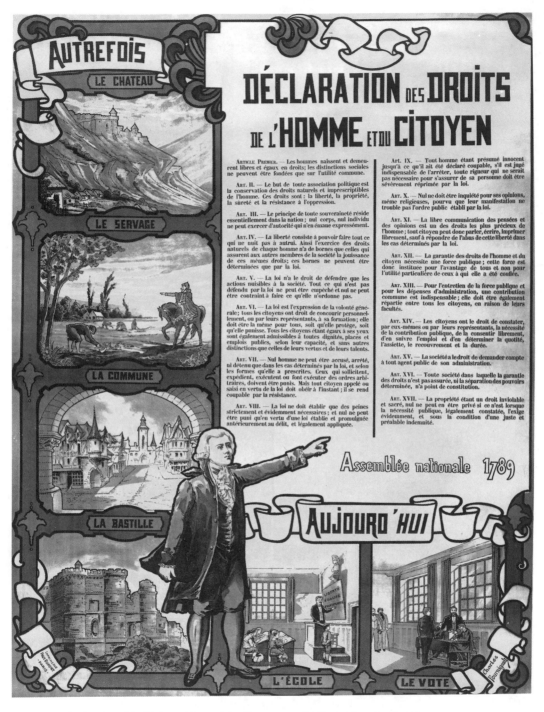

FIGURE 2.0 *Declaration of the Rights of Man and the Citizen;* poster by Charles Fournigault, 1905.

CHAPTER 2

The Ancien Régime and the Revolution

François Furet

If the French Revolution lies at the root of the political civilization in which we still live today, two hundred years after it appeared on the historical scene, it is primarily because the Revolution wanted it that way. Through the voices of its principal actors and the actions of a people, it thought of itself as a foundational event, a memorable occurrence if ever there was one: the regeneration of humanity through individual liberty at long last won from the hoary powers of oppression. The past that preceded it was nothing but an "Ancien Régime," a lapidary definition that erased from the national memory everything that came before, feudalism and monarchy alike. The Revolution thus occupied the whole space of history as the necessary instrument of its redemption. Henceforth there would be nothing but the Revolution itself to commemorate, honor, or celebrate, as if continually to ward off the return of what it abolished.

In order to measure how much this ambition—upon which Burke offers the most profound commentary—shook things up, we must restore its strangeness, which was to unite history with reason: the Revolution sought to reinstitute society in the manner of Rousseau, that is, to regenerate man through a veritable social contract. This universal ambition was akin in its abstraction to a religious message but different in its content, since regeneration was now without a transcendent foundation of any kind, and indeed claimed to take the place of transcendence. In the French Revolution not only was the religious distinct from the political, but there was a transfer of function from one to the other. The Church had given its hand to the monarchy, and it paid the price. More profoundly, the Revolution, quite apart from its effects on institutions, delivered human action from its subjection to higher authority of any kind, granting man full sovereignty over the ultimate ends of history: the revolutionary investment in the political thereby invaded the realm of the religious, replacing divine reward with its own earthly promise. Conversely, Catholic tradition became the bulwark of the Counterrevolution. It was this philosophical radicality that was the most profound characteristic of the French Revolution, the feature that distinguished it from both the English and the American Revolution.

The English Revolution of the mid-seventeenth century saved the nation from the corruption of the monarchy but did so in the name of the Holy Bible and Anglo-Saxon liberties. Finally, in 1688, the replacement of the old dynasty by a new one founded a durable regime based on a return to religion and tradition. A century later, just prior to the French earthquake, the American Revolution did indeed begin a new nation, but independence was acquired in the name of the inextricably religious and political values of the original immigrants, indeed as the faithful fulfillment of their wishes.

In order to understand, by contrast, the unique historical character of the French tabula rasa, one can still follow Tocqueville's inspiration and begin with the American event. Consider, for instance, how the insurgents of the Thirteen Colonies conceived of their own past. To do this, let us look at two relatively early texts in the history of the American Revolution, John Adams's *Dissertation on the Canon and the Feudal Law* (1765) and Thomas Paine's *Common Sense* (1776). Adams and Paine—the two names more or less mark the limits of the political scene of the time, on the right and on the left.[1]

Adams based his thinking on an idea of human history taken from Scottish philosophy: as man gains enlightenment, he moves from a barbarous social state to subservience to arbitrary rule before arriving at a form of government in which his freedom can flourish. This sequence, perfectly exemplified by English history, is in conformity with human nature and reason as God constituted them. Adams's thought thus combined the theme of English liberties with a providential model of history, a reconciliation through God of the particular and the universal. From the outset, the American version of English history was more universalist than the original.

In fact, there was an "old regime" in England. The words are not found in Adams but the thing is: it was inherent in the combination of canon and feudal law that was characteristic of medieval England. Although many forms of tyranny existed in the epoch separating barbarism from liberty, none was so miserable as the combination of spiritual and temporal oppression, at once clerical and aristocratic. Spiritual oppression availed itself of God's name to bestow absolute power on the Roman clergy, which sustained its rule through a carefully perpetuated obscurantism. Temporal oppression grew out of the domination of the barbarian populations by warriors and their chieftains. From this came vassalage among lords and servitude among the people. This period of darkness, during which freedom, enlightenment, and virtue all were trodden under foot, lasted until the Reformation: "From the Reformation to the first American settlement, Enlightenment gradually spread through Europe, especially in England. And with this progress, ecclesiastic and civil tyranny, that is canon law and feudal law, seem to have lost their strength and influence."[2] Eventually there was rebellion against both forms of tyranny under the reign of the "execrable" Stuarts.

It was this rebellion, this combat, that brought people to America. The Puritans who crossed the Atlantic, fleeing persecution for their love of enlightenment and their spirit of free inquiry, came to the New World to establish a civil and religious society that was the exact opposite of the clerical and aristocratic tyranny they left behind: it was a society led by men of learning, faithful to both the great lawgivers of antiquity and the teachings of Christ and in conformity with both reason and revolution. In the ecclesiastical sphere the Puritans destroyed the episcopal hierarchy, dispelled the ridiculous superstitions in which that hierarchy shrouded its power, and thus established an enlightened, virtuous clergy independent of the temporal power. In the civil realm they knew that "government is a thing without mystery, simple and comprehensible, founded in nature and reason and within reach of common sense."[3] They wanted nothing to do with the dependency of one individual upon another, such as had existed even in the democracies of antiquity but above all in the feudal regime. They established a government of free men, which for Adams was not the same thing as a republic, for a king was necessary, as were priests, as a brake upon the power of the people. And just as the founding of the American colonies was a consequence of the Enlightenment, so, too, was the Enlightenment responsible for an extraordinary improvement in the education of the people, a necessary prerequisite for the preservation of public as well as individual liberties.

As for the conflict with England, which formed the context of Adams's pamphlet, the reason for it was none other than the political and cultural gap separating the mother country from her American colonies. Seventeenth-century England had indeed been the theater of the great historical struggle between the "old regime" and liberty, but the country had been unable or unwilling to continue that struggle to the end. Upon the ruins of Catholicism it had reinstated a hierarchical church led by an archbishop with ties to the state. It had replaced the Stuart dynasty with another ruling family, faithful at first to the contract of 1688. But the Hanoverians had revealed their intention to return their subjects, the Americans first of all, to their former state of slavery. Why? Because the systems of canon and feudal law, "though largely undermined in England, are not yet destroyed." Traces of the old laws remained, and with them, the spirit of domination they embodied. The proof of this was George III's determination to rule America in that spirit.

Not only was there no "old regime" in the colonies, but the colonies must fight to keep from being contaminated by one, for that absence was their chief distinction, the very essence of their identity. In fact, the English Revolution of the seventeenth century had nothing like an "old regime" in the French sense either, since it was shaped in part by the biblical spirit and in part by memories of the Magna Carta. But John Adams constructed an old regime for it in order to bestow upon America the revolutionary privilege of the tabula rasa. For America was born of a desire to go a step beyond English liberty, to establish, in virgin territory devoid of all prior tradition, a homeland based on human rights and human nature. It was the best of English society transplanted to another clime, to a new land, and purified, as Louis Hartz recognized, of any of the old spirit's contamination by the journey itself: the new country was to have no past other than its passion for religious and political freedom.[4] America has no history but the history of an idea. Born in Europe, that idea had to cross the Atlantic in order to find the tabula rasa upon which it could flourish unopposed. It embodied itself in a new society, which for that very reason was not a nation in the European sense, slowly shaped by circumstances and the vagaries of princely ambition, but a community born subsequent to the discovery of liberty, which shaped itself and recruited its population in the light of that principle. In 1765 John Adams was not telling his compatriots anything radically new. He was simply repeating the original choice of the American colonists to oppose English tyranny.

As Adams saw it, the English "old regime" consisted of feudalism plus the Catholic Church. To that duo Thomas Paine added the monarchy, making a trio. He condemned the whole English constitution: not because that constitution had always been harmful (Paine agreed with Sieyès that it marked an advance over the dark age in which it came into being), but because it included oppressive elements such as a hereditary crown and an aristocratic House of Lords, both in contradiction to the principle of equality (as was the sacerdotal hierarchy). The republican component, the House of Commons, was not strong enough to compensate for the flaws in an overly complex system.

Thus Paine did not attack the English regime on the grounds that it was liable to be corrupted by forces that it had vanquished but not entirely destroyed between the Reformation and the "Glorious Revolution." He condemned it in toto on the grounds that it was incompatible with the rights of humanity. In this respect he was closer to the French Revolution than to John Adams, since he wanted to radically sever the American Revolution from the tradition of "English liberties" and turn the rebellion of the American colonists into a revolution, that is, a new epoch in the history of the world. Paine carried the idea of a radical break so far as to deny the filial relationship between England and her colonies, writing that "Europe, not England, is America's motherland." By that he meant that England was no better than the rest of Europe, since she, like other countries, had exported to America those whom she persecuted on civil and religious grounds.

But if America's revolutionary novelty had no precedent, no ancestor, the obstacle that it had to overcome was not, as in France, within itself, lurking in its innermost sanctuary to thwart its purpose. England was a foreign power in the strongest sense of the word: foreign because it was remote, and foreign too because it was of a different and hostile nature. All that was necessary to give the American plan a chance was to sever the ties between the colonies and the mother country. Paine's pamphlet therefore came to the same conclusion as Adams's treatise: the war of 1776 was merely a repetition of the act by which the colonies had been founded, a natural consequence of the emigration from Europe, a solemn reaffirmation of the break. The physical journey of the seventeenth century and the declaration of independence of the late eighteenth century were twin events, and the second therefore had no "old regime" to liquidate but only a foreign power to defeat.

Compared with the France of 1789, therefore, America had the good fortune of being able, without difficulty, to associate the radicalism of the tabula rasa with the circumstances of its history. From the beginning, it left behind, it relegated to the Old World, to England, the ghost of the "old regime" that has haunted French revolutionary culture and politics for two hundred years. The United States could face the future squarely without having to settle any scores with its past. It knew nothing of the anguish and conflict of a history severed in two, yet it enjoyed the revolutionary advantages inherent in the manner of its birth.

In the American case there was no contradiction between the existence of a past and the wish to rebuild society on an absolutely new foundation. The "revolution" of 1776 repeated that of the Mayflower. So far from being incompatible, American history and the tabula rasa were one and the same thing, for that history, whose beginnings were still, in the late eighteenth century, fresh in everyone's mind, originated with a spatial separation from the mother country and the founding of a new society on (supposedly) virgin territory. Thus the concrete history of the Americans, and of the Americans alone, satisfied the abstract criterion of democratic philosophy: the institution of society through the free will of the parties to a social contract. Hence the American tabula rasa, unlike the French, was not an abstraction. Indeed, it was the very historical origin of the United States, the heart of its identity, that distinguished it from Europe as a society and a nation.

European intellectuals sometimes see this paradoxical character of the United States as a consequence of the brevity of its history: Americans, it is alleged, lack a sense of history because their history has been so short. In fact, this kind of thinking misses the point. "Recent" histories can be very difficult to live with, and thus foster a tendency for individuals and nations to ruminate upon the past: think, for example, of the French obsession in the nineteenth century with the Revolution. What is unique about the American experience is that it had as its genetic code, so to speak, a *true* tabula rasa, a true recommencement of society—a unique historical experiment, an almost miraculous success of negativity. The American obsession is not with the past but with the "frontier"—that is, the future.

As a result, moreover, America was particularly well suited to found a society based on a contract freely accepted by the parties and guaranteed by law. In France, the men of 1789 wanted such a foundation as ardently as their American predecessors of 1776 and 1787 but had to contend with the formidable weight of the national past. By contrast, the American colonists had no history but that sanctioned by a voluntary contract among themselves and by the contract that tied them to the English monarchy until the king violated its terms. In emancipating themselves from a king who betrayed their confidence, the colonists restored the original conditions of their partnership. From there it was but a short step to formalizing its terms. That was the purpose of the Constitution.

In the France of 1789, as in the American colonies, the idea of instituting society *de novo* was also at the center of what would soon, by autumn, be called the Revolution. The most spectacular aspect of the event, that which contemporaries found most striking, was indeed the ambition to rise above the details of how the Revolution had come to pass, to abstract from the particularities of the moment in order to attain the universal. The men of 1789 wanted to emancipate not the French but man in general. In their attempt there was something akin to Descartes's rejection of everything that had been thought before him: a negation of what preceded them in the history of France, all of which was branded irrational and particular. The idea that society was to be made over from top to bottom, literally reconstructed, was in any case so intimately intertwined with French philosophical rationalism that it predated the Revolution. It could be found in the royal administration well before it became the weapon of the monarchy's enemies in 1789: among the Physiocrats, for example, and in the experiment that has come to be known as Turgot's ministry (1774–1776).[5]

The French idea of tabula rasa thus differs from the American in having been a philosophical view rather than an experience. The American colonists had invented out of whole cloth a society that did not exist prior to their arrival. The French revolutionaries of 1789 passionately wanted to create a new world, but on the ruins of a long history that had shaped their territory into an old nation and their community into a monarchy. Their project implied a negation of what was irrational and particular in their past and presupposed the birth of a new man, regenerated by the actions of a new public authority. Instead of repeating the origins of French society, the Revolution was to rescue that society from the curse of its past. Instead of an event to be relived in its original spirit, a whole history was to be jettisoned in order to create a new spirit. If the two revolutions share a common cult of will in the service of a universalist ambition, if both sought to invent a novel society based on the free consent of the contracting parties, the French project was beset from the outset by formidable tensions between the historical circumstances in which it came to pass and the abstraction inherent in its very nature.

The idea of a radical break with the past in the name of a rational reconstruction of the social was present from the first, even before the outbreak of the Revolution, for example in Sieyès's famous pamphlet *Qu'est-ce le tiers état?* of January 1789. The emergence of this idea coincided with the rapid disappearance of references to an ancient customary "constitution" of the kingdom, which were still quite common in pamphlets that date from the period 1787–1788. It was accompanied by calls for a completely new written constitution, which would set down in black and white the rules governing the organization and powers of the government. Furthermore, the idea of the tabula rasa was not limited to men of learning steeped in the rationalism of the Enlightenment. It was also widely diffused in the sensibility of the time. One sign of this is the number of people who, in the spring of 1789, began dating their letters "the first year of liberty." Nothing at the time compelled them to do so other than their perception of unfolding events and the mounting collective enthusiasm that drove those events forward. Four years before the Convention decided on a revolutionary calendar, in other words, people had spontaneously hit on the same idea. There can be no doubt that these people had a much more vivid sense of a rupture in the chain of time than did the Americans who had preceded them twenty years earlier, for it was their own history that they suddenly perceived as something separate from them and not, as had the Americans of 1776, the history of a metropolis that had little by little grown as remote as the maps said it was.

This powerful sense of a break in the continuity of time, which would give the idea of the Ancien Régime the peculiar force that it had in France, is inseparable from the rationalist, voluntarist radicalism of the men of 1789. What they undertook to do was to reestablish society, through their action, on a basis of reason. In this respect, as has often been noted, their project was less "prudent" (in the ancient sense of the term) than that of the American Founding Fathers, since they eschewed any reference to God and ignored Christian pessimism about the nature of man. Not only that, but they were also without the legal and constitutional moorings that the English common law and political legacy of Whiggery (including opposition) afforded the Americans. In what preceded it the French Revolution found neither Coke nor Bolingbroke nor a taste for, much less practical experience of, the balance of power; it found absolutism.

What did absolutism mean in this context? A first subversion of the "constitutional" tradition of the monarchy. Tocqueville is unforgettable as the historian of the pathological relationship between the French Revolution and absolutism. As he showed, the final two centuries of what the Revolution called the Ancien Régime witnessed the destruction of traditional society from within. For one thing, the growth of the state and the concentration of administrative as well as political power in one place drained the feudal hierarchy of meaning and stripped its authorities of power. For another, this dispossession of society by the state was accompanied by a continual readjustment of the statuses and ranks inherited from feudalism: the monarchical government, for instance, sold access to the nobility to the highest bidder, and nobility was henceforth defined solely in terms of privileges. The growth of the fiscal and administrative machine resulted in something like a "caste" society, composed of *corps* kept meticulously separate from one another and by their very nature unconcerned with the public interest.

In order for the absolute monarchy to occupy the whole space of public authority, however, it had to reduce its subjects to equal obedience: this was the condition of uniformity of its laws. Its actions therefore tended to have a leveling effect, even when, for financial reasons, it sought ever more ingenious ways to milk cash from an endless proliferation of minor differences of status (which, because they were devoid of any real content in terms of power, had all the more symbolic value in terms of self-regard). The monarchy continually re-created both equality and inequality and fortified each passion by what it gave to the other. According to Tocqueville, the absolutist state dishonored aristocracy without opening up a space for democracy. This observation explains what Burke failed to grasp: that the ancient monarchy had nothing to bequeath to the Revolution other than the pure negation of what it was. The tabula rasa of 1789 was born of this paradox: the French revolutionaries' passionate repudiation of history was itself a product of their history.[6]

One can imagine extending Tocqueville's analysis by approaching the subject from a somewhat different angle, closer to the symbolic than to the sociological. The monarchy developed as a power embodying the nation, the head of a "body politic" conceived of as something very ancient, fundamental to communal existence, and represented by the king of France (in the old sense of the word *represented*, meaning identically reproduced). It was this constellation of things that constituted the essence of what the Revolution would soon baptize the "Ancien Régime" and, in the few months from May to September of 1789, demolish once and for all.[7] It first abolished the organic society of orders, which in one night was transformed into a society of free individuals, and it then severed the king from the nation, making him simply its delegate. Henceforth it would be the deputies, the *représentants,* who would be charged, as the word suggests, with "incarnating" the nation, but on the basis of a society henceforth composed of autonomous atoms. Such an exercise would be difficult in any case, and all the more so because it was

FIGURE 2.1 *The Frenchman of the Past;* anonymous engraving, 1790.

FIGURE 2.2 *The Frenchman of Today;* anonymous engraving, 1790.

quite new at the time, but under the circumstances it was almost impossible, since it required combining the radical individualism of 1789 with a no less radical concept of the nation as a unitary body.

This difficulty illustrates the ambiguities and impasses into which the men of 1789 were led by their negation of the entire national past, aristocracy and monarchy alike. Consider, for example, the first great constitutional debate in late August–early September 1789, even as the deputies were planning the devolution to the people of the absolute sovereignty of the king—a devolution that had been in the cards since June 17, when the assembly of the Third Estate renamed itself simply the National Assembly, thereby accomplishing the first and most fundamental act of the Revolution. In this tremendously important debate, the right wing of the revolutionary camp, the first moderates of the Revolution, argued in favor of English-style co-sovereignty, with supreme power divided between the king and a bicameral parliament. But this idea of joining the national past to the Revolution by dividing power between the old monarchy and the new national representatives ran afoul of two impossibilities. First, the *Monarchiens* were appealing to a tradition, a monarchy, that either did not exist or, if it had even so much as begun to exist in France's past, no longer had any reality. And the attempt to "restore" it, along with a second chamber that would have revived the old specter of an aristocratic power base after two centuries of absolutism, was

FIGURE 2.3   *The Oath of June 17, 1789;* anonymous engraving.

made to seem even more unrealistic by the Revolution's radical condemnation of the "feudal" principle, which having existed before absolute monarchy, now outlived it.

In this sense, the radical part of the revolutionary camp was unwittingly more traditionalist than the moderate part: it took over the sovereignty that the efforts of absolutism had produced, whereas the *Monarchiens* sought to reinvent sovereignty in a novel form. The radicals gave the Constituent Assembly sovereign power to remake the body politic. But the peremptory affirmation of chronological discontinuity that gave the word "revolution" its new meaning was inextricably associated with the patriotic party's adoption of a concept of political sovereignty shaped by absolutism: the people took the place of the king, but it was the same place. Pure democracy supplanted absolute monarchy. Since there was no place in the old conception of sovereign power for anything but the monarch, there was no place in the new conception for anything but the people or its supposed representatives. Thus, in the idea of Ancien Régime that took shape precisely in August and September of 1789, there was a symbolic and practical overthrow of the throne masked by the reuse of the king as first functionary of the people, proclaimed as such by the vast majority of constituents.

The radical negation of the Ancien Régime quickly demonstrated its extraordinary power over people's minds as well as its power to mask the legacies of the past. In rejecting the tyranny of the Hanoverian kings and even in denouncing the principle of monarchy itself, the American colonists had no difficulty remaining faithful to English liberties: even Thomas Paine drew the essence of his political thinking from the English tradition. By contrast, it was against their will and without their knowledge that the French of 1789, bent on forgetting or wiping out all memory of previous centuries, were constantly digging up old constraints in new forms. They wished to make a clean slate of the past even though that was impossible. No people on earth were in less of a position to found a new society based purely on convention, neglecting the substance of their history. The French abolished aristocratic society on the Night of August Fourth, but that very abolition led them to reaffirm the unity of the new sovereignty all the more vigorously. Indeed, the specter of the Ancien Régime would continue to haunt the Revolution and drive it forward. The surviving monarchy would haunt it like its own ghost until it was finally exorcised on August 10, 1792, even before the execution of the king. It was then and then only that the Convention decided to begin time anew with Year I, relegating the first four years of the Revolution to the Ancien Régime, as if the national past had never stopped contaminating the great national recommencement.

To understand this, take, among a thousand other possible examples from the same month whose gist would be identical, a memorandum circulated by Roland, minister of the interior, to the municipal governments of France, dated August 19, 1792.[8] The purpose of this document, issued a little more than a week after the seizure of the Tuileries and the fall of the monarchy on the tenth, was to allow the minister to explain to local authorities the meaning of what had happened in Paris: nothing less than a new revolution, relegating to the corrupt past the years since 1789. To be sure, Roland conceded, "despotism was destroyed in 1789." But "1792 will be the epoch of the reign of *equality*." The popular insurrection of August 10 was necessary because "we were generally very corrupt, and the revolution, a consequence of Enlightenment, had to combat ingrained habits [*moeurs*]." In other words, the destructive habits inherited from the Ancien Régime had compromised the very establishment of the new regime and of equality among citizens. Strangely, however, this theme of the inertia of custom, which was destined to achieve vast influence later on, in no way limited the revolutionary reaffirmation of the Tenth of August: "The Revolution having just been completed, let us hasten to assure its beneficent effects. Our representatives have sworn to uphold liberty and equality. Never again shall the two be put asunder." For the next few weeks *Le Moniteur* and administrative documents would continue to be dated "the fourth year of liberty."

There followed a brief transitional phase, in which documents bore the inscription "the fourth year of liberty and first year of equality." But in the end, after the Convention reconvened, as of September 25, all official texts were to be dated "the first year of the French Republic."

In contrast to the United States, which has an enduring fundamental text, the covenant of the new nation, the French Revolution had several "Year Ones" and several constitutions. A series of commencements and recommencements, a work endlessly completed and rebegun, it offered those who came after it the idea of a tradition created ex nihilo and of an endless battle against a constantly renascent past: the Ancien Régime was what the Revolution, in order to fulfill its promises, would have to overcome now and forever. Always lurking within what the men of 1789 wished to invent, a curse hidden even from those who wished to abolish it, the Ancien Régime withstood the repeated annunciations of a new age. What is paradoxical about France is that a solemn rejection of the past was intimately intertwined with an obsession with history. The rejection of the past signified more than the tendency of modern democracy to build the future upon human will. It also reflected the Revolution's inability ever to achieve its ends.

Within the Revolution, as a result, the ghost of the past was always present, and the revolutionaries were obsessed with arriving at a destination they never reached. It would be impossible to list the men whose principal goal, or the moments whose principal theme, was to bring the Revolution to an end. First there was Mounier in July 1789, followed by Mirabeau, Lafayette, Barnave, the Girondins, Danton, and Robespierre—each, moreover, to his or their own advantage—and ultimately Bonaparte, who succeeded for a time, but only for a time (and only by allowing the Revolution, gone amok, to wreak havoc on all of Europe). In no case did the Revolution demonstrate any real capacity to found a new social order. The very number of attempts to do so in such an extraordinarily short period of time bring out the narrowly instrumental character and philosophical vanity from which all of them suffered. Even the Festival of the Supreme Being (June 1794), which was probably the Revolution's most pathetic effort to transcend the ephemeral and the immanent, never for one moment succeeded in passing itself off as anything other than an attempt at manipulation by a provisional government. The ambition inherent in the Revolution, which was of a fundamental order, never ceased to be a terrain of maneuver and suspicion. It never achieved any independent or higher existence, as if the Revolution as history could not overcome its own internal contradiction, which was to be at once political and a foundation of the political.

In effect, the French Revolution was never anything but a series of events and regimes, a sequence of power struggles: power was to rest with the people—this remained the unique and unchallenged principle of the whole business—but it was embodied in men and groups of men who, one after another, arrogated to themselves a legitimacy that, though elusive, remained indestructible, or at any rate was repeatedly reconstructed each time it was destroyed. Instead of arresting time, the Revolution accelerated and fragmented it because it was never able to create institutions. It was a principle and a politics, an idea of sovereignty around which unregulated conflicts developed: between that idea and the struggles for power there was nothing—an ideal formula for historical drift. No reference point in the past, no institutions in the present, just a future forever possible but always postponed. The French Revolution wavered endlessly between that which held it in place and that which propelled it forward. It legislated for eternity, and it was tightly constrained by circumstances. It was the Declaration of the Rights of Man but also July and October of 1789. It was the constitutional monarchy of 1790–1791 but also the schism in the Church, the king's resistance, the flight to Varennes. It was the Republic of September 1792, Year I, the Constitution of 1793, but also the de facto dictatorship and the Terror. Its true essence was finally captured in 1793, in the formula describing the government of the Revolution simply as "revolutionary." This tautology aptly expressed the incompatibility between the French revolutionary idea and any fixed or durable institutions. What was fixed or durable in the Revolution was its principle, together with the set of collective beliefs and passions associated with that principle: whence the infinite elasticity of the bids for power in the politics that it inaugurated, and the attempts to put an end to it, all in vain yet forever tried anew.

It was in the character of the Revolution, therefore, to snatch France from its past, which was condemned in toto, and to identify it with a new principle without ever being able to root that principle in institutions. This gave rise to two sets of antagonisms whose memory the French would meticulously keep alive. One of these centered on the fundamental opposition between Revolution and Counterrevolution, which would eventually take on the aspect of a religious debate over two conceptions of history and of the world. The French of the nineteenth century were a people who could not cherish as one what 1789 had put asunder: those who loved the Revolution detested the Ancien Régime, and those who loved the Ancien Régime detested the Revolution. But alongside that fundamental split, in relation to which the right and the left would define themselves, the clashes that took place between 1789 and the Empire left behind a second series of conflicts over the men and ideas of the Revolution itself. The revolutionary tradition consists not of unified homage to a common beginning but of a range of loyalties to legacies that are not just diverse but contradictory: the left is united against the right, but it has nothing else in common. The men of 1789, 1793, and 18 Brumaire may have embarked upon parallel careers in combat against the same adversary, but they bequeathed to their successors memories and ideas that, once deprived of the excuse of *le salut public*, proved to be incompatible.

FIGURE 2.4   *Allegory of the Rights of Man:* "Aristocracy and its agents are buried beneath the ruins of the Bastille. From these ruins rises Liberty, armed with a sword and trampling the hydra underfoot. Prisoners, the victims of arbitrary power, prostrate themselves in thanksgiving before the Altar of the Nation;" engraving, 1791.

FIGURE 2.5   *Allegory of Liberty:* "The King takes up residence in Paris. In the procession behind his family are the Deputies of the National Assembly. The Parisian Militia keeps the people in line in order to show that its mission is to maintain order and ensure that the Laws are executed;" engraving, 1789.

FIGURE 2.6   *Allegory of the Festival of the Supreme Being;* engraving, 1794.

The whole history of the century that runs from the French Revolution to the Third Republic attests to this reality. No nineteenth-century historian or politician attempted to explain his time without first casting an eye not just on the French Revolution itself but even more on the fact that its unpredictable events were continually being reenacted owing to divisions within France whose causes ultimately stemmed from the Revolution. The history of this period can therefore be organized in terms of two chronological cycles.[9] The first runs from 1789 to 1799 (or 1804 if one wants to include the creation of the Empire), the period that saw the creation of a repertory of political forms invented by the Revolution to institutionalize the new public sovereignty. Indeed, this prodigious inventiveness was the Revolution's quintessential trademark.

In the second, repetitive, cycle the French recast and in so doing crystallized for longer periods the same political forms, reborn from the same revolutions: two constitutional monarchies after that of 1789–1792, two victorious Parisian insurrections (July 1830, February 1848) and two insurrections smashed (June 1848, March 1871), a second republic modeled on the first, and even a second Bonaparte, even though the first had been taken to be a unique historical phenomenon. This series of repetitions was unprecedented: it reveals the extraordinary constraining influence of the Revolution on nineteenth-century French politics. In the middle of the century, moreover, the Second Republic, the most mimetic of all the nineteenth-century regimes, itself reproduced the whole cycle of the last ten years of the eighteenth century, except that it began with the republic and its Jacobin phase was stillborn (the June Days). But all the actors were present, lined up with their illustrious ancestors: farce followed tragedy, as Marx said. The fact that the play ended with a second Bonaparte demonstrated in almost insulting fashion how completely French politics was owned by the revolutionary tradition. What had seemed, in the second year of the nineteenth century, the product of a fortuitous encounter between exceptional circumstances and a peerless leader could now be seen, a halfcentury later, as the fatal consequence of revolutionary republicanism. The mediocrity of the beneficiary revealed the influence of a deterministic mechanism independent of human will: this mysterious but obvious fact became the focal point of the work of both Tocqueville and Quinet.

There was, however, one essential difference between the two great cycles of the French Revolution, that of the eighteenth century and that of the nineteenth. The first took place in the absence of stable, powerful administrative structures, since these had disappeared in 1787 with the last great administrative reform of the monarchy. This, in large part, accounts for the extraordinary fluidity of revolutionary politics, which never relied on powerful state structures. The Revolution, in 1789, settled into a space abandoned by the monarchy, and until the Consulate it never succeeded in reorganizing that space in a durable and systematic way. By contrast, the second cycle of the French Revolution, that of the nineteenth century, took place entirely within a strong and stable administrative framework: that created by Napoleonic centralization, which did not change throughout the century and which no revolution even attempted to transform. French political life in the nineteenth century was characterized by a profound consensus around state structures coupled with permanent conflict over the form to be taken by that very same state.

Why this consensus? Because these state structures were both a monarchical tradition and a legacy of the Revolution. This is what Tocqueville showed in unforgettable fashion: there was an Ancien Régime in France that the Revolution, for all its ambitions, was never able to extirpate and ultimately identified itself with. By contrast, the Revolution's only legacy to the living memory of the French con-

FIGURE 2.7   David, *The Triumph of the French People;* drawing, 1794.

sisted of doubts about legitimacy and conflicting allegiances. It was precisely because the crisis in France was more a crisis of legitimacy than of substance, moreover, that its solution proved so difficult: the consensus around the administrative apparatus of the state made revolutions technically easy, and the conflict over the form of the state made them inevitable. What is more, no one was aware of the consensus, including the political actors, while everyone, including those most indifferent to politics, endlessly dredged up old conflicts. This was because conflict was fueled not only by the memory of the Revolution but also by the belief that the Revolution bequeathed to the French—to all the French, left and right alike—namely, that political power is the key to social change. These two facts account for the oft-noted paradox that the French are at once a conservative and a revolutionary people. Through the Revolution the French love a far more ancient tradition, which is that of the monarchy; into that tradition they infuse equality all the more easily because the monarchical administration spent centuries laying the groundwork for it. But the Revolution also made the French a people that cannot love both parts of its history at once, as well as a nation that since 1789 has been obsessed with the reinstitution of the social. And they cannot build a new legitimacy out of fragments of their recent history, which has left them with building blocks that do not fit together properly.

For two hundred years the classical example of the replication of political confrontation within the revolutionary tradition has been the pitting of 1789 against 1793, of *quatre-vingt-neu-vistes* (eighty-nineists) against *quatre-vingt-treizistes* (ninety-threeists). For one side the problem is to pin down 1789, to root the new principles in stable institutions: in a word, as always, to end the Revolution. This was already Benjamin Constant's goal in 1797. It would be the goal of Guizot and Thiers a generation later, and of Gambetta and Jules Ferry at the end of the century. For the other side, by contrast, the problem is to deny 1789, to transcend it in the name of 1793, to reject 1789 as a foundation and celebrate 1793 as an anticipation whose promise has yet to be realized. Here we have two exemplary instances of the alternative that the Revolution continues to provide to those who invoke it as a reference. Either it must be ended or it must be carried on, evidence that in either case it is always open-ended. To end it, the only available stopping place is 1789, which saw the advent of political citizenship and civil equality, because that is the point of national consensus. What remains is to find a definitive form of government for this new society. To those who wish to continue it, however, the Revolution also offers a point of departure, provided that one is willing to look upon 1793 not as a temporary dictatorship in an hour of need but as an abortive attempt to go beyond bourgeois individualism and reconstitute a true community by transcending the principles of 1789.

Indeed, to the observer the French Revolution has the extraordinary property of being, in the sequence of its events and periods, the concrete embodiment of the theoretical critique of liberalism that Rousseau conceived thirty years earlier. It brings down to the level of actual history the quintessential philosophical problem of the eighteenth century: What is a society, if we are individuals? Classical "English-style" liberal philosophy escaped from this impasse by begging the question of the social character of the natural individual: that is the secret of the final order to which the interplay of the passions and the interests gives rise. But nearly a century before Marx, all of Rousseau's political work was a critique of such question begging: in order to move from natural man to social man, society must be "instituted" by denaturing the natural individual, erasing the individual of selfish passions and interests in favor of the abstract citizen, the only admissible party to the social contract. It is easy to understand how this conceptual scheme can serve as a frame of reference for 1793 as against 1789, provided that one ceases to see 1793 exclusively in terms of a response to an exceptional situation. Furthermore, the Jacobins themselves set the example, by isolating Rousseau from the century's other philosophers as the only thinker to deal with equality and citizenship. In order to establish 1793 as the central reference point of the Revolution, the negation-transcendence of the liberal individualism of 1789, the men of the nineteenth century did not have to go very far: they simply had to reread first Robespierre and then Rousseau. In tracing the Revolution back to philosophy, they could interpret the whole Revolution in terms of a clash between two contradictory principles that arose one after the other.

To end the Revolution or continue it. These two objectives or representations very soon gave rise to two admirably opposed yet complementary histories of the Revolution, which crystallized in the 1830s around the July Revolution.

The liberal generation of the 1820s was exemplary because it meditated on and even wrote the history of the French Revolution before moving on to practical work in July 1830. Thiers, Mignet, and Guizot invented historical determinism, the class struggle as the motor of that determinism, and 1789 and the victory of what they called the middle class as the crowning moment of this historical dialectic. The events of 1793 were but a passing—and deplorable—episode in this history of the bourgeoisie, an episode attributable to exceptional circumstances whose repetition was to be avoided: the "government of the multitude," to use Mignet's terms, was not part of the inevitable. The essential, in effect, the sense of history, was still the transition from aristocracy to democracy, from absolute monarchy to free institutions. In this respect the history of France was, along with that of England, one of two fundamental components of European identity, which is to say, of civilization itself. The advantage of the French over the English case was that in France the victory of democracy was more

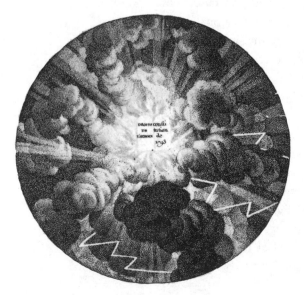

FIGURE 2.8   *Allegory of the Constitution of 1793,* engraved by Allais.

FIGURE 2.9   *Between Two Stools, Ass on the Ground;* caricature of the coup d'état of 18 Fructidor, Year V (September 4, 1797).

decisive, but France also had the disadvantage that free institutions took longer to develop there.

The reference to England expressed a deep kinship of values and ideas, particularly apparent in Guizot: the English conception of liberal individualism based on self-interest and property as well as the English wariness of political democracy, the

wish to borrow the British example of a free government rooted in history and supported by the propertied elite—these aspects of the English tradition appealed
strongly to this generation of French liberals, who drew many of their philosophical principles and convictions from the other side of the Channel.[10] But seventeenth-century England also presented them with a model of disciplined revolution:
1688 after 1648. It was the example of a people who, like the French, had executed
their king and experienced spiraling promises of egalitarianism as well as one-man
rule only to return to the old regime, but who then, forty years later, had hit on the
middle way of a conservative revolution out of which came a moderate parliamentary regime. To end the Revolution was thus also to adopt an "English" strategy.

In this respect 1830 marked a turning point, and Guizot, Thiers, and their friends
were quick to go to work. The *Trois Glorieuses* were supposed to mark a new 1789,
but the accession of an Orléans to the throne was to avoid another 1793. The *intellectual* "eighty-nineism" of the liberal historians of the Restoration was not radical,
because it allowed a place for the dictatorship of Year II, which it saw as a secondary,
and deplorable, necessity. But their *political* "eighty-nineism" *was* radical. The goal
was to avoid at all cost a repetition of 1793 by halting the Revolution in its initial
phase through recourse to Louis-Philippe. In short, the aim was an improved 1789
based on the 1688 English model, to be achieved by daring what the men of 1789 had
been unwilling to try: a change of dynasty, putting an Orléans on the throne and
thus founding a monarchy of the Revolution. This political strategy met with
apparent success, since it resulted in the July Monarchy, but at a deeper level this
success only concealed the inconsistency of the 1830 liberal interpretation of 1789.

That interpretation fell short first of all intellectually, for if all that had been
needed to avoid a terrorist dictatorship was a change of dynasty, the Revolution's
ever-mounting promises must have been rooted not in "circumstances" but in the
conflict with Louis XVI. It also failed as a matter of practical politics, because subsequent events showed that the accession of Louis-Philippe was not enough to stem
the Revolution's predilection for outbidding itself. The July Days were followed by
four years of brutal combat between the new government and the republican people
of the street, who felt cheated of "their" revolution. These battles, which the men of
July finally won, can in one sense be taken as testimony to their political realism;
their successful "1789" led only to an abortive "1793." But on the level of intellectual
analysis, it remains the case that this new "canonical" 1789 did nothing to prevent the
revival of street Jacobinism. On the contrary, the experience proved that without an
Ancien Régime monarch, without aristocrats, without foreign or civil war—in a
word, without "circumstances"—Jacobinism emerged from the July Revolution as
a river emerges from its source. If a radical eighty-nineism could exist in politics, it
could also exist in history: there is some of 1793 in every 1789. It was this unavoidable truth that the crushing of the barricades on the Rue Transnonain was meant to

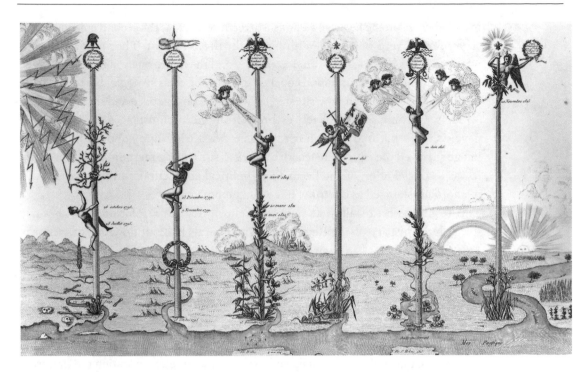

FIGURE 2.10   *Ah! Ah! This Is the History of France from January 21, 1793, to November 20, 1815. Look at It!* anonymous engraving, 1815.

exorcise, but how could it? The July bourgeoisie had replayed the process of memory in the street, proving that the dynamics of revolution are, at least part of the time, uncontrollable. Compared with their ancestors of *la Grande Révolution,* the men of 1830 had the advantage of their memories, as well as greater class consciousness, more political experience, and fewer humanitarian scruples, yet with the same uncertainties they rediscovered and dealt with exactly the same problem as Mirabeau, Brissot, Danton, and Robespierre, namely, how to stop a revolution.

Now at the same time, but for symmetrically opposite reasons, this radical eighty-nineism led to the crystallization of the contrary belief, that the Revolution can succeed only if it remains true to its own dynamic and runs no greater risk than that of being betrayed in mid-course. The Orleanist confiscation of *les Trois Glorieuses* gave rise to a dramatic and decisive confrontation within the national revolutionary tradition. It seemed almost natural to interpret that confrontation by analogy with the fall of Robespierre and the meaning of the Ninth of Thermidor. Indeed, no other date was available to symbolize a premature end to the Revolution. Its significance had been explored, moreover, well before 1830 by Buonarroti and the Babouvist tradition, which held that what happened on the Ninth was that a clique of wealthy bourgeois overthrew the hero of an egalitarian republic who looked favorably on the people's cause. The *juste-milieu* regime of 1830 that had installed itself on the heels of a Paris insurrection stood as the second episode in this saga of recurrent betrayal. With hindsight the Ninth of Thermidor was thus wrapped in the historical *ressentiment* of 1830 and the interpretation that surrounded the later event: an interpretation couched in terms of class struggle, borrowed from the liberal historians but now situated between the bourgeoisie and the people.

Thus a Jacobinism completely divorced from the circumstances that supposedly gave rise to it became fixed in revolutionary historiography and tradition. This image survived the entire nineteenth century as something far more than a memory: it was a constellation of intellectual and political convictions, an interpretation, a memory crystallized as doctrine. But what memory?

It resulted first of all in an important chronological displacement within and through the history of the Revolution. The liberals had put down their anchor in 1789. The Jacobins had their source in 1793. For them the crucial period of the Revolution was precisely the one that Mignet had dismissed as the provisional reign of the multitude, which he attributed to exceptional circumstances. What he had excused, they celebrated: among the necessities of the Revolution, 1793 occupied in their eyes not a secondary, derivative place but a central and decisive one. This was the period during which the Revolution escaped from its own clutches by crushing its enemies, internal and external, while at the same time adumbrating the first truly egalitarian image of the social contract.

FIGURE 2.11   Lordereau, *The Throne Burned;* lithograph, 1848.

Behind the celebration of *le salut public* there was not only patriotic investment in and retrospective love for a France threatened and saved but also, more simply, the cult of the state in all its forms: military, economic, political, educational, and even religious. In this respect it is significant that the great Jacobin historians of the Revolution were even more systematic proponents of absolute monarchy (up to

FIGURE 2.12   Allegory of 1848: *Year 33, Charity* (Christ); *1793, Faith* (Robespierre); 1848, Hope (Barbès).

FIGURE 2.13   Langelot, *Jesus the Montagnard;* lithograph, 1848.

and including Louis XIV) than their liberal predecessors, whose work they drew on freely. Like the liberals, the Jacobin historians admired the monarchy as the instrument of nation building and the embodiment, representation, and defense of the public interest above the various classes, but they also saw it as protecting the common masses from bourgeois individualism, selfish private interests, and the cruelty of the market. They reworked the whole Ancien Régime to bring it into line with 1793. In their eyes the Jacobin state carried on and magnified a tradition that Louis Blanc, for one, celebrated as well in Sully, Colbert, and Necker. Guizot, Mignet, and Thierry liked that aspect of the monarchy which paved the way for 1789: the alliance of the Third Estate with the kings of France to create a modern nation. Buchez and Louis Blanc admired only that which prefigured 1793: the incarnation, *le salut public,* the government of souls, the protection of the weak. Among the Jacobin historians "ninety-threeism" was absolute. Starting from a negation of 1789 (repeated and radicalized in the negation of 1830), they rejected all the work of the Constituent Assembly on the grounds that it bore the hallmark of bourgeois individualism and threatened to destroy the national community.

For liberal memory the Declaration of the Rights of Man was the most important moment of the Revolution, the charter of the modern citizen, the founding act of the new political civilization. Even Michelet—the Michelet of the *Histoire de la Révolution française*—who was not a liberal, much less an Orleanist, saw in the Declaration the quintessential meaning of the Revolution: it was the text that inaugurated a society based on law as opposed to favor. In Buchez's eyes, by contrast, the Declaration was the Revolution's great error, for the rights of man were not a principle capable of reconstituting a community. It was Jacobinism, rather, that was like a latter-day Annunciation, heralding the advent of a new eschatology in which socialism and Catholicism were inextricably intertwined. For Louis Blanc, the Constituent Assembly was the fulfillment of the program of Voltaire, which was that of the propertied classes; the Convention was the daughter of Rousseau, working on behalf of the toiling masses to pave the way for mankind's third age, after the ages of authority and individualism: the age of fraternity. Instead of a battle between the third estate and the privileged, the Revolution was transformed into a confrontation between the bourgeoisie and the people, which ran right through 1793. For Esquiros the Montagnards were the party of the proletariat as opposed to the Girondins, the prisoners or interpreters of bourgeois interests. Jacobinism was transformed into a precursor of socialism.

In this historiography, therefore, "circumstances" were not invoked, as in the work of Thiers or Mignet, to excuse the dictatorship of 1793 on the grounds that it was temporarily indispensable, because that dictatorship was now to be celebrated as fundamentally liberating. They were used only to distinguish the Terror, alleged to be a pure product of the exceptional situation, from Jacobinism or Robespierrism

as the case might be, these being the very embodiment of the Revolution's meaning. Thus the distinguishing criterion of nineteenth-century Jacobin historiography was not the theory of circumstances, a by-product of the theory of necessity, which the Jacobins in fact shared with the liberals. What characterized the Jacobins was the centrality accorded to 1793 as the most important period of the Revolution, or in any case the period most crucial for the future. The goal was to strip the bourgeoisie of its title to the revolutionary legacy, which it had irrevocably renounced in the deceptive game it played in July–August 1830. Jacobin history saw 1789 as merely marking the end of the Ancien Régime, whereas 1793 invented the future. (Quinet would argue precisely the opposite.) The Jacobin historiography that was born in the July Monarchy was the product of a chronological displacement that linked two powerful ideas: the Revolution as the power of the people, culminating under Robespierre and smashed on the Ninth of Thermidor; and the Revolution as a rupture in the fabric of time, as advent, as prefiguration of the future. The eighty-nineism of the

FIGURE 2.14   Patrioty, *The Republic That Decent People Do Not Want;* lithograph, 1848.

FIGURE 2.15   Alfred Le Petit, *The Two Republics;* 1871.

men of July was the acceptance of one kind of society and the quest for a government suited to that society. The ninety-threeism of those defeated in the July Revolution was the inventory of an aborted promise and of a society to be remade.

The July regime can thus be seen as the period when national memories of the French Revolution crystallized—remembrances, passions, and ideas all mixed up together and quite difficult to unravel. The July Days created legitimism, embodied in the vanquished party, giving the Counterrevolution an *appellation contrôlée* that would retain its rights until the death of the duc de Bordeaux. In the victorious party the July Revolution created Orleanism, but the heirs of 1789 would soon find themselves in the same situation as their predecessors: divided over the type of government likely to guarantee the famous principles the greatest stability, and threatened by republican outbidding. Not only did the substitution of Louis-Philippe for the republican dynamic of the *Trois Glorieuses* leave years of civil disturbance in its wake, but after a brief period of stability between 1835 and 1840 revolutionary agitation returned more vigorous than ever in the last eight years of the Orleanist reign. The republican and socialist ideals found their most brilliant interpreters in this period: Michelet and Quinet, Louis Blanc, Proudhon and Buchez. As is customary in France, works of history and literature preceded and heralded the fall of the regime.

February 1848 sounded the death knell of the monarchy of July 1830 and thus ended what amounted to the first systematic effort to bridge the gulf that had opened up in 1789 between the Ancien Régime and the Revolution. Before becoming its leader, Guizot had been the theoretician of the regime whose doctrine he had more or less set down in writing. As a result, the revolution of 1848 killed not only a monarchy but the ideas that had surrounded its inception. It thus gave renewed vigor to all that those ideas had sought to dispel. With the action in Paris in February, the new revolution reclaimed the fundamental heritage of French politics, even its birth certificate, namely, the ambition to begin society anew on the ruins of the past. As a result, democratic make-believe may never have enjoyed a finer moment than it did in the late winter of 1848 in Paris: with socialist utopianism adding its effects to those of the revolutionary tradition, practically anyone with a thought in his head set up shop selling the best of all possible societies. Some found the spectacle laughable, others touching, depending on their cast of mind. Among the former, Flaubert is without rival, but one could be just as moved by the social imagination set free by the fancied abolition of the past and abstract ideas about the future. In this respect February 1848 not only repeated 1789 but diversified it to the utmost, endlessly multiplying providential advents and felicitous combinations. There was, however, one big difference between 1848 and 1789: in 1848, proposals for a happier future greatly outweighed condemnations of the past. This was because the Ancien Régime of 1789, already defeated a second time in 1830, could not be recycled indefinitely:

rather than a presence or a threat, it was now a memory. The future, by contrast, was more than ever to be reinvented, since a solution to the "social question" was an even more pressing need than a solution to the question of government.

In fact, the particular importance of the revolution of 1848 in French history stems not from the novelty of its course or the talent of its political leaders or the brilliance of its achievements but from the fact that it restaged the great founding scene of French politics, the revolutionary rupture, with renewed vigor. In retrospect July 1830 had come to seem little more than a matter of some fiddling about by politicians. February 1848 aimed to be a reincarnation of illustrious ancestors. The proof of this can be seen in a comparison of the triumphant historians of 1830 with those of 1848. The former, Guizot above all but also Thierry, Mignet, and Barante, wanted to re-create a 1789 that could cap both the Ancien Régime and the Revolution, whereas the latter, Michelet primarily but also Quinet, Louis Blanc, and even Lamartine, had it in mind to begin the Revolution anew.

The French obsession with the tabula rasa by no means ended with the new revolutionary cycle of 1848–1851, which, like the first one, culminated with a Bonaparte. True, the positivist republicans who grew up under the Second Empire learned something from their fathers' utopian hopes. They would found a republic in the 1870s in part by forging an alliance with the Orleanists, in part by reinterpreting the whole history of France, monarchy and democracy combined, as hitched first to the

FIGURE 2.16   Rougeron Vignerot, *The Promised Land;* engraving, circa 1891.

rise of the Third Estate and then to the education of the people. The dream of an absolute new beginning migrated at this time to the socialist movement, where it prospered: *du passé faisons table rase,* goes the famous line of *L'Internationale.*

Not that this dream is necessarily inseparable from the socialist idea: to see this one has only to consider Marx's dogged efforts to distinguish himself from the utopians. In his work the collective appropriation of the means of production is made necessary by what goes before, above all by the formidable economic growth characteristic of bourgeois society. But Marx combined his concept of objective laws of historical development with a revolutionary messianism that, to the contrary, emphasized the role of human initiative in history: this reconciliation of science and will may lack intellectual coherence, yet it had an extraordinary power to seduce the intelligence. When the Bolsheviks seized power in October 1917, they gave immense power to this fragile synthesis by associating Marxism with revolution and by reviving, dressed up this time in scientific finery, the French idea of regenerating men through their own free will. No one can grasp the influence of the Communist idea in France from 1920 on without taking into account what that idea owed to its Jacobin precedent. Through the Communists, therefore, the left rediscovered the idea of the tabula rasa in the form of a recommencement of a first, abortive attempt remembered as a promise. Paradoxically, it was when the Communist Party sought to portray itself as the faithful heir of revolutionary history that it revived what was by definition ahistorical in the Revolution's legacy: the fiction of a purely conventional refoundation of society. The French left is revolutionary because of what is conservative in its makeup.

The idea of Ancien Régime even survived the decline of communism for a time, because in the 1970s François Mitterrand's Socialist Party regained its dominance of the left only at the price of shouldering the revolutionary heritage. Not only was the idea of a break with capitalism and bourgeois society the key to the Programme Commun, but anyone who was in France at the time can remember hearing the victors in the 1981 presidential elections refer to the presidency of Valéry Giscard d'Estaing as the Ancien Régime. Farce after tragedy, to borrow a phrase from Marx: this final farce pointed up the exhaustion of the formula, which had become an almost magical incantation for solving the problems that the left would have to face. The Ancien Régime and the Revolution died in an indifferent and prosperous nation.

FIGURE 3.0   The city hall and the church in Biot, Alpes-Maritimes.

CHAPTER 3

Catholics and Seculars[1]

Claude Langlois

On July 5, 1904, the National Assembly approved a law prohibiting members of Catholic "teaching congregations" from teaching in the public schools. The secular camp had at last emerged victorious from a long struggle, the stakes of which were portrayed in the March 19 issue of *L'Assiette au beurre*, with that satirical publication's usual ferocity. That issue bore the title "Freedom of Education," and in it Grandjouan and Roubille set up two opposing educational models, each countering the other, symbol for symbol and slogan for slogan.[2] As in a mirror, every image had its symmetrical counterpart. Two old crones tower menacingly over a small child. Both order him to show respect, though in each case to a different idol: "Kneel before the Savior!" or "Take off your hat to the Fatherland!" The crucifix or the flag, the catechism or the Rights of Man—the alternative is hardly one to gladden the heart. The women—a desiccated nun and an overstuffed, pop-eyed Marianne (symbol of the Republic)—egg the child on: "Go ahead, choose. You're free." Gone are heaven and hell, gone are the broad highway leading to perdition and the narrow path to salvation: ahead lie two identical roads.[3] Both rise steeply but toward the same capitalist hell, represented in one case by a church, in the other by military barracks.

A battle between proponents and opponents of religious education? Don't be misled by appearances! the magazine warned. In fact, the drawings insinuated, both sides are in it together. Teachers from both camps understand each other perfectly: "*Au revoir, mon cher collègue,* let's hope the children won't notice the change." At the center of a perfect circle two men shake hands, like horse traders at a fair, while the children remain prisoners. "The *grand séminaire* is dead, *Vive l'École Normale!* The curriculum hasn't changed." A pointless revolution. The morality of the state would replace that of the Church; the government's truth would replace the Vatican's.

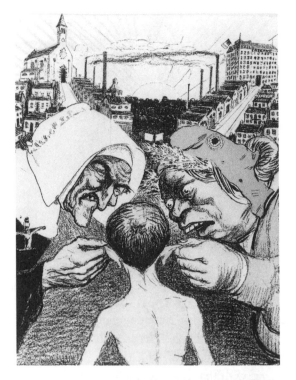

Rather than smash old idols, the Republic merely substituted new ones. In two adjacent sketches, fiercely didactic in their caricature, Grandjouan confidently unmasked the Republic's strategy for shoring up its nascent memory: the cult of the great leader from Joan of Arc to Carnot; the continuity of the nation's history from monarchy to republic, as contrasted with the wound inflicted on the nation's geography through the loss of Alsace and Lorraine; and last but not least, the new trinity of secular values, comprising Kant's morality, the immortal principles of 1789, and the fatherland. And all of this against a background of generalized Hugolatry—the adoration of the national poet, Victor Hugo.

In a country that could stoop to a sordid battle over the future of its children, liberty was dead. As if by instinct, Grandjouan recaptured the spirit of the caricatures of 1789, and instead of the lamentable political theater in which complicitous so-called enemies basked in each other's limelight, he offered France a new version of the *Réveil du peuple* from the early days of the Revolution.[4] Liberty, still female and eternally young but reinterpreted in the light of Swift and the Book of Judges, had turned into a giant chasing Lilliputians, laymen as well as priests. A female Samson, she brought down temples and smashed idols yet emerged unscathed. Freedom would come from socialism, or so the artist would have us believe.

FIGURE 3.1   Roubille, *Choose, You're Free;* drawing in *L'Assiette au beurre,* special issue on freedom of education (March 19, 1904).

FIGURE 3.2   Grandjouan, *Always Idols;* drawing in *L'Assiette au beurre,* special issue on freedom of education (March 19, 1904).

For *L'Assiette au beurre,* with its anarcho-syndicalist leanings, it was long past time to be done with the incessant quarrels of that decrepit couple, the Catholic and the secular (*le laïc*), who refused to admit that it was time to step aside. It was time to be done with these "sacristy quarrels" that simply made it possible, as the Dreyfus Affair had done earlier, to mask what was essential, namely, the class struggle. The apparent complicity of old enemies, stuck in roles they had already played a thousand times, is not, however, entirely convincing proof that this was simply a shadow theater. Quite apart from the ritual designation of enemies—Jesuits during the Restoration, Freemasons under the Third Republic[5]—the very excessiveness of the nineteenth-century polemic, the very extremity of the insults, the fantastic nature of the obsession, all point toward very real issues and distinct camps. The history is also filled with "affairs," whose character remained constant from one century to the next: from the Mortora children (1858) to the Finalys (1953), from Father Mingrat (1823) to the priest from Uruffe (1956),[6] along with forced baptisms of Jewish children and sexual crimes by members of the clergy. These attacks from the secular camp were met with equal vehemence from the Catholic side: there were attacks on the university, culminating under the July Monarchy, and on the Republic after 1880. And "mainstream" history was not immune from the consequences of this long antagonism: the alliance of Throne and Altar during the Restoration led to anticlerical violence in 1830, and the compromising favors that the authoritarian Empire handed out to the Catholic Church met with dramatic sanction in the execution of hostages by the Commune. The list goes on and on: the laws instituting secular education, the Dreyfus Affair, the laws forbidding members of religious orders or congregations to teach in public schools (a real confrontation), the Separation, etc. The "Two Frances" that Father Besse, in the wake of many others, saw in 1907 as naturally opposed do indeed exist: "Royalist and Catholic France, and revolutionary and atheist France."[7]

Notwithstanding its self-imposed blindness, *L'Assiette au beurre* forces us to focus on essentials, for the magazine in its own way raised several troubling questions that can help us get a better grasp of this major conflict in French history. On what battleground was the conflict really fought: ideological or practical? Was it a struggle for minds or a struggle for power? What bound the contestants together? If there are indeed *laïcs*, people of secular disposition, is *laïcité*, or secularism, an equally palpable reality? And finally, how are we to interpret the excessive prominence accorded these debates? Even if posed differently, the magazine's blunt question—"What does all this hide?"—remains pertinent.

The Age of Historians

After World War I, as the conflict was beginning to subside after a half century of incessant confrontation, a number of historians attempted to answer these ques-

FIGURE 3.3   Catholic ceremony in the Italian community of Marseilles.

FIGURE 3.4   Islamic ceremony in front of the city hall of Charvieu-Chavagneux (Isère), 1989.

tions. Three works appeared within the space of ten years. Their outlooks were quite different, even though all dealt with the same subject: secularism. The first came out in 1925, as the Catholics were mounting a "second rally" and just after the failure of Édouard Herriot, who had believed that it was still possible to hold the Cartel des Gauches together with the mortar of anticlericalism that had worked so well before the war. Georges Weill produced a work of impeccably intelligent erudition and careful objectivity, which extended his *Histoire du catholicisme libéral en France* (1909) and anticipated his *Histoire du parti républicain en France* (1928): the *Histoire de l'idée laïque en France au XIX*ᵉ siècle chronicled a battle that had truly ended with the armistice of 1905 and the peace of the Union Sacrée.[8] Ten years later, *L'Invasion laïque,* by the less irenical Canon Capéran, professor at the *grand séminaire* of Toulouse, inaugurated a series of books on "the contemporary history of secularism in France."[9] One year earlier, in 1934, Georges de Lagarde had published the first volume of his monumental *Naissance de l'esprit laïque au déclin du Moyen Age.*[10] The three authors not only had different attitudes about the desirability of objectivity but also chose to treat different subjects over different time periods: the secularization of thought, which began with the challenge of nominalist philosophy to scholasticism; the secularization of the state, which began with the Revolution; and the secularization of schools, which took place over the first few decades of the Third Republic.

The nature of the subject required all three authors to combine a structural with a genealogical approach. "Born of Christianity," Lagarde pointed out, "the word *laïque* follows it like a shadow. It adheres to it even as it thinks to be working itself free. It inevitably recalls what it claims to suppress. Its very rallying cry rivets it to the chain it wants to break as firmly as the prisoner's leg iron is riveted to its chain."[11] Yet a pair of terms that exist only in opposition and mutual dependence nevertheless have a history, and therefore an origin: in the fourteenth or the eighteenth century, but not in the sixteenth. It is instructive to find Canon Capéran, in 1957, invoking the names of both Jean Jaurès ("Our French genius withheld itself from the Reformation so as to preserve itself intact for the Revolution") and Ferdinand Buisson ("France is not Protestant but secular") to bolster his argument that the Reformation, despite the reproaches that Catholics traditionally heap upon it, should be left out of the inevitable investigation of paternity; indeed, he shares the classic view of his adversaries that the origins of the Revolution, and therefore of the secular idea, were necessarily philosophical.[12]

Historians thus first tackled the issue between the two world wars, as the conflicts surrounding it were subsiding. The new political situation after 1945 seemed to relegate the whole matter to the past once and for all: the emergence of the (centrist Christian-Democratic) MRP was thought to symbolize the reintegration of Catholics into French political life. But Vichy had revived the educational issue, by then dormant for forty years. This allowed the right, which resurfaced in 1951, to establish a permanent toehold as the opposition to the socialist–MRP (or lay-Catholic) alliance known as the Third Force (between the Communists and the right). In 1984 the Savary Law was intended to restore peace to the educational system. Instead, it revived old divisions: a huge demonstration on June 24, 1984, forced

President François Mitterrand to withdraw the bill and force the resignation of Prime Minister Pierre Mauroy.

But what was the significance of this most recent confrontation? It is tempting to dismiss it as a throwback, since the debate had moved onto new ground in the "thirty glorious years" of postwar growth: the new issues were democratization of education and post-1968 cultural change.[13] Was it a throwback, though, or a return of the repressed? It appeared that thirty years of calm had come to an end: old battles picked up where they had left off. One last time, in any case, left and right acted out the secular versus Catholic conflict on the familiar ground of education, although this was an area that had been extensively transformed since the advent of social democracy. The issue was no longer one of establishing secular public schools as in 1881, or of deciding whether specific groups of people had the right to teach as in 1904, but one of effective autonomy for recognized private schools, most of them Catholic, which received substantial state subsidies.

Of course anything can be explained. Consider, to begin with, the changes that had taken place within Catholicism. The situation in the 1980s was substantially different from that of the 1950s. Owing to a shortage of priests and lay brothers and sisters, the Catholic hierarchy no longer exercised effective control over its system of *écoles libres* (parochial schools), which were increasingly in the hands of their users, that is, the parents of their pupils. The dwindling number of practicing Catholics were ever more firmly attached to the right, whereas the more left-wing "militant" Catholics were on the decline.[14] The educational issue was thus still a political issue. Only one thing had changed over the course of the century, but it was an important thing: a hundred years ago the battle for secularism helped to consolidate the fragile unity of the republican side, whereas the battle over parochial schools under the Fourth and Fifth republics has served mainly to revitalize struggling right-wing parties. Nevertheless, this all too visible confrontation cannot by itself account for the enduring antagonism or for the reemergence of combative identities long buried in memory but never truly eliminated. Taking for granted that the secular camp's vitality and organization depend on the existence of a substantial and intransigent Catholic opponent, it follows that the decrease in the social influence of religion and the triumph, for the time being at any rate, of conciliar Catholicism have helped to reduce traditional antagonisms.[15]

We are indeed living in a period of change, but the source of that change is most likely elsewhere. The enduring Catholic-secular split that is so peculiar to France reflects the exclusive domination of Catholicism in the country after the revocation of the Edict of Nantes. The Revolution's proclamation of religious freedom and the organization of non-Catholic faiths under the Consulate and Empire did not alter the balance of power. Throughout the nineteenth and twentieth centuries Catholicism enjoyed a near monopoly simply because it was the religion of the vast majority (more than 95 percent) of French people and because it maintained a steady institutional as well as monumental visibility.[16] Neither Protestantism nor Judaism wished to or could take advantage of the system of religious organization to reinforce their stature vis-à-vis Catholicism. Indeed, both religions were far more affected by liberal influences in the nineteenth century than Catholicism was, and as a result many Protestants and Jews poured their energies into civil society and became the staunchest supporters of the new Republic.

Some would suggest that French Catholicism itself began to secularize under the combined influence of Vatican II and May 1968 and that in so doing it followed a course plotted by any number of new theologies. Several factors worked in the opposite direction, however. To begin with, there has been a revival of self-conscious Catholic identity, partly in reaction to the unchallenged domination of academic history and the resulting "secularization" of religious history.[17] While Protestants have found at least four opportunities since 1980 to repeat the celebration of their origins, Catholics have taken on the more difficult task of writing new "church histories" dealing with the complex burden of a two-thousand-year history.[18]

But other factors were more important. When Archbishop (later Cardinal) Lustiger of Paris spoke at a rally organized by the Parent-Teacher Associations of parochial schools in the Paris area on April 24, 1982, he had this to say about the history of religious education in France: "The system has not always been clearly defined. This ambiguity was essential to the delicate and difficult equilibrium of the French educational system. All things considered, however, we can pride ourselves on the fact that our culture has been able to accommodate the three religions that Emperor Napoleon I recognized: Catholicism, the Protestant Church, and Judaism. But what a difficult problem we face now with the unforeseen arrival of large numbers of French-speaking children of Islamic background!"[19] In fact, the change had begun much earlier: first the decolonization of North Africa and then the end of prosperity in Western economies together led to unprecedented changes in the French religious landscape.

First, decolonization, and above all the dramatic outcome of the Algerian War, led some 250,000 to 300,000 Jews to emigrate from North Africa to France between 1950 and 1970.[20] The short-term effect of this was to double the Jewish population of metropolitan France. More profoundly, the long-term effect was to change the nature of French Judaism, as large numbers of traditionally minded Sephardic Jews from North Africa joined the existing Jewish population.

This phenomenon went largely unnoticed, however, by a public much more keenly aware of the new presence of Islam on French soil. Gilles Kepel sees the birth of a new religion in France as a consequence of the economic crisis that shook the capitalist economies, leaving many North African immigrants as permanent residents of France.[21] Although other causes must surely be taken into account as well, it is clear that the number of Muslim places of worship in France increased sharply after 1975, proof that a minority of Muslims had become determined to satisfy the requirements of their religion wherever they happened to be living and raising children. Statistically, Islam has become France's second most important religion, as measured by the number of people living on French soil who claim to be of Muslim descent (some 3 to 4 million). This is a recent development, even though France has been involved in dealings with Islam since at least the conquest of Algeria, if not before. Indeed, the point is that France can no longer take a colonial attitude toward Islam, treating it as an alien, and inferior, religion. French Muslims will no longer tolerate being treated as second-class citizens.

The greater visibility of Judaism and the presence in France of an Islamic community that has yet to exercise its full potential power are entirely new ingredients in the situation.[22] Now, if it is true that the Catholic-secular split became established in France as a result of the failure of Protestantism and thus of the absence of true religious pluralism, it may well be swept aside as the religious landscape is transformed before our very eyes. Does not the "new secularism" that some have proposed as a solution to the parochial school issue that erupted in 1984 risk becoming a dead letter if it is envisaged solely as a way of resolving an old conflict between Christians and seculars?

The "Islam of a thousand mosques" is surely a fantasy, the result of a more or less deliberate confusion between a simple place of worship and the full-scale mosques complete with minarets that some see replacing village churches throughout France. Yet the fantasy is revealing of a new sense of vulnerability, for the construction of minarets would end Catholicism's long-standing monopoly of French religious architecture. In effect, modern Catholicism has portrayed itself as the sole legitimate heir of medieval Christianity. In the nineteenth century Catholics built many neo-Romanesque and above all neo-Gothic churches precisely to underscore that point, and in the twentieth century the Church has called upon modern architectural technology to promote a new sacred art. In terms of monuments, the lesson is clear: France is either Catholic or secular. There is no middle term.

Choosing Sides

It was when statues of Marianne were erected in republican town squares in deliberate opposition to statues of the the Virgin on the heights overlooking those same towns that the secular camp really made its existence known for the first time.[23] That moment is remembered in two symbols, one a text, the other a motto. The text is from Sainte-Beuve, an influential orator in the Bonapartist Senate, who in 1868 spoke out against Catholics who dared to challenge the materialism of the medical faculties by calling for an end to state control of higher education. In response to the threats of the clerical party Sainte-Beuve drew this portrait of the nascent secular world:

> There is another great diocese, Gentlemen, a diocese with no fixed borders, which covers all of France, indeed all the world, and which extends its branches and enclaves even into the dioceses of the honorable prelates...which comprises...minds emancipated to varying degrees but all in agreement on one point: that the greatest need of all is to be liberated from absolute authority and blind submission; an immense diocese (or, if you prefer, an indeterminate, boundless province); which counts among its members thousands of deists, spiritualists, and disciples of so-called natural religion, pantheists, positivists, realists...skeptics and seekers of all kinds, adepts of common sense and champions of pure science; this diocese...this great intellectual and rational province, has no pastor or bishops, it is true, and no consistory president or other designated leader authorized to speak in its name, yet each member in turn has the duty, when the occasion arises and conscience compels him, to recall the rights of truth, science, and free inquiry to the attention of anyone who might be tempted to forget or neglect them.[24]

An astonishing definition: Sainte-Beuve rejects Catholicism in toto in the name of individual autonomy and unfettered reason, yet at the same time he projects onto the lay camp that he is trying to define two caricatures borrowed from traditional religious controversies: one an image of Catholicism as wholly identified with the Jesuits, a body with many "branches and enclaves," the other an image of Protestantism, defined à la Bossuet as a source of continual sectarian proliferation.

In contrast to this convoluted self-definition we have the concise motto that Gambetta borrowed from Peyrat less than ten years later: "Clericalism—that is the enemy."[25] The terms *clérical* and *laïc* had already begun to take on connotations beyond their technical meaning (clerical and lay) during the Second Empire. The two adjectives always appeared together as opposites and were soon joined by the nouns *cléricalisme* and *laïcité*. As late as 1876 there was no such thing as "clericalism," only a "clerical" spirit, party, or policy; but on May 4, 1877, Gambetta made "clericalism is the enemy" the new republican war cry. One has to read the great orator's speech to understand what remains, after one hundred years, astonishing: that it was indeed the denunciation of clericalism that held the republican camp together, and that this was indeed the terrain on which Gambetta, having won an election, now sought to obtain the indispensable mandate of the people. For him, moreover, clericalism was not merely a periodic resurgence of a remote peril but a new and dangerous evil that threatened to weaken the state, undermine society, and destroy national unity. If the clerical party were to win, France would immediately face a military adventure, social peril, and counterrevolution.

This was in part pure fiction. The denunciation of clericalism was a convenient way for the republicans to invoke history, not only the avowable history of 1789 but also the unavowable history of 1870 and 1871—in other words, it was a way of raising two specters at once, that of a return to the Ancien Régime and that of a revival of socialism. Even more, it was a way of evoking an image of the battered nation. Eckmann-Chatrian typifies these bellicose fantasies.[26] Chambord's return, he says, would lead to conflict with Italy if France should attempt to restore the former papal states to the Holy See. "The Jesuits would saddle us with a religious war," in some ways like the war in the Cévennes, in some ways like the Thirty Years' War. Apocalypse would follow: France would be devastated, depopulated, and bled white. She would be delivered into the hands of the Prussians, who this time would exact an even higher toll: ten billion francs and all of Champagne. It would mean the breakup of France, with the south seceding from the north and the country dividing into four or five parts, in which the comte de Chambord would play the role of the king of Bourges, reigning over his capital and a country "the size of a garden." This nightmare—as in Lavisse's history textbook, but backwards, with history destroying France rather than building it piece by piece—was one that Gambetta continued to evoke, though in more restrained terms, as he availed himself of every opportunity to attack his enemies' aggressiveness and antinational outlook.

Fiction in part, but also reality, given the way in which the Republic did indeed come to power, in the wake of efforts to establish a new dynasty and of a war and the Paris Commune. In order to gain support, the republicans emulated Thiers's skill at embodying pacifism and conservatism, but they also backed the Orleanist parliamentary tradition: it was difficult for them to accuse their adversaries of resurrecting the "party of order" when that was precisely the role they wished to play themselves. In any case, there was no immediate dynastic threat, as both royalists and imperials were at least temporarily out of action. Only one thing united groups otherwise deeply divided over the proposed solutions, and that one thing was religious policy: the authoritarian Empire had manifestly supported Catholicism, and the Ordre Moral government, if it had failed to give France a king, nevertheless outdid its predecessor in supporting the Church. So the enemy was indeed clericalism.

But clericalism was more than just a convenient substitute for a missing political opposition. The term also designated a Catholicism that had undergone a thorough overhaul during the July Monarchy and another transformation in the 1860s: facing changes of many kinds that threatened both its place in society and the credibility of its doctrinal foundations, it responded by making the ultramontane, counterrevolutionary spirit of the *Syllabus* its own.[27] Gallicanism died, and with it went what was left of the spirit and practice of the Concordat. French Catholicism, which had in fact proved incapable of establishing a party of its own on the model of the German

FIGURE 3.5   Dumont, *Law on Public Ignorance;* engraving after Bertall, circa 1850.

FIGURE 3.6   Valery Muller, *The Last Idol,* for the Freethinkers Convention, 1905.

Zentrum, did manage to create numerous organizations of both clergy and laity with the ability to exert increasing influence on society and, as a result, on the state.[28]

The Republic, in effect, established itself just as old local solidarities were disappearing forever: the *fin des notables*[29] coincided with the *fin des terroirs*[30]—that is, the effective unification of once self-sufficient regions coincided with the collapse of local dynasties and the waning of memories of what those dynasties had represented. Meanwhile, experiments with monarchy and empire also failed, along with the history, old or new, that these attempted to emulate and the political and social patterns they embodied. At the same time, workers' organizations that had formed in the final years of the Empire were repressed, along with the legitimate memory of the nascent proletariat. In effect, the triumphant republicans had returned to the ideology of 1789:[31] the individual alone, isolated, without a past—the tabula rasa—but facing a Catholic Church riveted to its history and strengthened by state backing for its parish clergy and by the energy of its congregations of men and especially of women as well as by the active support of organized lay groups, most of which came to the Catholic camp from legitimism. Meanwhile, the state lost control of the secular clergy, who became ultramontane. Under the circumstances it is hardly surprising that there was a resurgence of the familiar figure of the "congregation," fraught with memories of the monks of the Leagues and of Jesuits

imposing their discipline on the nation's elites. There also appeared a new figure, a lay Janus, the convinced legitimist and assiduous benefactor, the *jésuite en robe courte* likely to lead a new "cabal of the devout."[32] What emerged from this unusual juncture and unique conjunction was thus by no means chimerical.

If the Republic was to achieve stability, it needed solid local roots. As republicans turned their attention to this task, they encountered Catholicism, both as an ideological model and as a social force. What they called clericalism was in fact the mobilization of an impressive apparatus of social control, together with a simultaneous denunciation of the paths that the new society hoped to take toward modernity. Under the circumstances it is not difficult to see how the schools became the prime battleground.

The conflict eventually engulfed the whole society, because republican attacks on the Jesuit *collèges* and efforts to establish secondary education for young women threatened to realign control of the elite and because the institution of secular public primary schools threatened to realign control of the masses. The struggle was nevertheless primarily ideological: revolution versus counterrevolution. Both camps were fond of these kinds of identifications. If the *Syllabus* reinforced the counterrevolutionary aspect of French Catholicism, the repression of the Commune led republicans to exalt the revolutionary heritage by way of compensation. As Claude Nicolet rightly noted, the battle over secularism made republicans aware of "the fundamental and ineluctable link between the political and the spiritual." For them, the anticlerical battle was the prerequisite of all political action; it was "literally the *motor* of history."[33]

That is why the process of educational secularization, affecting both teachers and curriculum, was so important. The reform process was begun by Jules Ferry and the Opportunist Party.[34] The first impact was on the curriculum: the catechism disappeared from the program, and under pressure from the Radical Party all religious instruction was eliminated from the public schools. Thursdays (later changed to Wednesday afternoons) were reserved for religious instruction, and the time lost was made up in Saturday classes. In recent years this has led to protests from parents upset about losing weekend time with their children, but as recently as 1991 the courts sided with the bishops, ruling that unless the whole arrangement were to be renegotiated, the existing compromise must be maintained.

In the short run the secularization of the curriculum had ambiguous consequences. For teachers, neutrality became the cardinal rule of behavior, not only because it made sense but because the authorities did not want to stir up trouble or put weapons into the hands of the enemies of secular education. In a famous statement Ferry warned teachers that nothing in their instruction should shock fathers who entrusted their children to the public schools.[35] Still, nothing in this admonition prevented the schools from inculcating the new republican values of nation, work, and science, as a result of which battles over textbooks flared up periodically.

Just as compulsory education in France marked the final stage in the long process of virtually eradicating illiteracy,[36] the secularization law completed a similar, and equally irreversible, evolution in primary education: traditional religious texts such as the Royaumont Bible and *Les Devoirs du chrétien* were replaced by new and more "functional" texts such as *Francinet* and *Simon de Nantua;* sacred history ("In the beginning God created the heaven and the earth") was replaced by profane history ("Our ancestors the Gauls"); and new disciplines such as geography appeared, in which curiosity about the things of this world took the place of the afterlife as the substance of children's lessons.[37] A good example of the change is the famous *Tour de la France par deux enfants* by G. Bruno, the provocative pseudonym chosen by a writer with a flair for teaching, whose work illustrates how the new curriculum supplanted a traditional religious program that was clearly outdated.

The secularization of the teaching staff came about somewhat later, as lay teachers trained in the new normal schools replaced Christian Brothers, who by now constituted only a minority of the teaching staff in public schools for boys, and teaching sisters of various orders, who still accounted for the majority of teachers in girls' schools. In boys' schools the replacement process began as early as 1860 and continued throughout the decade that preceded the new law (1886), so that compliance was almost immediate. In girls' schools, by contrast, the shortage of lay female teachers made it necessary to adopt a policy of gradual changeover, as Catholic teachers died off or quit their posts. In any case, the new law heightened antagonism in religious regions, where the public school and the church school often vied for pupils.

Reality is of course never neat. At the village level one wonders how many families like the Sandres continued to produce generation after generation of schoolmasters and -mistresses almost as if the law had never been passed.[38] In how many regions was there no battle of the schools at all, because there was no real opposition and no enthusiasm for conflict? How much real change was there in the Doubs, for example, where a majority of schoolmistresses were laywomen (that is, not sisters) before 1880 but were nevertheless practicing Catholics (hence not "seculars")—as indeed they would remain afterward?[39] Still, the Republic's "black *hussards*" were quite real: if the typical village schoolmaster of the early nineteenth century also served as choirmaster, usher, and sacristan, he was likely to be replaced at the end of the century by a man who doubled as mayor's secretary, town librarian, and local bandleader. An idea of the magnitude of the change can be gleaned from a glance at the government's budget. In the period 1875–1879 more money was allocated to religious functions (*cultes*) than to public education (55 million francs versus 46 million), whereas by 1885–1889 spending on the former had declined to 48 million versus 130 million on the latter. Minutes of parliamentary debates, for 1883 especially, show how republicans saw every decrease in the budget for religious functions as a direct contribution to the progress of public education.[40]

Secularization affected all levels of the educational system. Religious officials soon disappeared from the Conseil Supérieur de l'Enseignement Public, and theology faculties, already moribund to be sure, soon discovered that they were no longer welcome in the state university system.[41] The secularization process also involved other areas of public service: nuns, for example, left the women's prisons to which they had been systematically assigned after the 1839 reform.[42] By contrast, they remained at their posts in provincial hospitals, though not in institutions run by the Assistance Publique in Paris, where lay nurses replaced Sisters of Charity. The secularizing wave also swept through cemeteries and courts. In 1880, Sunday ceased to be an official day of rest: Was this political progress or social regression? In 1884 it ceased to be obligatory for assemblies embarking on new terms to solicit the "assistance" of God "in the churches and temples": God was discreetly outlawed at the cost of a slight modification to the Constitution.[43] Divorce was reinstated that same year, so that the Catholic conception of marriage ceased to be a universal requirement. But certain symbols had a more direct impact. When the Assumptionists inaugurated a new daily newspaper in 1883, they called it *La Croix* (The Cross), because, to the outrage of Catholics, the crucifix had just been banned from schools and hospitals.[44]

Catholic Science and Secular Morality

The schools were central to republican thinking not only because they were a strategic prize to be wrested from the clergy but also because education was directly implicated in two areas in which the war between Catholics and seculars was neverending, namely, science and ethics. As it happens, the vocabulary of the time is revealing: contemporaries spoke of "Catholic science" and "secular morality," as if both contenders were required to prove their mettle on the enemy's terrain.

"Catholic science" originated with the followers of Lamennais.[45] It was in no sense a precursor of Stalin's concept of "proletarian science" but rather the expression of a wish to reestablish a unifying theological discourse capable of incorporating the practice of science, which had achieved autonomy from theology in the seventeenth century and turned secular in the second half of the eighteenth century and during the Revolution. When it came to particulars, Catholic science also tended to favor those "scientific" concepts most closely aligned with traditional philosophy (advocating, for example, vitalism over materialism in medicine) or revealed truth (preferring monogenist to polygenist theories in anthropology). After 1860, and even more after 1870, discoveries in scientific disciplines ranging from German philology to Darwinian biology challenged biblical truth more and more directly. Meanwhile, scientists such as the illustrious Marcellin Berthelot were quick to throw their support to the Republic. Catholics found themselves in a defen-

BRANLY CROIT..! FOCH CROIT... PASTEUR CROIT...

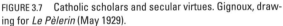

... mais M. Homais, lui, ne croit pas!

FIGURE 3.7   Catholic scholars and secular virtues. Gignoux, drawing for *Le Pèlerin* (May 1929).

FIGURES 3.8 AND 3.9   Grandjouan, The Secular Virtues; for *La Raison* (August, 1907).

sive situation, defended only by the still young science faculties of the Instituts Catholiques and reduced to issuing lists of scientists who were also believers in order to prove that science need not be atheistic: fortunately there was Pasteur. They were also obliged to refight old battles, as their enemies purposely raised again and again the trial of Galileo. Fortunately, anniversaries raised less predictable issues of contention. In 1892, for example, Europe celebrated the four-hundredth anniversary of the discovery of America by Christopher Columbus. But what exactly was being celebrated? Was it "the triumph of positive science over the chimerical science of theology?" Or was it the advent of a new missionary fired by an "almost supernatural desire to bring Christ...to the unknown peoples who waited so long for Him in the shadow of death?"[46]

The battle raged on at a more down-to-earth level as well, at times in rather picturesque fashion. In 1910, for instance, a teacher in Blajan (Haute-Garonne) offered this rather curious exercise in dictation in a course in hygiene:

> Those submissive to the clergy rarely bathe because their religion teaches them to prefer filthy modesty: one may not look at or touch certain parts of the body, the sexual parts for example....A great doctor set out to discover which religion has the greatest number of victims and the greatest variety of diseases of this kind [sexual disorders]. He found that it was the Catholic religion, which is understandable since this religion teaches no, or virtually no, principles of hygiene....I am speaking to you *scientifically*, honestly and decently but above all practically.[47]

In fact, at this late date, the *patronages catholiques*, or church youth organizations, then at their peak, paid particular attention to the physical development of the boys who joined them: it was through these clubs that soccer, and later basketball, came to France, and they also popularized all sorts of gymnastic activities.

If the Catholics were called upon to demonstrate their mettle in science, the seculars were obliged to do the same in the moral realm. Anticlericals were of course in the habit of responding to attacks in this area by pointing accusatory fingers at Christian Brothers found guilty of various crimes by the courts. And while republicans were only too glad to reprint Diderot's salacious novel of the religious life *La Religieuse*, they also knew that such tactics were useless at the grassroots level, where the "good sisters" were generally held to be above suspicion. By contrast, lay schoolmistresses, often isolated single women, were relatively vulnerable to attack on moral grounds, or at any rate more open to suspicion than their religious counterparts, as can be seen in Léon Frappié's novel *L'Institutrice de province* and the responses to it compiled by Francisque Sarcey.[48] That is why the officials of the Upper Normal Schools of Sèvres and Fontenay, which trained future female schoolteachers and principals, insisted that their young charges be morally beyond reproach, as Françoise Mayeur has pointed out. In the "gentle lay convent" of Fontenay, for example, particular attention was paid to "education of the conscience." At Sèvres, the first headmistress, Mme Favre, daughter of an Alsatian pastor and wife of the republican Jules Favre, inculcated a strict sense of duty in her female students, using the ethical writings of Epictetus, Kant, and Emerson.[49]

At its peak in the period 1860–1910, the antagonism between seculars and Catholics found visible embodiment in every village in France, where from 1880 on combined town hall–school buildings went up opposite clerical compounds (church plus rectory) renovated during the Second Empire; and in every city, where government buildings and statues of great men in the main squares counterbalanced the downtown church steeples and crowned Virgins looking down from the surrounding heights, or where Renaissance-style city halls competed with huge neo-Gothic churches built a few years earlier.

Not even Paris was exempt from this battle of symbolic architectures. For more than a century the two sides fought over Soufflot's neoclassical edifice: Was it a church or a pantheon? The issue was finally decided by the death of Victor Hugo (1885), which came at the right moment to weigh definitively in favor of the latter choice, today's Pantheon. But soon each side in the dispute would be able to claim a still more modern emblem: Sacré-Coeur for the Catholics, the Eiffel Tower for the seculars. Both drew criticism from within their own camps. Everyone knows of the hullabaloo unleashed by the construction of Eiffel's tower. But Sacré-Coeur had its Catholic detractors. Its Romano-Byzantine architecture (actually it was an extrapolation of the Romanesque of southwestern France) was hard to take. "Will Sacré-Coeur of Montmartre be built in our national style or in some foreign style?" It was a vexing question, and those who signed one protest petition were unanimous in their answer: the church should be French and Gothic and not a "mosque."[50]

Before long, however, these initial quarrels gave way to out-and-out antagonism between seculars and clericals. The construction of Sacré-Coeur was a "national vow" approved by the Assembly on July 24, 1873, that is, at the height of reaction. Those who made the vow had of course denounced the imperial feast and were reacting to the shock of France's defeat, both sentiments that republicans could share, but that made no difference: the shadow of clericalism that the new church would cast over Paris was intolerable. In 1881 the Radicals sounded the alarm in the Assembly:

CLEMENCEAU: We ask only one thing, and that is to repudiate the work of the clerical reactionaries in the National Assembly, to disavow it publicly.

ADMIRAL DE LA RONCIÈRE DE NOURY: No to the revolutionary spirit!

THE MARQUIS DE BELCASTEL: Catholicism is for all times—

M. CORDON: I beg your pardon. Catholicism did not exist before it existed and will not exist after it has ceased to exist.

THE MARQUIS DE BELCASTEL: It has existed since the first day of the world and will exist forever.[51]

And that was not the end of it. Before long it was being alleged that Sacré-Coeur had been built in expiation for the crimes of the Commune. This was not the initial intention, but the choice of site lent itself to this interpretation, which many Catholics did not shrink from proposing as a justification.

As for the Eiffel Tower, aesthetic debate should have been enough. But the Tower was built on the Champ-de-Mars, which Michelet had called the Revolution's only monument, on the occasion of the hundredth anniversary of

FIGURE 3.10   *The Christ of the Criminal Courts;* postcard, 1904.

FIGURE 3.11   *Christ Will Stay, despite the Sectarians;* engraving, *La Croix illustrée* (November 11, 1905).

1789. That was too much. To many outraged Catholics, the new monument was a
modern Tower of Babel that would sow confusion among those who had haughtily
dared to erect such a "hideous skeleton," such a "horrid piling," as opposed to
Sacré-Coeur, that "bastion of God" and "white citadel." The Breton publication
Semaines religieuses, from which these compliments were taken, even offered this
pastiche of Victor Hugo in mockery of the project:

> Nains de quatre-vingt-neuf, singez les grandes choses,
> Multipliez l'énorme, artisans, apprentis:
> Créez des tours de fer pour vos apothéoses,
> Mais vos rêves sont laids et vous êtes petits.
> [Midgets of '89, emulate great things;
> artisans, apprentices, copy what is immense:
> Create iron towers for your apotheoses,
> but your dreams are ugly and you are small.][52]

There is no need to multiply examples. No one denies that the antagonism was
fierce at the time the republicans came to power. Like it or not, Protestants and Jews
were forced to adapt to this Procrustean bed. Events also played a part. There were

many Protestants among the republicans, and their educational militancy worked miracles.[53] And what is there to say about the unfortunate Catholic Bank of the Union Générale, whose collapse was blamed on a conspiracy of its alleged Protestant and Jewish enemies?

In any case, the real antagonism that developed in the wake of the major secularization legislation of the 1880s dictated certain political positions but failed to impose a permanent structure on either the right (both Orleanists and Bonapartists being only sporadically pro-clerical) or the left (where anticlericalism was an issue of only moderate importance to the chastened Opportunists and even to certain socialists). That persistent antagonism did not prevent temporary realignments, however, as when Legitimists and Radicals found themselves on the same side in the Boulangist controversy, nor did it prevent many Catholics from offering their permanent support to the Republic. Nevertheless, the presence of vociferous activists and eager followers in both camps—the Assumptionists of *La Bonne Presse* on the right, for example or the editors of *La Libre Pensée* on the left—precluded any real effort to restore peace.

If we focus for a moment on the Catholic side, *La Croix* can tell us a great deal about the new state of mind among Catholics in the early years of the Republic. Founded in 1883 by Father Vincent de Paul Bailly in the spirit of *Le Pèlerin*, *La Croix*, which was aimed at a broad audience and spawned many local affiliates in order to extend its roots into the provinces, was a daily paper with an obvious zest for polemic: its choicest words were reserved for Freemasons obviously, Jews above all, and schoolteachers, "the teaching Republic's chain gang." *La Croix* attacked the secular state ("the state-god that expelled the real God and lives solely on universal suffrage"), parliament ("a chamber of disorder"), and above all the university, that "mortal illness," which "discovered a secret that had previously eluded humanity: how to increase the number of suicides by young people." Apart from polemic, however, the political battle never really amounted to anything: one can understand why the time was not ripe for "proper" royalist combat, yet despite Pope Leo XIII's injunction, rightists remained steadfastly opposed to accepting the Republic or forming a true conservative party. Catholics pursued the illusory goal of trying to unite people around Catholic interests alone, and they failed regularly in election after election. *La Croix* revealed a powerful capacity for invective coupled with a weak capacity for organization: up to the time of the Dreyfus Affair, this was the disconcerting public face of the Assumptionists' private newspaper.[54]

Thus the "separation of church and school" induced combative Catholics to wage ideological warfare without real contact with the new political realities.[55] On the educational battlefield, at any rate, it held its own. By the end of the nineteenth century both sides had reason to be satisfied. Seculars were pleased that secular education was a reality: nearly three quarters of all elementary school pupils attended secular public schools, and *lycées* and *collèges* for young women had become popular. The revitalized university system still enjoyed a near monopoly, with little competition from the five Instituts Catholiques thus far established. But the Catholic educational system (which now included most of the private schools in France) still had its strong points. In certain regions such as the west of France it held its ground against its competitors. Girls remained loyal to the Church: forty percent of female students were taught by religious sisters, and that figure understates the Catholic influence in both the lower and middle classes. Finally, a network of Catholic *collèges* with priests and monks as teachers attracted more and more students every year from 1887 to 1898, increasing its share of the male secondary school population from thirty-two to forty-two percent of the total.[56] In education, the battle strengthened both sides without designating a victor.

Hence something had to be done, and to the detriment of liberal principles a series of anti-congreganist measures were passed in the wake of the Law of 1901: France now enjoyed freedom of association for all except the "congregations," which previously were the only legal associations. What had been a privilege became grounds for discrimination; the exceptional status remained. To the detriment of the Concordat as well: from 1905 the Republic no longer recognized or assumed the cost of supporting any religion. The battle now shifted to new and more delicate terrain: not the school but religion itself. Was the Radical Party's Republic prepared to revisit the Revolution? Catholics saw a repetition of 1790 in the anti-congreganist laws and of 1795 in the separation of church and state. Despite the vociferous exhortations of extremists on both sides, however, the Republic did not revisit either 1791 or 1793. It sought neither schism nor dechristianization. Let *inventaires* turn to confrontation resulting in death, and Clemenceau would have the troublemakers arrested.[57] No new persecutions for a few candlesticks! Let the pope prohibit *cultuels*, and other procedures for the devolution of church property would be negotiated. The separation of church and state presented a paradoxical situation: because it was carried out under the searchlight of history, there was an obsession with the revolutionary precedent, but the end result was an amicable parting of the ways without dramatic incident. The "lesson of the Terror," recited throughout the nineteenth century, was not forgotten, even though the protagonists delighted in the heroic combats of their illustrious ancestors.

Then came the war, which changed nothing but confirmed everything: Catholics, like socialists, died to defend France and in so doing also defended the Republic. There was nothing like the uprising of the Vendée against the Revolution; indeed, "émigrés," actually banished clergymen, returned to France in order to take part in the war. Catholics marched to the front under the blue, white, and red of the Republic, although they might have preferred a flag embellished with an image of Sacré-Coeur. The dead had their caskets draped in blue, white, and red. In fact, most Catholics were outspoken in their outrage when the pope proposed in 1917 that peace be concluded without a winner or loser. There were a few false notes, however, as at the end of 1915, when a "vile rumor" circulated that the country harbored some "15,580 shirker priests." Verbal excess was always possible; images of revolutionary violence sprang readily to mind, even if it was only to deny their reality. *Le Bonnet rouge,* for example, began one polemic with this blast: "We have never insisted that conscript priests should have to die. We have no intention of refloating Carrier's scuttlable boats."[58,59]

Tactical errors of this sort did not stand in the way of reconciliation in the trenches. After the war the religious conflict seems to have come to a standstill, as the neither side was able to develop new themes. The Cartel des Gauches would learn this lesson the hard way when it attempted to rekindle the battle in 1924. Catholics plastered the walls with their answer: "We will not go."[60] Men who had worn the uniform and shed blood for France could no longer be exiled. All that could be said on the subject had been said, yet the battle was not yet over. The secular camp was probably never more highly organized than in the interwar years, and verbal clashes were not uncommon. Take the case of Joan of Arc, for example. In 1920 Rome canonized her, and a legislature filled with war veterans honored her as the "national saint." In 1929 the five-hundredth anniversary of the beginning of her adventures again put her in the public eye. A counterattack was inevitable, and it came in 1930 in a series of ten articles published in *L'École libératrice,* the organ of the Syndicat National des Instituteurs, in which Gaston Clémendot set out to topple "the idol of Domrémy."[61]

When Vichy legislation favorable to Catholic schools was overturned in 1945, proponents of the parochial school system began to organize. Their opponents revived such publications as *La Calotte, La Raison,* and *Les Cahiers rationalistes.* Breton priests gleefully denounced "the devil's schools," while seculars responded with the incontrovertible slogan, "Public schools, public funds." Had the entente between "those who believe in heaven and those who do not" failed to survive the Resistance? In any case, those who refused to lay down their arms enjoyed a marvelous second season.

The Revolution as Matrix

Where did this terrible family battle begin? If we ask those involved, we will come away with genealogies but not explanations. Perhaps there is a sign in the fact that when *La Calotte* resumed publication in 1945, it remained faithful to the republican calendar. Other secular voices invoked precursors from before 1789: the legists of Philip the Fair, the "freethinkers" of the Renaissance, the *philosophes* of the eighteenth century. Their adversaries followed a somewhat different route to the same

L'homme enfin satisfait d'avoir recouvré ses droits, en rend graces à l'Etre Suprème.

FIGURE 3.12   Pérée, *The Rights of Man;* engraving, 1793.

end, but their heroes and martyrs had different names. A glance at the history text-books used in Catholic and secular schools under the Third Republic is all the confirmation one needs.[62]

Everyone pointed to the Revolution, but was this really the origin of Catholic-secular antagonism? I prefer to call it the matrix—but in what sense? The two camps did not exist as such at the time, and the vocabulary was not yet fixed. Or at any rate, the noble vocabulary was not yet fixed; common parlance was something else again. The clergy were ferociously mocked. Indeed, political caricature was invented for the purpose of attacking the clergy: the debauched monk, the big, fat bishop.[63] The clergy were an early target of insults as well: the streets rang with shouts of "priests to the lampposts" as patriots emerged from the theater where the actor Talma thrilled crowds with his portrayal of the Saint Bartholomew's Day massacres in Marie Joseph Chénier's *Charles IX*. In November 1789, Camille Desmoulins inaugurated his soon-to-be-famous newspaper *Révolutions de France et de Brabant* with this lapidary summary of the situation: "The king is in the Louvre, the National Assembly is in the Tuileries...the mills are turning, the traitors are fleeing, *la calotte* [literally, the skullcap, that is, the clerical party] is prostrate, aristocracy is on its last legs." He happily adapted Voltaire's anticlerical polemics, including the famous slogan *écrasez l'infâme* (crush the vile thing!), to the needs of a daily struggle against the "swindling and stupid bonzes." When the first religious tensions arose in 1790, he came up with this formula, the first of a long line: "There appears to be a struggle to the death going on between the skullcap and the tricolor sash."[64]

The ferocity of such images and the impertinence of such words cannot be ignored, nor can the fundamental antagonism between patriots and aristocrats.[65] Still, historians seeking to understand what happened in 1789 and 1790 have their own way of putting things: it is possible, for example, to suggest that the Revolution initiated a twofold process of secularization, half of which succeeded while the other half failed. On the one hand there was the immediate, irreversible secularization of political space, which took place almost by consensus. Catholicism disappeared not only as the first order of the tripartite medieval system but also as the kingdom's leading landowner and primary source of legitimation of government power. The divine-right monarchy gave way to popular sovereignty. In the new political landscape the religious dimension had no relevance. In the new, regenerated France there were in theory no longer Catholics, Protestants, and Jews but only free citizens enjoying equal rights. No longer was Catholicism a fundamental reference. On the contrary, it was reduced to just another of those opinions open to public discussion, in the light of which individuals were free to choose how they stood.[66]

This unprecedented secularization of the political sphere—one form of the tabula rasa of which the revolutionaries were so fond—encountered no immediate obstacles among the deputies of the clergy, but the progress of the Revolution soon aroused an opposition whose goal was to defend the rights of both Catholicism and the monarchy, pitted against a clerical avant garde more inclined to explore genuine social equality than to draw the consequences of the new definition of liberty.[67] In any case, the clergy saw concretely that the installation of the new political order was in fact working out to their disadvantage: the Church's property was

Figure 3.13   *The Jehovah of the French;* engraving after Sauvage, 1792.

Figure 3.14   *God and the Head of the Church Protect Napoleon;* anonymous engraving. Note the ungrammatical legend (*protège* should be *protègent*).

nationalized to finance the Revolution, their religious vows were nullified in the name of individual freedom and public utility, and Catholicism was denied recognition as the national religion in the name of the brand-new principle of freedom of religion.[68]

But the Revolution, after creating an autonomous political space by excluding Catholicism as an integral component of the Ancien Régime, also attempted to secularize that very same Catholicism by incorporating it into the new administrative order that was beginning to be established by late 1789. "Secularize the Church": this paradoxical formulation is borrowed from Jaurès.[69] In the present context we may take this to mean the imposition on the Catholic Church of new "norms" established for the nation as a whole: the redistricting of space through the creation of *départements,* with which the Church's new dioceses were to coincide, and through the realignment of mainly urban parishes, which took more account of the population; and new procedures for choosing religious officials, primarily bishops and parish priests, involving the same multistage electoral system used for selecting administrative officials. What is more, the Civil Constitution of the Clergy also regulated the finances of the Catholic Church, offering more equitable and more generous compensation to the parish clergy generally and introducing reforms in church procedures desired by a majority, along with a pinch of Presbyterianism and a dash of Gallicanism.

This is where the rupture originated. Those who rejected the Civil Constitution of the Clergy also dismissed a reorganization of the Church along lines they considered too "secular," even though this would have replaced a system which, with its nonclerical *collateurs,* or patrons, also left a great deal to be desired. The repudiation also concerned the manner of the reform: the Catholic hierarchy in particular could not accept a reform without either agreeing to it itself, in accordance with Gallican tradition, or submitting the proposed changes to Rome for the customary negotiations. But the Constituent Assembly, in the flush of its new sovereignty, could not agree to a national council, which would have revived the Church of France, and did not wish to await the favors of Pius VI, who had been antagonized by the revolt in Avignon, was hostile to the Revolution anyway, yet who for the moment had chosen to refrain from action pending further developments. Faced with mounting troubles, particularly in the provinces, the Assembly took the initiative and forced all concerned priests, from bishop down to vicar, to take the oath (in common after February 1790) and assent to a Constitution that by now included the new law against which many clerics had protested.

What followed was the paradoxical spectacle of an oath, a sacred act of national unity, becoming instead a sign of national division, accepted by some and rejected by others among the 160 bishops and coadjutors and 50,000 curés and vicars of

France.[70] The Civil Constitution, which had laid down the implicit principle that Catholicism coincided with France—a state religion but not a national one—thus led, as a result of the oath, to the first perceptible sign of division at the national level, since the people were to one degree or another involved in the choices made by their clerics. The first secularization defined a political space outside Catholicism, whereas the second placed religion back at the heart of political debate. Until then the opposition to the Revolution existed only in the relatively vague form of the "aristocracy," but now it took on the precise outlines of Catholicism. The Third Estate had of course initiated the Revolution by refusing to maintain three distinct orders. But the Revolution was able to attach "figures" to the abstractions it excluded only by transforming the noble into the "aristocrat" and the priest into the *calotin*. The pejorative term *calotin* in fact combined three distinct images that would merge into a single image for posterity: the fanatic preacher of an intolerant and superstitious religion, the representative of the Ancien Régime who had lost his property and privileges, and, last but not least, the refractory who, by refusing to take the oath, excluded himself from the new civic order.[71] There is a direct line of descent from the Revolutionary *calotte* to the *cléricalisme* of the Republic.

Of course the Revolution never learned to deal with the religious conflict that introduced a crucial division into its history. The rest of the story is familiar: a renewal of secularization, this time directed at society as well as the clergy, coupled with dechristianization: by the end of the Terror, the Revolution of Year II had become vehemently antireligious. For collective memory, whether spontaneous or more often than not revived, the dominant image is not one of uniform hostility to religion but rather of different treatment for the two rival churches, the one refractory, the other constitutional, that grew out of acceptance or rejection of the Civil Constitution: on the one hand the martyred priest, on the other the clergyman who discarded his surplice and took a wife. The aureole and the stigma. And of course people would also remember the Vendée and the way in which a rural population organized an armed opposition to defend its faith and its king.

The crisis around the oath soon raised another related but distinct issue. It was not only that nonjuring priests found themselves at odds with the Constituent Assembly, but that Catholicism found itself at odds with the Revolution. The revolutionaries therefore sought to establish their own sacred ritual distinct from the Catholic liturgy, as evidenced by three highly symbolic acts that took place in 1791: the transformation of the Church of Sainte-Geneviève into the Pantheon, the purely "secular" celebration honoring Voltaire, and the exhibition of David's sketch exalting the Tennis Court Oath as the moment in which, pure of all clerical taint, the Revolution inaugurated itself in a unanimous outpouring. The great revolutionary scholar Albert Mathiez gave an excellent summary of the novelty of the situation in the conclusion to his thesis, written when he was still just a young man in 1903: nowadays, he explained, republicans

> no longer give any thought to dreaming up new religions. They do not care to establish a new church, but they have not given up hope of resolving the problem of democracy. Today, in order to impress the republican stamp on generations to come, we have free, compulsory, secular education....Our ancestors of the Revolution hoped to achieve the same goal of imparting a republican education by establishing a religion.[72]

Why do I bring up the subject of revolutionary religion? Because the effort to define the new cult brought out another type of tension between Catholicism and the Revolution: along with secularization went a transfer of sacrality. A century later Jules Ferry would set out to resolve practical questions: What kinds of teachers did the Republic need? What curriculum for its schools? The Revolution had much more utopian dreams for education, and these reveal the central issue at the heart of the debate over secularization in terms similar to those used by the young Mathiez: How were the people to be wedded to the new course of politics? How were free citizens to be persuaded to embrace the new system, founded on reason?

Those who took part in this thinking were unanimous in seeking a substitute for discredited Catholicism but disagreed about what that substitute ought to be. There were, however, two primary models. The first, more or less inspired by Rousseau, was implemented to a degree in Robespierre's project to establish a cult of the Supreme Being. The idea was that every society requires a common religious foundation as the basis of its morality. "Religion is therefore the first point I want to be stressed in primary education....What the primary schools must instill in their pupils is a religious principle, the essence and basis of all faiths—a religion as simple and grand as nature."[73]

This first model remained mainly theoretical; the second aimed above all at becoming operational. It began with the observation of the immense ability of Catholicism to "mobilize" the faithful; the Church, with its impressive liturgy and a theology that offered comfort even as it stirred feelings of guilt, clearly had the resources to indoctrinate large numbers of people.[74] When it came to training today's patriots or tomorrow's republicans, it therefore made sense to tap into Catholicism's sources of energy in order to generate genuine revolutionary enthusiasm. According to a well-known text by the pastor Rabaut Saint-Étienne, "National education consists in seizing the child still in the cradle, and even earlier, for the unborn child already belongs to the nation. The nation takes hold of the whole person and never lets go, so that national education is not an institution for the child but for a lifetime."[75] The new catechism, essential to the salvation of the future republican, is to be inculcated from birth.

These dominant positions—religion as the foundation of society and the adaptation of Catholic forms for the benefit of the republican regime—found a radical critic in Condorcet. "Fanaticism," Bouquier pronounced, following Rabaut's lead, "once had a temple in every commune. Let those temples now become the temples of liberty, of education."[76] But Condorcet replied that "if you call a school a national temple," you would introduce the principle of authority, the very basis of fanaticism, into education.[77]

> Neither the French constitution nor the declaration of rights should be presented to any class of citizens as tablets from heaven that must be worshipped and believed....As long as there are men who do not obey reason alone, who receive their opinions from an alien opinion, all chains will have been broken in vain. Even if those guiding opinions are useful truths, the human race would nevertheless remain divided into two classes, those who reason and those who believe, masters and slaves.[78]

Between the light of reason and the darkness of belief no compromise is possible.

Condorcet was even more vehemently critical of "revolutionary enthusiasm" in his *Mémoires*. Were some people advocating that students be taught the text of the Constitution? "If they mean that it must be taught as a doctrine conforming to the principles of universal reason or that one should whip up blind enthusiasm in its favor so that citizens will be incapable of assessing its true worth; if they are proposing to tell people that this is what you must worship and believe; then what they propose is the creation of a kind of political religion." Responding directly to Rabaut Saint-Étienne and others who hoped to form future citizens by controlling the education of the young, Condorcet strongly denounced those who "propose to seize the child in its very first moments in order to fill its mind with images that time cannot destroy, to bind individuals to the laws and constitution of their country by blind emotion and introduce them to reason only through the miracles of the imagination and the confusion of the passions." Were such people "more certain of their political truths than fanatics of all sects feel they are certain of all their religious delusions?...To declare it permissible to dazzle men rather than enlighten them, to seduce them in the name of truth...is to consecrate all the follies of enthusiasm, all the ruses of proselytism."[79]

Why dwell on the texts of an isolated thinker? The answer is that they set forth the ideological underpinnings of the Catholic-secular relationship in the most forceful of terms. If Religion and Reason are antinomical, a reasoned critique of religion cannot permit a religious administration of knowledge and power without contradicting itself. Condorcet's remarks are valuable not only in themselves but also because of Condorcet's strategic position as a link between the *philosophes* and the *idéologues*. Both directly, through his writings on education, and indirectly, through his influence in transmitting the legacy of the Enlightenment in the form of scientism, Condorcet transmitted to the Third Republic a message that would by and large be heeded,[80] despite recurring temptations to combat Catholicism with its own weapons, such as civic baptisms and weddings.[81] Condorcet made explicit what the Revolution in its early stages demonstrated: if politics is to be based on rationality alone and independent of all authority, then it cannot assume direct control of religion in any form. Condorcet's critique thus explained the imbalance that would emerge later in the relation between secularism and religion: the state tended to renounce religion (secularization) rather than appropriate it (secular religion).

Mediations

Of course the passage from the fundamental experiences of the Revolution to the later Catholic-secular split involved a number of mediations, three of which I shall discuss here. First, Napoleon brought stability to French society and its institutions. A postrevolutionary order emerged that included effective secularization of state and society through the Civil Code; the existence of multiple faiths was recognized, while the Concordat consecrated a special place for Roman Catholicism as the majority religion; and the university was given responsibility for managing public education under the control of the state. Catholic-secular antagonism was henceforth constrained by a system of institutions that, reflecting both the effects of revolutionary secularization and France's distinctive religious history, resulted in a high degree of stability. No matter whether Catholics sought to control the university or to rival it, the state's role in education had become irreversible. Seculars could try to overturn the Concordat, but Catholicism would nevertheless remain the majority religion sociologically and retain its Roman roots. Napoleon's aim was to achieve a stable empire through a utopian fusion of antagonistic traditions, as epitomized in Portalis's pithy phrase: "Philosophical without impiety and religious without fanaticism." The reality would eventually fall short of this unrealizable ecumenical ideal, yet the effort would help to make possible—and in a sense legitimate—the emergence of two traditions rooted in two antagonistic memories, which Michelet, for example, would transfigure in the Introduction to his *Histoire de la Révolution française* in the following terms: "Therefore, despite all the theoretical elaborations and new forms and new words, I still see only two great facts, two principles, two actors, two persons on the stage: Christianity and the Revolution."[82]

The second mediation is not institutional in nature but has to do, rather, with the implantation of a tradition. It has been said, rightly, that the Revolution created the Vendée as a region based on the memory of a murderous history.[83] Indeed, all of France continues to bear the stigma of revolutionary division. The most enduring and visible and therefore most profound of those divisions is religious in nature. A map showing the proportion of priests who took the oath to support the Civil Constitution of the Clergy in 1791 is strikingly similar to a map showing the frequency of religious practice just after World War II. Areas where a high proportion of priests refused to take the oath became areas where a high proportion of the population continued to go to church, whereas "constitutional" areas became "dechristianized." The problem is how to interpret these facts, and two errors in particular are to be avoided. The map of the oath already reflects a long religious history, as Timothy Tackett has shown.[84] Furthermore, the contrasts in religious practice are already noticeable in the nineteenth century thanks to episcopal surveys conducted under the July Monarchy and afterward.

The crucial factor, however, is what took place in each locality in the three decisive

FIGURE 3.15   For or against Catholicism after Thermidor: propaganda by engraving in 1797. Strack, *Atheism Tries and Fails;* engraving, 1797.

FIGURE 3.16   Strack, *The Magic Lantern,* 1797.

decades following the oath of 1791. The crisis surrounding the oath seems to reveal the existence of two distinct religious models, a traditional one in the refractory regions and a new one in the constitutional regions. In areas where the clergy, in accord with their flock, accepted the autonomy of the political and a degree of secularization of the church, they would have difficulty in the future maintaining its spiritual hegemony through preaching and confession among men who had largely committed themselves to the revolutionary process or simply benefitted from it. There was also another, more immediate, difficulty: the systematic destruction of the Constitutional Church, which got off to an effective start with the forced abdication of Year II, continued with loss of clergy to its rival during the Directory and with marginalization under the reconstruction that followed the Concordat, and ended with the elimination of the last surviving constitutional clergy during the Restoration. Of the many consequences of this systematic elimination of the constitutional clergy, two deserve explicit mention. Areas in which the constitutional clergy had dominated found themselves without any priests at all or, at best, with no priests of their "own." In some particularly hard-hit dioceses, up to forty percent of the parishes were therefore eliminated. These "devastated" regions were also, for obvious reasons, quick to become dechristianized, especially in view of the fact that, at the national level, the destruction of the constitutional church resulted in the total triumph of the refractory, of which revived nineteenth-century Catholicism was the direct heir. It is not difficult to understand how such a monopoly helped to perpetuate rather than attenuate hostility.[85]

One result of this forgotten "schism," lost in the silence surrounding the destruction of the constitutional church in which so many parties had a hand, was that old differences were preserved in the forms of religious practice itself. Was the cleavage really between "practicing" and "nonpracticing" Catholics? No, because each group had its own "version" of religion. The real difference was rather between, on the one hand, a Catholicism in which, as in the past, the clergy continued to monitor beliefs and control practice through the catechism, liturgy, sacraments, and above all confession, a Roman or ultramontane form of Catholicism that was also more intransigent and fundamentalist; and on the other hand, a traditional Catholicism sustained largely by the desire of the faithful to seek the sanction of the clergy for important moments in life such as birth and death, as well as to seek the direct aid of healing saints in facing life's misfortunes. The first of these two models is linked to the clergy, the second more directly to the laity. Thus the old medieval distinction between lay and ecclesiastic was revived within Catholicism as a result of the Revolution. Furthermore, this difference in religious practice served as the matrix within which a quasi-religious, quasi-political opposition between seculars and clericals could develop.

FIGURE 3.17   *The Revolution Today.* Above the entry to this church in Houdan (Yvelines), the text of 18 Floréal, Year II, can still be read: "The French people recognize the existence of the Supreme Being and the immortality of the soul."

The third type of mediation was the restoration of normal political life, which occurred in two stages: the first began in 1814–1815, with the institution of public debate within a constitutional framework, and the second in 1848, a year that marked the beginning of an irreversible process of democratization.

The Restoration brought with it the possibility of nonviolent political confrontation, although within a narrow framework. In fact the postrevolutionary equilibrium had to be left untouched in most essential respects; external constraints imposed by the allies in the wake of Napoleon's defeat had to be taken into account; and, last but not least, the fragile legitimacy of the new regime had to be maintained. Under these conditions both sides had little room to maneuver. It was legitimate, however, to debate the Revolution in historical or philosophical terms, just as it was also legitimate to debate religion by arguing about the role of the Jesuits or the Congregation or, better yet, grappling over educational issues. The very visible role played by influential Catholics in the new regime and the open goal of missionaries of working toward both a political restoration and a religious reconquest provided pretexts for adversaries to seize on. Thus the narrow scope of permissible debate combined with ideological and symbolic overinvestment in questions of the sacred and the laws concerning sacrilege and with the desire to return to the Ancien Régime to bring religion back in as a discriminating factor in contrasting political choices. It was the liberals versus the ultras, a situation that was in many ways a precursor of what would come to pass in the early years of the Third Republic.

One clear sign of this situation was the new importance of debates over education, over the role of the Jesuits and the teaching congregations, a pedagogical battle over mutual instruction (the monitorial system) that turned into a doctrinal battle in the context of new legislation concerning primary education.[86] Every occa-

FIGURE 3.18   Demonstration protesting the publication of Salman Rushdie's *Satanic Verses;* Paris, 1989.

sion was an opportunity for conflict. A new theme appeared with a long future ahead of it: the division of society resulting from two different educational systems. But whereas Destutt de Tracy, in Year X, as the Revolution was ending, still saw the dual system of education as a reflection of class division (working class and educated class),[87] in 1816, at the beginning of the Restoration, the rector of the academy of Rennes insisted instead on the ideological division within the elite: "Today," he wrote to a friend, "studies pursued separately and in institutions whose spirit is not entirely the same are a source of division in society. When young people leave their preparatory or church schools, they enter the world filled with serious prejudices against one another. They accuse each other of ignorance and impiety. They feel contempt and hatred without knowing one another."[88] Such ideas, common during the Third Republic, were still new in the Restoration, where it would be six more years before the liberal deputy General Foy would initiate public debate over the question.[89] As it happens, the quoted passage is from a priest with Jansenist leanings who began his career on the eve of the Revolution as the principal of the *collège* of Vannes after the expulsion of the Jesuits. Another case in which critical thinking simply leapt over the Revolution was the denunciation of the "priestly party" by Montlosier in 1826.[90] Montlosier was a Gallican who had somehow wandered off into the past of the Ancien Régime; he drew on the anti-Jesuit literature of the eighteenth century to compose pamphlets giving one of the earliest clinical descriptions of clericalism. It was an odd trick of memory: the Revolution remained present but chiefly in a historical mode, whereas everyday politics drew on the debates of the previous century. Never before had there been so many published editions of Voltaire and Rousseau. There were no seculars yet, nor were there clericals, but there were two camps that bore an uncanny resemblance to them.

Debate, however, remained narrowly circumscribed. It began to spread, however, after 1830 and especially 1848, affecting minor provincial *notables* like the pharmacist Homais (in Flaubert's *Madame Bovary*) and the elite of the urban working class like Pierre Proudhon, as well as rural people. In the end, with the establishment of universal suffrage, the people decided, once the issue was openly raised, as in 1877. But this outcome required not only the introduction of universal suffrage but a new politicization of Catholicism. The history of the former is well known, but the latter process is less well understood. In one département of east-central France (the Ain), Philippe Boutry has found that the clergy began to play a greater role in public debate after 1860. They spoke out on relations with Rome, the teaching congregations, schools, and even monarchy versus republicanism. By 1880, "a process of politicization had created a unified segment of public opinion in support of the Catholic faith, the Holy See, and the conservative parties."[91] Clerical and secular parties squared off in village elections. The curé of the 1870s ventured beyond the boundaries of the reservation to which the Concordat system had confined him, at the same time replacing the *notables*—prominent local citizens—whose power was on the decline. In any case, "the curés possessed the kinds of knowledge that politics required: historical, philosophical, and theological. No one was better equipped to deal with the issues facing civil society."[92] Indeed, clericalism reflected a desire to bring older modes of knowledge to bear on the political process, and this inevitably meant invoking a different set of memories to justify one's actions.

It is customary to portray the clash between seculars and Catholics as a uniquely French phenomenon, along with the variety of French cheeses and the insatiable French thirst for history. There have of course been clashes just as pronounced and outbursts of anticlerical sentiment even more violent in southern Europe and Latin America, but the enduring mix of radical secularism and Catholic dominance is no doubt unique to France. There is nevertheless reason to ask whether this unique heritage can survive the expansion of our horizons to embrace worldwide models and regional alliances.

Have we ultimately plumbed the deeper meaning of this novel couple? It is tempting to see it as the symptom of a structural imbalance, a sign of the modern coexisting with the archaic. What is undeniably modern in France is the affirmation of individual autonomy and the secular character of the state, the plurality of faiths and the privatization of religion. What is probably archaic is the internalization of civil war, the incessant "theologization" of political debate, and the persistent implication that the adversary is somehow illegitimate. This recurrent conflict has been internalized, but fortunately in some ways it has also been exorcised. Based on differences over the oath of 1791, exacerbated by revolutionary violence, the dispute was quickly institutionalized and soon civilized. From it derives France's unique partition of liberties: seculars enjoy those of 1789, while clericals enjoy freedom of religion and education. On the minus side of the ledger, one can blame the all-pervasive secular-Catholic split for the "absolute" Republic's inability to accept a legitimate opposition.[93] On the plus side one can put France's later allergy to the fascist virus.

Is the *laïque-Catholique* split beginning to fade? Is it one of the old-fashioned charms of a France that no longer exists? Surely it is too soon to draw any such conclusion. Events always send people back to the past in search of precedents. There will always be someone—and perhaps not the someone one expects—to invoke the ghost of that champion of anticlericalism, Émile Combes (1835–1921).[94]

FIGURE 4.0   Antiracist demonstration by the group S.O.S.–Racisme, November 1987.

CHAPTER 4

French and Foreigners

Gérard Noiriel

In recent years the French political scene has been disturbed by demonstrations concerning the presence of "foreigners" in France, and in a figurative sense the sound of those demonstrations can still be heard resounding in the streets of the country's major cities. *La France aux Français!* This old nationalist slogan, which the extreme right has made its war cry, has been countered by antiracist organizations with a slogan never before heard in France: "We are all immigrants of the first, second, third, or fourth generation."[1] A new front has thus been opened in the battle over immigration: the front of memory.

Reasons for the Repression

"Peoples always reveal their origins. The circumstances surrounding their birth and development influence them throughout their history."[2] This idea of Tocqueville's tells us a great deal about the contrary roles that immigration has played in the histories of France and the United States from the beginning. As Jeanine Brun points out, the very fact that the American nation was created by the migration of European colonists meant that "the United States was aware of the realities of immigration from the inception of its national history."[3] The American model of immigration even today still preserves aspects of its initial function of populating a territory. It was in the period during which the nation was born that Crèvecoeur originated the myth that in America a fusion of different peoples was giving rise to a "new man." From this it was for a long time assumed that every immigrant was a potential American citizen. This has given rise to a widely shared feeling that America is still an "unfinished country," to borrow a phrase from Nathan Glazer, who sees this enduring set of ideas as one of the main reasons why the United States is finding it so hard to stop illegal immigration.[4]

Immigration is also a part of the American myth of origins, and so it has always been an important topic in history books. For many people the American example is the principal if not the only historical model of immigration in the world. A glance at the statistics, however, is enough to see that since the beginning of the twentieth century immigration has had a proportionately greater impact in France than in the United States. After a massive influx in the first decade of the twentieth century, America established a strict system of ethnic quotas. Thereafter France became the world's leading immigrant host country, with a rate of increase in its foreign-born population of 515 per 100,000, compared with 492 for the United States (in 1930). Forty years later, at a time when Western economies were once again calling for massive influxes of immigrants, the percentage of foreign-born residents in France reached eleven percent; while it was less than six percent in the United States.

If, despite these figures, France until recently was not seen as a historic host country, it was because immigration did not coincide with the building of the French nation. On the contrary, the distinctive feature of the French model as compared with the American is that the purpose of immigration in modern times has never been to populate open territory. At the time of the Revolution, France was the most populous country in Europe, and its leaders were chiefly concerned with the emigration of French subjects to other countries. Furthermore, centuries of centralized rule had helped to bring about ethnic and linguistic unification, which in turn facilitated the implementation of strict revolutionary government. It was not until the second half of the nineteenth century that mass immigration began in France. At the time this immigration was seen as closely linked to industrialization, and this perception is corroborated by a comparison of curves of industrial activity with foreign population as well as by an examination of the areas in which the immigrant population was concentrated. At first, therefore, immigrants were seen not as future citizens but as a temporary addition to the labor force. Because immigrants were seen as part of a workforce, their activities were traditionally subject to close government regulation and police scrutiny, whereas the American authorities, obedient to the law of supply and demand, were far more liberal. In France, a whole system of identity cards and labor contracts was set up by the government to funnel immigrants into industrial areas where workers were in seriously short supply (most notably in heavy industry and agriculture). The authorities also saw to it that workers would be flexible by organizing a dual labor market: one for French workers (skilled and settled), another for immigrant workers (unskilled and mobile). As Gary Cross has shown, France thus invented the "modern" model of immigration, which other industrialized countries would adopt after World War II.[5]

Controlled by the necessities of big industry, the French model of immigration was also the product of an early democratization of the political system. The French economy was unable to find the proletariat it needed to expand (even though France was the most populous country in Europe in 1800) because most French peasants were not only immune to the charms of big industry but resourceful enough to elude its grasp. In my view this state of affairs was one consequence of the French Revolution that rarely receives the attention it deserves. By spreading the "passion for equality" and the urge for ownership into even the most remote rural areas, the Revolution not only encouraged the Malthusian behavior that manifested itself on a broad scale in France a century before it developed elsewhere in Europe, but at the same time discouraged peasants from fleeing the countryside for the city. Parliamentary democracy, which culminated in the adoption of universal (male) suffrage in 1848, gave working people the political tool they need to oppose proletarianization, a tool that their English counterparts as described by Marx sorely lacked.[6] Hence big industry had no choice but to seek the workers it needed through immigration. Surely it is no accident that the massive importation of foreign workers by other major European countries after World War II illustrates the same correlation between industrialization, Malthusianism, and political democracy.[7]

The importance of the Revolution for the French model of immigration is evident in many other areas as well. Two events were crucial in establishing the legal status of foreigners in France. As Jean Portemer has noted, the Night of August Fourth, when the Constituent Assembly abolished all privileges, simultaneously founded a national community with one constitution and one code of law for all. "From then on nationality was the criterion that defined the foreigner."[8] The other key event, which also took place in the summer of 1789, was the Declaration of the Rights of Man and the Citizen. This document is the source of the radical differences between the French and American conceptions of immigration. From the very beginning of the Revolution, in debates over Protestants, Jews, and "people of color" (to use the language of the time), the universality of the "rights of man" was repeatedly stressed by spokesmen for groups that had been relegated to inferior status under the Ancien Régime. On August 23, 1789, Rabaut Saint-Étienne based his case for the Protestants on the following logic: "Gentlemen, you would not wish to lay yourselves open to the reproach of having contradicted yourselves by declaring a few days ago that all men are equal in rights and today that they are unequal; of having declared previously that they are free to do whatever is not harmful to others and today that two million of your fellow citizens are not free to worship in a way that harms no one."[9] A few weeks later the "people of color of the French islands and colonies" filed a motion based on a similar argument, which earned them this reply from President Fréteau: "No part of the nation will ask the Assembly of its representatives for its rights in vain. Those who, by dint of the seas' expanse or prejudices concerning differences of origin, seem to be placed farther from its regard, will be drawn closer by these sentiments of humanity, which characterize all its deliberations and inspire all its efforts."[10] Still, if all individuals were recognized as having equal rights, it was on condition that the realm of religious and ethnic practice (which belonged to the "private" sphere, in which every individual was his own master) be strictly separated from the political arena, to which each citizen came divested of all traces of his origins. As Clermont-Tonnerre put it in his brief in favor of allowing Jews to occupy municipal and provincial offices, "we must deny the Jews everything as a nation and grant them everything as individuals. They must not constitute a political body or order within the state. They must individually be citizens.... If they do not wish to be so, let them say so, so that they may be banished forthwith."[11]

These few excerpts from the parliamentary debates of 1789 bring out an essential and permanent ingredient in the French conception of immigration. In the United States the immigration issue is invariably associated in theory, practice, and attitude with race and ethnicity, whereas in France the Declaration of the Rights of Man marks the triumph (or at any rate the legal triumph) of a repudiation of any form of segregation based on race, religion, or ethnic origin. In exchange, however, all cultural and religious practices were to be confined to the private sphere. Any political grouping based on cultural or religious criteria was prohibited. This is an essential feature of French immigration policy today. Even when the authorities were obsessed (as they were in the interwar period) by the idea of selecting immigrants so as to weed out those who appeared to be most alien to French cultural norms, they invariably came up against the "republican tradition," which precluded the adoption of ethnic quotas as in the United States.[12] For two centuries, officials have worried about the possibility that people of similar ethnic background would band together in pursuit of political ends. Even under the July Monarchy, France accepted refugees and even paid them subsidies, yet only on condition that they remain dispersed throughout France. A century and a half later, the government is still using a similar "policy of atomization" with regard to refugees from Southeast Asia.[13]

An exciting problem for social history would be to study the concrete modalities by which these traditions stemming from the French Revolution were transmitted. Philosophers all too often confine themselves to the analysis of texts, as if words by themselves were enough to fashion traditions capable of enduring for centuries. As recent polemics abundantly illustrate, one can, by confining one's attention exclusively to discourse, bring out an image of France as the "homeland of liberty" or, by using different texts, develop a picture of France as a testing laboratory for national socialist ideology. Yet a century ago Émile Durkheim showed that one could not understand political traditions by studying discourse alone. "Yesterday," he wrote at the height of the Dreyfus Affair, "everyone was all for cosmopolitanism. Today, patriotism has the upper hand. And all this turmoil, all this ebb and flow, takes place without the slightest change in the cardinal precepts of law and morality, *which are immobilized by their hieratic form.*"[14] Thus for Durkheim discourse becomes tradition only if it succeeds in embodying itself in legal rules, codes, or institutions. The numerous Declarations of the Rights of Man since 1789 and the great constitutional principles of the Republic are the true underpinnings of the French tradition.

In order to understand how those great principles affect the collective consciousness, however, we cannot rely on legal texts alone. We must explore the thousand and one material channels that, unconsciously and therefore all that much more effectively, orient our everyday perception of the social world. An excellent example to illustrate this point is the official statistical apparatus of the government. It has often been said, and rightly so, that statistics are the lenses through which modern man observes the society in which he lives. A comparison of U. S. and French immigration statistics is enough to demonstrate, once again, the importance of the French Revolution as a foundational moment. Until the 1960s, American immigration statistics were based on racial and ethnic categories (race, religion, language, parents' place of birth). By contrast, French statistics since the nineteenth century have incorporated the principles of

FIGURE 4.1   Game of the goose, circa 1790. The caption on the top card reads: "Foreigners who acquire National Properties in accordance with the Law are regarded as French." The bottom card says: "Non-Catholics under the Safeguard of the Law."

1789: hence there are no questions about religion or parents' place of birth, and the

most important criterion is the legal one of citizenship (French or foreign). A thorough comparative study would reveal the crucial effects of these initial differences in nomenclature in determining how the Americans and the French have perceived immigration over the past century and still perceive it today: on the one hand as an "ethnic" problem, on the other as a problem of "foreigners."

Important as the Declaration of the Rights of Man is, it is equally important to see its limits. In the debate that followed Clermont-Tonnerre's declaration in favor of the emancipation of the Jews, quoted earlier, one speaker pointed to a fundamental contradiction in the ideology of human rights. Abbé Maury justified his opposition to Clermont-Tonnerre by an argument based not on a racist or ethnic logic but on the same "national" ground on which the revolutionaries themselves stood. The Jews, he argued, were a nation and therefore foreigners on French soil, hence they could not become full-fledged citizens of France: "To call Jews citizens would be tantamount to saying that without letters of naturalization and without ceasing to be English or Danish, Englishmen and Danes could become French." This argument revealed a fundamental inconsistency in the Declaration of 1789, an inconsistency that has continued, as we shall see, to have an important impact on the treatment of immigrants in France to this day. In fact, as Tzvetan Todorov has pointed out, the Declaration of the Rights of *Man* and of the *Citizen* is a contradiction in terms. Although the universalist logic of the French revolutionaries was able to reconcile religious and ethnic origins through nationality, it inevitably ran up against the question of the foreigner, since the foreigner is defined precisely as one who does not belong to the nation. The blindness of the men of 1789 to this issue is all the more surprising in that the contradiction had not escaped Rousseau several decades earlier. In *Émile* he wrote: "One must choose between making a man and making a citizen, because one cannot simultaneously make both." Later he added: "Every patriot is hard on foreigners. They are merely men, they are nothing in his eyes."[15]

Revolutionary events would reveal the pertinence of this observation in dramatic fashion. As Albert Mathiez pointed out, universalist enthusiasm prevailed over all other considerations during the first years of the Revolution.[16] By virtue of the logic described above with respect to religious minorities, the foreigner living in France was seen primarily as a man and therefore as directly concerned by the Declaration of Rights. In August 1790 the right of escheat (reversion to the state of a nonnaturalized alien's estate) was unanimously abolished, because the deputies felt that it was "contrary to the principles of fraternity that ought to bind all men, no matter what their country and their government; that this right, established in barbarous times, should be proscribed in a nation that has based its constitution on *the rights of man and the citizen* and that free France should open its bosom to all the peoples of the earth by inviting them to enjoy, under a free government, the sacred and inalienable rights of humanity."[17] In subsequent years the revolutionaries continued to display generosity toward foreigners. In 1792, even though France was at war and its enemies were taking steps against French citizens within their borders, foreigners held (as they had under the Ancien Régime) important posts in the government and bureaucracy and even commanded troops. In August of that same year the deputies voted to approve the well-known decree declaring that all philosophers and freedom fighters throughout the world (such as Thomas Paine, Jeremy Bentham, George Washington, and others) were French. In November France offered "fraternity and aid to all peoples who wish to regain their liberty." According to Mathiez, it was not until the middle of 1793, following a series of military defeats, domestic troubles, and an economic crisis, that the attitude toward foreigners underwent a total reversal. Within a few months, as if no halfway measures would do, one logic replaced another. It was then that most of the ingredients that would recur in subsequent outbreaks of xenophobia were first seized upon: the issue of foreigners became a key element in Franco-French political struggle, each party accusing the other of being in the pay of the enemy. All the troubles of the moment were "explained" as the effects of a conspiracy hatched abroad. That conspiracy was political: foreigners were spies who destabilized the country. It was also economic: foreign gold was ruining the national economy. These arguments were used to justify increasingly authoritarian measures: revolutionary clubs with foreign members were banned, and noncitizens were removed from public offices and the army. Foreigners were also among the first victims of the Terror. Police checks were stepped up. Lists of suspects circulated, and many whose names appeared were ultimately guillotined despite their roles in the first years of the Revolution. The greatest champion of universal values, Anacharsis Cloots, was executed as a Prussian agent. Thomas Paine was thrown in prison. Even though most of these measures were abandoned after the Terror, they demonstrated the implacable logic of the forms of exclusion inherent in societies built upon national foundations.

The last essential aspect of the French model of immigration that can be explained by the Revolution has to do with historical amnesia. The very fact that republican rights and their concomitant statistical categories erased every last vestige of origin in the definition of the individual is important for understanding why the history of immigration remained invisible in France for so long. More generally, the myth of origin that was built upon the events of the Revolution made it impossible for "foreigners" to have a place in the collective memory of the nation. While many American textbooks celebrate the contributions to the American republic of the various communities that settled in the United States over the years, in France immigration is always approached as a question extrinsic to the country's history. It is seen as a temporary phenomenon, something fleeting and marginal. Similarly, while Ellis Island, through which millions of European immigrants passed in order to enter the United States, has became a museum, comparable sites in France, such as the Toul selection center, which processed most Central European immigrants in the interwar period, have been torn down, as if something dictated that a history so starkly at odds with the myth of the soil had to be magically erased.[18] It is hardly surprising that this repressed history has resurfaced in recent controversies.

The Great Battles

Albert Mathiez introduced his book on the Revolution and foreigners by saying that "if the present work has any usefulness other than the satisfaction of curiosity, surely it is to discover beneath changing appearances what is permanent, what remains, so as to distinguish it from what passes, what is accidental."[19] His purpose in this work—to highlight common features in French attitudes toward foreigners in wartime—could be expanded to include xenophobic attitudes in times of economic crisis. In fact, given the close relationship between immigration and industrialization in the "French model," every period of economic expansion (Phase A of the Simiand Cycle) leads to a massive influx of foreigners, and every economic downturn (Phase B) leads not only to unemployment and a halt to hiring but also to integration of recently arrived foreign workers. Labor-market competition intensifies French hostility toward foreigners, and this xenophobia makes itself felt at the political level. The issue of immigration then becomes a national problem.

It was at the end of the nineteenth century that this pattern was first noticed. The industrial expansion of the Second Empire led over a ten-year period to a doubling of the number of foreigners in France, to approximately one million in 1880. The majority came from neighboring countries, primarily Belgium (40 percent) and Italy, and they lived mainly in départements near the borders (Nord, Bouches-du-Rhône).[20] The importance of immigration for the French economy was already recognized by Paul Leroy-Beaulieu: "France," he wrote in 1886, "is a land of immigration, just as the republics of Argentina and Australia are. An average of forty to fifty thousand foreigners a year come here to settle and put down roots."[21] The Great Depression, whose impact on France was particularly severe, saw a leveling off of the foreign population at about one million. Competition was particularly fierce in the mining and construction industries, which had recruited large numbers of foreign workers during the Second Empire only to see them vie for jobs during the crisis with unemployed French workers. For the period 1867–1893, Michelle Perrot has found evidence of eighty-nine incidents in which French and foreign workers clashed; she also notes that xenophobic arguments were a particularly effective means of mobilizing French workers for strikes, petitions, and demonstrations.[22] In these clashes Flemish Belgians were the first victims. In the Nord every economic crisis since the July Monarchy triggered demonstrations against them. By the end of the century there were veritable anti-Belgian uprisings by the working

FIGURE 4.2   *Italian Emigrants in the Gare Saint-Lazare;* engraving, *Petit Journal illustré* (March 29, 1893).

class. In 1892 at the Drocourt Mines in Pas-de-Calais, Belgian workers, who constitutedthree quarters of the local workforce, were obliged to flee the commune in haste under threat from the French population. "Their return, which was nearly complete by 31 August, was accomplished under difficult conditions. Trains from France arrived crowded with large families of poor people carrying cheap bags. There were housing problems at their destination. They also had to find furniture to replace what the French miners had destroyed." An official Belgian inquiry set the losses of each family due to vandalism at forty to fifty francs.[23]

At the end of the century the target of xenophobia shifted to the most recently arrived immigrants, the Italians. In Marseilles in 1881 there were veritable riots for several days in the streets of the city. "At four in the morning," wrote a journalist for the *Petit Marseillais*, "brawls broke out between French and Italians in various parts of the city.... At five-thirty, as workers gathered at Belsunce for hiring, a gang of youths began chasing Italians, shouting at them and striking some rather hard blows. Faced with such a welcome, the Piedmontese fled in panic as their pursuers chased them into the Rue de la Couronne and the Rue de l'Échelle, ordering them to shout *Vive la République!*" Within days hundreds of Italians left the city.[24] Hatred of Italians reached a fever pitch at Aigues-Mortes in 1893. Following brawls between French and Italian laborers in the salt marshes, three hundred people armed with clubs, shovels, and branches set out after foreign workers. A convoy of eighty Italians being escorted out of town by gendarmes was attacked by rioters, and several people were left dead. Some of the injured were bludgeoned to death. The official toll was eight dead and fifty injured, but according to the *Times* the actual toll was fifty dead and a hundred and fifty injured.[25]

What was new at the end of the nineteenth century was that acts of popular violence against foreigners were increasingly related to the political climate of the time. Whereas popular brawls under the July Monarchy had been mainly of the "ethnic" variety (triggered by hostility toward Piedmontese, Auvergnat, or Flemish workers), hatred of foreigners was now most often justified in terms of the international situation. For example, the immediate cause of the attacks on Italians in the streets of Marseilles in 1881 was colonial rivalry between France and Italy over Tunisia.[26] Conversely, violent clashes between French and foreign workers found an immediate echo in parliament. Here, then, is another illustration of the link between mass immigration and democratic politics. Indeed, it was not until the parliamentary and party system began to flourish in the early years of the Third Republic that immigration really became a political "problem." Following a pattern first laid down during the Revolution and fully developed in the 1880s, the immigrant with no voice in policy making became a political football to be kicked about in polemics between the right and the left. Boulangism was the first major political movement to make systematic use of popular hostility toward foreigners for elec-

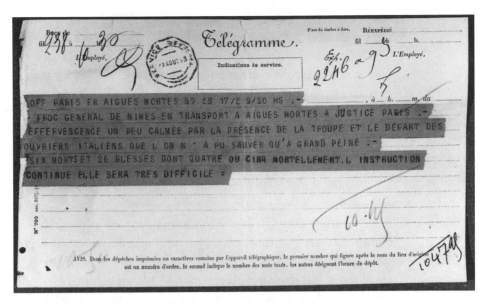

FIGURE 4.3   Telegram concerning the anti-Italian demonstrations in Aigues-Mortes in 1893.

FIGURE 4.4   *Disturbances at Aigues-Mortes: The Departure of the Italian Workers,* engraving from *Le Petit Parisien* (September 3, 1893).

toral purposes. That was one reason for its initial success in socialist ranks, which responded to Boulanger's defense of national employment and denunciation of large employers who used foreign workers and opposed any measures to expel them or reduce their number.[27] The respective positions of the left and right with respect to immigration did not really stabilize until Marxism gained influence in the workers' movement, French workers strengthened their ties to the Second International, the Ligue des Droits de l'Homme was created, and the conclusion of the Dreyfus Affair clarified the political situation: the parties of the right, harping mainly on the issue of security (which particularly appealed to the groups most affected by the crisis), emphasized the "national interest" and proposed vigorous measures against immigrants, whereas the left was more apt to invoke the "rights of man" in calling for equal treatment of French and foreign workers, while at the same time advocating strict measures to stanch the influx of new immigrants.[28]

The impressive growth of French industry in the 1920s, which was associated with postwar reconstruction, together with the wholesale slaughter of wartime, gave rise to an unprecedented need for immigrant labor. By 1930 there were three million immigrants in France, three times as many as in 1920. Workers were recruited over a much wider area than before. Belgian workers formed just one contingent among many, and if Italians were the most numerous, it was other nationalities, such as the Poles, that experienced the most rapid growth in their numbers.[29] Once again, the economic crisis that hit France in the 1930s halted the recruitment of new workers and led to a renewal of xenophobic speech and acts. What made matters worse now, compared to the prewar period, was that many of the new immigrants were actually refugees: Armenians, Russians, and German Jews. Many were people of professional background who sought positions in France comparable to those that they or their parents had known before their exile. Hence foreign competition on the labor market was not limited to the working class. This was one reason for the intensity of nationalist rhetoric in the 1930s, at which time nationalism enjoyed the support of a substantial segment of public opinion. Although the right in the early 1930s was once again "far more inclined than the left to make the issue of protecting the national work force an electoral warhorse," as Jean-Charles Bonnet has shown,[30] nationalist pressure was such that the issue gained in popularity even on the left, except for the Communist Party, which on the whole stuck to its internationalist positions until the Popular Front.

Many legal and bureaucratic measures were adopted against foreigners, a taste of what was to come under Vichy. Under pressure from lawyers and doctors, a bill to revise the Code of Nationality of 1927 was filed on June 22, 1934. Rushed to the floor within weeks, the new law was passed by the Chamber, including the Socialists, and went into effect on July 19, 1934, less than a month after it was first proposed! Keen to ban naturalized foreigners from the professions, the deputies established the requirement that newly naturalized citizens must complete ten years of training before being admitted to any position considered to fall under the rubric of *fonction publique*. And that was not all. Contradicting the entire republican tradition, the Council of the Order of Attorneys decided to reject applications for membership submitted by any individual naturalized before 1934, thus giving the new law a retroactive interpretation that was upheld by the Paris Court of Appeals.[31]

The third high point of French xenophobia coincided with the country's third major economic crisis in a century. The industrial expansion of the 1960s relied on a massive recruitment of foreign workers made possible by yet another enlargement of the zone of recruitment. For the first time the majority of new immigrants were non-Europeans from what was once the French colonial empire, primarily the countries of North Africa. A growing worldwide recession in the 1970s produced effects similar to those of earlier crises: a halt to the recruitment of new workers, settlement of immigrants already in the country, and hostility from some French workers, who called for immigrants to be sent back where they came from. Racist attacks proliferated, particularly against North Africans, reaching a peak of violence in the bloody summer of 1977, which left fifteen people dead in Marseilles. Various legal and administrative measures were taken to deal with the situation, from the "Fontanet memo" suspending immigration in 1974 to the Loi Bonnet of 1980 (allowing immediate deportation of foreigners without proper papers) to the Chalandon plan to revise the Code of Nationality in 1986–87. These measures themselves became the subject of endless polemics between the right and the left along much the same lines as in previous periods. And surely the most important consequence of these polemics was to have facilitated the rebirth of the extreme right in France in the 1980s.

To some it may be worrisome or incomprehensible that, in the very year in which France celebrated the bicentennial of the Declaration of the Rights of Man and of the Citizen, timeworn demagogic themes, such as "national preference" in employment, housing, and health or that miracle cure for unemployment, sending all foreigners home, could still attract a not inconsiderable segment of the electorate. But when Jean-Marie Le Pen justified this program of exclusion by asserting that "citizens have equal rights, not men," he put his finger on one of the Republic's oldest, deepest wounds.[32] Clearly France has yet to overcome the initial contradiction between the rights of man and the rights of the citizen.[33]

Beyond "changing appearances," the history of immigration illustrates another invariant, namely, an intrinsically French way of approaching the matter of "integration."[34] Recent arguments concerning North African immigrants begin from the premise that today's problems are new.[35] For some observers, what is novel about the present situation has to do with the unprecedented pace and magnitude of immigration since the 1960s. The minister of justice explicitly introduced the proposed revision to the Code of Nationality as a way of preserving "French identity" in the presence of such a destructive influx. "France, as is well known, is a country composed of foreigners, but the process took shape over centuries. Today we have to contend with accelerating change."[36] A more common argument for the novelty of today's problems has to do with the alleged "cultural distance" between the French and North African communities. There was no problem before, proponents of this view allege, because most immigrants were Europeans, hence similar in cultural background to the French: "France is a European nation, that is, a territory located in Europe and populated by Europeans, which has always remained open to its European neighbors.... Today's immigration, unlike that of the nineteenth century or the 1930s, is extra-European. The majority of immigrants are now North

Africans, Black Africans, Turks, and Indo-Pakistanis. In terms of background and cultural references, these foreigners have no connection with the major periods of European history: Antiquity, the Christian Middle Ages, the Renaissance, the Enlightenment."[37]

Let us now cast our eyes backward one century. Commentators were already referring to the "novelty" of the migratory situation and already proposing the argument that the sudden influx of foreigners posed a threat to the "national identity" and that the "cultural distance" between the newcomers and "native" Frenchmen was unprecedented. To be sure, Jean Laumonier asserted, using fashionable organic metaphors, France had experienced any number of invasions since prehistoric times, "but then our nationality was still in formation. Those invasions were necessary to the development and definitive constitution of a social organism. Indeed, they played the role that abundant and substantial nourishment plays in the growth of a young individual." Today, however, the French nation is grown up, and all those immigrants can no longer be "digested." If the influx continued, there was likelihood of "a social disorder analogous to the physiological disorder of poisoning."[38]

Fears for the future were often spelled out more explicitly. In 1883 a doctor stated that "if our population is holding steady or even increasing to a very slight degree, the reason is foreign immigration. It is the foreigner who is filling our empty spaces, and this introduction of generally hostile elements is an invasion in disguise, a threat for the future. A people that recruits abroad quickly loses, as a result of this commerce, its character, its customs, and its intrinsic strengths. Over time it loses its most precious possession, its nationality."[39] Twenty years later Vacher de Lapouge confirmed that "the French population as I have just described it will not last forever. Over the past half-century immigration has introduced more foreign elements than all the barbarian invasions put together.... Add a little yellow blood to top it all off and the French population would truly become a nation of Mongols. *Quod Dii omen avertant!*"[40]

At the time, of course, discussions of "cultural distance," that is, of criteria for measuring the foreignness of foreigners, did not rely on "European culture" as a standard of proximity. On the contrary, it was because the "enemy" was at our gates that the problem was said to be so serious. Some authors were critical of the naturalization of German immigrants in eastern France: "The naturalization of a family, if it is to be complete and definitive, requires not just interbreeding but the passage of two or three generations. The presence in the east of recently naturalized citizens, still attached to their former homeland by a thousand unconscious ties, therefore constitutes a danger the gravity of which must be obvious to any child."[41] Maurice Barrès played an essential role in the process of constructing difference by elaborating on Jules Soury's discussion of parents of whom "we are all only the substantial continuity, the still living thought and word with their train of gestures, habits, and hereditary reactions in virtue of which the dead contain the living; and the intrinsic ethnic and national characters, born of secular variations, that differentiate the Frenchman of France from the foreigner, are not metaphors but phenomena as real as the anatomical components of our nerve centers.... That is the foundation of our cult of the dead and of the earth on which they lived and suffered, the basis of the national religion."[42] Under these conditions the very concept of "European civilization" makes no sense. "Any foreigner living on our soil, even one who thinks he cherishes us, naturally hates eternal France, our tradition, which he does not possess, which he cannot understand, and which, precisely, constitutes nationality."[43] For Barrès, this irremediable "cultural distance" explained why Zola was "predestined for Dreyfusism": "Because his father and ancestors were Venetians, Émile Zola quite naturally thinks like a rootless Venetian."

The discourse of the interwar years was cast in the same mold, except that now a contrast was drawn between the troubling present and an idealized past, in which the immigrants of the late nineteenth century were seen as a positive model. Charles Seignobos, for example, argued that the foreigners who came to France before 1914 did not alter the anthropological character of the population because they were "our neighbors." By contrast, he insisted that the influx of Polish workers to replace soldiers killed at the front had given rise to a "new" problem.[44] "Before the war," Georges Mauco observed in terms repeated virtually word for word fifty years later by Albin Chalandon, "immigration was unregulated. It was a slow process, the result of individual decisions, and this allowed for rapid fusion with the population. Since the war, the arrival of homogeneous masses of people in a short period of time in relatively circumscribed regions has greatly encouraged the tendency of immigrants to band together in their land of exile and to reconstitute their social structures and communal life."[45] A few years later, another specialist went even further: "Our powers of absorption were still quite high in 1910.... It is no longer the same in 1940. Our absorptive capacity has been all but abolished because we are no longer faced with immigration by recruitment but rather with a sudden flood, which threatens to drown all that remains of the French race."[46]

Anxiety about the future can even be found in theses in political science written in the interwar period. "From the standpoint of maintaining political liberties," Jean Pluyette asked, "what effect has the immigration of 1.5 million Mediterraneans had? Doesn't such a massive invasion risk disrupting the national ethnic equilibrium in favor of one of its components? And won't it then promote the characteristics of that component in such a way as to alter our public customs?"[47] There was considerable anxiety about France's ability to assimilate newcomers, be they Russians, Armenians, or Poles.[48] The most respected authorities even drew up a list of inassimilable groups, whose "customs, cast of mind, tastes, passions, and age-old habits are in contradiction with the profound orientation of our civilization."[49]

The Memory of Origins: A Controversial Battle

> The secretary of the Conseil Général of Meurthe-et-Moselle, Maria Liberatore-Lefebvre, who grew up in Pont-à-Mousson, has just published a history of her family at her own expense. Entitled *Le Passé simple*, her book is a touchingly naïve account of her parents' arrival in Dieulouard from their native Italy in 1958 and of the birth and upbringing of their five daughters. She tells of the children's relations to one another and to their surroundings. The pace of the book is agreeable, and many of the situations are delicious. The author, aged twenty-nine, embarked on this literary adventure as a unique gift for her mother and father, who will celebrate their thirtieth wedding anniversary on January 22.[50]

Because immigration has not until now been a legitimate object of national memory, a whole segment of France's collective history has been relegated to the realm of private memoirs. Over the past few years, however, there have been growing signs that people who came to France from other countries want to make this officially neglected history public. The above example of an autobiographical work published by the author at her own expense is by no means exceptional. All across France one finds people from every immigrant group that arrived before World War II involved in similar efforts to rescue the past from oblivion and tell previously untold stories. The struggle to preserve the memory of one's forebears can take many forms. It would be useful to have an exhaustive summary. Many theses on the history of immigration are the work of descendants of immigrants, for example, and they are often explicitly described as a token of fidelity to the author's roots.[51] There has also been a sharp increase in the number of organizations whose stated purpose is to keep immigrant culture alive. Among French people of Armenian descent, for instance, especially in communities with large Armenian populations, one finds new newspapers and organizations supplanting earlier village-based groups.[52] At Issy-les-Moulineaux, to take one example, one finds the Centre de Recherche et de Documentation Arménienne and the Association Audio-Visuelle Arménienne.[53] A similar determination to hold on to memories of one's roots can be found among descendants of Spanish refugees in the south of France. At Bédarieux, for example, high school students and teachers have published an account of their history with a preface by the Communist mayor, Antoine Martinez, who did not hesitate to give his introduction the title "Spain at Heart" or to assert that his town bears "the indelible imprint" of Spanish immigration.[54] The Italians, who formed the first foreign community in France, appear to have been in the forefront of this effort to reappropriate the past. Thanks to the energetic efforts of its president, Pierre Milza, the Centre d'Étude et de Documentation de l'Émigration Italienne (CEDEI), founded in 1983, has funded

FIGURES 4.5–4.8   Billheads of the Giai bakery on the Rue Nationale, where it first opened for business around the beginning of the twentieth century.

FIGURE 4.9   Séraphin Giai and his family in front of their bakery in 1906.

FIGURE 4.10   Fernand and André, the children of Séraphin Giai.

FIGURE 4.11   Giai descendants return to Italy for a birthday celebration. The Usseglio-Giais, who have been bakers in Paris for four generations and nearly all of whom have taken French spouses, are perfectly assimilated into French society yet remain attached to their native village.

research, conferences, and exhibitions on the subject of Italian immigration. In the early 1980s the Ministry of Foreign Affairs listed more than 325 Italian associations in France, two thirds of them established since 1970. Of these, membership figures are available for 258, with a total of 52,000 members. Half of them are of French nationality (many having been naturalized). For participants in these groups, what counts most is not nationality but the fact of being "from somewhere." A study of the ties that have been maintained over the past century between certain towns in the Val-de-Marne and the Italian town of Casalvieri in Lazio finds that descendants of immigrants are more likely to join these kinds of groups and points up the importance of "bilateral references" among French people of Italian descent.[55]

This revival of memories should not be taken to imply that a communal life based on "culture" or "ethnicity" has managed to sustain itself over all these years, however. The time has come for an end to the false debate between those who, being rather too quick to embrace the republican view of the nation, continually idealize the assimilation of successive waves of immigrants without inquiring about either the nature of that integration or its cost, and those who wish to limit the discussion to a cursory denunciation of the Jacobin state by glorifying this or that memory or identity as the mythical refuge of all resistance to oppression. In order to do so, we must first step back from debates in which so many passions have been engaged. Rather than defend a cause, let us try to make an accurate assessment of the situation.

The study of French immigration points up the existence of a permanent process, and this must serve as our point of departure. Every group of immigrants, no matter where it comes from, tries to protect itself against the destructive

FIGURE 4.12   Interior of a Polish worker's home in the Pas-de-Calais.

effects of deracination by reconstructing a communal life. The language, culture, and customs that testify day after day to the group's "foreignness" are the most powerful instruments for preserving this memory of origins. First-generation immigrants are the ones most often accused by "native" French of "not being like us," and at least in the first few years of exile most immigrants look upon complete integration as an inaccessible goal—a fact that reinforces their tendency to withdraw into a community of their own and to cultivate nostalgic memories of the old country. Preserving those memories in the hope of one day returning home is a major concern of the group. From the Flemish societies of working-class Lille in the late Second Empire to today's Portuguese organizations, one finds the same concern with maintaining the community and preserving memory. There is no exhaustive study of this phenomenon: the number and type of such organizations remains obscure, as does the history of immigrant publications, holidays, and demonstrations.[56] The Polish groups are the ones about which we know most, thanks to the work of Janine Ponty. These groups were particularly active in the interwar years, and they often organized communal festivals as though they were joyous battles whose purpose was to preserve communal memories. "Celebrations were an important activity of these organizations. All the members took part, marching together with flags and banners, men, women, and children all dressed in regional costumes marching to mass and then moving on into the streets of town, led by a band. The day might end with a play or sporting event of some

FIGURE 4.13   Polish miners in Nœux.

kind."[57] Of course immigrant groups also offered members mutual aid and support, which the poorest members of the community often needed in order to survive. But a great deal of evidence suggests that the need to re-create a "homeland in exile" was a constant concern. This obsession with memory can be seen clearly, for example, in the words of Arnam Turabian, founder of the Office National Arménien, a group that aided new refugees in the aftermath of World War I: "In the future, when my daughter reaches the age of reason and finds a flourishing Armenian colony, she will be able to say with pride, 'Well, anyway, that is my father's work.' "[58]

Like all forms of collective memory, immigrant memory needs material forms in which to make itself concrete. Forms give permanence to the often intense emotions of exile. Yet no comprehensive inventory of immigrant places of remembrance has ever been compiled in France, despite the fact that there are many such sites throughout the country. There are Russian churches, for example, in Paris and Nice, Armenian churches in Paris and Marseilles, a Russian cemetery in Sainte-Geneviève-des-Bois, a Polish cemetery in Troyes, and monuments, like the one dedicated in 1979 in Lille, which bears the inscription: "To Polish men and women, with gratitude, the Nord–Pas-de-Calais region." Still, the bulk of the evidence concerning the history of immigration takes a much more modest form: the personal archives, furniture, photographs, and memories of immigrant parents and grandparents.

FIGURE 4.14   *Polish Miners Expelled from Escarpelle;* drawing by Damblans in *Le Pèlerin* (September 2, 1934).

FIGURE 4.15   Polish miners expelled from Escarpelle.

In the struggle by first-generation immigrants to hold on to memories of their roots, writing is frequently an indispensable instrument, particularly for those who were forced to flee their homelands for political reasons. They write lest others forget. Such is the justification most commonly invoked by those not accustomed to wielding a pen but who nevertheless feel compelled, often toward the end of their lives, to leave a record of their singular fate. Consider, for example, the Polish exile who lived under the July Monarchy and wrote a historical chronicle beginning with these words:

> Several thousand Poles are moldering in exile. One day history and prosperity [*sic*] will ask to know their names. Even today, compatriots of ours who remained on their native soil wish to know the names of those exiles who did not shrink from this sacrifice. To rescue these martyrs to the most sacred of causes from oblivion, to offer up their names for other nations to admire and to inspire hope at home—that was my purpose in publishing this *Historical Almanac: A Souvenir of the Polish Emigration,* which lists the names of Poles scattered abroad and chiefly in France, that noble France which, in the midst of our disasters, remembered its old friendship and took us into the shelter of its embrace.[59]

A hundred and fifty years later, it was the same desire to keep faith with his people by preserving their memory that drove Khoren Margossian, an orphan of the Armenian genocide and a copper engraver, to publish at his own expense the story of his life: "When I wrote this little book, my sole thought was of my sister. She was determined that I should tell the world of our misfortunes. That is what I have done."[60]

Yet the memory of origins is shot through with contradictions from the first generation on. Those who now insist on the "plurality of memory" and continually impugn the Jacobin state forget that many of the people in whose name they speak did all they could to stop others from reminding them of their past. "I am not afraid of living," Mary Antin, an immigrant living in the United States, proclaimed in 1912, "as long as I am not obliged to remember too much."[61] Similar feelings were not uncommon in France in the interwar years, particularly among refugees from pogroms against the Jews and from the Armenian genocide, who were keen to forget the trauma of their previous lives. Simone Signoret described this attitude in her last novel, in which she wrote of the steadfast refusal of her parents, Ukrainian Jews, to talk with their children about their experience of the pogroms.[62]

Another reason why memories of immigrant origins fade is that not all members of an ethnic group share similar recollections of the past. One constant feature of xenophobia (which one also finds among some champions of the immigrant cause) is to apply a uniform label to individuals whose histories may in fact be quite different and who may not even see themselves as members of the same group. Chicago sociologists long ago discovered that Sicilian immigrants did not discover that they were Italians until they came to the United States, where they were depicted as such by anti-foreign propaganda.[63] Under such conditions, what would a phrase like "Italian memory" mean? Similarly, the word *Pole* strictly speaking refers to the members of an ethnic group defined by a common language, a common religion (Catholic), and a common sense of coming from a martyred nation; but in a broader—and legal—sense a "Pole" is any citizen of Poland, including the third of the population that in 1919, according to Janine Ponty, consisted of minority groups, primarily Ukrainians, Jews, and Byelorussians. Such legal composites can of course be broken down into ethnic groups with memories of their own, but one then runs into other problems having to do with social and occupational background. In his memoirs, Giorgio Amendola, a leader of the Italian Communist Party in exile in Paris and the son of a Liberal Party minister who was assassinated in 1926, described the Italian immigrants who worked in the steel industry in Lorraine in order to show that he had nothing in common with them: "Generally speaking, they had no Italian culture. They spoke and wrote a Frenchified Italian, a Franco-Italian jargon full of French loanwords. Most of them were illiterate when they left Italy. Among themselves they spoke not Italian but a regional dialect."[64] Such social differences are further compounded by political ones. Practically all "immigrant communities" split along left-right lines, and these political differences are reflected in community organizations, further weakening the sense of belonging to a single group and fragmenting a collective memory no longer supported, in exile, by the nation-state. When a nation celebrates "at home," it is a way of affirming its sense of rootedness and continuity, but when immigrants abroad celebrate their "national" holidays it is primarily to keep alive the hope of one day returning to a home remote both in space and in time.

In contrast to "culturalist" approaches to immigration which isolate culture from its concrete context, it is important, I think, to recognize that immigrants are obliged to adapt to local conditions on a daily basis in order to survive, and that this adaptation in itself constitutes a kind of "betrayal" of one's origins. Seventy years ago, Robert Park pointed out that the cultural institutions of immigrant communities "are not purely inherited but the product of efforts by immigrants to adapt their past to American conditions."[65] The reconstruction of native cultural traditions is marked from the beginning by conflict between the (subordinate) norms of the native country and the (dominant) norms of the new homeland. In any case, collective memory is unwittingly dependent on a context composed of thousands of ingredients missing from or ill-adapted to the new environment. Traditional costumes may not be practical for new types of work. The ingredients needed for traditional cooking may not be available. Moreover, modern societies are individualistic in ways that affect many aspects of life from a person's daily schedule to the nature of housing, and such individualism may be incompatible with traditional communal customs.

Before looking at the role of the state in weakening immigrant culture, we must therefore note the many factors that contribute to the dissolution of group memory: the wish to forget, the pressure of dominant norms, and the need to adapt to a foreign setting are the principal among them, as we have just seen. Studies done in the early 1950s reveal the rapidity of cultural change. Take Italian immigrants in Haute-Garonne, for example. Although many of the immigrants in question were employed as farm workers and sharecroppers, hence often relatively isolated from the French population, men ceased to wear their traditional broad-brimmed hats after a few years and women gave up their scarves. French food gradually supplanted polenta. French words insinuated themselves into the vocabulary of everyday life. About the same time a survey conducted by Alain Girard and Jean Stoetzel among Italian and Polish workers who moved to various parts of France in the interwar period yielded statistical proof of the destructive effects of adaptation. Among Italian construction workers in the Seine département, 97 percent dressed entirely in the French manner; 94 percent of Italian merchants in the same region and 86 percent of farm workers in the Lot-et-Garonne had similarly adapted to French clothing norms. The same was true of 96 percent of Polish miners in the Nord. Dietary habits underwent a similar transformation. The percentage of those whose diet had become totally French ranged from 15 percent for the Italian construction workers to 82 percent for Polish farm workers in Aisne. Figures concerning the reading of newspapers tell a similar story. While 38 percent of the Polish farm workers in Aisne and 30 percent of the Polish miners in the Nord continued to read Polish papers, only 1 percent of the Italian merchants and 9 percent of the construction workers in the Seine read Italian papers, in stark contrast to the 28 percent of Italian farm workers in Lot-et-Garonne who continued to the scan the news from back home. Fertility rates also reveal a rapid adaptation to French norms. "One cannot help being struck," the two authors note, "by the birthrate decline that occurred in Paris in both groups of Italians that we observed, workers as well as merchants. Fertility fell to a level close to that of the French population of the city." Still, the clearest sign of a renunciation of the country of origin can be seen in attitudes toward naturalization. Among first-generation immigrants, the survey found that 13 percent of the masons and 41 percent of the merchants in the Seine and 18 percent of the farm workers in the southwest had already become French. Among Poles, the naturalization rate was 5 percent for farm workers and 23 percent for miners in the Nord. Thus after just twenty years in France, the decisive factor in determining behavior was already occupation as opposed to national origin.[66]

The French studies nevertheless point out that traces of the country of origin can never be completely erased in the first generation. Sociologists in Chicago had arrived at similar findings much earlier: "An individual can never completely shed all traces of belonging to his original group. Some sign, word, gesture, or sentiment gives him away."[67] This fact accounts for the tendency, observed among immigrants in both France and the United States, to distinguish sharply between public behavior, where one attempts to conform to the norms of the receiving country, and private behavior (whether within the family or among peers), where one can keep faith with native traditions, safe from prying eyes. Social psychology can help us to understand why first-generation immigrants bear traces of their original culture throughout their lives. It is during the first few years of life that individuals acquire the decisive (and often unconscious) dispositions that shape their future personalities: children learn their mother tongue, encounter the world for the first time, and experience things that will have a major impact in later life. These attitudes, which form the basis of one's sense of belonging to a particular group, are acquired in the future immigrant's native land, on home soil, which can never be entirely forgotten.

The collective memory of immigrant communities can therefore be analyzed as a never-ending struggle between what Émile Durkheim called "native dispositions," which impel the individual to turn back to his native traditions, and everyday life in a foreign land, which requires some form of adaptation, that is, a sacrifice of the past for the sake of the present and future.

Turning now to collective memory in the second generation, we find a much more pronounced withering away of the sense of community than in the parents' generation. Any number of citations could be adduced in support of this assertion. Three examples involving groups reputed to be profoundly inward-oriented will suffice. The authors of one recent study note, for instance, that their work confirms other work on "young Muslims born and raised in France: their acculturation and secularization has been much more rapid than the general public imagines."[68] Studies published fifteen to twenty years ago of second-generation Armenian immigrants in France came to similar conclusions. Parents complained of their children's indifference to traditional holidays, commemorations, culture, and monuments recalling the genocide. The explanation for this was said to lie in the "irresistible force that impels the sons and grandsons of immigrants to disappear into the French melting pot." Soon, we are told, "the family name will be the only remaining sign of their distant roots."[69] In the 1930s, even as French investigators were claiming that Russian immigrants were failing to assimilate, studies published by Russians complained of the impossibility of passing Russian culture on to the second generation. "The children speak Russian poorly. Most cannot read or write it. Neither their parents, at work all day, nor Thursday schools can do anything to alter the situation."[70]

The explanation for this indifference to or, in many cases, rejection of the parents' culture is fundamentally the same as the explanation for the first generation's attachment to its roots. For the members of the second generation, the crucial moments of early socialization take place in the country of their birth, the country they grow up in, which is the host country. For them, the memory of their family's roots can no longer draw on souvenirs of actual experience. The children of immigrants know the country of origin only by proxy, through the words of their parents. If the first generation's "conflict of memory" pits one phase of life against another, the conflict for the children occurs primarily in early childhood, when two forms of socialization, two value systems, clash. Through language, customs, gestures, and memories the parents transmit the norms of the country of origin, and the children become familiar with these early in life, but those norms are already crumbling because of the family's having been uprooted. The second generation soon discovers the dominant norms, moreover, which the host society conveys in a thousand and one ways, primarily through the educational system. These contradict and even discredit the culture of the original group. This situation is often a cause of inner conflict, from which many immigrant children suffer. Among numerous accounts of such difficulties, I shall cite two from different communities and different times in order to bring out the fact that what is happening is a general process not restricted to any particular group, although it seems likely that individuals belonging to groups that are the target of the worst xenophobic hatred will suffer the most severe effects of stigmatization. Benigno Cacérès in one of his novels describes a Spanish child living near Toulouse in the period before World War II. Because the child's classmates call him a "foreigner," he goes to the town hall to obtain a copy of his birth certificate in order to prove that he is French: "How, then, could he be a foreigner? Emmanuel stared at himself in a mirror, looking for signs that distinguished him from us. He found none. When he went to bed, he looked carefully at the color of his skin and saw nothing unusual." Finally he asks his teacher, "Why am I a foreigner?"[71] More recently, an architect of North African origin and French nationality wrote of a similar traumatic experience when he and others like him "discovered our difference from other children" and became aware of "the way in which the other children saw our parents. And since that image was often negative, we rejected our own parents and tried to make friends with the other kids. These problems continued throughout our school years, culminating at around fourteen or fifteen years of age, in adolescence, a time that for me felt something like insanity."[72]

These initial traumas (which occur at an age when, as many psychoanalysts have shown, the child has a profound desire to identify with "others," that is, with the dominant norms) are an extremely powerful factor in favor of internalizing the national culture. The term *internalization* is essential, for it indicates that what is going on is not an educational process, not a conscious acceptance of certain rules, but a mechanism that operates within the scene of psychic experience itself, in large part unconsciously but often with extraordinary effectiveness, as is clear from the ease with which immigrant children learn French even when their parents do not know a single word of the language. The fact that some people contest the immigrant child's right to call himself a citizen of his native land—for he is as much a "native" as the child descended from a "native French" family—only reinforces his identification with the values of the environment in which he grows up. The at times desperate struggle to be fully recognized as a member of a national group accounts for the frequent rejection of the parents' culture, which has no value in the child's eyes and therefore must be kept at arm's length.

It is therefore legitimate to speak of assimilation, in the sense of an appropriation of the dominant culture.[73] As Étienne Balibar says of language acquisition (the idea can be generalized), "the second-generation immigrant...inhabits the national language (and through it the nation itself) in a manner as spontaneous, as 'hereditary,' as imperious for the emotions and the imagination, as the children of one of our 'home regions' (most of whom only a short while ago did not even speak the national language at home)."[74] One must add, however, that the transmission of the national culture takes place through the mediation of the local milieu in which the immigrant child grows up, and this is usually a working-class milieu. Shared memories, tastes, and manners, including even tics of language (the ironic banter of Parisian street argot, the accent of Lorraine or Provence), reveal how deeply second-generation immigrants identify with their local models. When the archbishop of Paris, Cardinal Lustiger (who was born a Jew but raised a Catholic after his parents were deported), called himself a Polish Jew from the hills of Montmartre, he captured in a memorable formula the importance of the local environment in the assimilation of those who still harbor memories of the experience of deracination.

The very fact that for the children of immigrants "home" is France, a specific part of France, explains their loss of interest in the memory of the group of origin. But other factors reinforce this tendency, in particular the disintegration of the "community" due to social mobility, which is common in the second generation. The change in social status often results in a change of dwelling place, a move out of the "ghetto" in which most of the instruments of communal fervor are located. Mixed marriages have an even more corrosive effect. Studies have shown that the spouse of foreign origin and, to an even greater degree, the children generally adopt the customs and habits of the French-surnamed partner. Rare in the first generation, mixed marriages are far more common in the second, as table 4.1 indicates.

TABLE 4.1 PROPORTION OF MIXED MARRIAGES AMONG ITALIANS AND POLES
IN THE EARLY 1950S

	First Generation	Second Generation
Italians		
Seine (workers)	27%	56%
Seine (merchants)	44	84
Lot-et-Garonne	7	51
Poles		
Aisne (farm workers)	4.5	55
Nord–Pas-de-Calais (miners)	9	24

Based on the Girard and Stoetzel survey.

The figures show that the places most propitious to mixed marriage are either large cities, like Paris (which offers a great number and variety of ways for couples to meet), or small villages (where the number of immigrants is too small to form a "community"). By contrast, the presence of a dense foreign population (like that of Poles in the Nord) encourages endogamous marriage.

If the analysis is carried further, one finds that it is chiefly between the second and third generations that the objective criteria of membership in the group of origin collapse. Take the Armenian population of Décines, for example: the proportion of mixed marriages was 1.4 percent between 1925 and 1929; it rose to 6.4 percent in the 1930s, to nearly 52 percent in the 1960s, and attained a peak of 75 percent in 1970–71.[75] Similarly, a poll of people of Polish descent showed that in the third generation fewer than 10 percent spoke Polish and fewer than 7 percent could read the language.[76]

The Problem of Integration

Historians can contribute to the current debate over the integration of immigrants by analyzing the factors that aided the integration of previous waves of immigrants and showing which continue to be operative and which have become obsolete today. The first area for useful comparative study is the labor market. Upward social mobility is of course a powerful factor for integration. The study by Girard and Stoetzel that I cited earlier shows that the children of Italian and Polish immigrants who came to France twenty years earlier generally succeeded in rising to a higher social status. Among Italian workers in the Seine, for example, half the children of working age had moved out of the manual trades. Similarly, fifty percent of the sons of Polish agricultural workers in the Aisne had achieved higher skill classifications than their fathers. The survey's major finding was that in France the most important factors in integration were not ethnic or national origin but occupation and geographical location. No matter what their nationality, the children of immigrants living in the Paris region in the 1950s were much more likely to improve their social status than were those living in rural areas or in monoindustrial regions of northern and eastern France.[77]

A recent study published by INSEE (one of the few sources of quantitative data on our subject) enables us to compare second-generation integration in the 1950s and today. After examining immigrant families living in France for roughly twenty years, the authors found that "the common view of the social mobility of immigrants and their children does not fit the facts." In reality, "after eighteen years in France, the majority of the immigrants we studied fared as well as other workers and enjoyed an average financial situation. Most children born to them in France before 1968 moved into white-collar jobs and generally enjoyed a higher social sta-

FIGURE 4.16   Muslim immigrant family in Marseilles, 1988.

FIGURE 4.17   Two girls who attempted to wear veils to school, at home with their family, 1989.

tus than their parents." Another of this study's major conclusions, one that will no doubt surprise those who believe that North African immigrants do not assimilate, is worth quoting: among immigrant children, "the ones who were least successful were those whose fathers came from eastern Europe, perhaps because many of them lived in regions strongly affected by the recession (such as the Nord–Pas-de-Calais and Lorraine). The majority of the rest moved upward in society, including the second-generation Arabs. The second-generation Arab community is fragmented, however, because it includes both many individuals who have moved up and many others who have remained poor."[78] Further studies are needed before any definitive conclusions are possible. Still, the most likely hypothesis when one compares occupational patterns of integration over a forty-year interval is that the "French model" remains intact. In other words, the job market in France is such that it does not create ghettos to which the children of immigrants are confined on account of their backgrounds. The parents' occupation and geographical location count more than their national or ethnic origins. Even today, these are statistically the most important factors for explaining the fate of the second generation (as the case of children of eastern European immigrants in northern and eastern France confirms).

Although most recent studies show that the French model of immigration is not in crisis, it would be misleading to deny that recent immigration has given rise to problems that did not exist in previous decades.[79] The INSEE study cited above shows that what is unusual about the "Beurs" (second-generation Arabs) is not that the "community" has any special difficulty with integration but that it is fragmented into two groups, those who have risen and those who have not. What accounts for the *simultaneity* of these two contrasting fates? That is the real problem that today's immigration raises. Compared with the 1930s or the 1950s, the change, I think, has to do with a new conception of immigration.

Previously, xenophobia, as well as political discussion of immigration in general, was focused on foreigners, that is, on a group of people defined by legal criteria (since in general the second generation acquired French citizenship virtually automatically). Today, for the first time in the history of the French Republic, the whole debate around immigration is focused on the second generation, which is to say on people who are legally French citizens but who are stigmatized because of their "ethnic" origin. Over the past thirty years a number of factors have conspired to bring this about. A new social category has appeared since the 1960s, that of "youth," whose very existence confuses the old picture of social classes. Contrast this with the past, when the sons of immigrants passed imperceptibly from childhood to adulthood, generally moving easily into blue-collar jobs. The extraordinary urban development of France over the past thirty years has considerably heightened the visibility of this youth group. Cities, where life is more anonymous and family controls are weaker than in smaller towns and villages, generate their own pathology. Juvenile delinquency among the children of immigrants, already a central feature of Chicago sociology in the interwar years, became a problem in France with the advent of planned cities and large urban housing projects in the postwar period. The phenomenon was made even more visible by the media's preoccupation with social issues. Acts of violence against immigrants were far more frequent in the 1930s than they are today but were rarely publicized beyond the local press. Today such incidents can easily make the front page of national newspapers, lending additional credibility to the idea that immigration is a fundamental social "problem." The growth of the welfare state has had a similar effect, increasing the number of sociologists, social workers, and others whose jobs involve looking after the needs of immigrants.

FIGURE 4.18   Cover of *Le Grelot* (September 4, 1892), attacking Belgian immigrants.

FIGURE 4.19   Posters for the National Front; Marseilles, 1988.

FIGURE 4.20   Hansi, *My Village*, 1911.

FIGURE 4.21   Cartoon by Plantu at the time of the municipal elections of 1983.

This new vision of French society has been consolidated by another crucial development, the decline of the workers' movement. Whereas immigrant children were once seen, and saw themselves, primarily as "workers," today they are seen, and see themselves, increasingly as "Beurs"; that is, in terms not of what they do but of where they come from. It may be that this major break with the basic principles of republican ideology, while it may not yet have affected either the law or administrative regulations, is one of the main causes of the dual trajectories mentioned earlier (some second-generation immigrants rising in status, others not). On the one hand, the political importance of "integrating North Africans" has meant that considerable resources have been allocated to social assistance, the creation of new teaching positions, and other measures to aid the Beur community. Hence the most fortunate Beurs, who readily present themselves as spokesmen for the "community," have enjoyed an upward social mobility greater than that of young people from other immigrant groups. On the other hand, however, the discourse of ethnic identity has helped to establish the stereotype of the "Arab as problem" which underlies much of present-day French racism.[80] Hampered, whether they like it or not, by this definition of themselves, second-generation immigrants who are perfectly assimilated but unemployed or downwardly mobile are forced to resort to the available vocabulary to decry their situation.[81] In the 1950s that vocabulary was drawn from the rhetoric of Communism. Today, the unfortunate are apt to lay the blame for their misfortune not on capitalist exploitation but on racism ("the French don't like Arabs"). Following this logic, they may turn to Islam (as they know it) in search of the language they need to proclaim their rebellion. If, in spite of everything, this phenomenon remains of relatively minor importance, it is no doubt because it is far more difficult, in our disenchanted secular societies at any rate, to mobilize large numbers of people around ethnic or religious issues than it used to be to mobilize people around issues of class.

Figure 5.0   Joan of Arc Festival, Place des Pyramides, Paris, May 8, 1988.

CHAPTER 5

Vichy

Philippe Burrin

Vichy: the name is symbolic of a regime that lasted only four years yet is deeply ingrained in the memory of the French. This assertion needs no documentation, substantiated as it is by countless films, novels, political speeches, and works of history. Fifty years later the atmosphere still becomes charged with passion whenever conversation turns to this period. Even the calls for an end to the debate attest to the persistence of this particular memory.

There are obvious reasons why Vichy has been so difficult to forget. The regime was an exception, as the location of its capital indicates. Paris, which had been France's center through monarchy and revolution, was dethroned by a city previously noted chiefly for its medicinal hot springs. True, the so-called government of national defense also abandoned Paris during the Franco-Prussian War (1870–1871), but not for so long a period. And true, Vichy did not leave Paris of its own volition: Pétain wanted to return to the capital, but the Germans objected. Nevertheless, the obligatory encampment in central France accorded admirably with the new regime's rural-oriented "deep France" outlook.

Obviously Vichy is also remembered because it grew out of France's defeat at the hands of the Germans and coincided with a period of occupation, with its attendant division and suffering. Memories of that period are still vivid in the minds of many people living today, people in a position to influence both public debate and scholarly research.

Finally, and more fundamentally, Vichy is remembered because it offers a convenient contrast to other regimes. The Fourth Republic grew out of resistance to the German occupation and rejection of *L'État français* (as the Vichy regime officially called itself, in opposition to *la République française*). Similarly, the Fifth Republic reacted against the Fourth, but because the founder of the Fifth was General de Gaulle, the new regime contributed as much if not more to the condemnation of Vichy. Politicians often invoke the history of Vichy in order to marginalize antirepublican groups and, at times, to discredit political enemies of whatever camp.

Is there anything unusual about this? If memories of Vichy are alive today, is the situation any different from, say, that of the Third Republic in the late nineteenth century, when people looked back to the Second Empire? Or from the period after the revolution of 1848, with its memories of the July Monarchy? And Vichy itself, for that matter: the regime defined itself in opposition to the Third Republic, just as the Third Republic had defined itself in opposition to the Second Empire.

Indeed, this series of regimes can be followed all the way back to the beginning: the French Revolution was the major rupture, the matrix of all that followed. Within a period of a few years nearly all possible forms of government were tried. The experience left the stamp of historical conflict on French political culture, by which I mean that France has tended to conceive of its conflicts in historical terms and to conceive of its history in terms of conflict. It also made memory a key element in the definition of all subsequent regimes as they searched, in one direction or another, for a stable equilibrium.

Each of those regimes was obliged to situate itself in relation to the great founding event as well as to what preceded it and what grew out of it. Each carried with it the memory of a predecessor, whether as model or anti-model. The Revolution, animated by the Promethean ambition to create a new society and a new man, ended by placing an enormous burden on the future: the past became a dynamic agent, its divisions constantly replayed, with the result that all postrevolutionary regimes, including the republics, have been to one degree or another "memory regimes."

The Third Republic, which looked to the future, also forged a tradition for itself and worried about integrating the country's prerepublican past. Still, memory clearly played a more important and more central role in those regimes that can properly be called reactionary. The Restoration, the Second Empire, and Vichy were all attempts—each with its own distinctive features—to turn things around, to set the clock back, though admittedly each of these regimes was obliged to strike some sort of compromise with changes deemed to be irreversible. The success of these attempts at reaction diminished over time, moreover, to judge by the decreasing duration of each successive regime (1815–1848, 1851–1870, 1940–1944) compared with the lengthening intervals left to the Republic to establish its roots.

In this family of reactionary regimes Vichy nevertheless enjoys a place apart, which entitles it to be called *the* memory regime par excellence. Although it resembled its predecessors in seeking to tailor the future to the pattern of the past, it also differed from them in a number of important ways: it did not aim to restore a previous regime, it did not attempt to restore power to political leaders or social groups that had held it before, and it did not try to revive the glory of a defunct empire.

Vichy's memory was filled with pure representations, the quintessential one being "France," but a France that was no longer linked to God through a divine-right monarchy and even less associated with humanity by way of a universal form such as the republic. Vichy was a deliberate, persistent, and futile effort to organize reality around such a memory, to reconstruct a national spirit in which the memory of a mythologized past would shape the perception of the present to create a unified way of feeling, thinking, and acting.

An Ambiguous and Shifting Past

Before examining this project of Vichy's, however, we must digress a moment to recall briefly what the *État français* was and how it was perceived by contemporaries. We will then be in a better position to appreciate the subsequent work accomplished by memory, the way in which it in turn organized the reality of a period whose experience was ambiguous, shifting, and divided.

There was a great deal of diversity in the Vichy regime, and chronology cannot be neglected. The picture of Vichy that certain elements of the Resistance, especially the Communist Party, tried to paint in the immediate postwar period—that of a uniformly black regime, totally abject before the occupying power and completely united in its oppressive policies against the French—has been substantially modified by subsequent historical research.

In fact, the regime harbored a number of rival tendencies, to the point where Stanley Hoffmann has proposed calling it a pluralist dictatorship. Other scholars have noted various phases in the regime's sinister evolution, with Laval's return to power in April of 1942 marking one turning point, followed by another in November of 1942, when the extension of German occupation to cover all of metropolitan France placed the principal reins of government in Laval's hands. Still others have tried to connect Vichy with the prewar and postwar periods, noting the prevalence of xenophobia before 1940 and the increasing state intervention in various aspects of French life after 1945.[1]

It is now clear that Vichy was not a monolith. Nevertheless, despite its internal diversity and evolution over time, there are good reasons for seeing the regime as fundamentally unified. As often happens, the outcomes and consequences of Vichy's policies did not always coincide with the original intentions or calculations of the policy makers. Some programs went awry, while others veered out of control, but these failures were not all the result of unforeseeable circumstances, such as the fact that the occupation continued for four years during which the Germans demanded ever greater sacrifices as the fortunes of war turned against them. Some of the failures were ineluctable consequences of the logic inherent in the regime's initial choices and goals.

To put it in a nutshell, the outcome was a foregone conclusion from the moment Vichy decided not simply to accept the consequences of defeat but to attempt a national revitalization in its wake. Once it was decided that the war was definitively lost, the only thing left to do was to save what could be saved. When Pétain announced that the time had come for France to break with Great Britain and pursue its own national interest, he was in effect assessing the outcome of the policies of the interwar period as many others did: mutual security had failed and the alliances to which France had committed herself had proved disappointing, not to say dangerous. France, the marshal declared, was left "alone to face her destiny." She had no choice but "to free herself from so-called 'traditional' friendships and hostilities."[2]

In the short run the defeat made it possible to embark on a renewal of French institutions, perceived as the only guarantee of a better future. Because France's new leaders had become convinced of the need for such a renewal *before* the war, they were all the more inclined to believe that the judgment of the battlefield had confirmed their analysis. In launching their effort to revitalize the nation, they set forth their priorities. No one expressed those priorities more clearly than the radical right-wing writer Charles Maurras, despite the marginal role that he played at Vichy.

In *La Seule France*, a book that he published in 1941, Maurras drew the following parallel: in 1429, Joan of Arc chose to go to Reims and the king's coronation even though by continuing her military campaign she might "have shortened by twenty years—who can say?—the fight to drive the English out of France." But, "then as now," the military aspect of the situation was only one element. "As harsh as the English conquest was, it was merely the effect of more profound causes that would have remained even if the English had left. The conquest grew out of France's division, fragmentation, enfeeblement, and anarchy.... The war might have been ended, but not without breaking out again soon thereafter as a result of the new divisions that would soon have engulfed a France without a Leader."[3]

Maurras treated the military struggle against the occupying power as secondary. A thorough overhaul of the nation took priority over regaining control of French territory and full sovereignty within its borders. To be sure, Vichy's leaders, whose views were by no means uniform, never defined their task with such clarity and rigor. Nevertheless, their actions followed the lines that Maurras had sketched out. And given the unforeseen course that the war would take, it was this establishment of a link between acceptance of defeat and national reform that would turn out to be the crux of the issue.

Vichy had counted on a rapid end to hostilities, which would have allowed the government, though left to rule an admittedly grievously wounded and subjugated nation, to concentrate on building a new France. Despite the forecasts of a quick end to the war, however, the battle continued to rage. England refused to give up, and Germany, it turned out, lacked the power to force England to do so. The French government was obliged to accommodate itself to a continuing occupation, which exposed it to daily pressures from the occupying power. Instead of a regime obliged to accept a German-dictated peace, Vichy became the regime that collaborated with the Nazis.

In order to preserve what autonomy the armistice had allowed it, and above all to outmaneuver London and de Gaulle and hold on to the Empire, which, along with the fleet, was the principal guarantee of that autonomy, as well as to pave the way for peace on the most favorable possible terms, Vichy made the strategic decision to adopt a policy of collaboration, a choice that was a logical consequence of the armistice that its leaders had sought. The collaboration in question was to involve mainly economic matters; it was to avoid open conflict with London and alignment of France with the Axis powers. Yet it was based on a wager that the Third Reich would ultimately win, or at any rate that the British would certainly not win.

Vichy's leaders claimed that this policy was based solely on a "realistic" assessment of the situation. But their realism was hampered by their own domestic policy preferences, to

FIGURE 5.1   André-Paul and Louis Simon, *Long Live France, Long Live the Marshal;* poster.

FIGURE 5.2   *The Marshal Established the Peasant Corporation;* postage stamp, 1943.

which they clung even as the war raged on and which ultimately led the regime into a blind alley. If the government renounced the policy of collaboration, it would risk losing all remaining autonomy while remaining vulnerable to German retaliation. To quit France for North Africa in order to join the Allies would have meant giving up any chance of authoritarian reform in France for the foreseeable future.

The events of November 1942 proved that the leaders of Vichy, Pétain above all, refused to acknowledge the utter futility of their initial decisions. Instead, they clung to their policies, showing, to be sure, some signs of doubt and foot-dragging but never more than hinting at any possibility of fundamental change. Collaboration continued to be advocated and practiced, and while Vichy now bargained more than ever with the Germans, it nevertheless accepted responsibility for enforcing the recruitment of French workers for "compulsory labor service" in Germany (the so-called Service de Travail Obligatoire, or STO) as well as for deporting Jews.

Meanwhile, the National Revolution remained on the agenda, although much of the original enthusiasm had gone out of it. By the autumn of 1943, Pétain and Laval separately sought to revive the National Assembly. At the same time they turned to the Milice, a paramilitary national militia, to maintain order, and both leaders would back its oppressive activities right to the bitter end. By agreeing to remain in power after November 1942 and thus choosing to owe their political survival to the occupying power, they ended up being made to look like partners and accomplices to Nazi perfidy. Ultimately Pétain was reduced to claiming that he had wished to serve as France's "shield," a wretched end to a policy that began with very different ambitions.

Although Vichy's course was by no means predetermined, the lines of force that it eventually followed were present from the beginning. In hindsight the regime can be said to have been unified, which is just how it appeared to many resistance fighters and to much of the French population immediately after the Liberation. Vichy thus entered history as the antithesis of the republicain tradition, the anti-Republic. Simultaneously, people who now saw the regime in the blackest of terms forgot that initially, especially in 1940 and 1941, many contemporaries to whom the future still seemed opaque were quite ambiguous in their attitudes toward Vichy.

Indeed, the regime's very inception was ambiguous. Continuity and rupture coexisted. Pétain did not come to power in the manner of Louis Bonaparte, who dispensed with legality only after being duly elected. Nor did his government take power by proclamation, as the government of national defense did in 1870 in the wake of military defeat. In July 1940 the Third Republic voted itself out of existence and transferred full power, seemingly quite legally, to Marshal Pétain.[4]

After the war there were attempts in various quarters to challenge the legality of this vote on the grounds that it was not a free or deliberate decision by the deputies of the National Assembly. Nevertheless, the fact is that the deputies, none of whom protested the armistice, knew exactly what they were doing, and the vast majority of them were ready to trust their fate to the man of the hour, onto whose shoulders they were perfectly willing to shift responsibility for whatever ensued. Was this the result of a failure of nerve or of a deep sense of blame for France's failure? In any case the vote was an expression of the collapse of democratic values among the very people sworn to uphold them.

Vichy was in no sense an antirepublican conspiracy led by a seditious gang ready to take advantage of the country's disarray in order to impose their own counter-revolutionary beliefs. It was first and foremost an expression of the authoritarian metamorphosis that afflicted much of the republican establishment. More specifically, the regime grew out of ideas developed by a loose network of small reformist groups coupled with a widespread collapse of faith in democratic values that began in the 1930s and was completed by the defeat. The collapse of faith in democracy affected nearly the whole of the French elite and much of the population as well.

True, the new regime was to a large extent the revenge of the Republic's mortal enemies, along with all who had merely paid lip service to republican values. The extreme right could not restrain itself from applauding the overthrow of *la gueuse* (literally "wench," a derogatory term for the Republic) and quickly threw itself into the breach. Yet it failed to win places in the government for its leaders. Maurras was excluded, and such aspiring leaders as Déat, Doriot, and Bucard left Vichy to try their luck in Paris. It was not until early 1944, however, that Déat, Henriot, and Darnand joined the government under pressure from the Germans, indicating not that Vichy had become a fascist regime but that it now contained a notable fascist presence.

The Catholic Church, which had reluctantly acquiesced to the Republic, offered the new regime its enthusiastic support, especially during the first two years, a time of inflated hopes of a new role for the Church. But Vichy never allowed itself to be defined as a pro-Catholic regime. Although Pétain and Darlan allowed the Church a much greater role than it had recently enjoyed and harped on the old theme of a "Christian France," in the end they found it preferable to limit their concessions rather than revive long-dormant religious conflict.

In fact, Vichy employed officials of many stripes and drew support from a fairly broad segment of the political spectrum, including dissident left-wing fringe groups. A solid core of reactionaries and men who had been involved with the fascist-oriented extreme right of the 1930s, such as Benoist-Méchin and Marion, was joined by others of varied background and outlook, all convinced, however, of the virtues of authority after the doubly chastening experience of the Popular Front and the defeat. Among them were former liberals such as Flandin and Barthélemy, technocrats like Bichelonne, and even René Belin, a former leader of the anti-

Communist wing of the C.G.T. (Confédération Générale du Travail, a labor union), who was supposed to demonstrate that the new regime enjoyed backing among workers and was keen to enlist the support of all social classes.

Even if well-intentioned people had continued to join the government in numbers as large as in the summer of 1940, the regime still would have been far from establishing itself on a firm footing had it not received the support of people of more modest background but decisive importance: civil servants at all levels apparently felt no particular compunction, given the vacuum created by the legislature's resignation, about taking up the reins of a government at long last turned over to those with the "competence" to keep its machinery running smoothly. Defections in the first two years were rare, even in the diplomatic corps.[5]

Nor did the army withhold its approval. After hesitating for a short time after the armistice, it threw its full support to the new government, whose ranks swelled with military officers. The Army of the Republic helped to bury the Republic: Pétain, unlike Hindenburg, was not a monarchist who had agreed to serve a republican government against his innermost convictions. He had served the Third Republic and no other power throughout his long military career. In fact, he had been a distinguished military leader in the previous regime, just as Pierre Laval had been a distinguished civilian leader.

We see the same divorce between army and republic, but for diametrically opposed reasons, in the behavior of the first man to challenge Pétain's authority. After de Gaulle escaped to England, where on June 18, 1940, he issued a call to the French to continue the struggle against the Germans, he broke with a government—the Pétain government—that was duly constituted and at that point still represented the government of the Republic. The transfer of power was approved only three weeks later, and the ensuing inception of *L'État français* changed de Gaulle's status in a way that he could not possibly have foreseen when he rebelled. Gaullism sprang primarily from a rejection of the armistice, not of the National Revolution.

It was not just the elites and the bureaucrats of the Republic who welcomed the new regime with open arms. The desperate situation of France in the summer of 1940 inclined much of the population to accept a strong government. Given the disarray that followed the defeat, the widespread disaffection with parliamentary democracy, and the general relief at the cessation of combat, many people were only too glad to welcome a government that promised to get things back in hand. For many long months the resistance would have to grope its way in darkness.

Pétain was the chief beneficiary of this climate of opinion, as shown by his triumphal journeys through the free zone from the autumn of 1940 on. To judge by figures gleaned from the postal censorship records, the government and its ministers never enjoyed more than limited popular support. The National Revolution aroused little enthusiasm or even sustained interest. The people were primarily concerned with two things: food and the repatriation of French prisoners of war. Darlan and especially Laval bore the brunt of dissatisfactions to which Pétain alluded publicly as early as the spring of 1941, but he himself would remain exempt from the public's wrath for some time to come.[6]

And yet, immediately after meeting Hitler at Montoire, he had personally assumed responsibility for a policy of collaboration that would soon encounter considerable hostility: "I alone shall be judged by History." Once anti-English sentiments triggered by the massacre at Mers el-Kébir had dissipated, the majority of the French clearly hoped for a British victory; they rejected a policy of collaboration whose benefits were by no means evident but which raised the danger of a disastrous confrontation with France's former ally.

As in Nazi Germany, people in France distinguished to an astonishing degree between the leader and his minions, reviving the ancestral myth of the good king flanked by wicked advisors.[7] Pétain, to be sure, encouraged such confusion both by his acts—such as the dismissal of Laval in December 1940, which many people quite wrongly interpreted as a repudiation of Montoire—and by the image he created through speeches and public appearances.

He rarely, for example, struck a note of command, intimidation, or threat. An interesting exception occurred in a message delivered on August 12, 1941, in which, after denouncing the "veritable malaise" from which the French were suffering, he announced a series of harsh new measures. Citing his "duty to defend" France, he said: "I put an end to the mutinies in 1917. I put an end to the rout in 1940. Today I want to save you from yourselves."[8] As consent evaporated, the regime's repressive vein rose to the surface; the Milice was already in gestation.

Ordinarily Pétain used a very different tone: that of persuasion, exhortation, and preaching, filling his speeches with Christian references that were not without effect on a population still deeply imbued with Christian culture. He addressed the French as "my friends," "my dear friends," and even "my children," speaking as a father or a pastor.[9] He was at first the providential man, the honored savior, prepared to sacrifice himself: Pétain "gave the gift of his person" to France in its hour of greatest need. Later the father began to sound more like a grandfather, the savior more like a martyr. Six months after the "ill wind" speech of January 1, 1942, Pétain made a show of his chains in order to win his compatriots' assistance: "In the partial exile that has been imposed on me, within the limits of the quasi-liberty that I am allowed, I aim at doing my duty to the fullest possible extent. Every day I work to rescue this country from the asphyxiation that threatens it, from the troubles that lie in store. Help me."[10]

Pétain offered the French a range of perceptions and images. Some—a large minority—subscribed to the program of National Revolution that he set forth; as events unfolded, they would either withdraw into inaction or enlist in the Milice.

A

AMOUR

★ ★ ★ ★ ★ ★ ★

K

KÉPI

★ ★ ★ ★ ★ ★

Y

YEUX

★ ★ ★ ★ ★ ★ ★

FIGURE 5.3, 5.4, AND 5.5   "Love," "Képi," "Eyes"; three plates from *The Marshal's Alphabet* (1941).

The others—certainly far more numerous—felt for Pétain a loyalty, or at any rate a respect, that they believed he deserved because of his glorious past and advanced age, his image as the savior-martyr of his country, and his role as a symbol of national continuity. Over time this admiration and devotion turned to compassion and pity more often than hatred.

To many French people Pétain and Vichy were not at all the same thing. Because of their respect for the man, however, they were loyal in a sense to the regime he headed. This attitude, a product of various assumptions and expectations, slowly eroded without vanishing altogether, and surely it is a crucial factor for explaining some of France's later difficulties in coming to terms with the past. In September 1944 a majority (58 percent) in France felt that Pétain should be acquitted. In the summer of 1945, after the discovery of the Nazi concentration camps, their number had dwindled to 17 percent. But in the 1970s and 1980s it rose again to more than 30 percent (35 in 1976, 31 in 1983).[11] Vichy is condemned in toto, but Pétain is still judged separately.

Here there is a considerable gap between the judgment of the public and that of historians, among whom there is universal agreement that Pétain headed the regime until the autumn of 1942 and bore ultimate responsibility to the very end. Even at the time it was clear that the government of Vichy saw itself as something other than a Roman-style dictatorship for extraordinary times. Beyond purging the bureaucracy and stifling political life, the steady stream of measures that the regime adopted in its very first months heralded an ambition of global reform.

To take just one example, the "Jewish statute" of October 1940 can hardly be described as an ad hoc measure. It apparently pleased many people and was passively accepted by the majority, without noticeable opposition, in contrast to what happened in the summer of 1942 when the police began arresting and deporting large numbers of Jews. The widespread protests that erupted then stemmed from compassion for the victims combined with a now deeply ingrained hatred of the occupying forces.[12]

Furthermore, Pétain himself was constantly issuing messages and proclamations to explain his ambitions and goals. Indeed, his role in the articulation and formulation of Vichy's program was so central that it is hard to see how, in this respect, the regime can be separated from the man.

The "Reconstruction of the National Soul"

To pool energies and revitalize the nation: that was Pétain's goal, and he alone would establish the lines that that revitalization was to take, a road map to a radical utopia. In the present context it matters little how this project was carried out and to what extent its goals were realized. Because various tendencies coexisted within the regime, and because the war did not end and the occupation continued, certain corrections, detours, and amplifications were required.

The new order was to be based on so-called natural communities: family, commune, occupation, region. Revitalized, these would again become the nation's essential skeleton. The family, the "essential cell," the "very foundation of the social edifice," was to be restored by returning women to the home and encouraging a higher birth rate. Young people were to be better educated and disciplined in school. Occupations were to be organized, with cooperation among the various categories of productive workers being the touchstone of social harmony. And among those productive workers a special place was to be reserved not only for artisans but especially for peasants, who were once again to be France's backbone.

This strategy was designed to foil and defeat the nation's principal enemy, individualism, which eroded social bonds and sapped France's strength. It would restore the "concrete" reality of *corps intermédiaires*, organizations standing between the individual and the state and said to be the only real framework within which individual liberty made sense. The state, for its part, was to be the culmination of the hierarchy of natural communities, capping them without crushing them. A strong state was necessary, but Pétain rejected *étatisme*, especially in its extreme totalitarian form. "Family rights," he affirmed, "are prior and superior to the rights of both states and individuals."[13]

The strong state was to be a state "reduced to its genuine functions"[14] and based on principles of authority and hierarchy in accordance with a thoroughly military model. Such a state would need elites, who would have to be raised and trained without regard to social origin. At the summit one man would govern, taking advice from a select few and seeking the consent of the many. There was to be no place in this system for political parties, much less for a unique party. Pétain chose instead to have a single organization of veterans to convey messages between himself and the general public.

The goal of the whole enterprise was to revitalize the nation. Pétain stressed the role of the school in this regard, along with that of youth organizations, which were charged with instilling into French youth a team spirit, solidarity, a sense of service to the community and of obedience to the authorities. In place of a France undermined and divided by conflicts among parties and special interests, and, more profoundly, by individualism and materialism, there would arise a new France, its energies mobilized by a "new spirit," a "spirit of social and national communion."[15]

Pétain defined his project as an "organic realignment of French society."[16] The goal was to reattach those parts of the nation that had been severed from the main body, or, varying the metaphor, to bring back into the flock sheep allowed to stray by "bad shepherds." Along with the theme of inclusion, there was a parallel theme of exclusion that Pétain never discussed publicly: groups recently arrived and deemed unassimilable, such as Jews, were to be weeded out. The nation was to be brought together by persuasion if possible, but if necessary by force: the government would act for the good of the people, if need be against its will. Like any project based on an obsession with unity, Vichy's unification project incorporated the potential for exclusion and repression from the outset, and these tendencies would be strengthened as the unity of the people with its leaders was increasingly deferred.

Vichy's project is often characterized as counterrevolutionary, and the regime is sometimes taken to represent Maurras's triumph.[17] A coincidence of values and goals does not imply identity, however. Pétain had no intention of restoring the monarchy, nor was he concerned with expunging the French Revolution from history in order to bring back what it had eliminated.

Clearly the marshal's philosophy of man and society, according to which individuals need supervisory authority and are properly subordinate to the community, derived from the counterrevolutionary tradition. But the nationalists of the late nineteenth century had already integrated this aspect of counterrevolutionary thought into their own thinking, in addition to which they had made their peace with the Revolution, which was now an accepted element of the nation's past. Pétain, too, accepted the Revolution, though reinterpreted in the light of his own values.[18] If he continued to celebrate Bastille Day and kept France's tricolor flag, he replaced the old triad of republican values—liberty, equality, fraternity—with a new triad of his own: work, family, fatherland. Nevertheless, he did not condemn the old values outright, arguing instead that they needed to be limited and complemented by new ideals. Yet his words and actions in effect negated the core of the old republican values to which he continued to pay lip service.[19]

For late-nineteenth-century nationalists, monarchy was no longer viable, but republicanism was not up to what they saw as the essential task. They therefore invented "France," a timeless, eternal, ideal form that had found imperfect embodiment in a series of different regimes. Pétain was a fervent if unimaginative disciple of this line of thinking. What was central to his project was not the question of the type of regime but the question of "France." The purpose of *L'État français* was to protect and revitalize the substance of France, and this included a wish to purge France of all that was not properly a part of it or that claimed to transcend it.

It would, however, take more than institutional reform or a new governmental structure to revitalize "France." Beyond enumerating a series of fundamental principles, Pétain had strikingly little to say about constitutional reform. This discretion was only partly the result of circumstances, actual promulgation of the constitution having been put off until peace was concluded. Although the point has been little noted, the fact is that the precise organization of the state did not matter to him as much as social and national reform did, society and the nation being the only profound realities. Pétain's stated ambition was to "rebuild society" and "reconstruct the national soul."[20]

Underlying this vast project was the conviction that there existed an "eternal France," the bedrock of any possible salvation. The defeat provided a unique opportunity to rediscover that bedrock, and the best way to do it was to promote a return to the soil. In 1938, Pétain said that "prosperity, like victory, puts us to sleep," whereas "defeat always awakens the French."[21] He took his generation's experience from 1870 to 1940 and turned it into a philosophy of history. Defeat did not frighten him, and he was prepared to accept it for its virtues.

In so doing he explored an avenue first opened up by Ernest Renan, who, after France's defeat in 1870, asked if the country would "continue down the slope of national enfeeblement and political materialism as it had been doing" or "respond to the knife that had been plunged into its living flesh as Germany did in 1807 by taking its defeat as the beginning of an era of renewal." The comparison with Prussia in 1807 was a staple topic of conversation at Vichy, where the idea was again that war could be "more useful to the vanquished than to the victor."[22]

Thus the defeat was seen as an opportunity for reflection, a pooling of energies, and a new commitment to the essence of the national identity: Vichy was above all the memory of this mythical kernel, a concept that could not be formed until two Napoleons had tested the limits of national power. It was also a highly French concept, an exemplary expression of which can be found in the myth of Vercingetorix, which was so very different from the mythical soil from which the dreams of Fascist Italy and Nazi Germany drew their sustenance.[23] Could a nation that celebrated defeated warriors such as Vercingetorix and Joan of Arc as heroes kindle with passion for a "Thousand-Year Reich"?

The way to rediscover "eternal France" and, along with it, a promise of survival, was to return to the earth: the earth which does not lie, which "continues to be your solace," which "is the fatherland itself."[24] In order to restore the substance of France it would be necessary to "reroot, so far as possible, Frenchmen in French soil" by putting an end to those practices that led to "the best elements in every class" being "uprooted" and condemned to a life of "wandering in a bureaucratic desert" (nomadisme administratif).[25]

The land was a key category in the Pétainist vision, which was far more than an expression of nostalgia for the past. Evoking the future of France, which was to become "what it should never have ceased to have been, an essentially agricultural nation," Pétain added that "like the giant of myth, [France] would recover her full strength by reestablishing contact with the soil."[26] The earth had literally magical powers, which guaranteed that the nation would regain its identity and its strength.

Finally, history itself testified to the existence of an eternal France and offered its portion of comfort. For what was history but a series of successes and misfor-

tunes, with success in each instance growing out of misfortune? Pétain's senten-
tious, moralistic style, much given to the timeless present and to natural metaphor,
nicely captured his belief in "eternal certitudes."

"One day, a peasant, a neighbor of ours, sees his crop destroyed by hail. He does
not lose hope in the next harvest. He continues, with the same faith as before, to
plow the same furrow to receive tomorrow's seed."[27] The point of this little parable
was of course France's defeat, here reduced to a natural disaster that could be overcome by persistence, stubborn determination, and courage to "withstand the
inevitable staunchly and patiently."[28] Suffering not only brings redemption but
guarantees it: France is eternal because it persists even through the cycle of victory
and defeat.

Vichy's project was a radical one in the proper sense of the word, a search for
roots blessed with the power of eternal survival. Was this too vague to qualify as a
project? If the details were never really worked out, the central vision was clear
enough. Whatever vagueness there was came from the quaking emotion that
inevitably accompanies any dream of returning to a golden age.

Everything in Pétain's vision expressed a powerful aspiration to escape from
time: it was the reactionary utopia of a nation challenged by disruptive socioeconomic change and by more dynamic nations on the attack. Ultimately Vichy was a
regime that no longer wished to confront history, that wanted no further part of it
so long as history meant continuous creation. The destiny of France was to experience fortune and misfortune: What did Hitler and Nazism matter alongside such an
"eternal certitude"? Vichy's policy expressed nothing more than the wish to go on
living of a country that had retreated into its own backyard.

Nevertheless, the memory of a timeless France that Vichy hoped to turn into an
active presence was already dated: it was as old as Pétain. It was the memory, exalted
as myth, of a man and a generation: the memory of a vanishing society of craftsmen and peasants, of contested moral and political values (service and sacrifice),
and of a historical experience interpreted as a timeless paradigm (the cycle
1870–1918–1940). Last but not least, it was also the memory of a set of images
inherited from nineteenth-century nationalism, the imagination of a national community transformed into an eternal reality.

Paradoxically, it was through this reactionary memory that Vichy revealed its
modernity: ex-republicans attempted to restore not a regime but a substance that
transcended both monarchy and republic or formed their common foundation.
Benjamin Constant had seen the truth as long ago as 1814: any authority that
attempted to restore the Ancien Régime "would try to claim that it was merely
reviving ancient institutions. But those ancient institutions would simply be absurd
and unfortunate innovations."[29] The judgment applies to Vichy all the more in that
its primary ambitions were to rebuild society and reconstruct the national soul.

Vichy did not go so far in its efforts to modernize as to conceive of its project as the fascist regimes did, in totalitarian terms. To be sure, "reconstructing the national soul" implied a need for resolute action to transform both the society and the educational system. Consider, for example, the major importance that Pétain attached to schools and the values they were supposed to instill into the minds of French students. Or consider the steps taken to encourage folklore and popular traditions.[30] Reviving old costumes and forms of expression was supposed to rekindle interest in the communal experiences of yesteryear. Fundamentally, however, Vichy had blind faith in the belief that the "old" could be restored if traditional institutions were once again allowed to exercise their full influence on society.

Were the French fully aware of how utopian this project was? Did they even perceive that there was a coherent, overall plan? It was in fact quite easy to hear the official rhetoric as an echo of the kinds of things that people said at home or to interpret Pétain's words in the humblest of terms as befit the circumstances. He celebrated the earth at a time of shortages; he extolled the family in a time of separation; he appealed to authority in the midst of war. The radical goals of the Pétainist program could be obscured, the program itself reduced to a panacea for a time of trial, an act of faith in the country's survival, and, in its innermost but perhaps most comforting aspect, a profession of national identity. The continuation of the war, which prevented Pétain from carrying out his program, brought him a popularity that it would have been difficult for him to achieve in peacetime, but at the cost of misinterpretations and ambivalence.

A Vivid Memory

The Vichy regime did not revitalize France as it had hoped, nor did it restore the nation's independence and grandeur. Instead it first divided the nation, then united it in opposition to its policies of repression and collaboration, which chiefly served the interests of the Germans. Instead of "reconstructing the national soul" by filling it with memories of an invented "France," it left vivid memories of a very real France that continues to be a source of embarrassment and outrage. During Pétain's trial, Mornet, the prosecutor, spoke of "four years to be stricken from our history." The idea was bizarre and striking, especially in its expression of a fervent desire to forget. But the past that we try to forget has a way of coming back to haunt us.

The history of the memory of Vichy—or, at any rate, of its public memory—is a good example of this, as Henry Rousso has shown in a remarkable and path-breaking book.[31] There is no need here to go into the wealth of detail he offers about the phases of repression and activation of Vichyite memory or about the propagation of what he calls "the Vichy syndrome." It will suffice to note the overall pattern of evolution, especially the turning point that occurred in the 1970s, before moving on to consider the change in themes and perspectives as well as the issues that have been forgotten or obscured even as others were remembered.

When the war ended, Vichy was discredited, and along with it all the various factions of a right wing that was summarily identified with the regime. The trial of its leaders, the execution of Laval, the imprisonment of Pétain (in deference to the special status he enjoyed in the minds of many Frenchmen, a status that, as a result of this decision, he would go on enjoying) made it clear how the general public had chosen to remember the recent past. There were two main charges against the former head of state: that of having conspired against the Republic, culminating in the vote to transfer full power to Pétain on July 10, 1940; and that of intelligence with the enemy, since the policy of collaboration had been adopted in what was officially still wartime, the armistice having simply called a halt to armed hostilities.

A complex history was reduced to a basic scenario—an underground conspiracy, treason—whose one advantage was to limit the number of those responsible. Many people had reason to be pleased with an interpretation that defined Vichy exclusively in terms of the armistice and the July 10 vote. The left stressed the latter theme, as well as its continuation in the National Revolution. De Gaulle concentrated on the armistice: as a government Vichy was "null and void," and it had failed to mislead the French people, who had formed a united front in resistance to the Germans.

As the war receded into the past, French concerns turned to other matters. New political differences arose to obscure the old ones, laying the groundwork for the amnesties of 1951–1953. Formerly prominent figures not scared off by Vichy found their way back into government thanks to Cold War anti-Communism. Even de Gaulle was not averse to taking part in this effort at rehabilitation.[32] Meanwhile, Pétainists joined together after the marshal's death to defend his memory, appeal the verdict in his trial, and win permission to transfer his ashes to Verdun: the hero of World War I, it was hoped, would redeem the head of state judged guilty of injuring his nation.

In the first half of the 1950s the *résistants* were no longer alone on the political scene, nor did they enjoy the same unquestioning prestige as in the immediate aftermath of battle. But the Resistance itself remained a central reference that could not simply be tossed aside. De Gaulle's return to power gave it a second life. Gaullist rhetoric lent authority to an image of France as "Free France," a France from which a handful of traitors had excluded themselves only to receive their just deserts at the Liberation. France, Resistance, de Gaulle: together these three magic words substituted a glorious, mythic past for a complex, shifting, and divided one.

The myth, however, was already dying. De Gaulle's departure from power in 1969 and his death the following year led directly and indirectly to a major change in the public's memory of Vichy. With the general gone from the scene, it was in a sense possible for Vichy to die: not just the interpretation of Vichy that Gaullism had sustained but the universe of values from which de Gaulle had drawn just as much as Vichy. De Gaulle was steeped in the same late-nineteenth-century nationalism as Pétain; he, too, believed in an "eternal France," a France whose history was a series of fortunes and misfortunes but which was only truly itself in times of grandeur.[33]

Though nurtured on the same values as Pétain, de Gaulle looked at the way things stood in the summer of 1940 and drew the opposite conclusion. The grandeur and honor of "France" required that priority be given to the pursuit of combat rather than to the national revitalization that de Gaulle too believed was indispensable, but not until after the victory had been won. De Gaulle did not share Pétain's belief in the redemptive value of suffering, or his mystique of the soil, with its attendant ignorance of technology, or his dogmatic authoritarianism: he could live with the Republic, provided that it remained strong. In other respects he shared Pétain's views: a substantialist view of the nation and a belief in the importance of memory in shaping the future. In proposing his interpretation of the war and of Vichy, de Gaulle hoped to rally the nation around a single, unifying memory.

In 1970, however, the mirror was shattered, as Henry Rousso so eloquently put it. In part this was a reaction against the ideological straitjacket imposed by Gaullism; in part it was a sequel to the protests of 1968; and in part it was simply a reflection of generational change. Men and women born during the occupation or immediately thereafter wanted to know more about their parents' world. And so the past returned, heterogeneous and complex. Each person held a piece of the mirror, adding his or her own reflection to a memory that had become kaleidoscopic. Even those who had emerged from the war as losers had their word to add—the price to be paid for a liberating freedom of speech.

The Gaullist memory of Vichy was a state-centered memory, centered around an event that in any case was not strictly speaking the work of Vichy at all, namely, the armistice. Because of the armistice it found the Vichy regime guilty of dishonorable conduct and treason. The National Revolution was in a sense set aside. After de Gaulle's death, public memory of Vichy expanded to include the regime's internal policy and the attitude of the French under the regime.

The film *The Sorrow and the Pity* is the perfect symbol of the change that was under way. Shot in 1969 but banned from French television (until 1981) and not shown in theaters until 1971, this documentary film presented a scathing view of the occupation. The image of the French as a nation of resisters gave way to an image of a nation in which many citizens remained passive while others compromised themselves in relations of one kind or another with the occupying forces. In short, it portrayed a France without grandeur, preoccupied with survival above all else.

The remainder of the decade witnessed the airing of a series of long-suppressed versions of the past.[34] Children of collaborators such as Marie Chaix recounted their experience. Novelists offered fragmentary images of the period. The condemned part of the past also returned in the form of a fascination, not always innocent, with collaborationist intellectuals such as Pierre Drieu La Rochelle and Robert Brasillach. All of these things helped to shatter the Gaullist myth. Since then the occupation has been subjected to a variety of interpretations, with due attention paid to the diversity of individual situations. At times the pendulum has swung far in the opposite direction: Louis Malle's film *Lacombe Lucien*, for example, offers a stylized account of how one good-for-nothing loser became a collaborator.

In the meantime there was also a reawakening of Jewish memory, focusing on Vichy's role in the persecution and deportation of Jews. In the immediate postwar period the nation had bestowed its honors exclusively on those deported for political reasons. No distinction was made between concentration camps and extermination camps. The public took little interest in the camps anyway, and many survivors preferred to suffer in silence. For all these reasons, a veil was drawn over this aspect of the past and remained in place for a long time. Even French historians were unusually circumspect on the subject. Until recently the only available studies were the work of either survivors or foreigners.

A published interview with Darquier de Pellepoix in 1978, followed by the Faurisson affair the following year, focused public attention on the existence of people who denied that the extermination of the Jews had taken place. The reaction to this information, coupled with a television broadcast of the film *Holocaust*, helped to mobilize public opinion and galvanize the government. Additional impetus came from the assumption of power by the Socialists in 1981 and the reemergence of an extreme right behind Jean-Marie Le Pen, the leader of the National Front; growing pressure on the government to do something led finally to the arrest and trial of the former Gestapo officer Klaus Barbie.

Even more important, perhaps, was the initiation of investigations into the actions of certain French officials under Vichy. Among the high officials accused of involvement in the persecution of the Jews were Jean Leguay, Maurice Papon, and René Bousquet. Leguay died in 1989 before being brought to trial; Bousquet was assassinated by a lunatic in 1993; the case against Papon is still pending. Despite the long delays in prosecution, these cases signal a fundamental change in attitude on the part of the government.

In the past the authorities were careful to distinguish between French and German responsibilities. The Vichy leaders who were tried and convicted and the civil servants who carried out their orders ostensibly had no choice but to obey. But World War II was not a war like other wars: it was a conflict in which elements of the occupied nation joined forces with the occupying power to wage war on certain common enemies. The persecution of the Jews, so central to current memories of Vichy, has made it impossible to ignore certain truths about the past.

FIGURE 5.6 *Hitler and Pétain Shaking Hands in a Field of Ruins* (perhaps an unconscious echo of the handshake at Montoire?); fresco in the Salle Wagram for the "anti-Bolshevik exhibition" of March 1942.

FIGURE 5.7 Departure of soldiers of the League of French Volunteers, who fought on the German side in World War II. The soldiers salute the flag in the presence of German ambassador Otto Abetz, September 1941.

As a result, Vichy can no longer be seen as just Pétain and Laval and a handful of Parisian *collabos*. It was also a bureaucracy that went about its business "normally," drafting, commenting on, and enforcing the Jewish statute. And it was a population whose attitude was shot through with ambivalence, in partial (active or passive) agreement with certain aspects of the regime. Few French people desired or approved the deportation of the Jews, yet many acclaimed Pétain, who discriminated against the Jews and delivered some to the Germans.

Such critical scrutiny of the past can have the effect of driving judgment to the opposite extreme. As has been the case with Italian Fascism, Vichy, long seen as a diversion from the main stream of French history, has lately been transformed into the most authentic expression of that history,[35] and fascism, long said to be alien to France and its democratic traditions, has been portrayed as a quintessentially French invention.[36]

Vichy is today of more topical interest than at any time since the Liberation. The main reason for this obviously has to do with the existence of the National Front, whose recent successes have focused attention on Vichy as a regime of xenophobia and exclusion.

Paradoxically, the Front's leader, Jean-Marie Le Pen, cannot make any public appeal to memory. He cannot invoke Vichy or Pétain as models unless he wants to limit his party's base to a small group of nostalgic reactionaries, most of whom already back him. He is therefore obliged to adopt a strategy of forgetfulness, or else, when there is no other option, to hide behind word-play or minimize the gravity of the past. In either case his adversaries are naturally inclined to raise the issue of the past in order to shed light on the present.

Since the Liberation the memory of Vichy has remained a dark spot in French history, even as perspectives and emphases have changed. Today Vichy is remembered, and reviled, more for its repression and persecution of individuals and minorities than for having signed the armistice. Collaboration with the Germans is now a less serious charge than cooperation with the Nazis and contributing to their ideological war. We have gone, in a sense, from a regime guilty of harming a collective person, "France," to a regime guilty of infringing the rights of man.

Although the outlook has changed, the old view shares certain features with the new. Both emphasize certain aspects of Vichy (armistice, repression, persecution) while overlooking or ignoring the radical utopia that was at the heart of Pétain's project.

The Gaullist view minimized the importance of this aspect of Vichy in order to promote its own version of the past: that of a France reinvigorated by struggle and once again on the path to greatness. Today's view, fostered in part by the discredit now attaching to the great ideologies of the past and by a certain widespread rela-

MENSONGE

Je hais... les mensonges
qui vous ont fait tant de mal.

Ph. PÉTAIN

FIGURE 5.8   "Lie," from the educational card game
Life's Trumps, circa 1941. The card reads: "Lie: I
hate...the lies that have done you so much harm.
Philippe Pétain."

tivism, neglects Vichy's utopian program because it no longer makes sense to people brought up in an urbanized, individualistic society (and that includes the supporters of the National Front, with the possible exclusion of its Pétainist fringe). How can we understand the memory that inspired the Vichy program when its social underpinning has disappeared? All that remains is an old-fashioned and rather exotic image of a ruralist regime, capable only of provoking smiles or sarcasm.

Both views portray Vichy as a regime without roots or origins, a monolith whose crimes are ticked off and denounced but that seems to have come from nowhere, to have fallen out of the sky. It is worth remembering, therefore, that this authoritarian regime grew out of the Third Republic, that it was a product of the crisis of democratic values in the 1930s as much as of the shock of defeat.

The evolution of French society has made Vichy's project obsolete and consigned it to oblivion. The collapse of nationalism and progress toward European unity have made the armistice less plausible as the primary count in the indictment of the regime. It is unlikely that a similar fate will befall the themes that are currently at the center of public memories of Vichy, for those touch on the fundamental principles of democracy, the dignity of man and his imprescriptible rights. The memory of Vichy is therefore likely to live on as long as democracy lives. Its critical value will be that much greater if we heed the lesson it teaches: that the most dangerous threat to democracy is that which comes from loss of confidence in itself.

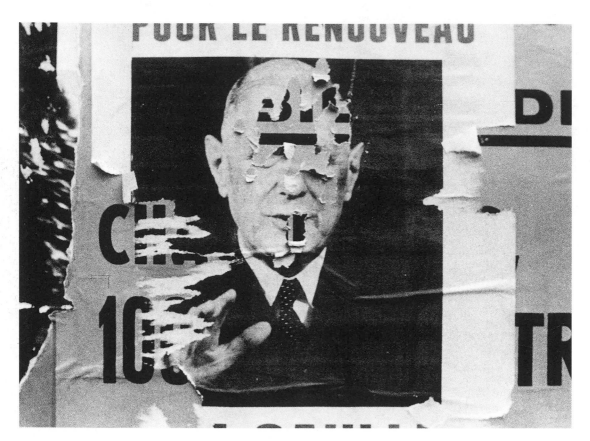

FIGURE 6.0   Wall poster from a 1965 campaign, photographed by Chris Marker.

CHAPTER 6

Gaullists and Communists

Pierre Nora

The Work of Time

"It's either us, the Communists, or nothing." Malraux's celebrated remark at the national convention of the nascent Gaullist party, Rassemblement du Peuple Français (R.P.F.), in 1949—a year in which it was the "nothing" that made the difference—has survived many ups and downs. Looking back, however, the two political forces that dominated French political life with their polarizing power from the Liberation to the mid-1970s have not enjoyed the same fate. The liquidation of Communism has been accompanied by a retrospective curse, a demonization, whereas Gaullism, its influence similarly eroded, has been wreathed in the sacred aura surrounding its founder.

The change has been prodigious. For anyone wishing to explore how, over time, the clash of Communism and Gaullism has turned into a *lieu de mémoire*, it is impossible not to notice the magnitude of the change that has occurred in less than twenty years: the moment of truth—perhaps only a provisional one—came in 1989 and 1990, when the historical collapse of Communism nearly coincided with the centenary of Charles de Gaulle's birth, which also became the occasion of his historical consecration. The negative has been flipped not once but twice, however: the price paid for the general's canonization was that his personal image has been stood on its head.

This is how things stand: according to all the polls, the statesman who, during his lifetime, was more hotly contested than any other has become, within twenty years of his death, the indubitable champion of French national memory.[1] The man who divided the nation more than any other has been transformed into the ultimate symbol of unity and cohesion. The man of the *coup d'état permanent* is remembered as the founder of the most universally approved French institutions of the past two centuries. The general whom many people suspected of harboring Boulangist imperialist pretensions now tops Victor Hugo, Jules Ferry, and Georges Clemenceau among the pantheon of republican heroes. The apostle of nineteenth-century nationalism and the man most hostile to a supranational European organization is hailed as the most skilled of artisans in the construction of Europe. The spiritual contemporary of Barrès and Péguy has become the visionary who foresaw the twenty-first century. *L'homme de la différence,* the glacial, taciturn commander, has become, thanks to the media—owing to the sympathy induced by caricature and the power of endless commentary—the cliché most easily digested by the popular imagination: *le grand Charles,* our national Asterix and Eiffel Tower. Meanwhile, Communism, only yesterday the future of the world and promise of a brighter tomorrow, and Stalinism, an insult worn as a badge of honor, an ideology experienced by its apostles as the soul of human warmth if not the milk of human kindness, today stands accused by its former champions of bureaucratic and totalitarian atrocities, of responsibility for the Gulag, of falsehood and perversity. Even if de Gaulle never entirely freed himself from classical authoritarian nationalism, no one today would interpret Gaullism in such terms: the phenomenon is now seen as having had the amplitude the general wished it to have. Nor would anyone today interpret Communism as a radical form of humanism temporarily gone astray, a characterization that survived even Solzhenitsyn's seemingly devastating critique and that once seemed ineradicable. Today the more common comparison is with Nazism, and in the hands of some writers Nazism seems almost the lesser of the two evils, for it at least did not hide behind the mask of liberating Marxism or order armored columns to roll beneath doves of peace. In both cases memory has effaced the gritty reality of history. The Communist credo has become a mystery, even—perhaps especially—to those who once believed in it and cannot help trying to understand why, while anti-Gaullists feel a retrospective need to justify themselves.[2]

This outcome is all the more surprising in that, viewed globally, Communism is undoubtedly the more substantial phenomenon, the one less bound up with local circumstances and an exceptional personality, the one more oriented toward the future and more saturated with history, in logic and in reason, in space and in time. Communism was a secular eschatology that entailed its own politics, morality, philosophy, science, aesthetics, way of life, and everyday behavior; and it was a *praxis* equipped with its Bible (Marx, Engels, Lenin), its Sacred History (that of the party), its Promised Land (worldwide revolution), and its Chosen People (the proletariat). How can one compare the grandeur of all this to Gaullism, which from the outset was afflicted with a narrow, backward-looking nationalism and by definition bound up with a purely individual political adventure? What one can compare and contrast is that which, from a political point of view, de Gaulle and the French Communist

Party (P.C.F.) shared in the form of intimate negative polarities: the lively vicissitudes of their confrontations, their duel and duet, in which both figured as confederates and accomplices.[3] One can also compare the aversion that each side felt toward the other: for the Communists the general with the particule could, at various times, be nothing other than a reactionary, a dictator, or a potential fascist, whereas for the champion of nationalism the Communists could only be "Moscowteers," separatists, or totalitarians. Yet between the two adversaries there was also a profound kinship, born of sharing the most deeply rooted traits of French political culture and tradition: a Jacobin patriotism, a haughty nationalism, a heroic and sacrificial voluntarism, a sense of the state, an understanding of the tragic in history, and a shared hostility to American modernity and the world of capitalism and cash. As to weight of historical memory and intensity of hope for the future, one cannot compare a great secular religion of the democratic age, which infused even primitive societies with the dynamic of class struggle and whose church, the French Communist Party, the French Section of the Communist International, envisioned its work as part of a worldwide strategy, with a simple "idea of France" and its "rank," an idea destined to disappear with the man who embodied it. Yet the Communist idea, that organic totality, has, despite the survival of a rump party, evaporated so completely that the rich memories once associated with it now seem comparatively artificial and meager, whereas Gaullism, completely dissociated from the political coalition that still lays claim to the name, has, through the miracle of de Gaulle, insinuated its memory deep into French consciousness, there eliciting the most profound echoes and so becoming the central reference point of France's present-day collective and national memory, at once an indelible mark and an unavoidable influence.

How much further will this divergence go? Will the future confirm today's interpretation or point up the need for a new one? Will the image of de Gaulle shrink to less invasive proportions, or will it survive in history and legend as the last embodiment of a grandeur forever lost? Will something new emerge from the purgatory in which the Communist saga has ended, or will Communism be consigned to the eternal damnation of the century's great black hole? If it is impossible to answer these questions, it is also impossible to avoid them. Indeed, they dictate the approach that I will take in the remainder of this essay. Before proceeding, however, it is important that we be clear about different possible levels of analysis.

To speak of Gaullist or Communist memory, or of Communism and Gaullism as *lieux de mémoire,* is to speak of several things at once. First, there are the memories that the two movements have left behind them, which we have just surveyed in the broadest of terms but whose detailed traces remain to be elucidated.[4] There is the intertwined history of these two major political forces, with their reciprocal strategies, their mirror images, their parallel lives, and their intersecting romances, whose endless vicissitudes form the subject of a political history that has for the most part been told, and quite well told at that; this will concern us only indirectly here. Yet there is also a very different aspect of the question: both political phenomena were, as it happens, in large part based on memory. Memory, that is, was an important dimension of the identity of each. It played a role, it occupied a place in the orchestration of both movements, far greater than in any other political groups or movements. Both fed on history. Both were scrupulously careful about their own histories. Both played powerfully on memory. Hence one can and should explore both Gaullist and Communist memories in all their wealth and distinctive individuality. Each has its own structure and baggage, its own technique and tonality, its own symbolism, didactic apparatus, rituals, instruments, and history.[5] These are not the things that chiefly interest us here, however. Most important of all, there is the fact that both Gaullism and Communism were, in themselves, phenomena of memory. They derive their very existence from memory. Both de Gaulle and the French Communist Party drew their appeal and power to mobilize not so much from their ideological coherence, the number of their supporters, or their relation to power as from the historical legitimacy they claimed to embody, from their ability to represent France, all of France, the true France.[6] Both were able to synthesize the two major themes around which the history of contemporary France has been built: Nation and Revolution. We thus have two versions of national legitimacy, two syncretic, rival, and complementary visions of France, whose opposition structures the historical memory of contemporary France in an emotionally intense way, which illustrates in particularly and perhaps ultimately striking fashion how politics in France is driven by the invocation of great memories and the emotional manipulation of the past. While other factors may contribute to the same end, it is for this reason and in this sense that Gaullism and Communism constitute a *lieu de mémoire* in the strict sense.

The details are important, all the more so in that the two phenomena offer what is probably a unique example of opposing trajectories in memory. A whole series of circumstances and mediations had to intervene before the Gaullian memory of Gaullism could reassert itself and consolidate its position in terms of celebration. The key element was the order of presidential successions, whose subtle and unexpected influence greatly favored the gradual amplification of the last strong image of French national identity: first came Georges Pompidou, the Louis-Philippard banker and industrialist, the closest in time to de Gaulle but the most remote in spirit; next was Valéry Giscard d'Estaing, the young technocratic economist who hoped to lower the level of tension in the country but whose image never came into clear focus and failed to resonate in the lives of ordinary Frenchmen; and finally François Mitterrand, de Gaulle's most implacable adversary yet the man actually most responsible for fixing his image. First, the fact that the general's most persistent detractor adopted the very institutions that de Gaulle had created and that those institutions were put to the test by the experience of "cohabitation" (in which a right-wing prime minister and legislature held power under a left-wing president) absolved them of any suspicion of partisan bias and bestowed on them the anointing of the nation: Caesar and Sulla became Solon.[7] Second, François Mitterrand himself became the artisan of a mirror-image consecration, joining his defunct rival in one of those summit dialogues filled with political and literary allusions of which the French are so fond, a dialogue implicit in the very notion of a two-party system and perfect for all sorts of exercises in symmetry.[8] Above all, Mitterrand's work made it possible and legitimate for the left to offer de Gaulle its posthumous support, which was the most important—and striking—element in the establishment of the general's image.[9] "Have we all become Gaullists?" Max Gallo asked even before the left came to power (at which time Gallo became President Mitterrand's official spokesman).[10] This major shift of opinion was reinforced by another, which also contributed significantly to recentering the general's image. Even as the collapse of proletarian internationalism revitalized the national idea, bestowing new youth on what now seemed to be the old law of the world, the rebirth in France of a nationalism of the extreme right, which had been thought dead since the end of World War II, purged as if by contrast Gaullian nationalism of its more caricatural traits, thus opening it up, making it more patriotic, and investing it with ecumenical features sufficiently undifferentiated to allow all political families and sensibilities—from Barrès to Péguy, from Michelet to Renan—to recognize themselves, and transforming Gaullism into a banner that could be honorably invoked in what was all in all a rather idealized fashion entailing no particular commitment. Meanwhile, the reduction of the revolutionary ethic to the philosophy of the rights of man, which would be the central focus of the bicentennial of 1789, made it possible to inflate the general's image with the whole legacy of the French Revolution. Thus the base of Gaullian memory was expanded in three directions: from individual adventure to constitutional inscription, from right to left, and from narrow nationalism to republican ecumenicism. This triple transgression of de Gaulle's natural historical space was intelligently managed by the high priests of a memory that was launched by the general himself[11] and paradoxically served by the right turn taken by his purely political heirs, thus rescuing the general from the confines of partisan opinion to place him very soon at the center of the national mythology.

Very soon indeed: for while the mythologization of General de Gaulle was a long-term affair, an integral part of a history that began when he first arrived on the public scene, it is clear in retrospect that his present image first crystallized and took hold in the eighteen months that elapsed between the general's repudiation by French voters in the referendum of April 28, 1969, and the worldwide apotheosis afforded by his funeral on November 12, 1970.[12] The orchestration of themes and acts was nothing less than magical. First there was the Retirement, a major theme modulated in three ways: in its historical and political significance, from the laconic communiqué of April 28 ("I am relinquishing my functions as President of the Republic. This decision takes effect today at noon.") to the no less laconic final message ("I shall say no more."); in its private significance, with the premortal burial at La Boisserie, which had already become the pilgrimage site for close friends and superloyal supporters of the felled "oak" (*Les Chênes qu'on abat*— "Felled Oaks"—was the title of a book that Malraux wrote about the general in this period); and finally, in its imaginative and quasi-metaphysical significance, in the retreat within the retreat, into that abyss, the Elsenor of Connemara, from which came the images, soon flashed around the world, of de Gaulle as mournful menhir. Then came the thundering publication of the first volume of the *Mémoires d'espoir: Le renouveau*, which sold 175,000 copies in three days (October 7–10, 1970), a fabulous success. And then, one month later, death, in the midst of this success and fraught with symbolism, for the end came almost instantaneously, as if a still-living saint had been snatched from earth by the hand of God. Finally, in accordance with wishes expressed in the general's will, drawn up in 1952, hence before his return to power, he was given two solemn funerals: one at Notre-Dame in Paris, with an empty coffin around which gathered leaders of all the world's nations except, for the greater glory of de Gaulle, the South Africa of apartheid and the Greece of the putschist colonels; the other at Colombey, with "the parish, the family, the Order; a knight's funeral."[13] It was thus a double ceremony, both intimate and global,[14] and topped off by the spontaneous homage of the anonymous crowd that gathered in the rain on the Champs-Élysées and all night long marched up the avenue where he had marched with another crowd on the luminous twenty-sixth day of August 1944. There, through an interplay of accident and will, at the intersection of presence and absence, between what was already no longer life but not yet death, there was enacted a symbolic sequence, an extraordinary theater of memory, whose miraculous plotting and precise gestural language seemed, though no one at the time was fully conscious of it, almost a counterpoint to that other celebrated staging of memory, the emotional explosion of May 1968. There one had had symbolic barricades reminiscent of the Paris of 1848 and the Commune, the black flags of anarchism mingled with the red flags of revolution, soon followed by the Grenelle Accords, which mimicked the accords between the Matignon and the Popular Front; one saw Communist memory wrested away from the high priests of Communism by the youthful outpouring, the spontaneous uprising of young students and workers. Here one had the great escape of the solitary man, the reemergence of another de Gaulle, forgotten during ten years in power: the rebel of June 18, the man who had crossed the desert alone, the author of the *Mémoires de guerre*, to whom time had offered, in the end, a chance to recover his true destiny.

This triumph of memory stands in striking contrast to the Calvary the Communists were forced to endure. The first thunderclap sounded with the Khrushchev Report to the Twentieth Congress of the Soviet Communist Party in February of 1956, in the wake of the acknowledgment of the Yugoslavian schism and on the eve of the crushing of revolt in Hungary by Soviet tanks.[15] To be sure, there had been no shortage of denunciations of official memory or analyses of its manipulations before that date. But for the first time Stalin's "crimes" and "errors" were attacked in the most official forum of the Communist hierarchy, and once Pandora's box was opened it could never again be closed. The spell was broken; Communist memory would never be the same. Indeed, Khrushchev's efforts to limit the indictment to the "cult of personality" would prove all the more damaging in France because the Stalinism of French Communist leader Maurice Thorez had always conceived of and presented itself as the perfected form of Marxism-Leninism. By striking at the keystone, the attack thus threatened to bring down the whole edifice. The idea that democratic centralism was inherently infallible in practice was permanently discredited. Faced with this central menace to the integrity of its memory, the party's official reaction was typical—and fatal. There was never any candid concession or public recantation or expiatory denial which might have threatened the core of the party's identity. Yet this was a world in which words had double and triple meanings, in which all language was coded; and beyond all the vociferous denials and protests of candor and unbroken continuity there were insidious shifts, structures that crumbled only to be shored up at once, and adjustments calculated to the last millimeter; the more intolerable rhetoric was gradually toned down, while certain new key words were surreptitiously introduced—it was a tried and true formula. The shock of 1956 would trigger a great diaspora, especially among intellectuals, which soon gave historical visibility to the category of "ex-members" of the Communist Party, but meanwhile the party would condemn itself for the next twenty years to hiding behind the formula of the "so-called report attributed to Comrade Khrushchev." It was not until 1977, at the height of the Union de la Gauche (or Socialist-Communist alliance around a Common Program) and the flirtation with Eurocommunism, in the context of a Twenty-Second Congress dedicated to the theme of a sham modernization of the party, and in the wake of a series of dark and ambiguous polemics initiated by Jean Ellenstein in *Le Monde* and by the television broadcast of the film *L'Aveu*,[16] that the politburo of the P.C.F. published in *L'Humanité* of January 13 one of those long, labored explanatory communiqués that can be deciphered only by initiates: "In the course of preparations for the Fourteenth Congress of the French Communist Party [immediately after the Khrushchev Report], in order to allow all militants to participate usefully in discussions of the problems raised by Comrade Khrushchev's report, the polit-buro asked the Central Committee of the Communist Party of the Soviet Union for the text of that report, whose contents were known to the members of certain Communist and workers' parties." Curtain. The shift from Georges Marchais's admission of "delays" in the reevaluation of "certain theoretical positions" in the period 1955–1960 to the general theory of "the complex and contradictory" so prominent in the explanation of what Roger Martelli, party historian and Central Committee member, finally in 1982 termed a "strategic blockage," leaves the heart of the matter untouched.[17] It was simply not in the party's nature to confront its past head on.

The Stalinist grip on the apparatus had the effect of compromising the funda-mental heritage to the point where it was ultimately claimed or challenged by oth-ers, who had freed themselves from Stalinist hegemony, and who threw the party onto the defensive and attacked it from two angles: socialists and social-democrats worked hard to escape Communist attempts to discredit them, while the ultra-left deprived the party of its monopoly of the revolutionary tradition and, with help from the Sino-Soviet split, Cuba, and the Algerian War, reinvested the legacy in Maoism and third-worldism, only to end up in the nebulous world of *gauchisme* with its many *groupuscules* and sects. Thus there was a vast shift of memory along two fronts. Before any socialist renaissance would be possible, and before the non-Communist left could, as the idea of revolution lost its hold on men's minds, cleanse itself of the endless allegations of "treason" that grew out of a Leninist interpreta-tion of history, a great cultural mutation had to take place. It came about—a devel-opment that I can do no more than evoke here—as a result of a conjunction, in the 1970s, of Catholic with Marxist doctrine. With the Second Vatican Council the Church had begun to change its direction, and for the first time the hierarchy was prepared to enter into a "dialogue" with workers' hopes.[18] Meanwhile, a multiform Marxism had flowered on the ruins of Leninist orthodoxy. It drew on the refur-bished tradition of Jaurès and Blum as reinvigorated by Gramsci to become, in a vague and diffuse way, the all-purpose reference of French-style socialism, which it remained until the political break with the Communists in 1983 (and even then it was never officially repudiated).[19] On the other front, among *gauchiste*, Trotskyite, and libertarian militants, a whole range of revolutionary moments once overshadowed by Leninist Bolshevism was systematically revisited both before and after 1968: from the sailors of Kronstadt to the Spartacist leagues, from Makhno to the work-ers' councils to the anarchists of the Spanish C.N.T., old movements were brought to light. The heroes and casualties of the "unknown revolution" were rehabilitated the better to discredit the monolithic official party history.[20] Indeed, that monolithic official history was itself so dull, so inconsistent, and so "revisionist" that propo-nents of a return to a more uncompromising orthodoxy advocated a rereading of the classics of Bolshevism, such as the lectures that André Ferrat had delivered to the cadres of 1930,[21] which for a long time remained the only history of the French Communist Party prior to the Popular Front.[22] Indeed, Communism's darker memory had become almost its only memory. It had lost across the board, to the point where it was jeered, misused, and caricatured even by its most vigilant guardians. *L'Humanité* had to have come a long way from the heroic days of yore to reach the point where, on the final day of the Mundial, it could deride once-sacred values by running this four-column headline: "This is the final struggle!"

This contradictory evolution has yielded two exemplary types of historical memory, which the contemporary historian rarely has the opportunity to study in such crystalline purity: a mythified memory and a historicized memory.

In the case of Gaullism, it is as if posterity, generally implacable, not only ratified an individual's policy and intention with respect to memory,[23] subscribing with overwhelming approval to the image that de Gaulle had deliberately forged for himself, but also seized upon certain elements of that image to extend it, illuminate it, enrich it with new material, and allow it to respond to posterity's needs by constructing an autonomous *lieu de mémoire*. With each new commemoration[24] and round of polls,[25] with each new wave of books,[26] collection of photographs,[27] and television series,[28] the personage was transformed. It was stylized by a gradual obliteration of memorially dubious periods: the R.P.F., May 1958, the Algerian War, May 1968. It was reduced to a stereotype by the addition of features not found in the initial version: good father, good son, good husband, good Christian. It was academicized as a subject for examinations[29] and institutionalized by the work of the Institut Charles-de-Gaulle.[30] Just as the publication of Marcel Proust's *Contre Sainte-Beuve* and *Jean Santeuil* provided background for the meteoric appearance of *A la recherche du temps perdu,* so the first of twelve volumes of *Lettres, notes et carnets* revealed a de Gaulle before de Gaulle, a man both prepared and not prepared for the striking entrance of June 18, 1940, while also illuminating the carefully hidden part of the edifice, the private man.[31] One sign and consequence of the rising power of the mythic figure is the regular failure of counter-memory offensives propelled by periodic revivals of the Algerian affair or the question of mass support for Vichy. The personage has assumed the dimensions of a Father of the French, who has not only taken his place in the portrait gallery of great ancestors but also been brought closer to home by humor, by the intimacy of derision, which Jean-Pierre Rioux felicitously calls the "privatization of fervor." In 1978, Claude Mauriac wrote a book filially entitled *Aimer de Gaulle,*[32] and twelve years later the now fraternal Régis Debray produced *A demain de Gaulle.*[33]

Yet despite the nearly 3,000 books that have been written about him (more than about any other figure in the history of France, including Napoleon), de Gaulle has not yet entered his historiographic age; he may even have escaped it altogether.[34] In all this enormous outpouring of books, most of them written by eyewitnesses, journalists, and political scientists, how many can really claim to be historical?[35] How, moreover, can one write the history of a myth without also writing the history of a counter-myth?[36] Nearly all the historians who have looked at some aspect of Gaullism or of the general's activity would probably concede that the case can be argued two ways. On every major issue, particularly since 1958, de Gaulle's achievement is subject to contradictory interpretations and judgments, starting with the return to power and the war in Algeria, but including as well Germany and Europe, the Constitution, France's attitude toward the United States, and even de Gaulle as writer. Even the sweeping general assessments vary between extremes: from the activist realist that François Goguel[37] sees in de Gaulle to the "artist of history" first brought to our attention by Stanley and Inge Hoffmann.[38] A historical treatment cannot consist in contrasting one de Gaulle with another, truer de Gaulle but must somehow place the undecidable ambiguity at the center of each historical problem. Meanwhile, among the possible interpretations, collective memory has chosen as the general would have wished, and that must be the starting point for the historian's work. Whatever historians do, they are caught in a fundamental dilemma: either they grant, from the outset, the Gaullist phenomenon and the personage of the general the status of absolute exceptionality that de Gaulle claimed for himself, and thus abandon the essential, which for the historian is to free himself from the grip of that in his subject which is still that subject speaking through him; or they must refuse that exceptionality at the risk of missing what is essential, which consists precisely in what was exceptional about Gaullism and de Gaulle. The best biographers—Jean Lacouture in particular[39]—have not avoided this dilemma, for they begin by interpreting de Gaulle in terms of categories and criteria by which he himself would have wished to be judged: those of the providential hero, the Lancelot rising to every challenge. Once that crucial concession is made, one can introduce all the qualifications and nuances one wants and still miss what for historians ought to be the central question: the personage is judged by self-imposed norms. It is the subject who dictates the rules of the game, as in a painting by La Tour or Vermeer, in which the light that seems to illuminate the scene comes from within the scene itself. This is not "ego history" but "echo history," which proliferates and branches out from a fundamental central source, developing ever more refined and ramified genres that invoke each other's works in a perpetual round, in which each witness calls forth a counter-witness and a corroborating witness, in which official commentary elicits private confidences, and in which the endless round of daily news reports calls for a periodic overview. The hierarchy of proximities obliges some to speak and others no less eloquently to hold their tongues. The uniqueness of the model elicits portraits and psychological analyses; its nobility sets the noblest of pens to paper,[40] its solemnity is a goad to caricature and to the publication of private witticisms, and its foreignness attracts the foreign eye: the escalation feeds on itself. Gaullology has its laws and its rhythms, its high priests and its choirboys; it even has its historians. Yet even then the history of Gaullism and de Gaulle can only be written from within a history itself "Gaullized" or "Gaullified." Here, then, is tangible proof that, appearances to the contrary notwithstanding, historical work is not always possible.

By contrast, it was on the terrain of history, and history of the most critical kind, history devoted to the establishment and comparison of facts, that Communist memory was attacked, undermined from within and without, and finally destroyed.[41] This was sensitive terrain, all the more sensitive in that the Communist Party had always abused history for strategic purposes. As a Marxist party, how could it avoid reverting to historical explanation at every turn? "History teaches us that...." As a people's party, a proletarian party, how could it deny the justice of educating memory on the broadest possible scale, through party primary schools, propaganda publishers, memoirs of revolutionaries, and constant celebration of working-class struggles and of clandestine attacks on the Nazi invaders—a deluge of edifying literature? Surveys have even shown that, at comparable levels of education, Communists know more history than non-Communists. In late 1938 the party appointed an official historical commission, and it was never reluctant to grace its official podiums with historians. What is more, no other party was so conscientious about its own historical portrayal, about the representation of its own history. No other party imposed the duty of remembering as such a key element of its identity. But Communist history was a very special kind of history, a "memory-history" with well-worn and regulated mechanisms.[42] Until the early 1970s there was no professional party historian. Whatever self-styled historical materials were produced came exclusively from party officials, foremost among whom was the nonpareil Maurice Thorez, "son of the people." The party's history was therefore purely official and politicized. Even when it did not emanate directly from party authorities or professional historians whom the party discredited by calling upon them to produce propaganda instruments (like *La Vérité sur 1939*, published by Jean Gacon and Jean Bouvier in 1954), it remained an "institutional expression," written with the "party spirit" in mind, a spirit still explicitly invoked in 1964 by those who contributed the preface to the first, long-awaited, and very disappointing textbook *Histoire du Parti Communist Français*[43]: "The basic principle of this study is the party spirit in science, this being the only approach that combines vigor with scientific honesty." It was a history that was all the more pedantic for being a close imitation of a model imposed from without, for the P.C.F. never looked back without keeping one eye fixed on a history that was not its own, whose standard and tone were set as early as 1937 by the celebrated *History of the Communist Party of the Soviet Union (Bolsheviks)*. It was essentially an interpretive, adaptive history, whose emphatic and peremptory rhetoric reflected an intrinsically ahistorical internal structure. It was also a totally linear and positive history, invariably a matter of going, as any number of titles hammered home, "From A to B."[44] It was a history of fixed elements and roles assigned in advance, with the imperialist bourgeoisie on one side, the heroic party of the working class, the true incarnation of the repudiated fatherland, on the other. This structure was so rigid and invariable that Georges Lavau went so far as to analyze it in much the same terms as Vladimir Propp analyzed folk tales. Even today some fine specimens crop up from time to time, the last remaining fossils of a particular style of history writing that Communists have slowly been obliged to abandon.

For the past twenty years, in fact, the party has had to deal with having its own memory thrown back in its face as that memory has been dismantled piece by piece in a series of assaults, each more lethal than last. In these sapper attacks, historians have drawn on the work of memoir writers—in some cases the historians and memoirists are one and the same. Firsthand accounts, reminiscences, and autobiographies of former party officials and ordinary activists have become a genre to be studied as such, a rich and diverse corpus of documents constantly replenished by the party itself, which has acted as a kind of filter, a locus of memory unto itself, an instrument through which Communism's official memory has been funneled into the minds of individuals, where it shaped private memories in blissful indifference to matters of truth or falsehood.[45] All in all the genre may have contributed more to the endurance of Communism than to its decomposition, but there were some sensational shocks (such as Edgar Morin's *Autocritique* in 1958 and Artur London's *L'Aveu* in 1968[46]) as well as a steady flow of timely information for analysis by the experts.

All sorts of things found their way into this literature, beginning with the conditions under which Communism was born.[47] Then there was the personality of Maurice Thorez.[48] Above all there was the dark period from the German-Soviet Pact of September 1939 to the German invasion of the Soviet Union in June 1941, which raised the crucial issues of revolutionary defeatism and the date when party leaders decided to join the Resistance.[49] No recess of memory went unexamined. The Communists were forced to acknowledge the secret protocol added to the German-Soviet Pact,[50] the fabrication of a phantom issue of *L'Humanité* dated July 10, 1940,[51] the requests to the Propagandasstaffel to allow the party newspaper to resume publication, and the letter from Billoux to Pétain asking that imprisoned Communists be freed.[52] All these were sore points that remained major issues within the leadership for a long time.[53] Communist historians are still fighting pitched battles over them today.[54] Annie Kriegel was the first historian to provide an overall framework for a critical reevaluation of the party, and she has since been joined by a battalion of historians whose ranks include members of the generations marked by the Algerian War, 1968, and Union de la Gauche. Communists have been forced to respond to their work. Although the Central Committee, meeting in Argenteuil in 1966, issued a timid proclamation that no official truth should be in contradiction with "actual history," the gap has slowly widened between what Marie-Claire Lavabre and Denis Peschanski have felicitously called "reference history," that is, the politics of the past, and "substantive history," which has been treated in a relatively autonomous way since 1970.[55] Once the "subject" of history, the party has now become an "object" of history.[56] The *Manuel* of 1964 was entirely controlled by the political leadership. This had ceased to be true of *Étudier le P.C.F.* (1979) or *Le P.C.F., étapes et problèmes, 1920–1972* (1981), two noteworthy publications by the Institut Maurice-Thorez.[57] Even the professionals among Communist historians remained imbued with a sense of the political issues at stake in historical research: as one has said, "even a sincere refusal of an essentially justificatory history must not entail a simple reversal of position that would induce the P.C.F. to quit a battleground important to itself and to the ideological battle."[58] This extends right up to the present day the limits laid down by Georges Marchais just after the Twenty-Second Congress, when, after stating that it was henceforth "unthinkable for us not to tell the truth on all subjects," he extended an invitation to historians "to issue a judgment on our past behavior" but then rendered that invitation rather Platonic by adding: "We are unanimous in our belief that, in the main, the policy of our party from its foundation to the Twenty-Second Congress has served the interests of socialism well."[59] However attached historians may be to old issues, the battle is virtually over now, having lost its polemical edge. Whereas Gaullist memory has taken the upper hand in the battle with history, the history of Communism has defeated its memory.

The passage of time has thus created two diametrically opposed situations. Gaullism offers the strange case of a mythified historical memory, and even historical analysis that aims to be scientific and "objective" must somehow deal with a history that coexists with a myth and cannot be understood without it. Communism offers the no less peculiar case of a fully historicized historical memory, to the point where the memory is no longer intelligible unless reconstituted by history. Without the history, the memory makes no sense. It was important to delineate these two "ideal types" of memory before exploring, as we shall do next, the ways in which they were parallel.

The Dual System of Memory

It began with exorcism and forgetting: the fact that Gaullism and Communism are "memories" as well as realities and necessarily twinned stems from the historical dream-state that both existed to create and sustain. This is the fountain from which springs the common capital that divides them, the inexhaustible foundational legitimacy that both derived from Free France and the Resistance.

The Second World War was not only a military and diplomatic operation but also an operation of memory. When it was over, France's shame had to be cleansed, the unprecedented humiliation of what Marc Bloch called the "strange defeat" and the trauma of national collapse had to be effaced, the general guilt of the summer of 1940 and the weight of German oppression had to be laid to rest. When Liberation came, the priorities were clear: a nation of wait-and-seers, prisoners, and finaglers had to be taught the lesson of its own heroism; a ravaged country had to be made to believe that it had liberated itself, virtually unaided, by virtue of the battle it waged inside and outside its borders; that country's "rank" had to be restored by making sure it had a place in the councils of the conquerors; it had to be persuaded, by means of a selective, controlled purge (*épuration*) of collaborators, that apart from a small minority of misguided individuals and traitors, the vast majority of Frenchmen had never wanted anything but what was best for France. The pillars supporting the two fundamental myths were erected even before the Paris insurrection was over. In an editorial published in the first issue of *L'Humanité* after it resumed publication (August 24, 1944), Marcel Cachin, referring to the German-Soviet Pact obliquely as "the event of 23 August 1939," set out to justify both the U.S.S.R.'s passivity and the patriotism of unjustly condemned Communists:

> *L'Humanité* was shut down because it denounced Hitler, the traitors, and those in favor of the Munich Accord. Bonnet promised the Germans that *L'Humanité* would be shut down, and it was shut down.... France has heard nothing but lies about the causes and circumstances of 23 August, the date when the Soviet Union thwarted a plot hatched by the appeasers against it and against peace.

The next day, August 25, 1944, General de Gaulle, speaking at the Hôtel de Ville, did not mention France's "cherished and admirable allies" until nearly the end of his speech:

> Paris outraged! Paris crushed! Paris martyred! But Paris liberated! Liberated by itself, liberated by its people with the cooperation of the armies of France, with the support and cooperation of all of France, of fighting France, of the only France, of the true France, the eternal France.

Two concurrent versions of "resistantialism" were thus quickly put in place.[60] De Gaulle's version denied the Vichy episode and insisted on the continuity of republican legitimacy. Hence his reply to Georges Bidault, on the same day and in the same place as the speech just quoted: "The Republic has never ceased to exist.... Why would I want to proclaim its existence?" De Gaulle's theme of a "thirty years' war" effectively obliterated the ideological content of the war while stressing its

significance in national and military terms. The Gaullist version of events also minimized the importance of both the Communist-dominated internal Resistance and
the collaboration, which in its legal definition was limited to "intelligence avec l'en-
nemi," so as to exalt the unity of a combative, patriotic France. By contrast, the
Communist version attached primary importance to the clandestine struggle waged
on French soil, out of which came the myth of the "75,000 *fusillés*" (men and
women allegedly shot to death by the enemy); to the antifascist nature of the war
and of a victory won primarily through the efforts of the Red Army, hence of the
F.T.P. (the Francs-Tireurs et Partisans, the principal Communist Resistance
group); and to the class combat implicit in that victory, which must now be carried
on and intensified "in the Resistance spirit" against all those who had betrayed
France. Over time these two versions gave rise to numerous variants, as details were
modified and adapted to new circumstances. They soon elicited fierce protests
within their own camps and fueled constant polemics: as late as 1964 passions ran
high among former Resistance members when it was decided to transform Jean
Moulin[61] into a symbol of the Resistance by transferring his ashes to the
Pantheon.[62] Nevertheless, these two versions provided the basic themes of a collective iconography whose mystique was continually reinforced by both academic
historiography and official commemoration. This iconography went virtually
unchallenged until the early 1970s. Once again 1968 marks a break with the past.
Over the past twenty years a once-solid illusion was blown to bits as France compulsively and obsessively revisited the darker aspects of the war, every year adding
new ingredients to what Pascal Ory called *retro-satanas*.[63] Yet its psychological and
institutional force can still be gauged by the magnitude of the furor unleashed by
the first challenges to the established view: the scandal stirred up by Patrick
Modiano's first novel, *La Place de l'Étoile* (1968), the polemics attending the publication of a French translation of Robert Paxton's *Vichy France* (1973), and the ten-
year ban on broadcasting the documentary film *The Sorrow and the Pity* (1971) on
French television.[64]

The compensatory mechanism and historical prestidigitation intrinsic to both
phenomena were by no means necessities of war. Regardless of whether one
stresses the realism of de Gaulle's policies or his intensive use of myth, it remains
the case that in thirty years on the national scene de Gaulle's historical genius presumably consisted in cloaking the actual diminution of French power in the
rhetoric of grandeur. He transformed, as if by magic, the most crushing of French
military defeats into a form of victory. He made France forget that it had been
forced to lower its flag in Algeria by ushering it almost simultaneously into the
club of nuclear powers. He hid the new constraints of Atlantic dependency
behind a mystique of independence and an exploitation of populist anti-
Americanism. He compensated for the abrupt arrival of the third industrial revo-

lution by an emotional appeal to eternal France, as if the French could confront the harsh trivialities of capitalism only if one spoke to them in a more exalted language. The old-fashioned illusionism may even have been the most charming thing about the memory of de Gaulle. "France is herself only when she dreams," Malraux once said on de Gaulle's behalf. This was an oracular way of saying that, in the long relationship between de Gaulle and the French, "what the French will be most enduringly grateful for is de Gaulle's having obtained for them the relief of amnesia."[65]

Amnesia: the word may, on the other hand, seem incongruous when applied to the action of the Communist Party, which always liked to see itself as closely aligned with the realism of working-class struggle. The more we know and the more we learn, however, the more clearly we can see that the phases of the struggle in which Communist energies were most fully engaged—the Popular Front, the Liberation, the Cold War—were in fact the times when the French Communist Party learned, both in regard to its credibility in Moscow and its actual capacity to influence events in France, the painful lesson of the limits of its power and so resigned itself to impotence. A close look at the year 1947 is particularly revealing in this respect.[66] With twenty-five percent of the vote, five ministers in the government, its legend and its prestige at their zenith, "France's leading party" never seemed more powerful or more menacing to the fragile new Fourth Republic. The insurrectional strikes of November had truly set the regime tottering on its new foundation. Yet from the dismissal of the Communist ministers in May to Zhdanov's condemnation of the French party leadership in September for "parliamentary cretinism," that year of endless turmoil, dominated by the "clandestine conductor" (*dixit* Paul Ramadier), was in fact nothing but a series of disasters in which the party repeatedly gave ground in every confrontation until it was forced to admit publicly that it was undertaking a "strategic withdrawal." The Communist Party never unleashed more of a storm than its congenitally cautious leadership could handle. As a revolutionary party, it was forever obliged to await the coming revolution, which was forever delayed, promised only to be postponed: the "objective conditions" were never right, and the leadership always chose to avoid real risks in favor of holding on to what it had, falling back on its secure internal identity. The outcome was really determined at the Liberation, behind the scenes, and historians have always wondered whether the party was not merely pretending to want to play a role.[67] It was then that the Communists lost the game once and for all—to de Gaulle. Thereafter the party ensconced itself in a purely ideological construction of reality—the general crisis of capitalism, the Soviet Union as agent of peace against American imperialism, Gaullism as "a presidential regime oriented toward personal dictatorship and opening the way to fascism," etc.—which forced it not only to speak a wooden language but to think and act in such wooden fashion that its incessant harping on the same theoretical points, its repetitious aggressivity, served only to divert attention from the past and surreptitiously erase it from memory. To what extent can we interpret French Stalinism's steadily increasing demands, its verbal excesses and outrages, as admissions of its inability to accommodate itself to reality, the price to be paid for the historical hesitancy it felt obliged to impose on its troops?

The compensatory mechanism did not work the same way in both cases, nor did it have the same meaning. With de Gaulle, word was made action; he exalted the poetry of legend over the prose of reality, France over those *veaux*, the French, historical will over "inevitable consequences." Stories about de Gaulle ranged widely in tone, from heroic narratives of the man prepared to face every maelstrom and respond to every challenge to small, Ubuesque anecdotes about the general's private life. Meanwhile, the P.C.F. worked to orchestrate forgetfulness; in this it was helped for a time by a rapid and massive generational turnover in its membership. For the Communists, the manipulation of memory was a technique of power and an instrument of mobilization, a way of hiding errors and changes in the party line, a form of terror and intimidation, and a way of consolidating party identity by forcing its members to forget. De Gaulle offered a projection with which all the French were invited to identify: "Everybody was, is, or will be Gaullist." The Communists offered a manipulation of the past that was binding only on those who agreed to subject themselves to it. But—fatality in the one case, finality in the other—both served the function of a historical exorcism, and this, far more than their respective ideologies or political capabilities, explains why both proved so attractive and powerful. In effect, this "counter-history," far more than the consistency or persuasiveness of their answers to history's contingencies, accounts for the success of both antagonists.

Two memories, then, both charismatic, combative, strategic, and associated with referents from which they derive some of their transcendental gravity *(la France, la Révolution)*. Yet behind their affinities the two are so radically alien, so different in their internal organization and existential economy, that one can easily oppose them term by term. Communist memory is militant, anthropological, and sectarian; Gaullist memory is contractual, symbolic, and ecumenical. One is open, the other closed; one eternalized, the other immobilized.

If there is such a thing as a true memory, produced by physical and mental conditioning of the entire individual, then Communist memory is it.[68] French Communism was a closed, self-sufficient world, with its local roots, its deeply ingrained customs and souvenirs, its rites, its codes, its traditions, its symbols, its language, its repetitive rhythms, its liturgy of the quotidian, its mental reflexes, its celebrations, and its key sites, foremost among which was the headquarters of the Central Committee at 120 Rue La Fayette, celebrated by Aragon in his 1933 poem *Enfants rouges*:

> C'est rue La Fayette au 120
> Qu'à l'assaut des patrons résiste
> Le vaillant Parti communiste
> Qui défend ton père et ton pain.
> [At 120 Rue La Fayette,
> The valiant Communist Party withstands
> The bosses' onslaught and defends
> Your father and your bread.]

No other political party or group created a universe so thoroughly mapped out, so reassuring, so full of signs and markers, so warm, protective, or comforting. Its principle was the principle of happiness: a history in which nothing happens,[69] a suspension of time, a reality of unrivaled intensity sheltered from all other realities. All the party's militant activity was taken up with the subtle and absorbing business of confining time to a present without hierarchy or perspective.[70] A glance at *L'Humanité*, or for that matter at *Pravda*,[71] is enough to reveal how time was segmented and compartmentalized, detemporalized as it were, because the purpose of the myriad small news items published in the party organ was always to repeat the same news, the good news, the good word of a brighter tomorrow. Each campaign effaced all memory of the previous one, because in each case the purpose was to galvanize militant ardor around the stated objectives of the moment, to give, through salvos of slogans, the illusion of the final battle. In each case it was the future of the fatherland of socialism that was at stake, and all progressive forces were engaged in the battle. In this hermetically sealed universe of blessed repetition, facts did not accumulate, because the good militant absorbed in his work was like a good student, for whom each moment of the present symbolically epitomized the whole of the past and the hope of the future. Indeed, the whole history of the Communist Party can be and has been written in terms of a dialectic of identity and change. "Has the Communist Party changed?" Answers to this eternally recurrent question can be collected almost all the way back to 1920. Now we can see why Communists were so inordinately fond of celebrations,[72] commemorations, funerals,[73] rituals of memory without any real remembering, celebrations of a participatory legend in which the essence of what makes up the Communist memory could be deployed. Important sites were marked out for visible appropriation by the masses: from the Wall of the Fédérés (where defenders of the Paris Commune were massacred by the French Army in 1871) to the Vel' d'Hiv (Vélodrome d'Hiver, the one-time bicycle racetrack that served as a holding area for Jews rounded up in the great sweep of

July 1942), from May Day to the metro station. The crowd in its togetherness is swelled by the presence of those who are no more, and the natural bombast of Communist speechifying with its wooden rhetoric is infused with the "living spirit" of the working class.[74]

Communist memory had great penetrating power. It struck deep roots and spread widely. Its force can be measured only as one measures the waves created by tossing a stone into water: by its effects, by what it touched. Take, for example, the traces that remain in the minds of so many people who no longer believe in the movement but who have retained something of its manner and intonation. If Mme de Maintenon invented "good posture" and Gambetta invented the rhetoric of the republican banquet, Thorez invented a language of gesture and phrasing, a special Stalinist bearing, compounded of working-class familiarity, aggressive, earnest didacticism, and a first person singular-plural, an "I-we," redolent of both the revolutionary past and the new world to come. Just as the Baron de Charlus's bizarre chuckle revealed to Proust the unconscious legacy of a great-granduncle the baron had never known, many former Communists of the golden years would be surprised if one pointed out to them how a certain tone of voice, a certain grandiosity of inspiration, a certain stiff optimism in argument, a certain whiff of bleating humanism or virile violence could betray, after an interval of twenty years, traces of their former allegiance. Their memory has literally been incorporated into their identity. "The *great* Russian Revolution," "our *great* enthusiasm," "the *immense tide* stemming from the social republic established in Moscow," "*that achievement*, the first of its kind in the history of the world": these are just a few early seeds taken from a speech by Marcel Cachin to the Congress of Tours. Before developing into the stereotypical images of the wooden rhetoric to come, such turns of phrase could find their way into the speech of a man so thoroughly steeped in the nineteenth century only because Bolshevism encountered a strong predisposition in its favor in the secular republican heritage. There would have been no *Fils du peuple* had there been no *Tour de la France par deux enfants*.[75] Bolshevism could not have grafted itself onto so distinctively French a mentality unless the party that claimed a monopoly of the republican legacy and sharpened certain of its features to its own ends had also duplicated its most general and enduring traits: Christian piety was converted into the patriotism of the French people; submission to state authority became democratic centralism; rationalist, secular humanism pointed toward the logic of revolution. It was this concentrated reinvestment of the republican legacy that gave Communist Manichaeanism such power to intimidate well beyond the limits of the party's sphere of influence, that gave it hegemony over the entire left and even beyond. Anyone exempt from the charge of "primary, visceral anti-Communism" more or less internalized something of the Communist point of view. The left respected the logic of Communist thought, recognized its political culture, and, because it shared some of Communism's baggage, implicitly accepted its frames of reference and norms of interpretation. Communist memory has its own purely national genealogy, but in the besieged citadel of socialism it became a barricaded memory, haunted by its constitutional relationship to the internal adversary and regulated by the law of orthodoxy and heresy, inclusion and exclusion. The earliest memoirs of former Communists,[76] those firsthand accounts and narratives of what Claude Roy has felicitously called "the long alienated season of our lives,"[77] were built around this passage: entering/leaving, conversion/apostasy. When one reads these accounts, including the latest, *Ce que j'ai cru comprendre* by Annie Kriegel,[78] when one views the television programs that have been based of late on such memoirs such as Mosco's *Les Mémoires d'ex*,[79] one inevitably feels a strange sense of distance in proximity and mystery in what is obvious. These ex-Communists tell all except what is essential. They give the facts but not the faith, the how but not the why. Memory has taken its secrets with it.

The world of the "companion" of General de Gaulle was nothing at all like that of the Communist "comrade." Based on the notion of loyalty, it revolved entirely around duration. It was a compound of filiation and affiliation, a dialectic of unanimity and solitude, of high times and low times. "Everybody was, is, or will be a Gaullist." Gaullist memory is a memory with eclipses, with ups and downs, with compressions and elongations, and the graph of waxing and waning political support reveals only the outer shell.[80] Its central principle is a strange and perhaps unique example of the telescoping of ultra-personification with absolute depersonalization. The commander's secret was of course to make a symbol of himself, and his historical course seems to run from opportunistic self-assertion ("I, General de Gaulle, currently in London...") to the anonymity of the constitutional text. Historical doubleness seems to have marked him from birth (by what providential chance did the father of a man called to such a destiny name him Charles?) to death, with his two funeral ceremonies and the homage of the world at Notre-Dame. It all began on June 18, 1940, as the solitary adventure of a man of forty-nine suddenly driven "beyond any known path,"[81] but also as history in the form of eternal France and the inextinguishable flame of the Resistance. Even as a man, de Gaulle was a troubling mix of uncommon individuality and astonishing conformism.

Nowhere is this counterpoint more visible than in the confrontation with nature, by definition the most ahistorical of phenomena. De Gaulle played powerfully on this image, as if to underscore his transition from submission to the "nature of things" to rapid historical decision, the agitation of the tempest, and the timeless significance of action. January 1946: "While meditating by the sea, I planned my departure." From Antibes on the Mediterranean to the west coast of Ireland, "in a wild place remote from any town, with access to a beach as deserted as possible,...bordering on or not far from a forest," this extraordinary setter of scenes always situated his action so as to place himself in profound harmony with the landscape, a description of which ends the first volume of his *Mémoires de guerre*: "From the corner room where I spend most of the day, I can see far off to the west...vast, untouched, mournful vistas; melancholy woods, meadows, fields, and wastelands; the relief of ancient hills, eroded by time and forlorn; quiet, not very prosperous villages whose soul and location have remained untouched for millennia. And so it is with mine...." The historical presence of the immemorial: that was the general's emotional geography, a spiritual culture of the neatly checkered landscape that reveals a great deal about the rich soil in which Gaullian memory is rooted.[82]

The same syncretic, combinatorial plasticity can be found in the historical register. De Gaulle possessed the gift not only of evoking the memory of great figures from French history but of embodying by turns the most contradictory personages: Joan of Arc and Louis XIV, Saint Louis and Clemenceau, Napoleon and Gambetta.[83] He could incorporate all the historical strata of nation building: Christian and medieval France, absolutist France, revolutionary and Napoleonic France, republican France. All the strands of the national tradition were combined in his person, and he knew how to pluck each string and make it sing: the military, the political, the literary. Thus Gaullist memory was a synthesis, a confluence, and therefore less interesting for its content, which reflected all of France and nothing but France, than for the manner of its construction.[84] It was a projective memory (unlike Communist memory, which was introjective), which consisted entirely in acts, in public expressions, and in demonstrations through action. It was not particularly interested in proselytism through education, yet it displayed itself exclusively through the middle range of the national imagination.

Gaullist memory was thus a permanent mixture of the personal and the impersonal, the particular and the general, the individual and the collective, the circumstantial and the transhistorical, as evidenced by the difficulty of selecting its most representative sites. There is no shortage of candidates.[85] A brief list would include various places outside France (Carlton Gardens, Algiers, Saint-Pierre and Miquelon, Brazzaville, Dakar), Parisian sites (Mont Valérien, the Champs-Élysées, the Rue de Solferino), and a number of coastal and border locales often cited in connection with the Resistance (the Ile de Sein, Bayeux, Bruneval, Lille, Strasbourg). The problem is that there are too many such places; they fragment the story into too many pieces to carry conviction. The only two genuine Gaullist *lieux de mémoire* clearly reflect the bipolar character of the whole Gaullian saga: the Constitution of the Fifth Republic, the epicenter of de Gaulle's legacy, and his country place, La Boisserie, which has become the true center of the memorial cult: "This is my home."

Both these memory machines therefore refer back to France, but to two types of France, two extreme forms of historical memory and national identity. One makes

France the promised land of revolution, projecting the rationalism of the Enlightenment onto revolutionary universalism and thus in turn onto the idealized Russian Revolution. The other returns repeatedly to the deep emotional sources of filial and religious patriotism, endlessly reaffirming the miraculous permanence and timeless essence of France. Both Communist and Gaullist—or in this case more precisely Gaullian—memory filter the national past and operate in a dualist mode, but the dualism is different in each case. For the Communists there is a good France and a bad France, and from the Franks versus the Gauls to the "multinationals versus the people of France" there is, based on this division, a consistent, simplified, Manichaean version of history whose high points include the medieval communes, Étienne Marcel, the seizure of the Bastille, the Paris Commune, and the Popular Front. In the Gaullist vision the dividing line passes instead between France and the French, between the stagnant periods of French history and the great redemptive outbursts of national energy, between the vicissitudes of history and the genius of the fatherland. On the one hand, a linear and dynamic France beginning in Year I of the Revolution; on the other, a cyclical and eternally reborn France. Yet both memories, the revolutionary and the national, share a common conviction of the singularity and exceptionality of France's destiny, of what there is in France by virtue of history or Providence that is unique, universal, and sacred. The song of the Union des Jeunesses Révolutionnaires de France, "Nous continuons la France," echoes the Gaullian theme of "France as an unclaimed legacy" (la France tombée en déshérence). "Take up the theme of history,...respond to something that lies deep within this nation that we are delivering,.... become necessarily a moment of eternal France": these phrases are not from the pen of General de Gaulle but from a celebrated editorial by Paul Vaillant-Couturier in L'Humanité of July 11, 1936, when, amidst the enthusiasm of the Popular Front, the headiness of popular marches, strikes, and factory occupations, the joy of the Matignon Accords and paid vacations, the tiny Communist Party of 30,000 revolutionaries swelled within the space of a few months to a mass party of 300,000 members and its leadership immediately set about celebrating the marriage of Lenin and Joan of Arc to the commingled strains of "L'Internationale" and "La Marseillaise." The major difference between the two memories was this: the rupture that the Communist Party desired and indeed represented in national memory and French tradition wreathed itself in the theme of continuity, whereas the essential continuity that de Gaulle wished to embody and secure could manifest itself only through an act of rupture. Yet both held an equally messianic vision of France, a vision intensified all the more by the fact that it was the Communist Party's mission to fulfill and reveal its revolutionary destiny and de Gaulle's mission to embody personally a moment of the eternal return.

This shared vision accounts for the power of these two forms of memory as well as for the unbridgeable gulf between them. Both arose out of the same anti-German reaction, both were spontaneously anti-American, both were hostile to the European Defense Community, both joined in opposition to the Third Force, both opposed the Secret Army Organization (O.A.S.) and the proponents of keeping Algeria French, both were hostile to a supranational organization of Europe, and both rejected the libertarian spirit and "bed-shitters" (*chienlit*: de Gaulle's word for the protesters) of May 1968—but never for the same reasons or in the name of a shared idea of France. This was because the memory of both sides consisted of two strands that seemed indistinguishable to the faithful yet quite distinct to the other side, and that distinction made all the difference. Once the decision was made to join in the Popular Front, Communist memory came to rest on the twin foundations of Jacobinism and Bolshevism: in the words of Thorez, "everyone has two father-lands, France and the Soviet Union." Because Gaullist memory was purely patri-otic, it was both national and nationalist. With these dual foundations the two sides inevitably shared common ground yet just as inevitably clashed. They shared com-mon ground because, while the Communists embodied "the dream of social jus-tice," according to Malraux, "we stand for fidelity to France in its legendary, which is to say exemplary, part."[86] Yet they inevitably clashed because they were locked in fierce, ongoing battle over the legacy of the past and in a radical conflict over legit-imacy.[87] "The Communists are neither on the left nor on the right, they are to the east": de Gaulle persistently exploited this neutralizing, disqualifying argument. Meanwhile, the Communist Party trimmed its strategy to suit its interests but was never able to get a theoretical grasp on Gaullism, a shortcoming in which it was by no means alone. Unable therefore to take the measure of the phenomenon, it spent the entire Fourth Republic trying to demystify the "heroic period" of Gaullism, and until the general's death it clung to the definition that Maurice Thorez gave in the summer of 1958, just before de Gaulle robbed him of a million votes: "Either Gaullism is nothing or else it is a political and social phenomenon, in which case de Gaulle is inseparable from the social forces that brought him forth and continue to drive him."[88]

The Communists were forced to engage in acrobatics to bring together the two parts of their heritage; Gaullism, on the other hand, was able to achieve symbiosis between its two components, which often were separated by only the thinnest of boundaries. In the end this led to a fundamental asymmetry between the two mem-ories, in the various senses in which we are using the word. Communist memory was constantly being touched up and refurbished. Going all the way back to the Congress of Tours, it was handicapped by scandal and dubious personalities whose role had to be covered up from time to time. Members were expelled or denounced as "traitors" and "renegades."[89] Skeletons emerged from closets, and stories were fabricated. Communist memory was clouded, moreover, by endless internal reor-ganizations and by the concoction of imaginary biographies, beginning with that of

Maurice Thorez. Whatever state arcana may have been concealed by Machiavellian Gaullists fond of invoking *raison d'état*, they are as nothing compared with the notorious "party secrets." Communist memory was never accountable to any authority but itself: its tactics had to be adjusted continually to accommodate an international strategy over which the French leadership had no control, indeed of which it was usually among the last to be informed: single front, Bolshevization, German-Soviet Pact, Khrushchev Report, repudiation of the Common Program— these were just a few of the more bitter pills that had to be swallowed. Gaullian memory has its dark spots, too, such as the executions of Pucheu[90] and Brasillach, but these are nothing compared with the difficult task of the Communists, who were constantly forced to hide or embellish the truth. The party maintains tight control over its archives and releases precious few documents, and then only when they are no longer of any interest or have been rendered utterly anodyne.[91] General de Gaulle saw to it that his papers were regularly handed over to the Archives Nationales.[92] His *Memoirs*, along with official and private documents, can be disputed by witnesses or contradicted by historians.[93] As one-sided as they are, there has been no need to publish repeatedly revised and corrected editions as there has been with the *oeuvres* of Maurice Thorez.[94] The diffusion of Communist memory, even when party influence was at its height, never extended beyond the limits of, if not precisely a sect, then at best a sector of public opinion, remaining alien even to much of the left. Gaullism, even in the darkest days of the R.P.F. or the "desert crossing," always benefitted from the prestige of the "most illustrious of Frenchmen" and his place in that most officially representative of national institutions, the army. No one protested the tricolor cover of his *Mémoires de guerre*. And few people were outraged in 1960 when the general referred to "the national legitimacy that I have embodied for the past twenty years."[95] And no matter how deep the ties that the Communist Party was able to forge with "the people of France" at the height of its communion with the nation, during July 1936 and the Popular Front or in the dark night of the Resistance, those bonds are relatively insignificant compared with a historical experience whose supreme moments and most celebrated images are part of every Frenchman's family album. Gaullism not only ruled the country for a long time but crystallized itself in institutions that are still in place today; it has become a part of the French national memory. Because of this asymmetry, Communism and Gaullism occupy similar yet different places in French historical memory.

Inside France's Historical Memory

We have emerged from the world of war, poverty, and revolution from which Gaullism and Communism derived their significance and influence. A long period of conflict has come to a close, including not just the "thirty years' war" that de Gaulle evoked at the Liberation so as to bury the disaster of 1940 in a broader memory of Franco-German conflict but also the Cold War and the threat of nuclear apocalypse associated with a bipolar division of the world, and the colonial wars in which the stakes were the material and symbolic substance of French power. It was war, which helped to revive the idea of revolution, that bestowed upon both Gaullist and Communist memories mobilizing power, lyrical grandeur, and a degree of sacredness. War runs through the one as through the other, from a time well before the key dates at which each attained maximal intensity to a time well after: all the way back to the Dreyfus Affair, the rise of French irredentism after the Franco-Prussian War, and the advent of international socialism, and forward to the Algerian War and its aftermath, the consequences of economic growth, and the rise of third-worldist *gauchisme*. This history thus covers the whole totalitarian age.

When did things begin to change? If a date has to be fixed, it would probably be 1965. It was then that de Gaulle failed to achieve an absolute majority in the first round of voting in the first election of a president of the Republic by universal suffrage in the history of France: a first chink in the armor of Gaullian infallibility, an anticipation of the chant that would be heard in 1968, "Ten years is long enough!" In that same year the Union des Étudiants Communistes, the weak link in the Communist chain, collapsed, in a parallel that seems striking now but was invisible at the time. Out of this micro-event came the host of *gauchiste* groupuscules that would become visible three years later in the events of May 1968.[96] Symbolically, moreover, 1965 was also the point of convergence of a series of economic, demographic, social, and cultural changes in which sociologists like Henri Mendras have taught us to see the beginning of a "second French Revolution":[97] a decline in the birth rate, a decrease in the workweek, a sharp rise in the number of working women, a return of the economy to the level predicted by a projection of the growth curve for the period 1900–1914, and the end of Vatican II, not to mention the widespread diffusion of paperback books, the discount store, and—why not?—the first appearance of nudity in magazines and films. It was the end of one world and the beginning of another, whose effects Mauriac anticipated when, for example, he asked in his *De Gaulle* of 1964 "what makes today's world, which de Gaulle's adversaries do not recognize, so different? .... In fact, the washing machine, the television, and the family automobile have become the visible signs of a paradise that manifests itself in the three weeks of annual paid vacation.... It was not de Gaulle, the last paladin of the old world, who invented this new one."[98]

This exit from *la grande histoire,* as the century's tragedy receded into the past, should have stamped both memories with the same sign of obsolescence, the paladin's more so than the Communists.' But de Gaulle's was lucky. He had a hand in two ages of French history and operated on two distinct levels: on the level of discourse with a rhetoric of national grandeur that was out of line with the historical reality of the moment; and on the level of reality, with the advent of a society that was completely alien to that discourse, indeed most apt to dissolve and subvert it, a society based on economic enrichment, hedonistic individualism, and consumer euphoria. Such was the ruse and irony of history: the wartime dinosaur emerged from the museum to which he had repaired to write his memoirs, memoirs that ended with the affirmation of a man who "never tired of waiting in the dark of night for the first glimmer of hope." By the miracle of another, equally archaic war, the Algerian conflict, this man presided over the birth of a new world, which ultimately rejected him but with which we still identify, a world that he equipped with institutions that his successors made viable if not fully democratic. Can we then say that de Gaulle was saved by "thirty glorious years" of postwar growth and the industrial policies of Georges Pompidou? There is nothing absurd about the notion, given the care that de Gaulle took after 1958 to leave the prose of necessity to his prime minister while reserving for himself the poetry of history, rich with memories of the great adventure. The idea can even be stood on its head: it was the "thirty glorious years" of postwar economic growth that necessitated de Gaulle's return to power, because the French could not bear the thought of building super-highways unless the task was presented to them in the language of the Crusades. By crystallizing Gaullism's political heritage around the modernizing, industrializing right, de Gaulle's half-approved, half-repudiated successor enabled the hero to "strike to his left," as the political wisdom of the Third Republic recommended, thereby hastening the transformation of the personage into the myth. To explain the periodic resurgences of Communism despite repeated historical defeats, some commentators have pointed to the replacement of one generation of militants by another, thus drawing a contrast between Communism and Gaullism, which was presumably bound up with one man and destined to vanish with him. All the successive brigades of forgetful generations were unable, however, to prevent the ideological collapse of Marxism or the sociological disintegration of its working-class base or the demise of the Soviet myth or the breakup of the internal Communist system, these being the main causes of the collapse of the French Communist Party. The hermetic nature of Communist memory has been compounded by the historical demise of Communism, which has made that memory even more enigmatic. We no longer understand the ardor, the rage of commitment, the logic of violence, or the passion that sustained it. The age of opulence has swept all that away, while in direct contrast allowing Gaullist memory, symbolized by de Gaulle himself, the possibility of survival.

Both phenomena drew their historical energy from the same source: the series of crises that beset France after 1914, which reached its apogee with the disaster of 1940, whose aftereffects would continue to be felt for another twenty years.[99] It was a period in which French morale and faith in democracy suffered grievous blows, and particularly hard on Captain de Gaulle, for whom France's humiliation could be traced back to the Treaty of Frankfurt, the national disgrace largely responsible for the decision by the Congress of Tours to affiliate with the Third International. The Great Depression led to the political crisis of February 1934, during which the Communist Party emerged from the shadows to mount the ramparts against fascism; meanwhile, a solitary Charles de Gaulle wrote two books in quick succession, *Le Fil de l'épée* (1932) and *Vers l'armée de métier* (1934). Then came the Czech crisis and appeasement at Munich in September 1938, a foretaste of the 1940 debacle that laid bare France's economic, political, and psychological unfitness for the modern world. It was a crisis of national identity, to which, broadly speaking, three kinds of response seemed possible: that of the national right, adaptive and technocratic; that of a segment of the right which was drawn into the orbit of counterrevolutionary and profascist revolution; and that of the revolutionary left. The Communists' time had come; de Gaulle's moment still lay in the future. Once the height of the crisis was over, however, the revolutionary right found itself discredited by the defeat of Nazism; the reformist right found itself discredited by its association with Vichy; and the only contestants left in the game were the two active branches of the Resistance. To the sense, hard to swallow, of national decline (whose only prewar expression had been the reactionary lament of decadence), to the urgent need for modernization to catch up with other countries, only de Gaulle and the Communists responded with plans, tempting yet in the end unacceptable, for France's rescue. Both expressed a will to rebuild, a radical approach, a faith in the revolutionary and universalist capacity of France, yet each believed in a different revolution, a different France, a different universal. The fact that the Gaullist solution won out no doubt stems not so much from the intrinsic advantages that with hindsight one can see in it, nor from its strategic superiority, but rather from historical realities that hastened the fall of the one and allowed the other to occupy the terrain.

In order to assess properly how the two phenomena were related and gauge correctly the likelihood that each would gain a hold on memory, we must first investigate how each stood in relation to the central fact of the republic. What strikes one immediately is that both Gaullism and Communism derived an essential part of their capital from their ability to present themselves as the syncretic reprise and ultimate synthesis of a number of major antirepublican traditions: Gaullism combined memories of monarchism, Bonapartism, and nationalism, whereas Communism incorporated revolutionary memory in its terrorist, socialist, and internationalist forms. Each was the revitalized embodiment of its respective tradition. De Gaulle, whose family was monarchist though not anti-Dreyfusard, long labored under the reputation of having been a Maurrassian.[100] At the Seventh Congress of the

International, moreover, just before the Communists abandoned the "class against class" strategy, the same Paul Vaillant-Couturier whose chauvinistic lyricism I quoted earlier expressed the official position of the tiny French Communist Party of Bolshevik agitators in *L'Humanité* for February 19, 1935: "Defend the Republic, says Blum? As if fascism were not yet the Republic! As if the Republic were not already fascism!"

Still, while Gaullism and Communism both battened on antirepublican memory, each took a radically different, if ambiguous, stance toward the republican tradition. Appearances were deceiving, moreover, since it was the man who embodied the memory of everything the Republic stood against who restored it twice,[101] while it was the party that claimed to be the Republic's natural child and ultimate shield that posed the most direct threat to its existence. Gaullism and Communism assumed their memorial legacies in very different ways. General de Gaulle never alluded to or acknowledged his manifest affiliations.[102] He allowed his adversaries to attach labels to him, to establish a continuity that certainly did not exist in his own mind, and to blur the contours of this past in a way that he never deigned explicitly to clarify. On August 25, 1944, at the Hôtel de Ville, he refused Georges Bidault's request to proclaim a Republic that in his eyes had never ceased to exist; in a press conference on May 19, 1958, he limited himself to the famous gibe "Who becomes a dictator at age sixty-eight?"; and he never scotched rumors of a possible restoration of the monarchy, alluding in admittedly private messages to the possibility of a dynastic succession.[103] Yet de Gaulle never claimed that the sovereignty of the executive could stem from any source other than universal suffrage.[104] Napoleon did not belong to his personal pantheon, whereas Carnot did, and what emerged from various references and allusions to the latter was his role not so much as the founder of a regime but rather as the man who consolidated the Revolution. In his memoirs de Gaulle devotes only a few lines to the R.P.F., which of all his ventures bears the most direct relationship to late-nineteenth-century nationalism.[105] His essential obsession was not to combat the Republic but to remedy its congenital weakness by "equipping the state with institutions designed to restore...the stability and continuity of which it has been deprived for 169 years."[106]

By contrast, the Communists aggressively wreathed themselves in the revolutionary heritage, while offering their own interpretations of both the French and Soviet Revolutions. They did everything they could—see the work of François Furet[107]—to fold '93 back into '89 and to denounce the formal democracy of the rights of man in the name of the proletarian vocation supposedly inherent in the Revolution, a vocation periodically frustrated by the victories of the capitalist bourgeoisie. What is more, they tried to bring all French history since the Gauls into line with the unwavering course of revolution.[108] They immediately latched onto the Bolshevik image of themselves as emulators of the Jacobins,[109] so much so that the twenty-one conditions imposed on the socialists before they could join the Third International influenced the Congress of Tours far less than the enthusiastic passing of the revolutionary torch evoked, for example, by L.-O. Frossard in his speech at the Cirque de Paris: "Lenin and Trotsky, the authorized representatives of the soviets, in bidding us to convey to you their greetings of socialist fraternity, said: 'It is inconceivable that the French proletariat in Paris, the sons of the Jacobins of '93, of the insurgents of 1830, of the revolutionaries of June 1848, of the heroic warriors of March 1871, should fail to understand that we are the heirs to all their revolutionary tradition.' "[110]

Ultimately, this blurring of distinctions in both camps, although denied by the Gaullists and loudly proclaimed by the Communists, served as the basis for a vague, ambiguous, uncertain relation to democracy and the republican regime, a relation that ranged from passionate identification to a spectrum of suspicion and was permeated by a strange dialectic of continuity and rupture, depending on whether the "republican tradition" was identified, on the one hand, with the "system" (by Gaullists) or "bourgeois power" (by Communists) and, on the other hand, with national defense and public safety. At times together, at times in opposition to each other, Gaullism and Communism were thus able to portray themselves as either the gravediggers of the Republic or its ultimate defenders; they could share and yet vie over the prize of being its true representatives. Take, for example, the 1947 municipal elections, in which the P.C.F.'s 30 percent and the R.P.F.'s 40 percent of the vote reduced the legitimacy of the Republic to its lowest level in history. Or take 1958, when the Communists demonstrated in defense of the Republic on the Place de la République in May, and the Gaullists did the same in September. Or 1961, when Communist battalions, responding to a call from the president of the Republic, made ready to defend the Republic against the threat of parachutists launched by rebellious army generals in Algiers—a revival of the taxis of the Marne. Or 1965, during the first campaign for the election of a president by universal suffrage, when André Malraux, speaking at the Vel' d'Hiv', berated the Communists' ally François Mitterrand: "Sole candidate of republicans, let the Republic sleep!" At all times, even times of institutional or revolutionary rupture, both Communists and Gaullists wanted to and were able to represent necessary, ineluctable, natural continuity. Both were as plausible in the role of champions of continuity as the rival republican tradition.

The point is that, on the one hand the Gaullist, or rather Gaullian, refusal to identify with the legacy evoked by their leader's personal history, on the other hand the Communist adherence to the revolutionary ideal, respectively account for the hegemony of each, for their resistance to any attempt to reduce or dilute their substance, and for the impossibility of marginalizing either one even in the worst moments of shared fury against republican centrality or the darkest days of mutual ostracism.

These features, even more than the services that each rendered to France during the war, are most responsible for legitimizing both Gaullism and Communism. The degree of their legitimacy is not measured by their respective party memberships or by the size of their votes in any particular election but rather by the effective role that each played in the national imagination: in one case a subtle reinvestment of the monarchic image in support of the democratic system, in the other a forceful reinvestment of the revolutionary idea through projection onto a worldwide revolutionary movement temporarily limited to the Soviet Union. These were vacant places in the national memory just waiting to be filled, and the memories that filled them thereby acquired a kind of magisterium.

The two sides exercised that magisterium in very different circumstances, however. The Communists relied on repeated protestations of undying loyalty to the revolutionary promises of the national past, while the Gaullists claimed to be pursuing something radically new in politics, guided by a providential leader who had nothing in common with other "providential leaders" of the past. The Communist Party was wholly absorbed in preserving the sacred legacy that made France, the promised land of revolution in the nineteenth century, the eldest daughter of world Communism and that turned intellectual Marxism into a secular clerisy. This task was made easier by the fact that the P.C.F., unlike other Communist parties in Europe, enjoyed a long and continuous legal existence (interrupted only by World War II). It was also made easier by the good fortune of its having been allowed to bask in opposition, thereby avoiding any compromise with the bourgeois Republic. Yet that task was entrusted to the most sectarian, dogmatic, fiercely Stalinist party apparatus in Europe, an apparatus that was also more dependent than any other on its heritage of souvenirs and traditions, and this in the end led to stalemate. The P.C.F. immediately met every historical and social change with a ready-made interpretation based on the assumption of a worldwide crisis of capitalism which, in its ultimate phase, would inevitably lead to imperialism and fascism.[111] During its lifetime the party had to face three historically new phenomena, namely, Hitlerian Nazism, postwar economic growth, and Gaullism, yet in each instance it responded, undaunted, with its usual reflex reactions: the struggle of class against class, the Cold War, the absolute pauperization of the working class, the denunciation of Gaullism as a "personal and military dictatorship imposed by force and threat...by the most reactionary, chauvinistic, and colonialist elements of the *grande bourgeoisie*."[112] Every effort to open things up, such as Waldeck-Rochet's, for example, was nipped in the bud.[113] The party quickly lost touch with reality and ensconced itself in a frozen memory.

The process by which the figure of the sovereign was revitalized within the republican system was quite different. Unplanned, it depended on two factors, one psychological, the other institutional: the personality of Charles de Gaulle and the

Constitution of the Fifth Republic. The executive was certainly uppermost in the general's political and constitutional thinking, yet he made no attempt to restore royal prerogatives. A strong executive was simply the remedy, advocated by every reformer since the end of the nineteenth century, to the weaknesses of a regime dominated by the legislature and with a long tradition of limiting presidential powers. As applied to the Fifth Republic, "presidential monarchy" was simply a metaphor, almost a form of folklore.[114] It was a spontaneous reaction to a man who assumed the trappings of a king without possessing a kingdom and who was personally appreciative of the forms and magnificence of monarchical style, so much so that the Constitution of 1958 and the Law of 1962 providing for the election of the president by universal suffrage seemed not so much the source and confirmation of his powers as a regime tailor-made for the general (with, as the keystone, the famous Article 16, granting special powers that were never invoked) plus a royal gift. It is true, nevertheless, that the shift of the center of gravity of the political system to the chief executive has allowed and fostered the development of regalian practices whose style each new president must define and whose forms and limits are open to experiment.[115] The image and place of the king in the national memory and imagination are ambiguous, a matter of pure fantasy, a mixture of magic and nostalgia.[116] They can be revived only through empirical reacquaintance, allusion, and symbolism careful not to violate invisible boundaries. They are essential to the system and yet peripheral, entirely a matter of nuance and almost of smiles. What made General de Gaulle a constitutional "king" was the fact that he occupied a place that by tacit accord, and only after the sanction of universal suffrage, was acknowledged to be his and his alone, and as long as he did occupy it there was no one who could take it away from him. That is why the electoral joust with François Mitterrand in 1965 seemed so strange and yet so familiar: it was David versus Goliath. But once the students took to the streets in May 1968 and began shouting "Ten years is long enough!" His Royal Majesty lost his footing. And when Georges Pompidou said in Rome on January 17, 1969, that he would be a candidate for president "whenever there is an election," sacrilege had been committed and the general's exile followed soon thereafter. The Gaullian "king" was a two-stage mechanism. Initially it functioned as a kind of time machine, moving quickly back through the centuries in a manner that was not so much threatening as amusing: this was symbolized early on by a well-known column in the satirical weekly *Le Canard enchaîné* entitled "The Court." After the general left office, however, the contraption began to function as a memory machine, spewing forth images with which all of de Gaulle's successors would have to cope in one way or another, either by competing with him or distancing themselves from him. As a result the memory of de Gaulle remains in a sense curiously incomplete, and paradoxically that incompleteness has played a role similar to that of the closure of Communist memory: de

Gaulle allowed the French to reconstruct their past history, whereas the Communists allowed the "people of France" to live history in anticipation.

Therein, ultimately, lies the long-term significance of both phenomena: to have contributed in symmetric, opposite ways to the conclusion of the vast historical cycle initiated by the French Revolution. Gaullism lodged the republican idea deep in the culture of the right, whereas Communism integrated a previously segregated working class into the French nation. Gaullism was the route by which a patriotism still unreconciled to postrevolutionary France opened itself up to democracy. Communism was the route by which the universal values of the Revolution, embodied in the proletariat, were integrated. These may seem modest achievements, but their effects on memory were powerful and of lasting consequence.

Neither of these two operations was deliberately premeditated, but Gaullism and Communism provoked them, went along with them, and at times orchestrated them. Four factors helped right-wing memory to accommodate itself to the republican idea. First, the traditional parties of the right vanished through the trapdoor of the Liberation, an unprecedented disaster from which a segment of the right would recover only thanks to the R.P.F.[117] Second, although the mechanisms of growth and the effects of the third industrial revolution were in themselves politically neutral, they had the effect of transferring to the traditionally backward-looking right the values of realism and modernism that the left, with its unrepentant anticapitalism, seemed to abandon. Third, de Gaulle worked to bring Catholics back into the orbit of the Republic and, with the Debré Law of 1959, to secure what he hoped would be peace on the educational front. Fourth and most important of all, although the general never acted as a party leader except with reluctance, and although Gaullism had many components, including some from the left, the general was able to unite all the parties of the right, excluding extremists, under one authority, de Gaulle's.[118] Gaullian republicanism exonerated the right of the charge of antirepublicanism that Vichy had incurred (see "Vichy," by Philippe Burrin, in this volume). Meanwhile, the Communist Party's representation of and symbiosis with the working class broadly coincided with a long period of economic growth and expansion of labor, which had established a solid base in heavily industrialized regions and remained structurally quite stable from the early 1930s to the late 1960s. It was this working-class world that erupted in the Popular Front, when strikes and factory occupations symbolized the newfound public role of those whom Simone Weil described as "foreigners, exiles, uprooted refugees" in their own country, on behalf of whom Léon Jouhaux and the representatives of the C.G.T.U., awkward in manner and openmouthed in astonishment, nevertheless successfully negotiated the first labor-management agreements with employers who had until then ruled by divine right; when red bastions grew in northern France and the Paris region; when the new young workers born of the second industrial revolution developed the political, trade-union, and symbolic instruments with which to represent themselves; when the "metal worker" of Marcel Carné's *Le Jour se lève* and the films of René Clair became an object of fascination for intellectuals and artists; when the legendary epic of Billancourt began and the working class evolved a memory of its own, with its own fictitious but remarkably influential genealogy.[119] One historian has called this "the singular generation."[120] Or rather generations, for it was the same working class—one animated by a now forgotten combative violence and tightly disciplined by the C.G.T. and P.C.F., whose carefully monitored demands shrewdly combined calls for greater prosperity with political objectives—that for thirty years supplied the manpower for Communism's battalions and shock troops: from this world came the Francs-Tireurs et Partisans (F.T.P.) of 1943, the nationalizations of 1945, the insurrectional strikes of 1947, the demonstrations against Ridgway-the-Plague in 1952,[121] the anti-Gaullist marches from Bastille to République in 1958, and even the Grenelle Accords of 1968. The symbolic integration of this working class was achieved with Jacques Duclos's candidacy for president of the Republic in 1969, shortly after de Gaulle's departure from power, and just before the old working-class base began to fall apart under the impact of deindustrialization and social realignment.

This dual and parallel process of acculturation cannot in any sense account for the end of political and social violence or head-to-head conflict, nor can it explain the partly invisible resurgence of class struggles that one might have thought to be a thing of the past. It does, however, mean that these phenomena must assume new forms, for they now unfold within what can only be called a democratic or republican frame of reference. The mode of political expression has also had to change as France has developed a new political culture in response to the withering away of both Gaullism and Communism and to the simultaneous embrace of and estrangement from the memory of de Gaulle himself, a political culture that gives fresh currency to ideas and words hitherto alien to French tradition: consensus, pluralism, and constitutional review.[122] The change has brought joy to some people, who see in it the end of a political culture of conflict and exclusion, as well as of a national messianism of which Gaullism and Communism were extreme forms, grandiloquent parodies of an already transcended historical reality. Yet it has also brought despair to others, for whom these ultimate forms of French grandeur, singularity, and universalism are survived by nothing but mourning and melancholia. For the French feel an emptiness, a sense of a void, born of the retrospective discovery that if Communism and Gaullism did not occupy the whole of the political sphere, they had at least achieved the miracle of occupying the whole of the political imagination, and perhaps also of a sense that the day may not be far off when this sharing of the imagination even by two parasitic phenomena may well be looked back upon as a blessed time of tranquil democracy. One thinks of Michelet, for whom the Revolution-Revelation was the swan song of *L'Histoire de France*,[123] and of the pages of *Mémoires d'outre-tombe* in which Chateaubriand described the insipidness of Restoration political society after the fall of Napoleon: "I blush to think that I must now drone on about a host of insignificant creatures, myself among them, shady, nocturnal people on a stage from which the great sun had disappeared."[124]

For the historian the metamorphosis may be of a different order. Communism and Gaullism represented two extreme and fully developed forms of the French historical and political model, the product of a longer, more continuous history than that of any other western country, and of a country that long believed itself to be rational and therefore superior. This model both imploded and exploded. Fundamentally national and state-centered, it exploded on contact with new realities for which it was not made: the transition from the status of great power (which it had been) to that of middling power; the end of imperial consciousness; the need to adjust to a world controlled by two systems beyond France's influence; the aspiration to build a regionalized, decentralized society; and the uniformity required by France's membership in the European Community. Fundamentally logical and rational, the model also imploded because, in response to these external forces, the

FIGURE 6.1   Wall posters in Paris in the year (1970) of Costa Gavras's film *L'Aveu,* starring Yves Montand. Photo by Chris Marker.

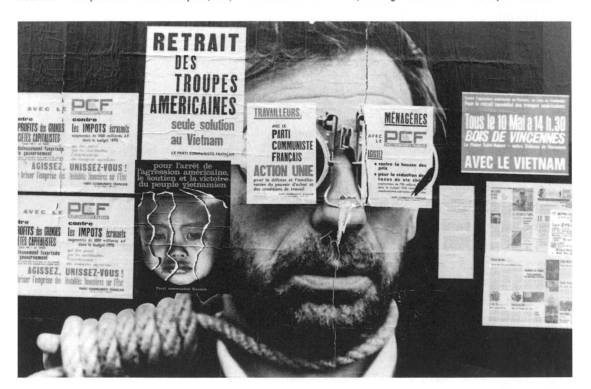

Communists pushed Enlightenment rationalism to the point of perverting it into something totally absurd, while the Gaullists reverted to an ideal France, a France they imagined as a sort of sleeping princess lost in the forests of history. Both gave the French powerful illusions to live by: for some the illusion of a revolutionary break and new beginning, for others the illusion of a periodic epiphany of redemption. Today all have awakened, sober yet nostalgic in the aftermath of two such exhausting dreams, to discover how strange yet special the French historical model was in itself and what kind of rationality was bound up with the country's sense of singularity and special relationship to the universal. This is a moment in which historians must pause to take stock: we must look at the history of this century with a fresh eye and reexamine all of our political traditions and representations. We must "reconceptualize" the Revolution and pursue a new exploration of "French identity." This calls for a vast reformulation of our relation to the past and a thorough inventory of our memory, which the present work is intended in its way both to demonstrate and to embody.

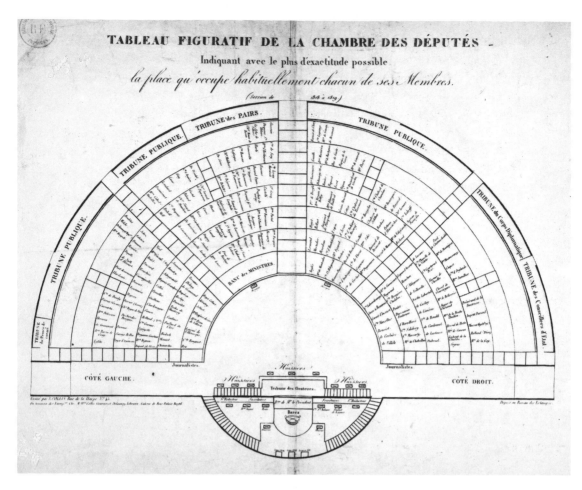

FIGURE 7.0   Public consecration of the left-right division during the first Restoration: parliamentary topography becomes a news item. This "Tableau" is one of the first of its kind, and there would be many other attempts to visualize the precise distribution of parliamentary forces and positions.

CHAPTER 7

Right and Left

Marcel Gauchet

It should come as no surprise that so little has been written on the history of the couple "right and left," paired terms firmly ensconced in the intellectual and symbolic workings of contemporary societies. Thinkers are never keen to reflect on that which enables them to think.

Countless definitions have been attempted. There are essays that do a remarkable job of clarifying the terms of the opposition. A rich political history has taught us to recognize and follow the various components of right and left on the French scene. What all these works have in common is the assumption that the terms themselves are well understood and that their classificatory role is accepted. As for their origin, it is presumed to be enough to refer in ritual fashion to the French Revolution. In fact, a great deal of water flowed under the bridge between the Revolution, when people hesitantly spoke of the assembly as divided between a "right side" and a "left side," and the Restoration, when the terms were permanently enthroned in the parliamentary lexicon. And it is an even bigger jump from the jargon of the Chamber of Deputies to the quintessential emblems of political identity, the fundamental categories of democratic confrontation, that *right* and *left* have become for us—usages that were not firmly established until the beginning of the twentieth century. Yet we are so accustomed to organizing political opinions and differences in terms of the left-right dichotomy that we apply it to the past without noticing its absence, at least in the fully developed sense it has for us, from the speeches and representations of contemporary actors. Indeed, this is all the more true in that the idea caught on in part because it suggests a continuity of struggle that can be traced all the way back to 1789. The pairing of right and left signifies a permanence of division that discourages us from looking into its origins. On the other hand it encourages us to examine the fluctuations and metamorphoses of the content of the notion, an avenue of inquiry that promises to be fruitful. If the established terminology covers up its past, the purpose of this essay is to examine the process by which it became established. It will add nothing to our knowledge of the electoral, social, anthropological, cultural, or geographical realities that the left-right division overlaps. Here, our only interest is in the system of denomination. Tracing this dualist representation of political reality through the pages of the lexicon may not be a bad way to learn more about the forces governing that representation. From the inception of representative government to the era of mass parties, this survey in a sense condenses a complete memory of democratic development. Furthermore, it directly confronts the difficult problem of the universal applicability of French history. Indeed, one of the most mysterious aspects of the left-right dichotomy is the way in which it has been taken up by countries around the world. The goal is to understand why it caught on in some places and not in others, and why the specific conditions under which it emerged could elicit a response general enough to permit such identification. The history of right and left: how the French, with the aid of a history unlike any other, produced a simplifying symbolism whose widespread applicability suggests that it contains some secret of modern politics and citizenship.

The Revolutionary Assemblies and the False Start

As indicated above, it is rather superficial to say that right and left leapt fully armed out of the Revolution. The terms did appear there and did gain some acceptance but remained narrowly circumscribed. The story might well have ended there without originating a tradition.

The terms *right* and *left* were actually used much earlier to denote the parts of an assembly. They occur, in fact, in a 1672 translation of Chamberlayne's account of contemporary England, *L'Estat présent de l'Angleterre,* in which the author describes the members of the House of Commons as arrayed "on the King's right hand and the King's left hand."[1] It is doubtful, however, that there was any connection between this and the revolutionary usage of the words, which appears to have been reinvented for the purpose. This is not to say that the English example was necessarily without influence on the de facto choice of a spatial arrangement of deputies in those confused weeks of the summer of 1789 when the National Assembly began to meet. It is well known that the term "Commons" was chosen by the representatives of the so-called Third Estate to replace an appellation that to them seemed insultingly inappropriate. Arguments about the rules of debate turned on discussion of British forms. Mirabeau proposed the British example as a model but it was rejected.[2] British influence was nevertheless perceptible in such earlier propositions as the "provisional rules of order" of June 6, for example in the stipulation that "those who speak may address themselves only to the chair."[3] In the end a different rule would prevail: the speaker, rather than remain in his place to have his say, was required to mount the podium, from which he would harangue the entire assembly—a point of some consequence for our subject. In general what is interesting about the English precedent is how the French case differed from it in important ways. It is not inconceivable that it was the squaring off of government party and opposition that inspired the bipartite division of the National Assembly that gradually solidified in July and August 1789, but it was precisely to the extent that the two segments of the legislature diverged from the logic of government versus opposition that they developed into right and left.

It took time, however, for the situation to clarify itself and even longer for names to be applied. The idea may actually have originated somewhat earlier, in a form of voting briefly adopted by the Third Estate in the early days of the Estates General. Indeed, on May 8, when it came time to vote on rival proposals by Mirabeau and Malouet concerning the combination of the orders, the deputies apparently decided to count heads "by inviting the assembly to divide itself in such a way that those of Malouet's opinion should pass to the right and those favoring Mirabeau should array themselves on the left."[4] Such a procedure was too cumbersome to be used often, however, and it was of course a long way from there to the crystallization of a stable political geography. Unless, that is, we imagine that this was an occasion for the minority in particular—since "the greater number" moved to the right—to discover itself and regroup. That could be what happened, assuming we can rely on retrospective testimony which, without mentioning the episode, dates the division of the assembly into "two sections separated by the chairman's desk" from the time of the "chamber of the Third," before the three orders were combined. "Whether by chance," we are told, "or because shared feelings impelled the friends of the people to band together and separate themselves from those who did not share their opinions, it was clear that they favored the left side of the hall and never failed to gather there."[5] To this one should perhaps add the fact that after the three orders began meeting together, the clergy returned to their original place in the Estates General, which may have furnished the right side with its core.[6] In any case, it was toward the end of August, in the debate over the rights of man and the royal veto, that the phenomenon first called itself to the attention of observers. Significantly, Duquesnoy remarked it in connection with the session of August 23, the occasion of a clash over the clause concerning religious freedom in the Declaration of the Rights of Man: "It is remarkable," he wrote in his diary, "that the hall is divided in such a way that in one part sit men who no doubt hold exaggerated opinions at times but who in general hold a very high idea of liberty and equality."[7] He does not say which part, being struck only by the division, and the first prominent feature that leaps to his eye is the unnamed "left." "The other part," he continued, "is occupied by men whose less exalted ideas and less pronounced opinions give them a character of weakness and pusillanimity most unfortunate under the present circumstances." This tendency for a group to form on the left, gradually pushing its adversaries to the right, appears to be corroborated by notes made a few days later, on August 29, the day after the assembly began discussion of the royal veto, by a right-wing deputy, the Baron de Gauville, who remarked on the completion of the process: "We began to recognize each other: those who were loyal to religion and the king took up positions to the right of the chair so as to avoid the shouts, oaths, and indecencies that enjoyed free rein in the opposing camp." The most revealing part of his account, however, is to be found in the recital of his own peregrinations: "I tried to sit in different parts of the hall and not to adopt any marked spot, so as to remain more the master of my opinion, but I was compelled absolutely to abandon the left or else be condemned always to vote alone and thus be subjected to jeers from the galleries."[8] Here the baron reported not only the fact of the division but also the reason why he would continue throughout the Revolution to oppose granting any kind of legal status to it: his dislike of being compelled to follow the crowd. This was not a personal trait but a consequence of the fundamental political ideal that would continue to define revolutionary experience to an almost obsessive degree. There were supposed to be only private interests and the general interest, according to the celebrated formula of Le Chapelier, hence in deliberation all opinions were supposed to be strictly individual, for there was no other way to arrive at the authentic general interest. In other words, there were to be no "parties" or "factions." The unity and universality of collective representation would emerge naturally, it was believed, from the diversity of individual points of view. Yet from late August 1789, revolutionary assemblies would always be divided. They adjusted to this fact in practice without ever acknowledging it as a normal or even significant aspect of their operation.

There was also a certain delay between the clarification of the division as participants observed it and its public designation. Pierre Rétat has reviewed the contemporary press and determined that news of the division did not appear before September 12: "The first clear but isolated reference to the localization of the parties appeared in the *Nouvelles politiques* of Berne, in a definition of the 'Palais-Royal corner': 'This is the term applied to the left side of the hall, where this party usually gathers.' "[9] The idea did not really catch on until December, when Camille Desmoulins for the first time gave "substance to both sides of the hall." In his report on the session of December 19, which saw the creation of *assignats* (paper currency) backed by church property, it was no longer the right side but "*the right* of the chair" that Abbé Maury urged to withdraw, and it was no longer the left side but "the left" that clapped its hands "as it did when Mounier resigned." Whereupon, Desmoulins continued, "*the right* preferred not to let the matter drop but raised a hell of a ruckus, and the priesties shrieked like banshees."[10] Although the historian's reverence for beginnings compels me to call attention to this instance, I am bound to add that similar usages remained quite rare. A few cases can be found. Duquesnoy, for example, remarked early in 1791 on "the extraordinary conduct of some members of *the right,*" and a little later observed that "*the left* is divided into two quite distinct, quite opposed parties."[11] A close topographical association with a *side* or *part* of the chamber, however, remained the rule, even when the expression was used as a synecdoche. Thus Chabot told the Jacobins in September 1792 that he "had seen all *the right sides* of the national assembly come almost fawning on him."[12] The geographic influence remained apparent, moreover, even after the "right part" evolved into the somewhat more abstract "*right party.*"[13] It was still felt in 1791 in the tense final months of the Constituent Assembly, which witnessed the emergence of the *left extremity,* at first as the *left extremity of the left part* but later in the abbreviated *extremity of the left part* and subsequently in even more simplified forms.[14] Essentially, however, the applications of these terms were limited to descriptive accounts of parliamentary proceedings.

Meanwhile, these divisions had become an accepted part of assembly practice, as became apparent after the Legislative Assembly met. The Constituent Assembly having declared its members ineligible for reelection, the Legislative Assembly was filled with new faces. Furthermore, the old structure of orders, which had left its impress on the Constituent, was now a thing of the past. It was not unreasonable to assume that the traditional cleavages of the old order would vanish along with the men involved in that particular historical episode. Instead, the division of the assembly into left, right, and center immediately reappeared. "The places on the left side that had been occupied in the Constituent Assembly by the true champions of liberty were invaded and seized by the most spirited innovators," according to one participant, the *Feuillant* Mathieu Dumas. "A far larger number of enlightened men of moderate opinions, reputed to be wise and almost indifferent observers, hastened to the center, where their mass and packed ranks might, by dint of numerical weight and strength, take on in their own eyes the appearance of an immense majority, comforting to them in their timidity. There remained to conscientious friends of the constitution only those places on the right which in the previous assembly had been occupied by the defenders of the *ancien régime.*" The reader will have grasped that our witness ranged himself among these "patriots," now transformed in the eyes of the people into an "aristocratic minority" by the sheer force of geography. "Thus the pattern of the Legislative Assembly was set in its first sessions," he concluded, "and nothing in this local disposition was changed as long as it continued to meet."[15] It was as if a law of legislative seating had been established. In reading these lines one cannot help being struck by a sense of witnessing an accelerated repetition of what had happened in the summer of '89. It was the left that took the initiative, with the right reacting after a sizable centrist reflex had asserted itself. The latter point was omitted from our earlier account, yet it bears emphasizing. Duquesnoy, for example, noticed more than just the polarization of the hall on August 23, 1789. He also observed the significant position of those who "occupy the middle": "They are in favor of everything that is being done," he says, "but they would like to see it done more slowly and with less disruption."[16] The *Impartiaux* would be an important part of the structure of the Constituent Assembly and of the political tradition that in a rather confused way it prefigured. The conceptual dichotomy of right and left is closely related to an actual tripartite division articulated around a center.

The same scenario apparently repeated itself when the Convention met. The left of the Legislative Assembly, minus its "left extremity," became the "right side" of the Convention. For a period of several months tensions were often high between the two parts of the assembly. But following the coup d'état of June 2, 1793, and the arrest of the Girondins, a novel situation developed: the right vanished. According to Thibaudeau, "the summit of the Mountain, which passed for the highest level of republicanism, absorbed everything; the right side was deserted once the Girondins were rooted out; those who had sat with them, being too conscientious or too frightened to become Montagnards, took refuge in the *belly*, which was always ready to receive men who sought their salvation in its indulgence or nullity."[17] The place thus liberated was ostensibly reserved for "envoys of the people": on August 12 one Montagnard proposed "placing the right side of the hall at the disposition of deputies from the primary assemblies; they will purify it, while only the left side deliberates."[18] Thermidor would restore symmetry between the contending forces. This was a time of high expectations, during which the division of the assembly took on special significance, as can be seen particularly in the crisis of Germinal and Prairial, Year III, which ended in the exclusion of the most visible representatives of the "left extremity." In keeping with a custom that can be traced back at least as far as the early days of the Convention, the confrontation among the deputies was mirrored in the galleries, where spectators also arranged themselves according to their political views. On 12 Germinal, for example, the petitioners who invaded the assembly "marched to applause from members and galleries of the left extremity."[19] It is all the more remarkable, therefore, that despite this polarization we find no greater identification with the vocabulary than in previous periods. "Right side" and "left side" at this point reflect a well-established, smoothly running parliamentary practice, but they were not yet terms with which people identified. Even within the walls of parliament, where the opposition of right and left had become a de facto rule, it was not perceived as the inevitable expression of deep leanings but as the pathological product of unfortunate discord that a healthy organization would not tolerate. Thus the Convention's last word on the subject would be to dismiss it. The

Constitution of Year III was capped off by a code of rules for future assemblies expressly designed to "break up the party groups that treat the legislative chamber as a battlefield on which a number of armies are engaged in a bitter struggle for victory."[20] On September 14, 1795, La Revellière-Lepeaux spoke at length on the "extremely serious drawbacks" of a situation in which deputies were obliged to express not their own wishes but those "that the public and the members of the assembly themselves believed ought to emerge from the place we occupied."[21] At his instigation the deputies voted that seating would be determined by lots to be drawn every month. Thanks to this frequent rotation, he explained, deputies would get to know each other better yet remain freer from influence: the resulting opinions, being more distinctively individualized, "would merge more easily into a truly general opinion."[22] So while it may be true that the French Revolution introduced the terms *left* and *right* into the language of politics, it protested strenuously all the while. True, there were a few surprising people, Sieyès among them, who drew a different lesson from the experience, concluding that the phenomenon was inevitable. Had not Sieyès gone so far as to concede, on July 20, that "the existence of two parties similar or analogous to those that are known elsewhere as the ministerial party and the party of opposition is inseparable from any kind of representative system. Let us tell the truth: they occur everywhere, regardless of the form of government"?[23] He was wasting his breath. The dominant view, in the waning days of Thermidor, was to bestow practical consecration on the fundamental philosophy of unity that Sieyès in his day had done so much to establish. It is not enough, therefore, to say that the Revolution created our favorite political categories; we must also say that it did its utmost to abolish them. This was not so much a beginning as a false start.

The Restoration and the Origins of the French Parliamentary Tradition

The true beginning was the Restoration. In this area it was the Revolution's worst enemies who completed its work. In 1815 the ultraroyalists were in command. Their impatient initiatives led to the resurgence of "parties" in the so-called *Chambre introuvable*. These formed groups and organized, not without raising anxieties in the mind of a public still traumatized by the Revolution. "Shortly after the chambers began meeting," one contemporary observer reported, "word spread among the public that deputies were meeting in several groups known as clubs. The two principal ones were named.... The mere idea of these clubs spread alarm among those who recalled the unfortunate influence that clubs had wielded during the Revolution, and indeed from its very outset."[24] And it was not just the bad memories; at bottom there was a prejudice in favor of the "noble independence that should be the first characteristic of a deputy." The same observer continued: "People asked how it would benefit the public interest if a deputy sacrificed to a party by adopting an opinion not his own." The quest for unity on one side forced opponents to band together. Moderates counted heads to gauge their strength vis-à-vis the ultras. Two months after the session began, on October 7, 1815, the fracture appeared to be irreparable: "The battle was on, the parties were set; in the chambers there was a constituted majority and a constituted minority."[25] Crucially, the ultra majority, after "a moment of doubt," according to Duvergier de Hauranne, "ultimately decided to take up its position on the right."[26] It certainly would have been world-shaking if the ultras had decided to sit on the left! As is well known, increasing dissension over the next few months between a ministry compelled to adopt a basically realistic attitude and overzealous champions of the monarchy would force the king to dissolve the legislature in September 1816. The ultras were severely beaten in the October elections, and the ministry thereafter sought the support of deputies favoring compromise in the spirit of the Charter, who were known as "constitutionals" and who soon became "the center." This happened after the elections of 1817, which led to the emergence of a group of "Independents" large enough to constitute an opposition on the left, which gained strength in the elections of 1818 and especially 1819. Given a regime with a government of the center faced with opposition on both its left and its right, the crystalline simplicity of the English two-party system no longer captured the reality. As late as August 1816, Vitrolles, one of the ultra leaders, could still call for the adoption of the British party system.[27] By 1820, Louis XVIII could only look back, sadly nostalgic, to a vanished ideal: "O Tories! O Whigs! Where are you?"[28] The logic of the French parliament was very different, and much more difficult to manage because of the possibility of shifting coalitions. It was this unique distribution of political forces that gave meaning to the appellations left and right. The period 1815–1820 was thus crucial in establishing the ultimate sense of the two terms.

The establishment of the couple required, if I may put it this way, a preliminary *ménage à trois*. Left and right were the product of an anomaly relative to "the normal state of parliamentary government, whose mechanism runs more smoothly if there are only two parties present." Yet, Duvergier de Hauranne continued, "how could there be just two parties, when one was hostile to the Charter and the other hostile to the Dynasty? A ministry faithful to both the Charter and the Dynasty was of course obliged to keep its distance from both and pursue a middle course."[29] With this double secession, ultramonarchists on one side and intransigent liberals on the other, France entered a period of fixed positions: alternation of the parties in power was impossible, and there could be no rotation of ministries. The system was therefore one in which the positions of the parties took on intrinsic significance, since the government necessarily defined itself in relation to them. In order to obtain a working majority, the government was usually forced to seek a coalition between its natural centrist constituency and at least a faction of one party or the other. At the end of 1818, for example, Decazes and de Serre tried to govern "in the sense and with the support of the left, although the left was not represented in the government," whereas in 1819 they changed their orientation and tried to govern "in the sense and with the support of the right, although the right had no part in power."[30] Some "constitutionals" consequently favored alliance with the right and others with the left (or at any rate with those factions of the right and left capable of parting company with the *exagérés* in their own camps). Deputies were therefore inclined to seat themselves with extraordinary subtlety so as to express the nuances of their position relative to both the extremes of both parties and the center defined by the action of the government. Since this position was the key to the political game, it became a matter of public knowledge. The revealing topography of parliament was publicized in a series of *Statistiques, Tableaux,* and *Plans,* such as the *Plan figuratif de la Chambre des députés indiquant avec exactitude la place qu'occupe chacun des membres,* a title sufficiently eloquent to make commentary superfluous.[31] The editor of one *Statistique* (for the session of 1819) took the trouble to explain that it was not enough to pay heed to the three major portions of the hemicycle, for not only were right and left both divided into two "sections" but each of these sections itself revealed significant differences: "The deputies who sit in the second section of the left, the second section of the right, and in the center are placed in such a way as to indicate the division of the assembly toward which they lean." What is more, the horizontal order of the chamber was supplemented by a vertical order. "The three columns are divided imperceptibly into three degrees."[32] In order to describe this exquisitely mapped terrain one needed a terminology capable of capturing not only the major divisions but the internal variegation as well. The terms *right* and *left* were thus supplemented by *extreme right* and *extreme left, center right* and *center left.* "But these classifications," an observer would comment somewhat later, "are far from indicating all the nuances of the parties that compose our assemblies. How many diverse complexions there are from the extreme right of the center left to the extreme left of the center right!"[33] Note in passing that this is surely one of the sources of the power of the left-right couple: it allows one to conceive simultaneously of both radical opposition and a continuous, infinitely subdividable spectrum.

The 1819–20 session of parliament marks one of the great moments in the history of political vocabulary. The whole lexical system was apparently clarified and consecrated at this time. Newspapers, pamphlets, and private correspondence all confirm that the terms *left* and *right* now began to be used not just in isolated instances but in a consistent and regular fashion. To be sure, the circumstances were favorable. The first part of the session witnessed the perfection of the system of government through shifting coalitions. After the liberals made a good showing in the September 1819 elections, Decazes reversed direction, dropped his pro-left policy, and formed a center-right ministry seeking allies on its right. Inevitably he ran up against the hostility of the *irréductibles*. Villèle, who conducted the negotiations, declared in December 1819 that "Fiévée and La Bourdonnaye would indeed like to raise a banner of their own on the extreme right."[34] The logic of the process dictated a policy of isolating the extremes. In that vein, *Le Censeur européen* noted two months earlier the discrepancy between "the praise heaped on the left and the blame leveled at the extreme left."[35] But such a policy of course created the possibility that the extremes would join forces, a phenomenon with important implications for the coalescence of the semantic system that was beginning to emerge. The elections offer an excellent example: the regicide Grégoire won election thanks to the support of ultra voters, a fact that caused an enormous scandal. An advocate of the policy of ultimate victory by making things worse in the short run, the ultraroyalist *Quotidienne* asked if, "rather than reject the regicide, it might not be better to allow him to sit in the middle of the left, to rise with it, and thus by his presence to enlighten doubting royalists as to the dreadful intentions of the Revolution."[36] By contrast, after the election was declared invalid, the *Bibliothèque historique* expressed outrage that "an elderly man honored by sixty years of virtues did not find one champion in the left."[37] When the time came to vote on the budget, however, the same *Quotidienne* did not shrink from calling for a union of opposites: "The left and the right should come to an understanding in order to manifest their common outrage against M. Decazes."[38] In lieu of an agreement, there was at least a common enemy, the ministerial party, which drew gibes from both sides. The *centre* was scornfully dismissed as the *ventre* (belly), reviving a play on words inherited from the Revolution. Writing of the 1819 session, Béranger lampooned the *ventru*, the deputy made plump by all "the dinners the ministers threw for him," for having "learned his lesson and taken up his place ten paces from Villèle and fifteen from d'Argenson." (It is interesting to note the familiarity with parliamentary topography that the writer assumes on the part of his audience.[39]) Then, in February 1820, the Duc de Berry was assassinated, and the ensuing reaction disrupted the subtle game whose rules were in the process of being established. It was back to the simplicity of head-to-head combat. The government joined forces with the ultras to pass a series of restrictive laws. Liberals of every stripe, reunited by adversity, engaged in a delaying action that provided a great opportunity for the display of oratorical eloquence. The parliamentary debates were followed with passionate interest in Paris, where students made a much-noticed entry onto the stage of political action. The bitterness of the debate by no means diminished in the wake of the November 1820 elections, which gave the ministerial party and the right an overwhelming majority. The eighty liberal survivors fought the counter-revolutionary onslaught tooth and nail in a session that Duvergier de Hauranne characterized as "civil war." Meanwhile, some liberal forces went underground.

Surely this polarization of attitudes played a part in persuading the public for the first time to identify itself with political positions expressed in terms of parliamentary geography. Take, for example, Paul-Louis Courier's account of the 1820 elections: "Among us the prefect called upon three sorts of men: men of the right, easily counted, men of the left, equally few in number, and men of the middle, a bunch."[40] Stendhal took yet another step in 1824, when in describing the Salon exhibition of paintings that year, he said that his "opinions in painting are those of the extreme left," whereas in politics they were "center left, like those of the vast majority."[41] The language of taking sides was thus emancipated from the electoral context in which Courier still used it; indeed, it had attained sufficient expressive generality to support a metaphorical extension. But it was not simply the intensity of parliamentary combat that made symbolic substantivization possible. Tacit recognition that the terms *left* and *right* expressed the underlying reality of a historical situation was also needed. The context puts the matter in a clear light. The conflict between liberals and ultras could not be mistaken for a relatively artificial factional struggle for power. It was plain to everyone that this was how the country was and would remain divided. One of the great differences between this situation and that of the revolutionary period was, moreover, the clearly intelligible contours of the confrontation, an intelligibility in fact created by the memory and legacy of 1789. With hindsight what had been at stake in a confused battle was now clear. No one had the slightest doubt that the old and the new France were now squared off face to face, and the question was whether compromise was possible between "two nations." Meanwhile, Montlosier on the reactionary side and Thierry and Guizot on the liberal side provided historical interpretations that took the long view, seeing duality as inevitable in a France "condemned by its history to form two rival and irreconcilable camps."[42] To the extent that political division thus seemed to everyone justified, ineluctable, real, and persistent, it made sense to identify with it, to transform the distribution of parliamentary forces into a concept, to convert the accident of their spatial disposition into something essential about French political reality. Historical dramatization plus political subtlety formed a volatile mixture in 1820, and the resulting explosion blasted the terms *left* and *right* indelibly into the political bedrock of France. The goal of restoration revived the cleavages of the Revolution with new clarity, and party identification lent gravity to the situation. Nevertheless, the outcome depended on the prior incorporation of the antagonism into a complex political game whose descriptive semantics came into wide use.

The result was further reinforced by what happened in 1828. There was extensive debate in the parties and the press about how to respond to the elections of November 1827, debate that once again brought the language of political classification to the forefront. Interest in the subject had subsided somewhat after 1824,

owing to the right's overwhelming domination of the so-called *Chambre retrouvée,*
even though the talents of the fifteen opposition deputies huddled in their fortress
on the extreme left, and even more dissension within the majority, divided between
the hotheads of the extreme right and the moderates of its "left," were sufficient to
sustain lively parliamentary discussion. In 1827 the antigovernment coalition was
revived, and it was back to the tripartite situation of the Decazes era. The ministerial party, reduced to 180 deputies, faced opposition on both flanks, with 70 royalists on its right and 180 liberals on its left. Thus the issue of forming coalitions capable of sustaining a majority was once again on the agenda. Should the ministerial
center right join forces with the center left? Some people thought so, arguing, as
Stendhal had done a few years earlier, that "the general opinion of France and the
spirit of the age lies there: *all of France is center left.*"[43] But this proposal drew vehement criticism from both the right and the left, each side insisting on unity as the
guarantee of its own hegemony. The *Journal des débats,* for example, argued that
"the cabinet should march with the entire left.... It would be madness to wish for a
union of the center right and center left strong enough to withstand the attacks of
the two extremities."[44] Similarly, Benjamin Constant denounced as utopian any
attempt to sever the center left from "what is called the extreme left." "The left will
remain united," he said, "even though it has in its ranks some who are impatient and
others who are resigned."[45] The young men of *Le Globe* confirmed this, disdainfully dismissing "the distinctions of center left and left, relics of 1819.... The true
elements of the majority are on the left, without distinction as to center or extremity."[46] On the right, however, the Vicomte de Saint-Chamans, an influential pamphleteer, sought to prove in quite parallel fashion "that the alliance between the center right and center left is impossible, and that there is more distance between the
most moderate man of the center right and the most moderate man of the center left
than between either one and the most ardent man in his party."[47] He therefore
favored an "alliance of the right with the center right."[48] In support of his thesis he
advanced the interesting argument that "the four parties and their delicate shadings
really exist more in the Chambers than in the nation," where by this time "only
clear-cut opinions of the right and left have any power."[49] In practice, Martignac's
center-right ministry would venture, throughout the year and a half of its existence,
to keep open precarious lines of communication with the left in the hope of an
unlikely "fusion" with moderate liberals. This was a perilous course to take, for it
left the government at the mercy of a concerted opposition, which in the end
brought it down. The result, ultimately fatal to the regime, was to hazard "the folly
of a ministry of the extreme right," as Villèle had warned.[50] In any case, the
episode, which entailed a general revision of terminology and tactics, contributed
to the definitive enthronement of terms describing parliamentary divisions as categories of political understanding.

The Era of the Masses: From Topography to Identity

We now turn our attention to understanding how right and left became the primary categories of political *identity*. This was a long, drawn-out process that lasted more than three quarters of a century, until the first decade of the twentieth century. It transformed the specialized language of parliament into the basic idiom of universal suffrage. The exemplary clarity of the early Restoration did not last. After 1830, the words *right* and *left* remained, but the political deck was reshuffled. It was no longer the case that the division of the National Assembly accurately reflected the issue facing the country: to preserve the gains of the Revolution or accede to the counterrevolution. With the victory of liberal Orleanism, the scene became more complicated, the mirror turned cloudy. Old antagonisms waned as extreme royalism, which had served to harden everyone's position, disintegrated. "Since the July Revolution," one pamphleteer wrote in 1842, "a dozen honorable members, leftovers of legitimist opinion, have found themselves scattered among deputies of every stripe. As a result, the words *right* and *right side* no longer refer to a political party."[51] Politics was increasingly a matter for professionals, in which rivalries between individuals and cliques mattered more than doctrine. Official debate became rather esoteric because the two great issues of the day, the republican question and the social question, were studiously avoided. The descriptive terms *right* and *left* remained by force of tradition, but they lost much of their appeal, much of the identificational power they had had during the memorable battles of the 1820s.

Thus when universal suffrage arrived in 1848, the right-left language did not spring spontaneously to mind. The words were too closely associated with the internal workings of parliament to lend themselves readily to the description of fundamental divisions in public opinion. They were institutional terms, words for assembly minutes or political analyses. But when Proudhon, for example, sketched a typology of the parties in his *Confessions d'un révolutionnaire*, he was careful, after establishing the need for two middle-of-the-road parties to occupy the space between the two parties of the extreme, to clarify his meaning by invoking a different but familiar vocabulary: "in parliamentary terms, a center right and a center left."[52] As it happens, the vocabulary adopted to describe electoral competition and party politics took a different turn entirely. The elections of May 1849 (which, as is well known, set the pattern of political confrontation in France for a long time to come) pitted what ordinary people referred to as the *démoc-socs* against the *réacs* (democratic-socialists against reactionaries). The banners flown by the opposing parties also established a very powerful symbolism of colors: *reds* versus *whites*. The red-white opposition would remain the key distinction between the two camps for the next half century. In the Breton village of Plozévet in the 1960s, Edgar Morin found that these two colors were still the primary symbols of party affiliation.[53]

Well into the twentieth century, long after the terms *right* and *left* had taken hold, red and white banners were still flown in times of tension, indeed at moments when there was a need to emphasize the stark character of the choice. "I am for the forces of revolution and against the forces of counterrevolution. There are whites and reds, and I am with the reds!" proclaimed the radical Malvy at a 1923 demonstration in favor of the Cartel des Gauches.[54] And in 1936 there were still candidates who referred to the "eternal struggle" between the "red bloc" and the "white bloc."[55] The importance of this cannot be overemphasized. Universal suffrage immediately created an enormous need for political identification. Everyone was called upon to choose sides. People did so at first by identifying with either the red or the white. It was this opposition that both simplified the terms of conflict to the utmost and allowed people to indicate immediately where they stood. It was not until later that right and left supplanted white and red. The symbolism of color had established deep roots, even insinuating itself into folklore, especially in certain parts of the south. The symbolic battle developed its own panoply of costumes, masquerades, and ritual clashes of color. And of course red and white, both rich in symbolic overtones, were ideally chosen to speak to the imagination and the heart. In the end this makes it all the more mysterious that right and left, despite their cold abstractness, could have achieved the same emotional resonance, the same earnestness of identification or repulsion.

Perhaps the first thing that this shift points to is the success of the parliamentary regime. By the beginning of the twentieth century the institution had taken firm hold. Not only did people by now conceive of politics in terms of parliament, but they measured social forces in terms of electoral power. Even the regime's worst detractors spoke its language. It had taken thirty years to achieve this result, thirty years (1871–1900) during which democracy in fact adapted itself to France. It may well be that the vicissitudes of the political vocabulary can themselves shed light, as from within, on some of the psychological aspects of this process.

The words *right* and *left* came back into circulation with the liberalization of the Second Empire, or, more precisely, with the legislative elections of 1869. According to one journalist, the ninety deputies of the opposition "will oblige the assembly to revert to old definitions: left, extreme left, center left, center right, extreme right."[56] He was right about the new dynamic, as can be seen from the open letter that Gambetta dispatched two weeks later "to the voters in the first district in the Seine département," in which he tried to clarify how things stood on the left: "The present left," he said, "should be divided into two parts," a center left (although he did not use the word) and a true left. What he wanted to do was to give the word *left* its "precise, definite, exact meaning: it refers to and defines a political party of homogeneous composition, of identical origin, of common principles," a party consisting of all those for whom the emancipation of universal suffrage must ultimately lead to democratic institutions.[57] The text can be seen as a turning point. On the one hand it looks forward to the idea of a modern political party, that is, a group unified by acceptance of a common doctrine: "We must organize a left consisting solely of citizens in support of a common set of principles." Yet its conceptual world is essentially that of parliamentary debate, as can be seen from the following passage: "A checkered, heterogeneous left comprising opinion of all sorts can harangue, criticize, and verbally harass the common adversary, and that is a great deal; but in action it will always amount to nothing."[58] This limitation would continue to be the rule for many years to come. The revival of the terms *right* and *left* thus came about in the midst of war, the fall of the Empire and the collapse of the Commune, and then the return to normal with a parliamentary regime capped by the approval of the new Republic in 1875. The February 1871 elections introduced a Republican Left, a Center Right, and a Center Left as official parties in the National Assembly.[59] To these were added an Extreme Left in 1876 and a Radical Left in 1881. In 1885 the Extreme Left formed a group in the Senate with a manifesto that says a great deal about the familiarity of these labels: "The characterization 'extreme left' is a sufficient indication of the motives behind the formation of this group."[60] After the 1885 elections a Union of Rights was formed in the chamber. In the following year Raoul Duval took the initiative in creating a Republican Right, a name later taken over by Jacques Piou in 1893 for the former Constitutional Right. In parliamentary discourse and political analysis, a genre whose development was greatly fostered by the growth of the press, *right, left,* and derivative terms flourished and became indispensable. There were two circumstances in which their use was almost inevitable: in the heat of polarized political debate, and in the cold light of political analysis of the strength of opposing camps, especially the internal structure of the various parties composing rival groups. In the latter vein the earnest commentators for *Le Temps* are an inexhaustible source. In 1873, for example, one of them deplored the fact that "not a single of the right's advantages was not created by some imprudence on radicalism's part."[61] A year later the same paper observed that "the left and center left are infinitely more united than the right and center right."[62] Examples were no less numerous in the realm of language to describe tension. In July 1876 the Bonapartist Cassagnac proclaimed that "we have republican intolerance to thank for bringing total unity to the right." In January 1879 the radical Floquet called for a union of the left in what was perhaps the first use of that formula: "What saved the Republic was the Union of the Left.... The Union of the Left—therein lies the truth."[63] Allowances must of course be made for the phenomenon of coalition between extremes, which earned Gambetta the chairmanship of the budget committee in January 1877: "It was the right that settled the issue between two roughly equal factions of the left," according to one Bonapartist journal. "It voted almost unanimously, and openly, for the radical candidates, whose victory it was delighted to see."[64] This was a common enough tactic for Jules Ferry to make it a central issue of his 1881 campaign, whose goal, he said, was to eliminate enough intransigent monarchists to "protect the government desired by the majority from coalitions of the right and the extreme left."[65] The resulting "republican concentration" was to be safe from extremist minorities, and it was this context that gave rise to one of the most famous dicta of Opportunism, inaccurately attributed to Ferry himself: "The peril is on the left." Ferry was content merely to make the point by implication, as in a speech at Le Havre on October 14, 1883, in which he discussed the "partial successes of the intransigent party": "The peril of monarchy no longer exists, but it has been replaced by another, which we must face head on."[66] It was his enemies who took it upon themselves to recast and popularize the slogan. On the eve of the 1885 elections, the *Manifeste de la commission du congrès républicain radical socialiste* branded him a "pernicious man who, forgetting our eternal enemies in his hatred of radicals, did not shrink from telling the country that the peril is no longer on the right, it is on the left."[67] Any number of additional examples could easily be cited. For the sake of balance I shall quote a statement of Raoul Duval, made in a period when former Bonapartists and monarchists were throwing their support to the conservative republic (1886–87): "If I turn to the left [of the Chamber], I see mistrust and suspicion. If I look to the right, I see many colleagues who for fear of a word [Republic] shrink from openly backing the policy that in their hearts they find most reasonable."[68] Thus ready-made labels and traditional divisions no longer corresponded to the actual situation: this, too, was a theme with a great future ahead of it, the inception of which is worth noting.

This flurry of examples risks creating a misconception. All remain closely associated with parliamentary politics and reflect its specialized vocabulary. The only difference is that with political stability achieved and new means of publicity in place, the news circulated more widely. If we focus on elections, however, the left-right distinction pales to insignificance. Militants mobilized around other categories, and voters identified with other themes, although left and right do reappear after the voting in analyses of the results. The Commune revived the colors of 1848. In particular it attached an ineradicable luster to the word *red* (and in consequence to *white*)—a positive identification for some, a repellent emblem for others. Revolution itself became "red" for its proponents, while "reds" were the very embodiment of bourgeois fears.[69] In fact, the language of denunciation would continue to draw on the Commune for decades, and the language of denunciation would play an important part in familiarizing people with the friend-enemy vocabulary that went along with elections. As for the more tranquil matter of the labels claimed by each side (and recognized by the other), the period was dominated by the contest between "conservatives" and "republicans." Under the electoral system adopted in 1875, each district elected a single member by majority vote in two stages, and in the second round, voters, in accordance with their allegiances, cast their votes for the surviving conservative or republican candidate. This was the system that would finally bring republicans to power after the decisive elections of October 1877, and it remained in effect throughout the 1880s, despite a temporary return to voting by list in 1885. We have a unique instrument for appreciating the value of this system, an anthology of professions of faith by victorious candidates; the radical Barodet sought and won approval for the compilation of such an anthology in 1881, in order to determine more accurately what wishes the voters were expressing through the ballot box.[70] And in that respect the texts are indeed quite eloquent. Until the late 1890s *right* and *left* did not figure in candidates' statements to the voters. When the terms did appear in a platform, appeal, or proclamation, it was in a purely parliamentary sense, as for example when General de Frescheville explained in 1889 that he, "together with [my] colleagues on the right, have done all that it was within the power of a minority to do," or when Montgolfier explained to the voters of Tournon that "the platform I wish to place before you is the platform of the right."[71] These terms are relatively neutral compared with more inflammatory labels such as "the reaction" or "the reds," applied to the opposition, and the more laudatory labels of "republicanism" or "conservatism" attached to one's own party. These were the primary categories in use in the early days of the Third Republic.

Things changed about 1900, at the time of the "republican defense" and the major conflict triggered by the Dreyfus Affair. *Right* and *left* would soon establish themselves as *the* terms for describing the two Frances that clashed so passionately over the most fundamental issues of truth, justice, religion, nation, and revolution. By the eve of World War I, their fundamental role was established once and for all. Parliamentary topography became the primary reference in terms of which citizens expressed their political beliefs. The change was already apparent in the 1902 elections, which saw the victory of none other than the Bloc des Gauches. It assumed its full dimensions in the elections of 1906, even though the period of most acute confrontation, of "*bloc* against *bloc*," over the religious issue had ended with the fall of the Combes government the previous year. It would survive the vicissitudes of the alliance of Radicals and Socialists in the years to come. Circumstances ceased to matter. From now on, no matter what was happening internally in terms of relations among the various constituents of right and left, the competition for votes would be played as a contest between right and left, for this was the language of the voters even more than of their representatives, hence the language the candidates were obliged to speak.

We must now try to understand the minor psychological revolution behind this shift in vocabulary. In my view the change largely reflects the advent of democracy in the modern sense and what this implied in the realm of *representation*. In addition, this profound transformation of the political order was powerfully affected by certain accidental features of a very specific historical moment. Structural changes and conjunctural factors were inextricably intertwined. The subtle interplay of these various forces is what we must now try to unravel, taking the linguistic symptoms as our starting point. To reduce the answer to simple, if rather schematic, terms, the adoption of the right-left dichotomy by the mass of voters simultaneously solved three main problems: how to deal with change in the very grounds of confrontation, resulting from the continual emergence of new parties; how to cope with contradictions, given the differences within each camp as well as between them; and how to cope with the interchangeability of actor and observer, when representation portrayed itself as an objectification of social divisions.

The moment was of course defined most of all by the civil war of the mind that began in early 1898 with the polemic over the guilt of Captain Dreyfus (Zola's *J'accuse* appeared on January 13). For seven years the conflict of opinion took a particularly bitter turn, first with the rise of nationalist sentiment, followed by a republican riposte and later an anticlerical offensive by the Combes government. It was in this tense atmosphere, so favorable to the emergence of dualist categories, that the shift we are interested in mainly occurred. Still, the vehemence of public debate by itself explains nothing. The existing categories were perfectly adequate to express the divisions, and the situation could easily have solidified the opposition between republicans and conservatives or reds and whites. Indeed, it was under the banner of "defense of the Republic" that the left and extreme left joined forces to confront nationalist agitation in 1899, from the demonstration of June 11 to the inauguration of Dalou's *Triomphe de la République* on November 18. Yet instead of reinforcing the existing categories, the situation substituted a different one. In order to understand this, we must consider the evolution of the political forces, which sapped the strength of some and led to the realignment of others. In this connection the central fact was of course the emergence and growing power of the Socialists. What Jaurès called "the dawn of 1893," the breakthrough the party made in elections in which the social question was the central issue, brought full visibility. Although the new party was divided and still limited in its electoral and parliamentary influence, its arrival was the crucial new factor that changed the rules of the political game. It was in relation to this development that other changes took on their full meaning. To begin with, the advent of the Socialists illustrated in striking fashion the law that André Siegfried would discover in 1913, that French politics moves from left to right, "tending to squeeze the parties, to drain them of their left-wing energy and propel them toward the center, the paradise of the satisfied," while at the same time spurring the development of new forces of protest on the left.[72] The replacement of the Opportunists by the Radicals offered a first, spectacular illustration of this law, and the arrival of the Socialists seemed to corroborate it. The elections of May 1914 produced this strange portrait of a chamber in which "the entire left half of the hall was occupied by groups born within the past third of a century and bearing the epithet socialist (unified socialist, republican socialist, socialist radical)," while "all the groups that kept the name left (radical left, left republicans, democratic left) were seated in the right half; the two progressive groups formed from the debris of the old (1880–1898) republican majority were forced all the way over to the extreme right."[73] This picture shows the degree to which the old labels were discredited. Not only did parties labeled "left" sit on the right in parliament, but the term *right*, once reserved for monarchists irretrievably on the wane, now became confused. Clearly, the appropriation of the terms *right* and *left* by the public went hand in hand with dissatisfaction with the way in which the words had been used in the National Assembly since 1871. The terms were not simply transferred or extended from one domain to another but redefined. Meanwhile, other identifying labels were also affected. For example, the term *republican* was challenged by the Socialists for its political narrowness, and it lost some of its defining resonance after some former conservatives became supporters of the Republic. The embarrassment is apparent in campaign literature from 1902, much of which was given over to denunciation of counterfeit republicanism. "Unite against all the parties of the right that fraudulently deck themselves out with the name 'republican,' " proclaimed, in typical fashion, one Radical candidate in Lyons.[74] What is more, the same conservatives showed a new readiness to concern themselves with social issues, as illustrated by Piou's creation of the Action Libérale Populaire in 1902. Meanwhile, other conservatives rallied under the banner of nationalism, a "new word that deceives no one," according to an often repeated allegation.[75] These two factors further confused the issue of party origins. All these processes of erosion and destabilization led in the end to a need for identification: the resulting void was filled by the opposition of right and left. We can see now what gave the terms their newfound force: they restored a stable identity to the confrontation, at the price of a relativization of the opposed terms.[76] They registered the shift that had occurred thus far and protected the principle of division from further changes yet to come. Instead of replacing more or less obsolete doctrine with new doctrine, the new opposition abstracted the fact of conflict from its ideological content. It separated the permanent principle from the random variability of its substance. The wonderful power of right versus left comes from the infinite openness of the terms, whose meaning can always be added to or altered. The search for an ultimate meaning is thus inevitable yet pointless, since it was the very latitude of the pair that allowed it to take hold. In their abstraction *left* and *right* functioned as memory notions through which historical continuity could be maintained. They allowed people to believe that political conflict is political conflict, that from the Girondins versus the Montagnards to the nationalists versus the socialists by way of the liberals versus the monarchists the story was always the same. That is why it has been so difficult to pin these terms down as products of history: words that help us find our way through history come to seem coextensive with it.

There is a phrase from the 1890s that can be credited with a definite role in helping the new system to establish itself: "no enemy on the left." This was the slogan of young reformers from the Radical group who joined forces in 1894–95 to push for an alliance with the Socialists.[77] They deliberately stood the Ferryist slogan of the previous decade on its head. Indeed, according to one of the reformers, this was the slogan of those who refused "to see a peril or threat on the left" but only "friends, brothers in democracy."[78] It captured the prevailing mood of the Radical Party convention of 1901. A memorandum from the Comité d'Action pour les Réformes Républicaines, which organized the convention, explicitly acknowledged it: "In confronting the common enemy, it will eliminate whatever may divide republicans and, in accordance with the Committee's formula, the convention will see no enemies to its left."[79] The success of this slogan takes us straight to the heart of the second set of factors that favored the shift to right versus left: the need for symbolic unification of deeply divided political groups. Of course splits "on the left" did not begin when the Socialists came on the scene. But the arrival of the Socialists dramatized old divisions, many of which could be traced all the way back to the Revolution, after which they were rediscovered in 1848 and revived by the Commune. The development of the workers' movement and the language of class gave new substance to these old divisions and provided new terms for interpreting them. Understood in terms of faction and social struggle, they came to seem insuperable obstacles, and the concrete results were obvious when "republican discipline" failed to ensure that votes cast in the first round for "left-wing" candidates were transferred in the second round to "bourgeois" candidates (Clemenceau paid the price in 1893). What made alliances with the new parties problematic was not so much intransigence in matters of principle as their very nature as class-based parties. Meanwhile, "on the right," particularly in the Catholic camp, the divisions were no less profound but of a different nature, as the elections of 1898 and after made clear. Some on the right had rallied to the Republic, others remained uncompromisingly antisecular, and still others were nationalists; the result was profound doubt and fierce disagreement. Under Waldeck-Rousseau and Combes the religious issue became a matter of bitter conflict, which as a result of these internal divisions took on paradigmatic significance. It was not simply, as is so often said, a resurgence of the fundamental antagonism of Ancien Régime and Revolution in the new guise of clericals versus anticlericals. What deserves just as much attention is the way in which the battle led to the realignment of two camps divided as they had seldom been before. If the basic conflict was irreconcilable, the forces in contention were fundamentally divided: despite the "duality of tendencies," as François Goguel puts it, there was a "multiplicity of parties and groups."[80] These two dimensions of the moment make it the perfect epitome of the tradition inaugurated by the French Revolution, in which the simplifying polarization of the central conflict is equalled only by the complex heterogeneity of the parties involved. Specifically, the need for unity against a background of tension in each camp is what the sacralization of the right-left opposition conceals. The factors we find at work here are the same as those discussed earlier from another angle. In particular, the abstract neutrality of a classification in terms of spatial poles adepts nicely to a situation in which no single party is capable of forcing its camp to identify with its key symbol. In other words, if there had been only two major parties in France, the lexical need for *right* and *left* would not have existed. The terms caught on precisely because there was in reality more than one right and more than one left. The official nomenclature reflected this, moreover, in designations ranging from the *délégation des gauches* that was supposed to coordinate parliamentary action under Waldeck-Rousseau to the Bloc des Gauches organized to wage the election campaign of 1902.[81] The more lefts (and rights) there were in actuality, the greater the need for an ideal left (or right). Within this unifying power, however, it was always possible to discern potential divisions, as when Vaillant told the chamber in 1907 that "the right begins for us much further left than you think." Another benefit of the purely formal and therefore infinitely reproducible distribution was that the terms of union were also the terms of division. It is significant that it was in the 1906 elections, when *right* and *left* were mobilized as signs of identity, that they found their way into the Barodet anthology mentioned earlier.[82] On the one hand were the accomplishments of long years of intense struggle, which surely helped the new terminology to catch on. But on the other hand there was the recurrence of division on the left. After the Congress of Amsterdam condemned the policy of class collaboration in 1904, the Socialists, rebaptized the Section Française de l'Internationale Ouvrière (S.F.I.O.), adopted a new line, rejecting any alliance "with any portion whatsoever of the capitalist class." This was a warning that had to be taken seriously, particularly because the governmental axis had, after the fall of the Combes ministry, shifted noticeably toward the center. Nevertheless, the elections took place with republican discipline in effect, but these menacing noises surely were not unrelated to the fate of the new unifying categories in this campaign. Consider these revealing snippets of rhetoric: "Vote against the right bloc and for the left, more compact and unshakable than ever"; "The unshakable unity of the parties of the left must be affirmed in the first round"; "I plant my flag in the center of the bloc, with those who recognize no adversary on the left and who will accept no compromise on the right."[83] To be sure, this was shortly after the tempest stirred up in early 1906 by the "inventories" provided for in the previous year's law separating church and state, a law that had not met with unified opposition from Catholics but that, given its relative moderation compared with the

"Combesian spirit," had rather revealed certain hesitations, doubts, and divisions. As far as the flourishing of our dualist system is concerned, the equation was therefore ideal, with mobilizing tension (resulting in the highest voter turnout since 1877) offset by just enough relaxation to allow differences to emerge. The combination of bipolar antagonism with internal contradictions in each camp could thus produce its full effect.

A third set of factors having to do with a profound transformation of the political system also contributed to the consecration of right and left as categories of political identity. These factors were connected with the development of a new economy of representation connected with modern democracy. *Right* and *left* were the words that would result in a change in the function of the representative scene and, with it, a change in the way in which citizens located themselves in the political realm.

Once again, the emergence of the Socialists offers a good way into the subject. Both aspects of the new situation were most clearly visible in the socialist camp: true political parties were born, and their inception was connected with a demand for social representation. These were not the first or the only parties in France. Unification, as we have seen, did not take place until 1905, whereas the Radical Party had been constituted, admittedly in a rather loose fashion, since 1901. On the right, Piou's Action Libérale Populaire, whose organization, interestingly enough, was based on that of the German *Zentrum*, was born in 1902. Nevertheless, the S.F.I.O. was the only prewar political organization to practice exclusive identification of the parliamentary group with the party. In any case, the party phenomenon in France was far weaker than in Germany or Great Britain. (Recall, in passing, that the two great books on the emergence of modern political parties, written as the phenomenon was taking place by Ostrogorski and Michels, appeared in 1903 and 1911, respectively.[84]) The meager influence of the parties in reality must not be allowed to create the impression that the symbolic break was unimportant. It was extremely important, particularly since French tradition had been hostile to parties since the Revolution for powerfully articulated reasons.

The purpose of representation, in the French tradition, was to reveal the general will, which was in essence unified. For that reason the deputy had to remain an absolutely independent individual. Only if his opinion reflected his true conscience could he validly exercise his function, which was to speak as a universal representative of the entire country. Representation, in other words, was the nation's means of expression, since for reasons both practical and "mystical" the nation could not formulate its will in person. In return, the nation had no other voice than its representatives; they were its sole organ. The ambition to make the law the emanation of the body politic as a whole thus led to an identification of the nation's representatives with the nation, which was in fact a substitution of one for the other. Election was an act of delegation of the collective will to an individual, who, once that transfer was made, was in principle entirely free vis-à-vis his constituents.

The new forms of political organization and discipline struck at the very foundation of this whole conceptual framework, the core of the French republican tradition. What makes the French case unique and interesting is that in France democracy was obliged to constitute itself in opposition to the Republic. The mere existence of political parties pointed to an organization of society outside of its representation and, potentially at least, an inversion of the relationship that was supposed to reveal the general will: the deputies of the parties would then simply transfer into the field of power a preexisting system of organizations, which would determine the result in advance. The idea of a class-based party, or, more generally, the idea of a party as the organized expression of specific interests and groups, only reinforced this quality of exteriority and anteriority. The image and very nature of representation were thus transformed: instead of a monist image of revelation of the unified collective will, one now had a dualist image of a correspondence to be established between two distinct spheres. To represent had meant to give face and body to an entity incapable of expressing itself in any other way; henceforth it would mean to reflect adequately the complex realities of a structured society, politically and in other ways, through the free initiative of its members— and once again, the secession of the working class proved decisive as an example. Accordingly, demands for just representation began to be voiced at the same time. The vigorous campaigns for proportional representation that began in 1902 were the most visible illustration of this. They brought conservatives and Socialists together but failed in the face of opposition from the Radicals. Proposals for professional representation that surfaced in this same period should also be placed under this head. So should the violent antiparliamentarism of the end of the decade, which stemmed from frustrations due not so much to governmental instability after years of rule by the Bloc as to the spectacle of an assembly left to its own internal machinations. In negative terms this reflected a wish to see parliament reflect a reliable, stable image of the country's own divisions and debates—a desire that would be incorporated, timidly, into the 1910 reform making parliamentary groups official and requiring deputies to affiliate exclusively and publicly with one group. This search for a faithful match between a dynamic society and the defining locus of its political identity forms the common substance of these various protests and expectations. What people wanted was a parliament that would be not a substitute for the body politic but a mirror capable of giving an accurate reflection of the diversity of views and multiplicity of forces, not to say the division of labor, in society itself. This parliament was not to be a closed body removed from the community the better to arrive at an image of the general will but a reflective body in every sense of the word, open to society in order to make disputes and difference visible and conceivable and thereby to allow bargaining and compromise.

In this context the meaning of the act of voting itself changed. It ceased to be simply a matter of delegating a substitute to work in behalf of the voter's views and became a way for the voter to define himself, to identify himself, to situate himself on a political terrain whose salient features were recognized and understood. In other words, the voter became not just a participant in but an analyst of politics, though in an elementary mode to be sure, and this is probably the secret of the vote's symbolic efficacy. Democracy, which first began to emerge in its developed form at the beginning of the twentieth century, is more than just de facto and de jure coexistence of the contending parties. It consists above all in the pacifying representation of the existing correlation of forces as epitomized in the structure of parliament. Its heart lies in that singular process of competitive objectification whereby each person becomes a spectator of a division in which he is also an actor. The citizen-voter is in fact a split personality, in whom political commitment coexists with the detachment of the observer who records results, evaluates their consequences, and orients himself with respect to the map that emerges.

Left and right—terms fraught with passion yet at the same time neutral markers—would prove to be appropriate landmarks in this twofold process: they made it possible to assert a clear-cut partisan identity while at the same time reckoning one's position on the overall political battlefield. Indeed, it was because the terms *left* and *right* lent themselves to such dual functionality that they enjoyed a decisive advantage over other pairs of contrasting terms such as *red* and *white*. Because of the very intensity of their contrast, red and white were excellent symbols for implacably opposed camps. But the problem now was not so much for allies to recognize one another and estimate their strength vis-à-vis the opposing force. More fundamentally, it was to understand the reasons for battle in a setting where the opposing forces were constantly taking each other's measure. Now we see why the vocabulary of parliamentary division corresponded to the vocabulary of political affiliation. The unique subtlety of *right* and *left* in characterizing relative positions was an amazing marriage of radical simplification with the possibility of broadening nuance. When social warfare, instead of developing its own categories by widening the gulf between the spontaneous signs of social division and the prevailing code in the political arena, ultimately adopted the pre-formed language of representation as its principal language of action, democracy had taken a definitive step toward establishing itself in people's minds. From now on, democracy was conceived of as a means of domesticating conflict by organizing the major players on a vast scale and by ritualizing their clash down to its very vocabulary. The replacement of red versus white by left versus right implied acceptance of the reversible two-sided relationship of party supporter and political analyst over the one-sidedness of the partisan.

This entry into the age of permanent, irreducible, institutionalized political conflict would prove terribly traumatic, however, and its chain of negative effects would become the tragedy of the twentieth century. There was something extremely ambiguous about the antiparliamentarism I described earlier: on the one hand it was associated with the misguided search for a representativity not guaranteed by the classical forms of parliamentary government, while on the other hand it was part of a broad refusal to accept the prospect of an irreparably fractured public space. Indeed, that fracture symbolized nothing less than the collapse of a very deeply rooted cultural bias that made it impossible to conceive of society other than under the sign of unity. The culture of unity sprang from at least three roots. The traditionalist current left its imprint on the founders of French sociological thought from Comte to Durkheim before being reinvented, significantly, at the turn of the century by Charles Maurras, who saw the organic solidarity of communities, corporations, and ranks as a necessary condition of collective cohesion. The Jacobin current treated the active identity of people and power as the supreme republican ideal. In addition to these two sources of cultural unity, there was the loss of certainty that conflict would come to an end. When republicans were battling with monarchists, the objective was clear; both sides believed that when the goal was achieved, the adversary would simply disappear. But now the goal was achieved: the republicans had won conclusively if without great enthusiasm. Nearly all political forces in the country had pledged to support the Republic and found their place in it. Yet conflict continued. More than that, it had become a constitutional rule of the Republic itself. Come what may, there would always be division and discord between a right and a left—such was the promise of perpetual conflict that the two terms in their deepest sense conveyed. Looking back, it is not easy to appreciate the disorientation that many people felt at this prospect of being imprisoned in conflict, which seemed to contradict deeply rooted beliefs and certitudes about the nature of the good society. Out of this disorientation grew a powerful reactionary movement, to which the disaster of 1914 and its aftermath brought emotional amplification. This reaction took two opposed forms, one on the extreme right based on backward-looking rejection, the other on the extreme left based on future-oriented transcendence. The extreme right believed that intellectual dissension and clashes over material interests were signs of a pathological deviation, in response to which society must seek to recover its former solidarity, for which the natural context was the *nation*. Meanwhile, the extreme left believed that society's contradictions must be played out to the end, not because they were good in themselves but because they promised, through *revolution* to bring reconciliation. Between these two extremes there were all sorts of hybrid positions, from reactionary modernism to revolutionary nationalism. Note, by the way, that we have here, in this discussion of extremism, the key to the asymmetry in the attitudes of right and left toward the existence of the right-left division. Clearly the division was promoted by the left, while the right, which had little use for it, tended to deny its existence or refuse to acknowledge it. This is because the left in general, even the moderate left, sees division as a driving force and hope for a future of concord, whereas the right sees it as damaging, artificial, and a distraction from the essential, which is the quest for unity and harmony. Yet these two dissimilar ways of dealing with division are in fact quite similar at bottom when it comes to rendering the idea of division less scandalous. If we refine the actor-observer distinction, we can say that the right, suppressing its instinctive repugnance, treats the right-left division as a subject for cold analytical reason, whereas the left sees itself as protagonist and opts for enthusiasm, only to encounter that much more difficulty in trying to reduce the phenomenon to normal intellectual dimensions. Yet these attitudes are not the permanent results of some sort of political characterology. They are the products of a well-defined historical moment, when the liberal image of the representative process gave way to our democracy of parties and conflict. Perhaps the clearest sign of the change is the shift in attitude on the right toward the term *right*, which was easily accepted through the 1890s only to be rejected, for the most part, after 1900. Not that the right had changed, only the sense and scope of the denomination. It caused no difficulty as long as it referred only to a location in parliament. It began to encounter resistance when, wedded to its antagonist, it introduced the certainty of interminable discord. It would take several decades of convulsive history for the right to learn to live with this redoubtable truth of democracy, which, when it came in with the new century, was mostly seen, even by those who welcomed it, as an anomaly to be overcome.

The Age of Extremism and the Rites of Division

"A mystique of the pure left, a religious character attached to the word *left*—do these things exist today in the sense in which they existed during the militant republic's battles against clericalism?" It is interesting to find so astute an observer as Albert Thibaudet asking himself such a question in 1931. "I do not think so," he answered, adding a warning to "wait for the elections of 1932."[85] Healthy caution. The question was provoked by a famous survey initiated by the monarchist publicist Beau de Loménie on the theme "What do you mean by right and left?" It was in response to the same survey that Alain came up with a formulation that had a bright future ahead of it: "When people ask me if the division between parties of the right and parties of the left, men of the right and men of the left, still makes sense, the first thing that comes to mind is that the person asking the question is certainly not a man of the left." The author of *Propos* was already, even in his prewar debut, an excellent example of the essentialization of right and left. Yet Thibaudet's observation rings true for the time, for there was a certain vagueness about the left-right opposition in the period after World War I. A firm fixture of the landscape, it was nevertheless perceived for a time as an old-fashioned legacy with which the forces of the new were not obliged to encumber themselves. The *cartel* of 1924 rekindled the flame somewhat after the great collapse of old structures brought on by the war and the lengthy interval of Union Nationale. It did not generate enough heat, however, to overcome doubts and objections to this dusty symbol of the old Radical Republic. The problem was not simply that the left-right split no longer aroused the same passions and fever as in the past but that it was actually denounced. On the extreme left it was attacked in the name of the proletarian revolution and on the extreme right in the name of national restoration. What had been an embryonic tendency in the first decade of the century now took the form of formal doctrine and organized political forces whose first imperative was to do away with the harmful and foolish political game symbolized by the pseudo-rivalry of right and left. In the end, however, this double rejection of the right-left opposition led to its reinforcement. Five years after Thibaudet's diagnosis in 1936, it was more vital, more central, and more sacred than ever. It had become, in a word, ineradicable. The Communists, who had originally attacked it from the left on the grounds of rigorous class analysis, helped to consecrate it by joining the Popular Front. Meanwhile, pro-fascist ideologues and movements insisted on their symmetric proscription, "neither right nor left," which only helped to consolidate the position of the two terms as definitive markers.

In fact, what happened with the Communists was the same thing that had happened with the Socialists before 1914: protest led to integration. The vehement insistence on separation ultimately reinforced the need for unity. At first the Communists were even more intransigent about refusing to play the "republican game." The new revolutionary party that emerged from the schism of 1920 was not content merely to pour scorn on class collaboration; it rejected outright both traditional contenders as "two factions of the bourgeoisie."[86] In the 1924 elections, the first major elections in which it took part, the Communist Party could not find words harsh enough for the "bloc of newly rich bourgeois" that was running as the "left" against the "bloc of satisfied bourgeois."[87] In opposition to the incumbent Bloc National and alongside the revived "union of the left" in which Radicals and Socialists joined forces as the Cartel des Gauches[88] after the disappointing results of 1919, in which the parties had taken their case to the voters separately, the P.C.F. ran a *Bloc Ouvrier et Paysan*, whose propaganda focused on denouncing the false political alternative being offered to the voters, an alternative that masked the only real division, that between capital and labor. "Right-wing capitalists and left-wing capitalists are the same."[89] The left was merely another face of the right: "Behind two masks, one face: On May 11 you will not be faced with a single National Bloc: there will be two, one on the right, the other on the left."[90] From this came the definitive campaign, which was repeated like a leitmotif: "No to the rightist National Bloc and no to the leftist National Bloc."[91] Yet one cannot help noticing that the rejected categories played an extraordinarily significant role in the culture and even the practice of the new party. At the Congress of Tours, delegates were seated according to the old parliamentary divisions of right, center, and left. The official minutes noted "applause from the center," "protests on the right," and "turmoil on the left" just like the most routine bourgeois assembly. At the moment the decisive vote was taken, we learn that "the left sang *L'Internationale*. The right repeated *L'Internationale*. Shouts on the right: *Vive Jaurès!* Shouts on the left: *Vive Jaurès et Lénine!*"[92] Even more significant, the inner councils of the party were divided along the same lines. In November 1924, Monatte, Rosmer, and Delegarde published an open letter to party members in which they complained of being labeled "right-wing" by party leaders: "We are quite certain that we do not belong to the right of the party." They insisted on being put down as members of "a tendency that might be called the workers' left" rather than of "the pestilential right" to which the leadership wished to assign them.[93] Party leaders repeatedly proclaimed the need to do battle on two fronts, against "right-wing opportunism" on the one hand and against "self-styled radical leftist practice" on the other. All these signs attest to

FIGURE 7.1   Another example of the "representation of representation." The date, April 1820, is no accident. The Duc de Berry had just been assassinated, an event that triggered an offensive by the forces of reaction and resistance by liberal speakers. Because of this sharp antagonism and passionate commitment to the issues, the 1820 session played an important role in crystallizing the left-right distinction and leading different sectors of public opinion to identify with parliamentary factions.

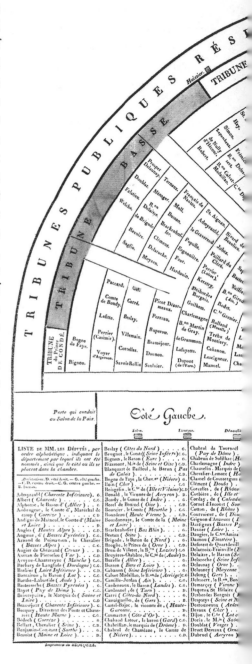

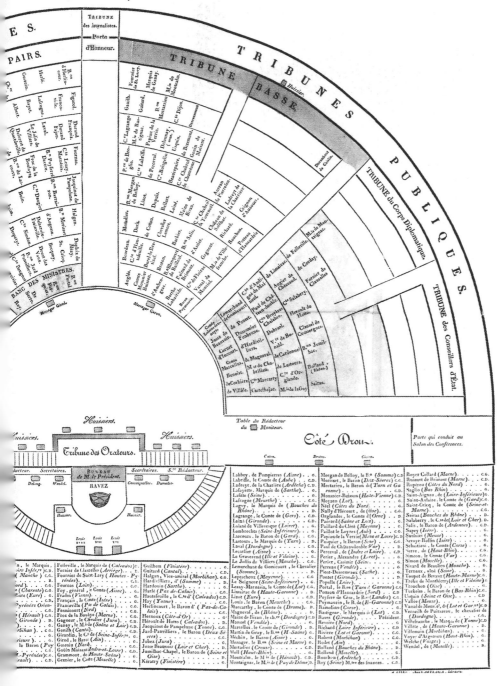

DE LA CHAMBRE DES DÉPUTÉS,

place qu'occupe chacun des Membres qui la composent.

(Avril 1820.)

the deep inroads made by the new organizational geography. Even if the left-right distinction was declared meaningless in the official elections, it was inevitably in terms of that distinction that one oriented oneself politically and thought about the party's own everyday activity. Hence it should come as no surprise that the Central Committee deplored the force of left-right identifications in the 1928 legislative elections. In the meantime the election laws had been modified. The proportional system used in the 1919 and 1924 elections had made it fairly easy for a candidate to run as his own man. The return to uninominal voting by district once again raised the delicate problem of whether a candidate should remain in the running in the second round or drop out and throw his support to another candidate. The Communist leadership was under no illusion: "Many workers still see the Party as the farthest left of all the parties," so that a "mechanical tactic of resignation in favor of the best-placed 'left-wing' candidate ahead of the Communist candidate allows people to assume, despite our statements, that the Communist Party is the extreme wing of the Cartel des Gauches or a participant in some neo-cartel."[94] This made it difficult to bring out the uniqueness of a party that, "by its very essence, is steadfastly opposed to all political formations of the bourgeoisie," because the psychological mechanism of the vote, by this point firmly established in the public mind, inevitably imposed the prevailing symbolism. In order to break out of this traditional encirclement the Central Committee proposed the "proletarian formula *class against class*" as opposed to "the republican formula *reds against whites*."[95] The Communist tactic of systematically maintaining its candidate in the second round led to a series of three-way races from which the right profited, although some Communist voters defied party orders to vote for the candidate of the "republican left." Tradition would ultimately prove stronger than the will to secede. The 1932 elections revealed the limits of the "class against class" strategy: the Communist Party vote declined from 11.3 to 8.3 percent. The party nevertheless insisted, rather half-heartedly, on maintaining its candidates, but this time 500,000 of its 800,000 voters broke ranks and voted for the better-placed left-wing candidate. This spelled the end of the attempt to defy established polarities in the name of class conflict. Despite their rhetoric of social difference, the Communists were integrated into the established political opposition. On the whole, even "class-conscious" proletarians identified with an all-inclusive left opposed to the right more than they saw themselves specifically and exclusively as proletarians opposed to the bourgeoisie.

This is not the place to recount the story of how the P.C.F. ultimately decided to follow the lead of its own voters. I will not retrace the obscure path that Maurice Thorez followed between February 6, 1934, when he vilified "fascist gangs" and "left-wing ministers and deputies" in the same breath as "the cholera and the plague,"[96] and October 10, 1934, when he first pronounced the words "popular front." If the party had been firm in its will to secede, it was even more fervent in support of the "triumphant union of the lefts" of 1936, a marriage around which a veritable mystique developed. The left was reinvigorated by the extreme left: the 1936 Barodet was notable for the number of expressions linking "the left and the extreme left," both positively and negatively. In the March 1934 issue of *Marianne*, Emmanuel Berl noted the contrast between "the strong sentimental significance" that the words *right* and *left* continued to have in the country and their vagueness and therefore lack of effectiveness on the political level.[97] It seems accurate, moreover, that the challenge to the right-left dichotomy from two sides—on the one hand the very small but intellectually influential extreme right and on the other hand the very isolated but socially representative extreme left—seriously hindered its practical usefulness. The realignment of the left, which took place against a background of antifascism, greatly clarified the situation. Thorez was thus correct to distinguish between the prewar Cartel (and its 1920s offshoots) and the Popular Front: "One sometimes hears or reads," he said in his report to the Villeurbanne Congress early in 1936, "that the Popular Front is nothing but the old Cartel des Gauches expanded to include Communists. This is not correct." There is no need to go into the obvious reasons why he felt obliged to clear himself of the charge of class collaboration, which presumably had been the fatal defect of these earlier alliances: "The Cartel des Gauches was a segment of the working class hitched to a bourgeois clique.... The Popular Front is the working class through its own activity influencing the workers of the middle classes and dragging them into battle against the bourgeoisie, capital, and fascism."[98] Beyond the stereotypes and the wooden language, an important idea emerges from this. The Popular Front was not a mere extension of a well-honed set of preexisting alliances. The participation of the Communists led to a realignment of the left and a recasting of its identity to transcend the diversity of its concrete components. In that recasting, events played an important part: Léon Blum became the first Socialist to serve as president of the council, and the Communists nearly doubled their vote. Once again the same mechanism was at work: a unified identity was reestablished by integrating a force that had previously seemed unintegrable. More precisely, class difference was digested and metabolized into political affiliation; whether that difference was real or imagined is of little importance here, because it was representations and symbols that were at stake. Having long thundered against the "left," the P.C.F. would soon hold the key to the "real" left, and for a long time to come. To that end it received powerful help from memory and history. Its reintegration into the nation at the time of the Popular Front allowed the party to benefit from the unique legitimacy attached to the heritage of the Jacobin Revolution: it availed itself of a primogeniture that accrued from "having breathed the spirit of the people back into *La Marseillaise*," as the celebrated "Letter to Daladier" put it in October 1936.[99] World War II and the Resistance then added the credit attaching to defense of the endangered fatherland. Standing at the intersection of the national past with the future of mankind as embodied in the Bolshevik Revolution's fulfillment of the promises of 1793, the party of the proletariat ostensibly became the standard of reference against which left-wing values were measured, for all that the party's political behavior raised doubts and for all its own ambiguity about the term "left," which was cultivated precisely because it symbolized a broad coalition but which was therefore always used with caution by a party bent on preserving its own revolutionary distinctiveness.[100] But all this simply amplified and deployed the effects of the formative operation of 1936, the last and ultimate of its kind. The symbolic unity of the left worked in favor of the partner which for fifteen years had embodied implacable division. More precisely, unity bestowed symbolic mastery of the situation on the party that had embedded social division within political division and that could always undo what it had done.

Once again the left had the initiative in this process. It would be artificial to proceed by symmetry with the right. It was on the left that the division between right and left was affirmed, underscored, and dramatized in parallel with the redefinition of the left as left. Under pressure the right set itself up as the party of resistance. Its reluctance even to call itself "the right" concealed an even stronger distaste for the antagonism that the left was now so keen to emphasize. Significantly, the right's campaign rhetoric was far more likely to denounce the left than to assert its own identity as the right (or even simply to call itself by that name). Rather than promote itself, the right preferred to blacken the name of the opposition and to forecast disaster "if the lefts should triumph."[101] In doing so, however, it played the game of division that it liked to denounce, if only in the mode of denial. It is as instructive, perhaps, as it is paradoxical that the militants of the extreme right, who insisted that they had no use for either right or left, did not shrink from using the term "right." To be sure, they generally did so in order to mark their distance, unambiguously, from those closest to them in the political spectrum, for whom they felt nothing but contempt. In March 1936, for example, Brasillach launched a memorable attack on the "cuckolds of the right" for their public disapproval of a physical attack on Léon Blum by militants of the Action Française: "The real scandal in what has to be called the Blum Affair...is the attitude of the deputies of the right."[102] In more measured terms Thierry Maulnier made the same point a few months later when he warned "the traditional right" that it had best not count on the support of "stalwart and hopeful youths."[103] To compel the right to recognize itself as such was to rescue it from the torpor into which it had sunk with "the amorphous mass of moderates." Hence this ought to be the first action of those on the right who wished to react against its "bankruptcy." Sometimes the appellation was accepted in the name of realism only to be treated with a hint of disdain if not held at arm's length with scare quotes. Take Jean-Pierre Maxence, the founder of the pro-fascist journal *L'Insurgé*, who began one article with a summary of the grounds for abandoning hope in the "organized right," the "bourgeois right," and the "corporalist right" (*droite capo-raliste*). In those dark weeks of December 1936 and January 1937, he went on, *L'Insurgé* wished to align itself with the reaction against "the disillusionment, discouraged solitude, and impotent rage of the best in the face of the collapse of the 'right.' "[104] The difference was between the moderates who hoped to remain ignorant of what was troubling them and the activists determined to take a cold, hard look at reality because they intended to transcend it. Moderates were still trying to deal with real divisions abstractly, whereas activists were determined to abolish them and so had no difficulty naming them. Sternhell dates the first use of the slogan "neither right nor left" about 1927. Georges Valois was supposedly one of the first to use it in his book *Le Fascisme*.[105] Note, however, that this was some time after the Communist dismissal of the two "bourgeois blocs," with which it has a great deal in common, except that for the Communist Party the idea was to denounce a false division that was supposed to conceal a real division of class, whereas for the ultra-right the point of rejecting the artificial opposition of the parties was to restore the nation as the supreme unifying principle. What is more, the Communists in the end would consecrate the division by appropriating it, while their most implacable adversaries would seize upon this as grounds for clinging to their refusal of the whole notion.

This phase of extremist protest was a crucial moment in annealing the opposition of right and left. It made the pair's status more complex: the reference became indispensable, yet its relation to reality was relativized. It emerged from these various challenges on the whole stronger than ever. The Communist turn infused it with new energy. The rejection by pro-fascists helped in a roundabout way to preserve it: even those determined to escape its hold could not do so. To reject the right-left dichotomy was still to define one's position in relation to it, if only in the hope of transcending it. Those who proclaimed its disappearance dug themselves into a hole. In a general sense, the revolutionary promise to restore unity, whether in the form of a classless society or an organically unified nation, tended to corroborate the notion that political division is intrinsic to the present era. Criticism did have its effects, however. It altered the relation of the terms decisively. By forcefully focusing attention on the wide gap between political categories and social ones, critics showed that *right* and *left* were conventional appellations, and this in no small way helped to make them more flexible and adaptable. It was understood that the boundary between right and left did not coincide with the boundary between proletariat and bourgeoisie. It was accepted that citizens of one nation could oppose one another as right and left. In other words, political division was one dimension through which realities of a different order could be represented by means of a constructed language. It was precisely because *right* and *left* were artificial constructs not precisely coincident with social realities that they could be manipulated in such a way as to subsume those realities. On the one hand, in a climate of combat and revolution, the right-left opposition was pregnant with meaning and importance, while on the other hand, under the influence of similar absolute visions of earthly salvation, it was the political relativity of the pair that stood out, to the point where suspicions, at times ironic and at times indignant, of a false left or pseudo-right became intimately bound up with the use of the terms in the 1930s.[106] The two developments might seem contradictory if we were not duly warned about the split functioning of these identifying labels. In fact they were complementary, one in the realm of involvement, the other in the realm of observation. The whole secret of the right-left couple lay in its ability to attract militants while simultaneously providing analytic distance. Magical adherence to sacred names and wariness of being taken in by misleading labels or abstractions actually reinforced each other. From this came the full deployment of a system of definitions whereby actors could deal simultaneously with their convictions and calculations.

The dramatic polarization of Communism and Fascism ultimately reactivated the structural factors that had helped to root the right-left dichotomy in the heart of French political life. In this respect the convulsive decade leading up to World War II was the culmination of a long history. Although conditions had changed radically, the age of mass politics and totalitarian passions continued to exhibit the same interplay of unity and division, the same dialectic of center and extremes, that once drove the constricted parliamentary politics of the Restoration. In 1935 the scale, content, and stakes of the political contest were no longer what they had been in 1815, but the order of battle was formally analogous. Hence the game did not destroy the old left-right opposition but actually reinforced it. What was crucial was for a radical division of public opinion to coincide with a political game in which there are more than two players. If there are only two parties, then there is no need for any additional identification beyond party name. People can identify themselves as "Democrats" or "Republicans" as in the United States. If there is to be a left and a right, there must also be a third term, a center. But if there is a center, then each of the lateral parties is itself subject to radical tendencies. Hence there are at least two rights, a "right right" and an "extreme right," and similarly there are at least two lefts. What is more, the attraction of the poles divides the center into a center right and a center left. This division of opinion, insofar as it complicates the situation of each camp when it comes to power, has the practical political result that left, right, and center all become virtually tripartite. This is the basic configuration that leads to the adoption of *right* and *left* as basic terms of identification. It is the result of an untenable bipolarity, a bipolarity so intense that it cannot be contained within a two-party system, so that factions tend to multiply rather than unite. Now, it was this basic logic that the historical situation revitalized with particular clarity after the

Bolshevik Revolution and the triumphs of Mussolini in Italy and Hitler in Germany. Not that right and left had ever disappeared in France: as we have seen, the combination of conflict with fragmentation had remained a permanent feature of French politics, the defining characteristic of its style. But the radical movements of the twentieth century restored a clarity to the pattern that circumstances had at times obscured.

What helped to clarify matters most of all was the unprecedented prominence of the extremes, which achieved ideological dominance in this period. (Significantly, the Larousse dictionary records the first use of the term *extrémisme* in 1922.) I say *ideological* dominance because while the clash between revolution and a newly revolutionary counterrevolution inundated public space with its symbolism, it was a long way from such omnipresence on the social scene to political predominance. To be sure, the million and a half votes received by the Communists in the 1936 elections made them a third force to be reckoned with on the left, slightly ahead of the Radicals and still far behind the Socialists. But they remained outside of the political game, and their ability to influence their own partners in effective political terms remained quite limited, even though it was their vision of society's future that obsessed everyone who thought about such things. The disproportion was much more flagrant on the right, where the Action Française received relatively few votes despite the far-reaching intellectual and moral influence it had achieved over bourgeois opinion. Then there were also explicitly Fascist groups, which were able to make very little political capital out of the increasingly marked sympathies on the right, and particularly in the right-wing press, for the regimes they admired. Indeed, this disparity between left and right is a large part of the story. It was responsible for the dual dynamic of head-on confrontation coupled with factional tendencies in both camps. The prevailing rhetoric of combat made party competition seem like an ineluctable confrontation of two hostile blocs whose absolute divergence on all issues offered two stark historical alternatives to the human race. Nevertheless, in the moments of greatest tension it was not Communism and Fascism that squared off but, once again, indeed more than ever, left versus right. This was because the two camps were so divided internally that they had to be held together metaphysically, and no single party was in a position to impose its own name or distinctive trademark. Those who dominated symbolically did not wield effective power, and those who were politically powerful were symbolically subordinate. Hence the division was as indeterminate as it was fervent and clearly delineated. Right and left prevailed as ideal identifying categories in a situation in which it was impossible to identify the terms of political division with concrete protagonists. Unifying labels were needed to achieve the intensity associated with the duality of friend and enemy; those labels could not be borrowed from the name of any particular party; hence people resorted once again to the abstract neutrality, to the infinite flexibility, as well as to the drastic simplification of right versus left.

Contrary to what a superficial view might suggest, then, Manichaean dualism actually feeds on fragmentation of the political contest. Manichaeanism does not occur in two-party systems, where the center is generally the main battleground, but in a system in which the camps are irreducibly composite. If France has been the scene of clear-cut, dramatic political contests that have earned it a reputation as a *locus classicus* of political conflict, the reason is that it has always been a country in which a considerable variety of political thought, opinion, and parties have flourished. This is particularly clear in the 1930s, a time of veritable dissociation between the sphere of realities and that of political identities or, if you will, between politics as thought and politics as practice. A tacit division of labor was established between the conduct of political affairs and the governance of political consciences. In practice moderates for the most part continued to collude, centrists continued to share power. Exceptions to this rule were rare and short-lived. This did not prevent the doctrinaires of the extreme right and the extreme left from gaining the upper hand, however; indeed, it was grist for their mill. The compromises of the moderates only pointed up the rigor of the extremists (while conversely the intransigence of the extremists justified the inglorious malleability of the moderates). The ideologues did not determine how people behaved but did determine how people defined themselves. Political identities were determined, not primarily by the prosaic choices associated with the administration of things as they are, but by options as to society's ultimate salvation.[107] Thus the influence of ideological panjandrums with no stake in electoral politics but a lock on symbolic mastery turned the political arena into a pitiless battlefield of good versus evil, light versus darkness. Yet this implacable and virulent dualism not only did nothing to prevent dissension and irreparable splits in each of the armies so pathetically at grips, it actually grew out of and lived on that dissension. One can even say that dualism and internal opposition constituted a system: within each camp you had governmental centrism and utopian extremism. And this kind of system becomes more active and visible when the historical situation is such as to encourage extremes.

Let us look a little more closely at the distribution of forces and the composition of the two camps. In the totalitarian era the tension between center and periphery comes to be associated with a very clear issue: the acceptance or rejection of democratic coexistence. Both the extreme right and extreme left propose a permanent solution to the political division of the present: unification either in the bosom of a unanimous nation or in the form of a classless society. In such a situation, that of a democracy living with the challenge to its own right to exist, one has a schism of principle on both the right and the left between a party for which preserving democratic competition is paramount and another party which engages in that competition (with sufficient ardor, moreover, to dominate it) for the sole purpose of doing away with it. There will most likely also be an intermediate party attempting to strike a compromise between the ideological aspiration for a definitive solution and democratic realities. In other words, there will be three lefts and three rights. A radical (in the French sense of the relatively moderate Radical Party) left, trusting in the Republic by itself to resolve the social question; a Communist left, committed to revolution and the socialization of property; and, between the two, a Socialist left hoping to marry doctrinal collectivism with republican practice. On the right there will be a liberal right (again in the French sense of *libérale*) fervently supportive of free enterprise and the free market; a traditionalist right, preoccupied with the need to restore a hierarchical order undermined by individualism (and itself divided between *anciens* and *modernes*, classical reactionaries nostalgic for the monarchy and fascists more confident in the nation and the leader than in the king as sources of organic cohesion); and between the two an authoritarian right, anxious to reconcile popular sovereignty with the supreme imperatives of government.

Note that in this distribution the divisions on the right are potentially more serious than those on the left. The various lefts share a similar idea of the opposition and a similar faith in the necessity and fruitfulness of struggle, which helps to bring them together. The radical may regret the Communist's brutal language of class yet be ready himself to resort if need be to denunciation of the clerical peril, and so the two can manage to wage war as comrades. On the right, however, distaste for the very idea of antagonism is reflected in a sharp divergence between extremists and moderates. Even the most conciliatory have no choice but to confront opponents on the attack, but the tendency on the right is to characterize one's opponents as sowers of a discord that would not otherwise exist. This is expressed in another way by the refusal to avow explicitly that one is on the right, even if one's outspoken hostility to the left is tantamount to declaring one's colors by contrast with the enemy's. The reason for such refusal is that to do otherwise would be tantamount to admitting that there are structural reasons for division and discord within what one would prefer to think of as a harmonious collectivity or a united nation. If sharpened and radicalized, the same idea can be used to justify the opposite behavior, however: denial turns into frantic accusation. Given the belief that the existence of the community ultimately depends on absolute unity, the totalitarian spirit derives its identity from a constitutive menace and a fatal enemy, for which blame is invariably imputed to the undermining efforts of some alien element (there being no possible internal cause of dissension): often that enemy is unmasked, with elective anguish, as that unassimilable yet indistinguishable presence, the Jew. To the extent that there is combat—the inevitable combat required if the national organism is to survive—there are camps that the militant persuaded of his mission does not hesitate to join. This explains the frequently observed fascination of the extreme right with the rhetoric and methods of the extreme left, where it found more useful models for its disputatious tendencies than among its natural allies. However deep the gulf created on the left by the debate over democratic forms, there was a common left-wing culture of conflict capable of overcoming political differences in the name of a shared identity. On the right, however, the free-marketer's tendency to minimize contradictions was at the opposite extreme from the Fascists', and even the authoritarians', absolute repudiation of democratic conflict; the differences in outlook, language, and style seemed almost insurmountable, even inconceivable. Ultimately, however, this did not prevent ideological cooperation in the name of an ideal polity free of the pernicious ferment of division. It did, however, make it all but impossible to forget the underlying differences, even in times of coalition. In short, while the left was at least mythically one, the right was in practice divided. This difference derives in large part from the contrast between a symbolism of implicit unity and an irreducibly plural identity.[108]

This approach may also offer a new perspective on the difficult question of whether, as René Rémond suggests, the plural forms of the right in the nineteenth century stand in a relation of continuity to the several currents of the right in the twentieth century.[109] To what extent did legitimism, Bonapartism, and Orleanism extend their influence through the ultra-nationalist, authoritarian, and free-market sensibilities that dominated in the realignment of the right that led to the flourishing of new parties after 1900? The question can also be raised in regard to the left, as the often-asked question of the relation of Jacobinism to Communism shows. While I do not pretend to resolve this issue here, I think that it is possible to shed light on what it is that makes this question so profoundly important. If there is continuity, it is primarily a consequence of structure. What remains relatively intangible is the rule of distribution in consequence of which there are always (roughly) three ideal types of right and left. Since representative government was established in France under the sign of radical conflict—from the outside in the name of a tradition to be maintained, from the inside in the name of the social content to be imputed to the new regime—its concrete political realization implied a more or less permanent division between moderate proponents (whether of monarchical or republican leanings) and resolute adversaries (including those determined to wipe out the new regime and those determined to move beyond it), in addition to which, the starkness of this opposition gave rise to reconciliatory tendencies on both sides. Very quickly the Napoleonic regime gave remarkably durable force and influence to this need for synthesis, ending the Revolution by combining nostalgia for personalized authority with a plebiscitary legitimacy stemming from the revolutionary past. From the Girondins to the *démocs-socs* of the Second Republic, the search for a balance between greater liberty and the demands of collective sovereignty in economic and social matters certainly occupied many minds. Of course the location of the main battle lines did not remain stable. The pendulum having swung in a reactionary direction, public debate between 1815 and 1848 returned to the narrowly political issue of monarchy versus republic. Nevertheless, even within the restrictive framework of the institutions of that period, there was room enough for political forces to array themselves in what might be called their "classical" pattern, with a centrist government facing opposition from both extremes, at once separated and bound by mixed forms intended to bring together the idealism of the *doctrinaires* with the realism of the possible. The important point is that the revolutionary legacy defined the extremes once and for all in a way that would remain surprisingly untouchable for almost two centuries. As a result, the "advanced liberals" of the 1820s, who did not even go so far as to call themselves republicans, nevertheless carried the burden of being identified with Jacobinism. This was not merely a polemical ploy: the identification had real symbolic value stemming from the primal scene to which all political action had to be related in order to be understood. Hence the development first of republicanism and later of socialism within and alongside the republican movement would also be interpreted in terms of the same primal scene. The same can be said of the advent of the Communists. Despite the reservations of Marxism about Robespierrism's bourgeois limitations, the Communists did not hesitate to make all they could out of the comparison. Thus despite the formidable "leftward shift" entailed by the democratization of French politics over the course of the nineteenth century, the symbols marking the limits of the political domain, from ultraroyalism to ultra-Jacobinism, would remain remarkably constant. This was an important element of continuity, the significance of which must be measured in conjunction with the persistence, over the same period of democratization, of tripartite organization in both the party of order and the party of change.

In this respect the political recomposition that has taken place since the beginning of the century is exemplary. With the parallel reformulation of both the revolutionary project and the counterrevolutionary program, it was as if the twentieth century was going to repeat or replicate the nineteenth. It seemed that democracy had become an accepted part of political life. In a deep sense it had: its principle of legitimacy was sufficiently well established for even its adversaries to be obliged to respect it. Yet even in victory it spurred two utopian challenges, one backward-looking, the other forward, which would subject it to an assault of unprecedented magnitude. Under the pressure of these challenges a new family of political views emerged, a family quite similar in structure to that which the Revolution bequeathed its successors. In terms of content, of course, continuity is illusory, even when it is explicitly claimed. Whatever Charles Maurras may have believed, he had little in common with his royalist predecessors of the nineteenth century, from whom he was separated by a crucial event, the conversion to nationalism. Nationalism obliged the right to redefine itself around an image of collective power, which propelled it in spite of itself into individualistic modernity. The recycling of nostalgia for the Ancien Régime as ultranationalism brings us to the "age of fascisms." Make no mistake: I am not claiming that the reference to the past played no real role. On the contrary, if one wants to understand how the Action Française, one of the first expressions of fascist sentiment, differed from the more virulent expressions that followed it in Italy and Germany, one has to give careful consideration to this commitment to the past. Indeed, there was something like an inverse proportion between totalitarian intensity and the determination to uphold tradition. If the common objective of all fascisms was to ensure unity through authority, it is also true that the greater the degree to which social forms were explicitly borrowed from the monarchical, hierarchical, organic past, the less comprehensive and violent was the associated totalitarianism. By contrast, the less powerful the faith in tradition, the greater the need for power and the rivalry with Bolshevism (most notoriously in the case of Nazism, the reinvention of the nation as a force united for war around a leader and a race), and the more likely it was that totalitarianism would veer out of control. In France it was probably the vigor of the counterrevolutionary spirit and the cultural prominence of the Ancien Régime model that limited the spread of fascisms of the Mussolinian or Hitlerian type.

As far as collective symbolism is concerned, it was a matter of some importance that the new was so strongly linked to the old, to the point where all that was new about the twentieth century was submerged in the changeless conflict launched in 1789. The same was true on the left, despite the desire for a break with the past, and even allowing for the importance of the tradition of the workers' movement in Bolshevism. The Leninist party was indeed something new, not only as an instrument for seizing power but even more as a bridge to the classless society. Yet this image of perfect military unity of minds, wills, and actions, of precise subordination of every cog to the overall doctrine of the machine—a unity destined to extend to the entire collectivity once the party subsumed the state—was easily assimilated in France into the rich imagery of '93, the Committee of Public Safety, popular unanimity, and the necessary Terror. In a strange way, because of these multifarious roots, the age of totalitarianism would be an almost classical period in French political history, reviving the most canonical distribution of forces while at the same time infusing new vigor into basic historical emblems. Under pressure from the implacable and systematic enemies of democracy, the division within each camp over the question of liberty would be reduced to its elementary simplicity, complicated by the inevitable attempt to avoid the dilemma. On the left the configuration of the parties corresponded almost exactly to the ideal tripartite pattern, with the Socialists holding the balance between those worried champions of individual rights, the Radicals, and those uncompromising worshipers of social power, the Communists. There was nothing comparable on the right, not even the extreme right, where parties as a rule were fragmented and ill-defined. Our typology proves useful in this situation, however, for with it we can identify three broad allegiances roughly comparable to legitimism (systematically hostile to an individualistic world view), Orleanism (willing to accept a version of modern industrial society and representative government), and Bonapartism (obsessed with the need to transform popular sovereignty into authority). Of course these labels apply only if we are not too insistent on demonstrating any actual connection with their historical bearers, the credibility of which depends entirely on the apparent (and fundamentally misleading) analogy with intransigent royalism.

What actually persists and counts, however, is the structure that imposes these symmetrical tripartitions. While the content and issues may change, the central question remains the same, and with it the range of possible fundamental choices. What the structure determines is of course not parties or even "spiritual families" in Thibaudet's sense.[110] It is rather a probability that opinion will form itself into certain clusters whose content is relatively indeterminate but whose configuration is remarkably stable. This framework of opinion establishes a political infrastructure, upon which the pressure of circumstances, the impress of historical experience, and the influence of individuals works to create relatively complex and shifting political alliances that to one degree or another reflect the underlying pattern. Yet not everything in the public arena can be traced back in a simple way to this structuring kernel. There are authentic spiritual families that grow out of specific situations or concerns and cannot be explained in terms of infrastructure. One such family is associated with industrialism, which Thibaudet rightly singles out. It arose in response to the peculiar difficulties that France, starting with its elites, had in converting to material modernity. Another example is the Christian Democratic family and its representative effort to make a place for religious consciousness in the world of liberty. Indeed, this second example points up the inadequacy of the notion of "spiritual family" when it comes to answering the question we have posed. The idea deserves credit for introducing an essential distinction between what is unstable and what is permanent, which in turn helps to clarify the high degree of stability of currents of feeling and thought behind the ceaseless revision of party programs. In pursuit of such deep historical continuities, however, it confuses phenomena of different levels under a single head based on a single, too narrowly descriptive criterion. Not all of what persists is of the same order. Spiritual families exist, and they are characterized by a combination of psychological embeddedness and semantic inertia, but these factors cannot account for the powers of permanence evident in the truly fundamental divisions in the political realm. That permanence is rooted in the internal coherence of the positional system. It stems from the logic of a mode of definition of political duality that divides each camp in two before effecting a final realignment into three. The lines of force determined in this way are therefore relatively independent of the historically specific content. All this remains within the limits of the basic question: Where does liberty stand between revolution and counterrevolution? Not only does the question remain the same, but so do the extremes in opposition. But if the continuity of attitudes and mentalities over time in part reflects what we know in general about the viscosity of representations and passions, it is also in part an optical illusion. In reality it is the rule of distribution that it is invariable: despite the changeless language of tradition, the forms in which the various components express themselves change profoundly. Since the framework is fixed, however, one has the largely illusory impression of watching the metamorphoses of a singular object. Out of this comes the interminable debate between the proponents of discontinuity, whose attention is focused primarily on the huge shift in the nature of politics over the past 125 years, and the advocates of continuity, who focus more on the perpetuation of certain regular patterns in the midst of change. There is no point in trying to settle the issue. It is better to try to understand how such a dilemma arises out of the interaction of structural constraints with a prevailing symbolic system.

The obsessive centrality of the right-left pairing, whose culmination came in 1939, was therefore not a product of chance but the epitome of a history. It is by no means inconsequential that these two words possess the astonishing property of absorbing and reducing everything to one common denominator: their elementary Manichaeanism is in effect a concentrate of the twists and subtleties of an entire political tradition. They offer a simple formula to sum up the complex algebra of a system of many variables. Their simplifying dualism is the result of combining at least two overlapping triples: the tripartite internal structure of both the party of order and the party of change, and the tripartite rule that governs the structure of political space around a governmental center with opposition on two flanks. Features of this system that may seem contradictory at first sight are actually perfectly compatible. It may seem strange, to say the least, that such a simplifying opposition can coexist with the irreducible (and conflict-ridden) plurality of supposedly simple essences. And it may seem astonishing that the discourse of confrontation that dominates at the ideological level can coexist with accommodation at the practical level. In fact, these are different aspects of a single system, the system engendered by the conditions under which representative government found its embodiment in France.[111] In the aftermath of the Revolution opinion was so torn that the only way to establish a government of opinion was for power to be shared among the various camps, each of which found itself inexplicably faced with conflict between extremists and moderates within its own bosom. This was the basic situation in which the French developed a system of political definition with three distinctive features: 1) in contrast to the two-party system, the government-opposition polarity is reproduced within each camp; 2) as a result, an evolving rule of internal distribution ultimately takes the form of a tripartite structure; 3) politics as thought is consequently dissociated from politics as practice, because control over identity and boundaries is ceded to the extremes. To the extent that political life is organized around a fixed central pivot rather than an alternation in power of two blocs, the right-left terminology is likely to take hold. To the extent that the system reflects a radical division dependent for its vitality on the extremes, only a drastically simplified opposition will do (although further divisions within this basic system are by no means excluded). And finally, to the extent that such a system can take shape only in a coalition in which no single party dominates, neutral denominations are necessary: unlike party names, these denominations must be acceptable to all yet impossible to appropriate. Dry terms of classification, *right* and *left* were thus able to rise to the rank of ultimate identifications, quivering with passion and laden with memories. It is a rare thing indeed for so many passions, events, and ideas to have been poured into two meager words to disappear as into a melting pot. Each word encompasses the soul, the memory, of a way of political being. The ubiquitous use of these terms expresses what is most paradoxical about them: the primacy of identification over membership. To speak the language of right and left is to identify with a camp without belonging to a party—but it is difficult to belong to a party in a world where motivating issues are always dividing against themselves, and it is this difficulty that has redounded to the benefit of the right-left opposition, the indubitably expressive totem of a society strange in so many ways, not least for having combined a traditionally high degree of politicization with chronically weak political organizations.

On the Dualist Organization of Contemporary Societies

Two sets of questions remain. First, what exactly is the role of the right-left opposition in a world profoundly different from that in which it first took hold? What significance does it still have, and how likely is it to survive? These questions are not unrelated to the second set. Indeed, the right-left opposition has in the meantime become a universal idiom, and this fact has naturally had an impact on its use. How did such a quintessential product of what is most singular in French history become a universal figure of speech adaptable to any context? Did this occur at the price of a distortion of the pair's original meaning? Or did the peculiarities of French experience have the effect of bringing to light a truly universal dimension of modern political experience, hence one that could easily be appropriated and incorporated into a range of political categories?

Superficially, it might seem that French politics in its traditional form has simply persisted since 1945. It continues on its old course, and the right-left division has survived with it. To be sure, the extreme right all but disappeared, destroyed by the defeat of fascism. What is more, the traditional right emerged from the trial deeply discredited. As its opposition it faced a left wreathed in victorious heroism, more than ever inclined to identify itself as "the left," and more than ever dominated by the Communist extreme. For there to be a left, there must be a right. The symbolic and moral domination of the left normally would have helped to perpetuate the strength of the old division. Of course that division was rejected more vehemently than ever by the supposed right, whose traditional reluctance to identify itself as "the right" was reinforced by its determination to separate itself from a dishonorable past. The Gaullist current was ideally placed to herald this view. Even the presidential phenomenon (since 1962) has not diminished the right-left opposition. It has, however, altered one of the chief factors that contribute to maintaining it by giving an absolute parliamentary majority to one party, the president's party, on several occasions. At the same time it has helped to harden the right-left opposition by turning it into the basic fact about the supreme election, the iron law of presidential politics. The voting system—the winner must receive an absolute majority in the second of two rounds of voting—promotes a system in which many parties run candidates in the first round only to group into two "Manichaean" blocs for the final battle: the tried and true formula of republican discipline. The multiparty system survives, and it is only the pooling of all the votes on the "right" or the "left" that elects the president. The de Gaulle years shook the system, for the majoritarian logic implicit in the selection of the chief executive by plebiscite seemed irresistible, so that "between the Communists and us" everyone else was "nothing" and had no choice but to accept that position of insignificance. But the revival of the Socialist Party and the emergence of the Union of the Left in the 1970s ushered in an era particularly rich in celebrations of the fundamental antagonism. Politically, the center all but evaporated, yet the recurrent insistence on the need to find an "opening" to what was left of it shows that the basic structural tropism remained intact. As one president (Valéry Giscard d'Estaing) revealingly put it, "France wants to be governed in the center." The moment he chose to say this was also interesting: it was a moment when the Socialist renaissance on the left and a split between the presidential party and the Gaullist party on the right had established a clearly quadripartite structure in France. With four parties the basic mechanism that we have identified was safe: right and left resulted from coalitions between parties fated to come to some kind of agreement, given that one side had a lock on power while the other seemed almost inevitably drawn to the role of opposition. Indeed the mechanism survives virtually intact if one considers the president's place in the system. His job was to locate the center in such a way as to provide a firm basis for governmental action. The location of that center did not have to be politically consistent to be symbolically quite powerful. The result was that in an institutional setting profoundly at odds with long-standing republican traditions, the most traditional formula for the distribution of political forces once again found favor—further evidence of France's invincible fidelity to her traditions.

Yet something changed in 1945. Something new began to make its way quietly at first, then more noisily, until at last it erupted to reveal the full range of its consequences. The date 1945 is somewhat arbitrary. It is chosen to draw a contrast between two postwar periods, which differed in both overall ambience and direct political impact. The reader hardly needs to be reminded that 1918 saw the emergence, on the heels of the Bolshevik Revolution, of a Communist movement in France, which led to a radicalization and eventually complete realignment of the left. The same year marked the radicalization of the extreme right, even if its themes already existed in embryo before 1914. The terrifying experience of total war provoked new outbursts of old fears. By contrast, 1945 marked the beginning of a new era, even if it took a long time for it to be noticed. It was the end of France's leftward drift, of the notorious *sinistrisme* that had determined the direction of French politics since 1815. No new force would emerge to the left of the Communists to move the whole mechanism one notch to the left. For a brief moment after 1968 it seemed as if some such development might be taking place under the influence of various *gauchiste* sects. But this time the fire on the left was only a flare-up, not a conflagration, and it prefigured a radical change of direction even on the part of the very same individuals who participated in it. It would not be long, in fact, before the *gauchiste* critique of Communism turned into a liberal critique. This time it was not simply another case in which the old well refused to yield new water. It was the beginning of an erosion, a folding inward of the extremes, most strikingly illustrated by the spectacular decline of the Communist Party during the 1980s, even as the Soviet system was beginning to lose its direction and finally disintegrate. It would be a mistake, however, to focus on the most evident aspect of the crisis without attempting to discern its more general implications. A similar though less flagrant disintegration could also be observed on the right. The Catholic "isolate" fell apart, the values of an industrialized, market society were broadly embraced, and more modern social norms were accepted: whatever remained of reactionary loyalties and hostility to egalitarian, capitalist, democratic modernity on the right suffered a setback no less serious than that inflicted on the extremism of the left. Perhaps the most telling example of this was the fact that the xenophobic extreme right, which has regained some of its strength in recent years, itself subscribed to an ultra–free market ideology imported from the United States, a doctrine that would never have passed muster with earlier nationalist extremists. The Great Depression heightened totalitarian passions and whetted the appetite for power. The long economic recession that began about 1974, which to be sure followed three decades of glorious growth and expansion of the welfare state, was reflected instead in a new sacralization of the individual, an aggressive return to liberal principles, a profound embrace of pluralist values, and a marked disillusionment with radical programs based on the primacy of the collective over the individual, whether reactionary or progressive. This was true to such an extent that the Revolution, as the 1989 Bicentennial revealed, had ceased to function as the primal scene of French politics. There was no longer any significant family or force prepared to claim the traditionalist heritage. The influence of the last remaining champions of Jacobin dictatorship and of public safety through overwhelming governmental authority appeared to be on the wane. For the first time in two hundred years, the principles of a liberal polity went unchallenged in France, safe from extremist challenges. If this change proves durable, it will certainly alter the classical uses of the left-right opposition in essential ways, because it strikes directly at that opposition's fundamental principle. In the absence of extremes well enough defined to influence the structure of politics in general, France may well move toward a two-party system, with two major political forces clashing in the center without pronounced ideological differences. *Right* and *left* would then become mere vestigial labels, drained of the spirit that once gave them life, a spirit born of an overriding need to unify irreparably divided forces. Yet culture becomes a second nature that must be reckoned with: even as politics moves toward the simplicity of a contest between a party of government and a party of opposition, are there not new parties emerging on the extremes? Political analysts once claimed that the resurgence of nationalist, xenophobic sentiment was but a flare of protest not likely to have long-term influence, yet it seems to have left a mark on the political landscape that may well be permanent. Similarly, the ecological movement was not supposed to develop into more than a marginal, if not unwelcome, influence, yet it has already acquired the dimensions of a true "spiritual family." If so, we may only be in a transitional period, about to cross a threshold not unlike the one we saw in 1900, when growing acceptance of the democratic principle refocused political debate around the question of how best to embody democracy. Ultimately this led to a resurgence of the traditional distribution of political forces, albeit in a new guise. Reform or rupture? The question typifies the major uncertainties affecting French identity today, as that identity remains as always torn between the continuity of its history and "the end of an exception" that would reduce the nation's past to pure memory.

Come what may, right and left now have a life independent of the matrix in which they first developed. They have conquered the planet to become universal political categories. They are among the basic notions that shape the functioning of contemporary societies generally. To conclude, I will investigate this prodigious good fortune. Why these words in particular? It is not enough to note, as people often do, the tendency of democratic elections to come down to a choice between two alternatives. One must also explain why this reduction is generally expressed in the language of right versus left, though more so in some places than in others (more in Europe than in North America, for example).[112] A common argument runs like this: universal suffrage requires an extreme simplification of the choices offered to citizens. Suppose for the moment that this is true. There is no shortage of binary oppositions capable of symbolizing such two-way choices: examples abound in the histories of particular countries as well as in the world's stock of symbolism. We saw an excellent example earlier with the rise and fall of the pair "red and white." Of all the possible oppositions, why did "left versus right" finally win out, and not just by supplanting the others but by establishing itself as the last resort, the epitome of all other oppositions, whether democrat versus republican, labor versus conservative, socialist versus bourgeois, or progressive versus reactionary? Another common argument is the following: In forward-looking societies open to history, societies that know they are changing and debate the issue of how they are to change, it is inevitable that a party of the past will emerge in opposition to a party of the future. Proudhon put it well after 1848: "Since humanity is progressive, and since it acts only on the basis of memories and predictions, it naturally divides into two great classes: one that is more affected by the experience of its forebears and reluctant to march forward into the uncertainties of the unknown; and another that is impatient of present ills and inclines more toward reforms."[113] This split between conservation and change is a fundamental, constitutive dimension of societies whose members believe themselves to be in the grip of change. In that case, however, why not "order versus change," which François Goguel's studies of the Third Republic show to be the opposition most relevant for understanding voting patterns in that regime?[114] Although "order versus change" fits the facts and captures a basic aspect of life in contemporary society, it remains a scholarly category with no resonance in the general public. At most it may have infiltrated the realm of social representation in the form of "reaction versus revolution." And despite the fact that "right versus left" has little inherent capacity to express duration or convey temporal tension, this spatial opposition has been able to subsume the central rift between love of established tradition and hope invested in what is new. What feeds this multifarious expressivity?

A convincing explanation would require a patient study of the spread of ideas from country to country. Among many important cases to be examined, it would be very useful, for instance, to study how right and left came to Great Britain, from the 1906 elections, which first established the Labour Party as a third force on the political scene, to the moment when Labour supplanted the Liberals as the number-two party in the interwar period. A series of comparative studies would help to reveal the factors that allowed "right versus left" to supplant whatever national divisions were previously in place. But such a project is well beyond the scope of the present essay. Since I can do no more than outline a research program, I shall instead venture to suggest two hypotheses, or, rather, a two-part hypothesis concerning the reasons for the universal acceptance of "right versus left." The first part of the hypothesis has to do with the subjective roots of the opposition, the second with its objective place in the political sphere as defined by certain fundamental principles of contemporary society. One major reason for the success of "right versus left," I submit, is that it allows political actors to identify in a physical way with the groups to which they adhere. Indeed, the right-left division is a substitute for the age-old organic symbolism in which society is depicted as a body, a substitute that takes hold in modern societies which, unlike their predecessors, can no longer be represented in organic terms. The second reason is quite different in origin. It is a consequence of the logic of democratic legitimacy and of the antinomies inextricably associated with it. In a society that recognizes no basis other than individual rights, not only is there inevitable conflict over how to translate those rights into practice, but there is, as I shall attempt to prove, no political position based on the claim to be carrying out such a translation which is not itself riven by internal contradiction. And this takes us back to reason number one. The right-left identification permits each individual to subsume the whole symbolically and to embody these internal divisions. In my view it is therefore at the point where the two forces intersect—the requirement that society be representable by the individual and the requirement that it be possible for the individual to embody the contradictions implicit in our fundamental social values—that the source of this omnipotent and omnivorous lateralization of politics resides. Right and left, in other words, belong among those primary reference points that enable us to live in the world.

Indeed, one of the fundamental requirements of any political symbolism is to justify the identification of the individual with the collective. The singular actor needs to be able to find his place in the whole; he needs to feel a part of a larger structure that makes sense in a way he can understand. For millennia this was the function of images of society as a *body,* in all their countless variants and ramifications. This organic symbolism had a very clear architecture. It was inseparable from a religious organization of the world. Its cornerstone was the union of the tangible community with its invisible foundation, from which derived the corporeal cohesion that bound the members of the community together. To put it in somewhat different terms, organic symbolism was natural to what Louis Dumont has called the holistic model of social organization. When the whole takes primacy over its parts, when the principle of collective order is prior to and takes precedence over individuals, then the imperative of belonging necessarily finds itself represented in terms of encompassment within a body. The bond between men can be symbolized as an organic one so long as it is metaphysically posited as being above their will. In many societies, and especially powerfully in the West, this expressive economy found its ideal support in the person of the king. The king's body epitomized the entire body politic, and by holding out a mirror to his subjects allowed them to represent the physical solidarity that held them together as subsumed in a materially and mystically defined individual. We must bear this root in mind if we want to understand the once all but ineradicable nostalgia for monarchical personification. What was at stake was more than a carefully considered belief; it was the possibility for individuals to achieve a stable, comprehensible representation of their society. The advent of individualistic, historical, and democratic modernity involved a break in the symbolic order, which took the form of an ineluctable loss of incorporation of the social. All dependence on a divine source evaporated, along with any sacred mooring; all at once society became something subject to change. The bonds between individuals were loosened, as the innate autonomy of each was recognized as the only possible source of order. Impersonality was ascribed to a new form of power, which emanated from the will of citizens. When unity ceased to be the defining characteristic of society at every level, it became impossible to conceive of contemporary societies as bodies. As a result, it soon became clear that modern societies were subject to a major problem of identity, by which I mean a problem of identification for society's own members. Not for nothing would these societies be challenged by waves of protest and radical subversion in many guises, yet all similar in their desire to reestablish the communal cohesion, clear self-definition, and holistic consciousness essential for individuals to represent to themselves the society in which they live—the kind of reassuringly inexhaustible, straightforwardly comprehensible representation that throughout much of human history the organic image provided. Not for nothing, too, did revolutionary (and counterrevolutionary) passions come to a head in this century, when it became clear that the realization of democracy involved the explicit division of society and institutionalization of conflict, and, more specifically, when it became clear about 1900 that the tacit model of democracy was no longer the unifying revelation of the general will but the staging of civil discord. Claude Lefort was quite right to see a fantasy of reincorporation, of restoration of the social as body, as one of the underlying goals of totalitarianism, a restoration in which the investment in the egocrat, the intense repersonification of power, also played a decisive role. If, on the other hand, democratic societies have, after so much difficulty, enjoyed a remarkable period of calm since 1945, a stability quite striking when compared with their prior history, much of the credit must go to the establishment of a symbolic apparatus capable of responding to previously frustrated needs. Was the old organic and sacral organization finally forgotten, thus making it possible for people to accustom themselves to increased activism, to the internal externality of the state, and to continual conflict? Or was it because people found the resources necessary to deal with those aspects of collective experience that had been sources of rebellion and scandal? Was that why the primitive model to which desperate people had wittingly or unwittingly clung suddenly lost its attraction and disappeared? In any case, the age of nostalgia seemed this time to have come to a close; the rupture was complete. For the first time democratic societies seemed to have discovered a foundation firm enough to permit them to live in harmony with themselves—a harmony that included, among other things, an acceptance of discord. In this evolution the development of a series of symbolic responses to the basic uncertainties inherent in a society of individuals played an important role. These responses were contained in various practical measures, whose impact as reforms has often been stressed but generally without their significance on the level of collective representations being measured. The welfare state was a response to concrete needs for protection, but it also had the effect of giving tangible form to the abstract cohesiveness of a society lacking the natural sense of belonging and solidarity that had made social cohesion immediately tangible in the past. More than that, it revealed the hidden law of our world, which is society's responsibility in the production of individuals. The reinforcement of the executive does not simply make representative regimes more governable. Through the personalization of power that goes along with it, it ends the bewilderment induced by the inconceivable notion of anonymous government. It affords citizens an identifiable grasp on the agency that is supposed to embody the collective will. Similarly, the development of an information society, which parallels that of a regime of public opinion, represents not just a technical achievement but a new way of shaping the demands implicit in the functioning of democracy, namely, the need for public control of governmental actions and for a clear expression of the general will. The universalization of right and left is one aspect of this process. It is part of a process of creating a frame of reference whose purpose is to make the underlying order of society more legible, more intelligible, and more acceptable to its members. In this process the left-right distinction occupies an important place. It symbolizes membership in a society whose law is division. It provides the symbolic vector that makes possible what would otherwise be highly improbable: identification with a fragmented collectivity. For a long time that fragmentation made the collective impossible to grasp as a whole, apprehendable only in parts. But the left-right couple relates division to a deeper organic unity. It provides a way of conceptualizing an organically integrated dualism. This was not the reason the pair first gained currency, and it was not primarily used in this way in French politics until recently. But this new fact does explain why the pair was so widely embraced, why it became a universally acceptable cliché. This symmetrical dichotomy made it possible to symbolically reduce social division to the dual indivisibility that characterizes each of us in our individuality. For millennia the body had stood for the supposedly unbreachable unity of the community; now it was mobilized to represent the community's constitutive division. I can easily and without risk project myself into this division because it already runs through me and defines me. What appears as fragmented in public space is something I carry whole within myself. If from the standpoint of politics I place myself either on the right or on the left, within myself I can be simultaneously right and left; I can switch momentarily from one to the other; I can at any moment explain the division to myself. This, by the way, amounts to saying that the expansion of the categories right and left has taken place in a climate very different from that which prevailed during most of the period in which they were used in the French tradition. Ordinarily the pair implied Manichaeanism and a spirit of exclusion. But lately, in contrast, they have spread as tokens of an ultimate solidarity of opposing terms. I can be on only one side at a time, but it is inevitable, indeed necessary, that there be two sides. Here, then, is yet another of the pair's resources: a flexibility that enables it to stand not only for conflict of the most radical sort but also for a regulated system whose parts happen to be in conflict. Right and left were once banners for the most extreme political passions. Now they are embarked on a second career as emblems of moderation. As the two terms take on this organic sense, they inevitably lose some of their virulence, or so it seems. Only the future can tell, for it seems highly likely that this symbolic reconstitution of individual commitment to an organic society marks the beginning of a new historical epoch that will endure for a long time to come.

This embodiment of conflict takes on its full meaning only when we relate it to the underlying expansion of the feeling that the contradiction is a part of social reality, indeed to such an extent that it is refracted in each of us. This vague perception takes us close to the source of the fundamental change of climate that is occurring in modern societies in the post-totalitarian age, which is to a large extent a change in the social actors' spontaneous representation of what the normal form of society is. The driving force behind totalitarianism was the feeling that contradiction was somehow a scandal to be eliminated, and on the subjective level this went along with a misapprehension of one's own contradictions. This was particularly clear in the Communist case, where the expansion of collective power soon proved to be at odds with the individual emancipation it was supposed to help bring about. But the contradictions, if less apparent, were no less real on the fascist side, where a covert affirmation of the individual distorted the restoration of the nation's organic primacy. Ideology posited the necessary return to Oneness in the form of a theory of history. If there was change, it must be moving toward some end. Fascists had an impoverished conception of that end, as a simple restoration of a communitarian and racial truth obscured by materialist and revolutionary modes of thought. Communists had a more powerful conception, as the ultimate reconciliation to be achieved at the end of the human species' long march toward self-consciousness of its production of itself. The sense of the journey from present to future was nevertheless fundamentally the same: the future inevitably meant an end to today's intolerable divisions. Bear in mind that it was by way of such myths, in which the future figured as the solution to all of today's problems, that the idea of history gradually insinuated itself into the collective consciousness over the past century. It is therefore impossible to overstate the importance of the "crisis of the future" that suddenly, under the impact of the great crisis of the 1970s, discredited all these images of reconciliation, whether reactionary or progressive, radical or moderate.[115] What evaporated in this moment of crisis was all prospect of an "end of history." Suddenly one faced a future with no end in sight. The gaping void of the unknown accounts for the return to the doctrinal sources and legitimating principles of our world: human rights, liberalism, individualism. What gives meaning to this revival is the idea that no transcendence lies in store, but rather that an open-ended creative process is possible on the basis of these existing principles and rules. Along with this goes the intuition that the insurmountable oppositions that beset modern society are rooted in these same principles. Those oppositions do not merely divide the public mind; they are also refracted into contradictions within each of us. Events generally reveal things that have been in gestation for a long time. Lucid, unfettered thinkers long ago observed the effects of these irreconcilable forces on themselves. Paul Valéry, for example, made this note at a most interesting moment, in 1934: "Ego— *right* by instinct; *left* by spirit; *right* among the lefts and *left* among the rights. Here the ideas repel me, there the type."[116] He goes on, in a variation of the same thought, to flesh out his views: "My political opinion? I have none. But if I question my instinct—I find contradiction in all of them. Anarchy. Monarchy."[117] This shows that the development of which I speak has been a long time coming. But the whole complexion of the matter changes when what was once a flash in a single mind becomes an integral part of a belief system and shared mentality. The discovery then ceases to be a mere exercise of intelligence marginal to reality to become a force capable of transforming practice; it begins the long, slow process of changing attitudes, behavior, and expectations, ultimately perhaps giving rise to a new way of relating to politics.

It would be an error at this point to attribute to psychological disposition what actually stems from an objective social logic. The contradiction does not come initially from individuals; individuals feel its effects, but the original contradiction is inherent in society's defining axioms. It is an intrinsic, insurmountable feature of any society of individuals, of any society that recognizes no other foundation or source of rights than the original independence of its members, than the liberty and equality of originally separate beings. In the most general possible terms, the contradiction is inherent in the structure of any society that tends to mistake its social nature and therefore finds itself torn between the requirements of its explicit ideology and the constraints implicit in its systemic functioning. Put slightly differently, it is a contradiction between the visible and the hidden face of the individualist principle of legitimacy. The society that thinks of itself and (with what potent effects we well know) behaves as if it were a society produced by the will of individuals is also in reality a society whose basic norm is to have individuals as members, individuals whose reproduction is therefore society's task. In the first case, however, it is up to each individual to assume his own responsibilities in a situation in which the public sphere is to be limited as much as possible, whereas in the second case the collective authority is charged with instituting and protecting its subjects in their very status as individuals, with all that that implies in the way of expansion of that authority's competence and resources. Therein lies the deeper meaning of what would explode as the "social question" after the Industrial Revolution but which in fact had already arisen as part of the political transformation initiated by the French Revolution. There was no coherent, fully achieved liberal order that workers somehow modified or imposed social correctives on through their struggles. There was rather an internal dilemma within the liberal order, between its public face, governed by the principles of liberty and individual self-interest, and its hidden face, which in the service of the same goals called for extension of social power. Hence the compromise achieved in one way or another between these two logics, which resulted in the welfare state, was the inevitable and normal destiny of liberal societies (regardless of what libertarians might think). It is not enough to say, as Louis Dumont argues, that the holistic dimension must necessarily survive, if only in a diffuse or unacknowledged form, in the reconstruction of society brought about by the ideology of individualism. It not only survives but transforms itself and, more than that, in some respects multiplies. The redefinition of the whole on the basis of individual wills is also the source of a dynamic of collective power whose consequences in terms of coercive membership can be devastating. The example of the nation is proof of this assertion. Recognizing individual liberty as the supreme value opens unlimited possibilities for the expansion of social authority, since individual independence is apt to be converted into a popular sovereignty virtually extended to everything. The holistic society was one whose parts all functioned according to an identical logic, the logic of subordination. The individualist reversal leads to divergence between the individual and the collective points of view, thereby giving rise to two intimately associated yet antagonistic logics, a logic of emancipation and a logic of socialization. These are intellectually exclusive yet inseparable. The impossibility of keeping the two dynamics is what determines the pattern of political contradictions in modern societies. Both dynamics will repeatedly appear, intertwined yet opposed, in various symmetrical and inverse versions.

It is important to be clear about the connection between the demand for independence and the obligation of membership as it relates to Dumont's analysis, because Dumont gives a very interesting interpretation of the left-right polarity.[118] In substance, Dumont proposes looking at the left as the party of the individualist ideology that grew out of the French Revolution. The right, on the other hand, is supposed to represent the party of the holistic imperative, which necessarily survives. Thus the ideological domination of the left is presumably balanced by the real powers that the right continues to wield within the society. The result is a conflictual expression of hierarchical complementarity by incorporation of opposites, whose rules Dumont elucidates.[119] This interpretation has the considerable merit of deriving political division from the very principle on which modern societies are based and of shedding a great deal of light on the resulting social tension. But the formulation is too sweeping, and it results in a one-sided view of both the right and the left by seriously underestimating the internal contradictions within each. To fit the historical material, each term of the model must be made more complex: the tension between the two components is also found within each party. Dumont's interpretation actually fits the starting point of the history that concerns us here: it gives a more or less accurate image of the distribution of forces in 1815. The "left" (insofar as such an anachronistic substantive can be used) corresponds to the principles of 1789, to the "bourgeois" liberties, whereas the "right" stands for tradition, hierarchy, and ascriptive social position. By the second Restoration the picture had changed, however, and in 1848 it became unrecognizable. Socialism brought into being a left concerned primarily with collective organization and capable of conceiving individual emancipation only in the framework of a clearly materialized primacy of the general interest. In other words, a lasting split developed on the left between those who gave priority to political liberties and those who ascribed absolute necessity to social authority. This split also appeared in the form of an internal contradiction on the extreme left, which found itself ineluctably divided between a desire for individual emancipation through an end to the alienation of labor and the impossibility of conceiving of such a goal without coercive organization, as Élie Halévy rightly diagnosed in 1936.[120] On the right, meanwhile, similar complexities evolved. The expansion of industry gave rise to an entrepreneurial wing of the right, committed to the values of individual initiative and competition, whose coexistence with the proponents of a stable hierarchical order proved to be highly problematic. Between libertarianism and conservatism, between the language of self-interest and devotion to the spiritual, between the mobile power of money and the ideal of a landed community unified by ancestral loyalties and natural hierarchies, the internal tensions of the right were no less significant than those of the left.[121] Hence it was no longer a party of the individual confronting a party of the whole. One party did in fact trace its origins back to the rights of the individual, but its history had forced it to confront from within the persistent issue of collective primacy. And the other party had indeed come into being in order to preserve authority, but its history forced it to acknowledge the ineluctable requirements of economic actors. In the end, two versions of individual preeminence confronted two versions of hierarchical order. The left emphasized the values of freedom of consciousness and individual choice, while the right promoted self-interest and entrepreneurial efficiency. In opposing this emancipation of self-interest, the left insisted that self-interest must be subordinated to the will of all. And against the anarchy of opinion and the atomistic dissolution of social bonds the right mobilized spiritual authority, moral constraint, family ties, the force of tradition, and the benefits of communal roots. Of course neither camp was monolithic, and each of these points became in turn a source of new divisions. There is a right which, in the name of heredity, community, and true hierarchy, detests money, industry, and the market, and there is a right that the logic of the marketplace tends to move farther and farther away from conservative authoritarianism. And there is a left which, in its collective intransigence, feels nothing but contempt for the miserable demands of the bourgeois ego, just as there is an individualistic left which is highly suspicious of the means of government. If there is to be conflictual complementarity, it is by way of such splits that it introduces itself into the system.

It is in relation to the development of this network of contradictions within and between camps, as exacerbated by historical change, that we can begin to understand the rise of totalitarianism. Totalitarianism is nothing other than a desperate attempt to escape the contradiction within oneself through murderous violence toward one's enemy. It stems from a kind of dim awareness of the inner fragmentation caused by conflicting demands whose sting precipitates a flight of avoidance. Individual autonomy through total collectivism, fusion of citizens into a single nation as a means of authentic liberation—antinomy erected into solution by way of annihilation of the enemy: this was the historical driving force behind the violence toward reality and human beings that has dominated this century. The historical process continues; ideals once opposed to an intolerable degree have now become intimately intertwined to reshape our world. The phase of rebellion is over, and we stand on the brink of a period of peaceful resignation, a time in which social actors will begin to discover the solidity of the system of which they are a part. We are beginning to understand the connection between our own inevitable contradictions and the inexorable opposition we encounter in the political sphere, and we are also beginning to grasp the higher solidarity that holds this bundle of dissensions together. I cannot avoid contradiction, and I cannot avoid being contradicted. It is impossible to affirm the prerogatives of the individual without being forced to recognize the need for collective inscription, and to that extent it is impossible to avoid coming face to face with an antagonist who confronts you with a mirror image of your own dilemmas. Those on the right who dream of a diminished role for the state also insist on a central government strong enough to ensure law and order. And those on the left who detest coercion and repression nevertheless hope to extend public control over the economy. They want open borders when it comes to immigration, while the right would put the national interest first. We cannot help wanting both, yet we are impelled to choose one goal over another. Yet what we are powerless to hold together takes on global coherence through confrontation with adversaries no less implicated in contradiction than we are. This makes it meaningful to identify with the whole range of interchangeable positions, even as we recognize that the focal point of contradiction is within ourselves. We are of the right *and* the left to the extent that at any given moment we can only situate ourselves on the right against the left or on the left against the right.

For more than a century political struggle had the air of a battle between past and future, between Ancien Régime and Revolution, between monarchy, hierarchy, and privilege on the one hand and the Republic on the other. What compromise was possible between two strictly incompatible systems of thought and value? After the Republic emerged victorious, the basic requirements of social coherence and integration were completely transformed. Although those requirements were no longer expressed in the language of the old society, they continued to exist, and it became impossible to miss the fact that they were part of the democratic world-view. As the contrast with the Ancien Régime faded and it became increasingly apparent that the crux of the conflict was the organization of society, people began to believe that we were on the verge of deliverance from all conflict. This belief mobilized formidable energies, ravaged the century, and turned the world upside down, yet conflict remains, unchanged, even as our entire frame of reference has changed: conflict is indeed an intrinsic part of our world. It has become difficult to ignore its constructive role. Our growing awareness of this is exemplified by the new status that has gradually been conferred on the right-left pair. We are in solidarity with our enemies in two senses: first, it is through opposition that the truth of our world is revealed, that truth which by nature can only come to rest in a unique position; second, what divides us from our enemies is also, in principle, what divides us within ourselves. This helps to explain why central issues can so easily move from one side to the other, the shift of the national theme from left to right being only the most famous illustration of this.[122] Contrary to what skeptics believe, this inconstancy is much less an argument for relativism or for the inconsistency of the opposition than it is an argument for its solidity: although positions on this or that point are apt to be exchanged, the gap remains. It is a unique property of the left-right opposition that it allows simultaneous expression of both dimensions. That expression gives form to the final solidarity of the antagonists while echoing the division within each. It allows me to formulate within myself a coherent image of what is given outside me as fragmented, but at the same time points up the inner division that each individual experiences as a consequence of being part of a larger whole. Through a miracle of the body which effects a conversion of objective space into subjective space, by the grace of an endless conversion of mutual exclusion (in objective space) into reciprocal integration (in subjective space), right and left become the vehicle of the symbolic reversibility of the individual and the collective. They become the cognitive tool through which the dualist organization of modern society and the concomitant necessity of mobilization through dissent become organically apprehensible and intelligible. And thus they constitute the basic frame of reference in terms of which the law of contradiction of the world in which I am destined to live is at once epitomized and resolved within myself, since I can thereby both embody a contradiction and transcend it, take a stand on one side of a divisive issue and yet embrace the whole.

Clearly, then, it is illusory to assume that the calm that has come of late to political life betokens an imminent disappearance of the split between left and right. To do so is to mistake the surface for what lies beneath it in both functional and symbolic terms. True, the Manichaean magnetism of left and right has lost something of its mobilizing intensity. But what has been lost in passion has been gained in functionality. The deflation of combativeness has gone hand in hand with anthropological implantation. If the emblems have lost some of their luster, the opposition now underpins one of those identifications that enable social actors to achieve symbolic mastery of their world. The role of right and left can no longer be measured in terms of attraction and repulsion. Their new vocation is to make a world structured in terms of contradiction representable. Just because contradictions now manifest themselves with less violence than in the past, it does not follow that they are destined to disappear. Moderation of expression is one thing, fundamentality of principle is another. Issues may seem to lose their importance, and the substance of conflict may appear to become confused over time, yet the core logic that governs the distribution of antagonistic positions remains intact. That logic is a feature of the structure of modern society itself. To the extent that our world is built on individuals, politics will take the form of confrontations around the always problematic relation between private powers and public authority. The resulting, ever-recurring contradictions will not vanish overnight. Even if negotiation takes place at the center, moreover, it seems likely that we will continue to conceptualize those contradictions in terms of right and left for a long time to come.

The nature of the metamorphosis is such that it will be felt peculiarly acutely in the country that invented the left-right identifications as names for what was inexpiable in its internal discords. In France the cooling of the passions associated with these terms seems to herald, more than it does elsewhere, their imminent relegation to oblivion, when in fact it means, as elsewhere, simply that the role of these designations has changed. In any case, this ultimate revival gives the terms *left* and *right* a special status in France, at the cusp between the past and the present. Right and left epitomize the era in which French politics thought of itself as universal politics precisely because of the clarity of the alternatives for which it provided the theater:

1815, a choice, yet again, between Ancien Régime and Revolution; 1900, a choice between faith and enlightenment, between human rights and the nation; 1935, a confrontation between fascism and socialism. Three key moments in which the opposition crystallized around the immutable primal scene of 1789, three moments in which debate revolved around ultimate choices and fundamental issues. We have seen how the uniquely French nature of the apparatus ensuring the preponderance of ideological universalism was translated into the primacy of the categories right and left. That universalism was in a sense corroborated by the worldwide acceptance of its fetish terms. But the diffusion of those terms was part of a general process of democratic stabilization, which led in France to a questioning of the belief in an exceptional status that caused the French to project themselves into the universal arena. If France's peculiar idiom became the language of the entire world, it was by way of a shift in the meaning of *right* and *left,* which now referred to the ordinary, insurmountable coexistence of opposites rather than to the relentless antagonism they once signified. The spread of the terminology actually reflected a decline of the model. As France's terminology conquers the world, France itself rejoins the ranks of other nations, accepts its unexceptional status, and increasingly becomes a democracy like other democracies. By dint of comparison the country is also learning to see what French historical figures in general understood as universally exemplary as having been instead singularly insular. The achievement of true universality compels us in retrospect to appreciate the consummate singularity of a tradition that saw itself as universalistic. This has created a tension between past and present which now permeates the notions of right and left and turns them into memory-notions. They actively refer to the past precisely because they remain alive, but in a function that acts as a continual reminder of the difference between their present and past grounds for existence. They serve today as one of the forces working to bring France into the mainstream. But France cannot rejoin the ordinary without reminding itself of its former exceptionalism. The more the terms *right* and *left* come to evoke the new norm, the more they will also serve to evoke the unique past of dissension and struggle that made France, once the eldest daughter of the Church, for many years the chosen homeland of the political.

PART II

MINORITY RELIGIONS

FIGURE 8.0 Philippe de Champaigne, *Mother Angélique Arnauld.*

CHAPTER 8

Port-Royal: The Jansenist Schism

Catherine Maire

At the gates of Versailles, in the depths of a marshy glen surrounded by forest, the ruins of the abbey of Port-Royal des Champs stand in strange contrast to the sovereign magnificence of the nearby palace and its park. Only the pigeon house, barn, and a part of the outer wall built at the time of the Fronde have escaped the destruction ordered by Louis XIV in 1711.

Even the *hôtel* of the Duchesse de Longueville, sister of the Grand Condé and soul of the first Fronde, who liked to take her retreats, accompanied by her entire entourage, in proximity to the monastery, was completely razed. The Gentlemen's Lodge, erected in 1653 at the behest of illustrious friends of Port-Royal, suffered the same fate.

Yet by some irony of history nothing could destroy the impression of "solitude," "desert," and "hermitage" (Thébaïde) that so struck Mme de Sévigné. The foundations of the Cistercian abbey built in the early thirteenth century by Robert de Luzarche, the architect of the cathedral of Amiens, remain gaping heavenward, while a few avenues of trees hint at the cloister's outline.

The cemetery is completely empty. On orders of the king the bodies were exhumed when the abbey was destroyed, as if, not content to demolish buildings, the absolute monarch wished to erase the monastery's invisible roots, the cult of its dead, the circle of its friends. Anything likely to evoke the spirit or memory of the place was ruthlessly obliterated.

Nevertheless, not only is the memory of Port-Royal still alive today, but even more astonishing, it has remained continuously alive since the seventeenth century. The monastery's archives, miraculously saved from destruction, the works of the seventeenth- and eighteenth-century Port-Royalistes that were destined to keep the abbey's memory alive, the entire literature of the long Jansenist struggle, nearly fifty thousand volumes in all, were patiently assembled in an authentic *lieu de mémoire* that replaced the abolished physical site: the Bibliothèque de la Société de Port-Royal, which also owns the ruins of Port-Royal des Champs.[1]

The society in fact styles itself the direct heir of the *boîte à Perrette*, a relief fund founded by Pierre Nicole himself. Throughout the eighteenth century the fund was constantly replenished and passed on through an ingenious system of inheritance to a number of "friends of truth." These friends were called upon to make good use of the fund in the battle against the Roman Constitution or papal bull *Unigenitus* of 1713 and in defense of persecuted clerics.[2] After the Revolution, the fund was reconstituted in the form of a mutual annuity, the Réunion Catholique. During the nineteenth century, the society, which took the name Société Saint-Augustin in 1845, gradually became the repository of the Jansenist archives. One of its members, Jean-Amable Pâris, secretary of the Conseil d'État, bequeathed it the library of the Jansenist lawyer Louis-Adrien Le Paige, whose heir he had become during the Revolution.

Throughout his long life, Le Paige, bailiff of the Temple and advisor to the Prince de Conti, strove to assemble his library of "witness to the truth," collecting every available record of the battle waged by the adversaries of the bull *Unigenitus*, not only the so-called *appelants* who made their appeal to the Concile de la Nation but also the *convulsionnaires* and, later, the *parlementaires*. He collected some 2,500 volumes, including 228 thick compilations containing some 12,000 printed and handwritten documents. All in all, some 15,000 documents were represented, covering more than two centuries of France's religious and parlementary[3] history, from Port-Royal to the Revolution. It was also Le Paige who recovered most of the copies and originals from the archives of the destroyed monastery, roughly 150 volumes' worth.

This exceptional collection forms the core of the library, which has been enlarged through the addition of other Jansenist collections. It is located today at 169 Rue Saint-Jacques in Paris. In particular, the library of Port-Royal contains a large portion of the archives of Abbé Grégoire, who represented the spirit of Port-Royal during the Revolution. With the purchase of the ruins in 1868, the symbolic patrimony of Port-Royal was gathered together under the auspices of the Société Saint-Augustin, rebaptized the Société de Port-Royal in 1954.

Over the course of the nineteenth century the Jansenist controversy that had long raged within the Catholic Church gradually abated. It survived in the form of a spiritual ancestry and sensibility. But Jansenism survived even more importantly as a cultural memory, as evidenced by the creation, after World War II, of another, larger group, the Société des Amis de Port-Royal.

Looked at closely, this seemingly unified memory actually consists of two distinct strata. There is "Port-Royal" and there is "Jansenism." Sainte-Beuve consecrated the idea of Port-Royal as the epicenter of French classicism. Port-Royal is often portrayed as a rosette of classicism, with Pascal, Saint-Cyran, Racine, Boileau, Philippe de Champaigne, Antonin Arnauld, Nicole, Duguet, Mme de Sévigné, and Descartes as its petals, touching every facet of the seventeenth century. Port-Royal is also celebrated for the pure French of its translations, the modernity of its *Grammaire*, and the intelligent teaching methods employed in its Petites Écoles.

"Jansenism" means resistance to absolutism. Powerful images have found their way into history texts: the confessor Saint-Cyran's opposition to Richelieu's policies based on *raison d'État* and the refusal of the nuns of Port-Royal des Champs to sign a document condemning the five propositions taken from Jansenius's *Augustinus*. On the right the Jansenists are suspected of somehow having instigated the French Revolution. On the left they are associated with the development of republican ideas. Sometimes they are even regarded as the precursors of "a heightened awareness of the rights of the person, and above all of personal thought, in the face of absolutisms of authority."[4]

The different images actually hide a judgment of different epochs. What the clichés make it difficult for us to see is the difference between the two Jansenisms, that of the seventeenth century and that of the eighteenth. Though seventeenth-century Jansenism survives thanks to its writers, the political Jansenism of the eighteenth century is little known or has had a bad press. Port-Royal is the incarnation of Jansenism in its moment of greatness, as opposed to its "unfortunate" evolution in the battle over *Unigenitus* and the affair of the *convulsionnaires*. Sainte-Beuve did a great deal to forge the image of this divorce. He attempted to preserve the mythical purity of the monastery's golden age under Saint-Cyran by portraying it as gradually overtaken by a disputatious, caviling spirit which was first introduced by Arnauld and which he alleges ultimately led the movement into complete decadence in the following century.

The paradox, however, is that it was the political Jansenists of the eighteenth century who constructed the memory of the Port-Royal du Grand Siècle for the needs of their cause. Sainte-Beuve followed in their footsteps and read their books. He relied on their sources and completed their work. He excluded them from history, yet he completed their design. One of the novel features of Jansenism in the century of Enlightenment was the role that the battle over history played in its development. It may be that the whole Jansenist movement can be reinterpreted by examining the ways in which it has been remembered.

The Enigma of Jansenism

There is something enigmatic about Jansenism. Few religious sects have given rise to so many contradictory views of their nature. For such typically French dissidence to break out within the Catholic Church in modern times remains mysterious.

It constitutes one of the major cleavages in the history of France, the ramifications of which were central to public life for a century and a half, and yet the significance of the sect and the details of its development remain baffling and have given rise to endless interpretive controversies.[5]

The difficulty of grasping Jansenism probably has a great deal to do with its being intimately intertwined with the whole theological and political structure of the French Ancien Régime. It accompanied absolutism in its course and followed its phases, from its establishment to its collapse. It is absolutism's profoundly revealing double, its religious mirror, its ghost. It refracts the difficulties of the modern religious consciousness within the framework of absolutist construction. Jansenism opposed the political religion of *raison d'État* with its own religious politics, that of God as absolute.

Theologically, the movement began in Louvain in the context of discussions, following the Council of Trent, concerning free will and grace in reaction to the Protestant schism. The Jesuits gave it a name, based on that of Bishop Jansenius, whose *Augustinus* (1640) was the most elaborate expression of the doctrine that would eventually trigger the controversy. In opposition to Molina, the theologian of the Jesuits, Jansenius pointed to man's fundamental corruption and God's omnipotence. But since the battle was now being waged on two fronts, not only against the Jesuits but also against the Protestant doctrine of predestination by grace alone, Jansenius also stressed the necessity of good works on the part of Christians: in the work of salvation constant effort and total conversion were indispensable. In opposition to the Protestant tendency toward desacralization, Jansenius reaffirmed the sacraments in precisely the same spirit as the Counter-Reformation.

In any case, it was in France, through Jansenius's great friend Duvergier de Hauranne, abbé de Saint-Cyran, that the Jansenist movement in the strict sense found its true home. There, theological rigorism encountered the problem of politics in the form of Richelieu's policies of *raison d'État*. Things came to a head around 1635. Jansenius published *Mars Gallicus,* a pamphlet that explicitly attacked the policies of the cardinal, who did not shrink from forging an alliance with Protestant countries to serve France's needs in its war with Catholic Spain. Saint-Cyran, who in that same year, 1635, became the confessor of Mother Angélique, the mother superior of the Port-Royal convent, assumed the symbolic status in this context of leader of the religious party and defender of the rights of conscience. For Richelieu, he became an enemy to eliminate, especially since he attracted proselytes. Saint-Cyran, meanwhile, had actually begun recruiting *solitaires,* who had made up their minds to withdraw from the world under his spiritual guidance and to live henceforth only for the purpose of "making it to heaven." The first of these was an *avocat* with the Parlement of Paris, Antoine Le Maître, soon joined by two brethren, the priest Antoine Singlin and the grammarian Claude Lancelot. The three men lived as "Christian friends" in buildings attached to the convent of nuns of Port-Royal, temporarily located at the Hôtel de Clagny in the Faubourg Saint-Jacques. The nuns had a history of their own. The first reform of Port-Royal des Champs, undertaken by Mother Angélique in 1608, when she was just seventeen, actually pre-dated Jansenism. The convent followed the Cistercian rule and was influenced by a peculiarly French brand of spirituality associated with Bérulle and Saint Francis de Sales. The future of the convent was determined, however, by Angélique's encounter with Saint-Cyran and later, under his influence, with other Jansenist directors and confessors such as Singlin, Le Maître de Sacy, and Arnauld. The nuns would become at once the focal point of the Jansenist movement, the eye of the ensuing storm, and the quintessential repository of Jansenist memory.

It was in 1638 that Port-Royal des Champs became the Port-Royal that we know. Saint-Cyran was arrested. The "gentlemen" then moved to the original site of the monastery, which the nuns had abandoned ten years earlier in favor of a healthier home in the capital. The *solitaires* undertook to drain the land and improve the property, after which some of the nuns, whose numbers had grown too large for the new convent built to Lepautre's plans in 1646 in the Faubourg Saint-Jacques, returned to the old abbey. The *solitaires,* their ranks significantly expanded after the sensation created by the publication of the great Arnauld's *Fréquente Communion* in 1643, then retired to the hillside farm. The history of Port-Royal de Paris parts company with that of Port-Royal des Champs in 1665, the dramatic moment when the nuns fell under royal repression. Because of their refusal to sign a document condemning five propositions from *Augustinus,* as required by the Assembly of the Clergy in 1655 and reaffirmed by the king in 1664 and 1665, they were punished. Leaders of the opposition, such as Mother Angélique de Saint-Jean, the niece of the convent's foundress, Mother Angélique, who died in 1661, were dispersed to vari-ous convents in Paris and its environs. The rest of the company was confined to Port-Royal des Champs. From 1665 to 1669, eighty "rebellious and disobedient" nuns were obliged to live in custody under the authoritarian command of the nuns of the Visitation, cut off from all contact with the outside world and, worse still, deprived of the sacraments. In 1666, Louis XIV legally severed the property of the two houses and, to consummate the rupture, appointed as abbess of Port-Royal de Paris one of the *jureuses,* or nuns who had agreed to sign the document. The con-vent in the Faubourg Saint-Jacques would have nothing further to do with the fate of Jansenism. There, the royal policy proved successful: the building, today a maternity hospital, bears no trace of the party whose soul and fortress it was for thirty years.

From the beginning the Jansenists were suspected of being, in Louis XIV's famous jibe as reported by Saint-Simon, "a republican party in church and state." It is true that the kind of obedience to temporal authority that they advocated consid-

erably underplayed the power of great lords and even in a sense desacralized the monarch in comparison with the one valid absolute, that is, Jesus Christ. In a state whose affirmation repressed the Reformation, Jansenism in a sense represented Catholicism's crisis of individualism. How was Catholicism, a religion of mediation, to be reconciled with modern religious experience, the *devotio moderna*, rooted in

FIGURE 8.1   Madeleine de Boulogne, *View of the Abbey of Port-Royal des Champs;* after an engraving by Magdeleine Horthemels.

individual consciousness? This was the fundamental question from which Jansenism's contradictory nature arose. It was constantly torn between affirmation of the principle of authority within the visible Church and the development of invisible personal belief, brought on by the individualizing process of God's absolutism, the other face of "divine right," distinct from that invoked by the monarch.

Similarly, the theology of "the hidden God" expressed the contradictory search for a God active among but incomprehensible to human beings. The God of the Jansenists was therefore both present and absent at the same time. Outside the world like the God of the Protestants, he nevertheless continued to act and bear witness to his presence in the world, in particular by the distinctive means of miracle.

The internal tensions of Jansenism were most intense in regard to the Church. Jansenism aspired to reform the Church but from within, as opposed to the Protestant challenge from without. For Jansenists, the Church was capacious enough to incorporate the insistence on faith within the broad spectrum of conflicts that could not fail to arise from the integration of what one might, at the risk of being provocative, call the "Protestant spirit" into the Catholic structure.

The potential for conflict is particularly clear in the area in which "Jansenism" probably exerted its greatest influence on French religion and culture, an aspect of the question that has strangely enough been neglected by historians until now: namely, the translation and distribution of the Bible and other religious works. After 1660 the "gentlemen" published not only such fundamental works of Christian spirituality as *De l'imitation de Jésus-Christ* (1662), the *Psaumes de David* (1665), Mons's *Nouveau Testament* (1667), the *Histoire du Vieux et du Nouveau Testament* (known as the Bible de Royaumount, 1670), and the Bible de Sacy (1672–1708), but also a series of texts that brought the liturgy within reach of ordinary Christians: service books, books of hours, missals, and breviaries. Like the Protestants, the Jansenists encouraged people to read the Bible in the vulgar tongue and in the original text rather than a paraphrase. What differentiated them from the Protestants was the role accorded to the priest, in whom was vested the meaning of the text. It was his job to help others to understand that meaning.

Moreover, it was probably this sacralization of the priestly function, which is quite accentuated in the *Nouveau Testament en français avec des réflexions morales* by the Oratorian Quesnel,[6] that crystallized the consciousness of the lower ranks of the clergy, who became such an explosive force in the early eighteenth century. Quesnel's commentary on the New Testament was in a sense the epitome and culmination of all Port-Royal's efforts to put the Bible in the hands of ordinary people. In highly didactic fashion Quesnel discussed Sacy's translation, the so-called Bible de Mons. It was this commentary that drew the fire of Rome and that was condemned in *Unigenitus,* the 1713 papal bull. A tenth of the condemned propositions pertained explicitly to the right of ordinary Christians to read the Bible in the vulgar tongue.

The anathema was thus pronounced at a time when most of the major translations were already widely available in France. It is easy to understand why many parish priests would have felt outraged by an anathema from Rome challenging what they had come to consider as their most eminent priestly function: teaching Scripture and explaining the word of God.

The Sacrament of Memory

Port-Royal's grip on posterity cannot be accounted for simply by pointing to the indelible traces of Jansenist disputations or the enduring memories of persecution of the convent's nuns. And while I have no wish to detract from Angélique Arnauld's reputation for courage and determination, the famous "day at the grille" of September 25, 1609, which Sainte-Beuve transformed into the first act of a tragedy, was not the kind of extraordinary event that leaves an ineradicable imprint. The young abbess's decision to return to the old Cistercian rule and honor the cloister was typical of a Catholic revival movement whose effects were widely felt after the beginning of the seventeenth century.[7]

The roots of Port-Royal's enduring hold on the imagination are to be sought rather in the sect's novel insistence from the beginning on the importance of memory. The nuns and *solitaires* looked upon themselves as a community of saints, exemplary in their humanity and destined to edify others through their charitable acts. In order to set an example for others, those acts had to be recorded and publicized.[8] In addition, Port-Royal held to a distinctive mystical interpretation of the Eucharist, of a nature to reinforce this commemorative inclination still further. When the nuns moved to the new convent in Paris, they were given the name "sisters of Port-Royal of the Holy Sacrament." Distinguished by splendid scapulars of white serge emblazoned with a scarlet cross, they practiced a fervent, and not merely external, adoration of the eucharistic body of Jesus: they became literally "Christ-Bearers," to borrow a formula of Saint Cyril's that was incorporated into their *Constitutions*. They thought of themselves in eucharistic terms, "as bearing Jesus Christ in their hearts and exposed to the view of others." The latter expression is characteristic of Jansenist theology with its fondness for a dialectic of the visible and the invisible, the exterior and the interior, the hidden and the veiled. It is easy to imagine how the kind of devotion peculiar to "the daughters of Christ's passion" predisposed them to embrace the theme of martyrdom and flourish in persecution. It is also easy to see how, even before the persecution, anyone associated with Port-Royal could become worthy of memory through the mystery of the Eucharist. One of the distinctive features of Port-Royal as a spiritual environment was its passion for hagiography.

It was out of determination to rescue the memory of such spiritual guides as Saint-Cyran, Le Maître de Sacy, and Arnauld d'Andilly from oblivion that *solitaires* such as Lancelot, Fontaine, and Du Fossé wrote their memoirs. It was for the same reason that nuns such as Marie de Sainte-Claire Arnauld, Catherine de Sainte-Agnès Arnauld d'Andilly, Catherine de Sainte-Suzanne Champaigne, and, later, Elisabeth de Sainte-Agnès Le Féron piously set themselves the task of retranscribing the works of the illustrious "gentlemen." The case for the canonization of Mother Angélique was tried, so to speak, during her lifetime.[9] Under Singlin's direction, Mother Angélique was obliged to begin her own autobiographical narrative as early as 1654, albeit "with such distaste that one could not persuade her to finish it."[10] Some of her letters, in particular those to the queen of Poland, were spirited away for copying before being dispatched to their intended recipients.

In creating the legend of Mother Angélique, her niece and disciple Mother Angélique de Saint-Jean played a fundamental role.[11] While Antoine Le Maître transcribed his edifying conversations with his aunt, the niece set out to compile the memories of the older nuns even before her aunt's death. For more than twenty

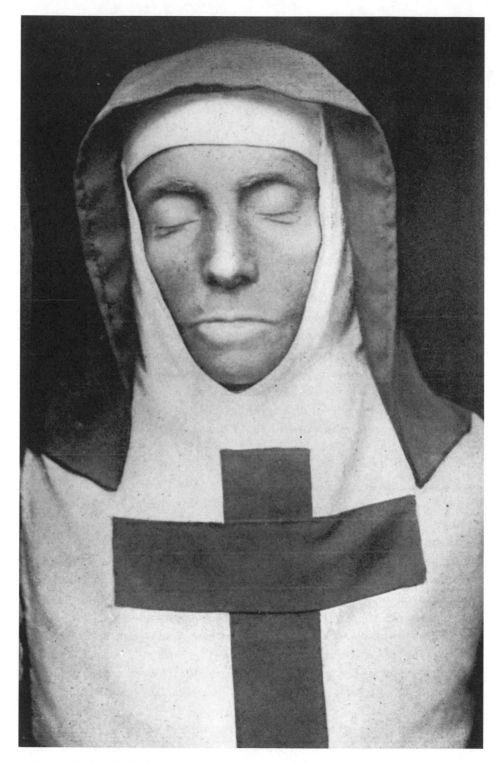

FIGURE 8.2   Death mask of Mother Angélique.

years, from 1652 to 1673, she gathered accounts of the foundress's life, which she stored in secure places outside the convent during the period of persecution. When calm was restored, she relied on this source along with her own memory in writing a history of the life and works of the order's foundress up to the time when the Paris convent was established.[12]

During the long, patient years of archival work and composition, external circumstances—namely, the order to sign the document condemning the propositions of Jansenius—led to a change in the work's primary objective: it became an apologia for a successful and complete effort of reform. The sanctions compelled Angélique de Saint-Jean to recount the history of a martyrdom, the unjust persecution of reform. There was a shift from the mystery of the Eucharist to the theme of the Passion, a shift also evident in diaries and journals of captivity written in this period by nuns dispersed to various convents or confined at Port-Royal from 1665 to 1669. A certain uniformity of style in these accounts suggests, moreover, that all were revised by Angélique de Saint-Jean. Her *Relation de captivité* (1711) and *Réflexions sur la conformité de l'état des religieuses de Port-Royal avec celui de Jésus-Christ dans l'Eucharistie* (1710) contain the seeds of the heroic myth of Port-Royal, a myth that would be developed later by any number of writers from Quesnel to Montherlant.

Not that this form of apologia was Angélique de Saint-Jean's personal invention. The same model also shaped the writings of other *solitaires,* such as the *Apologie pour les Religieuses* of 1665 and even the prophetic letter from Lancelot to his master Louis-Isaac Le Maître de Sacy dated January 1, 1665. That letter clearly demonstrates the Port-Royaliste conviction of belonging to a community of saints and martyrs whose fate would one day be to edify the entire Church: "The ruin of Port-Royal is its glory. It is the salvation of the souls it contains, it is the edification of the Church through the centuries, and it is the protection of all virgins that God will in consequence offer through his Church, for no one will hazard this kind of attack in the future if people see that the nuns remain unshakable to the end."[13]

Persecution was the cornerstone of Port-Royal's memory, because it allowed the heroic potential implicit in its mystery of the Eucharist to realize itself. It also offered the support of a social function by justifying a recourse to public opinion. It overcame scruples that might otherwise have hindered the keeping of journals of captivity, a practice not at all consistent with the Cistercian rule of silence and modesty. Arnauld invoked the persecution as a justification, moreover, at the beginning of his *Apologie pour les religieuses du Saint-Sacrement,* which was published in 1655 as a contribution to their defense. And it was owing to the imminent destruction of the convent that Quesnel in 1711 withdrew his objections to the publication of Mother Angélique's *Relation de captivité.*

Two years later the condemnation of his *Réflexions morales* in *Unigenitus* gave new significance and a new destiny to the Port-Royal archives. This precious repository was seized in 1790 by d'Argenson, the *lieutenant de police,* but was later restored owing to some mysterious scruple of conscience. It was this hagiographic treasure that enabled the Jansenists of the eighteenth century to erect a monument to the glory of the abbey and its spiritual enterprise. After being buried or hidden for more than half a century, these invaluable archives would enter history in the wake of the struggle over the Roman Constitution of 1713. By the middle of the eighteenth century nearly all the primary documents in the Port-Royal repository—letters, memoirs, journals, narratives of captivity, obituaries—were published. This first batch of published documents served as the basis for the great histories of the second half of the eighteenth century.

The survival of these manuscripts is almost miraculous, given the king's express wish to annihilate every last vestige of Port-Royal. It was in fact the work of two women, Françoise-Marguerite de Joncoux (1648–1715)[14] and Marie-Scholastique Le Sesne de Théméricourt. The former was the key figure in the reorganization of the Jansenists at the beginning of the eighteenth century. She was in contact with both centers of the "Jansenist party": the theologians of the Saint-Magloire seminary and Quesnel, Fouillou, and Petitpied in the Netherlands. Modest in her appearance, she wore no color other than "that of very darkened tree bark" and a black scarf with none of the "then customary trimmings," yet she was regularly received by the archbishop, at court, and by several high magistrates. She had already exerted herself in defense of the nuns even before their forcible eviction. It was to her that d'Argenson, who valued her greatly for her works of charity, returned the seized manuscripts, whereupon she hastened to have copies made and distributed to several of her friends. Meanwhile, she made efforts to collect various documents that relatives and friends of the nuns had been able to assemble. In her will she bequeathed the originals to the library of the Benedictines of Saint-Germain-des-Prés. These documents were probably used by the Benedictine Rivet de la Grange for his *Nécrologe de Port-Royal* as well as by the author of a *Histoire de Port-Royal,* the Benedictine Dom Clémencet.[15] Following Mlle de Joncoux's premature death in 1715, the work of copying and collecting documents was carried on by a former inmate of Port-Royal who had been expelled in the second major wave of persecution in 1679: Marie-Scholastique Le Sesne de Théméricourt, who was aided in her work by several anonymous copyists.[16] She was the first

FIGURE 8.3   Shell reliquary in memory of Deacon Pâris and Port-Royal. The deacon's portrait is in the center.

cousin of Jean-Baptiste Le Sesne des Ménilles d'Étemare, the principal theologian involved in the battle against *Unigenitus*. In 1740, informers employed by the *lieutenant de police* kept watch on his home in the Hôtel du Petit-Luxembourg near the *montagne Sainte-Geneviève* in Paris, "the trash heap of the *convulsionnaires*," where "the fabricators of miracles," that is, the leaders of the Jansenist party, "used to gather."[17] Most of the copies produced by the Théméricourt workshop found their way into the library of Le Paige, the archivist of the struggle for the appeal to a council. In the meantime it has now been established that the manuscripts circulated among Jansenists, especially in the Netherlands, where several of them were published through the efforts of various exiles.[18] All these efforts reflect the passionate fervor with which the documents, the authentic witness to the life of Port-Royal, were preserved, completed, copied, and passed on.

The Emblem of Resistance

The history of Port-Royal's commemoration and exaltation after 1720 divides into two main phases. Before that date, a series of texts concerning the expulsion of the nuns, the destruction of the abbey, and the memory of the illustrious foundress Mother Angélique had found their way into print.[19] But this publishing venture was limited in its scope and modest in its influence. By contrast, the publication of the abbey's hagiographic treasure that began fifteen years after its destruction and ten years after the promulgation of *Unigenitus* was massive and systematic. It would continue for the next thirty years, into the 1750s. Memoirs and fragments of memoirs, letters, diaries, narratives of captivity, obituaries, and autobiographies were piously and methodically printed.[20] Around the middle of the century this commemorative enterprise entered its second phase: no longer content merely to publish documents attesting to the memory of Port-Royal, scholars now sought to capture the history of the abbey and set it down on paper according to the scholarly norms of the day.[21] During this process of exhumation, the image of Port-Royal's destruction took on a new significance. What had been relics constituting a memorial to sanctity now acquired the status of examples of resistance to the Roman Constitution. An emblem of a new struggle was gradually constructed around the image of an abbey and its venerated foundress. Had it not been for the quarrel over *Unigenitus* and the needs of the battle waged by the heirs of the Grand Siècle dissidents, the moral reliquary of Port-Royal would no doubt have remained in the utmost oblivion.

The few histories of Jansenism published in the final years of the seventeenth century would not have sufficed to keep the fading memory of Port-Royal alive.[22] They represent the rump of old polemics, their chief object being to establish that the so-called Jansenist heresy was nothing but a "ghost" fabricated by the Jesuits.

FIGURE 8.4   Procession of nuns of Port-Royal during the feast of the Blessed Sacrament in the cloister of Port-Royal; engraving by Magdeleine Hortehmels.

In fact, even before the first shovelfuls of dirt had been thrown over the remains, Port-Royal was nothing but a shadow of its former self. The great *solitaires* were gone, and there remained only twenty or so elderly but still determined nuns. Indeed, it was an act of resistance on their part that led to the destruction of the abbey. They refused to sign a new document required by the bull *Vineam Domini*. The response was sudden and disproportionate. But the nuns' removal, followed by the razing of buildings and the exhumation of bodies from 1709 to 1711, met with relative indifference. Before the bull no more than fifteen short briefs had been written in defense of the nuns.[23] Thus the destruction of the abbey by itself was probably not enough to trigger the building of the memorial monument to Port-Royal that was soon to come.

The briefs defending the nuns may not have had much impact at the time, but they did play a nonnegligible role in the crystallization of a new theme: they began to shift attention away from the Jansenist movement as a whole and toward the *site* of Port-Royal. Henceforth the imperative was to remind people of the existence of Port-Royal des Champs. To answer the challenge of the moment, the Jansenists revealed certain unpublished texts of Mother Angélique de Saint-Jean concerning the most painful episodes of the "past troubles."[24] The first of these, published in 1710, was the *Réflexions sur la conformité de l'état des religieuses de Port-Royal avec celui de Jésus-Christ dans l'Eucharistie*, written at the time of her captivity with the *annonciades*. In the following year Quesnel himself provided a preface to the *Récit de la captivité*, in which he developed the theme that the nuns were "martyrs of truth and Christian sincerity" whose deeds deserved to be recorded. Sites became relics. Just prior to the demolition, the former secretary and biographer of Le Nain de Tillemont, Michel Tronchay, declared, in his *Histoire abrégée de l'abbaye de Port-*

Royal, which appeared just after the removal of the nuns in 1710, that "the very ruins of this place, so worthy of veneration, will as it were raise their voice and stand as eternal witness."[25] It was in this spirit that the *Mémoires sur la destruction de l'abbaye de Port-Royal des Champs,* published in the Netherlands by Fouillou in 1711, offered the first detailed description "of the inside and outside of Port-Royal." Sold as separate sheets, this series of small engravings by Magdeleine Horthemels, the widow of a bookseller on the Rue Saint-Jacques and a friend of the abbey, portrayed Port-Royal from every possible interior and exterior angle. The image of the site was henceforth sacred.

Thus the stage was set for the transformation of Port-Royal into an emblem of the coming battle. But still nothing might have come of the new imagery, which could well have been nothing more than a final flare-up of an obscure ecclesiastical controversy from the age of Louis XIV, soon to be forgotten. It was the promulgation by the pope of the bull *Unigenitus* against Quesnel's *Réflexions morales* in 1713 that turned a mere possibility into a reality. The bull launched a second wave of Jansenism, of far greater amplitude than the first wave. This time the controversy was not confined to a narrow elite but spread to all classes of society. The bulk of the clergy in Paris and various other dioceses backed the appeal initiated by the Jansenist bishops. Ordinary Christians became passionately involved in the "affairs of the day." It was in the midst of this collective passion that the *convulsionnaires* went so far as to exhibit their own twitching bodies as witnesses to the truth.[26] Lawyers and *parlementaires* wedded the cause of God's rights in this world. From 1713 to 1775, Jansenist dissidence would provide a religious theater for a protopolitical opposition, which also served as a matrix for the unequivocally political opposition of the *parlements.*

It was in the service of this important cause that the memory of Port-Royal would be mobilized. Proposed as models of conduct in the "time of troubles," troubles associated with a Constitution that posed a challenge to the fundamental truths of Scripture, the lives—outwardly obedient but inwardly free—of the nuns and *solitaires* of Port-Royal were now made available to a broad public. The *Nécrologe* published in Amsterdam in 1723 and the "journals of captivity" published clandestinely in Paris in 1725 praised Port-Royal for exhibiting an attitude said to be exemplary for a large community consisting not only of nuns and *solitaires* but also of "outside friends." There was nothing extraordinary about these lives: they offered models with which any Christian could identify, successful examples of resistance within the Church. Anyone, without distinction as to estate or class, could see himself or herself in these stories. In the preface to the *Nécrologe,* the Benedictine Rivet de la Grange introduced these accounts as "sure rules," "the sincere actions of individuals who have sanctified themselves in our own time, who lived in a manner of speaking before our eyes and in our own country." The community of saints was national. Port-Royal was praised for giving France "an advantage over the other countries of Christendom" thanks to its "purer faith, less fettered by human traditions and superstitions," its "more enlightened piety," its "taste for reading Scripture and pious works," and its "augmentation of the educational level of the people and Clergy."

These edifying texts were more than just weapons in the spreading opposition to *Unigenitus*. They were the result of a careful, deliberate strategy adopted by the "Jansenist party" leadership gathered at Saint-Magloire. Indeed, this Oratorian seminary in the Faubourg Saint-Jacques became, in addition to the Quesnel group in the Netherlands, a second center of loyalty to Port-Royal, led by Duguet, the other great latter-day Jansenist theologian. The seminary did more than just provide theological and clerical instruction to Oratorian students; it also welcomed other priests and members of the elite in a position to assume high offices in the future. One of these, the Abbé Le Sesne des Ménilles d'Étemare, later became, along with his contemporary the philosopher Boursier, the leading theologian and driving force behind the campaign promoting the "appeal to the national council."

The theologians of Saint-Magloire were well prepared to respond to the Roman Constitution from the moment it was announced. In the summer of 1712 Duguet and his faithful disciple d'Étemare had inaugurated a series of lectures on a question of exegesis: the need for a figurative interpretation of the Bible in order to preserve the concordance of the Old and New Testaments.[27] At the time Duguet had ventured to put forth an idea that would prove to have serious consequences for his student. This was connected with the prophesied conversion of the Jews, which traditionally was postponed until the end of time. Duguet suggested that it might come much sooner. Perhaps the time had already arrived. D'Étemare, generalizing and systematizing this suggestion, developed it into an exegetical system that his adversaries characterized as "figurism." It involved interpreting events in the history of the Church, including very recent ones, in the light of their prophetic figuration in sacred texts. Nothing that happened nowadays was without its biblical precedent. The persecution of the Jansenists and the Roman Constitution were simply manifestations of the "iniquitous conspiracy" that was to precede a broad and general reestablishment of the Church.

In this exegetical system Port-Royal was to occupy an important place. When read in the light of Scripture, the history of the Church in fact showed that it had always been divided into two opposed camps. Like Rebecca, it bore within its own body two hostile peoples: Jacob and Esau, Saint Augustine and Pelagius, Jansenius and Molina, Port-Royal and the Jesuits. Within the Church there existed an uninterrupted series of repositories of truth, Augustine's community of saints. That tradition of truth culminated in Port-Royal and its cause, which stood to become the foundation of a new lineage.[28] Thus emboldened by the idea that they were the only branch of the Christian family in which the sap of God's chosen people continued to flow during the time of troubles, the "figurists" of Saint-Magloire ardently embarked on the mission of bearing "witness to truth," as indicated by the title of a programmatic work published by one of them, Father Vivien de la Borde, in 1714: *Témoignage de la Vérité.*

Their novel strategy actually built on earlier Jansenist efforts to make the Bible available to a broad public. Since the papal bull, in the view of the Jansenists, questioned the truth of the fundamental sacred texts, it, too, must be brought to the attention of as broad a public as possible. Public opinion was the best tribunal for deciding where the true word of God was to be found. The appeal to a council within the body of the Church, an appeal orchestrated in every way by the Saint-Magloire group, was thus accompanied by a campaign to educate the general public of ordinary Christians. This propaganda campaign was redoubled after the failure of a second appeal in 1721, which had attracted much less support among parish priests than the earlier petitions of the four Jansenist bishops.[29] It therefore became even more important to carry the message over the heads of the priests and directly to their flocks. This was the background behind the launching of a new campaign in the form of Rivet de la Grange's *Nécrologe.* From 1728 to 1735 a large number of texts, intended to be clear statements accessible to even the humblest of readers, were circulated to the public.[30] The best example of this desire to inform the general public about the background and evolution of the religious controversy was the creation in February 1728 of the *Nouvelles ecclésiastiques,* the first newspaper of broad social impact, with a circulation estimated at 6,000.[31] Meanwhile, figurists published a series of works intended to be read by parish priests, so that they might in turn give currency to a theology of history capable of saving them from discouragement despite their "small number."[32] So the history and doctrine of Port-Royal were presented to the general public in the form of a figurist interpretation of sacred history, one of continuous resistance by the defenders of truth within the Church. From now on the appeal to a general council would forever be confounded with the cause of Port-Royal: the general public made no distinction between the two.

This educational effort had unintended consequences, however. The *convulsionnaires* drew their own practical conclusions from the figurist lessons they received in a number of Parisian parishes. They believed that their own bodies had become "corporeal figures" of martyrs to persecuted truth. The ensuing episodes of "convulsions" and figurative ceremonies divided and plunged into disarray a Jansenist party already weakened by actions taken by the new minister Fleury.[33] The Jansenists now sought to disassociate themselves from the present and preserve intact, in the past, the golden age of the *sainte maison.* This nostalgic turn eventually led to changes in the business of exhuming accounts of the abbey's edifying period of greatness. The most important documents in the historical record were published between 1735 and 1750, and it is difficult to grasp their point outside the contemporary context of the defeat of the Jansenist party. It is the defeat that accounts for the interest attached to these glorious attestations at a time when the party had split over the issues of convulsionism and figurism. It was in the same period, moreover, that the Jansenists began to think of writing a history of Port-Royal, as is indicated by the titles of a number of works, such as the *Mémoires pour servir à l'histoire de Port-Royal*. Members of the group that had organized the pro-Appeal campaign bore the cost of printing these works under the ironic pseudonym "Aux dépens de la Compagnie" (that is, at the expense of the Jesuits). Much of the burden was assumed by Jansenists who had fled to Utrecht, especially Nicolas Legros, the author of the *Renversement des libertés gallicanes* (1716).[34]

Besides the nuns' personal narratives, the published texts consisted mainly of accounts of the lives and spiritual itineraries of the great *solitaires*, written at the behest of surviving members of the community for their own edification. Fontaine, Sacy's secretary, while in Melun for his last retreat (1696–1700), painted for posterity a portrait of the master translator and other *solitaires*, basing his text on papers in his possession. He also included several invented dialogues, such as the celebrated "Conversation between Pascal and Sacy," which is supposedly based on a text by Pascal.[35] Even earlier, at the behest of Sacy himself, Lancelot, whom Sainte-Beuve called the "teacher par excellence," compiled souvenirs of that *directeur de conscience* par excellence, Saint-Cyran. Lancelot so revered Saint-Cyran that he divided the inmates of Port-Royal into two groups: those who were "of the time of M. du Verger" and those "who knew not Joseph."[36] And in 1697 and 1698, five or six months before his death, Du Fossé, who continued Sacy's work of explaining the books of the Bible, obedient to the wishes of the Jansenist Théméricourt family (we have already encountered the son, the Abbé d'Étemare, and his cousin Mlle de Théméricourt), had recounted his education at Port-Royal by Le Maître as well as the everyday life and cultural pursuits of the illustrious men who had preferred solitude to the world.

Since these authors did not write in order to be published, they contented themselves with collecting various kinds of information: details of conversions, retreats, portraits, pious exercises, travels, intellectual work, polemical works, waves of repression, marriages and exiles. These were assembled in more or less chronological order and in a manner befitting the relatively limited perspective they brought to the task. The editors therefore had not only to correct and rework the texts but also to collect additional documentation to supplement what was already there. These works continue even today to form the basis of any study of Port-Royal. The 1740 *Recueil d'Utrecht*, for example, was originally conceived as a "supplement" to the previous memoirs of Fontaine, Lancelot, and Du Fossé. It contains a large number of miscellaneous documents concerning, in particular, a number of *solitaires* about whom too little had been said in earlier works, including the famous "Mémoire sur la vie de M. Paschal," based on papers of Pascal's niece, Marguerite Périer. The preface to Fontaine's *Mémoires* indicates that some changes were made "for correctness of style and to avoid repetitions." In order to compensate for the lack of chronological order, particularly flagrant in the work of Sacy's secretary, the editors preceded his work with Tronchay's *Abrégé de l'histoire de Port-Royal*. Either in footnotes or in the body of the text they also indicated the dates of various events, and they compiled an "index of persons and subjects." An appendix included three short documents to complement the account of the daily lives of the "gentlemen."[37] Finally, in 1742, all the nuns' accounts and documents concerning the foundress of the order were collected in a three-volume set with a uniform style.[38]

All this effort reveals a determination to preserve, clarify, and exalt the memory of the great personages involved in the history of Port-Royal. The memory of the abbey was envisioned as a sort of "portrait gallery," and one could add new portraits or rearrange existing ones to tell a clearer story. Conceived in terms of a perfect unity among nuns, *solitaires,* and "outside friends," Port-Royal became synonymous with true piety, which was to be saved from oblivion. Given the disarray of the movement, the very identity of the Jansenists was at stake in this transfiguration of Port-Royal. As Abbé Goujet put it in his preface to the first *Mémoires pour servir à l'histoire de Port-Royal* of 1734, "men have indeed been able to destroy the substance of Port-Royal, to disperse its society, to prevent its continuation, and to destroy its walls, but it is not in their power to deprive it of its spirit or to dispel the fragrance of life that it gave off, and it is to that spirit that we must devote ourselves."

After being used as a living emblem in the service of an ongoing struggle, Port-Royal began to be relegated to the past, though for the time being that past remained quite abstract, almost atemporal, a link in a chain of examples drawn from sacred history. Idealized as belonging to a golden age reminiscent of early Christian fervor, the exemplary lives of nuns and *solitaires* would ultimately lead to "the triumph that truth must sooner or later win over errors that are allowed to gain credence temporarily only so that their eventual defeat may seem that much more impressive." The memory of Port-Royal solaced the appellants for their defeat and enabled them to cling to an ideal of purity unsullied by the vicissitudes of the age.

Writing History

It was the great conflict between king and *parlement* triggered by the dispute over the *billets de confession* that provided Jansenist authors with the perspective and overarching theme needed for writing a sustained, systematic history of Port-Royal. History was repeating itself in a most peculiar fashion: the "refusal of the sacrament" in the middle of the eighteenth century was reminiscent of the episode

L'ANTIPATHIQUE

Un Magistrat de la 2ᵉ des Requêtes exposa avec une éloquence mâle, e³ digne de l'auguste Sénat à qui il parloit, combien il étoit fâcheux de se voir arrêté dans un objet aussi important. (Il rappella) les principes sacrés de cette obéïssance primitive à laquelle les Magistrats doivent déférer plutôt qu'à l'obéïssance momentanée. (Il représenta) qu'il s'agissoit ici de la tranquillité de l'Etat, de celle des Sujets du Roi, et de la conservation de la Religion même. Le Schisme (ajouta t-il) se déclare manifestement dans la Capitale du Roïaume. Des Magistrats qui sont revêtus d'un Sacerdoce sacré et qui doivent par état veiller au maintien de la Religion e³ de la Paix, peuvent ils s'y opposer avec trop de zele ? Si on vouloit les empêcher d'agir, ce Seroit les anéantir. Rien ne doit donc empêcher leur zele et leur activité. C'est sur l'usage des Billets de Confession que l'on fonde ce Schisme. Poursuivons à jamais ce prétendu usage, qu'on fait servir à des nouveautés si dangereuses. Dit en Parlement le Lundi 27. mars 1752.

FIGURE 8.5   *The Refusal of the Sacraments;* engraving, 1752.

in which the nuns of Port-Royal were denied all the consolations of religion in 1664. It became possible to compare two distant epochs, setting each in perspective.

Once again the memory of Port-Royal was implicated in an ongoing religious and political struggle. This time, however, it emerged detached from its religious context, perhaps even somewhat secularized, and thus as a gleaming pendant to the dark myth of a "Jesuit conspiracy" that Jansenist authors concocted in the same period. The virtues and vices of the two religious adversaries tended to become secularized in the heat of a parlementary battle in which both were implicated as symbols. Published between 1752 and 1754, the three great histories of Port-Royal, by Clémencet, Besoigne, and Guilbert, coincided exactly with the unfolding of this latest controversy, the final offspring of the battle over *Unigenitus*.[39]

In the hope of flushing out Jansenist sympathizers and suspect priests, Christophe de Beaumont, the new archbishop of Paris, introduced a system of so-called *billets de confession* in 1749. A person suffering from a life-threatening illness was required to show the priest a *billet de confession* (or confession certificate) signed by a non-Jansenist confessor before the administration of viaticum or extreme unction or authorization of burial in consecrated ground.

These measures triggered a huge scandal in Paris. For the *parlement*, which had already taken up the defense of clergy persecuted for their rejection of the papal bull, this was an opportunity to intervene in a major way by pointing out that the Constitution could not be an article of faith since it had not received the unanimous approval of a council. The constitutional bishops were therefore abusing their authority. By 1750 the courts were taking action against priests responsible for refusing the sacraments to dying individuals, and several vehement remonstrances were addressed to the king. In the "great remonstrances" of April 1753, which would result in the *parlement*'s being exiled to Pontoise and replaced by the Chambre Royale, the *parlementaires* (among whom an active Jansenist group was led by the *avocat* Le Paige) resorted to an expression that *le grand* Arnauld had used in his *Apologie pour les religieuses de Port-Royal* to characterize their enemy: the heresy of domination.[40] The characteristic forms and diction of the seventeenth-century Jansenist resistance thus resurfaced in the midst of the parlementary struggle.

In this context Port-Royal served as an image of sincerity, of constant devotion to the truth in the face of persecution, of the cultural wealth of the nation, and of the value attached to the individual through education; this was contrasted with the "party of disguise and dissimulation," as the *Nouvelles ecclésiastiques* termed it.[41] All the histories share a common subtext: the tale of an enormous injustice, of a "rape of the laws," to borrow Guilbert's phrase. The political machinations had been secretly organized long before by Jesuits contemptuous of the fundamental laws of France. Not once, however, was the king named as the person responsible for the destruction of Port-Royal.

The meaning of the three historical narratives emerges from the chronological perspective they establish. For the first time these three texts dare to recount the history of the abbey as one long tale of arbitrary persecution met by heroic resistance. Three great waves of sanctions hit Port-Royal one after another until it is completely obliterated. "There is nothing in history more astonishing than the virtually constant vexations visited upon this *sainte Maison* until it was utterly destroyed," wrote Jérôme Besoigne (1680–1763), the first historian of Port-Royal as well as a doctor of the Sorbonne and important member of the "Jansenist party."

The abbey now had a history of its own, independent of sacred history. The task now was to establish the facts of the matter according to the rules of Benedictine scholarship rather than to cast the history of Port-Royal as yet another example in the timeless tableau of the defenders of truth within the Church. All three authors carefully quote from the printed sources. Guilbert (1697–1759), the preceptor of Louis XV's pages and defender of the *convulsionnaires*, even went so far as to express doubts about the printed sources and advocate a systematic use of manuscript documents only. He criticized the religiosity of those who viewed the abbey's archives as relics, on the grounds that they contributed to the fragmentation of the record by scattering invaluable manuscripts all over the place. His scholarly passion drove him to initiate a violent dispute among the three authors, even though all were on the same side in the struggle, over questions of sources, narration, and interpretation. Of the three he was the only one to draw the full chronological consequences of treating his subject independent of sacred history. Although he began, like his rivals, by recounting the abbey's history from the reform of 1608 to its destruction, he chose to trace the history all the way back to the foundation of the abbey between 1204 and 1350, convinced as he was that the spirit of the place could be found even in the etymology of its name, "Porrois," a soggy, uncultivated patch of land. His account of the intervening years (which would no doubt have caused him great difficulty) was never published.

The project of writing the history of Port-Royal was not an isolated phenomenon. In the same period other Jansenist writers concerned themselves with the history of their hereditary enemy, the Jesuits, in a form different from the traditional compilation of the past century's worth of grievances. Le Paige, for example, together with Boursier's student the Abbé Coudrette, wrote a vast history of the Jesuits, the second part of which dealt with their political theology.[42] The allegation of a cabal, traditionally (since the Fronde) raised against the Jansenists, was now turned back against the Jesuits, who were suspected of hatching dark plots and of seeking "to establish themselves as a monarchy or, rather, a universal despotism." The heroic image of resistance in the name of obedience developed in the various histories of Port-Royal had its dark counterpart in the myth of the "Jesuit conspiracy" that other Jansenist authors elaborated simultaneously. Guilbert, in his first volume on the founding of the abbey (published in 1758), included a long digression on Damiens's attempt to assassinate Louis XV, which he compared to the horrors of the Ligue. It was of course the Jesuits who accused Port-Royal of entering into leagues, factions, and other conspiracies against the sovereign. Guilbert countered that "the heirs to the sentiments of Port-Royal" had always respected the king, preferring, "in perfect fidelity, to endure prison and exile, to suffer the uttermost misery and privation of all temporal solace during their lifetimes and of all spiritual assistance at their deaths." Dom Clémencet (1703–1758), a Benedictine of Saint-Maur celebrated for his *Art de vérifier les dates,* also contributed to both the anti-Jesuit myth and the glorification of Port-Royal. Both perspectives can be found in his *Histoire générale de Port-Royal,* which might have been called "the century of Port-Royal." Even as "the century of Louis XIV" was becoming an object of veneration in the wake of Voltaire's eloquent account, Clémencet pointed out that the true splendor of the age was to be found in Port-Royal, which was responsible for advances in education and culture in general, criticism, history, and the enrichment of the language. Of the three Jansenist historians, it was Clémencet, the author as well of a "Histoire littéraire de Port-Royal" that remained in manuscript, who did most to point out the central cultural contribution of Port-Royal, which he saw in some respects as a spiritual precursor of the Enlightenment. He placed particular emphasis, for example, on the attention paid to individuality in Port-Royal's theory of education, a conception totally opposed to the Jesuit precept *perinde ac cadaver.* He also arranged for the publication of the *Conférences de la Mère Angélique de Saint-Jean* in Utrecht in 1760, as a sort of counterpoint to the *Constitutions* of the Company of Jesus which were subjected to such close scrutiny by the *parlements* in the same period.

When the Company of Jesus was expelled from France, Port-Royal, at the culmination of this decisive phase in the recording of its history, became an "official" pilgrimage site, complete with a *Manuel des pèlerins de Port-Royal des Champs,* which recommended an itinerary including several stops, and was published in 1767 by that fierce enemy of the Jesuits the Abbé Jean-Antoine Gazaignes (1717–1802), known by the pseudonym Philibert.[43] Designed to serve as a pocket guide, the book also contained prayers, an obituary list, and an abridged history of Port-Royal des Champs along with a bibliography of works by the *solitaires.* What Gazaignes magnified even more than the examples of piety was a set of lay virtues, "the testimony to a clear conscience," "the cradle of our attachment to truth and of our courage and steadfastness in its defense," and "the love of justice." "In their state of servitude," he went on, the saints of the Société de Port-Royal "found the secret of how to become free."

This politicization of the image of the two principal, and antagonistic, religious groups of the seventeenth century played an important part in determining the course of events themselves. The united *parlements* scored their first major victory against the Jesuits, putting an end to a century-old dispute.[44]

The histories of Port-Royal were far more than a mirror image of the *parlement*'s remonstrances and decrees, which in turn drew censure, oversight, and orders of exile from the king and his ministers. If the struggle over the *parlement* played such an important role in the construction of Port-Royal's history, it was because the *parlements* had already taken up the religious ideal defended by the Jansenists in the ecclesiastical sphere and carried it over into the political sphere. Like the Port-Royalistes, the *parlementaires* advocated resistance in the name of obedience, not only to God's absolutism but also "to the fundamental laws of the Kingdom," which transcended the person of the king. The nuns, *solitaires,* and appellants were the "repositories of truth in the Church," and the *parlementaires* saw themselves as "defenders of the repository of laws in the State." In order to grasp fully what was new about the resistance to *Unigenitus,* it is not enough simply to invoke the conciliar tradition or the traditional liberties of the Gallican Church. It was the Augustinian and figurist ecclesiology of preserving a "deposit of faith" in the Church through the community of saints, including both clergy and laity, that initially fueled the appeal to the national council and later guided the interventions of the *parlements.* As the religious struggle shifted to the political arena, it was simultaneously secularized within the framework of figurist theology. The role of the *parlements* as guardians of the law was legitimized, much as earlier the appellants were sacralized because they had taken up Port-Royal's sacred combat within the Church. The *parlementaires* and the appellants shared the same attitude, one of intransigent opposition in the name of obedience to the truth, whether in church or state. The example of Port-Royal shaped the course of parlementary politics, as if the abbey's history did indeed prefigure that of the *parlements.*

The Archivist

After the Appeal, the resistance of the *parlements* too thus became an integral part of the history of Port-Royal itself, one of its continuations. The archives of the "battle for truth," whether waged by the appellants or the *convulsionnaires* or the magistrates, became as precious as the moral treasure of the abbey itself. These additional documents were now collected and published with the same concern to bear witness to exemplary conduct.

When the *Nécrologes* were published in mid-century for the purpose of exalting the memory of the principal appellants much as earlier necrologies had exalted the memory of the Port-Royalistes, certain *parlementaires* were included along with them.[45] In addition, important documents bearing on the *parlementaires*' struggle began to appear in religious works. The fifth volume of Cerveau's *Supplément au*

FIGURE 8.6 *The Evils of the Constitution in Parlement;* engraving, 1732.

Nécrologe, the most important compilation of obituaries of the "defenders of truth," included the Paris Parlement's principal remonstrances before 1764. In other words, these legal documents were treated as the equivalents of the great ecclesiastical attestations of the Appeal. The *Recueil général des actes d'appel inter-jettés au futur Concile général* by Nivelle, a pupil of Boursier's, included "decrees and other acts of the Parlement of the Kingdom which have to do with these matters." The figurists' key work of historical vulgarization, the *Catéchisme historique et dog-matique* by the Abbé de Fourquevaux (one of d'Étemare's Saint-Magloire disci-ples), was revised by Troya d'Assigny (the first editor of the *Nouvelles ecclésias-tiques*) to include an appendix on the "progress of the dispute" through 1760.[46] The *Nouvelles ecclésiastiques* reported in great detail on the debates that took place in the chambers of the Parlement of Paris. Its 1760 index contained 318 columns in fine print recapitulating "measures taken by Parlement for the public good and means used to oppress this illustrious Company." "Editorials" regularly interpreted recent events by setting them in a historical context that began with the destruction of Port-Royal, which became the universal cause of all the woes of church and state. In 1790 the Revolution itself was interpreted as a logical consequence of the perse-cution of the abbey and the appellants, which had opened doors for the first time to the impious spirit promoted by the Jesuits and the *philosophes.*

One man would devote his life, with remarkable devotion and abnegation, to the immense effort of preserving this historical record: Louis-Adrien Le Paige (1712–1803). As party spokesman he would hail the Constituent Assembly's eccle-siastical reforms. His efforts led to the assembling of an imposing archive of docu-ments concerning the history of Jansenism from Port-Royal to the revolutionary crisis: more than 15,000 printed and handwritten documents intended to pave the way for restoring truth within the Church. This modest figure, all but unknown to history, was nevertheless one of the principal actors in the parlementary politics of the eighteenth century. Overshadowed by his voluminous polemics and occasional historical pieces, a single book constitutes Le Paige's claim on posterity: the *Lettres historiques sur les fonctions essentielles du Parlement,* the one visible product of an enormous output, much of it anonymous. It was published in 1753 under the same imprint ("Aux dépens de la Compagnie") used previously for the publication of the *Mémoires pour servir à l'histoire de Port-Royal.* Fired by the belief that he alone was the repository of the history of one of the most important affairs involving church and state, the humble attorney secretly pulled strings and successfully manipulated the outcome of the political struggle over the *parlements.*

Le Paige himself was the link between the figurists of Saint-Magloire and the Jansenist group in the *parlements.* His career demonstrates how it was possible to move from figurist religious beliefs to political action. His education took place at the height of the struggle against *Unigenitus,* when the lawyers joined the battle to defend the Jansenist bishop Soanen after he was deposed by the Council of Embrun

FIGURE 8.7   Louis-Adrien Le Paige, after a drawing by Mlle Hélène Dehaussy.

in 1727. Three of his uncles, including M. Hideux, a syndic of the Sorbonne, were
fervent appellants. Having become intimately familiar with the figurist message
through his reading of Jansenist propaganda, Le Paige was quick to wax enthusiastic about the miracles of Saint-Médard, of which he recorded several eyewitness
accounts. Along with some forty companions, he became a regular participant in the

figurative ceremonies of the *convulsionnaires*. He continued to follow the sect's activities and ascetic practices right up to the time of the Revolution.

Le Paige the attorney was encouraged to enter into public affairs by his belief that he was representing the defense in the "trial of God's cause." In 1732, when he was just twenty, he was already bold enough to defend the *Nouvelles ecclésiastiques* after their condemnation by viaticum, the archbishop of Paris.[47]

His great chance came at the end of 1756, when he was nominated bailiff of the Temple, a post that would guarantee him immunity from prosecution and allow him considerable freedom to maneuver. He was appointed to this position by the Prince de Conti, the grand prior of Malta, who, having quarreled with Louis XV, gave up his post as head of the king's Secret Council and assumed leadership of the parlementary opposition. He no doubt chose Le Paige to head his staff because the lawyer had already proved his worth in the affair of the denial of the sacraments.[48]

FIGURE 8.8   Diagram showing the distribution of the *Nouvelles ecclésiastiques,* 1728–1803.

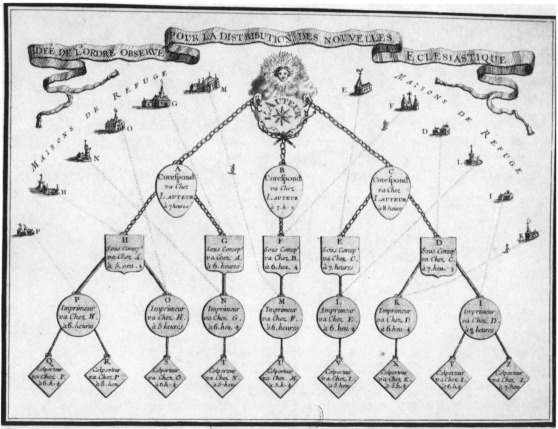

From 1750 to 1774, in the thick of the struggle over the *parlement*, Le Paige played a leading role as the chief theoretician of the Jansenist magistrates. He occupied a key position in the party structure, maintaining relations with Presidents Durey de Meinières and de Murard, the head of Conti's council, with party theologians such as Gourlin, with canonists such as Maultrot, with the editors of the *Nouvelles ecclésiastiques*, with Harlay and Montazet, the bishops of Cambray and Lyons, and with provincial *parlementaires*. Not only was he the author of major works on the history and background of the various *parlements*, he also participated in drafting the "law of silence" as well as various proposals to bring peace to church and state by eliminating *Unigenitus* as a rule of faith.[49] He also developed the main political arguments against the Jesuits and coordinated the decrees of the various *parlements* at the time of their expulsion. During the Maupeou revolution, he was credited with being the author of any number of pamphlets that thwarted the chancellor's efforts to reform the monarchy. Suspected of having a hand in the drafting of a pamphlet entitled *Correspondance [de] Maupeou avec son coeur Sorhouet* and of operating a clandestine printing shop within the Temple walls, he was obliged in 1772 to go into hiding for two years in Beauce. The magistrates appreciated the extent of his historical knowledge and above all his collection of documents, reputed to be one of the most comprehensive of the age, as can be seen by a glance at the article entitled "Parlement" in the *Encyclopédie* (attributed to Boucher d'Argis). Le Paige provided several notes and excerpts from parlementary decrees of centuries past to the committee that drafted the Great Remonstrances of 1753. He readily lent out his books and documents and revised or completed texts written by a number of magistrates. He was "the Parlement's secretary."[50]

Without the figurist theology of history that provided the impetus for his activities, it is impossible to understand either Le Paige's perseverance as a collector or the size of the collection he amassed. His 15,000 documents were concerned exclusively with "affairs of the day" relevant to the Jansenist controversy, excluding for instance all contemporary historical works not written by friendly hands. Le Paige's collection made him the trustee, secretary, and archivist of God's cause. This was his secret lifelong battle, which earned him the *nom de guerre* the *chevalier de Jérusalem*.

He began both his career and his collection in 1732, at a crucial moment in the religious and political crisis, during the strike of the Paris Parlement and the related emergence of the *convulsionnaires*. In a note drafted in his minuscule hand in 1733, he described his method of classification, which was both chronological and thematic. His initial collecting bore on the question of miracles and, later, of convulsions, which elicited an outpouring of books, pamphlets, and drafts of speeches. He also collected documents connected with the parlementary controversy that was erupting at about the same time, but they went into a separate category of the collection that received no greater emphasis than the archives of the *convulsionnaires*. What made these documents worthy of belonging to a single archive was that all were strands of a single historical thread. Here we see a clear sign of the influence of the *Nouvelles ecclésiastiques* and of the figurist theology of history on the *convulsionnaire* attorney, who followed all the ins and outs of the *Unigenitus* controversy and scrutinized events as so many signs of God's will: "Compilations of this sort are nothing but storehouses in which one finds the indicated documents, which form a historical unit (*corps d'histoire*), arranged according to the time of their appearance in the *Nouvelles ecclésiastiques,* which connects the various documents to one another and would, had I stayed with my original intention, have served as an index."[51] Le Paige kept no diary or register. His outlook was not that of an author; on the contrary, he considered himself a modest observer caught up in the providential course of history. His personal notes, outlines, and projects, recorded on separate sheets, can be found scattered throughout his collections of documents. Often he covered printed or handwritten documents with notes that served as reminders in his own reflections. He did not make judgments but sought to understand, to gather all the available information, as if in the final analysis the ultimate meaning of all these earthly records would be left to the one infallible judge, who, when the time came, would render his verdict to humanity.

Safe behind the walls of the Temple, Le Paige indefatigably documented all the important religious and parlementary controversies through 1789. After Conti's death in 1776, however, his enormous, systematic compilations seem to thin out somewhat, only to disappear mysteriously about 1785. In fact, despite his growing blindness, Le Paige was still collecting printed documents. He must have lent out the final volumes, having to do with the Turgot edicts, the parlementary troubles of 1787 and 1788, the Assemblies of Notables, and the Estates General of 1789, because the Archives Nationales recently regained possession of them. During the Revolution, driven from the Temple, ruined, and almost completely blind, he probably lacked both the money and the physical capacity to purchase pamphlets, yet he carried on, at his home in the Rue Charlot, organizing and annotating his work during the very height of the Terror, still convinced that he was working for "the future of the Church."

The question of the origins of the Jansenist dispute was of course one that interested Le Paige passionately. He gradually worked his way back into the past, first collecting pamphlets and other texts from the early stages of the Appeal, then moving back toward Port-Royal, the *petites lettres,* the controversies over grace, and finally the treatises of Jansenius himself. It was Le Paige who collected the bulk of the manuscripts in the so-called Théméricourt Collection, probably with the assistance of d'Étemare, who had inherited many of the documents from his cousin in 1745. At the end of the century Le Paige even managed to purchase the original of the *Vérité des miracles démontrée,* the very copy that its author, the Jansenist and *convulsionnaire* magistrate Carré de Montgeron, had been so bold as to place into the king's own hands in 1737, in defiance of all the rules of etiquette.

Le Paige's many connections, together with his willingness to lend volumes from his library or provide references on demand, made it possible for the whole Port-Royaliste tradition of resistance, preserved in document after document, to transmit its influence to the *parlements* themselves. And as that tradition inspired any number of parlementary texts, they were in turn added to the collection. Thus the Le Paige collection became the source of Port-Royal's future image. Even historians who work today on the history of the *parlements* are in Le Paige's debt, for the archives on the Rue Saint-Jacques were used to prepare the critical edition of the *Remonstrances of the Paris Parlement*.[52]

Opposition in the name of obedience to the truth, insistence on sincerity in the face of all opposition, adherence to inward freedom in spite of outward constraint, the exemplary heroism of Port-Royal: all these were omnipresent in the behavior and language of the principals in our tale, whether they be called appellants or *parlementaires*. All saw themselves as the direct spiritual heirs of the nuns and *solitaires* of Port-Royal. Because the ideal of Port-Royal was so deeply implicated in some of the major intellectual controversies of the last seventy-five years of the Ancien Régime, it was inevitable that after 1789 people would raise the question of Jansenism's responsibility in paving the way for the Revolution.

Port-Royal and the Revolution

It was during the revolutionary period that the myth of the Jansenist party's subversive political activity reached full maturity. In fact, Jansenism had all but disappeared as an active force by 1774. The number of publications of works from or about Port-Royal also dropped sharply.[53] The allegations of a "Jansenist conspiracy" or "Port-Royal republicanism" thus stemmed not so much from any obvious Jansenist involvement in the politics of the Revolution as from the fact that the intimate connection of Jansenist issues with political matters earlier in the century had left profound traces. Jacob-Nicolas Moreau, the last royal historiographer, expressed this suspicion of Jansenism quite well in his *Souvenirs*: "Anyone who has followed the chain of events will readily agree that the controversies over the Constitution Unigenitus, in which the ministry repeatedly took such unreasonable and untenable positions, led by degrees to the terrible disputes over our Political Constitution."[54]

It was a revolutionary figure, and one of religious background at that, who lent credence to the view that Jansenist political theology had a republican coloration: namely, the Abbé Henri-Baptiste Grégoire, friend of Blacks and champion of the "regeneration" of the Jews, constitutional bishop of Blois, and defender of freedom of religion. In his *Ruines de Port-Royal*, written in 1801 in the wake of the Concordat, which put an end to all the Constitutional Church's hopes of reconstruction, the École de Port-Royal was cast in retrospect as the embodiment of the true revolutionary tradition. This republican transfiguration of Port-Royal, which cast the abbey's *solitaires* as theoretical proponents of popular sovereignty, would be echoed by a number of voices in the nineteenth century, and most notably by certain historians of the Revolution: Jules Michelet, Louis Blanc, Henri Martin, and Jean Jaurès.

After the parlementary Jansenists succeeded in thwarting the monarchy's attempts to reform itself under Chancellor Maupeou, the opposition movement lost much of its political *raison d'être*. Ten years earlier it had destroyed the principal underpinning of its religious existence by expelling the Jesuits. After the chancellor closed the *parlements* in 1772, Le Paige, at once lucid and fatalistic, foresaw the consequences of the governmental stalemate: "The State has come to such a degree of evils through the abuses that have corrupted its excellent constitution that its ruin is almost inevitable.... I see only too clearly that the government's present course will end sooner or later in either the ruin of the State or some spectacular reform, which may go too far."[55] Once the *parlements* were restored, the *Nouvelles ecclésiastiques* lost much of its foothold in the political news of the day. Its pages increasingly seemed nostalgic for the golden age of the battle in favor of the Appeal, while tirelessly continuing to hurl accusations at both Jesuits and *philosophes*, said to be the chief culprits in the rise of impiety. The taking of the Bastille was simply ignored.

The Jansenist party's last theologians were much weaker metaphysicians than their predecessors. Gourlin (died 1775) and Bon-François Rivière, known as Pelvert (1714–1781), were unable to respond to the new questions of the day. Even worse, they fell to bickering over the most crucial issue in Christianity, the nature of the eucharistic sacrifice. The party's learned canonists proved more influential: Mey (1712–1796), Jabineau (1724–1790), and Maultrot (1714–1803). But they pursued a secular path that moved ever farther away from the Port-Royaliste tradition, incorporating elements of natural-law thinking. In the end Maultrot, after affirming, as early as 1775, the nation's right to convoke the Estates General, became openly critical of Arnauld and Nicole's arguments in favor of absolute monarchy.[56] In contrast to what one might have expected, this group, which was generally considered to be the enlightened, "progressive" faction of the party, was the most vehemently opposed to the religious reforms attempted by the Constituent Assembly.

The Civil Constitution of the Clergy that was adopted on July 12, 1790, reduced the clergy to a corps of civil servants subject to the strict authority of the people and local officials. Both prelates and parish priests were to be chosen by election. The political at last took full precedence over the spiritual: Louis XIV himself would never have dared to hope for such a total victory. To register their disagreement, Maultrot, Jabineau, and Mey created an oppositional newspaper under the title *Nouvelles ecclésiastiques ou Mémoires pour servir à l'histoire de la Constitution prétendue civile du clergé*, which appeared from September 1791 to August 10, 1792. After heated attacks on the "despotism of the bishops," they contradicted their own earlier writings by reaffirming the political independence of the spiritual authorities.

Having argued for the nation's rightful authority over the monarch, they now condemned the king's deposition.[57]

The Jansenists were among the first to be taken unawares by the Revolution, which completed their division by forcing them to take positions on the issues of the day. The party's canonists, who had explicitly transported the religious reasoning of the Gallican and conciliar tradition into the political domain, now drew back, terrified at the thought of completely depriving the Church of any independent jurisdiction and breaking the mold of monarchical representation. The only exception was the Jansenist attorney Camus, who fully accepted the king's death. By contrast, the figurist faction of the party associated with the *Nouvelles ecclésiastiques* as it was run by d'Étemare's students, though suspected of "fanaticism," accepted the transformation of the Gallican Church through the Civil Constitution of the Clergy as a sign that the long-awaited reform or "regeneration" of the Church had at last begun. Since the Church's only power was spiritual, it was essential to confiscate the property of wealthy ecclesiastical despots in order to compensate for past abuses. The suddenly revolutionary tone of the paper's editorials after January 1790 is surprising. The early steps toward the reorganization of church and state were naturally interpreted within the framework of the theology of history that the paper had embraced ever since its inception. These recent developments were consequences of the destruction of Port-Royal, of the promulgation of the Constitution, of the persecution of the appellants, of the rise of ignorance and impiety, and of the spirit common to both Jesuits and *philosophes*. Despite their opposition to the Enlightenment, the Jansenist broadsheets had indeed in their own way laid the groundwork for the emergence of a kind of revolutionary mentality.

Perhaps the contradictions inherent in the movement throughout the eighteenth century erupted in this revelatory moment of crisis. The "political" strand of Jansenism, involving reflection on public law, unwittingly laid the groundwork for popular sovereignty, but in the final analysis it could not conceive of itself outside the framework of monarchical representation and a politically independent Church. The more "religious" branch, involving the figurist theology of history, fought the *philosophes* throughout the Ancien Régime yet readily embraced the new political constitution as a manifestation of history's providential course. In both cases, but most strikingly in the most religious of the Jansenists, Augustinianism with its insistence on the absolute rule of God had the effect of countering hierarchy and promoting secularism.

Where there is smoke, there is fire. There is some basis to the myth of the Jansenists' spiritual responsibility for the new organization of the Church despite the negative findings of historians. Research has in fact shown that there were at most a tiny number of Jansenists among the deputies of the Constituent Assembly and that only four of the attorneys on the ecclesiastical committee responsible for drafting the Civil Constitution of the Clergy can be considered Jansenists, and then only with respect to the nature of their training in canon law: Durand de Maillane, Martineau, Lanjuinais, and Treilhard. Nevertheless, rumors of a Jansenist plot began circulating immediately after the vote. In the *Découverte importante sur le vrai système de la Constitution du clergé décrétée par l'Assemblée nationale,* which was published in 1791 and which the *Nouvelles ecclésiastiques* attributed to Abbé Barruel, the Civil Constitution was denounced as an amalgam of Richerism, Calvinism, and Jansenism, the latter being the supreme heresy subsuming the two others. The Jansenists, it was alleged, had hidden behind the ecclesiastical committee, "in accordance with their custom of always making themselves invisible."[58] The Comte d'Antraigues also accused them of making common cause with the Protestants and *philosophes* for the purpose of destroying Catholicism in France.[59] On May 27, 1791, Sieyès himself reproached "certain" members of the ecclesiastical committee, whom he refused to name, for seeing "the Revolution as nothing more than a perfect occasion to apotheosize the spirits of Port-Royal."

Only after the wave of dechristianization had subsided did the abbey regain its positive political image. Port-Royal was reborn as a precursor of the Constitutional Church that Abbé Grégoire attempted to revive in the wake of Thermidor. And so, for example, on Corpus Christi in 1796 the bishops who were working to reestablish religion in France[60] went to Saint-Médard, the only parish church open at the time, to celebrate a solemn service intended to make amends for the insults heaped upon Jesus during the Revolution. Interestingly enough, the objects used in the ritual ceremony came from Port-Royal des Champs.[61]

In a similar vein, the members of the Société de Philosophie Chrétienne, a "religious and republican society" founded by Grégoire in 1797, which counted Le Paige among its members, made a pilgrimage to the ruins of Port-Royal des Champs every October.[62]

As things began to look worse and worse for the Gallican proposal put forward by the Constitutional bishops, Port-Royal was invoked more and more often as a symbol. After the 1801 ratification by Napoleon and Pope Pius VII of the Concordat, which restored the authority of the Holy See over all French Catholics, Grégoire went to Saint-Lambert to meditate prior to submitting his resignation. There he composed a brief pamphlet entitled *Les Ruines de Port-Royal,* a sort of visitors' guidebook.[63] The *rêverie du promeneur* around the ruins of Port-Royal of course owed much to the preromantic vogue for poetic ruins and cemeteries, but its nostalgia was more political than religious. Although Grégoire cannot be termed an unambiguous Jansenist on the basis of any of his initiatives within the Constituent Assembly or Convention or even of his pastoral work at Blois, when the Revolution was over he became an adept of a sort of utopian Port-Royal based on the same alliance of revolutionary and Christian ideals that had inspired his political action. His Port-Royal was that of the good Revolution, of the liberal, republican, moral, and Christian tradition. Unlike the party newspaper, the abbé was not content simply to associate the events of the Revolution with the history of the Jansenist controversy. He found the principles of the Revolution within the very political theology of the "École de Port-Royal." All the theologians of that school had raised "a double barrier against the encroachments of political and ultramontane despotism." Grégoire admired the "splendors of republicanism" not just in the eighteenth-century writers Maultrot, Legros, and d'Étemare but in the very first text by Jansenius, the *Mars Gallicus*. In Saint-Cyran's *Question royale* he saw "the principles of popular sovereignty." He even found traces of the same idea in Pascal and pointed to a text in which Arnauld attacked William III, the Prince of Orange, as a "tyrant" and usurper.[64] He was nevertheless obliged to concede that Maultrot had been right to combat the celebrated theologian's "less liberal ideas concerning monarchy." In an error that says a great deal about his desire to see Jansenism as a precursor in the battle for "the superiority of the Estates over the king," Grégoire attributed the Protestant Jurieu's *Soupirs de la France esclave qui aspire à la liberté* to an "adherent of Port-Royal."

Port-Royal became an intellectual focal point of the Enlightenment. It took part in the "progress of the human spirit" through its useful contributions to educational theory and practice as well as works such as the *Grammaire générale* and *Logique*, which won the admiration of the editors of the *Encyclopédie*. In addition, the organizational structure of the *Nouvelles ecclésiastiques* served as a model of how to circumvent the vigilance of the "French Inquisition." Grégoire went so far as to compare the history of Port-Royal to the situation in his own day, "when a number of European governments, joined in a conspiracy against the freedom of the press, are attempting to tighten the irons in which their people, their dethroned sovereigns, are held." Eventually, of course, Grégoire came to meditate over the ruins of the Revolution. He could not dismiss the swerve into terrorism and dechristianization. Even if Port-Royal had not been destroyed by Louis XIV, it would have been assailed by "vandals" with axes and torches. Grégoire would have liked to see society reborn "along the lines of that of the children of Bérulle" but knew that his wish was "fanciful." For the first time the memory of Port-Royal, which until then had functioned as an emblem of combat, consolation, or hope, offered no prospect on the future. Grégoire's text ends on a highly nostalgic note. Port-Royal was reduced to nothing more than a utopia, yet he immortalized that utopia and in so doing laid the groundwork for a new republican and secular posterity.

The Quintessence of the Grand Siècle

In the nineteenth century Jansenism was no more than a shadow of its former self, and what little life remained in the movement was all but snuffed out by the Vatican

FIGURE 8.9   *The Pilgrimage of Piety,* Firmin-Louis Tournus, priest, and François de Pâris, deacon of Port-Royal.

Council of 1870. The Loi Falloux, which restored the Jesuits' right to teach, followed by the promulgation of the doctrine of papal infallibility, marked the final defeat of Gallican forces. Yet even as the last vestiges of the Jansenist sensibility were being eliminated, Port-Royal was enjoying its most illustrious period as a cultural icon. Instead of fading into oblivion, Port-Royal entered the cultural sphere, where it was exalted as the quintessence of the Grand Siècle. The latest transfiguration carried with it an implicit value judgment concerning the history of the movement that had sustained the abbey's memory. The literary and spiritual Port-Royal of the seventeenth century would forever after be identified with all that was best in Jansenism. The "other" Jansenism, the political Jansenism of the eighteenth century, was discredited and consigned to oblivion.

Traces of the Jansenist presence in the nineteenth century are diffuse. There were of course pilgrimages to the ruins of Port-Royal, which drew sympathizers from all over the world, from the Italian Jansenists of the Risorgimento[65] to English feminists who looked upon the nuns of Port-Royal as their own sisters.[66] Shortly after the Revolution a Jansenist philanthropic society was established, and much of the movement's remaining resources and energies were funneled into it, but its activities were limited to the realms of charity and education as well as to perpetuating the memory of Port-Royal.[67]

Apart from this last gasp of militancy, there was one final outbreak of Gallican versus ultramontane emotion during the Restoration. In opposition to the ultramontanes Bonald, Lamennais, and de Maistre, who advocated restoring the prerogatives of the Holy See and the ecclesiastical hierarchy, liberals and Gallicans joined in a coalition against the ultraroyalist Villèle ministry and denounced backstage manipulations by Jesuits and the "priestly party."[68] Included in this group were a few descendants of important Jansenist families such as Royer-Collard, Barante, Molé, Pasquier, Rémusat, and Montlosier, but it is impossible to find any sort of doctrinal coherence within this rather ill-defined group of occasional allies.

In this spooky atmosphere, marked by the resurgence of old disputes, the inveterate enemy of the Jesuits picked up the banner of liberty, and the old fantasy of a Jansenist plot resurfaced. Villemain, in his "Tableau du Grand Siècle," painted Arnauld's and Pascal's struggle against the Jesuits as a precursor of liberalism's struggles in his own day.[69] Conversely, de Maistre completed Barruel's portrait of the origins of the French Revolution by including the Jansenist "sect" among those responsible for the upheaval and casting Jansenius as a disciple of Hobbes.[70] Lamennais went even further, denouncing the Jansenists as a "dangerous faction" highly reminiscent of Calvinism, "especially in its energetic genius, incapable of submitting to obedience and always ready to rebel."[71]

Yet this last stirring of Jansenists reduced to Gallicanism soon fizzled. Under Napoleon III, and following the proclamation of the dogma of the Immaculate

Conception, ultramontane ideas, widely publicized by Veuillot's *L'Univers,* emerged victorious. Priests in training would henceforth be required to read new textbooks that portrayed the Jansenist writers and even the Benedictines of Saint-Maur as direct disciples of Calvin and Luther combined.[72]

If the spirit of Port-Royal could not be passed on, an idealization of its image could be saved. After 1830, thanks to critical studies and scholarly editions, a new picture of the seventeenth century began to emerge. In this construction of French "classicism," Port-Royal would figure as the period's finest flower. The emblem of Port-Royal lost its polemical and political edge as it was transferred to the cultural sphere. The most important stage manager of this transformation was surely the literary critic Sainte-Beuve.[73] Of the many nineteenth-century figures from Chateaubriand to George Sand who daydreamed of monarchy, he was far from the only one to take an interest in Jansenism. The history of Port-Royal also attracted the interest of historians. At the Collège de France, Jean-Jacques Ampère offered a course in France's early seventeenth-century religious awakening. Antoine Latour, in his *Esquisses historiques* (1834) devoted to the nuns and *solitaires* of Port-Royal, explained why his contemporaries were so interested in the subject: "Our century, which is as much literary as political, loves Port-Royal for having reminded national studies of past sources of genius."[74]

Fashion alone, however, cannot explain the success of Sainte-Beuve's interpretation. Previously Port-Royal had been inextricably associated with Jansenism. For Sainte-Beuve's contemporaries the abbey was most celebrated for the persecution it had suffered and for Jansenist support of Gallican liberties. Sainte-Beuve's originality was to sever political Jansenism on the one hand from spiritual and literary Port-Royal on the other. The author's distaste for theological disputation was already apparent in Amaury, the hero of his novel *Volupté*. In Lausanne, where he was invited by people associated with the Protestant "awakening," Sainte-Beuve gave a course of some twenty intensive lectures, from the autumn of 1837 to the spring of 1838. In them he sketched the outlines of a classic drama. It began with the "day at the grille," continued with scenes devoted to Saint-Cyran and Pascal and several other distinctive *solitaires,* and culminated with Racine's *Athalie.* The conclusion of the tragedy was cast in the form of a long autumn, a period of decline, a desiccation already apparent in the overly disputatious Arnauld. Port-Royal's theologians were treated more as writers than as men of religion engaged in a battle to reform the Church from within. This central aspect of the Cistercian monastery's activity is strikingly absent from Sainte-Beuve's account. Sainte-Beuve denied that he was writing a history of the abbey like others that had gone before. He claimed instead to be painting a "portrait of Port-Royal" whose purpose was to reveal the soul of this august "personage." What interested him was discovering the abbey's spiritual and literary contribution to French classicism. The gallery of portraits of Port-Royal authors is therefore psychological, cut off from Jansenist controversies as such and omitting much of the eighteenth-century historical sequel: "What I wanted to create was a History not of Port-Royal but of the Spirit of Port-Royal, and, within that spirit, of what was pure, rare, unique, and eternally worthy of memory—the spirit that flowered in *Athalie* and not the spirit that went to the grave with Deacon Pâris."[75] Sainte-Beuve's stated purpose loses some of its apparent originality when one begins to examine his sources. His library in fact included all the histories of Port-Royal, including the manuscript literary history of Clémencet as well as the compilation by the Oratorian librarian Adry (1749–1818), which contains a great deal of information on the Petites Écoles. We also know that Sainte-Beuve read six volumes of records of *convulsionnaire* ceremonies, which apparently so frightened him that he ever after spoke only of the "ignominy of the convulsions" and withdrew his admiration for the theologian Duguet. His documentation mentions almost none of the works of Quesnel and not one document from the abundant polemical literature against *Unigenitus*.[76] Indeed, by using his predecessors' work uncritically, Sainte-Beuve only fulfilled the aim of the eighteenth-century Jansenists on whom he relied, which was to exalt the example of the illustrious men of Port-Royal in order to draw a discreet veil over the subsequent theological defeat. Perhaps part of the reason for the success of his work was that it was the realization of this century-old project. Even Sainte-Beuve's accentuation of character study simply continued and reflected the concern with the uniqueness of exemplary figures that was such a distinctive feature of Jansenist historiography. The first volumes of Sainte-Beuve's *Port-Royal*, which came out in 1840 and 1842, enjoyed only modest success.[77] It took longer for the work to establish itself as a new way of approaching religious history, with a mixture of respectful sympathy and detachment, but its influence was certainly felt by Renan and by Taine, who characterized the work as one that explored the "vast province of human psychology."[78] It was not until 1904, however, in ceremonies marking the centenary of Sainte-Beuve's birth, that Brunetière honored the work as a "masterpiece of French criticism."[79] As the fortunes of Sainte-Beuve's book rose along with the study of French literary classics in the schools, Pascal—in a case unique in the whole history of letters—became the modern man *par excellence*, the figure with whom readers identified. Victor Cousin, who launched the vogue for philological studies of Pascal manuscripts with his celebrated 1842 report to the Académie Française "Sur la nécessité d'une nouvelle édition des *Pensées*," caught the spirit of this identification most eloquently. He too hoped to distill the pure Pascal from the altered texts of Jansenist editions prepared with polemical intent: "Our skepticism and our exaltation, our discouragements and our pride, our need to believe and to love and our difficulty in doing so—he felt all of this."[80] *Esprit de finesse* and *esprit de géométrie*, sublime misanthrope, frightful genius, pessimist, ironist, precursor of impiety, skeptic, apologist, scientist, Protestant, Catholic, ascetic, victim of hallucinations, rationalist, moralist, anguished soul, existentialist: Pascal's projective plasticity is astonishing. Rarely have the enigmatic ellipses in an author's unfinished work elicited so many contradictory interpretations.

FIGURE 8.10   Louise Conte and Simone Valère in Henry de Montherlant's *Port-Royal* (1989).

The Secularized Heritage

By 1850 the principal components of the memory had been defined. Little would change afterward, apart from the revival of one or the other face of that memory: the republican political version or the cultural icon of classicism. We are still living off this divided, secularized legacy, which was established once and for all when Port-Royal's literary butterfly emerged from its Jansenist cocoon.

Not only did Port-Royal in its cultural form enter the university, but its new image changed Jansenist society itself. Under the influence of a new director, Augustin Gazier, a professor from the Sorbonne, the Société Saint-Augustin and the library on Rue Saint-Jacques took on a new, more scientific and cultural orientation. It was Gazier who opened the bulk of the Port-Royal ruins to the public and whose historical note to visitors presented the history of Port-Royal as that of "liberal and intelligent Catholicism."[81] He also built a museum-oratory on the premises and placed a bust of Racine there in 1899, on the occasion of the second centenary of the playwright's death.

In fact, Gazier was by no means a stranger to the Port-Royal tradition. The fortuitously named Augustin was born in the parish of Saint-Séverin, in the shadow of the Jansenist bell-tower, in 1844. His father, named president of the Société Saint-Augustin in 1863, had been a student and later a teacher at the Écoles Jansénistes de Charité in the Faubourg Saint-Antoine. He married a former pupil of the Sisters of Sainte-Marthe, an order founded in the eighteenth century in imitation of Port-Royal and which his sister Louise joined.[82] Gazier recounts in his "Souvenirs" that after the shock of the Franco-Prussian War and the Commune, the library, which had ceased to be the meeting place of the Société Saint-Augustin, had been virtually abandoned, left to be tended only by the spinsters Sophie and Rachel Gillet. Daughters of a wealthy entrepreneur who belonged to the Société Janséniste, the two women had devoted themselves entirely to the cult of the ancestors. Somewhat earlier, around 1860, they had even published figurists and eschatological texts in Abbé d'Étemare's own hand, texts that had never seen the light of day before (one wonders for what audience they were produced now). In 1872, however, Gazier took charge of the library with all the joy of a scholar discovering an unexploited gold mine, and it became the basis of his many learned publications. Like his great rival Bremond on the Jesuit side, Gazier created a center for the scholarly study of Jansenism to serve the new disciplines of religious and literary history at the turn of the century.[83]

Although Port-Royal's classicism became the dominant image, the republican interpretation of Jansenism did not disappear entirely. It, too, entered the university, where it played an important role in the educational battles over the republican school under the Third Republic. Earlier in the nineteenth century, the hostility of leading academics to "Jesuitism" had laid the groundwork for the coming battle over secularized education. Jules Michelet devoted his 1843 course at the Collège de France entirely to the Jesuits, for whose teachings he came up with some striking descriptions: "the spirit of death," "moral mechanism," a "police mentality applied to religious matters," a "spirit of pious intrigue and sanctimonious slander." In the same year his colleague Edgar Quinet also indicted the practices of the Company of Jesus, contrasting the "spirit of servitude" with that of "liberty and democracy" and perpetuating the tradition of republican anti-Jesuitism. Under the Third Republic, amidst the ambiance of secular faith that animated the school of Jules Ferry, Port-Royal recovered some of its symbolic value. Indeed, the abbey had the virtue of allowing republicans to encroach upon the territory of their Catholic adversaries. Port-Royal embodied the good side of Christian education, "the glorious conquest of the modern spirit, the abhorrence of intolerance and respect for liberty."[84] Two anthologies of texts by the masters of the Petites Écoles appeared in 1887. They were published by Félix Cadet and Irénée Carré, both Inspectors General of Elementary Education, who hailed the texts as veritable treatises on educational theory.[85] They praised Nicole, Lancelot, Coustel, Guyot, and Wallon de Beaupuis for having fostered individual development and independence and conscience and critical acumen. The *Logique* "clearly and boldly set forth the rights of human reason as against the pretensions of authority." They sought to retain only the secular aspect of Port-Royal's educational system while rejecting its theology. Carré contributed several articles on Port-Royal to Ferdinand Buisson's *Dictionnaire de pédagogie*. While expressing reservations about the "somber doctrine" of a system that treated education as "a drama of salvation," Carré admired the Jansenists' "profound respect for the human person, and particularly for the soul of the child, their religious awe at the enigma of the child, who may grow up to become either a saint or a demon."[86] He also noted the elitism and intimacy of small classes as well as the exceptional gifts of the Port-Royal teachers, "apostles of a kind who do not appear in every age." Nevertheless, he urged his readers in search of "experimental precedents" and authentic continuity of inspiration to look to Port-Royal rather than to the Jesuits, who failed to foster "a sense of personal dignity."

Despite the anticlericalism of the republicans, Port-Royal was a fundamental reference for the founders of French secular education, particularly such liberal Protestants as Steeg, Pécaut, and Buisson, who sought to establish "a lay religion and moral ideal without dogma, catechisms, or priests."[87] Pécaut, who, according to Buisson, wanted to be a "secular republican Saint-Cyran," took his students to visit the ruins of Port-Royal after being appointed to the post of *directeur d'études* at the École Normale Supérieure of Fontenay-aux-Roses in 1880.[88] A similar atheist admiration for Port-Royal can be seen in the Union pour l'Action Morale that Paul Desjardins founded in 1892 on the basis of Jules Lagneau's program "for social pacification through education." This philanthropic organization considered itself to be "a small-scale, purely rational trial of Port-Royal."[89] The many other groups in which Desjardins subsequently played a role, from the Union pour la Vérité (so renamed after the Dreyfus Affair) to the Foyer d'Études et de Repos de Pontigny, would also partake of the memory of Port-Royal and its fondness for the shadows.

From after World War I until about 1960, Sainte-Beuve's work remained the implicit basis of all studies of Port-Royal. The image it established remains influential, but increasingly it is no longer Port-Royal but Pascal as its finest and most robust incarnation who draws most of the attention. Pascal has been the subject of countless essays by authors from Barrès to Péguy to Mauriac. The three-hundredth anniversary of his birth in 1923 and of his death in 1962 occasioned fervent acts of homage to the man. The expansion of the universities after World War II stimulated the production of innumerable theses. The geometer obsessed with the abyss evinced an attractive intensity of mind born of an unusual combination of aesthetic gifts with spiritual concerns.[90] In 1952 the sale of the Les Granges estate, that is, of the Petites Écoles (which the nineteenth century mistakenly took to be the *maison des solitaires* with "Pascal's cell" often reproduced in postcard images), provoked such an uproar in the press that the government decided to turn the property into a museum. The first expositions of the mid-1950s, on "Racine and Port-Royal," "Pascal and *Les Provinciales*," and "Philippe de Champaigne and Port-Royal," drew on the Sainte-Beuvian image of the abbey as the cradle of literary classicism. Only Montherlant dared to venture gingerly beyond the boundary separating the "great" Jansenism of the seventeenth century from the "other," more political Jansenism, in a play presented for the first time at the Théâtre-Français on December 8, 1954, which met with considerable success. Based on the *Récit de captivité de la Mère Angélique de Saint-Jean,* the tragedy represented the difficult personal and political issues involved in the choice between resistance and obedience. Structuralism, with its interest in discourse, turned the spotlight on yet another Port-Royal, but one that also belonged to the seventeenth century, namely, the Port-Royal that produced the *Logique* and the *Grammaire*, texts that were reprinted and hailed as major milestones in the founding of the queen of sciences, linguistics.[91]

Since then, the image of Port-Royal has been fading, and reference to it is increasingly limited to scholars. Yet something of the Port-Royal spirit remains indomitably alive, even if only in the form of a diffuse influence on the French sensibility that extends well beyond its original religious setting. One might examine this by studying the semantic filtering that has kept the adjective *Jansenist* in the psychological and moral vocabulary while gradually pruning away its historical and spiritual roots. Not that the latter have disappeared entirely. Long after the last vestiges of the Jansenist "party" disappeared, there remains a distinctive strand within the French religious tradition notable for the austerity of its independence. A sort of Jansenist piety has survived doctrinal Jansenism. The connotation of religious rigor is powerful enough for the language to have preserved the word *Jansenist* to denote an inflexible self-discipline. This quality may be associated with other forms of severity, whether internal or behavioral, as when Leszek Kolakowski characterized Georges Sorel as a "Jansenist Marxist."[92] In this connection *Jansenism* joins puritanical intransigence with the virtuous activism of the Jacobin. But there is also another sign of the deep imprint that this Catholic protest left on French society: Jansenism is also the name of an aesthetic ideal. Indeed, the construction of Port-

Royal as an icon of classicism established this "Jansenist" ideal as one of an extremely purified form of classicism, the mythical figure of an art concentrated on the essential, extremely spare in its resources and style. Thus for Paul Valéry, Degas and Mallarmé are the "Jansenists of painting and poetry,"[93] while Blaise Cendrars spoke of "the messianic spirit and Jansenist demeanor of the N.R.F." (the *Nouvelle Revue Française*),[94] and André Bazin praised "the Jansenist direction" of filmmaker William Wyler.[95] Words have a memory of their own, and their fate is to continue indefinitely to spell out a history that one might have thought to be on its last legs.

Yet even as I write, as the bicentennial of the French Revolution is being celebrated, the political dimension of Port-Royal has once again reared its head, made topical by Tocqueville's analysis, according to which the French Revolution originated within the very structure of the monarchy. As a central element in France's distinctive religious and political configuration from the wave of reforms and counter-reforms to the revolutionary outburst of "dechristianization," the enigma of Port-Royal is once again a topic of major interest.[96] Perhaps posterity will soon again be able to see the Jansenist struggle in all its historical fullness and complexity.

APPENDIX I

A Short Critical Bibliography of Studies of French Jansenism

Jansenism has given rise to a vast literature as well as to the most contradictory interpretations, examination of which would have led us quite far afield. I have therefore chosen to give, in this separate appendix, a brief but organized survey of major developments in recent research.

It should be borne in mind that those who considered themselves to be "disciples of Saint Augustine" always rejected the reality of Jansenism. For Arnauld it was a mere "phantom" (*Fantôme du jansénisme*, Cologne, 1686).

"Réforme ou Contre-Réforme?" asked Jean Orcibal of the early Port-Royal (*Nouvelle Clio* [Brussels, 1950] 138–280), thus stressing the ambiguity of the movement. Jean Laporte called Jansenism "Catholicism in its purest form" ("Le Jansénisme," *Histoire générale des religions* [Paris: Quillet, 1947], 4: 195–218), whereas the *Dictionnaire de théologie catholique* brands it a "singular heresy": in a jest destined to become famous, Mazarin once called it "warmed-over Calvinism."

In the first historiographical reflection on Jansenist studies from the early 1950s, "Qu'est-ce que le jansénisme?," *Cahiers de l'Association internationale des études françaises*, nos. 3, 4, 5 (July 1953): 39–53, Jean Orcibal concludes that historians must give up the idea that there is any "substantial unity" to Jansenism. Indeed, attempts to reconstruct the doctrine since the turn of the century had contributed to fragmenting it into several distinct tendencies, each associated with different Jansenist personalities: Jules Paquier, *Qu'est-ce que le jansénisme?* (Paris, 1909); Albert de

Meyer, *Les Premières Controverses jansénistes en France* (Louvain, 1917); Jean Laporte, *La Doctrine de Port-Royal: Saint-Cyran* (Paris, 1923), *La Doctrine de Port-Royal: Les vérités de la Grâce* (Paris, 1923); *La Doctrine de Port-Royal: La morale d'après Arnauld*, 2 vols. (Paris, 1951–1952). The publication of documents concerning the history of the Jansenist movement by Father Ceyssens revealed the existence of several distinct periods: *Sources relatives aux débuts du jansénisme et de l'antijansénisme* (Louvain, 1957), *La Fin de la première période du jansénisme, sources des années* (Louvain, 1968), *La Seconde Période du jansénisme, les débuts, sources des années 1673–1676* (Brussels, 1968), *La Seconde Période, sources des années 1680–1682* (Brussels, 1974), *Autour de la bulle Unigenitus* (Louvain, 1987). There has been no attempt to synthesize any number of regional monographs, which in any case may not lend themselves to any kind of generalization.

For a summary of regional studies, one can consult the already somewhat outdated bibliography of Préclin, *Les Luttes politiques et doctrinales aux XVIIe et XVIIIe siècles*, 2 vols. (Paris, 1955–1956) 1: 235 and 236 (the work constitutes vol. 19 of the *Histoire de l'Église depuis les origines jusqu'à nos jours*, ed. Jean-Baptiste Duroselle and Eugène Jarry), as well as Émile Appolis, "L'Histoire provinciale du jansénisme au XVIIIe siècle," *Annales ESC*, 7 (1952): 87–92. The old survey by Jean Carreyre in *Introduction aux études d'histoire locale*, 3 vols., ed. Victor Carrière (Paris, 1934–1940), 3: 513–635, is still a useful source of interesting avenues of research.

One major object of controversy involved the question of Jansenism's role in the decline of mysticism and the baroque aesthetic and, more generally, its contribution to "dechristianization." Whereas Bremond, in the fourth volume of the *Histoire littéraire du sentiment religieux* (Paris, 1932), was harsh toward Port-Royal, which he held responsible, through the controversy it instigated, for the "retreat of the mystics," Orcibal saw Duvergier de Hauranne, the abbé de Saint-Cyran, as belonging to the mystical tradition and as a devotional descendant of Bérulle and Francis de Sales (*Jean Duvergier de Hauranne, abbé de Saint-Cyran et son temps*, 2 vols. [Paris, 1947–1948]). For Louis Cognet, the ascetic and antimystical strand in Jansenism could be traced back to Mother Angélique herself (*La Réforme de Port-Royal* [Paris, 1951]). In *Morales du Grand Siècle* (Paris, 1948), Paul Bénichou emphasized the "demolition of the hero" that he saw at work in Pascal, La Rochefoucauld, and Nicole, but René Taveneaux saw "the heroism of sanctity," a compound of poverty and charity, as the basis of Jansenist piety (*Héroïsme et création littéraire sous les règnes d'Henri IV et de Louis XIII* [Paris, 1974]).

In *Études de sociologie religieuse*, 2 vols. (Paris, 1955–1956), Gabriel Le Bras blamed the spare Jansenist notion of piety for the "dechristianization" so apparent in several of their bastions: the Paris basin, Sens, Troyes, Châlons-sur-Marne, Reims, the Beauvaisis. But René Taveneaux's monograph *Le Jansénisme en Lorraine* (Paris, 1960) brought to light a notable exception: "old-fashioned Augustinian

Jansenism" remained as alive in eighteenth-century Lorraine as it had been in the seventeenth century. In a searching review of Taveneaux's book, "Jansénisme et frontière de la catholicité," *Revue historique*, 227 (1962): 115–138, the Protestant historian Pierre Chaunu proposed an interesting hypothesis distinguishing between Jansenist regions "on the frontiers of Catholicism"—Lorraine, perhaps Normandy owing to a strong Protestant presence there, the Spanish Netherlands, the United Provinces—and Jansenist regions sheltered from interconfessional conflict, where Jansenism was ultimately transformed into a political and Presbyterian tendency in the eighteenth century. In the confrontation with the Protestants, Jansenism could reveal its true function, which was both to convert Protestants and serve as a substitute for Augustinianism. Dominique Dinet is currently pursuing research on the secularizing influence of Jansenism in certain of its bastions ("Le Jansénisme et les origines de la déchristianisation au XVIIIe siècle, l'exemple des pays de l'Yonne,"in *Du jansénisme à la laïcité* (Entretiens d'Auxerre, 1983; Paris, 1987).

In the wake of Sainte-Beuve, the eighteenth century, marked by "the ignominy of the convulsions," was for a long time deemed unworthy of inclusion in the history of Jansenism. Edmond Préclin's thesis, *Les Jansénistes du XVIIIe siècle et la Constitution civile du clergé* (Paris, 1929), restored the full historical importance of the appellants' struggle against *Unigenitus*, which he saw as laying the groundwork for the ecclesiastical reforms of the French Revolution. Taking a "history of ideas" approach, his thesis rests on a fragile foundation, however: "Richerism." Why and by what avenues would a conception of the Church developed by university syndic Edmond Richer in the context of early seventeenth century Gallican-Jesuit struggles—a conception of the Church as an aristocracy moderated by pastors instituted by Christ—have suddenly spread through the clergy in the early eighteenth century, when it was ignored by Jansenists at the end of the previous century? Jacques Parguez's thesis, *La Bulle Unigenitus et le jansénisme politique* (Paris, 1936), highlighted the problem of "parlementary Jansenism."

The second phase of studies of political Jansenism was strongly influenced by the Marxist model. Lucien Goldmann's *Le Dieu caché*, published in Paris in 1956 and hailed as an event in *Le Monde* on September 25, 1956, though criticized by some Marxists (e.g., Michel Crouzet in *La Nouvelle Critique*, 79 [1956]), remains controversial even today: see Gérard Ferreyrolles, "Un Age critique: Les trente ans du *Dieu caché*," *Commentaires*, 34 (summer 1986). Goldmann's essay continued a German historiographic tradition. Although Max Weber neglected Jansenism, which he saw primarily as a mystical movement that rejected the world, Marxist intellectuals were drawn to the subject after World War I. Bernard Groethuysen, whose *Origines de l'esprit bourgeois en France* was translated for the first time in 1927, used Jansenist literature from the early eighteenth-century campaign against *Unigenitus*. He was the first to the note the ambivalent nature of Jansenist apologetics: "In fighting for God's cause, they helped to bring about its defeat." His colleague Franz Borkenau, in a study of the "history of philosophy in the manufacturing period" in *Der Ubergang vom feudalen ʒum bürgerlichen Weltbild* (Paris, 1934), specifically attributed Jansenism to a group that he called the French "gentry," a comprehensive but anachronistic term according to Lucien Febvre ("Fondations économiques et superstructures philosophiques: Une synthèse," *L'Esprit du mécanisme,* Cahiers STS-CNRS [1985], 81–85). The French *noblesse de robe,* it was argued, played a role in the genesis of modern thought because modern thought was a product not just of capitalism but, more significantly, of the contradictions within capitalism. Pascal was thus the inventor of modern dialectics. Jansenism's failure and the triumph of the irreligious spirit in the eighteenth century were consequences of the consolidation of the bourgeoisie with its alleged emphasis on capitalist rationality. Following a similar line of reasoning but working more with literary evidence, Goldmann attempted to reconstruct the paradoxical Jansenist *Weltanschauung* from the works of Pascal, Racine, Arnauld, and Nicole, which he interpreted as nothing other than the tragic worldview of *officiers* (venal officeholders, who purchased their offices and could not be removed) thwarted in their social ascension by a bureaucracy of *commissaires* (salaried employees who served at the king's pleasure). The flaw in Goldmann's argument, however, was that he failed to provide any detailed sociological study of just which families were Jansenist sympathizers and which sided with the Jesuits. Roland Mousnier quite pertinently pointed out that two attitudes and two career patterns were equally prevalent among *robins*: preservation of the religious conscience by withdrawal from the world coexisted with engagement in affairs of state. These objections were restated in a note on pp. 115–116 of Goldmann's thesis (see also Mousnier, "Le Conseil du Roi," in *La Plume, la Faucille et le Marteau* [Paris, 1970], and the special issue of *Dix-septième Siècle,* 122 [January–March 1979]). The Jansenist group, moreover, was far from being exclusively pessimistic and fatalistic with respect to action in the world: one of Goldmann's own disciples, Gérard Namer, has shown that after 1661, Jansenist circles expanded to include, alongside the Barcosian group and the Arnauldian centrists, an extreme intramundane faction around Abbé Le Roy and the bishop of Alet, Nicolas Pavillon, who promoted a spirit of uncompromsing struggle (*L'Abbé Leroy et ses amis: Essai sur le jansénisme extrémiste intramondain* [Paris, 1964]). An indirect refutation of Goldmann's thesis can be found in Paule Jansen's *Le Cardinal Maʒarin et le mouvement janséniste* (Paris, 1967), which shows how much the Machiavellian Mazarin himself contributed to shaping the negative image of Jansenism to serve his diplomatic maneuverings vis-à-vis the Holy See. Richard M. Golden has posed a further challenge to the Marxist view by demonstrating that a high proportion of Parisian curés were Jansenists in the seventeenth century, and that many of them took the side of Cardinal de Retz in the religious Fronde of the 1650s (*The Godly Rebellion: Parisian Curés and the Religious Fronde, 1652–1662* [Chapel Hill, N.C., 1981]). Even the evidence concerning the close ties between early Jansenism and the *parlement* has been cast in a new light by Albert N. Hamscher, "The Parlement of Paris and the Social Interpretation of Early French Jansenism," *The Catholic Historical Review*, 69 (1977): n 3–4.

Over the past ten years historians have once again turned their attention to the role of Jansenism in the cultural origins of the French Revolution, a subject pioneered by the work of Daniel Mornet. For Alexander Sedgwick, early Jansenism was already a political oppositional movement and must be studied in the context of the Fronde: see his *Jansenism in Seventeenth-Century France: Voices from the Wilderness* (Charlottesville, 1977). Similarly, Robert Kreiser relates the episode of the miracles and convulsions to the great religious and parlementary struggles against *Unigenitus* in the first third of the eighteenth century (*Miracles, Convulsions, and Ecclesiastical Politics in the Early Eighteenth Century* [Princeton, 1978]). Dale Van Kley notes the influence of the parlementary "Jansenist party" in the second half of the eighteenth century (*The Jansenists and the Expulsion of the Jesuits from France, 1757–1765* [New Haven, 1975]). Pursuing an interpretation of the political theology of Jansenism put forward by René Taveneaux, *Jansénisme et politique* (Paris, 1965), and Antoine Adam, *Du mysticisme à la révolte* (Paris, 1968), Van Kley has called attention to the influence of Jansenist conciliar thinking on prerevolutionary politics ("The Jansenist Constitutional Legacy in the French Prerevolution, 1750–1789," *Historical Reflections/Réflexions historiques*, 13, no. 2 and 3 [1986]; "The Estates General as Ecumenical Council: The Constitutionalism of Corporate Consensus and the Parlement's Ruling of September 25, 1788," *Journal of Modern History*, 61 [March 1989]: 1–52). The political theology of Jansenism has also attracted the interest of Monique Cotteret, "Aux origines du républicanisme janséniste: Le mythe de l'Église primitive et le primitivisme des Lumières," *RHMC*, 31 (January–March 1984): 99–115, and Yann Fauchois, "Jansénisme et politique au XVIIIe siècle: légitimation de l'État et délégitimation de la monarchie chez G. N. Maultrot," *RHMC*, 34 (July–September 1987): 473–491.

Timothy Tackett's book on the oath of 1791, *La Révolution, l'Église, la France* (Paris, 1986), demonstrates the geographical coincidence of Jansenist regions with regions receptive to the Civil Constitution of the Clergy. It thus demonstrates the structural influence that this religious cleavage had on French society into the nineteenth century and perhaps beyond.

APPENDIX 2

Eighteenth-Century Memorials of Port-Royal

Le Nécrologe

Rivet de La Grange (1683–1749), Nécrologe de l'abbaye de Notre-Dame de Port-Royal des Champs, ordre de Cîteaux, institut du Saint-Sacrement qui contient les éloges historiques avec les épitaphes des fondateurs et bienfaiteurs de ce monastère, et des autres personnes de distinction qui l'ont obligé par leurs services, honoré d'une affection particulière, illustré par la profession monastique, édifié par leur pénitence et leur piété, sanctifié par leur mort ou par leur sépulture (Amsterdam, 1723).

Journals

Divers actes, lettres et relations des religieuses de Port-Royal du Saint-Sacrement, touchant la persécution et les violences qui leur ont été faites (1725).

On the foundress and the nuns

Abbé Goujet (1697–1767), *Mémoires pour servir à l'histoire de Port-Royal*, 3 vols. (1734–1737): Contains stories of the nuns of the Arnauld family, "le recueil de la Mère Angélique de Saint-Jean Arnauld d'Andilly," and the "Mémoires pour servir à la vie de la Révérende Mère Marie-Angélique de Sainte-Magdeleine Arnauld, réformatrice de Port-Royal."

Mémoires pour servir à l'histoire de Port-Royal et à la vie de la Révérende Mère Angélique de Sainte-Magdeleine Arnauld, réformatrice de ce monastère, 5 vols. (Utrecht: Aux dépens de la Compagnie, 1742).

Angélique Arnauld, *Extraits de Lettres*, part 1 (Leyden, 1734).

Lettres de la Révérende Mère Marie-Angélique Arnauld, abbesse et réformatrice de Port-Royal, 3 vols. (Utrecht, 1742–1744).

Entretiens ou Conférences de la Révérende Mère Marie-Angélique Arnauld, abbesse et réformatrice de Port-Royal, (Brussels, 1757).

Discours de la Mère Angélique de Saint-Jean Arnauld d'Andilly, appelés "Miséricordes ou Recommandations faites en chapitres de plusieurs personnes unies à Port-Royal des Champs" (1735).

Discours sur la Règle de Saint Benoît de leur Révérende Mère Angélique de Saint-Jean, Abbesse de Port-Royal des Champs (1736).

Réflexions de la Mère Angélique de Saint-Jean pour préparer ses soeurs à la persécution, conformément aux avis laissés sur cette matière par la Mère Agnès (1737).

Sister Eustoquie de Brégis, attrib., *Relations sur la vie de la Révérende Mère Marie des Anges* (1737).

Pierre Leclerc (subdeacon of the diocese of Rouen, champion of the *convulsionnaires*, in refuge in the Netherlands), *Vies intéressantes et édifiantes des religieuses de Port-Royal et de plusieurs personnes qui leur étaient attachées*, 5 vols. (1750–1751).

Idem, *Histoire des religieuses écrites pare elles-mêmes* (Utrecht, 1753).

On the solitaires

Histoire de l'origine des Pénitens et solitaires de Port-Royal des Champs (Mons, 1733).

Relation de la retraite de M. Arnauld en les Pays-Bas en 1769. Avec quelques anecdotes qui ont précédé son départ de France (Mons, 1733).

Relation du voyage d'Aleth contenant des mémoires pour servir à l'histoire de la vie de messire Nicolas Pavillon, évêque d'Aleth, par Monsieur Lancelot, dédiée à Mgr l'évêque de Senez, exilé à la Chaise-Dieu (probably about 1728).

Abbé Goujet, *Vie de Nicole*, in *Continuation des Essais de Morale*, vol. 19 (Luxembourg, 1732).

Relation de plusieurs circonstances de la vie de M. Hamon, faite par lui-même sur le modèle des Confessions de Saint Augustin, 1734, in-12.

Mémoires de Messire Robert Arnauld d'Andilly, écrits par lui-même, 2 vols. (Hamburg).

Le Febvre de Saint-Marc, *Supplément au Nécrologe de l'abbaye de Notre-Dame de Port-Royal des Champs* (1735).

Mémoires pour servir à l'histoire de Port-Royal par M. Fontaine, 2 vols (Utrecht, 1736; 2d ed., Cologne, 1738).

Mémoires touchant la vie de M. de Saint-Cyran, par M. Lancelot, pour servir d'éclaircissement à l'histoire de Port-Royal, 2 vols (Cologne: Aux dépens de la Compagnie, 1738).

Mémoires pour servir à l'histoire de Port-Royal, par M. du Fossé (Utrecht, Aux dépens de la Compagnie, 1739).

Barbeau de la Bruyère, attrib., *Recueil de plusieurs pièces pour servir à l'Histoire de Port-Royal ou Supplément aux Mémoires de MM. Fontaine, Lancelot et du Fossé* (Utrecht, 1740): known as the "Recueil d'Utrecht."

Jean Racine, *Abrégé de l'histoire de Port-Royal, par feu M. Racine, de l'Académie française*, part 1 (Cologne, 1742): the complete work would appear in Paris in 1767 and 1770.

The "outside friends"

Villefore, *La Vie de Madame la duchesse de Longueville, première partie*, and *seconde partie*, 2 vols. (1738).

Villefore, *La Véritable Vie d'Anne Geneviève de Bourbon, duchesse de Longueville, par l'auteur des Anecdotes de la Constitution Unigenitus*, 2 vols. (Amsterdam, 1739).

La Vie de Messire Félix Vialart de Herse, évêque et comte de Châlons en Champagne, pair de France (Cologne, 1738).

A Port-Royal bibliography by Augustin Gazier appeared at the end of a new edition of the *Abrégé de l'histoire de Port-Royal* (Paris, 1908).

On the history of the publication of the complete works of Antoine Arnauld, see Émile Jacques, "Un anniversaire…1775–1783," *Revue d'histoire ecclésiastique,* 70 (1975): 705–730.

On the fate of Pascal's manuscripts and anthologies of printed texts, and in particular on the work of Mlle de Théméricourt and the Jansenist milieu, see Jean Mesnard, "La Tradition pascalienne," in Pascal, *Oeuvres complètes* (Paris, Desclée de Brouwer, 1964), 1: 27–394.

FIGURE 9.0 The Musée du Desert, Mas-Soubeyran.

CHAPTER 9

The Museum of the Desert:
The Protestant Minority

Philippe Joutard

For the past eighty years, on the first Sunday in September, several thousand Protestants have gathered in the Cévennes region of France (Gard *département*) a few miles from Mialet, in the hamlet of Le Mas–Soubeyran, the birthplace of Roland Laporte, one of the two great leaders of the Camisards. In the morning they perform baptisms at various locations in the surrounding forest of chestnut trees, and then they attend services, just as in the days after the Revocation of the Edict of Nantes, when French Protestants held clandestine services "in the Desert." Toward the end of the morning the worshipers visit the Museum of the Desert, which is in the very house that Roland lived in. They pause for a long while before the list of those condemned to the galleys for their faith, and some point out to their children the name of an ancestor. They purchase Huguenot crosses and religious and historical literature before sitting down to picnic lunches. The afternoon is devoted to lectures on a topic chosen annually, usually to mark the anniversary of some great event (such as the edict of tolerance in 1987), celebrate a major Protestant figure (Farel in 1965, Guizot in 1974, Cavalier in 1981), or consider other matters of interest to the community (such as family day at the Museum of the Desert in 1973, the Refuge in 1986, or women and the Bible in 1982). At intervals during these sessions the group will sing hymns favored by the Camisards, such as Psalm 68: "Let God arise, let his enemies be scattered." Other favorite songs include the *Complainte des prisonnières de la tour de Constance* and especially *La Cévenole*, a veritable hymn of regional identity. Among those attending this day of remembrance are not just Cévenols and Languedocians but Protestants and descendants of Huguenot refugees from all over Europe.

As a site of remembrance, a place for families to gather, the home of the Museum of the Desert, and, for a time, home as well to a publishing house, Le

Mas–Soubeyran is today a focal point of French Protestant memory—a fact that is paradoxical in two senses.

History and Protestant Culture

The first paradox has to do not just with the choice of the Museum of the Desert but with the very existence of Protestant *lieux de mémoire*. Calvinism, the source of much of French Protestantism, is of all Christian theologies the least hospitable to the existence of a profane as opposed to a sacred memory. The only historical event worthy of recollection is Christ's sacrifice, memorialized in the sacrament of the Lord's Supper. Because human works play no role in salvation, they do not deserve to be remembered. The Calvinist refusal to worship saints was another obstacle to commemoration. The location of Calvin's grave is not known. Calvin was afraid that his followers might wish to honor his memory, and in any case sixteenth-century Protestants were wary of burials: the Ecclesiastical Discipline of the Reformed Churches of France states that "ministers shall not offer prayers or sermons during burials, in order to ward off superstitions."

Yet French Protestants have a longer memory than any other religious group. The name by which they like to call themselves, *Huguenots,* comes from the sixteenth century, presumably from *eidgnossen,* or confederates, a term that originally referred to Swiss Protestant soldiers and that French Catholics applied to their adversaries during the Wars of Religion. They have a historical culture that is closely bound up with their religious culture. For that reason many Protestant pastors in the early part of this century thought it useful to supplement their teaching of the catechism with lessons from history textbooks such as the *Histoire abrégée des protestants de France, textes et récits à l'usage des cours d'instruction religieuse,* by Jean Bastide. Clearly inspired by the *petit Lavisse,* this work consists of brief lessons divided into numbered paragraphs followed by a story and a list of questions. The goal was also quite similar to that of the Lavisse, as the preface made clear: "Our Reformed Church is, for us Protestants, a second homeland: you must know it, love it, and serve it as you would France."[1] Along with textbooks, Protestants also produced a wide range of historical literature for children, such as Henri Lauga's *Fleurs du Désert,* C. Duval's, *Récits des guerres cévenoles,* and Charlès Bost's *Le Théâtre pour la jeunesse.*[2] The fact that a pastor who developed a scientific approach to Protestant history and who was the author of a thick treatise on Protestant preachers also wrote five books for young people shows the importance that the Huguenot community attached to history.[3] Indeed, every Protestant publisher of edifying works, from the Société Religieuse des Livres of Toulouse in the late nineteenth century to La Cause in more recent years, has published numerous works on the "heroes" of the Huguenot adventure.

This saturation in history goes far beyond religious education, however. It suffuses all of Protestant culture, as can be seen from an examination of oral legends: comparison with Catholics is significant in this respect. Take Mont Lozère. Cévenols are well aware that this peak at the southern end of the Massif Central is a major religious boundary: "Papists" live on the north slope, Huguenots on the south. Clearly both sides of the mountain have witnessed the same tormented history over the past four centuries: Wars of Religion in the sixteenth century, disturbances after the Revocation of the Edict of Nantes, and in 1702 the outbreak of the Camisard uprising with the murder of the Abbé du Chaila at Pont-de-Montvert on the banks of the Tarn. At the end of the eighteenth century the northern slope of the mountain was the scene of a Cévenol Vendée. And the inventories of 1906 led to the most recent incidents. Catholic peasants have forgotten all this: they tell wolf tales and horror stories that sometimes include bits and pieces of memory but only after it has been transformed into folklore and stripped of all historical connotation. Protestants, on the other hand, never tire of commemorating their war. The American journalist Caroline Patterson discovered this in doing a piece for *National Geographic*: retracing Stevenson's journey through the Cévennes a century later, she found herself on the slopes of Mont Lozère. "We were invited to a picnic in the yard of Mme Turc, a venerable widow whose whitewashed stone house enjoys a magnificent view of the mountains across the river. As she pointed to the summits, her first words were that these were 'battlefields during the war,' by which she meant of course the war of the Camisards."[4] Her experience was the same as that of her Scottish predecessor, who in visiting Florac a century earlier had been astonished to "see what a lively memory still subsisted of the religious war." Stevenson went on: "These Cévenols were proud of their ancestors...; the war was their chosen topic; its exploits were their own patent of nobility.... They told me the country was still full of legends hitherto uncollected."[5]

Similar examples from other places could easily be adduced. Speaking of the Ardèche group, André Siegfried pointed out that "in the middle of the twentieth century one found, barely attenuated, the same passions that sustained the religious wars; people there still breathe the air of the sixteenth century."[6] Marc Bloch found the same thing in Montpellier: "Was the worthy headmaster of the Languedocian lycée in which I experienced my baptism by fire as a teacher so wrong when he warned me, in the gruff voice of a captain of learning, that 'here the nineteenth century is not so dangerous, but when you come to the Wars of Religion, be very careful?' "[7]

Apparently the Protestant capacity for commemoration extends beyond religion per se. In the Drôme, for example, they are more likely to recall the resistance to the coup d'état of December 2, 1851, than are their Catholic compatriots, even when the latter's ancestors were more active.[8] Furthermore, when French Protestants aban-

FIGURE 9.1   Re-creation of a Bible reading in a home in the Cévennes in the eighteenth century. Here the museum curators are trying to emphasize the family-centered nature of the Protestant resistance. One finds this as well in the construction of Protestant memories and what is called "Huguenot loyalty."

FIGURE 9.2   *Desert Assembly;* engraving, 1775. Such images were an early form of commemoration, even before the Protestant community had been officially recognized.

don religious practice or even give up the faith, their historical culture remains. The oral tradition is as rich among nonpracticing Protestants as among practicing ones and a source of fierce loyalty to the community: "I never set foot in church, but if anyone tried to destroy it I would take up arms." This oft-repeated phrase is in part explained by another that is heard just as often: "The church is a piece of history."[9] Huguenot culture produces its own private *lieux de mémoire,* which serve a community much as Protestantism is built around local churches. But the choice of a single site to represent the entire Protestant community of France was another matter entirely: it was a long-range project.

The Creation of Institutional *Lieux de mémoire*

In the beginning was the Société de l'Histoire du Protestantisme Français (S.H.P.F.), founded in 1852 by Charles Read, a high civil servant and *chef du service des cultes non-catholiques*. Earlier Protestant leaders were primarily preoccupied with restoring their own churches, and for this they were criticized at the society's first meeting: "If we are not mistaken, French Protestantism earlier in this century was misled by other interests and apparently failed to realize how important it was to know its own history. In some ways it therefore deserves criticism for having neglected if not altogether abandoned its major share in the common legacy of our country's history."[10] The founding of the society was not an isolated phenomenon. Six years earlier an important biographical anthology of *La France protestante* had been published, and in 1850 a pastor by the name of Gaston de Félice published the first major *Histoire des protestants de France*.

At a time of stormy debate between liberal and orthodox theologians, the newly founded society united the rival factions in a defense of Protestant history, as can be seen from the makeup of the first committee, which included both Félix Pécaut, a future collaborator with Jules Ferry and an extreme liberal, and Adolphe Monod, known for his uncompromising orthodoxy. This concern for reconciliation around history and for equilibrium among the various religious sensibilities within the reformed church would be a constant feature of the society's activities. In the year it was founded it began publishing a *Bulletin*, twenty-four years before the still-extant *Revue historique* (1876). The society also initiated a series of commemorations, at first through the intermediary of the *Bulletin*, which published articles on various anniversaries. The first, in 1859, honored the first national synod of 1559, which prepared final versions of French Protestantism's theological doctrine (the *Confession de foi*) and organizational structure (the *Discipline*). In 1866 the committee proposed the inauguration of a Reformation Festival modeled on that of the churches of the Augsburg Confession, which every year celebrated the anniversary of the day on which Luther posted his theses in Wittenberg (October 31, 1517). It suggested the first of November, "a holiday adopted by our brethren of the Augsburg Confession. Every section of the Evangelical Church should associate this pious anniversary with commemoration of events from its own history, so that from the variety of memories a unity of spirit might emerge."[11] This proposal was accepted by both the liberal and the orthodox factions, and by November 1866 several churches, mainly in the south, were holding Reformation Festivals with the same basic structure that would later be incorporated into the ceremony at Le Mas–Soubeyran: several pastors officiated, sermons were given on the lessons that could be drawn from the history of Protestant forebears, and various psalms and songs were sung. At Uzès, for example, the congregation sang this song:

> A la mémoire de nos pères
> Nous venons consacrer ce jour.
> Seigneur exauce nos prières
> Rends-nous avec leurs moeurs austères,
> Leur foi vivante et leur amour.
> [We devote this day
> To the memory of our fathers.
> Lord, grant our prayers,
> Give us back not only their austere customs
> But also their living faith and their love.]

Sometimes the crowds were so large that the festival was held in the open air, thus directly recalling the assemblies of the Desert. In Bréau, near Vigan, where the evidence showed numerous clandestine meetings to have taken place, "in a few minutes, armchairs, benches, and seats were transported or improvised in a vast and magnificent old chestnut forest, and beneath the vault formed by those magnificent trees the God of our fathers spoke once again through the mouth of his servants."[12]

A further step was taken with the first provincial annual general assembly in 1883. Significantly, the committee chose Nîmes and the Cévennes, thus inaugurating those geographic sites as fountainheads of memory. In Nîmes the participants first listened to the *Complainte des prisonnières de la tour de Constance* by the *félibre* (Provençal dialect) poet Bigot. The next day they went to Aigues-Mortes, and the day after that to Le Mas–Soubeyran to visit the birthplace of Roland Laporte, which the society had just purchased from his last surviving descendant. There they held an open-air meeting as in the Desert: texts were read from Roland's old Bible, and a liberal pastor, Viguié, gave a sermon commemorating the Camisard leader. That night, an orthodox pastor, Bersier, honored the memory of Coligny.[13] Thus the program largely anticipated that of the "first Sunday in September." It would be another twenty years, however, before things were finally settled.

In the meantime commemorations proliferated, beginning with the bicentennial of the Revocation of the Edict of Nantes. In Paris this was an opportunity for Protestants to give a loud and clear declaration of their loyalty to the nation in a period of heightened nationalism: of the five speeches given at the Temple de l'Oratoire, four ended with a celebration of France strangely intertwined with prayers of thanksgiving. The liberal Viguié told his listeners that "we are preserved by God for the good of France," while Senator de Pressensé, speaking for the

Independent Churches to which the most orthodox Protestants belonged, implored heaven in these terms: "Cloak of ignominy and glory, descend, descend upon our shoulders, so that we may be ready for any duty, for any struggle, wherever God has placed us to glorify Christ, revive the fatherland, and save souls."[14]

In the Cévennes the commemoration was more closely connected with Protestant history. At Saint-Roman-de-Tousque, for example, the Free Evangelical Churches gathered two thousand people on August 23. The site, on one of the royal highroads created by Bâville to keep an eye on Protestants, was chosen for its central location in the heart of the Camisard stronghold in the Cévennes. The date, the eve of Saint Bartholomew's Day, was also chosen as a reminder of past persecutions. The keynote speaker "rapidly retraced the major events of the Camisard War, mentioning the places where each had occurred." Then *La Cévenole* was sung for the first time. The song was composed by an Evangelical with Baptist leanings, a native of Saint-Jean-du-Gard named Ruben Saillens. The text had already been published under a headline that read, significantly, "Patriotic and Religious Song" in the first issue of a newspaper published by the Free Evangelical Churches, *La Cévenole,* whose express purpose was "to rescue from oblivion any number of instructive facts about the glorious history of our mountains and valleys" and to be "a humble, discreet messenger among all friends of evangelization in our ancient and beloved Camisard homeland."[15] The very wording shows how difficult it was to distinguish between regional attachment and religious loyalty. Note, too, that the initiators of the movement in the Cévennes were the Evangelicals most loyal to the thought of Calvin, whose misgivings about the exaltation of heroes have already been mentioned.

The words of *La Cévenole* bear out what has been said thus far. From the first lines the poet establishes a close connection between a landscape and a history:

> Salut, montagnes bien-aimées,
> Pays sacré de nos aïeux,
> Vos vertes cimes sont semées
> De leur souvenir glorieux.
> Élevez vos têtes chenues,
> Espérou, Bougès, Aigoual,[16]
> De leurs gloires qui montent aux nues,
> Vous n'êtes que le piédestal.
> [Hail, beloved mountains,
> Sacred land of our forefathers,
> Your green peaks are sown
> With their glorious memory.
> Raise your hoary heads,

Espérou, Bougès, Aigoual:
You are but the pedestal
Of their glories, which rise to the clouds.]

The Camisards and the earlier and later nonviolent resistance were also honored:

Les uns, traqué de cime en cime,
En vrais lions surent lutter;
D'autres, ceux-là furent sublimes,
Surent mourir sans résister.
[Some, tracked from mountain peak to mountain peak,
Fought like lions;
Others, sublime, found the courage
To die without resisting.]

And the final verse is a prayer:

Cévenols, le Dieu de nos pères
N'est-il pas notre Dieu toujours?
Servons-le dans les jours prospères
Comme ils firent aux mauvais jours;
Et, vaillants comme ils surent l'être,
Nourris comme eux du pain des forts,
Donnons notre vie à ce maître
Pour lequel nos aïeux sont morts.
[Cévenols, is not the God of our fathers
Still our God?
Serve him in these prosperous days
As they did in harder times.
And brave as they were,
Like them nourished on the bread of the strong,
Let us give our lives to the master
For whom our forefathers died.]

This hymn met with immediate success. It was published again in 1906 in a very popular collection of hymns, *Sous les ailes de la foi*. Hence it is not surprising to find that it was featured in the first congregation held at the Museum of the Desert.

Two years later the liberals, who did not want to be left behind, seized on the hundredth anniversary of the edict of tolerance to organize a major gathering of their own, on the plane of Fontmort, another high plateau on which combat took place during the Camisard War. There they erected a huge monolith with the following inscription: "On the occasion of the centenary of tolerance, the sons of the

Huguenots have erected, on the former theater of combat, this monument to religious peace and to the memory of the martyrs."[17] Evangelicals and liberals refused to allow partisan ceremonies, however: "You have also learned that the great lessons of the past...are not addressed to a few individuals or to the members of one particular denomination," *La Cévenole* pointed out, and *Le Foyer protestant* urged "all our Protestant brethren to forget that they belong to this or that religious denomination."[18]

Finally, on September 25, 1910, the society's acting president, the historian Frank Puaux, came to Saint-Jean-du-Gard to celebrate the 350th anniversary of the founding of the Reformed Churches of the Cévennes. Along with his childhood friend Edmond Hugues, he visited the Laporte home, in which a distant grand-nephew of the Camisard leader had died in 1891:

> The house was empty, dilapidated, abandoned. Was it possible to leave the poor and rarely visited rooms in such a state, rooms that contained the indomitable captain's old bed, kneading trough, pitchfork, and Bible? No, it was essential to turn this sacred spot into a vibrant center and to create a sort of museum that would collect souvenirs of the time when our church was "under the cross," days of mourning and suffering of incomparable grandeur.[19]

Within a year the two men had established a first museum from their own private collections together with gifts from various families. It consisted of four rooms, each bearing the name of one or more heroes symbolizing one of four Desert periods: Brousson, the age of preachers; Roland and Cavalier, the Camisard War; Antoine Court, the reconstruction of the church after 1715; and, finally, the calmer Desert of Paul Rabaut. The museum was dedicated on September 24, 1911, before an audience of 2,500.

Puaux and Hugues were not content to leave it at that, however. At the second assembly, Puaux proposed "a memorial of the time when our churches were under the cross" to be located next to the museum. This was completed after the war, in 1921. The contrast with the museum was deliberately stark: alongside the traditional Cévenol home rose an impressive marble sanctuary in the neoclassical style complete with stained-glass windows. Each of the four halls was dedicated to a different category of victims: executed pastors and preachers; exiles; galley slaves; and other prisoners, male and female. In the center were lists of names and dates that gave meaning to the adjacent rooms. A library was added, and families developed the habit of bequeathing their still-rich religious archives to the museum, including Bibles, psalters, hymnals, and prayer books.

In addition to the museum-memorial, Puaux and Hugues succeeded in institutionalizing the annual commemoration ceremony. Except for the war years 1914,

1916, 1917, 1939, and 1944, Protestants have gathered at the end of every summer since then to celebrate their history. In 1928 the date of this ceremony was fixed as the first Sunday in September, and in the following year the organizers decided that a specific theme would be chosen every year.[20] The event caught on with the public: in the 1920s there were already five to six thousand people in attendance; after 1945 the number rose to around 10,000, and after 1960 to 15 to 20,000.[21] The Museum of the Desert became the great annual meeting place for Huguenots.

In turn, as the Museum of the Desert gained autonomy from the society that created it, it spawned other *lieux de mémoire* by posting commemorative plaques in various locations, each of which helped to revive memories and create places where open-air assemblies gathered on the model of the first September Sunday services. In 1921, Edmond Hugues presided over the posting of a plaque commemorating the first synod of the Desert in 1715 at Monoblet, which restored clandestine Protestantism after the tortured episode of the Camisards. Between 1921 and 1962, twenty-four additional ceremonies followed this one in lower Languedoc and the Vivarais, with one incursion into the Deux-Sèvres commemorating the days of the Camisards with twelve inscriptions.[22] Radio and television broadcasts amplified the museum's role.

Meanwhile, another set of commemorations grew up around Marie Durand, who was imprisoned in the tower of Constance at age thirty-eight and who was the author of the celebrated inscription "Register, Résister" on the stone walls of her cell. Through her both Huguenot women and nonviolent resistance were honored. Commemoration of her began at about the same time that the Camisard sites were rediscovered in 1883 with the visit to Aigues-Mortes and Bigot's lament. In 1925 Edmond Hugues organized a ceremony at the birthplace of Marie Durand and her brother, the pastor Pierre Durand, at Bouschet-de-Pranles in Ardèche. Two pastors serving in Ardèche then took it upon themselves to arrange a service on the site every year on the Monday after Pentecost. In 1930 the ceremonies at Le Mas–Soubeyran alluded to Marie Durand's imprisonment in the tower of Constance. To top it all off, there was the commemoration in 1968 of the two-hundredth anniversary of the liberation of the last female prisoners, first at Bouschet-de-Pranles, where the Protestant museum of the Vivarais was inaugurated in the Durand home, then at Aigues-Mortes, and finally at the Museum of the Desert, where the audience exceeded 25,000.[23] Since that time the Vivarais museum has drawn four to five thousand visitors annually. The commemoration of Marie Durand has been a counterpoint to the exaltation of the Camisards. It gained in popularity as pacifism increased after World War I and especially with the success of the idea of nonviolence after 1945.

Other sites associated with Protestant memory have proliferated in recent years, each intended to celebrate the history of a particular community: at Poet-

FIGURE 9.3   Inauguration of the Musée du Désert in Mas-Soubeyran, September 24, 1911.

FIGURE 9.4   Protestant gathering at Mas-Soubeyran in 1987. The two photographs show the importance of the "great ancient chestnut" trees in this September meeting.

Laval, for example, for the Dauphiné and at Bois-Tiffrey in Vendée for western France. But these places remain obscure, and none can really rival the Museum of the Desert. Despite the diligent efforts of volunteers, these places draw no more than three or four thousand visitors annually, only a tenth to a twelfth the number of Le Mas–Soubeyran. The most surprising case is the Musée Calvin in Noyon, located in the birthplace of Calvin himself, which in 1988 drew fewer than three thousand visitors.[24] Even the Rue des Saints-Pères in Paris, where the Société de l'Histoire du Protestantisme has been located for the past hundred years, is less well known, even to Protestants, than the Museum of the Desert. Of course the Paris site serves a different clientele (pastors, scholars, and Protestant leaders), whereas the Museum of the Desert attracts not only average Protestants but also people of other religions, for many of whom it provides an initial lesson in the historical peculiarities of French Protestantism. But this sociological difference is not the only reason for the museum's success, which also reflects certain choices from the Protestant past—choices that constitute a second paradox in French Protestant memory.

A Paradoxical Historical Choice?

Initially, the society's plan was to cover the entire history of French Protestantism, according just as much space to the sixteenth century and the origins of Protestantism as to the so-called Desert period of clandestinity. This much is clear from the society's early recommendations of work to be done. Among the high points in the Protestant past, Charles Read mentioned, in his third report of 1855, "the conduct and actions of the *parlements* at the beginning of the Reformation and in reaction to it..., various incidents related to Saint Bartholomew's Day and the Revocation of the Edict of Nantes, those two great moments that are the supreme questions of our history, then the abjuration of Henri IV, an important problem and the crux of our modern history (as we are beginning to understand today), and finally the assemblies and synods of the Desert, those noble gatherings of Protestantism beneath the Cross."[25] Indeed, the early summaries published in the *Bulletin* from 1852 to 1902 reflect this concern with balance. The figures who aroused the greatest interest were all from the sixteenth century, from Calvin, by far the leader, to d'Aubigné, with Court appearing only in sixth place and Rabaut *fils et père* in eighth and tenth places, respectively. True, the table of subjects gives a somewhat different impression: the sixteenth century is no longer dominant, with the clandestine assemblies in first place, galley slaves in third place, and the Revocation in fifth place, with Saint Bartholomew's and the national synods in second and fourth places respectively.[26]

RANKING BY SPACE IN THE *BULLETIN* (IN PAGES AND FRACTIONS THEREOF)

Persons	Pages
1. Calvin	5.25
2. Bèze	3.25
3. Coligny	3
4. Henri IV	2.5
5. D'Aubigné	1.6
6. Duplessis-Mornay	1.5
7. Court	1.5
8. Rohan	1.4
9. Rabaut Saint-Étienne	1.4
10. Rabaut, Paul	1.3

Themes	Pages
1. Clandestine assemblies	4.2
2. Saint Bartholomew's Day	3.2
3. Galley slaves	2.6
4. Synods	2.3
5. Revocation	2.2

The museum, which was housed in a room in the library from 1885 to 1923, reflected this program in the amount of attention devoted to the sixteenth century and Henri IV and the relatively limited attention devoted to the period of the Revocation, which received only one-eighth of the display space and one-quarter of the document space.[27]

The decision to establish the Museum of the Desert in the home of a Camisard leader reflected two choices, to focus on the period of the Desert and, within that period, on the Camisards. These chronological choices implied a shift in geographical focus as well. The balanced presentation had made it possible to focus on the north of France as well as the south. Calvin hailed from Picardy, and the first national synod, to say nothing of the Saint Bartholomew's Day massacre, took place in Paris. The Desert was essentially south of the Loire, and the Camisard War was confined to the Cévennes and lower Languedoc. To be sure, the commemorations at Le Mas–Soubeyran sometimes touched on matters outside the Desert period, but such occasions were relatively rare. It was not until 1930 that they first dealt with Agrippa d'Aubigné and the Augsburg Confession. The assembly of 1959 celebrated not the four-hundredth anniversary of the first synod, the true founding act of the French Reformed churches, but the abduction of children and their placement in convents under Louis XIV. All in all, there were fewer commemorations of events outside the Desert area than there were strictly Camisard celebrations: in the sixty-three years for which we have data, the former numbered twelve, the latter sixteen.[28] The regional connection became clear when the Museum of the Desert chose to mark the early years of Protestantism in 1960, a date commemorating the advent of the Reformation in the Cévennes, as well as the fiftieth anniversary of the museum's founding.

The Museum of the Desert even influenced the society, to judge by the concerns reflected in its *Bulletin:* although sixteenth-century figures such as Calvin, Bèze, Coligny, and Henri IV remain in the lead, the names Cavalier and Roland appear in the list of Camisard leaders. As for subjects, the Revocation has taken the lead over Saint Bartholomew's Day. Beyond any doubt the Revocation has become, if I may put it this way, the founding event of French Protestantism as a whole. True, the society marked the four-hundredth anniversary of the massacre with a major international colloquium out of which came an important book, but virtually no other notice of the occasion was taken apart from the congregation at Le Mas–Soubeyran. As for 1959, another important anniversary for French Protestants, it went entirely unnoticed except for a few articles in the *Bulletin.* By comparison, the three-hundredth anniversary attracted attention from well beyond the professional community of the S.H.P.F. and museum staff, indeed from outside the Huguenot community.

Initially, the only event planned was a major historical colloquium, to be organized of course by the S.H.P.F. For ecumenical reasons the Protestant Federation of France was not in favor of other commemorations. But some people were not satisfied with a purely scholarly approach, particularly since descendants of the Huguenots in the countries of refuge were already preparing to celebrate this anniversary in a more public fashion. One academic, Jean Beaubérot, called for a "modernizing commemoration" of the Revocation in an article published in March 1979 in the Protestant weekly *Réforme:* "It is essential, I feel, that this reminder of the infringement of liberty and justice suffered by most French Protestants of the time should be an occasion for the Protestant community to interrogate itself and the rest of the country about how things stand with liberty and justice today."[29] In 1982, Beaubérot joined with several Protestant groups in organizing the Protestantism and Liberty Committee, which in the end persuaded the Protestant Federation of France that a formal commemoration of the Revocation would be useful. The magnitude of the event exceeded even the most optimistic predictions of its promoters: following a formal opening ceremony at UNESCO on October 11, more than 6,000 people attended two days of meetings on "Protestantism and liberty" during which present-day implications of the Revocation were discussed. Meanwhile, countless colloquia and exhibitions were held in the provinces. A spate of books appeared, offering further evidence of interest in the event: more than thirty titles were published, ranging from reprints of classics (such as works by Michelet and Vauban) to show catalogs to scholarly monographs and popularizations.[30]

The choices mentioned earlier remain surprising. That of the Camisards to begin with: for a long time they were despised and disavowed because of their violence and weakness for prophecy. To be sure, the general attitude toward them had changed completely since the middle of the nineteenth century.[31] But even the monopoly of the Desert raised problems for some Protestant institutions and leaders. Bear in mind the connection that existed between Protestantism and the emergence of nation-states. In Germany and England the secular ruler took the place of the pope and became the supreme spiritual authority. Everywhere Protestants used, in place of Latin, the language of the state, which was not, despite what is often said, necessarily the language of the people: in southern France, for example, services were conducted not in Occitan but in French, which some people understood better than others. The royal expulsion was a traumatic event from which the French Protestant community has only recently recovered, which explains the nostalgia for the sixteenth century and the emphasis on participation in the national life and government. It is highly significant that for the commemoration of the bicentennial of the Revocation, the Temple de l'Oratoire was decorated with the names of "the most famous Huguenots," among whom the men of the Desert were a small minority (five out of fifteen); the organizers clearly preferred artists (Palissy, Goudimel, and Goujon) and even more statesmen and military leaders (Coligny, Mornay, Rohan, and Duquesne).[32] That is why the first Protestant to be honored with a statue was Coligny (whose image stands near the Louvre), and it also helps to explain Charles Read's remark that the abjuration of Henri IV was the "crucial event of modern history."

Why, then, should Protestants stubbornly persist in commemorating primarily their period of exclusion from national life? This attitude is even more surprising given the general tendency of memory to seek the earliest possible founding events.

Memory, Force of Identity

At several points the commemorators betrayed their awareness of the contradiction between the celebration of one's ancestors and a theology that attributes glory to God alone. Many justified themselves on religious grounds, as the orthodox Babut did at the time of the first assembly in 1911: "Remembering our ancestors should lead us to measure the extent of our infidelities and the depths to which we have fallen." The Baptist Ruben Saillens alluded to possible errors in 1922: "To be obedient to God...it is not enough to be an assiduous participant in Huguenot pilgrimages; to be a true child of God, one has to have experienced the same inward, personal revolution as our ancestors." Pierre Bourguet put it even more clearly in 1954: "Protestants, beware! Here we are caught between the magnificence of a memorial and the just appreciation of the acts in question in the light of the Gospel of Jesus Christ; between our duty to grant legitimate recognition to martyrs and our obligation to worship God alone!... No servant, moreover, can hold a candle to the divine

master. We are not here on a pilgrimage in the strict sense. And we do not worship 'saints.' "[33] The most forceful formulation of the difficulty was given by the present conservator of the Museum of the Desert, Dean Carbonnier, in an article significantly entitled "Le Désert, lieu de mémoire?": "Sons of the Reformation, has not the Reformation caused us to forget?... Our churches broke with the apostolic succession, and from each of them we expect a new birth. Can and should the past mean anything to Protestants? Are they not theologically ahistorical?... Are not our Protestant commemorations and Desert Assemblies constantly in danger of becoming hagiographic?"[34]

Such feelings led some Protestants to oppose the creation of the Museum of the Desert itself, as Frank Puaux pointed out: "Glorify the champions of freedom of conscience? Why not canonize them? You are trying to create Protestant saints! What discouraging responses our first appeals received!"[35] After World War II, many pastors, influenced by Barth's teachings and hoping for a revival of

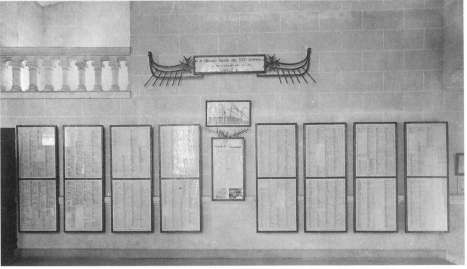

FIGURE 9.5   The Pyramid of the Camisards on the peak of Fommorte (also known as Fontmort). The official commemoration of the site merely reinforces a long oral tradition.

FIGURE 9.6   In the Musée du Désert, lists of five thousand galley slaves who died for their faith from 1684 to 1775. Here, individual, family, and collective identities come together.

Calvinism's original inspiration, refused to pay homage to the Huguenot heritage. The same sentiment contributed to early doubts about plans to commemorate the three-hundredth anniversary of the Revocation of the Edict of Nantes.

The amplitude of the commemorative phenomenon grew despite the reservations, however. The vocabulary used, at least until the 1960s, by those who spoke at Le Mas–Soubeyran is unmistakable: the terms most commonly employed in connection with the period of resistance in the Desert were *giant*, *hero*, and *epic*. There were even some explicit allusions to the cult of the saints, as in this statement by Rev. Trial (though an Evangelical) in 1912: "Those who take these venerable relics as the goal of their pious pilgrimage will feel as though they had been transported into the midst of the Desert and share a few moments of the experience of the Desert heroes."[36] Protestants were a tiny minority in France, scarcely two percent of the population at the end of the eighteenth century: could they preserve their identity and therefore their existence without a historical memory? Of course the doctrine of predestination, the idea that they, the elect, constituted a small flock, was already a powerful support, but it was not enough in a society for which the notion of unity presumed an end to difference.

The recourse to the past was already an important stratagem in the controversy in which educated Protestants were invariably enlisted, as Élisabeth Labrousse has noted of the eighteenth-century: "The Huguenots were such a small minority and so constantly persecuted that any educated man among them was a potential controversialist.... For more than a century the exigencies of debate had led Protestants into serious debate concerning not only the exegesis of biblical and patristic texts but also the history of the Church through the ages as well as of the still recent Wars of Religion, which could so easily be presented in such a way as to discredit the French Reformation. Every cultivated Huguenot was at least an amateur historian."[37] Gaston de Félice had a similar goal in mind when he published his *Histoire des protestants de France*, the first major work in that field: "In the opinion of the nation Protestantism has suffered the fate of minorities, and of defeated minorities. The moment people ceased to be afraid of it they no longer deigned to learn about it, and abetted by such indifference prejudices of all kinds grew up and took hold. Protestantism should not accept this injustice and must strive to overcome the misfortune."[38]

To use history in this way seemed quite abstract to the vast majority of French Huguenots, however. Personal and family memories were much more effective in linking the humblest of Protestants to an ancestor who long ago summoned up the courage to make the "right choice." Such sentiments go back a long way: one finds signs of them as early as the seventeenth century, and even in men like Pierre Bayle. When Bayle reverted to Calvinism after a period as a Catholic, he did not invoke theological motives or arguments from general history of the kind he was accustomed to using in his discussions; in his journal, the *Calendarium,* he simply noted "ad paternam legem redit" (he returned to the religion of his fathers).[39] Three centuries later we find the same sense of loyalty to a family tradition in these thoughts of a Protestant from Luberon: "If our parents, our great-grand-parents, chose this ideology, I think that we, as descendants, can be proud of what they did."[40]

One reason why French Protestants spontaneously choose to remember the eighteenth-century Desert period rather than the sixteenth-century Wars of Religion, and the Revocation rather than Saint Bartholomew's Day, is that these choices help to form family as well as communal memories. The Wars of Religion were fought by great nobles and princes of the blood, illustrious figures far from everyday life and further estranged from the average Protestant by the role they played in French national history. It was just this feeling that Puaux and Hugues evoked in their appeal for contributions to help build the Protestant memorial: "In Paris, opposite the Louvre and a short distance from Saint-Germain-l'Auxerrois, a statue of Coligny stands by the apse of the Oratoire. The obscure host of unknown martyrs who for a century, from the Revocation to the edict of tolerance, died in order to preserve and perpetuate the Reformation in France still await their monument."[41] The long repression of an entire population had given rise to a large number of oral traditions piously transmitted from generation to generation, so that every Protestant felt that his or her ancestors had been historical actors. Take, for example, one peasant woman from the Nîmes region who described her distant forebear in these terms: "She was taken to the church and as she stood on the threshold grabbed the wooden door frame. It seems that her nails dug into the wood, and the gendarme who was prodding her was so moved that he let her go, uttering words to the effect that he had 'seen enough.' In our view she saved the dynasty [*dynastie*], because if she had been baptized a Catholic, all who came after her would have been Catholic.... That is the story we were told, even though it goes back several generations, so it must have been told and retold.... What I know I told my children, and they still know it, and my grandchildren know it, and so it will go on, it will go on, and where it will end no one knows."[42] The humblest of Huguenots thus knows that he is the heir to a religious lineage to which he must remain loyal: in this respect the use of the word "dynasty" speaks volumes.

The force of this memory comes from the fact that it is constructed, like French Reformed Protestantism itself, of family networks: some people use the popular image of the *tricot protestant*: "If you pull one strand, the whole skein comes with it." Intermarriage has allowed this very small minority to survive. Symbolically, the Museum of the Desert itself is the product of two family traditions. That of Frank Puaux was recalled by his son Gabriel, the ambassador, to the 1949 assembly in the Desert:

It is with a sense of filial piety that I come today to commemorate this great past with you. The name of Frank Puaux remains, along with that of Edmond Hugues, closely associated with the Museum of the Desert.... My father set himself the task of preserving an attachment to the historical traditions of this church in Protestant thinking.... If he illuminated the Huguenot epic, it was in truth with light from a torch passed to him by his predecessor in life. When he rose to speak to the inaugural congregation on September 24, 1911, his first words were in honor of the memory of his father, François Puaux, the popular historian of French Protestantism in the time of the Awakening, a man with a talent for providing our Protestant churches with a vibrant and colorful account of their past. Among my childhood memories I still have an image of the man whom Auguste Sabatier called "the last and most authentic representative of the old Huguenot type..".. When I used to listen to him telling his grandchildren stories from our history...I tried to imagine the face and demeanor of Claude Puaux, our direct ancestor, who in 1585 was Vallon's delegate to the Protestant Assembly at Privas. Will I be worthy, I used to ask myself, of being a link in the chain?[43]

Edmond Hugues was also the son of a pastor who wrote a history of Anduze. His son, Pierre-Edmond, would later become conservator of the museum and an organizer of assemblies, and today his son-in-law, Jean Carbonnier, performs the same functions, even though the S.H.P.F. is officially the owner of the museum.

Traditions were more readily established if they could be related to familiar features of the landscape: the cave in which the underground preacher hid, the hidden valley where the clandestine congregation gathered, the hiding place for the Bible in the big house, and various markers that stake out the individual geography of each Protestant family's private memories. Such features cover a wide area, although the highest density is found in the Camisard stronghold of the Cévennes and lower Languedoc. The Vivarais, Dauphiné, upper Languedoc, and Poitou all contain numerous reminders of the Desert period. There are also folktales and laments from all these regions dealing with the martyred preachers and pastors of the eighteenth century, men who were "heroes" yet at the same time closer to ordinary Protestants than a Coligny—heroic cousins of the faithful. The tone of certain verses leaves no doubt about this feeling of closeness, as in the opening lines of this lament, which does not even mention that the hero Désubas, executed in 1745 at the age of twenty-six, was a minister:

> Chers protestants de France,
> Venez pour écouter,
> La sévère sentence
> Qu'on vient de prononcer

Contre un de nos chers frères,
Dit Monsieur Désubas,
Qu'une main meurtrière
Vendit à nos soldats.
[Dear Protestants of France,
Come hear the severe sentence
Just handed down
Against one of our dear brothers,
Known as M. Désubas,
Sold to our soldiers
By a murderous hand.][44]

When oral tradition dwindles or disappears, family historical legend can draw on other sources, beginning with the old Bible in which births, marriages, and deaths were recorded, as well as copies of prayers, catechisms, and poems piously preserved to the present day.[45] What Puaux and Hugues foresaw was the day when even those sources might fail, and so they created the Memorial at the Museum of the Desert in which every Protestant family can find its galley slave on the wall. Such aids are increasingly necessary in an age when rural societies, which had kept the old traditions alive, are disintegrating. But the intuition of the museum's founders was even more profound: by bringing all French Protestants together in one place, they transformed family memories and melded what had been separate fragments into a unified whole, as Jean Carbonnier points out: "Commemoration transformed them into a people, the Protestant people, which has a reality in space and time."[46] Scholarship and institutionalized commemoration have thus maintained the link between Protestants and their glorious past. Group memory, family memory, and local memory mutually reinforce one another.

The Revocation and the Desert: Multiple Meanings

The memory of the Protestant minority has not been at odds with French national memory since the nineteenth century. First liberal and later republican historians treated the Protestant resistance, and especially the Camisard War, as a precursor of the revolutionary struggle for liberty in 1789: these events fit neatly into the republican tradition. Thus for Michelet the Revocation was an event of concern not just to Protestants but to all Frenchmen: "The place that the Revolution occupies in the eighteenth century was occupied in the seventeenth century by the Revocation of the Edict of Nantes.... The whole century gravitates toward the Revocation." The author of *L'Histoire de France* felt desperate: "The desire to turn back to France's great love and great pity." The Revocation was in effect the triumph of the anti-

Revolution, of fate, and the Camisards were the first adepts of "the new church of modern times," the church of the "Holy Revolution founded on justice and liberty": "The thing was absolutely democratic and popular...it was national.... Nowhere was France greater or more terrifying."[47] Edgar Quinet went even further in *La Révolution* (1865), a work that caused quite a stir when it appeared, triggering a violent polemic in the republican camp because of its condemnation of the Jacobin dictatorship.[48] Not only did Louis XIV's intolerance and 1685 prefigure the Terror and 1793, but the Revolution, Quinet argued, failed to live up to its principles because France in the sixteenth century had been unable to complete its religious revolution. The republican philosopher thus became the leader of all who saw Protestantism as the form of Christianity best adapted to modern times and 1789.[49] He launched a theme that would enjoy a certain success in years to come: that France did not fully succeed in modernizing because it failed to become Protestant. A century later Alain Peyrefitte would take this idea up once more in his best-selling book *Le Mal français* (1971).

In commemorating 1685 and celebrating the resistance to absolute monarchy, Protestants were no longer in danger of calling attention to the difference between them and the majority of Frenchmen; rather, they cast themselves in the role of an avant garde, a prefiguration of contemporary France.

Before 1914, however, there was by no means unanimous agreement about including Huguenot memory in France's national history. Republicans favored inclusion, but Catholics and royalists accused Protestants of being in the pay of foreign governments. Consider the words of one Languedocian priest, the Abbé Rouquette: "Always false, Protestantism, which is essentially an antinational political party, has tried to pluck strings that strike deep into the human soul in order to elicit pity for the greatest of crimes. It was in the name of freedom of religion that they betrayed the fatherland and sold our ports to the English."[50] Matters progressed slowly until 1950. Abbé Dedieu was still emphasizing political relations between Huguenots and foreign powers in the thick volume he published in 1921, *Le Rôle politique des prostestants français de 1685 à 1715*. But in *Camisards et dragons du Roi* (1950), Agnès de La Gorce made no attempt to hide either the length of time during which Protestants were persecuted in France or the harshness of the repression. Five years later, the celebrated *Histoire religieuse* of Fliche and Martin cast no doubt on "the fundamental patriotism of the Huguenots."[51] And the very well known Catholic historian Daniel-Rops wrote in 1965 that "in its most powerful, most noble aspect French Protestantism is a religion of the persecuted, of martyrs for a faith."[52] Since then the distinction between Protestant and Catholic historiography has become increasingly tenuous, as the former has abandoned its hagiographic perspective while the latter is no longer willing to justify the policies of Louis XIV.

The tercentenary commemoration marked the culmination of these developments. Catholic periodicals such as *La Vie, Témoignage chrétien,* and *Notre histoire*
published lengthy articles on the events, and prominent Catholic historians took
part in the occasion through books, colloquia, and debates. The presence of
Cardinal Lustiger, the archbishop of Paris, at the UNESCO ceremony was highly
symbolic, as was the communiqué issued by a combined Protestant-Catholic committee on March 21, 1985:

> This commemoration is for us an opportunity to reflect together on a history
> that at once unites and divides us and on the conflicts that marked it.... Today,
> in the eyes of all, the Edict of Nantes of 1598 marked the search for a peace-
> ful, progressive solution. Its revocation was an act of intolerance and an insti-
> gation to persecution.... We today have a duty to maintain a vigilant eye on the
> inalienable right of religious freedom for individuals and communities, and
> every majority group has an obligation in all circumstances to respect the
> expression of religious and cultural minorities.[53]

More broadly, this three-hundredth anniversary was a truly national commemoration, unlike the two previous centenaries of the Revocation.[54] For one thing, it was
included in the official list of commemorations drawn up by the Ministry of
Culture, as a result of which the National Archives organized a major exhibition
that drew many visitors. Far more significant, however, was the extensive coverage
in the press, from *Le Monde* to *Le Figaro,* and including *Libération, L'Express, Le
Point, Télérama,* and *Le Nouvel Observateur.* "Minor Protestant Music" and "The
Return of the Huguenots" were among the titles featured in newspapers that rediscovered the importance of this minority group in French history, an importance that
far outweighed its tiny numbers: "The Protestants were a major influence, and their
traditions and values have left a deep imprint on today's society."[55] Even more symbolic of the national recognition accorded to the occasion was the participation of
the President of the Republic, François Mitterrand, in the evening commemoration
at UNESCO. Appearing with him were a number of government ministers as well as
representatives of other religious groups, as well as numerous descendants of
Huguenot refugees from various countries in the world. Paradoxically, it was this
international dimension that gave the anniversary its national importance, as if
French memory were willing to recognize as fundamentally important only events
recognized as world-historical beyond its borders.

In this respect, too, the tercentenary marked the culmination of a trend that
began in Le Mas–Soubeyran before the end of World War I. In July 1918, Edmond
Hugues invited the American pastor Mac Farland to preside over the assembly at the
museum, and on Roland's Bible the American speaker took an "oath of allegiance
to Huguenot France" and begged God to "choose him as His humble instrument in

bringing about a spiritual rapprochement between the French and American churches."[56] Clearly the museum's promoters no longer feared the accusation of complicity with foreign powers, which had paralyzed the 1885 commemoration and practically precluded the presence of foreign delegations. Six years later, the Huguenot New Netherland Commission organized a "Huguenot pilgrimage" to Europe in honor of the three-hundredth anniversary of the founding of New Amsterdam (New York). The travelers visited the sites of recent battles as well as sites of Protestant resistance, including the galleys of Marseilles, the tower of Constance, and the house of Roland, where they took part in the eleventh assembly at the Museum of the Desert. From then on descendants of Huguenot refugees regularly participated in the ceremonies. The movement gathered strength after World War II, particularly in connection with "army pilgrimages" in which Protestants from various NATO nations participated.

This internationalization was based on the idea that the Huguenot resistance was a precursor not only for France but for all humanity. At the 1924 assembly, a Boston clergyman named Leete proclaimed that "nearly 250 years ago these parts witnessed one of the greatest events in history. Here your parents died for the right to worship as they pleased. Here they fought for you, for us, and for the whole world.... For two hundred years you have been our inspiration. You have preached by example."[57] The rise of totalitarianism and the outbreak of World War II fueled this idea, which could be glimpsed in several speeches as early as the assembly of 1935, which commemorated the 250th anniversary of the Revocation: those who were persecuted for their faith were compared to the early victims of the Nazis. After 1940 the commemoration was deliberately oriented toward the present by the choice of themes: in 1941 it was "Under the Cross," in 1942 "Loyalty," in 1943 "Freedom" (with a focus on Rabaut Saint-Étienne as one who had championed freedom during the Revolution), in 1945 "Resistance," and in 1946 "Restoration." The assembly of 1942 went even further in the direction of reliving the past, for it actually served as a cover for helping persecuted Jews to escape from Nîmes and find hiding places in the Cévennes; chartered buses were used for the purpose. During the ceremony the clergyman Boegner asked all present to act as "good Samaritans" toward Jews, and that night he was even more explicit in a speech to pastors, whom he informed of the death threat hanging over the Jews and urged to do whatever was possible to help save them.[58] Many members of the underground resistance in the Cévennes were of Protestant background and eager to proclaim themselves the heirs of the Camisards. Among them was Jacques Poujol, the young leader of the Aigoual-Cévennes resistance unit, who wrote this hymn:

> Les fiers enfants des Cévennes
> Réfractaires et maquisards,

> Montrent qu'ils ont dans les veines
> Le sang pur des camisards.
> [The proud children of the Cévennes,
> Noncooperators and resistance fighters,
> Show that the blood in their veins
> Is the pure blood of the Camisards.][59]

Memory thus helped to create history.

After the war the Desert period served as a symbol for various forms of totalitarianism and repression. In 1968 various speakers at Le Mas–Soubeyran referred to the Prague Spring and the subsequent crushing of the Czech liberation movement by Soviet tanks, and the same theme was of course the centerpiece of the UNESCO commemoration in 1985, as is clear from the conclusion of President Mitterrand's speech:

> The *dragonnades*, the galleys, the Camisards—are these ancient history? Not at all: they are today's history all over the world. Everywhere minorities are excluded and rejected, and there are those who would expel—to what refuge?—those who live with and among us.... From the memory of what was, I say again, one of the bloodiest persecutions in our history, we can draw lessons of fidelity and courage. There is a generation—my generation—which in its youth experienced another drama of exclusion: a choice of death against conscience or of death with conscience. How can we forget what we went through? Only one duty remains: to teach it to those who will follow us.[60]

Yet the multiplicity of meanings implicit in the Desert period does not end there. In the late 1960s, when many people became concerned with their "roots" and various regionalist movements developed, the Protestant resisters of the south proved far more attractive than the memory of Saint Bartholomew's Day in Paris. The sixteenth-century Wars of Religion lacked the local identification of the Camisard guerrillas, which the veterans of May '68 saw as a kind of prototypical people's liberation movement, while the proponents of nonviolence preferred to look back to Marie Durand, the prisoner of Constance.

Conditions therefore favored the emergence and lasting success of a memory of the Revocation and the Desert rather than of Saint Bartholomew's Day and the battles of the sixteenth century. The latter memory left Huguenots trapped in defeat and misfortune with no prospects for the future. Victims in 1572, French Protestants could not even cling to the Edict of Nantes, because 1685 wiped out 1598: all they had was the Cross without the Resurrection. Then, too, the Revocation made victims of the Huguenots, but their resistance turned them into a "triumphant people": "Under the Cross, Triumph." Even in the violent form of the Camisard War, the Desert offered another advantage over the Wars of Religion so far as memory was concerned: in the latter Protestants were one of the "factions" who fomented division and civil war, whereas in the former the persecuted, rejected minority became a precursor of liberty. The message, which in the nineteenth century was a message for the French nation, became international in the twentieth century with the rise of totalitarianism. The Refuge gave the event a European dimension that made it even more topical. It was in this context that the Museum of the Desert achieved its success, thus firmly implanting a memory that was a product of oral tradition, of a century of historical literature, and of the feelings of a community that saw itself not just as a federation of families and churches but as a people.

Meanwhile, national consciousness was following a parallel path. The Revocation, like Saint Bartholomew's Day, was the result of a political miscalculation by the government, and the average Frenchman found it easier to identify with the victims of and resistance to misguided policy than with the policy itself. For the past twenty years, moreover, French culture has sought to become less uniform and more diverse though not quite multi-cultural. The Protestant minority offers a form of diversity that French culture is capable of accepting.

FIGURE 9.7   Stamp commemorating the two-hundredth anniversary of the freeing of the Huguenot prisoners from the Tower of Constance in Aigues-Mortes (1968). Does this memory compete with or complement that of the Camisards?

FIGURE 10.0   Philippe Garel, *Léon Blum;* Place de la Mairie, 11th Arrondissement, Paris.

Grégoire, Dreyfus, Drancy, and the Rue Copernic: Jews at the Heart of French History

Pierre Birnbaum

In the early 1980s various administrative and political authorities in Paris refused one after another to provide sites for statues of Captain Dreyfus, Léon Blum, and Pierre Mendès France, three Jews who at one time or another found themselves at the center of Franco-French conflict and thus the object of the most violent passions. It was unthinkable that the head of the École Militaire, where Captain Dreyfus was dramatically stripped of his rank, should be forced to make amends by allowing a statue of the man who was deported to Devil's Island to be placed in the famous courtyard. As for Blum and Mendès France, only the most patient of pedestrians would have been likely to stumble upon their statues, at one time hidden in out-of-the-way nooks of the Jardin du Luxembourg and later in the Tuileries.[1]

In an area somewhat farther from central Paris, a determined visitor may catch a glimpse of a small marker, located between two modern high-rises and next to a gas station, indicating the site of the old Vel' d'Hiv (Vélodrome d'Hiver), the one-time bicycle racetrack that served as a holding area for Jews rounded up in the great sweep of July 1942. Later, during the Fourth Republic, the same spot was the scene of a rally in support of the extreme right-wing populist Pierre Poujade, during which the most vile anti-Semitic outbursts could be heard to emanate from the crowd. This place of remembrance *par excellence* has simply vanished. Even worse, there is apparently no surviving photograph of the July 1942 roundup to preserve a visual record of the event. The camp at Drancy through which nearly 70,000 Jews passed in total destitution on their way to Auschwitz and other death camps is today just a station on the suburban express railway. Recently a barrier of tall bars was erected around an area within which stand a few buildings that were once part of the concentration camp. A strange monument bears witness to this fact, but already, in this highly urbanized setting, the memory is fading.[2] The same is true of the other camps in which, as early as 1939, so many foreign and, later, French Jews lived in dreadful conditions before eventually being deported (in nearly all cases). Argelès and Saint-Cyprien are pleasant summer vacation spots. "Rivesaltes has built its fame on the flavor of its muscatel, and cows graze around the Noé water tower. No sign indicates that there were once camps here."[3] Beaune-la-Rolande and Gurs are of course exceptions, but broadly speaking the camps in which the most tragic moments of the contemporary history of French Jews unfolded are not the objects of any particular commemorative attention.

Physical sites of Jewish memory in France are quite rare. Jewish memory often takes a different form: vestiges of the ancient past such as religious objects and manuscripts are housed in museums and libraries. In various cemeteries largely unknown to the public, including those at Haguenau, Rosenwiller,[4] and Carpentras, steles, some of them dating back to the fifteenth century, are slowly sinking into the earth, and their Hebrew inscriptions, almost entirely effaced, recall the existence of Jewish communities that have long since vanished. In other cemeteries of more recent vintage, also located in the east, near the battlefields of the two world wars, stars of David mark the graves of fallen Jewish soldiers, but here, too, time has already begun to do its work, slowly erasing these symbols of a tragic history. The few ancient synagogues in France, such as those in Mende (twelfth century), Carpentras, and Cavaillon, are little more than historical monuments for guided tours. In many small towns in eastern France travelers may still happen upon a busy *rue de la Juiverie*, but many of these one-time ghetto streets have been turned into picturesque tourist traps.

Traces of Jewish memory are thus the exception in the landscape of France, a profoundly Catholic country dotted with abbeys and churches. The *fleur de lys* rid France of heretics as well as serpents, as one poet noted:

> Le royaume très chrétien
> Où la foi est enluminée,
> Où n'habite ni juif ni païen.
> [The most Christian kingdom,
> In which the faith is illuminated,
> And no Jew or pagan dwells.][5]

Even today in the cathedral of Strasbourg the Synagogue is clearly represented as a blindfolded figure, symbolizing the permanent blindness of the Jews. Although the triumphant Republic curbed the public expression of purely Christian values, its heroes were champions of omnipotent Reason, hence monuments honoring them evoke only faith in the Nation or in Progress. The national myth in its various versions pays little heed to representations of any particular group, and those who cannot claim a privileged relation to a specific area, to memories rooted in a particular region, are more or less excluded from the national scene: no public *lieu de mémoire* gives them substance. In 1953, moreover, when Jews themselves broke with a long tradition of hostility to monuments and respect solely for books to build in the heart of Paris the Memorial to the Unknown Jewish Martyr, they chose an architectural style that avoided any reference to a specific tradition, and the dedication ceremony was patterned after the austere ritual of the republican "cult of the dead" and secular tradition.[6]

Absent from the memory of the kingdom and of the nation, French Jews themselves often behave as if suffering from amnesia. Their memory is almost entirely identified with that of France. They have forgotten the events of their own history. At best their past is hidden away in books of reminiscences. Until quite recently almost no French Jews were aware of the splendid work of the eleventh-century rabbi Rashi of Troyes, who wrote authoritative commentaries on the Bible and Talmud in the local dialect, Champenois, but with the aid of Hebrew characters; or of the massacres of Jews in Blois and Occitania, in Toulouse and Verdun, when the Pastoureaux passed through in June 1320;[7] or of the Carrières in Avignon and so many other episodes, happy or unhappy, in the history of the various Jewish communities that one after another have thrived on French soil over the centuries.[8] For Yosef Yerushalmi all that remains is transhistorical memory, the memory of the Exodus from Egypt and the destruction of the Temple, the memory contained in daily rituals and annual holidays and in moments of passage from birth to death, during which collective prayers nurse for a brief instant the illusion of time as a continuum unaffected by history.[9] This atemporal memory, with its ignorance of the many episodes that shaped the destiny of the Jews in France, has also been fading, however, as the general secularization of society proceeds under constant pressure from the state. The collective consciousness of France has long since been transformed by a secularization of customs and values. This slow erosion of ritual practices is surely weakening the faculty of memory at a time when everything, or nearly everything, has already been forgotten.

The Negative Imagination

Since time immemorial the Jews have been a subject of myths of all kinds, and French memory of them from the Middle Ages to the present is filled with caricatural images. Peasants have never gotten over the fear of the wandering Jew, who, dressed in rags and starving, anxiously roams the countryside. On seeing him dogs bark and children run wild. Condemned by Christ to wander about the world, he is the author of countless crimes, which the peasants of eastern France recount endlessly. Accused of pilfering, the Jewish hawker also symbolizes the outsider, the person who comes from some far-off land and whose mere presence poses a threat to order and to age-old tradition. Rural and Catholic France sees him as a demon, a devil whose tricks are to be feared, a sorcerer whose presence is so corrupting that he deserves to be burned. Though sometimes received courteously, the wandering Jew is usually driven mercilessly from one region to the next. He turned up unexpectedly in Beauvais in 1604, while folktales from other regions have him haunting the countryside of Brittany or the mountains of the Alps, destroying crops and riches as he goes. Popularized in the early nineteenth century by Béranger's lament and boulevard theater, he entered the realm of legend thanks to Eugène Sue, who etched the image of the wandering Jew into the national consciousness.[10] A magician accused of ritual crimes, he was repeatedly expelled like the Jews as a group: the history of the French monarchy was inextricably intertwined with ruthless repression of the Jews.

In the late nineteenth century Édouard Drumont was still pointing an accusatory finger at "this race of nomads," and barely half a century ago other anti-Semites were still pursuing his relentless campaign against "the tribes of Israel.... Beware Ahasuerus, you wandering Jew! The people's awakening will be terrible." Many anti-Semitic pamphlets treated Léon Blum as the incarnation of the "wandering Jew, the destructive Jew" who must once again be expelled. For Maurice Bedel, "the President of the Council comes from a wandering race and landed in France only by chance, when fortune might just as easily have taken him to New York, Cairo, or Vilna." And Marcel Jouhandeau had this to say right at the start of *Le Péril juif*: "Although I feel no sympathy for Hitler, Blum inspires a far deeper repugnance in me. The Führer is where he belongs, whereas Messrs. Blum and Benda do not belong among us." The same image was used repeatedly to describe such figures as Georges Mandel and Pierre Mendès France; of the latter it was said that he is "presumed to be camping now somewhere between the Atlantic and the Pyrenees." According to one myth, repeated as recently as 1960 by the *Petit Larousse*, Blum's real name was "Karfunkelstein," and Mendès was often called "Mendès Bessarabia," "Mendès Jerusalem," "Mendès Palestine," and even "Mendès anti-France." In the 1980s one heard the term *tribu Fabius* (Fabius tribe) applied to associates of Prime Minister Laurent Fabius, who was Jewish.

Forbidden to own land and therefore without ties to it, Jews performed functions of which the Church disapproved: in traditional imagery they were identified with usury, speculation, and manipulations of all kinds made possible by their lack of fixed abode and permanent nonintegration into tightly cohesive social groups. From age-old Alsatian legends to the novels of Balzac, Jews were depicted as greedy bankers shamelessly mocking their poor Christian victims. In *L'Argent*, Émile Zola paints a terrifying portrait of "unadulterated Jewry, that implacable, unfeeling conqueror" that makes itself "master of the earth" by means of gold,[11] while Maurice Barrès in *Les Déracinés* railed against the corrupting power of money with which Jews could buy the government, and Pierre Drieu La Rochelle in *Gilles* self-indulgently dwelt on the unhealthy degeneracy of his Jewish banker father-in-law. Even Proudhon, Fourier, and Pierre Leroux, theorists of French-style socialism, founders of anarchism, and bold utopian architects, helped to propagate the symbolism of the Jew as a corrupter of Frenchness and the human race.

Counterrevolutionary literature was just as likely as socialist tracts to pour unrelenting scorn on the Rothschilds, the very embodiment of evil and symbol of the domination of Jewish money. Georges Dairnwaell recounted the *Histoire édifiante et curieuse de Rothschild Ier, Roi des Juifs*, Jacques de Biez denounced *Rothschild et le péril juif*, and Jules Guesde, the author of "A mort Rothschild," blasted the "evil Jew from Frankfurt who for nearly a century has been living like a giant octopus in the heart of France, sucking its blood through his countless suckers."[12] The myth of "the two hundred families" further magnified this alleged plot by the great banks, from which the Jews were allegedly the first to profit. In the period between the two world wars, *La Flèche, Gringoire,* and *L'Humanité* pointed an accusatory finger at Rothschild, the personification of big Jewish capital, along with his putative allies of *la grande banque protestante*. As far as Paul Vaillant-Couturier was concerned, all of France, "from the Capetians to the Communists," including many of the nation's industrialists, would do well to band together to outlaw all trusts. And the chief of all the trusts, according to André Marty, was none other than Léon Blum, the "intimate friend of the greatest cosmopolitan financiers." Maurice Thorez meanwhile described the socialist leader as "a repugnant reptile, a jackal...with long, crooked fingers,...closely tied to monopoly capitalism," and Florimond Bonte simply called him "the bourgeoisie's pet...the reptile who, when angered, lifts its head and spits venom."

The leaders of the Communist Party, who frequently identified Jews with international capitalism, would later shift the brunt of their attacks to other prominent Jews such as Pierre Mendès France or François Bloch-Lainé. Their language is astonishingly similar to that of the extreme right-wing writer Hector Ghilini, for whom "the allure of the golden calf explains Blum's shift toward the *mur d'argent* [the moneyed interest]." The myth that the leader of the Popular Front dined on silver dishes was a key image of the period, during which the Action Française tirelessly assailed "little Blum, the silverplate Jew of the Conseil d'État." In a symbolic system that was widely shared, the image of the filthy-rich Jew was often completed by that of the eternal Jew, the revolutionary who from Léon Blum (note the versatility of the symbolism) to the underground militants of the Mouvement d'Ouvriers Immigrés (M.O.I.) to Alain Krivine provoked fears, and was indeed still a source of alarm when Henri Krasucki took over as head of the Confédération Générale du Travail (C.G.T.). Different images could run together, as in the case of

Pierre Goldman, the pro—Third World revolutionary and bank robber, who became an object of public fascination, and the idea of revolutionary Judaism could become threatening, as when crowds marched through the streets of Paris in support of the May '68 student leader Daniel Cohn-Bendit, chanting "We are all German Jews" as they marched.

In the French political imagination, revolutionary Jews thus coexist easily with their capitalist coreligionists. Both are modern transformations of the image of the wandering Jew, which is deeply rooted in the collective memory, and both fuel the fear of a plot of outsiders to undermine the specific identity of French society. Jews are accordingly perceived as outsiders availing themselves of the most varied strategies to ensure their own domination. Under the circumstances, it is not surprising that the notorious *Protocols of the Elders of Zion* should have been produced in late nineteenth century France, given the extent to which the text alludes to traits peculiar to that society. While the *Protocols* have traveled around the world and been translated into every language, their acceptance in France was rapid, particularly since they reinforced firmly rooted beliefs.[13] And there are those who have attempted to preserve those beliefs right up to the present day by seeing to it that the *Protocols* continue to be published: in 1990, *Révision* and *Lectures françaises*, two periodicals associated with the extreme right, published the full text.

Aliens to *la France profonde*, instruments of corrupting capitalism, money masters who pervert morals, instinctive revolutionaries responsible for every social upheaval, the Jews were almost always spurned by Catholic tradition with its organic and conservative conception of society. From Abbé Barruel to the liberal and progressive François Mauriac, Catholicism produced countless pamphlets and textbooks in which the Jew was caricatured as a doomed malefactor. The Jews threatened to dechristianize France, and for Bonald, for example, their necessary punishment, following the divagations of the French Revolution, heralded a redemptive return to the France of an earlier era. In the minds of many Catholics a latter-day Passion was a prelude to the triumph of Christ. In his *Journal* of 1892, Léon Bloy recorded his "contempt for the filthy, venomous yids who poison the world." In 1901, Louis Veuillot offered this outburst: "I, a Catholic Christian of France, as old as the oaks and with roots just as deep...I am governed by vagabonds in spirit and custom. Renegades or foreigners, they have none of my trust, my prayers, my memories, or my hopes. I am a subject of the heretic, the Jew, the atheist, and of a mongrel of all those breeds who looks a lot like a brute."

Despite an attitude that led him in the end to recognize Jewish values, Paul Claudel believed that Jews, by rejecting the Gospel, had excluded themselves from humanity and that their values were mostly incompatible with the values of the French. Many of his plays contain highly critical portraits of Jewish characters, and he often expressed vehemently anti-Semitic sentiments: on the Jews' flight from

Egypt, for example, he said, "Israel came out of Egypt as one says of smallpox that it 'came out.'"

Even Catholics with relatively liberal political views who were outspoken opponents of anti-Semitism often accepted many of the clichés put forth by Drumont and his followers. The pro-Jewish, pro-Protestant Anatole Leroy-Beaulieu, for example, did not hesitate to paint a portrait of Gambetta that Drumont would have had no trouble claiming as his own: "Take Gambetta's profile, with its pronounced Judaic line: there the Jew's narrow face broadens out into a leonine mask." More than a half-century later, François Mauriac, as much a philo-Semite as Anatole Leroy-Beaulieu, remarked in 1937 that "for a Catholic anti-Semitism is not just a sin against charity. We are connected to Israel, we are united to it, whether we like it or not," before going on to say that the Jews "cannot monopolize international finance without making nations feel dominated by them. They cannot pullulate wherever one of them happens to get in [viz., the Blum ministry] without arousing hatred." Time and again even the most benevolent Catholics avail themselves of anti-Semitic images dredged up from the depths of their memory. Even Emmanuel Mounier, who in 1939 courageously fought against the anti-Semitism of *Je suis partout*, which he considered to be "of foreign origin," nevertheless conceded that "there are other Jewish problems, in that Jews at times have a tendency toward clannishness if not secession, toward forming foreign bodies [*induration*] within the national community. The cinema, as a matter of fact, is infested by a particularly shady group of Jews. Higher education before the war was to some extent monopolized by a particular category of Jews, the rationalists and sociologists. M. Blum imprudently included in his entourage too many men drawn from a subgroup of politicians, the Jewish socialists." During this same period, just prior to Vichy and the statutory exclusion of Jews from the national community, the novelist Georges Bernanos, who would intervene on behalf of the excluded, seemed to be thinking back to the message propagated by the newspaper *La Croix* in the 1880s. Still celebrating the importance of Drumont's political thought, Bernanos proclaimed that "the Jew is the enemy: that has been the Christian cry from Golgotha to the present." And Jean Giraudoux, the author of a strange *Judith,* denounced, also in 1939, the "horde" of "hundreds of thousands of Ashkenazis escaped from the ghettos" only to find himself officially charged with the mission of defending the French race.

Even in the writing of authors who prided themselves on pacifism and toleration, the Jew often figured as a corrupting influence afflicted with various congenital physical defects. In *Jean-Christophe,* for example, Romain Rolland associated Jewish characters with "the ironic, corrosive spirit that gently attacked...religion and country." Furthermore, "Parisian Jews (and Judaized Christians), so numerous in the theater, had introduced that mishmash of sentiment that is the distinctive feature of degenerate cosmopolitanism." Rolland mocked his character, Sylvain Kohn, "the little German Jew, the oaf [who] had made himself the chronicler and arbiter of Parisian elegance." Similar stereotypes can also be found in the work of Jacques de Lacretelle, a writer as well-intentioned as Rolland: his hero, young Silbermann, is "small and outwardly unprepossessing.... His complexion was pale, verging on yellowish; his eyes and brows were black, his lips thick and cold in color." The "little Jew" at times transforms himself into the "Messiah" and ultimately decides to go to America "to make money," leaving the narrator to total up the damage: "It was in our foyer that Silbermann's devastation was most noticeable. All my gods were overturned. Once-honored ideas, our minor domestic laws, our conception of the beautiful—everything had lost its prestige."[14] André Gide himself had this to say about Blum in his journal for January 27, 1914: "The qualities of the Jewish race are not French qualities." In 1925 he judged Blum's book *Du mariage* to be evidence that "the Jews are past masters in the art of disrupting our most respected and venerable institutions, institutions that are the very foundation and cornerstone of our western civilization, for the sake of I know not what licentiousness and looseness of morals, which fortunately is repellent to our sensibility, our good sense, and our instinct for Latin sociability." Twelve years later, in quite a different tone, to be sure, Louis-Ferdinand Céline poured forth a torrent of scatalogical and sexual insults in his *Bagatelles pour un massacre,* in which he accused the Jews of perverting the pure but naïve women of France.

The beautiful Jewess was the female equivalent of the rootless, poisonous Jew. A sorceress and seductress, she posed a threat to the French male. Over the centuries Judith symbolized the danger to Christian France. From Balzac to Zola, Maupassant, Alphonse Daudet, Romain Rolland, and Pierre Drieu La Rochelle, beautiful Jewesses ready to prostitute themselves in order to deprive Frenchmen of their manhood were a staple of literature and therefore an obsession in the minds of any number of men. They embodied a fatal attraction, which according to Drumont led straight to "the circumcision of all Frenchmen," an idea reformulated by Paul Lapeyre in his book *La Sociologie catholique,* in which he lashes out at the "demons of the Talmud with their pruning shears." For Alfred Fabre-Luce, Proust and Léon Blum were both "courtesans." Léon Daudet applied the nickname "Fifille" to the leader of the Socialist Party, a "Hebrew Adonis who wets his bench in the Chamber," while Charles Maurras made fun of "Fleur-Bleue, baptized with a pruning shear." The historian Pierre Gaxotte caricatured Blum as an "old Palestinian mare, forever neighing, moaning, writhing, and fainting." Modeled after Léon Blum, Lucien Lévy-Coeur, one of the central characters of Romain Rolland's *Jean-Christophe,* was supposed to be drawn to pornography and a stranger to "all that is virile, pure, healthy, and popular," yet he got on "admirably with the perverted ingénues of bourgeois society, idle, wealthy women." In recent years the extreme right-wing press of Jean-Marie Le Pen's Front National described Prime

Minister Laurent Fabius as a "sexual bomb" with a "mouth such as one might find on a fat odalisque in the harem of the Sublime Porte."

Franco-Judaism and the Dissolution of Jewish Memory

The survival and periodic resurgence of stereotypes like these is astonishing, indeed almost incomprehensible, for if there is a country in which Jewish assimilation has been successful, it is surely France. Indeed, France produced a cultural synthesis, Franco-Judaism, more complete than that achieved anywhere else: the term implies a complete unification of values and destinies, a mutual permeability of world-views, and an identity of behavior. Even in the German Reich, in which the symbiosis of German and Jewish culture was so intimate that it yielded in some sense a common culture that only Nazism was able to destroy, Jews could never fully identify with the profoundly Christian structure of the state and of society as a whole. In despair some Jews converted, while others became ultra-patriots or rebelled by subscribing, for example, to Marxism or quit the Reich for Palestine or the United States. Those who remained, clinging in spite of everything to their faith in the Germany of the Enlightenment and of civilization, ultimately experienced the horror of the camps. Despite an entirely different history, many French Jews met with the same fate. Indeed, it was their identification with France, and more precisely with the Republic, that placed them, as we shall see, at the center of Franco-French conflict, revived the primitive virulence of archaic anti-Semitic stereotypes, and cast the Jews as absolute enemies of all antirepublican and antidemocratic forces.

The Jews' real encounter with France dates from the events of 1789. At the time most Jews lived in tight-knit communities in eastern France and virtually governed themselves. The vexations they had to put up with were mainly local, and they had little contact with the central government. The far smaller number of Jews who lived in Bordeaux[15] or Bayonne were already participating in French society as individuals, but their integration often meant that they lost some of their own identity. The marriage of France and the Jews thus took place as Enlightenment values were gaining the upper hand: the authorities' increasing determination to unify the country required a pool of equal citizens entirely beholden to the liberating state.

Abbé Grégoire hoped to complete the "regeneration" of the Jews, to rescue them from "moral depravity" and the "sewer" so that they might permanently escape the condition of "parasitic plants." A man of the Enlightenment and a faithful follower of the Jacobins and their centralizing practices, Grégoire, like Robespierre, aimed to do all he could to "dissolve the Jews in the mass of the Nation." "Let us take the generation that has just been born, that is growing into puberty," he proposed, "and guide them into state schools," so that they might acquire "healthy ideas" that will make them forget their "esprit de corps."[16]

FIGURE 10.1 *The True Portrait of the Wandering Jew,* popular image of the eighteenth century.

It was part of the explicit plan of the revolutionary government to eliminate out-dated particularisms by strictly requiring students to absorb the civic language and morality. Jews "are people like us," Grégoire pointed out, "before they are Jews." Once they learn to stop awaiting the arrival of the Messiah, as they had been doing for so many centuries, they might be willing to "convert" to some hybrid of Catholicism and Protestantism compatible with the fraternal ideals of 1789.

The revolutionary government thus took up the Jewish cause in the name of a liberating messianism of its own, a messianism that was admittedly destructive of communal institutions, traditions, and values yet ready to adapt itself to the messianism of the Jews so long as they did not seek to embed it in institutions of their own. While Mirabeau hoped that microsocieties with cultures of their own could be preserved within the new nation, the revolutionary proposal that established the contract setting the terms of Franco-Judaism's existence was prepared to accommodate the messianic hopes of the Jews provided that the Jews in turn were willing to transform those hopes into a rationalist deism acceptable to all citizens.[17]

Throughout the history of modern France, the foregoing conditions would serve as a normative basis for a French-Jewish symbiosis that would over the course of two centuries arouse the enthusiasm of large numbers of Jews. The Jews of revolutionary Paris made no bones about their commitment: "A single goal dominates and preoccupies our souls: the good of the Fatherland and the desire to devote all our strength to it." Once Jews became citizens, they declared themselves ready to submit "to a uniform plan of public order and jurisprudence." For the next two centuries it was taken for granted that Jews from Adolphe Crémieux to Joseph Reinach, Émile Durkheim, Marc Bloch, and Raymond Aron would unreservedly subscribe to Franco-Judaism thus defined. Whether practicing or nonpracticing, countless French Jews fully identified with the emancipatory goals of the Revolution. "France," one of them wrote in 1791, just after the vote on emancipation, "the first country to extinguish the shame of Yehudah, is our Palestine; its mountains are our Zion."

In a similar vein, Adolphe Crémieux, who served as a minister in several governments, also drew a parallel between France's mission and the messianic vision: "To the God of Abraham, Isaac, and Jacob we give our adoration; to our France of 1789 we give our filial admiration; to the Republic of 1870 we give our absolute devotion. This is our great Trinity."[18] For Crémieux, who in 1870 proposed extending French nationality to the Jews of Algeria, the France of 1789 truly embodied "a divine flame" that had since become the expression of Judaism itself. When the deputy Camille Dreyfus celebrated the hundredth anniversary of the Revolution in 1889, he too naturally reverted to the same religious vision: for him, "the men of the Estates General had, to the sound of thunderclaps, demolished the old law and founded the new.... You were the Christs of the new passion and the authors of the new humanity."[19] Similarly, according to the historian Marc Bloch, "the time of the Messiah came with the French Revolution." And Théodore Reinach straightforwardly declared that "any Jew today with heart and memory has for his second homeland, his moral homeland, the France of 1791."[20] From now on the "memory" of the Jews would thus trace its beginnings back to the events of 1789.

Even the rabbis were quick to look upon the French Revolution as a divine message incarnate. In their patriotic speeches French rabbis liked to draw a parallel between the Revelation of Mount Sinai and the Revolution, with France in the role of a "second Moses." Rabbi Abraham Bloch stressed the degree to which "the principles of 1789 protect us...we live in the land of justice and equality, and in our hearts we know that we have done all that was expected of us." Rabbi Kahn of Nîmes declared that for him the Revolution was "our exodus from Egypt...our modern Passover," while Rabbi Hermann of Reims drew the ultimate consequences from this religious rapprochement when he stated that France had been "chosen by Him who guides the destiny of mankind to work for the emancipation of all the oppressed and to propagate throughout the world the great and beautiful ideas of justice, equality, and fraternity that were formerly the exclusive heritage of Israel."

"Israelites," Grand Rabbi Aron of Strasbourg wrote in 1848, "the flag that today flies above the national courtyard of the French Republic is the sacred banner that the Eternal One entrusted to Moses.... It is the symbol of the rights of humanity, which our prophets courageously proclaimed." Jews thus literally identified with France. French memory and Jewish memory merged, leading to a kind of religious syncretism that made it easy for many Jews to "convert" to the ideology of the Republic and for a far smaller number to convert to Catholicism, the dominant religion in the emancipatory France that Jews so adulated.[21]

As a result, and even discounting the extreme of conversion to Catholicism, Jewish life in general was profoundly altered. In a meeting of the Grand Sanhedrin it was decided that Jewish consistories would become "appendices of the state." Their mission was to strictly monitor Jewish activities in France in close consultation with the Ministère des Cultes. For the Grand Sanhedrin "it is the religious duty of every Israelite born and raised in a state...to regard that state as his or her homeland.... His interest absolutely must not be separated from the public interest." Napoleon's Civil Code henceforth took precedence over specific religious laws.[22] The "Frenchification" of the rabbis can be gauged by their choice of models from French history as well as the Bible, by their official participation in events of national importance, by their passionate sermons on behalf of the fatherland, by their new costumes, which made them look more like Catholic priests, by the introduction of organs into synagogues whose facades offered no particular distinguishing marks to passersby, by changes in religious services, and so on.

At the beginning of the twentieth century, proponents of liberal Judaism even considered changing the Sabbath from Saturday to Sunday as well as dropping certain central rituals. For Théodore Reinach, "the religious costumes of the Jews...are delaying their moral fusion with compatriots of other religions."[23] And Benoît Fould told the Chamber of Deputies, "in the name of those who profess the religion to which he has the honor to belong, that they are ready to sacrifice the Sabbath day of rest on the altar of the nation."[24] More traditionalist, the rabbis of eastern France tried to slow such transformations of Judaism, but after the Rabbinical School of Metz was moved to Paris and the Central Consistory imposed (as one can see by reading the record of its internal deliberations) draconian controls on its provincial subordinates, nothing seemed capable of halting the process.

Later, the gradual extension of secularizing legislation, which was supported and in part shaped by numerous Jews from Camille Dreyfus to Paul Grunebaum-Ballin, was at first opposed but subsequently accepted by the rabbinate. These laws would contribute to the suppression of public displays of religious particularism, which would not be revived until Jews from eastern Europe began to arrive after the beginning of the twentieth century and again when more traditionalist Jews from North Africa came to France in the aftermath of decolonization. Secularism symbolized the victorious Republic, which had at last succeeded in imposing its order on a society previously dominated by the Catholic Church. By removing religion from the public sphere and relegating it to the private, and by transforming the educational system, whose teachers, steeped in rationalist and positivist doctrines, joined in the combat against religious forces, secularism, as some rabbis had feared, further eroded Jewish attachment to communal structures and groups.

The decline of religion, which accelerated over the course of the nineteenth century, also led to a decline of a peculiarly Jewish form of collective consciousness and opened the way to further assimilation, with its reductive effects on both memory and history.[25] Paradoxically, however, this very assimilation, which was so intimately connected with the very nature of Franco-Judaism, can also be seen as an inverted form of Jewish messianism, with France as the new Zion.[26] This led, in Germany as well as France, to a positivist science of Judaism, which, by historicizing it, stripped away the mythical significance of its unique destiny, which was an essential ingredient of a specific Jewish identity that could be passed on from one generation to another. "Jewish science," which understands Judaism purely in terms of moral values, destroys memory: Jews are seen as the bearers of universal values which predispose them to form a "community of the spirit" rather than "of blood" or even merely a specific social entity.

In the 1860s a certain number of Jewish scholars, some of whom had attended the École Normale Supérieur and passed the *agrégation* required to teach particular subjects at the higher levels, gained access to important academic positions at the

Collège de France and the École Pratique des Hautes Études. Salomon Munk, Adolphe Franck, Joseph Derenbourg, did nevertheless participate in various religious and educational activities in the Jewish community. Many of these same scholars, including Derenbourg and Munk, had also attended major German universities, where they studied with teachers like Leopold Zuns. When they returned to France they brought with them the positivist and rationalist methods developed by the German scholars who had pioneered the new "Jewish science." Franck, for his part, was trained in France in the similar methods of Victor Cousin. These scholars helped to found the Société des Études Juives, where they joined Théodore Reinach. All gave positivist interpretations of the major Jewish texts.[27]

Pursuing this line of thought, Joseph Salvador attempted to analyze Judaism historically as a "positivist religion" which took its inspiration from the French Revolution, whose efforts to institutionalize equality Salvador deemed similar to those of the ancient Hebrew republic. James Darmesteter, who taught at the Collège de France, also embarked on rigorous research into the intellectual foundations of Judaism since the emancipation, stressing from the outset that "I am a biblical scholar and only the tiniest bit a Jew." Rejecting, as Renan had done, the Mosaic Law, he argued that "there is no place in France for a history of the Jews; there is nothing other than a history of French Judaism, just as there is a history of French Calvinism or of French Lutheranism—nothing other and nothing more." For Darmesteter, France was the very goal that Judaism had always set for itself in its prophetic and universalistic vision, the logical consequence. Paris was in the end the place where Judaism could flourish, for the republican synthesis had finally achieved a reconciliation with Christianity. For the Jewish academic elite of the period, as for many rabbis, Jewish universalism was simply conflated with republican universalism, thereby relinquishing any claim to a collective historical incarnation of its own.

In this connection, the creation of the Alliance Israélite Universelle, in which many of these same scholars and rabbis participated, further reinforced the symbiosis whose legitimacy was such that it found itself exported beyond France's borders into North Africa, the Ottoman Empire, and the Middle East for the purpose of continuing the work of regenerating unemancipated Jews undertaken by the Revolution and Abbé Grégoire: here too, French universalism, which furnished the mold within which Jewish educational efforts operated, helped to obliterate the cultures and memories of the various communities whose values, practices, and rituals were deemed to be anachronistic.

In furtherance of the struggle against the "fanaticism," "superstition," and "obscurantism" of the rabbis, teachers of the Alliance followed the French model of accelerating the secularization of these Jewish societies, seeking for example to combat local "jargons": "Jargon must be wiped off the slate," one of them said in

Casablanca in 1898, unwittingly adopting the perspective of Abbé Grégoire's Jacobin report on *patois*, "translations must be defended, and the French form must be insisted on." The founding charter of the Alliance had this to say in 1860: "Israelites...if you believe...that the influence of the principles of '89 is omnipotent in the world and that it is desirable for the spirit of '89 to make itself felt everywhere...join us, give us your cooperation." In this way the Alliance was perpetuating the ideas of the Haskala, the Jewish movement in the Enlightenment, which also influenced the pioneers of Jewish science. It used those ideas to denounce traditional Jewish cultures in the name of emancipation, which alone was capable of engendering new citizens.[28]

Jews in the Republic

The enthusiasm of Jews for the principles of the Revolution as codified in the Declaration of the Rights of Man, along with their identification with France, cannot be separated from their actual integration into French society, in which they increasingly came to occupy positions of prominence. In the July Monarchy certain Jews achieved considerable visibility in the economic sphere: the Pereire brothers, for example, were active supporters of Saint-Simon and played a role in creating a banking system adapted to the needs of an industrializing society. Little by little, they, along with the Eichtals, the Foulds, the Rothschilds, the Mirèses, and many others, acquired a public role by way of their role—actually not all that extensive—in the business world and upper-class society. The press described the receptions, galas, and balls they attended in the company of the highest aristocracy and even, at times, the king or, before long, the emperor. These Jews were so visible that the popular perception of them changed. Where Jews as a group had once been thought of as vagabonds and beggars, they were now increasingly seen among people of power. This new image was blurred somewhat by the frequent conversion of Jews in the public eye. In a sense only the Rothschilds continued to be seen as "court Jews," at once close to the ruling authorities and in solidarity with other Jews, and for a long time they were therefore the target of much of the new anti-Semitic animosity.

After the Third Republic triumphed, other Jews suddenly entered the public arena and slowly established the image of the republican Jew devoted both to the new political ideal and to the rationalist philosophy that formed the bedrock on which that ideal rested. Adolphe Crémieux was the first to typify the new Jewish statesman: after serving as minister of justice in 1848, he briefly became the head of government in charge of the national defense after the fall of the Empire. Tocqueville in his *Souvenirs* characterizes him as an "eloquent louse" and notes his ugliness and "disheveled" look a few lines after remarking of Goudchaux that "nothing in his face betrayed the Jew in him, though both his father and mother

MOTION
EN FAVEUR DES JUIFS,

Par M. GRÉGOIRE, Curé d'Embermenil,
Député de Nancy ; précédée d'une Notice
hiſtorique, ſur les perſécutions qu'ils
viennent d'eſſuyer en divers lieux, no-
tamment en Alſace, & ſur l'admiſſion
de leurs Députés à la Barre de l'Aſſem.
blée Nationale.

A PARIS,
Chez BELIN, Libraire, rue Saint-Jacques,
Nº. 27.

1 7 8 9.

FIGURE 10.2   *Motion in favor of the Jews* by Abbé Grégoire (1789).

were Jews."[29] Closely associated with Gambetta, who had worked in his office as a young lawyer, Crémieux unwittingly played a crucial role in the birth of the anti-Semitic myth of the "Jewish Republic."[30] It was rumored that a clever plot had been hatched, under which Crémieux, working in Gambetta's shadow, would seize control of France. To replace the old elites, which remained hostile to the Republic, the

Vue du château de Ferrières,
sidence du baron de Rothschild,
visité par l'Empereur
le 16 Décembre 1862.

L'Empereur plantant
l'arbre commémoratif
de sa visite au château.

FIGURE 10.3   Adolphe Crémieux (second row, second from the left), with other members of the provisional government, 1848; lithograph by Maurin.

FIGURE 10.4   *Visit of Napoleon III to the Rothschild Estate at Ferrières* (1862); engraving from the Five-Hundredth Anniversary Brochure of Rothschild Brothers.

leader of the Opportunists did in fact turn to new groups among whom there were Protestants and Jews. One of his closest friends was Joseph Reinach, who became secretary of the government in the *grand ministère;* Gambetta even entrusted Reinach with the publication of his writings.

With the triumph of the Republic, Jews took advantage of the meritocratic route to social advancement, entering the École Normale Supérieure and the École Polytechnique and going on to climb toward the highest positions in government. A new image of the Jew developed: the Jew as an "examination grind" quick to conform to the principles of a rationalist and positivist Republic. Joseph Reinach's brother Théodore offers an excellent example. He won eighteen prizes in the Concours Général, more than any other student of his generation; he could play Sophocles in the original and went on to become a brilliant numismatist who published any number of learned works on ancient Greece and was elected to the Académie des Inscriptions et Belles-Lettres. The "learned" Jew was born, yet another caricature often found in novels from the end of the nineteenth and beginning of the twentieth century.[31]

Many Jews were now successfully taking the recruitment exams for the civil service, embarking on military careers after graduating from the École Polytechnique or Saint-Cyr, becoming magistrates, joining the prefectural corps, passing the *agrégation,* teaching in the university, and even being honored by invitations to join the Collège de France or the Institut. Some became prominent figures in French history: along with Joseph Reinach, a leading political figure before going on to chronicle the exploits of the French Army in World War I, there was Abraham Bloch, the rabbi famous for dying in the same war while holding out a crucifix to a fatally wounded soldier, a deed that earned him the enthusiastic approval of Maurice Barrès himself; David Raynal, a close friend of Lépine, the prefect who ordered a crackdown on anarchists at the beginning of the century; Abraham Schrameck, prefect of Paris, who also became famous for quelling another demonstration, this one by the Action Française; Georges Mandel, who established an image of himself as the tough Jew, showing even right-wing nationalists how to be firm; and the pitiless strikebreaker Jules Moch. A far cry from literary and artistic Jews such as Offenbach and Proust and Henry Bernstein, these men and others like them changed the public perception of the Jew because, along with other politicians who favored strong methods, they came to symbolize the quintessence of republican order.

Of course the image of the Jewish intellectual dedicated to truth and beauty was also current in France in this period, in large part thanks to the work of Charles Péguy. It was Péguy who opened the pages of his *Cahiers de la quinzaine* to Jewish writers such as Edmond Fleg, Julien Benda, and André Spire, who created an image of the Jew as a quasi-mystical being, rendering traditional stereotypes anachronistic. The election of Henri Bergson as the first Jewish member of the Académie

Française in February 1914 bestowed institutional recognition on the new figure of the Jewish thinker. A few other Jews would be similarly honored, from André Maurois, whose Judaism was as ambiguous as Bergson's, to Joseph Kessel, who succeeded the Duc de La Force in 1962. To his adversaries, led by Pierre Gaxotte, Charles Maurras's erstwhile secretary and the driving force behind all the anti-Semitic campaigns, Kessel said: "To replace the companion whose magnificent name has gloriously resounded in the annals of France for a thousand years, whose ancestors, great soldiers, great lords, great dignitaries, friends of princes and kings, occupied an illustrious place in France's history—to replace this man, whom have you chosen? A Russian by birth, a Jew to boot. A Jew from eastern Europe."

Even before the massive immigration of east European Jews in the late nineteenth century once again confused all the conventional images of the Jew, the symbiotic period gave rise to the "Israelite," for whom the various kinds of state Jews served as prototypes. Not only the prefects and generals but also important professors at the Collège de France such as James Darmesteter and Jacques Hadamard, members of the Institut like Salomon Reinach, and a host of Sorbonne professors including Émile Durkheim, Lucien Lévy-Bruhl, Léon Brunschvicg, and Marc Bloch changed the perception of Jews in intellectual circles and perhaps also in the public at large. Some were almost charismatic thinkers who exercised considerable influence on their contemporaries. Later, Jews honored by the Collège de France from Marcel Mauss to Claude Lévi-Strauss to Raymond Aron would exert a moral influence on generations of students and researchers: in the 1980s Lévi-Strauss and Aron were among those considered to be the leading "master thinkers" of the age.

Take the example of Émile Durkheim. His image was that of a Jew of severe mien, a zealous proponent of secularism and positivism whose teaching influenced generations of teachers. A proud patriot and earnest moralist, this son of a rabbi became the symbol of the rationalist Republic, and in countless pamphlets down to the time of Vichy he was denounced as the very embodiment of "Jewish science," whose cult of reason was blamed for the decadence of organic France. Marc Bloch, the Jewish historian of the Middle Ages who along with Lucien Febvre founded the celebrated journal *Les Annales*, was also the author of a celebrated and poignant testament composed on the eve of his execution by the Germans for acts of resistance. In this text he proclaims, one last time, his love of France and his refusal, as a man steeped in French culture exclusively, to be buried in the presence of a rabbi: "I die as I lived, a good Frenchman."

More recently, Claude Lévi-Strauss and Raymond Aron have been seen by their fellow citizens as important teachers capable of unraveling the mysteries of primitive cultures and understanding the burning issues of the day. Men of rigor and learning, they came across on television as scholars of whose Jewish origins not a trace remained other than their names. Crowning achievements of Franco-Judaism, these great men almost succeeded in making their fellow citizens forget that Jews were in any way different from themselves. Similarly, when René Cassin was interred in the Pantheon along with Abbé Grégoire, the Republic was in effect bestowing the ultimate recognition on its state Jews, who were now admitted into the most highly symbolic of mausoleums, a monument that unifies the national imagination around its *Grands Hommes,* even if it is still capable of arousing the indignation of the extreme right.

Henceforth the official national memory would virtually erase the Jews from France's history: their assimilation into the nation was such that their disappearance seemed inevitable. Historians of the contemporary period are all but silent on the subject, at best casting a quick, neglectful glance at Jewish matters. In any number of conferences and multiauthor works on French identity in the second half of the twentieth century Jews are purely and simply ignored. Even scholarly works on the Popular Front and Vichy periods used to maintain a discreet silence about the role of Jews in those crucial moments in French history. Many historians wrote about Pierre Mendès France as though he had no specifically Jewish dimension. Because Jews were assimilated into the Republic, official history avoided any mention of their origins, almost as though there were something unseemly about the topic.

As a result there is a danger of failing to notice that on the eve of World War II there were precious few Jews among candidates for the *agrégation;* or that Jews were for a long time barred from the Quai d'Orsay, the Inspection des Finances, and the Cour des Comptes; or that many top-notch social clubs still refuse to admit Jews. This same taboo leaves the way clear for foreign scholars, especially Americans and Israelis, to raise the questions that their French colleagues shy away from. Within France the history of the Jews in modern times is not a recognized area of study. Jews can be studied in antiquity or at the latest in the Middle Ages, but modern Jewish studies, which have been flourishing in many countries for years, have almost no legitimacy in France. Foreign historians come to consult the archives about the history of the Jews of Bordeaux, say, or Alsace, subjects on which few scholarly works have been published in France. Until recently, moreover, it was mainly foreign scholars who led the way in producing professional studies of the Dreyfus Affair, the history of the violently anti-Semitic radical right, Vichy, and even the Poujadist Movement of the 1950s—major episodes in French history in which the Jews played a central role.

At the Heart of Franco-French Conflict

The strikingly successful assimilation of Jews into French society and their integration into the state were achievements paradoxically made vulnerable by the close association of Jews with the fate of the Republic. The emancipation of the Jews by the French Revolution created an unbreakable tie between the fate of the Jews and

FIGURE 10.5   René Vincent, *Philosophy Lesson Amid Flowers* (Henri Bergson's first lecture at the Collège de France after his election to the Académie Française in 1914).

that of the revolutionary tradition from which the Third Republic still saw itself as drawing its inspiration. The very fact that the Declaration of the Rights of Man and of the Citizen was often presented as symbolizing the Tables of the Law was enough to convince some observers that the events of 1789 were the result of a conspiracy of Jews, Protestants, and Freemasons bent on destroying the Catholic soul of

French society. From Abbé Barruel to various nineteenth- and twentieth-century right-wing groups, the enemies of the Revolution and the Republic repeatedly directed their hostility at the Jews in particular, and the very repetitiousness of the caricatures inevitably shaped the consciousness of certain of their fellow citizens.

From General Boulanger to Jean-Marie Le Pen, enemies of the Jews have depicted them as playing a major role in French history. Jews have consequently been thrust into the limelight in such a way as to foster any number of contradictory myths. As the *Archives israélites* perceptively observed, "Caesarism, Boulangism, nationalism—in short, all the movements that have opposed the Republic and against which it has had to defend itself—have drawn on the enemies of Israel in recruiting impassioned spokesmen and valuable, energetic agents. Militant anti-Semitism has been involved in all the conspiracies whose aim has been to rid France of the regime of liberty that it had chosen." In 1914 the same newspaper added: "All that anti-Semitism has managed to achieve thus far with its abominable campaign of slander has been to direct the Israelite vote to the republicans and socialists, for Israelite voters have a natural interest in voting for the side that poses the least threat to the conquests of 1789." The conclusion was self-evident: "Nationalism, Boulangism's heir and successor, inevitably arouses tremendous suspicion among French voters."[32]

Of course not all Jews shared this view. It was the rare Jew, however, who actively campaigned for the Republic's enemies. Apart from Alfred Naquet, the faithful friend of General Boulanger; the pro-royalist journalist Arthur Meyer; the lawyer Edmond Bloch, who sat in parliament alongside Maurras and Doriot in the interwar period; Pierre David, a passionate supporter of the Action Française who died while paying his last respects to Charles Maurras; Maurice Sachs, whose shady activities during World War II brought him to the edge of collaboration; and a few Jewish supporters of Jean-Marie Le Pen—apart from these, nearly all French Jews supported the Republic. This was true of the Reinachs during the Panama scandal, of Bernard Lazare and the Reinachs during the Dreyfus Affair, of Léon Blum and Jules Moch during the Popular Front, of Pierre Mendès France and Jean-Jacques Servan-Schreiber during the Algerian War and Poujadism, and at the present time of Robert Badinter, Simone Veil, and Lionel Stoleru, favorite targets of the National Front.

French nationalism, whose main features were fixed in the aftermath of the defeat of 1870, was rooted in unshakable anti-Semitism, which satisfied the need to blame the nation's failures on a scapegoat. Édouard Drumont raised anti-Semitic propaganda to a new level, fashioning and reinforcing stereotypes with such meticulous care that he left an unmistakable imprint on the national consciousness. Although very few French historians have bothered to take any notice of Drumont,[33] he undeniably succeeded in transforming the nature of Franco-French conflict by offering a single answer to all of France's social anxieties, a single key to the solution of all problems, a single remedy for the many conflicts that pitted Frenchman against Frenchman to the benefit of their common adversaries: the Jews! Drumont and his many successors captured the French political imagination, introducing new themes that have been tirelessly repeated ever since. From Dreyfus to Vichy to Le Pen, the same leitmotif has been sounded. The same old tune has been sung steadily by the extreme right and occasionally by the extreme left, and it has even been taken up at times by the moderate right and reformist left: the gist of the message is that a Jewish conspiracy is to blame for France's degeneracy, decline, misfortunes, and military defeats. This refrain has had an irremediable impact on the place of Jews in French memory. The problem has been compounded by the fact that traditionalist Catholics *(intégristes)* and, in a different register, some progressive Catholics have also heaped obloquy on the Jews: By imposing rationalist values that poisoned the country's spiritual heritage, were they not ultimately responsible for all that corrupted Christian France and undermined its true identity?

Drumont's *La France juive* was a best-seller in its day, sold in the millions throughout rural France with priests often promoting the work. The book combined various ingredients of the new nationalism affecting different levels of France's shared memory. Echoed as well by *La Libre Parole* and *La Croix,* two mass-circulation newspapers with several regional editions daily, the corrosive theme of the Jewish conspiracy served as the foundation for a "national Catholicism" whose goal was to undo the emancipation of the Jews undertaken by the French Revolution; the movement drew support from socialist "national populism" as well. The Barrès episode was emblematic: Maurice Barrès, the "prince of letters" adulated by no less a figure than Marcel Proust himself, argued that "French nationality is intimately associated with Catholicism," which he called "the expression of our blood." The image of the Jews was like the negative of that expression: not only could they not understand *Bérénice* however cultivated or educated they might be, but this foreign "race" must, for all its assimilation, be rejected because it was fundamentally a source of perversion.[34] In *Mes cahiers,* Barrès apostrophized Drumont in these terms: "I love you above all because I was born a nationalist." And he frequently paid homage to Drumont's "true genius." Intransigent Catholicism, nationalism, socialistic populism, and anti-Semitism melded into a single prism, which ultimately affected most aspects of French historical consciousness. Charles Maurras once remarked that "the nationalist formula was almost entirely the work of Drumont, and Daudet, Barrès, and all the rest of us began our work in the light he shed." Maurras, the theoretician of the Action Française and pitiless scourge of the Jews, could easily have extended the variegated list of Drumont's successors, who came from all parts of the ideological spectrum.

The Drumont-Barrès-Maurras alliance set the stage for future Franco-French conflict, pitting the powerful Leagues against the republican state, which was

FIGURE 10.6   Alfred Naquet. A very active political leader and author of the divorce law, which gave rise to violent polemics, Naquet played an important role in Boulanger's campaign and was the target of continual anti-Semitic attacks.

FIGURE 10.7   Joseph Reinach. A leading figure of French Judaism, Reinach, one of the preeminent "state Jews," was detested by the nationalists. He was one of Gambetta's key advisors and later a leader of the battle to save Dreyfus.

accused of being a slave to Jews, Protestants, and Freemasons, united by a common will to destroy French identity for the benefit of foreign and cosmopolitan interests. From Barbey d'Aurevilly to Rodin, from Cézanne, Renoir, Toulouse-Lautrec, and Degas to Céline, Lucien Rebatet, and Marcel Jouhandeau, Gaxotte, Montherlant, Massis, Morand, Drieu, and Autant-Lara, the adepts of a pure France of the people, a France embodied by Joan of Arc, Bayard, and Pétain, wished that all the demons perverting her soul might be consigned to hell. Their fantasies were fed, moreover, by the ravings of Bernanos and Léon Bloy and other writers of their school. In many respects the most official institutions of legitimate culture, such as the Académie Française and the Institut, were often tainted by their influence. And a moderately scrupulous reading of the great French writers of the twentieth century would reveal any number of embarrassing thoughts and statements from artists of the stature of André Gide, Paul Valéry, Maurice Blanchot, Jean Giraudoux, Emmanuel Mounier, Anatole France, and Romain Rolland, proof that the stereotypes invented by the far right had a considerable unconscious effect where one least might least expect it.

Take one of the most surprising cases, that of Anatole France: the plot of *L'Orme du mail* revolves around a prefect, M. Worms-Clavelin, the husband of one Noémie Coblentz, whose father's name was Isaac. As host to his friend Abbé Guitrel, the prefect, whom the author has several times identified as an "Israelite," "felt in a confused way that, in the presence of this clergyman of peasant stock, as French in his priestly manner and type as the blackened stones of Saint-Exupère and as the old trees of Le Mail, he was become more French himself, naturalizing himself, shedding the cumbersome remains of his Germany and his Asia. The close friendship of a priest flattered the Israelite functionary. In it he unwittingly savored the pride of revenge. To master and offer protection to one of these tonsured heads, for eighteen centuries bent by heaven and earth on excommunicating and exterminating the circumcised, was for the Jew an invigorating and flattering success." Thus the amiable liberal author of *La Rôtisserie de la reine Pédauque* and of *L'Ile aux pingouins* was the creator of a portrait of a Jewish prefect that men like Drumont, Daudet, and Gaxotte would have had no difficulty claiming as their own. And leave it to dear old Anatole France to lay it on still thicker: "His large, fleshy nose, his thick lips...his receding forehead above large pale eyes, betrayed a resistance to all moral delicacy. He pressed his points and offered Masonic arguments against Christian dogma." Clearly Anatole France shrank from nothing. To finish off his portrait, he added that his Jewish prefect "had inherited no faith from his parents, who were as much strangers to all superstition as they were foreigners in every locale," and that if they had any religion at all, it was the "religion of money."[35] Nothing is left out, and much to our astonishment we find France, for a moment at any rate, in the same camp as Drumont, Maurras, and Céline. Even Jean Jaurès could lapse long

FIGURE 10.8   General Léopold Sée. Another prominent Jewish official, Sée became the first Jewish general in the French army, in November 1870.

enough to write an article in which he said that "if Drumont truly had the clairvoyance on which he used to pride himself every morning, he would have confined himself to denouncing the doings of the Jews as a particularly acute form of the doings of capitalism.... Such socialism tinged with anti-Semitism would have aroused few objections among free spirits."[36]

Beyond any doubt, it was the collapse of the Union Générale in 1882 that brought radical economic anti-Semitism, whose roots can be traced back all the way to the Middle Ages, once again to the forefront. The explosion of finance capitalism transformed Shylock into an omnipotent monster gnawing away at France's wealth. The case was comprehensible: people believed that Jewish bankers had maneuvered to do in the Catholic bank, deliberately plunging millions of small savers into despair. *La Croix* wrote that "the Jewish banks have triumphed on the Paris market.... The Jews are the kings of finance."[37] A few years later the Panama scandal accredited the image of the Jew as stockjobber and unscrupulous influence-peddler. As a people's capitalism came into being, that image spread to the humblest peasant cottage. Cornélius Hertz and Baron Jacques de Reinach would henceforth haunt the imagination: the latter's surprising suicide only made the scandal that much more sensational. *La Libre Parole* issued daily calls for murder. *La Croix* screamed for vengeance against the Jews, while Henri Rochefort, a brilliant polemicist for *L'Intransigeant*, denounced Jews day after day as "traitors and influence-peddlers."[38]

These various economic disasters were particularly hard on traditionalist Catholic France: anxiety and panic were the result, as thousands of stunned savers discovered they had been wiped out in the collapse of a Catholic bank. This happened at the same time as crowds, portrayed by sociologists such as Le Bon and Tarde as emotional and wild, seemed to surge into the public sphere.[39] This first full-scale economic crisis occurred just as the "era of the crowd" was undermining traditional norms, and this made it easier for the image of the Jew, allegedly responsible for all these misfortunes, to fix itself in the popular imagination, especially since the Jew was perceived as a foreigner concerned solely with his own interests. "Kill the Jews," shouted thousands of ruined savers, joined by those who seized on the situation to advance themselves and, they hoped, bring down the Republic. "Kill the Jews": the words resounded in the streets of Paris and large provincial cities and even in out-of-the-way villages. Panama rekindled the fears of rural France, reinforced the identification of Jews with capitalist modernity, and, through a series of bankruptcies, trials, and resignations, assigned them a demonic role.

Panama prefigured the Dreyfus Affair.[40] It was the latter, however, that dealt a fatal blow to the idea that many non-Jews held of their Jewish fellow citizens: from now on it was assumed that the danger came from within the government. If republican meritocracy could allow treason to insinuate itself into the military, the upholder of order and guardian of tradition, the very foundations of the nation-state were in jeopardy. The fantasy of a Jewish conspiracy was intensified because the state was seen as a kind of foster father on whom all its citizens depended. The all but timeless, virtually universal image of the Jew as simian, oriental, thick-lipped, greedy, and fond of Christian blood no longer applied; the danger now came from the state's loyal servants, those assimilated Jews who had attended the best schools, who had learned a strict code of discipline, who were steeped in the ethic of public service, and who retained virtually no trace of their origins. From now on it was these state Jews who became the object of popular hatred; it was against them that vengeful fists were raised.

The dramatic events that marked this crucial moment in the history of Franco-French conflict, from the arrest of Captain Dreyfus to the trial, deportation, and ultimate rehabilitation, spanned a decade on either side of the turn of the century. This period, during which France entered modernity, was marked by powerful popular anti-Semitic actions growing out of the Affair all over France, by an avalanche of hostile literature affecting even the normally calm pages of local papers in the quiet provinces, and by calls for murder issued by people ranging from the humblest of scullery maids to Paul Valéry himself. The Dreyfus Affair created a new image of the Jews, which led as if logically to a new expiation, this time that of the nation: whence the "divine surprise" of Vichy.

FIGURE 10.9   Méaulle, *The Degradation,* a "great French allegory for the punishment of Dreyfus," after Lionel Royer, published in *Le Journal illustré* (January 6, 1895).

Under constant critical pressure from Drumont and his countless followers, the French political imagination became a battleground in a clash between nationalist and universalist ideas, a battle in which the Jews were hostages and perhaps victims. The involvement of intellectuals, which began with the Dreyfus Affair, further accentuated the new symbolism of the Jews, who were now rejected by nationalist thinkers as well as considered foreigners to soil, region, and nation by organicist theorists. It was all rather like boulevard theater written not by cheery fellows like Offenbach or Halévy but by Corneille and Racine as revised and corrected by the haughty, indefatigable Barrès. France seemed about to embark on a new epic with new traitors and heroes. The dramatic scene in which Dreyfus was stripped of his rank in the courtyard of the École Militaire by itself inflamed the imagination; endlessly reproduced and caricatured, it left a deep imprint on France's collective consciousness. For many people, perhaps, Devil's Island, to which Dreyfus was deported, was ideally named to evoke any number of associations and memories. Zola's "J'accuse," a forceful plea on behalf of the captain, threw people into still more consternation, further accentuating the rigid, antique character of this modern tragedy. Dramatic events followed in quick succession, with a series of unexpected and astonishing deaths and suicides. And there was also an almost burlesque or melodramatic side of things, such as the discovery of Col. Henry's forgery, his suicide, leaks from certain figures in the case, duels, slaps. The Dreyfus Affair became a paradigm for all French political theater.

In the memory of French Jews, the Dreyfus Affair remains even today as the symbol of their always-precarious status as citizens. The fact that a Jewish officer could so easily be tossed to anti-Semitic mobs calling for his blood throughout France and even in Algeria, even though he had diligently satisfied all the rules for integration, was absolutely loyal to the army, and was thoroughly steeped in patriotic values, defied understanding and weakened the fundamental contract on which Franco-Judaism was based. The notorious degradation of Dreyfus remains deeply embedded in Jewish memory, for the state was not just punishing a captain but publicly denying its Jews, even as the army he had served enthusiastically came together as one to repudiate his fellow Israelites.

In 1898 there were several hundred anti-Semitic riots throughout France, from Paris to cities and towns of all sizes. They occurred in nearly every *département*, thus defying the usual explanations in terms of political geography. Crowds of thousands, drawn from all social classes, gathered to shout "Kill the Jews!" Sometimes they attacked synagogues or destroyed Jewish homes and stores. Scenes of rare collective violence, bordering on general hysteria, erupted here and there in an atmosphere that *La Libre Parole*, *La Croix*, and many local papers further poisoned day after day. The most sordid forms of anti-Semitism were on display in city streets, on walls, in printed matter, in poems, in songs, and in widely distributed postcards. Well-known artists did not hesitate to lend their talents to the movement. Degas, who delighted to hear his maid Zoé read to him out loud from *La Libre Parole* while he ate lunch, was an all-out anti-Dreyfusard, and joining him in that camp were Cézanne, Forain (who drew ferocious caricatures of Dreyfus's supporters), Toulouse-Lautrec (who did illustrations for anti-Semitic papers), Rodin, and Renoir.

An analysis of the justifications offered by the 25,000 people who contributed to the fund established by *La Libre Parole* to build a monument in memory of Col. Henry, the man who forged the document used as evidence against Dreyfus and who, when found out, killed himself, gives further evidence of the extreme character of French anti-Semitism at this stage: one butcher's apprentice said that he "would gladly spill Reinach's guts"; a lowly priest in Poitou said that he "would happily chant the Requiem for the last of the yids"; while other contributors poured venom on "Jewish vermin," "Jewish microbes," and "the Jewish cancer." Some said that the Jews should be drowned as opponents of the Revolution had been drowned in Nantes, while others said that they should be broken on the wheel as in days of yore. The most merciful simply called for the expulsion of noncitizens. More than 4,500 members of the armed forces contributed to this fund, along with many deputies, university professors, students at the top schools, and professionals. Among France's leading intellectuals, Paul Valéry contributed. Indeed, the poet, in speaking of Captain Dreyfus, allegedly said to Paul Léautaud, "Let's shoot him and stop talking about it."[41] Equally striking is the repetitive nature of the desire expressed by any number of professional organizations and political parties that Jews should be expelled from the army, the bureaucracy, the legal and medical professions, and so on. These calls marked the beginning of a long series of vehement protests that would bear fruit later, under Vichy, but which would henceforth continue to fill the pages of the national and local press to say nothing of countless tracts and pamphlets. Hundreds of examples could easily be cited: invariably these articles named names in demanding that Jews be expelled from France and that a large number of occupations henceforth be reserved exclusively for "native" Frenchmen.

While older forms of anti-Semitism based on religious, economic, or racial motives sometimes proposed that Jews be banned from society, political anti-Semitism focused its energies on the republican state, calling for an end to the recognition of Jews as equal citizens on the grounds that such egalitarianism was incompatible with respect for an organic national identity. This rejection of meritocracy in any form led straight to the idea of a *Judenrein* state, a state that would at last be suitable to a still Catholic France. Between Dreyfus and Vichy, Léon Blum became the chief scapegoat of this political anti-Semitism, particularly in the Popular Front period. A graduate of the École Normale Supérieure, member of the Conseil d'État, and brilliant literary critic, he was the quintessential assimilated Jew. He became

FIGURE 10.10 *A Clear-Cut Case;* caricature published in *Le Grelot* (October 9, 1898). Justice outweighs Drumont and his allies.

FIGURE 10.11 *National Tramway;* caricature published in *Le Grelot* (June 12, 1898), depicts the "Franco-French" war between right and left.

the object of a ferocious, insane hatred, and his presence at the summit of political power swelled the ranks of the anti-Semitic movement, which grew so powerful that it almost succeeded in bringing down the republican regime. As in the days of the Dreyfus Affair, two concepts of legitimacy clashed: one based on the idea of a rational, secular, Jacobin state open to all citizens, the other based on an idea of "Frenchness" understood in terms of local roots, of an organicist localism said to foster a virility capable of overcoming the decadence brought on by effeminate, cosmopolitan humanism. From Barrès to Maurras, Gaxotte, Léon Daudet, and Henri Béraud, the proponents of a return "to the land and the dead" spoke out against Jews as wandering nomads drunk on Christian blood, branding them perverse seducers as well as incipient homosexuals and revolutionaries. Marx Dormoy to the contrary notwithstanding, a Jew was not worth as much as a Breton, who naturally embodied the whole history of France. Not only Blum but also Jules Moch, Georges Mandel, Pierre Mendès France, and any number of Jewish prefects, judges, and generals were quick to learn this lesson, so immense was the hatred that most of them had to face. Anti-Semitism grew stronger in the society as a whole even as it flourished in numerous national and local newspapers across the political spectrum as well as in songs, poems, and chants at countless meetings throughout France, during which huge crowds gathered and marched. It was also rampant within the government itself, as the personnel files of many high functionaries can attest. Long after the official separation of church and state, these internal administrative documents continued to identify individuals explicitly as "Jews."

Vichy

The defeat of June 1940 and the subsequent establishment of the Vichy regime—which Maurras called a "divine surprise"—marked the end of the republican regime that had long amazed both assimilated Jews and more recent immigrants from Germany and eastern Europe. Jewish history and memory no longer coincided with the history and memory of other French citizens. Even before the defeat, in 1939–40, German Jews, including some 5,000 children, were interned in camps like the ones at Saint-Cyprien, Rieucros, Gurs (where more than a thousand German Jews died of hunger, dysentery, and typhoid), and Vernet, where conditions were even worse than those in German camps at that time.

After Montoire, camps sprang up all over France, from Beaune-la-Roland to Pithiviers, Noé, Les Milles, and above all, after August 1941, at Drancy. The French police handed German Jews over to the German police. Vichy issued explicit orders to begin a ruthless hunt for French and immigrant Jews, almost exclusively carried out by the French police, which also maintained order in the camps themselves.[42] Excluded from public offices by the Jewish Statute of October 1940, Jews lost all their legal protections.[43] Subject to capricious orders, they were required to wear yellow stars sewn to their clothing and to register with the authorities. Those who complied were turned over to the Germans and deported. Nearly 70,000 eventually ended up at Drancy, where they lived under French police guard in dreadful conditions before being shipped off to death camps.

The expulsion of Jews from public office and the various roundups, including the largest of all, conducted in Paris on July 16 and 17, 1942, were carried out by the French police and bureaucracy, which lent their services to a Gestapo that had very few agents on French soil. The prefectoral corps was of great help to the Germans. A very active role was played by members of other *grands corps,* including the Conseil d'État, which with the help of such illustrious law professors as Joseph-Barthélemy, Achille Mestre, Julien Laferrière, Georges Ripert, and others, provided a legal basis for the exclusion and repression of Jews.[44] Of all the functionaries charged with carrying out the state's anti-Jewish policies, virtually none resigned, and the efficiency of the French bureaucracy earned it the admiration of local Gestapo officials. All these things prove that the republican regime was over, that it had been transformed into an authoritarian system. The new regime dreamed of striking its roots deep into the immutable farmland of France and of focusing the national memory exclusively on its most Christian kings.[45] Quite apart from the German occupation and its policy of racial persecution, Jews henceforth had no place in France's future. Vichy was not only the end of the process of Jewish emancipation begun by the Revolution, it was also the brutal destruction of Franco-Judaism.

With their most cherished values under attack, state Jews nevertheless could not bring themselves to believe that they were being sold out by the very government in which they vested all their hopes. They blamed the Nazis for the ostracism that made them so bitter. Thus Georges Wormser, a one-time collaborator with Clemenceau, wrote to Marshal Pétain on August 1, 1941, in these terms:

> On December 7, 1792, in Soultz, a small town in Alsace, my great-grandfather Abraham Bloch, "chief" of the Israelites as his father and his father's father had been before him, took a solemn civic oath, on behalf of all the people he represented, as the first mark of the emancipation they owed to the tireless efforts of Abbé Grégoire. A century and a half has gone by. Yesterday I had to endure, along with my wife and four children, the humiliation of signing a statement separating us from the French community. I should forfeit all dignity if I failed to make my protest known to you in the strongest possible terms.... Disavowed today, reviled as a group in ways we do not deserve, we appeal to the Soldier, the Chief of State. Because we have brought our children up to believe in our pious heritage, will these innocents be deprived of the only lasting source of contentment there is, that of serving one's Country?[46]

René Cassin also observed that "in supposedly free France the work of Abbé Grégoire and the Declaration of the Rights of Man are trodden underfoot." To the Jews he said that "no sacrifice—none—will be too great to pay back in part the debt of emancipation by helping France to regain her liberty and greatness." Similarly, the deputy Pierre Massé, interned at Drancy before being deported to Auschwitz, wrote Marshal Pétain on the day after Jews were ordered expelled from the French Army:

> I would be obliged if you would tell me if I must remove the stripes from my brother, sublieutenant of the 36th Infantry Regiment, killed at Douaumont in April 1916; from my son-in-law, sublieutenant in the 14th Dragoons, killed in Belgium in May 1940; from my nephew Jean-Pierre, killed at Rethel in May 1940. May I allow my brother to keep the medal he won at Neuville-Saint-Vaast, with which I buried him? Finally, can I be sure that no one will take away my great-grandfather's Sainte-Hélène Medal? I want very much to abide by the laws of my country, even when they are dictated by the invader.

A delegation of eighteen veterans with a total of twenty-five wounds and fifty-six citations, led by General Boris, had this to say in 1941 to Xavier Vallat, then commissioner in charge of Jewish Affairs:

> Those French Israelites who gave their lives or who, wounded, gave their blood or who survived to wear their crosses did not believe they were doing so for a country that would renounce them. The fathers and progeny of our dead, our survivors, our maimed, and our wounded, declare through us that, far from renouncing France in spite of all they have endured, they intend to add their silent sacrifice of today to their gallant sacrifices of another time. In this way they hope to be doubly deserving, in a juster, freer future, of the title *Français,* which in their hearts they will never give up even if it be taken from them by force.

Upon learning of proposed laws excluding them from the French community, another group of Jews, including Léon Lyon, honorary councillor of the Cour de Cassation; Louis Halphen, member of the Institut; Robert Debré, member of the Academy of Medicine; and Léon Rheims, brigadier general, wrote Marshal Pétain in June 1941:

> We, Israelites by religion or descendants of Israelites but almost all of old French families, many with more than a century of history behind them, wish to state that, born French, we are French and will always remain French. We constitute neither a race nor a population (*peuplement*) but an integral part of the nation, from which nothing can separate us. That is why we unhesitatingly call upon the venerated Leader, in whom the idea of the nation One and

FIGURE 10.12   A Jew who lost his leg fighting the Nazis in 1940 is exempted from having to wear the yellow star, while his daughter, being above the age of six, must wear hers.

Indivisible is today embodied, and with anguished consciences urge him to intervene in order to avoid the tragic consequences of the cruelest of decisions.

In February 1941, Senator Moïse Lévy sent Pétain the following letter: "I protest in the most strenuous terms against the law of October 3, 1940, which was imported from abroad. In the Homeland of Liberty, the French will one day regain their freedom of conscience."[47] Forced to register as a Jew, Paul Grunebaum-Ballin, who had played a crucial role in drafting the laws concerning the separation of church and state and who became president of the honorary section of the Conseil d'État, said this: "We refuse to see ourselves as members of the Jewish religious community, the only community to which we belong being the French nation." Addressing the prefect, he added this:

> Yes, Monsieur le Préfet, for any truly French heart, the violation of the principles that have progressively been distilled from the noble, centuries-old tradition of this country, that the French Revolution proclaimed and spread throughout the world, and that the royalist Charter of 1815 preserved in their totality, is a source of pain that nothing can assuage.... The only comfort that we are allowed is that which stems from an unshakable confidence in an ultimate return to the true spiritual destiny of this "eternal France," this "standard-bearing" Nation in defense of which so many of my kin met with death or captivity on the field of battle and that I, for my modest part, have humbly served for almost half a century with passionate love.[48]

Excluded, persecuted, and in many cases exterminated, these state Jews remained confident in France and its leader, mistakenly ascribing sole responsibility for the atrocities that they and so many other Jews would suffer in these dark times to Hitler's Germany. And yet, not only did Laval propose on his own to "deport children under sixteen as well," as Dannecker wrote to Eichmann in July 1942, but Pétain, an adherent of Maurrassian ideology, directly associated himself, through his "lawful" collaboration, with the bloody repression of the Jews and the Resistance.[49]

Meanwhile, the entire government embraced the policy of its leaders, going so far as to withdraw French nationality from those who acquired it under the law of 1927, including nearly half of all Jews, thus deliberately increasingly the likelihood that these people would be deported.[50] The Church and its spokesmen ceremoniously sanctified the marshal and for a long time said nothing about the fate of the Jews, until Monsignor Saliège, Cardinal Gerlier, and Monsignor Théas courageously broke the silence.[51] The most celebrated writers and artists carried on with their activities, which often brought them into direct contact with the occupying forces.[52] Leading publishers agreed to publish a number of violently anti-Semitic works.[53] And for most people life continued peacefully enough, virtually the only

FIGURE 10.13 AND 10.14   Georges Moran, *Drancy:* the arrival of a boxcar full of children and the showers. Dedicated by the artist "to the memory of the twelve thousand Jews deported to Germany and exterminated, to hostages martyred in France, to the precious few companions who escaped, and to the 'friends of the Jews.'"

FIGURE 10.15   Drancy, symbol of the Jewish genocide, was a concentration camp that served as a staging area for the shipment of Jews in death trains to eastern Europe. Conditions in the camp were dreadful.

disturbances for several long years being the work of the foreign, mostly Jewish "terrorists" of the Mouvement d'Ouvriers Immigrés.[54] While all this was going on, a campaign of ruthless terror was being waged by regular French government agencies and police before it was taken over by the Milice, Vichy's paramilitary militia. Every day saw new Jews enter the camps for shipment to Drancy and eventually to death, and nothing interfered with the operation of this finely tuned mechanism.[55] Not one train transporting Jews to Germany was sabotaged, and not one Resistance attack intentionally targeted one of these death trains on French soil. In August 1942, four thousand Jewish children separated from their parents were deported in two weeks from Drancy to Germany in trains that were guarded by French gendarmes until they reached the German border. How could Jewish memory not crystallize around such tragic moments, which had the further effect of relegating the blessed time of emancipation to the distant past?

Nevertheless, this "second Inquisition," this Saint Bartholomew's for which so many anti-Semites had devoutly wished since the Dreyfus Affair, failed to shake the faith of most French Jews in the basic contract of Franco-Judaism. Confidence in France the emancipator almost prevailed, as it gradually became clear that outside the government and its elites a segment of the population repudiated the policy of annihilation as early as the 1942 roundups[56] As in the time of the Dreyfus Affair, when the efforts of Zola, Bernard Lazare, Clemenceau, Péguy, Lucien Herr, and, after a brief delay, Jean Jaurès inspired those who supported the Republic and equality among citizens to confront the other France, anti-Dreyfusard France, and ultimately to restore justice and save the threatened union of France and the Jews, under Vichy, when the political and intellectual elite played far less of a role in a struggle for liberty whose stakes were far higher, it was often more modest folk who did not hesitate to come to the aid of hunted Jews, despite the fact that much of the public remained, if not always anti-Semitic, at best indifferent to the Jewish plight. Ordinary policemen warned Jews of impending raids, peasants and priests hid them, Protestant communities offered them protection. With the belated but crucial statements by church dignitaries[57] and the actions of a host of civil and religious associations decisive aid came from the depths of French society and not from the government, which had given up its claim to embody universal values. After the war, memories of that aid opened up new possibilities for contacts between Jews and non-Jews, yet differences remained in the recollections of both sides.

A "New Deal" for Franco-Judaism?

Despite the magnitude of the trauma, nothing changed overnight when the war ended. The uniqueness of the fate reserved for the Jews was swallowed up in condemnations of Vichy. It took nearly fifteen years for Auschwitz to take on symbolic

FIGURE 10.16   Ceremonies commemorating the roundup of Jews and their confinement in the Vel' d'Hiv' on July 16, 1942, held in Paris on July 16, 1969. Rabbi Kaplan, the chief rabbi of France, is speaking.

FIGURE 10.17   Paris, July 16, 1992. Robert Badinter is speaking at ceremonies attended by the president of the Republic.

value. Significantly, it took the work of independent and foreign historians in the early 1960s to reveal the specific French responsibility in the persecution, exclusion, and martyrdom of more than 70,000 French Jews in a way that began to gnaw at the national conscience. Indeed, it can be argued that the revelation of the genocide and the legal proscription of incitement to racial hatred in the immediate postwar period restored and solidified the terms of the Franco-Jewish consensus as a normal part of French reality with deep historical roots. After the rehabilitation of Captain Dreyfus, the *Archives israélites* stated in July 1906 that "the Dreyfus Affair is over as far as Israelites are concerned. Its conclusion only makes us love our country all the more, if such a thing were possible." Similarly, the sociologist Georges Friedmann, whose encounter with Israel in 1965 was to be the real shock and whose participation in the Resistance he said only deepened his roots in French soil, observed in retrospect that "it was not France that drove me out of its schools and insulted me, it was Hitler and Goebbels.... *Civis gallicus sum*, I am a French citizen. I am so and shall remain so, come what may."[58] It was as if the wound had healed in a general climate of forgetfulness. No more attention was paid to the final squeals of the few remaining anti-Semites, people like the journalists of *Rivarol* or Maurice Bardèche, than to the first accounts of the deportees, who went unnoticed despite their numbers. Night and fog shrouded what was to become Alain Resnais's *Night and Fog* (1956); silence surrounded the Holocaust about which Claude Lanzmann would make *Shoah* (1985). No one wanted to hear what the deportees had to say. The parenthesis had been closed. It was taken for granted that Vichy was in no way representative of the real France, only an unfortunate excursion. There was deep repression of two kinds: much of France repressed its guilt, and French Jews repressed knowledge of the ultimately inexplicable fate that had been visited upon them. Such was the force of the French-Jewish symbiosis, so powerful was the consensus around the triumphant Republic, that in France, the country in which Zionism was born, few Jews felt much enthusiasm for the Zionist solution beyond contributing to charitable funds intended to allow persecuted Jews from eastern Europe to make their way to Palestine; and not even the creation of the State of Israel in 1949 had much effect on the adherence of French Jews to the values of integration.[59]

The earliest signs that an autonomous Jewish memory might be possible began to emerge while this consensus was still in effect. For example, the word *Jew* began to replace the euphemism *Israelite*, as if an insult were being turned into a form of self-affirmation, and this in itself reflects an abrupt and widespread resumption of a heavy legacy of identity.[60] A new solidarity developed among Jews, both French and non-French, who through misfortune had suddenly been reminded, if they had forgotten, that even without a native community, a historical community, or a community of belief, a community of destiny was always possible to bring them together with coreligionists of whatever background or nationality who remained

FIGURE 10.18　Transfer of René Cassin's ashes to the Pantheon: the symbolic interment of a "state Jew" in the Pantheon of the Republic.

Jews. Sartre's stinging *Réflexions sur la question juive* opened up an extrareligious space of legitimacy for Jewish identity: "The Jew is perfectly assimilable by modern nations, but he is defined as the one whom nations do not wish to assimilate. The Jew is a man that other men take to be a Jew." This view is today considered to be outmoded, but at the time it had a powerfully liberating effect: it provided a first explanation of what had just happened. Although it did not yet formulate any kind of "right to be different," it portrayed anti-Semitism not as something for Jews to endure or disarm but as something for non-Jews to overcome in order to achieve humanity. This new set of issues became in a sense official at a time when the last overt and covert barriers to the social and national integration of Jews were disappearing; at a time when the law itself prohibited fomenting racial hatred or discrimination; when the Church, thanks largely to the efforts of Jules Isaac, was renouncing the "teaching of contempt" in the form of the idea that the Jews were a deicide people, and beginning the evolution that would culminate in the Second Vatican Council; and finally, when the young state of Israel, with its *kibbutzim* and farmer-soldiers was once and for all dispelling the negative image of the cringing, wandering, money-grubbing Jew not only among non-Jews steeped in anti-Semitic mythology but even among Jews still vaguely influenced by what Heinrich Heine referred to as "self-hatred." André Schwarz-Bart would make use of this new positive sensibility in *Le Dernier des justes* (Prix Goncourt, 1959), the first Jewish novel to offer most Christian France a specifically Jewish dimension of its own history, the first book to attach flesh and blood to a still skeletal memory.

It was under these circumstances that the outbreak of the Six-Day War was able to crystallize a new attitude. The renewed specter of a total destruction of the Jewish nation gave rise within days or even hours to an outpouring of solidarity. For one thing, a latent memory, which neither the Dreyfus Affair nor Vichy had truly shaken, suddenly came to life, allowing for historic reawakenings whose roots lay outside France. For another, General de Gaulle categorically condemned the Israeli offensive, imposed an embargo on military shipments to Israel, which depended mainly on France for its supplies, and in a vocabulary laden with symbolic language stigmatized not just the Jewish state but the Jews as an "elite people, sure of themselves and domineering." This language was particularly provocative and ill-chosen given the fact that the end of the Algerian War had recently brought to France, among one million repatriated citizens, fifty thousand Jews who at that time had few reasons to feel particularly sure of themselves or domineering and for whom the specter of expulsion evoked recent and still painful memories. A fissure began to develop.

Even René Cassin, one of the first Gaullists and the most honored of state Jews, suddenly expressed the view that "France is identifying with injustice"[61] and split with the general, whom he accused of being unfaithful to Abbé Grégoire's emancipating vision. Even Raymond Aron, who as spokesmen for the most assimilated secular Jewish opinion was a man above suspicion, voiced his worry and anger, seeing the beginning of "a new period in Jewish history and perhaps in the history of anti-Semitism. Anything is possible now, everything is coming back. Persecution, of course, is out of the question, only malevolence. It is a time not for contempt but for suspicion."[62] That suspicion had a name: dual allegiance. It suggested a hypothetical "memory" whose frame of reference no longer coincided with that of France or the Republic. Later, after a bomb exploded in front of a Paris synagogue on the Rue Copernic, Prime Minister Raymond Barre aroused further suspicions when in a strange lapse he distinguished between the Jewish victims of the explosion and the "innocent French" victims.

A new period? In fact, the period between the Six-Day War and the Yom Kippur War (1967–1973), or between May 1968 and the oil crisis of 1974, or between de Gaulle's departure from office and the presidency of Valéry Giscard d'Estaing, witnessed a series of events which, without altogether undermining Franco-Judaism, tested its premises in a way that led to changes in three of its traditional tenets.

It is surely an exaggeration to say that assimilation was intended ultimately to lead to the end of Judaism. In centralized Jacobin France, however, it was supposed to remain a purely private religious practice. When it expressed itself in other ways, moreover, it was either in secular humanist terms perfectly compatible with the positivist Kantianism of republican ethics or in the form of a revolutionary messianism voluntarily or involuntarily blind to its Mosaic component. This compartmentalization now broke down, however, giving French Jewish life, history, culture, practice, sites, and expressions a more palpable, visible presence than ever before. The collapse of revolutionary utopianism in its Communist and *gauchiste* forms, which took place in the 1970s, led two generations of disillusioned socialists to rediscover their religious roots. This did not always lead to a revival of religious practice and faith but sometimes to the rediscovery of philosophical and cultural traditions long obscured by secular rationalism, beginning with the Bible, which the Congrès des Intellectuels Juifs de Langue Française made the center of its program for the first time in 1982.[63] The rediscovery of Judaism took many forms, from traditional religious observance to public rallies, from a sharp increase in the number of Jewish schools to a flourishing of Jewish organizations and celebrations, all expressing in one way or another a return to Jewish roots and an extension of Judaism beyond its traditional religious and institutional setting.

A second change had to do with a shift in the composition of the Jewish population with the arrival of large numbers of Jews from North Africa. Previously, the primary tension within the French Jewish community was between Jews of French origin (whether from Alsace, Bordeaux, or Provence) and immigrants, chiefly from eastern Europe, who came to France either at the end of the nineteenth century or in the 1920s and 30s. Now a new tension developed, as austere, discreet Ashkenazi

Jews lost power within the Jewish community to active, flamboyant Sephardic Jews. The Sephardim were much more likely to observe the traditional injunctions of Jewish law and were also largely unfamiliar with the French consensus. Like other repatriated North Africans, moreover, they were more or less consciously resentful of metropolitan France for failing to defend them. And they were steeped in community traditions and had learned from long experience of anti-Semitism how to defend themselves. Sephardic Jews were therefore likely to openly declare their solidarity with Israel and to invest the genocide with intensely sacred status. They also taught French Jews without a real communal identity the true meaning of "community." During the 1970s, Sephardim gained control of most of the representative organs of the French Jewish community, which until then had played little or no real role in public life because few Jews participated in them. It was mainly young Sephardim who led the Jewish revival and organized major public demonstrations in which the Israeli flag was openly brandished, including the Twelve Hours for Israel (1980), the reaction to the bombing of the synagogue on the Rue Copernic (1980), and the reaction to the desecration of Jewish graves in the cemetery at Carpentras (1990). If the Jewish community, like the Jew, was still "imaginary," demonstrations that spilled over into the public sphere, though not in violation of the laws on secularism, could be seen nonetheless as a threat to accepted norms.

The third change in classical Franco-Judaism was connected with the suspicion of dual allegiance, or, if you will, the idea that a visceral Zionism is in one way or another responsible for the actions and opinions of French Jews. Here again, as long as Israel, in the era of left-wing Zionism, could be seen as acting in the tradition of the national emancipation of oppressed peoples, in keeping with the ideals of revolutionary France, the in any case rather sentimental and idealized Zionism of most French Jews presented no obstacle to the more or less spontaneous philo-Israeli sentiment of the national majority. But the same factors that transformed French Judaism affected Israel as well, at the same time and for the same reasons but with far more serious consequences because of the closed nature of Israeli society and the seriousness of the external threats to its existence. Labor Zionism was supplanted by a national and nationalist Zionism, and in the meantime the religious parties grew more powerful and the populist right also made gains. The image of Israel changed from that of a potentially emancipating country to a power that was in some respects oppressive: no longer did the waters of the Seine and the Jordan flow inevitably in the same direction.

This metamorphosis of the classical terms of French Judaism is at once extremely important and beside the point. Extremely important because, having developed over a period of fifteen years, it may eventually give rise to an explosive situation, particularly as the last survivors of the Holocaust die out, for the memory of the genocide remains the black hole around which a specific Jewish memory has

FIGURE 10.19   Attack on the Rue Copernic synagogue, December 1980.

FIGURE 10.20   Demonstration against racism and anti-Semitism after the desecration of a Jewish cemetery in Carpentras, May 1990: Grand Rabbi Sitruk together with Jean-Pierre Soisson, Charles Millon, Pierre Méhaignerie, Pierre Bérégovoy, Georges Sarre, and Yvette Roudy.

been organized. Jewish memory is going through a period of enthusiastic reaffirmation associated with the need to preserve, understand, and above all transmit a patrimony threatened by the fatal erosion of time. At the same time, the lifting of French culpability, which was the primary instrument through which that memory was recovered, has raised fears that banished demons may return in new or more resistant forms.[64] The exceptionality of Jewish history has been questioned in ways that threaten the sacred status of Jewish memory. And there have even been attempts to deny the reality of the extermination.[65] Yet the metamorphosis is also beside the point because it has taken place within the now definitively established framework of the French Republic. A long-neglected history is neglected no longer. A majority consensus exists, and to repudiate that consensus would be all the more difficult in that centralizing Jacobinism is no longer as strong as it once was and, furthermore, the Catholic Church is striving to develop a more positive relationship with French Jews.

Figure 10.21   *Jews Considered to be French in Accordance with the Law;* from a game of goose of the revolutionary period, circa 1790. Emancipated by the French Revolution in 1791, the Jews became active citizens for the first time.

Basic changes are at work, and Jewish memory is experiencing those changes both as recognition of a hard-won legitimacy and as a threat to Jewish identity. This paradoxical situation is quite illustrative both of the ambiguous place that Jews have occupied and still occupy in French memory as a minority that history has placed at the heart of the national identity and of the role that France has played—that of a central laboratory, from Grégoire to Dreyfus to Vichy—in the destiny of the Jews.

PART III

DIVISIONS OF TIME AND SPACE

FIGURE 11.0 *A Street in Landerneau,* from Nodier, Taylor, and Cailleux, *Voyages romantiques dans l'ancienne France: La Bretagne;* lithograph by Ciceri after Gaucherel, 1846.

CHAPTER 11

Paris-Province

Alain Corbin

On November 27, 1796, the Théâtre-Français performed *Les Héritiers* by Alexandre Pineu Duval. In the play the valet Alain learns that an officer thought to have been lost at sea has unexpectedly returned home, much to the dismay of his family, which has been busily dividing up his property. The action is set in a castle in the Finistère region of Brittany, and several of the valet's lines provoked the mirth of the Parisian audience: "His death caused a stir in Landerneau" (scene 1); "It's good for at least a week's conversation" (scene 2); "Oh! There will be a scandal in Landerneau" (scene 18); "Oh! What a fine turn of events! I won't say anything, but *it will cause a stir in Landerneau*" (scene 23).[1] The expression "will cause a stir in Landerneau" entered into common parlance.

The actor who played Alain, Baptiste Cadet, was much appreciated by vaudeville audiences for his remarkable knack of milking the comedy of repetition. That alone cannot account for the force of the sketch, however. By the late eighteenth century, a script like this could count on certain long-standing comic conventions. Along with Pézenas, Carpentras, Brive-la-Gaillarde, Pontoise, and Quimper-Corentin, a Landerneau of the imagination was one of a long list of towns whose mere names sufficed to provoke mirth in Parisian audiences. At that date none of these comic places had been truly described. They existed in that ill-defined space known as *la province*. What fueled the comedy was the supposed inanity of the talk to be heard in such ridiculous places. Pineu Duval hammered the point home: the lost sailor's return, he noted, was "good for at least a week's conversation."

Obviously the gap that justified Parisian laughter was not simply geographic. The notion of *la province*, moreover, was not an analytic one based on some form of difference or inequality; it depended, rather, on the perception of a deficiency, an estrangement, a privation—the absence of the capital. North and South might be separated by a concrete line of demarcation, but Paris and *la province* were defined by their mutual relation.[2] So conceived, *la province* is not to be confused with "the countryside" *(la campagne)*, nor does it coincide with "the provinces" *(les provinces)*, which were territorial units with their own history, privileges, institutions, and forms of administration, whose geographic identities were just beginning to be defined. The *province* that concerns us here is not the sum total of France's several provinces; it takes the form, rather, of a highly complex sociocultural reality, a reality that, remarkably enough, evolves in large part independently of political history. In other words, the history of *la province* tells one story of how France has been represented, a story different from the political history of provincial imagery.

La province first appeared in French literature in the mid-seventeenth century, as the taste for heroism waned and the vogue for the baroque subsided. Its inception coincided with an "extreme constriction of ideal space,"[3] whose dimensions would ultimately be dictated by the limitations of the Parisian stage. Semantically, *la province* was associated with the centralization of both the representation and the reality of power; based on exclusion, it therefore had connotations of derision from the beginning. *La province* figured in, indeed tended to monopolize, a certain comical representation of space. "In the singular," Father Dominique Bouhours wrote in 1692, "one can scarcely say `he is a provincial' without laughing,"[4] and the *vis comica* of the places evoked in Scarron's novel *Le Roman comique* could be felt only by contrast with Paris.[5]

In this period *la province* also denoted an experience of a particularly intense and vivid kind. Born of curialization, it was defined as a space deprived of the king's radiant presence—the hell of disgrace, the banishment of internal exile, the obsessive fear of oblivion. *La province* was defeat; there one was in danger of withering on the vine, of being contaminated by rust (Bussy-Rabutin) or mildew (Mme de Sévigné). It was identified with lethargy and hibernation or, worse, symbolic death. *La province* was where one went to be "buried alive." "You people of the court," Bussy-Rabutin wrote to Benserade, "count the people of *province* as dead," while Mme de Sévigné characterized provincials as "people of the other world."[6]

At best *la province* could become the "desert," that is, a place of refuge devoted to contemplation, a theater where inner life developed beyond "disillusionment," where, borrowing Stoic images of retreat, one waited in triumphant renunciation in anticipation of the heavenly beatitude to come.

When exile was not voluntary, the irreparable rupture stemming from disgrace triggered the provincial metamorphosis. Thereafter, if the banished individual returned to grace, it could only be as a figure of ridicule or a person so broken that a decision to renounce the world must soon follow. Well-known examples of this painful experience include Bussy-Rabutin, who, having been banished by the king only from Paris and the court, at first suffered, then resigned himself to his fate; and Mme de Sévigné, who was forced periodically into exile in Brittany in order to preserve her modest fortune.

Remote from the society of the Place Royale, the salons of Paris, and the Academy, *la province* meant privation of proper usage and refined discourse. It was the opposite of preciosity. The involuntary provincial expected to be condemned to an absence of conversation and to endure the inevitable patois. One's command of language was therefore in danger of being lost, and Mme de Sévigné feared that just such a calamity would befall her owing to the mediocrity of the company available in Vitré. For the provincial exile the only hope lay in the joys of hospitality or the good fortune of finding a great lord sojourning on a nearby estate; short of that, the best one could do was to befriend the more erudite residents of the larger provincial towns, although such scholars were apt to be woefully out of touch with the latest fashions. No Parisian could hope to sustain his or her linguistic facility on such learned commerce for very long, not even with the supplement of correspondence, that essential substitute for genuine conversation that was in those days a crucial element of the Paris-*province* relationship.

The provincial who settled in Paris and hoped to gain recognition there was in turn obliged to renounce all ties to the milieu from which he sprang. Disparagement of *la province* was an obligation incumbent on anyone who wished to win the confidence of the City.[7] Molière himself begged the king's pardon for having exercised his art so far from Paris for so long. He knew that any portrayal of the provincial was apt to provoke the laughter of the court. The necessity of self-denial reinforced a notion of *la province* that was by no means limited to the Paris-born.

La province, which at the time meant estrangement from both the court and the City[8] and whose strangeness impressed itself on people's minds more and more vividly, did not denote any well-defined piece of territory. Racine never actually described the city of Uzès in which he was condemned to live and which he saw above all as a place inhospitable to the Muses.[9] *La province* was perceived as a vague intermediate space between the center of action, which was in Paris, and an exotic fantasy world.

Yet French soil was not all provincial to the same degree. Remoteness from Paris heightened provinciality. Caen, the Norman Athens and seat of a prestigious academy as well as the home of such distinguished sons as Huet, Segrais, and Moisant de Brieux, all familiar names in the capital, basked in and reflected the light of the City.[10] By contrast, France south of the Loire, especially the Midi, symbolized a sort of exacerbated *province*. The inhabitants of that remote territory epitomized the height of bad taste. Their language was mere gibberish. Gradually these figures were "carnivalized" and became unreal, like the caricatural puppet Gascons that amused a Paris eager for symbolic revenge against the once overbearing men of

Navarre. In this golden age of the *gasconnade*, the depiction of the boasts, oaths, and jabbering of these "Gascon" figures elicited laughter from spectators unconcerned with the realistic portrayal of manners.[11]

Between 1650 and 1670, the theater and to a lesser degree the novel elaborated a catalog of stereotypes that constituted a portrait of the provincial, whose ridiculousness stemmed from remoteness from the sources of power, if not knowledge.[12] But we must be careful: the provincial was not the same as the rustic. He (or she) was not one of the countless Parisian domestics sprung from the rural populace. They, too, were objects of laughter but not as representatives of *la province*. They never so much as ventured to utter a well-turned phrase, and the artificial language that was imputed to them draws on other sources of comic energy. Nor should *la province* be confused with those still rustic places close to Paris—Auteuil, Passy, Vincennes, Vaux, Fontainebleau—places semantically identified with *la campagne*, the countryside.[13] Owing to a sort of extraterritorial privilege, moreover, the château of the seigneur with a solid position at court was exempt from provinciality, as was that other temporary refuge of Parisianness, the spa town.[14] The characters in Florent Dancourt's *Eaux de Bourbon,* for example, are exempt from the ridicule ordinarily aimed at devalued provincial space.[15]

The minor provincial nobility, still immune to the allure of the court, now became the focal point of Parisian mockery. The curialized aristocracy sought to discredit the manners of this group along with its evident devotion to old values. On the stage, such local worthies as the bailiff and his spouse, the wife of the alderman, the provost, the notary, the tax collector, and the magistrate peopled the reviled *province*.[16] Nobles were given ridiculous names whose characterological connotations triggered laughter: M. de la Dandinière, de la Prudoterie, de Sotenville, de Pourceaugnac, le Baron de la Crasse.

The same basic traits recur frequently. The local worthies invariably yearn to be gentlefolk, people of quality. They burn to know, to understand, and to imitate Paris. They hunger for recognition. They are eager to show off their good grammar and refined speech. And needless to say, they are doomed to failure. After enduring, along with M. de Pourceaugnac, repeated disappointments and suffering from an obsessive fear of being duped, they eventually return to *la province*, which they should never have left in the first place.

In the eyes of the Parisian, the provincial was characterized first of all by his appearance, his "provincial look." Yet the impatient newcomer's first wish was to rid himself of his embarrassing cloak in order to "live in the Parisian style"—an impossible dream.

The provincial was further characterized by extreme pretentiousness. In every sphere he betrayed himself by excess, a consequence of insufficient self-control, incomplete mastery of the necessary codes, and lack of discretion and tact in the use of artifice. To counterfeit society and pass for something other than what one is: these were the provincial's principal goals, and it was of course child's play for the Parisian to outwit him. Molière's *précieuses ridicules* are foolish rustics who put on airs of intelligent refinement.

The final defining characteristics of *la province* are narrowness and backwardness. The provincial lives in a constricted space. His gaze is limited. His interests are petty. His circle of acquaintances is narrow. The major events of his life unfold within a narrow ambit. In M. de Pourceaugnac's Limoges, everyone knows everyone else and all their business. And Dorine's portrait of provincial marriage in *Tartuffe* is well known.

While suffering from the slow diffusion of news, *la province* lived in slow motion. The delay in receiving the news and the impossibility of taking it in close to the source engendered avid curiosity in people condemned to live as remote spectators and forever forbidden to be actors on the central stage. And the women of the provinces, try as they might, would always remain one step behind the latest fashions.

The men, for their part, continued to partake in some vague way of the surrounding rusticity. They were inappropriate and improper: their crudeness, "thickwittedness," and rages fatigued the Parisian, and La Bruyère for one did not fail to pour scorn on them for that very reason.

Over the years the catalog of stereotypes grew longer, the gamut of traits widened, and the definition of ethnotypes became more precise. Images of the provinces enriched the image of *la province*. One result of the neo-Hippocratic vogue in medicine was the constitution of a portrait gallery of provincials as their characters were etched by different climates and bearing even in their physiognomies the stamp of the local patois. As early as 1665, Raymond Poisson paraded a series of ethnotypes before the reader of his *L'Après-souper des auberges,* and this was soon augmented by Dancourt. Humorous place-names only added to the ridiculousness of Banneret de Kergrohinizouarne, M. de Kerbabillard, the Norman Vivien de la Chaponnardière, and the Gascon Fourbignac.[17]

Fascinated by the City and the court, in thrall to a desire for acceptance, immobilized by the expectation of correspondence from Paris, *la province* offered no counterimage to oppose the disparaging figures of satire, patiently allowing the erudition of its scholars and prestige of its jurists to be mocked for the amusement of court society. So eager were provincial academies for the grant of letters-patent from Versailles that they allowed their growth to be regulated and subjected to scrutiny and modeled their very activities after Parisian exemplars. Until 1715, at any rate, the spread of the academic movement may well have signified, in Daniel Roche's words, "the slowing of a provincial dynamism."[18] The academies proclaimed their adherence to the norms of the capital. The academic movement contributed to the spread of French and the liquidation of baroque culture. Like satire, the academies no doubt figured in a strategy whose purpose was to domesticate the provincial nobility.[19]

What is striking about this period—the end of the Great Century—is the success of an image of *la province* at first decreed by the center but later accepted, if not actively internalized, by the very people that image was intended to disparage. The attitude that emerged then would continue to regulate the Paris-*province* relationship for a long time to come: an attitude of docility, acceptance, even voluntary submission on the part of provincials who recognized themselves and identified with the image they saw in the mirror held up by the City. As early as the seventeenth century, according to some sources, Gascons experienced a desire to make their attitudes coincide with an image imposed on them by others, a literary trope. By making themselves accomplices in the strategy, they hoped to free themselves from their condition; what they got instead was "institutionalization of the trope."[20] Indeed, Philippe Joutard finds that the people of Marseilles exhibited an astonishing desire to embody an ethnotype rooted in fiction. The basic desire to conform, which manifested itself on the periphery, thus deepened the division without any deliberate intention on the part of the central power.

Meanwhile, another factor added further complexity to the configuration of provinciality. In 1666, Furetière, in his *Roman bourgeois*, invented a fictional *province* that, strangely enough, was also Parisian. He describes residents of the Place Maubert quarter of Paris, who, cooped up within the narrow confines of their neighborhood and subjected to the scrutiny of their neighbors, inaugurate a process whereby noble ridicule is transferred to the narrow-minded petty bourgeois, soon destined to become the central figure of provincial society.[21]

By the end of the seventeenth century, the notion of *province*, whose contours had been firmly outlined some decades earlier, lost its clarity. The shrinking of space had reached an extreme: Paris was no longer interested in anything but Paris. Owing to this blinkering of vision, the eighteenth century is less fundamentally important to our subject than are the middle years of the Great Century. The semantic history of *la province* owes relatively little to the later period. The perceived identity and range of sentiment associated with provinciality did not change profoundly. For the time being, Paris, the countryside, and the château were the favored settings. To be sure, the notion of *province* survived and was periodically reinterpreted. After Regnard, Marivaux, for example, examined the character of the stupid provincial fascinated by the capital and an easy prey for Parisians.[22] But *la province* was no longer central to the representation. It came to be seen more and more clearly as a space that threatened nobility with contamination by the trivial interests, values, and codes of the rising bourgeoisie.

Several important phenomena affected this relatively recent trope, however. First was a shift in the social center of gravity. Paris once again became the center of high

FIGURE 11.1 Gavarni, Illustrations for the *Physiologie du provincial à Paris,* P. Durand (1842).

society. Scholars in any case have probably overestimated the loss of prestige that Paris suffered when king and court moved first to Saint-Germain and later to Versailles. Hélène Himmelfarb has shown that the king's sojourns followed a complex pattern, even after 1682.[23] Robert Mandrou observes that the City, a fertile hotbed of fashion blessed with numerous salons, academies, and people of talent, had always set itself up as a competitor to the court.[24] And in the eighteenth century, as Marc Fumaroli points out, Parisian cliques determined who was talked about and who won election to the Académie.[25] This primacy of the City bears emphasizing, because until the end of the nineteenth century it was here that the system of representations and emotions that defined *la province* took place. For a long time it was in high-society conversation in Paris that the Paris-*province* split was defined as well as experienced and there, too, that the provinciality of the individual was most easily gauged.

Around the beginning of the eighteenth century, however, a centrifugal process was set in motion, a process that would continue until the fall of the monarchy. Little by little the capital began to criticize itself. Hints of denigration of the city are already perceptible in Lesage and Montesquieu, and these would be reinforced by denunciations of urban pathology launched by neo-Hippocratic physicians well before Louis-Sébastien Mercier contributed his hallucinatory diatribe.[26] Denunciations of the City stimulated idyllic discourse. Indeed, it was not *la province* but *la campagne*, the countryside,[27] that most obviously profited from the hunger to escape.[28]

The degree to which the academic movement spread outside Paris in the Age of Enlightenment might seem to point toward a successful effort of emancipation or even a cultural primacy of *la province*. Without denying the novelty of developments that in some cases demonstrate real initiative on the part of provincial actors, Daniel Roche's important study suggests a need to modify this positive interpretation.[29] Indeed, the academic movement spread by perpetuating a social model inherited from the Great Century. Furthermore, "a person who frequented the academies of his province and the salons of Paris was, however devoted he may have been to his city, governed more by Paris than by his provincial academy."[30] In this connection the example of Montesquieu is revealing. While it is true that a genuine desire for independence from Paris developed in this milieu between 1715 and 1750, that desire subsided in the second half of the century, when the thirst for local power was on the rise. The resulting accentuation of regional consciousness sharpened the contours of the provincial image. Anything that fostered local pride reinforced Parisian difference and heightened the uniqueness of the City that transcended all regionalism. By the same token, anything that helped to promote the several provinces tended to devalue *la province*.

Retouching the portrait of *la province* in countless ways, some more subtle than others, the Revolution reshaped the conception of the Paris-*province* relationship. The first thing to look at in this regard is the effect of the Revolution's creation of the départements and the resulting spatial rearrangements.[31] On the eve of the convocation of the Estates General, the concept of *la province* as a territorial and administrative entity remained on the whole rather vague. The territorial redistricting carried out by the Constituent Assembly had the paradoxical effect of spurring provincial consciousness. People began to delve deeper into provincial identity in their efforts to resist the abolition of the provinces. I shall have more to say presently about this process, which began under the Constituent Assembly.

At the same time, the emergence of a départemental identity, followed by its gradual refinement and promotion by a prolix literature, ultimately led to a profound upheaval in the system of territorial representation. This proved to be a decisive episode in the history of the spatial imagination and its relation to nature.

To be sure, the elaboration of a new départemental identity did not in itself radically transform the image of either Paris or *la province*. Immediately following the reform, the adjective *départemental* naturally inherited all the stereotypes associated with *provincial,* and no doubt those stereotypes became even more deeply ingrained. In fact, départemental identity established itself so forcefully that it accentuated the consciousness of belonging to this or that locality. Contrary to the intentions of those behind the new administrative map, who hoped to weaken the grip of territorial imagery, individuals over time became more intensely identified with their départements.

The creation of the new entity and the reflection it encouraged marked an important page in the history of "the relationship of territory to power."[32] The debates that accompanied the new division of territory, which was carried out on the basis of data concerning political economy, geography, and biology, revealed the existence of hostility toward Paris. They provided an opportunity for *la province* to vent long-suppressed bitterness.

The scope of this diatribe remains to be ascertained, however. Marie-Vic Ozouf and Ted Margadant have analyzed the provincial discourse in depth.[33] They show clearly that the initial hostility was associated with an anti-urban bias of more general import. It was one aspect of an ongoing polemic that pitted small towns against "capital cities," countryside against devouring metropolis. In addition, the drawing up of a new administrative map rekindled old interurban conflicts, whose remote roots have been unearthed by historians studying urban networks and hierarchies.

It is not enough, however, merely to note the revival of such conflicts. The administrative reform led to a rapid expansion of the Paris-*province* relationship, which had previously been confined to the sociocultural realm. As the capital, Paris tightened its grip on the rest of the country by turning itself into a symbol of harmony between the parts and the whole. The new territorial division gave the capital clearer authority over the totality of French territory. The city benefitted from the psychological importance of the notion of centrality, from the new desire to turn France into a single ontological entity, a nation whose greatness would be measured by the prestige of its capital. The revisions of the administrative map carried out first by the Montagnards and later under the Consulate and Empire merely clarified a centralizing tendency already apparent in the work of the Constituent Assembly during the final quarter of 1789. Of course the members of that body were already aware of the risks that the capital's new preeminence entailed, as is apparent in the lucid report prepared by Target as secretary for the Constitutional Committee in the fall of 1789. The balance that would have to be struck, he noted, was not between Paris and each of the provinces taken singly but between Paris and *la province* in its entirety.[34]

The creation of the départements and the new images of centrality imposed by the reforms were by no means the Revolution's only contribution to the new relationship between Paris and *la province*. We have yet to identify the consequences of a complex political history. To that end, we must keep our eyes fixed firmly on the chronology of events. The summer of 1789 made Paris the capital of the Revolution.[35] The center of the Enlightenment became the city of Liberty. The Fourteenth of July bestowed upon Paris an "immediately central role." By taking the Bastille, Parisians won the right to set themselves up as guides for all of France. As *Le Moniteur* noted at the time, "everyone felt that Paris ought to be regarded not as an individual city so much as the general meeting place and common city of all the French."[36]

The lapse of time between events in Paris and provincial reactions to those events attests to the capital's preeminence. In any case, it was Paris that would henceforth confer meaning on episodes of municipal revolution dispersed throughout the territory. The capital, perceived as the source of public opinion, tended to restrict *la province* to a receiver's role. The network of political societies, together with their associated procedures of affiliation and correspondence, established the figure of an initiating city. The press in the capital established a highly Parisian image of *la province*. The journalists of the big city set themselves up as sentinels. They saw themselves as the educators of the rest of France, whose inferiority they implicitly proclaimed.

The Festival of the Federation on July 14, 1790, gives us a clear view of the modalities of the relationship just then being established between Paris and *la province*. This occasion was a sort of "national investiture," conferring a new sacred status on the capital. The travels of the *fédérés*, Mona Ozouf observes, were experienced as a form of "national education," a glorious "federative pilgrimage" to the "sacred birthplace of the Revolution."[37]

In fact, the occasion showed that representations of Paris and *la province* were quite complex. There was a kind of tension between two conceptions of space: in the course of their travels to and from Paris, the *fédérés*, Ozouf notes, hoped that by experiencing "topographical egalitarianism" for themselves they could establish both the "sacredness of the center" and the concomitant sacredness of French territory as a whole.[38]

A new balance was struck in 1792. Unlike July 14, 1789, August 10, 1792, was not strictly speaking a Parisian event. Provincials, most notably from Brittany and Marseilles, took part in the capture of the Tuileries. The imagery became more complex than ever. In this instance the crucial point is surely not, as is often stated, the increased centralization of Jacobin France. In this area, as we have seen, the work of the Montagnards merely continued a process begun by the Constituent Assembly. What was decisive, by contrast, was the near identification that was established between the democratic populace of Paris and the national image.

In the eyes of provincial patriots who recognized that the people of Paris felt called to take upon themselves a mission of revolutionary surveillance, incitation, and initiative, the capital long remained the center and sentinel of the Revolution. The Thermidorians themselves would attempt, at least initially, to legitimate their actions by invoking the image of a populace blessed with a gift for thwarting conspiracy.

To my mind, the crucial development was the introduction of a new system of representations. The Girondins had developed a type of discourse which the Thermidorians, once victory was assured, were content to recycle as often as the circumstances required. What the provincial felt toward Paris was no longer simply a vague hostility but a deep and specific hatred. From the summer of 1792 to mid-June of 1793 the diatribe was at its most intense. Federalism, which built on a départemental base, developed a range of stereotypes whose influence on political representation would endure for some time. Alan Forrest, Mona Ozouf, and Raymonde Monnier see this system of images as a caricature intended to deprive Paris of its sacred status[39] The dialectical relation between the capital and *la province* was thus based on an evolving dialectic of good and evil. Paris, accordingly, was nothing but a blind, rebellious, faction-riven city. It was a center of intrigue and conspiracy, anarchic, turbulent, even tumultuous, much as Rome had been in the final years of the Republic, or better yet, under the Empire, when it was obsessed with the demands of the plebs.

Paris also showed itself to be an arrogant city, at once slavish and domineering. The Girondins denounced the dictatorship of the despotic city, obviously aiming their criticism at the Paris of the Commune. Marat, the quintessential Parisian, was seen as both symbol and scapegoat.

Against such a monster the only possible form of federation was one of hostility. *La province* was not to blame for the federalist crisis. As the Girondins saw it, Paris itself had long been trying to secede from the rest of France. Parisians had no sense of political legitimacy. "Destroy the imperious federalism of the Paris sections," read a petition from the Republican Society of Champlitte that arrived on June 20, 1793. "Nationalize this immense city, so that it may at last learn to obey the sovereign will of the people, to cut itself down to the level of the départements."[40] Some even called for the designation of a new center: the sections of Bordeaux proposed that this role be assigned to Bourges.[41]

Yet the summer of '93 was of course the point at which the political influence of the Parisian people in arms was at its height. It was Thermidor—July 1794—that led to the collapse of the power of the capital, which was soon deprived of its municipal government.[42]

However important this process may have been, the essential changes that were made at this time to the system of representations that concerns us here cannot be summed up under the heading of increased administrative centralization. The revolutionary period established the sacred character of the capital as the cradle of Liberty and gave a firm foundation to memories of the struggle between the people of Paris, invested with that sacredness, and the all too often helpless representatives of the nation. For years to come, conflicts of legitimacy based on this duality would continue to govern the political imagination, the consciousness of identity, and the pattern of revolutionary violence.

Over the course of the nineteenth century the real and imaginary relationship that wedded Paris to *la province* while sharply differentiating one from the other underwent numerous changes. Nevertheless, the range of stereotypes elaborated in the aftermath of the Fronde continued to define the deep structure of the relationship. All the dictionaries of the period—Bescherelle's, Littré's, Larousse's—illustrated their definitions with quotations from Molière, La Bruyère, and Mme de Sévigné. Deprivation, denigration, and ridicule remained the crucial semantic components, although a new sense of propriety may have somewhat moderated the denigration and mollified the diatribe.

At the beginning of the century derision was still paramount. Vaudeville gave wide currency to the motifs of classical comedy and the bourgeois novel. The intention was to make the provincial the butt of laughter for a broad audience of common people. The extension of Parisian complicity to a wider class of people is the chief feature of comic characterization in this period. The provincial lout visiting the capital and making a fool of himself became the paramount theme, supplanting the comedy of pure geography.[43] In 1802, Paris made a triumph of Picard's *Les Provinciaux à Paris,* which depicted the members of the Gaulard family from Ligny, a group of "nice folks who repeatedly allow themselves to be swindled." Vaudeville tacitly consented to the disappearance of M. de Pourceaugnac; there was no longer any need to poke fun at country squires.[44]

Under the July Monarchy the foolish provincial visiting Paris remained popular, but over the years the characterization of the ethnotype acquired new depth. Perpetually harassed, swindled, and robbed, forever deceived, quick to fall into every trap, the provincial suffered an endless series of "tribulations." In 1842, Eugène Guinot, writing under the pseudonym Pierre Durand, enumerated them in a humorous vein in a work entitled *Physiologie du provincial à Paris*.[45] In 1844, Delphine Gay, Mme de Girardin, attempted a further refinement of the portrait, meticulously describing "the inhabitants of *la province* prey to Parisian emotions." "Scarlet-faced" and with "a busy air,"[46] the provincial scurried about his business if he did not actually run through the streets. His gestures, manners, and gait all pointed up his clumsiness. Provinciality was a somatic reality, a fact well understood by petty criminals.[47] In 1837, Balzac noted: "The most obvious signs of provincial life are to be found in gesture, behavior, and movement, which suffer a loss of the agility that Paris continually communicates."[48]

The provincial belonged to a strange "species" that was utterly ignorant of the City, and his efforts to satisfy his curiosity were inevitably in vain. Paris eluded the grasp of provincials, who, Mme de Girardin tells us, stood no chance of discovering its reality because they saw only "its public pleasures" and "knew nothing of its high society."[49] Situated at the confluence of public and private, the inaccessible places frequented by the 2,000 individuals who made up "society" constituted the only theater in which a metamorphosis was possible; the rest was mere illusion, a counterfeit integration into the ways of the City. Ignorant of the city's codes, provincials committed errors that were not just foolish but "frightful." Having no contact with genuine Parisians, they copied one another: "A lady from Grenoble admires the stole of a lady from Beauvais, whom she mistakes for a lioness of Parisian society.... An elegant fellow from Cahors covets the jacket of a dandy from Abbeville.... It would be too cruel if they were to return from the capital with the latest fashions from Alsace or Berry!... After this trip, they will have seen Paris, no doubt, but let them be under no illusion: they will not have seen Parisians." Like M. de Pourceaugnac and the Gaulards of Ligny before them, these bewildered provincials have no choice but to go home.

Ridiculous though such visits to Paris were, they could nevertheless serve as a kind of initiation. The provincial who visited Paris somewhere retained "a trace of his pilgrimage, the indelible mark of a more or less complete experience." According to the Parisian, in fact, the provincial, "having once touched the streets of the capital, loses his primitive character, his départemental naïveté."[50]

Meanwhile, of course, a new consciousness of the primacy of the center was developing; Paris's relation to the *provinces* (plural, as opposed to *la province*) was being reshaped. Michelet made this explicit in his *Tableau de la France*. The process has been analyzed by Marcel Roncayolo and Jean-Yves Guiomar.[51] The new conception of a foundational center would henceforth determine the picture of the nation. The search for the local genius of each province suggests that consciousness of being French lay not in a mere summation of local qualities but in the "transcending of the constituent elements in [the nation's] center, Paris." In Michelet's words, "the center knows itself and knows all the rest." The provinces, on the other hand, "see themselves in [the center]. In it they love and admire one another in a superior form."[52] This semantic imperialism brings us to a fundamental paradox of this analysis: anything that heightened provincial individuality, anything that smacked of regionalism or localism (in this period a favorite pastime of local polymaths), increased difference and, owing to ignorance of the national, implicitly exalted Paris. The capital, which rose above the local genius of each of its components even as it marveled at their diversity, transcended the provinces. It emerged as the cornerstone of French unity, as the exclusive space of national expression and consecration.

The mapping of the territory and fabrication of regional images that took place at this time were carried out in accordance with this transcendence. Initially these projects were shaped by the discovery of the strangeness of the provinces. An astonished Parisian elite was eager to understand the resistance to reason demonstrated during the Revolution: the surprising, vexing, or just simply amazing attachment to old beliefs, superstitions, and prejudices, to the antique calendar, to outdated weights and measures, and to local patois. The investigation that Chaptal ordered prefects to undertake,[53] the research conducted by the Celtic Academy,[54] the venture organized by Charles Nodier and Baron Taylor, and the proliferating geographical narratives exemplified by *L'Ermite en province* were all organized implicitly with reference to the center. Regional images emerged in the capital. Between 1820 and 1835 the Parisian elite imposed its tragic view of Armorican Brittany.[55] In 1829, Jules Janin popularized a plutonic image of the city of Saint-Étienne.[56] Under the July Monarchy tourists from the capital sketched the portrait of the Pyrenean savage, studied by Jean-François Soulet.[57] And the portrait that was painted of the peasants of the Limousin mountains owed a great deal to Parisian readers of Walter Scott's Waverley novels. In 1842 three of the nine volumes of the important series *Les Français peints par eux-mêmes* offered a provisional summary of all that had been learned about provincial ethnotypes. Their images could be compared with those of the Parisians depicted in five other volumes of the series. The importance of the division that interests us here emerges strikingly from this ambitious work.

Local elites soon developed their own counterimages, about which I shall have more to say presently. Brittany was particularly quick in its response. Backed by a talented bourgeoisie, native nobles attempted at the height of the July Monarchy to establish the figure of the Arcadian Arcoat, exalted by Brizeux. This is not the place, however, to delve into a broad process that interests us only to the extent that it was influenced by the complex relationship among Paris, *la province*, and *les provinces*.

More important in the present context was the ambiguous emergence of a new fictional figure in the 1820s followed by a sudden explosion of interest in the subject after the Revolution of 1830. The small provincial town became an object of literary interest. Nicole Mozet has provided an excellent analysis of its rise, which reflected the primacy of the petite bourgeoisie in provincial imagery.[58]

The new precision in the topographical description of small towns paralleled the rise of archaeology.[59] As the fascination with the exotic temporarily waned, *la province* became a museum, a vast antique gallery. Balzac, one of the creators of the new imagery, even planned a moral and social archaeology based on the study of a small provincial town.[60] The Parisian reader was invited to embark on a journey in both space and time. The national past would emerge from the remains discovered through excavation in the open air. Paris was a surface on which it was easy to read a present perpetually in the process of creation, whereas the countryside was still an entity distinct from *la province*. Compared with either of these, the small provincial town was far more successful at preserving the vestiges of the past. Each of them offered the key to reconstructing vanished centuries. A fictional provincial itinerary—the imagination's counter to the erudite travels of Prosper Mérimée—was a way of recovering the national past, of grasping the stages in the creation of France.

This ambitious archaeological project transformed the image of *la province*. The latter was no longer a comic space peopled by fools so much as a static vacuum "of emptiness, boredom, negativity"[61] and "mediocrity of ideas,"[62] where women withered in "eternal virginity" and "non-life."[63] It was a trap, suggesting imprisonment in the infinite triviality of the everyday. Bussy-Rabutin's image of rust and Mme de Sévigné's of mildew were reinterpreted in the light of an archaeological project that contributed new figures to the social imagination and reflected the redistribution of power.

At the same time the small town of fiction became the theater of a new kind of tragedy. Here, close to nature, artifice had yet to draw the sting of vigorous passions as in Paris. Here the violence of desire, further exacerbated by the scarcity of opportunities, the mediocrity of available partners, and the length of the wait for love's impact, accounted for the vehemence of the act[64] and the alacrity with which the torment of dishonor is embraced.[65] It is because he is a Breton from Guérande that Calyste du Guénic attempts to hurl pretentious Béatrix from the top of a cliff.

A fatherless world at a time when the king's exile had reawakened memories of regicide, the imaginary *province*—an empty stage on which the only actors were boredom and "buried" love[66]—tended to be seen as a feminine place. A gulf of sex thus separated Paris from the small town. For the rest of the century *la province*, jealous in any case of a city that sought only to exploit it, fell for the seductiveness

of Paris.[67] The capital resorted to a variety of tactics to fan the flames of desire that it kindled. Like the Illustrious Gaudissart, clever image makers set out to seduce *la province* the better to swindle or even conquer it. Many people—salesmen, journalists, fashion designers, novelists, politicians—shared the same goal, as we shall see in a moment. In novels, the simple provincial woman, ardent but neglected, could be portrayed, at least until she acquired a "stock of foolishness"[68] and renounced coquettishness for confitures, as the ideal prey for the dandy or tired genius worn down by the harsh and unremitting warfare of Paris society.

This enrichment of the imagery, which reshaped the Paris-*province* relation in contemporary minds, was also reflected—the point is important—in a fundamental reversal of the figures of exile. *La province* no longer connoted only disgrace,

FIGURE 11.2   Gaudissart, a fast-talking Parisian flimflam artist, sets out to conquer the provinces. Gaudissart's renown suggests something of the complexity of the Paris-*province* psychology. Illustration by Piau for Balzac's *Scènes de la vie de province*.

FIGURE 11.3   Illustrations for the cover of L. Reybaud's *Jérôme Paturot à la recherche d'une position sociale* (1845). Representations of social ascent were inseparable at the time from the idea of a circulation between Paris and the provinces.

estrangement from the center, and the staleness of existence. Its feminization allowed it to become a "spatial metaphor for the mother figure."[69] The obligatory youthful sojourn in Paris turned *la province* into a refuge. Back to one's "roots": the romantic sensibility fostered such regressive tendencies, and the anxious expectancy of mothers and sisters made young men all the more impatient to return, however briefly. Private diaries and letters reveal the intensity of the exchanges that traveled back and forth between the young scholar's Paris and the sweetly feminine *province*.[70] In those exchanges the capital found yet another occasion to mold the woman who waited frozen in anticipation; the epistolary relationship that developed between brother and sister allowed the young man to play Pygmalion.[71] In contrast to the youthful, masculine Paris, boiling over with revolutionary ideas and eager to mount the barricades, *la province,* which became a place of initiation, was apt to become a focal point of reactionary interpretation.

In all of this the real and the imaginary were inextricably intertwined. Novels offered a new mirror to provincial female readers eager to discover their identity—and we know that their numbers were large. Literature fostered a new consciousness of provinciality and instilled a desire to conform. It was no longer a matter of embodying an ethnotype, like the Gascons of old, but merely of conforming to an image of oneself produced by the capital.[72] The care with which novelists described the private sphere when evoking the atmosphere of a provincial town surely made it easier for female readers to identify with the text.

Meanwhile, Paris was also developing new attractions. The collapse of the educational system and its subsequent reorganization and centralization under the Revolution made it necessary for ambitious young men who in the past probably would have remained in their native provinces to come to Paris to study. Nicole Mozet rightly calls attention to the intensity of the experience of deracination for young men who came of age between 1795 and 1810.[73] The prestige of the slowly reestablished academies as well as of the Sorbonne and the lycées of the Latin Quarter, the founding of the *grandes écoles*—in short, the entire state policy for training elites (and, later, the establishment of *conférences* for young men interested in going into politics[74])—made Paris an obligatory stop on the ambitious youth's itinerary for years to come.

Such deracination was pleasing to individuals eager to jump into the social swim and convinced that *la province* did not provide a grand enough stage for their inner selves. New forms of social mobility coupled with the rise of individualism helped refashion the relationship between Paris and *province*. The effect was a new division, if not a fracture, within the heart of each individual, at once keen to get to Paris and nostalgic for the provincial refuge.

The capital more than ever became the focal point of all ambition. All images of social and emotional success were centered in it, the culmination of every career. *La province,* formerly the hell of exile, stood out more and more clearly as the theater of failure: the provincial overcame hurdles and waited anxiously and achingly for Parisian promotion only to return in failure to a static life of disappointment and resignation. What was lacking was no longer the king's presence but a sense of progress; the provincial was a man of thwarted ambitions who had the sense of being trapped in a net.

For the young provincial-born student still innocent of failure's torments and disappointments, Paris was the favorite place to acquire a sentimental education. The plentiful opportunities for affairs, the liberated ways of a society of young people delighted to be free of familial and provincial restraints, a certain nonchalance characteristic of Paris society, the possibility of leading a bohemian life and of temporarily setting up housekeeping with a *grisette* (working girl) capable of calming senses inflamed by deferred desire for a prestigious mistress, the abundant varieties of male camaraderie—all these things made Paris the ideal place to learn the difficult arts of making love with finesse and boasting of it afterward. Within this space of freedom, moreover, one could, without great risk, provoke the bourgeoisie. At times the capital also offered, in its theaters and even in its streets, the intoxicating inducements of political turmoil.

In this Paris of juvenile tribulations, even as young scholars flocked to the city and the "younger generation" emerged as a distinct reality, provincial martyrs discovered new forms of suffering.[75] The youth who arrived in the capital from Grenoble or La Côte-Saint-André found that it was not easy to gain acceptance. Poverty beckoned; the pleasures of the capital were subtly undermined by the bitter certainty of some day being forced to swallow one's ambitions and return to a mediocrity that was both bourgeois and provincial.[76] Novels depicting small-town life meanwhile reveled in the pleasures and torments of the Parisian apprenticeship. In 1829, Gustave Drouineau's *Ernest ou le Travers du siècle* enjoyed a huge success. The wretched fate of the hero, who had come to Paris from La Rochelle to study law, drew attention to the misfortunes of young people uprooted from their native soil.

The problem was that a stay in Paris by itself was not enough to complete the provincial's initiation or metamorphosis. The indispensable skills of the true Parisian included knowing how to present oneself, mastering the capital's codes, a certain nonchalance in demonstrating that mastery, familiarity with fashionable places, habituation to the rhythm of Parisian life, and a capacity to decipher allusions quickly enough to make easy conversation. Such skills could be acquired only through contact with "society," proximity to which was the only way to learn what true superiority looked like, discover the real social hierarchy, and devise plans and tactics based on that knowledge. In other words, an assiduous immersion in society was the only way to gain a clear image of what success was and how to achieve it. A narrow but active circle of people determined who would be blessed with favor and recommendations.[77] Success depended on meeting the right people, even for the young man of talent or the genius awaiting anointment. Refinement of one's manners, progress in one's sentimental education, and realization of one's ambitions: there is little point in attempting to make hard and fast distinctions, for apprenticeships in all these areas were closely intertwined.

In this connection it is important to distinguish between two levels of provinciality. The provinciality of the vaudeville character lost in the Parisian tempest, the heir to a comic ethnotype with an already lengthy tradition behind it, should not be confused with the subtler, more discreet provinciality that only the hidden pitfalls of high-society conversation could flush out. Once again, however, it is difficult to distinguish the imaginary from the real in view of the tremendous influence of literary models and the acuity of contemporary social observers. Characters such as Rastignac, Jérôme Paturot, and Prosper Chavigni[78] exerted a direct influence on readers who studied and interpreted their behavior and perhaps even on those who served as models for these characters.

What happened, in sum, was that provincial elites were not so much supplanted as they were nullified by Paris. No longer was there such a thing as a provincial elite, because the talented provincial metamorphosed into something other than a provincial, whereas the elite Parisian who ventured outside the capital enjoyed a privileged exemption from provinciality.[79] So long as they did not overstay their welcome, the aristocrat in his château and the wealthy bourgeois in his country house remained Parisians. The high-ranking functionary serving in the provinces was a pawn manipulated by Paris and in no danger of contamination by his surroundings. Nor was his wife, the *femme administrative* whom Balzac so carefully distinguished from the *femme de province*.[80] Genius, by dint of a sort of immaculate conception, could not be reduced to the status of provincial. Eugène Guinot refused even to recognize as provincial the individual who arrived in Paris by postal coach.[81] A few decades later, Pierre Larousse's *Grand Dictionnaire* stretched the privilege of Parisian citizenship to include anyone arriving in central Paris by express train.[82]

The point is that the Paris-*province* distinction had become less geographical than ever. Provinciality, defined as backwardness, immobility, unavowed boredom,[83] archaic customs, petty intrigue, or sensual timidity—the "horticulture of vulgarities"[84]—had established itself in the center of Paris. Each quarter of the city had its own subculture, and there were bourgeois who continued to take their meals according to the old timetable. The Marais, for instance, was "a separate province that has nothing to do with Paris proper, and its inhabitants are in general less familiar with things Parisian than are the citizens of Quimperlé or Castelnaudary."[85] The judgment would be repeated a quarter of a century later in Larousse's dictionary: "The resident of the Chaussée d'Antin hardly distinguishes any more between a *rentier* of the Marais and an impeccable notary from Carpentras. The Marais is now *la province* in the very heart of Paris."[86]

For the true Parisian the danger of provincial contagion was quite real. Just how dire was the risk? To answer the question we must hark back to a social practice that can be traced all the way back to seventeenth-century *préciosité*. "Society" implies the absence of any belatedness or backwardness, a permanent harmony between the individual and the emerging present, a perception of fashion even as it evolves, a firm grasp on ceaseless but ever-shifting currents. Social commerce flourishes in conversation, which feeds on the effects produced by reporting and commenting on fresh news. But commentary on the news is a senseless activity unless one is situated close to the source. *La province,* being remote from that source, is perforce reduced to awaiting eagerly the news from Paris, only to greet that news with commonplaces and "retarded humor."[87] It is difficult if not impossible to be witty in Sancerre.

Delphine Gay had some intelligent things to say on this subject in the "Paris Mailbag" column she published in *La Presse.* The purpose of the column was precisely to provide the frustrated provincial with brief reports on Parisian fashion. According to Gay, a brief stay in the provinces was enough to create a dangerous gap. "We no longer feel in harmony with the ideas of the moment. Society seems wildly strange when one returns to it after a lengthy absence." "We arrive...and are soon asking what we should do, what we should see, what we should say, because we are as ignorant as can be about the interests of Parisians." "This is because Parisian life is a study that takes years" and implies "the habit of society." "What rock did you crawl out from under?" people ask the Parisian who has stayed away from the capital too long. "*It's impossible to talk to you any more.*"[88] It will take "many days to regain that tireless activity, that elasticity of character, that agility of judgment, that constant presence of mind, that perpetual courage in every detail that constitutes the Parisian intelligence."

Here I must digress a moment. These words were written during the July Monarchy, a time when the necessities of parliamentary politics actually tightened the links between Paris and the provinces. The *doctrinaires,* following Guizot, hoped that through representative government the nation would transform itself and produce new elites at an accelerated pace, drawing even upon the masses buried in the depths of *la province.*[89] In fact, this decanting of the superior portion of the provincial population more than ever required a metamorphosis of the provincial.

Political convictions aside, the Chamber consisted of three types of deputies. The first was the Parisian who seduced a small provincial town, the seat of an electoral district. An immeasurable distance separated this deputy from his constituents. For the time being the elected representative felt no need to tailor himself to fit the provincial mold. The voters of less fortunate districts did not need to be seduced. They deliberately chose representatives already belonging to the national elite, men close to the center of power and ready to serve as mediators.[90] Saint-Marc-Girardin never lifted a finger to please the loyal voters of Saint-Yrieix; prefects complained bitterly about this. Émile de Girardin—to confine ourselves to examples from the Limousin[91]—seems to have been a perfect stranger to Bourganeuf, which he served as deputy.[92]

The restoration of universal suffrage in March 1848 made it necessary for would-be deputies to appeal to the voters. Many aristocrats who lived in the Faubourg Saint-Germain and who in the past had simply gone through the motions of enduring from time to time a brief provincial exile now found it opportune to emulate the example of Alexis de Tocqueville, who cultivated the sympathies of voters residing in the district where he had his estates.[93] Meanwhile, the leaders of the Club des Clubs and later the Montagnards again sent eloquent speakers on missions into the vast heathen territory of *la province*. This soon provided the capital's vaudeville with new comic material, as it treated, in what could only be a derisory manner, the spread of Parisian political fashions and debates to provincial territory.[94]

The second type of deputy in the Chamber was the man who, though a provincial native, was nevertheless possessed of talent. After undergoing a virtually instantaneous metamorphosis, he joined cabinets, participated in central political debates, infiltrated the networks of power, patronage, and intrigue, and if need be manipulated elections. For such a figure the crucial talent was oratorical eloquence, which made it possible to stand out in a Chamber packed with ridiculous provincials but dominated by powerful speakers. Men such as Berryer, Guizot, and Lamartine turned the Chamber into an important place on the social circuit, one of the most fertile sources of conversational material. In the evening, assiduous frequentation of this or that salon allowed these renowned speakers to consolidate their successes on the podium.

The third type of deputy was the *notable de clocher*, the local worthy who managed to win an election and thus became the oafish bourgeois deputy who fell asleep in the Chamber beneath Daumier's ferocious gaze and who was a regular fixture at the mirth-provoking "bust-ups" (*cohues*) that made the Tuileries and the *hôtel de ville* under the July Monarchy places that society ladies were loath to visit.[95] Under the Second Republic the ranks of these anonymous provincials would be swelled by the kinds of *candidats ambulants* ("carpetbaggers" in American parlance) and *orateurs de tréteaux* (tinpot gasbags) at whom Tocqueville poked fun.[96] In 1852, however, the Prince-President and his friends introduced reform: they reduced the number of deputies, eliminated the speaker's podium, and prohibited public debate in the Corps Législatif.

During the first half of the nineteenth century, the established relationship between Paris and *la province*, through its profound impact on countless individuals and subtle portrayal and analysis in fiction, gained in both refinement and depth. For a particularly illuminating example of the richness of this experience and the inter-action between reality and fiction, we may turn to the *Mémoires* of Marie Cappelle.

Marie, having been born into the aristocracy of Picardy, spent many years in Parisian society before being exiled to the depths of the Limousin at the age of twenty-three. A cultivated though not very wealthy orphan, she felt nothing but contempt, occasionally tempered by pity, for the boorish fellow she was obliged to marry, a man by the name of Lafarge. Accused of poisoning her husband with arsenic and sentenced to life in prison, she recounted her sad experience of provin-cial life.

Her case was unusual, and her knowledge of *la province* went far beyond that of any tourist. Through marriage Marie Lafarge joined a provincial clan. She was obliged to endure the horrifying experience that Dorine had promised Marianne: social intercourse with the petty bourgeoisie of Tulle and Uzerche. Anxious to exonerate herself, Marie hoped to move her Parisian readers to pity by feeding them stereotypes of the fictional small town. The tactic was evidently effective, because this "poor flower lost among the brutes of the Limousin" won the sympathy of Parisian society.[97]

La province as she described it was by no means *la campagne*. In portraying the peasants and blacksmiths of the village adjacent to her manor, the sinister Glandier, Marie adopts an idyllic tone. She is careful not to disparage the few aristocratic châteaux in the vicinity: these she described as oases of Parisianness, places where good manners flourished and where she was able to sample the pleasures of "return-ing to the civilized world."[98] A few talented bourgeois, such as the attractive attor-ney Lachaud, who so brilliantly managed Marie's defense, also escape her scathing commentary. By contrast, the lengthy visits to Uzerche immediately after her mar-riage are recounted as though they were tantamount to a Sadeian torture. Marie Lafarge experienced a sense of extreme strangeness upon discovering the bour-geoisie of that small town and all the "incredible new things" surrounding it.[99]

To begin with, she was flabbergasted by the uncivilized and archaic customs: "I was shocked by the things I was obliged to see and hear." The local manners are rudimentary at best: guests are received in the kitchen, hugs are exchanged, no tea is served, the *tête de veau* is served *au naturel,* wine is offered as a refreshment. But this "degree zero" of civility is less appalling than the content of the conversation, or "Correzian chatter," as she calls it. The women unabashedly discuss the quality of the silver and question her about her servant's wages and the price of her clothes; they shamelessly question her husband about the size of her dowry. At night, at what passes for a ball, these scarlet women "could neither appreciate nor understand my simple gown of India muslin trimmed with twine."

Tulle, like Uzerche, utterly lacked a social life: "There is no society; everyone stays home and entertains no one else." The tragic setting is thus subtly portrayed.

Le Parisien passe avec dédain devant les monts d'Auvergne, magnifiques mais entièrement peuplés de porteurs d'eau, au dire des voyageurs.

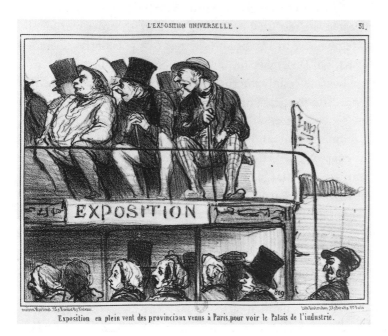

Exposition en plein vent des provinciaux venus à Paris, pour voir le Palais de l'industrie.

FIGURE 11.4 Veyron, *The Parisian in the Provinces;* lithograph, circa 1860. The caption reads: "The Parisian disdainfully drives past the mountains of Auvergne, which are magnificent but, to hear the travelers tell it, populated exclusively by water carriers."

FIGURE 11.5 Daumier, *The Exposition Universelle;* lithograph, 1855.

The sense of stifling imprisonment transmitted to the reader is more persuasive than a lengthy plea. The text successfully conveys a sense of the Paris-*province* cleavage that is the subject of this essay; it shows just how disorienting the distance between Parisian society and small-town provincial society could be.

The gap was again reshaped in the second half of the century. The restoration of universal male suffrage and the slow process of familiarization with the new political system altered the Paris-*province* relationship yet again by raising a challenge to Paris's imperial domination over what *la province* now implied, namely, the rest of France. The problem was keenly felt as early as February 1848, when the provisional government was being formed. Lamartine, Garnier-Pagès, Marrast, Marie, and Dupont de l'Eure felt that the establishment of the Republic ought to be ratified by the provinces. Lamartine prepared a proclamation to that effect. Louis Blanc, Ledru-Rollin, Albert, and Flocon, on the other hand, felt that Paris was sovereign in this instance and that the rest of the country, less politically aware, had no right to undo what the people of the capital had decided. If Louis Blanc is to be taken at his word, he carried the day because he enjoyed the backing of armed revolutionaries.[100]

The subsequent introduction of universal suffrage, however, transferred political predominance to the provinces as early as April 1848. The suppression of the June riots in Paris reflected the rest of the country's desire for order and for the defense of republican legitimacy; by this point "the rest of the country" included the suburbs of Paris itself. On December 10, Louis Napoleon Bonaparte's election as president of the Republic was rightly interpreted, by no less a commentator than Karl Marx himself, as proof of the peasantry's new role in politics.[101] In December 1851, while the "yellow gloves" hissed at Louis Napoleon on the boulevards, thirteen départements constituting what might be called *la province rouge* rose in rebellion at the news of the coup d'état, as if the domination of the provinces by Paris was about to be overturned. Ted Margadant has shown that the insurgency flourished in the very same small towns, many of them subprefectures, that figured so prominently in contemporary fiction: Béziers, Bédarieux, Clamecy, Marmande, Forcalquier.[102] After September 4, 1870, Paris would no longer be able to make and unmake political regimes. Thanks to universal suffrage, *la province*—here defined as the rest of France—slowly asserted its power over the nation as a whole. Through the ballot box on February 8, 1871, and then, in late May, through its support of the army, *la province*, the guardian of legitimacy, overcame the revolutionary desires of a considerable segment of Parisian society.[103] It would of course be a mistake to analyze these episodes in terms of the perception of the Paris-*province* gap as it existed in an earlier period. In such tumultuous times, the vast majority of Parisian "society" is apt to discover that, despite internal divisions on both sides (especially among youths), class-consciousness militates in favor of unity with the previously reviled *province*.

Meanwhile, however, new developments helped to reinforce provincial fascination with "Parisian life" and thus increase the intervening social distance. The new railway system was designed expressly to serve the needs of the capital. The invention of the telegraph meant more rapid dissemination of the news. This, together with new modes of social control and a powerful national police (first organized during the Second Republic and completed under the Second Empire[104]), reinforced centralization. Haussmann's urban planning forced provincial city fathers eager to embark on projects of urban renewal to accept the Parisian model.[105] Paris, now the "city of grocery displays"[106]—one immense, illuminated shopwindow as well as the site of world's fairs in 1878, 1889, and 1900—adapted to the reign of the commodity.[107] Nowhere else were the rites of modernity so handsomely celebrated.

The exalted spectacle of the capital was further heightened by new ways of dramatizing power. During the Second Empire a cosmopolitan court was assembled. (The novelty of this court deserves further analysis.) The sovereign once more became the focal point of fashionable society. The process of senatorial nomination consecrated new symbols of superiority. Shows, parades, receptions for foreign guests, and birthday celebrations kept the streets noisy. This extroversion, spurred on by artists who anticipated the image of the modern city[108] while decried by republicans who viewed the "imperial feast" with austere contempt, altered both the trope of provinciality and the image of "Parisian life," whose animation it revealed. The primacy of the private sphere gradually gave way to immodestly ostentatious rites and pleasures.

Hundreds of thousands of provincials flocked to Paris for the "Expo," the *caf' conc'* (or *café-concert*, which provided music hall entertainment along with drinks), and the funeral of Victor Hugo. First Carnot and then Loubet invited all the mayors of France to vast federational banquets. In an era fascinated by exploration, a trip to Paris was like a tour of the world. The 1860s clearly marked a major turning point in the history of the desire inspired by the capital. The tendency, prevalent in all fields in the 1880s, to adopt a pedagogical attitude only temporarily slowed the convergence of the city with the idea of hedonism, preparing the way for the excesses of the Belle Époque, which in symbolic terms was perceived as an essentially Parisian phenomenon.

New techniques of fascination perpetuated the contrast. Compared with the hedonism of Paris, *la province* more than ever evoked images of hibernation. Cities were now ranked according to how "Parisian" they were, that is, how alive or dead. Hippolyte Taine, who traveled throughout "greater France," took morose pleasure in provincial mustiness. Listen to him describe Poitiers, which he knew well from having spent considerable time there: "Narrow, twisting streets, steeply sloped, with old cobblestones and grass growing in the gaps between, punctuated every so often by a street lamp whose light trails off into the night, lugubrious blackness, a dismal solitude after eight o'clock and more often than not all day long...carriage gates on hinges that seem frozen in place, moss between stones, silence, and a vague impression of countless stale, cloistered lives." "One would not feel more alone in a city that had died at a single stroke, that had been caught unawares and emptied of inhabitants by some sudden epidemic." "The temperament of the region is flabby and inert," and "this species of moral inertia is painted on people's faces," including the "stupid and ignorant" faces of the young.[109] For Taine, *la province* meant the "attenuation of the individual," who was condemned to "kill time."[110]

The theme of social fragmentation would remain a stereotype until well into the twentieth century. François Mauriac was still harping on it as recently as 1964: the provinces, according to him, were ignorant of the pleasures of conversation and of "enrichment through closeness to others."[111] For the owner of the country estate Malagar, provincial life meant first of all "bitter separation from society" and therefore an obligatory retreat into home and family. Here the hypertrophy of the private, the secret, contrasts with the extroversion of the capital. The theme forms a leitmotif in the work not only of Mauriac but also of André Maurois and Marcel Arland, but it was Hervé Bazin who finally exhausted the last of its possibilities.

Meanwhile, the tragic figure of the fictional *province* took on dark new tones: *la province* was a place where people "knew how to hate," the stamping ground of long-nursed vengeance as well as violent desire. Here things moved slowly enough for an individual to be "more apt to hear the groaning of his flesh."[112] Accordingly, there is in Mauriac's work a moral frontier separating Paris from *la province*.

All of these feelings were intensified by an objective reality: the rural exodus. It was not only the peasantry that was affected but also the aristocracy, which, as Michel Denis has shown in the case of Mayenne, suffered from declining rents.[113] Toward the end of the nineteenth century many nobles abandoned their châteaux for good, some to try their luck in the colonies or other exotic places, others to live in nearby cities, and still others to embark on a career in the army or diplomacy or simply to squander what remained of their fortune in the whirl of Parisian life. The respectable rural and small-town bourgeoisie, a favorite target of parody in the fiction of an earlier period, was also affected. Further study is needed in order to shed light on the mobility of this group, which found it increasingly difficult to survive on its inherited capital. Taken together, the many varieties of exodus further impoverished *la province*, nipped early stirrings of a more animated social life in the bud, led to the closing of theaters, hindered the spread of learned societies, and, more irrevocably than before, consigned the cultivated elite to the secondary task of reproducing what was created elsewhere. René Bazin, who traveled in the provinces in 1893 at the behest of the *Journal des débats*, stressed the "decadence" of local societies, the decline of "social life in the evenings," and, more generally, the thinning of audiences.[114] By the end of the century, while rural villages, disencumbered of the heavy burden of poor laborers, were enjoying a revival of solidarity and a new wealth of organizations, festivals, and recreational activities, many small provincial towns languished and withered, looking forward to the day when Poincaré would threaten to deprive them of their subprefectures.

Meanwhile, the lengthening of vacations did nothing to lower the barriers between Capital and *province* but actually increased the intervening social distance. The ostentatious presence in isolated places of a Parisian society eager to witness the spectacle of nature but still indifferent toward if not contemptuous of *la province* stirred envy and heightened irritation. As the habit of vacationing spread to all segments of society, the Paris-*province* split became firmly rooted in the social subconscious. The Parisian cousin instilled a sense of social distance even in the peasantry. *La campagne*, the countryside, was provincialized. Maids and nannies who returned to their native villages brought with them a longing for the capital, images of which furnished their dreams. The wife of the rural town grocer emulated the doctor's wife by employing the services of one of the seamstresses whose numbers proliferated as women's magazines popularized "patterns" based on the latest Paris fashions. Once a *campagnarde*, she became a *provinciale*.

On the Parisian scene the ethnotype changed as well. "The old-fashioned, suspicious provincial who arrives in Paris with one hand on his watch, the other on his double pockets, and who, whether riding in a carriage or sitting in a theater, eyes his neighbors anxiously in the belief that since leaving Faucigny-les-Oies his every movement has been followed by a gang of thieves; who resolves never to sleep in his bed at the inn and who comes down with a fever and colic the day after arriving by the Messageries Laffitte et Caillard; who dares not mingle with the crowd or stop in front of a shop or enter a restaurant and who is swallowed up in the Parisian tempest without comprehending what it is all about—that provincial is virtually nonexistent nowadays except in the memory of habitués of the Palais-Royal or the Variétés."[115] Provincials no longer experienced the fear of visiting the capital that once drove them to draw up their wills before departing.

Many provincials keen to discover Paris were now willing to content themselves with a brief visit, a sort of pilgrimage. All they hoped was to catch an external glimpse of the city in all its brilliance. Unlike the ambitious youth of old, most no longer hoped to penetrate to the city's secret core, access to which remained difficult. They did not aspire to visit the laboratory from which Parisianness radiated. Often they came in groups, traveling on pleasure trains. In Paris "they talked of home even as they trod the asphalt pavement; they brought Carpentras with them."[116]

This ridiculous touristification, which Labiche mocked in *La Cagnotte*, produced a new comic figure to light up the pages of the ordinarily serious *Dictionnaire Larousse*. Paris in fact continued to rely on the same tactics to keep its distance and

FIGURE 11.6 *The 1900 Banquet of Mayors—View Inside the Huge Tent Set Up in the Tuileries on September 22*. The inset shows President Loubet reading his speech, flanked by Waldeck-Rousseau, Fallières, and Deschanel. The Third Republic took root because it managed to capture the sense of locality and weave together distinct regional identities. Here, the provinces came to Paris in a spirit of fraternity linking the mayors of all the country's *communes*.

even widen the gap. Listen to the prestigious dictionary's description of the new influx of tourists. Provincials now poured in through the capital's railway stations. It was a strange new *species* that stepped onto the station platforms, a species admirably symbolized by "the rubicund gentleman arriving on the train from Bordeaux." Drunk with desires inspired by the tales of "cousin Michel" and keen to have stories of his own to tell upon his return, he scurried about with his heart aflutter and "bulging eyes" firmly fixed on the ladies' ankle-boots. For him, Paris, the Great Babylon, meant above all *Fââmes* (women). The eroticization of the capital's image increased between 1860 and 1900, as manners loosened and clandestine prostitution spread. For the provincial on a binge, Paris was *the* place to go to escape from social and marital constraints, the ever-fascinating theater of moral decompression. The rentier dreamed of the house of assignation.[117] Montmartre, the capital of pleasure, shaped the provincial's very idea of hedonism. Less well-known singers from the Parisian cafés-concerts brought fashionable tunes to the music halls of Carcassonne and thus revived the traditional folksongs of Aude valley workers.[118]

FIGURE 11.7   Félix Vallotton, *The Café, or the Provincial* (1909). The timid provincial has come to be devoured. He is about to become the victim of a woman of Paris, symbolically more a sphinx than a creature of dreams.

Parisian tourism took on a certain ritual quality. This calmed visitors' anxieties but made each visit less of an individual adventure. The provincial tourist tended to follow a fixed schedule and itinerary: a dinner for forty-five sous at the Palais-Royal; a visit to the Invalides, the Vendôme column, and the Jardin des Plantes; some purchases from the stalls of La Belle Jardinière; and the "odd encounter with the orphan girl willing to let a stranger buy her a ticket to *L'Ambigu*"[119] taught the hesitant hayseed a thing or two about the ways of the big city. A brief stay in Paris taught the provincial visitor a whole new scale of sizes, values, and ranks. He experienced Paris, our dictionary tells us, as a "vast diminution of himself." He suffered a "kind of annihilation." Discovering the national sphere tended to relativize provincial hierarchies. It was a changed individual who returned home "with a little of the mud of our advanced civilization sticking to the soles of his shoes." In short, according to Larousse, the chief result of the trip to Paris was a heightened awareness of an infinite distance.

Meanwhile, however, a provincial riposte was being elaborated, the nature and effectiveness of which we would do well to measure. One positive new factor was a growing reluctance to disparage *la province*. The authors of the articles in *Larousse*, though subtle analysts of the cleavage that concerns us here, worked hard to deny its very existence. To take them at their word, the Revolution established national unity and thus abolished the provinces; *la province* simultaneously ceased to exist. The word remained as an archaic artifact of language. Obviously the republicans, whose most solid bastion was for a long time Paris, had plenty of reasons until well into the summer of 1871 to display bitterness toward a rural and provincial France that had first sustained the Empire and then elected conservatives.[120] They nevertheless felt a certain embarrassment at accepting the old cleavage, which first came to prominence, after all, under the monarchy, as anything other than an outdated, amusing, and on the whole nonsensical relic of the past.

This new sensibility emerged just as counter-images, developed by regional elites determined to do battle against the imperialism of the Parisian gaze, were coming into their own.[121] Let us pause for a moment to examine a minor, relatively late example of this effort of rehabilitation. In 1874, J. F. Daniel, a historian from Landerneau, protested against the connotation that his city's name had taken on in common parlance. He attempted to prove that "over the past few centuries" the city had been the oldest in the province and the place where the prominent men of the region gathered. Already "mired in luxury and pleasure" in the seventeenth century, it was seen as the "Sybaris of Brittany on the eve of the Revolution."[122] Thus nothing could be famous unless it was known in Landerneau. "In speaking of something memorable, people said, then as now, that it will cause a stir in Landerneau, a common expression that has no intrinsic meaning."[123] This use of history as justification, this mistaken fabrication of a prestigious etymology intended to draw the sting of mockery, to stand the contemptuous jibe on its head, was a common provincial tactic. Was it not said in Limousin that M. de Pourceaugnac, forced to emigrate during the Revolution, had never returned, and that people were glad of it? The reference to luxury and pleasure in the implicit argument is also significant: J. F. Daniel borrows these elements of superiority from the description of the capital in order to protect Landerneau from mockery.

Somewhat later, when scholars began meticulously recording the tales and rituals of folklore, other historians would attribute the popular expression to the fact that Landerneau was regularly the scene of the raucous popular demonstrations known as charivaris.[124] On "Low Sunday after vespers, blindfolded men with clubs would smash various kinds of earthenware pottery hung from ropes in the town's squares."[125] Until 1920 or so, the mayor and other prominent citizens used to march through the streets to the sound of drums collecting money for the poor while shouting *en guin an ed*. It was argued, in other words, that "the stir in Landerneau" was simply a matter of fidelity to ancient customs.

Certain malevolent Parisians, among them the author of the article in *Larousse*, suggested that the raucousness of Landerneau's charivaris was a consequence of the large number of cuckolds in the city. Mockery was thus reinstated. In any case, noisy Landerneau became a tourist attraction. Charles Monselet admits to having set out from Paris to visit the Breton city on account of the popular expression. He was of the opinion that Landerneau's comic reputation stemmed from the moon affixed to the bell tower of its old church.[126] In short, the counterimage does not appear to have been totally effective in this case.

There were other kinds of rehabilitation as well. Following the vogue for the rustic novel (which enjoyed great popularity between 1836 and 1856), the rise of agrarian ideology[127] stimulated research into provincial identity and sharpened the fictional portrait of village life.[128] The agrarian movement, which flourished in the final decade of the nineteenth century under the progressives, and later under Vichy, relates to the subject of this essay only indirectly. Writers who sang the praises of the soil, including that champion of the extended family, René Bazin, as well as Gustave Thibon and Pierre L'Ermite, hoped to restore traditional values and structures and to tar Paris, the modern Babylon, with a black brush.[129] But this ideology, which extolled closeness to the forces of nature and called for closer bonds among the cosmic, the animal, the vegetal, and the human, was rooted more in ancient pastoral than in the themes of provinciality.

Nevertheless, the very scope and vigor of the agrarian movement paradoxically increased yet again the distance between Paris and *la province*. Agrarian ideology posed no threat to Parisian transcendence. It was the capital that chose the leading talents among the regionalist writers, bestowing a national renown on the few lucky enough to enjoy its favor.[130] Essentially nostalgic, the agrarian movement reinforced the identification of *la province* with the past and with conservatism. It gave an even firmer footing to old-fashioned values, customs, and attitudes and elicited a counterimage promoted most notably by Zola, Maupassant, and Huysmans. Once again the old disparaging stereotypes were reinterpreted. Far from the capital, the idle Parisian succumbed to boredom and slowly destroyed himself.[131]

At the end of the century, even as agrarian literature was triumphing in the provinces, the capital was feasting on mockery of the village mayor,[132] the village fireman,[133] the *piou-piou* ("doughboy"),[134] and, before long, the servant Bécassine.[135] These figures were attacked because for Parisians they embodied oafishness as well as rusticity. By 1880 new hygienic norms also tended to devalue the man of the soil.[136] In other words, as *la campagne* turned increasingly into *la*

FIGURES 11.8 AND 11.9   A naïve provincial girl goes to her death in the modern Babylon, the victim of its venomous pleasures, while rejection of the capital is rewarded by lucid happiness and a healthy life. Illustrations by Damblans.

province—by which I mean that the countryside increasingly opened itself up to the dream of Parisianness—it became the butt of ever more aggressive mockery.

Historians specializing in the Third Republic have long emphasized the growing influence of *la province* on political life. The gradual decline of the process of choosing official candidates, often selected in Paris, and of the efficacy of mediation by citizens of great prominence led, we are told, to a transfer of power to new provincial elites and the *nouvelles couches,* or new segments of the population, that they represented.[137] Indeed, Jean Estèbe has shown that the number of government ministers born in the provinces rose sharply between 1870 and 1914, while the relative number of Parisian ministers fell. Estèbe also showed what an important role politicians born in the south and east of France played in shaping the future of the Third Republic.[138] On the eve of World War I, Jules Lemaître, Jules Delafosse, and the Quercy native Maurice Colrat attacked the outsized political influence of the Midi.[139] In Parisian circles passions were further heightened by the feeling on the part of traditional elites that they had somehow been shoved aside. These displaced wheeler-dealers were strongly critical of provincial deputies who, unlike the provincials who had served as intermediaries in an earlier period, had ceased, so they believed, to partake of Parisianness.

Christophe Charle, meanwhile, has shown how the "political-administrative sys-tem" composed of ministers, prefects, and high magistrates—all elite groups affected by republican purges—was also provincialized.[140] Candidates were thus obliged to take more care than before in demonstrating their compliance with local customs; they had to assume the characteristic traits of an ethnotype, to prove their provinciality. There is no denying that these things were true at a time when, owing to the absence of party organizations, deputies were forced to rely on personal con-tacts to "hold" their districts.[141]

But was the fundamental configuration of the Paris-*province* relationship altered as a result? No simple answer can suffice. New procedures ensured that the roads to success still passed through Paris. The École des Sciences Politiques, the Inspection des Finances, the Conférence du Stage, and the ministerial staff appointment became the approved stepping-stones to political careers. In addition, Parisian con-tacts became increasingly essential, and Parisian salons and high society remained as important as ever. Sons born into politically prominent provincial families were henceforth obliged, Gilles le Béguec points out, to take a detour by way of Paris. It was more important than in the past for the future politician to legitimate his posi-tion by acquiring the proper credentials. The result was the establishment of subtle interlocking networks "based on a complex system of provincial support and Parisian contacts."[142] What is more, the provincialization of the political elite was countered by the Parisianization of the upper civil service (the Conseil d'État, Cour des Comptes, ministerial chiefs of staff, and Ponts et Chaussées) and, even more dramatically, of the economic elites, which now contributed much more than in the past to the animation of Paris society.[143] Paris reaped the benefits of the centraliza-tion of large businesses and the common practice of private companies' hiring for-mer top civil servants. Meanwhile, the intellectual elite avoided provincialization altogether. Paris remained the culmination of every career. While it is true that many engineers who graduated from the *grandes écoles* married provincial women, this was because, as recent graduates, they were assigned to the least attractive posts, those located far from the capital.

At the beginning of the twentieth century as in the past, no debate of national importance could begin anywhere but in Paris. *La province* merely reinterpreted what the capital invented. As seen from Paris, national issues recast in local terms seemed to lose some of their dignity.

Central to our topic in this connection were organizations of provincials living in the capital. It takes some time to appreciate the importance of these mediating bodies, which have often been interpreted as representing a form of provincial revenge. At the end of the nineteenth century entire districts of the capital were given over to Auvergnats, Limousins, Bretons, and Rouergats. People from these groups saw each other socially; they published their own newspapers and ran their

FIGURE 11.10   Groups of provincials living in the capital popularized folkloric images of their native regions, while, conversely, anything that sharpened the contrast with the provinces made Paris that much more distinctive. Poster by Le Mouël for the Exposition of Bretons of Paris, 1895.

own employment offices; they organized celebrations of holidays and banquets and helped families realize their matrimonial strategies.[144] Gone were the days when the provincial who came to settle in the capital could be seen as a lonely victim, an exile from his native land. People now looked to their provincial roots with a kind of vague nostalgia fostered by extended vacations, but such feelings were far less intense than the homesickness of a previous generation of immigrants.

To be sure, the president of a group of "Limousins de Paris" could help to mediate between Paris and the home province. Such groups turned mockery into a force for mobilization and helped change the provincial image. But at the same time they insidiously reinforced the ascendancy of the capital and ensured the continued disqualification of provincial elites. They allowed certain Parisians to claim provinciality on ancestral grounds; they sometimes chose local candidates and helped "carpetbaggers" win elections back home. Gilles le Béguec has shown, for example, how Correzians living in Paris influenced political life in their native region.[145] Associations of provincials living in Paris sometimes allowed candidates to claim counterfeit provincial roots, enabling outsiders to defeat entrenched local elites. In 1964, François Mauriac went so far as to assert that the provinces had no way of taking stock of themselves other than from the vantage point of Paris.[146]

Le Béguec's extensive research has also established the growing political influence of Parisian lawyers during the period between the two world wars, along with the declining influence of their colleagues in the provinces. Broadly speaking, Le Béguec's work points up the gradual decline of local elites in the face of a new model of political competence, a model exemplified by the remarkable success enjoyed by veterans of the Paris bar's Conférence du Stage.

In the meantime, however, many journalists remained blind to the capital's growing role. Jacques Fourcade, for one, helped to perpetuate the hoary stereotype of the "provincial Republic" by publishing a series of essays under that title in *Le Temps*. In these articles he portrayed *la province* as a place of pure opinions and strong views. Once elected, however, the "party men...shed their doctrinaire opinions much as sheep leave their wool on the brambles along their path." Periodically, therefore, they must "plunge back into their districts," where they are once more caught in "the vise-like grip of their electoral clientele."[147] Fourcade's derisory portrait of political life as perceived from a small-town Café du Commerce only helped to shore up Parisian predominance. His work perpetuated the satirical portrait of the hapless provincial deputy proud of his southern accent, such as Claudius Pégomas in Édouard Pailleron's *Les Cabotins* or Arnaud Tripier in Octave Mirbeau's *Foyer*, both published before World War I.

Over the past thirty years, *la province* has become more sensitive and Paris has learned to moderate its tone. Disparaging references to the provinces are no longer as tolerated as they once were. *La province* has benefitted from this new sensitivity. The very term is becoming obsolete. Mail slots in Parisian post offices no longer distinguish between Paris and *province;* now there are three slots rather than two, marked, respectively, Paris, *banlieue* (suburbs), and *autres départements*.

Nevertheless, many traces of the old stereotypes remain. They are faithfully preserved in the standard dictionaries. For example, the *Grand Larousse de la langue française* (1976 edition) borrows this definition from a 1935 edition of the dictionary published by the Académie: "*Province*. Invar. adj. Fam. and pej. Said of a person or thing whose characteristics contrast with the refinement, elegance, or vivacity typical of the capital. 'Il a un air province; il est très province.' " Or this: "*Provincial*. Noun (1640. Guez de Balzac), sometimes pejorative.... Elsa Triolet: 'fatigués des provinciaux même quand ce sont des intellectuels [tired of provincials even when they are intellectuals].' " In other words, the provincial is no longer an object of laughter, at least not openly, but he can be portrayed as a person who thinks, acts, and expresses himself without grace or genuine distinction, a person who bores or tires the Parisian and elicits her pity.

Indeed, behind the emergence of new sensitivities associated with a restructuring of the realm of decency, there has been a profound transformation that, once again, has reshaped the old cleavage without abolishing it.

Leaving aside the counterfeit provinciality associated with certain vacation spots (Deauville, Avignon, Aix, Cannes), cities eager for cultural decentralization (such as Grenoble, Lyons, Toulouse, and Tours) have tried, not without success, to create for themselves an image capable of rivaling that of the capital. The delay involved in the transmission of information is dwindling, and this was once a fundamental factor in establishing the Paris-*province* split. The media carry the news simultaneously to everyone, thereby tending to Parisianize the totality of the national territory. Provinces once obliged to await anxiously the arrival of the news can now revel in the delights of immediate commentary. There has been no concomitant abolition of the delay in the transmission of fashions, however.

This Parisianization of the provinces is counterfeit, however, insofar as the ready availability of information confers no corresponding power to initiate, to participate in the circles from which innovations emanate. Accordingly, Jean Planchais sees not an identification of *la province* with Paris but a gradual dissolution of the notion of *province* in the featureless expanse of "Greater Paris."[148] This is just another way of noting the continued concentration of the nation's elites in a capital now readily accessible from a good half of the territory. This new mode of domination is exemplified by the "turbo-prof" (who commutes to a provincial teaching job by high-speed rail) and the difficulties that universities in provincial cities such as Amiens, Reims, and Orléans face owing to the attraction of nearby Paris. Consciousness of the uniqueness of Paris remains acute. The tempo of life in the capital continues to be more rapid than elsewhere. *La province* and *la banlieue* (the suburbs) are still defined by a different relation to time, by the need that people residing there feel to justify their choice of residence, often, nowadays, by some form of ecological argument.

All in all, the most significant change in the relationship has been the result not so much of the promotion of *la province* as of challenges to the role and position of the capital. The decline in Parisian imperialism has gone hand in hand with a reduction of France's importance in the world, an internationalization of channels of information, and a broadening of debate to encompass the entire planet. The 1984 edition of *Le Grand Larousse* records the manifestation of these developments in the cultural sphere: "The Landerneau of something, said of a constricted environment closed in on itself and perpetually agitated by trivial squabbles: for example, 'le Landerneau de la littérature parisienne.' "

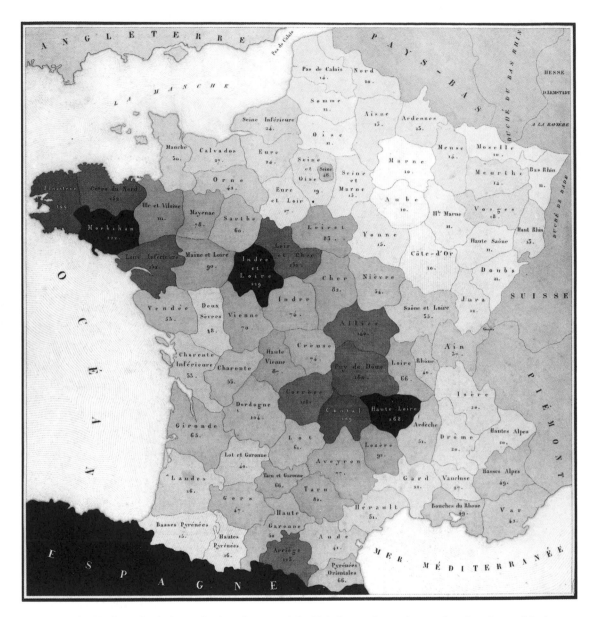

FIGURE 12.0 In 1826, Baron Dupin drew a line from Geneva to Saint-Malo "separating northern and southern France." On the map, "enlightened France" is all white, and "dark France" is gray and black. *Map Representing the Level of Education of the French Populace* (1826).

CHAPTER 12

The Saint-Malo–Geneva Line[1]

Roger Chartier

Over the past thirty years, few itineraries have been more traveled by French historians than that which leads from Saint-Malo to Geneva. Taking this journey has become a convenient way of pointing out the major contrasts between the two Frances that join along a line drawn between these two cities. On either side of this diagonal, which cuts the map of France in two, things appear to be different wherever one looks: whether at agrarian landscapes or at technology, at the distribution of communication or of manufacturing, at individuals' heights and weights or their mastery of the written word. The litany of such disparities, doggedly extended over the years, has revealed the contrast between northern and southern France as an enduring phenomenon, and one whose effects are often still perceptible.[2] Compiling and comparing new or refined indices—or both—is thus a permanently essential requirement for anyone who would bolster or, more recently, challenge this basic division of French national territory.[3]

Here, however, I shall take a different tack: my purpose will be to survey past perceptions of France in order to understand how, at various points in time, people conceived of the country's differential geography. In examining the (no doubt incomplete) evidence, I was guided by two fundamental concerns. First, I hoped to shed light on our national heritage: the "two-France" motif is by no means a recent invention, nor is it the work of historians. Tracing its genealogy can thus help to clarify the ideological factors that allowed it to emerge and that it in turn reinforced. Second, the study of geographical representations is an excellent way to demonstrate how the development of the social sciences was linked to the political and economic debates that absorbed the French elite from Louis XV to Louis-Philippe. Understanding how and why a divided France was constructed can give us a better grasp of what progress meant and what stakes it involved. Hence I have chosen to work backward in time, emphasizing first the period of the July Monarchy, during which the "two-France" theme triumphed in a variety of forms, then moving on to the second half of the eighteenth century in order to pinpoint the various groups that first became conscious of meaningful spatial divisions within the kingdom's boundaries, while at the same time examining the question of why interest in the theme at that time remained limited.

The history of a divided France began in 1822, buried in the pages of a book by the prolific Italian geographer Adrien Balbi. In volume two of his *Essai statistique sur le royaume de Portugal et d'Algarve comparé aux autres états de l'Europe* he included an excursus on the French monarchy's efforts to establish public schools, which was accompanied, without comment, by a table indicating the number of pupils and faculty in royal and communal secondary, primary, and boarding schools in each academic district. These figures were then compared with the population of each district in 1821.[4] Twenty years before Villemain,[5] this compilation thus offered a new statistical indicator, for which Balbi received due credit, as in this appreciation offered by Guerry in 1832: "This work by the learned Venetian geographer contains the first published documents concerning the state of public instruction."[6] Published but not exploited: indeed, it was Konrad Malte-Brun, a Danish geographer who settled in France during the Empire, who was the first, in a review published in the *Journal des débats*, to use Balbi's figures to think about geographical contrasts in France.[7]

What made Malte-Brun's innovation possible was the fact that the academic statistics fell neatly into two broadly homogeneous groups. By comparing the number of boys in school at various levels to the size of the male population, Malte-Brun discovered that "if we divide France into two parts, one to the north and east, the other to the south and west (and excluding, if you will, Paris), we have two very different results." In the first area, which contained twelve academies per thousand males, 123 boys for every thousand males attended school; in the second, with thirteen academies per thousand males, only 49 boys per thousand males were in school. From these data emerged this fundamental diagnosis: "Public education in southern and western France is to that in the North and East as 1 is to 2′." Malte-Brun's article did not indicate any clear boundary between the two Frances whose educational systems were so disparate; indeed, he included in the totals for northern and eastern France the academies of Orléans, Lyons, and Grenoble, veritable outposts in southern territory. But he had taken the crucial step: that of construing provincial or regional inequalities as a dichotomy. Rather than subdivide the perception of differences into a myriad of small contrasts, a clearly decipherable and rationally treatable order had been constructed.

Malte-Brun not only originated the basic division of the country into two parts but also touched on a number of themes that would figure in the work of later thinkers. To begin with, he situated France in a European context: "We would never have imagined that several parts of southern and western France stood at the level of some of the least-schooled countries in Europe, while the north of France is progressing shoulder-to-shoulder with the most civilized countries in the world." Because the line that divided Europe thus passed through France, the kingdom could be taken as a microcosm, in which contrasts that existed throughout the continent could be studied on a smaller scale. In his discussion of Austria, moreover, Malte-Brun reiterated the conviction of certain Enlightenment writers that improvements in education were linked to a decline in criminality: "Certain recent administrative reports note with pleasure that the number of crimes decreases in proportion to the increase in the number of primary schools." So far as Malte-Brun was concerned, however, this observation, which would later become controversial, was not of crucial importance. What mattered most to him was the relation between education and "administration." The effective use of power depended on a certain social homogeneity, but the figures showed that France was by no means uniform and that vast cultural disparities existed between provinces. Politicians, he cautioned, should pay heed to these differences, which careful study showed to be systematic rather than random.

In 1826, Baron Charles Dupin traced the frontier that divided the two Frances identified by Malte-Brun. Having marked on a map for each *département* the ratio of the population to the number of male primary school pupils, he made the following point at a lecture delivered at the Conservatoire des Arts et Métiers:

> Note the dark line that runs from Geneva to Saint-Malo, which separates northern from southern France. North of this line one finds only thirty-two départements and thirteen million inhabitants; south of it, fifty-four départements and eighteen million inhabitants. The thirteen million inhabitants of the north send 740,846 young people to school; the eighteen million inhabitants of the south send 375,931 pupils to school. It follows that, for every million inhabitants, the north of France sends 56,988 children to school, and the south, 20,885. Thus primary instruction is three times as extensive in the north as in the south.[8]

Charles Dupin was thus the inventor of a line that was to receive a great deal of attention in subsequent years, but for which another man would receive the credit. He was also the first to designate the northern part of the country as "enlightened France"[9] and, somewhat later, the south as "dark France." His text, less innovative perhaps than has sometimes been claimed, calls for two remarks. First, it shifted the ground of the debate over popular education from the political to the economic. For Malte-Brun, the value of elementary education as a "means of civilization" ultimately depended on the authority of the government: "Knowing how to read, march in a straight line, and shoot a rifle accurately are skills that, whether in a democracy or in a monarchy, can be either useful or dangerous, depending on whether the government does or does not know how to control the public mind." For Dupin, the significance of popular education was very different: it was the prerequisite for progress in general, both economic and intellectual. "Enlightened France" was in fact the richer of the country's two parts, as evidenced by taxes on both real estate and professional activities, as well as the more fertile in talent, as evidenced by the issuance of patents, the granting of degrees by Parisian *collèges*, admissions to the École Polytechnique, and the membership of the Académie des Sciences. The fact that the various indicators that Dupin examined yielded concordant results north and south of the decisive dividing line was sufficient to demonstrate the benefits of public education, which he proposed as a crucial factor in explaining the uneven economic development of the kingdom.

Although Dupin systematized the opposition of north and south, his lecture also proposed another spatial interpretation, one that would be somewhat neglected in *Forces productives et commerciales*. Southern and western France, it turns out, did not constitute a unified region: thirteen of his départements, in the regions of the Rhône, Languedoc, and the Pyrenees, constituted a "more industrious and opulent" section of the south because public education was "least backward" there.[10] This interpretation implicitly designated parts of Brittany, the Loire region, and central France as a less culturally and economically advanced zone, a dark wedge driven into a relatively enlightened region. This division, which contrasted an eastern France that penetrated southward proceeding from the English Channel toward the Mediterranean, with an Atlantic France that pushed far into the interior, would prove less successful than the contrast between north and south. Yet it did not go unnoticed, not only by Edward Fox,[11] but even earlier by Stendhal: "A minister of the interior interested in doing his job rather than engaging, as M. Guizot does, in intrigues with the king and in the Chambers would do well to ask for an allocation of two million a year for the purpose of raising the educational level of the population living in the fatal triangle bounded by Bordeaux, Bayonne, and Valence to equality with that of the rest of France."[12] But Dupin's success in quickly focusing attention on economic inequalities ultimately blurred this more subtle geography and established the dualist interpretation in its place.

Dupin devoted the sixth book of his great work, *Forces productives et commerciales de la France*, to a "Parallel of Northern France and Southern France with All of France," in which he treated the country's internal differentiation in terms of developmental models.[13] He correlated statistics published by Chaptal in 1819, as well as ones gleaned from various government agencies (such as the Contributions Indirectes, the Direction Générale des Forêts, and the Direction Générale des Mines), with the educational data and interpreted the results in much the same dualistic terms as in his lecture of the year before. In so doing, he raised a new question: How, in spatial terms, was the nation's economy organized? Previously, imperial administrators who relied on prefectural statistics had formulated their own conception of geography, which drew on two distinct modes of spatial representation, one sensitive to the infinite diversity of reality, the other firmly wedded to the idea of national unity.[14] In the summaries of J. Peuchet, prefectural statistics were presented in a series of juxtaposed descriptions of départements and regions; the data were never arranged so as to bring out broader internal contrasts in the empire as a whole.[15] By contrast, for Jean-Antoine Chaptal, the unitary vision was paramount: even if his figures were arranged in tables by département, his favorite descriptive categories were "everywhere" and "nowhere," indicative of a homogeneous conception of French territory.[16] Between these two extremes there was no room for thinking on an intermediate scale: differences were either dispersed in a host of local and départemental findings or aggregated into a portrait of national unity (now in the economic rather than the political sphere).[17] This observation helps to make clear what was new in the contribution of the Restoration "arithmeticians."

Reasoning in terms of the value of agricultural and industrial products, average income per inhabitant, and public revenues, Dupin concluded that northern France enjoyed an undoubted lead over southern France: the Saint-Malo (or Cherbourg)–Geneva Line clearly divided two distinct economic universes. Underlying this conclusion one can make out the broad outlines of an explanation based on three factors. First, northern France reaped the benefits of its natural advantages: at the beginning of book 7, for example, which is devoted to internal transport, Dupin stresses northern France's advantages in natural waterways and consequently in canals. But this factor could not have been decisive, because the south enjoyed natural advantages of its own, including a climate that permitted growing crops unsuited to the north.[18] Hence other factors were needed to account for the inequality in economic development. Dupin was discreet about one of them: history. On the problem of peasant income, he wrote: "The earnings of farmers in southern France are barely enough to keep them alive so long as they retain their strength and health, but if they fall ill or are injured or grow old, they sink into distress and can no longer support themselves or their families without private charity, the refuge of the hospital, or what have you. *Such was the deplorable situation of peasants everywhere in the kingdom prior to the Revolution*" (emphasis added).[19] Here the argument is based on history, moving from the determination of a disparity to a process of differentiation. History has stopped, as it were, along the Saint-Malo–Geneva line, and the nondevelopment of the south has become, owing to the progress of the north, a question of underdevelopment. The key to such an evolution is cultural: not only is elementary education more widely available in the north, scholastic competition is also harsher there. For every hundred pupils admitted to the royal *collèges* there were 15,980 children in primary schools in the north but only 6,931 in the south: "Thus subjects taken from the common class to be elevated to the superior schools are chosen from among a much larger group of competitors in the north than in the south. This, in my view, is the reason for the superiority of the northern French in letters, science, and the arts."[20] One might add, moreover, without being false to the spirit of Dupin's argument, that this superiority was limited to those activities and businesses dependent "not on the fertility of the land but on the knowledge of its inhabitants."

This pre-Darwinian version of "educational Darwinism" was Dupin's basic explanation for northern France's lead, and Dupin therefore held the north up as an example for his "compatriots of the south" to follow. The purpose of his two-volume work, *Forces productives et commerciales*, was thus to develop a model for those who ignored economic growth or had seen it pass them by. The work began on a solemn note: "Compatriots of the south, it is to you that I dedicate this description of northern France. For your generous emulation and reflective imitation I offer a model of one part of the realm."[21] He then takes his readers on an imaginary journey through the thirty-two *départements* on the more prosperous side of France's internal frontier. Their advantage is most evident in the area of industrial development, one result of which is inequality in the terms of trade between the two Frances:

Considerable trade flows between northern and southern France. The south sends huge quantities of wine, spirits, oil, livestock, wool, silk and silk products, and so on. In return it receives wrought iron in a thousand forms, objects of the goldsmith's art, jewels, fine furniture, woolens, spun and woven cotton, books, engravings, and many products of the arts. Thus the south ships primarily agricultural products, while the north ships mainly manufactured products to the south, some of which, such as woolens, are made in part of raw materials from the south.[22]

Dupin thus outlines one possible analysis of French inequalities in terms of the geography of underdevelopment. He cannot deduce all the corollaries of his thesis, however, because he sees the imbalance in the structure of trade between north and south not as the cause of the disparity between the two regions but merely as the symptom. For him, what matters most is not how the south is exploited by the north but rather how the north can set an example for the south to follow; the north's lead, as he sees it, can be imputed to the proximity of other advanced industrial nations. Northern France is "favored above all by the proximity of peoples advanced in industry and very happy in their institutions, such as the British, the Swiss, and the Batavians." By contrast, southern France's only neighbors are "the peoples of Spain and Portugal, Sardinia and Africa, long backward and degraded by bad laws and bad governments."[23] For Dupin, the two-France motif served to bolster a stirring plea in praise of manufacturing and celebration of parliamentary institutions. The model of development lay to the north, in England and Scotland, where a new and optimal equilibrium had been established between agricultural and industrial populations. By heeding the lessons of this example, northern France would enjoy still further progress and southern France would begin once more to move forward and close the gap. Once the surplus agricultural population was shifted into industry and public education became available to all, the Saint-Malo—Geneva line would disappear, and all of France, unriven by internal boundaries, would enjoy the benefits of England's good fortune.

The two opposed pairs, enlightened France and obscure France, prosperous France and poor France, were now joined by a third, which transformed the geography of values. The publication in 1827 of the first *Compte général de l'administration de la justice criminelle* introduced a new set of statistics into the picture, heightening the debate over the various "influences" likely to account for criminal behavior.[24] These new statistics were soon widely publicized, as evidenced by their inclusion in a pamphlet published in 1828 by Adrien Balbi under the title *La Monarchie française comparée aux principaux états du monde.*[25] Even more important, they became the basis of the new science of "moral statistics," which the Académie des Sciences in 1833 would "rank first among the branches of general statistics." It was in this area that the lawyer Guerry set out to do research that made him one of the first to explore the field of criminal geography.[26] Guerry proceeded to aggregate the data contained in the *Compte général* by using what he considered to be neutral geographic criteria: "We shall therefore divide France into five natural regions: the north, the south, the east, the west, and the center, each composed of seventeen contiguous *départements*. There is nothing arbitrary about this grouping, which does not favor any system, because it is entirely geometric, and the extent of each district is determined by that of the four others."[27] Guerry's plan is interesting for two reasons. First of all, his explanations are aimed at reconciling nature with geometry and at justifying a purely theoretical division of French territory, one that draws its lines in perfect freedom on a neutral surface with reference to a permanent feature, in this case, the obvious existence of "natural regions." In this we perceive a concern not unlike that of Dupin to identify his two Frances with what "our ancestors called the regions of *langue d'oïl* and *langue d'oc,*"[28] and perhaps also an echo of the tensions that had influenced the division of the country into *départements* in 1790.[29] The will to reshape space, whether by drawing boundaries on the ground or defining territories on a map, is hard put to it to deal with an absence of natural or historical guarantees. By dividing France into five parts, moreover, Guerry disturbed the simple symmetry of the Saint-Malo—Geneva line and the whole system of values that went along with it.

Indeed, the geography of criminal behavior, based on data taken from the *Compte général* for the years 1825 to 1830, turned out to be governed not by a single law but by different laws for each type of crime. In crimes against persons the south ranked

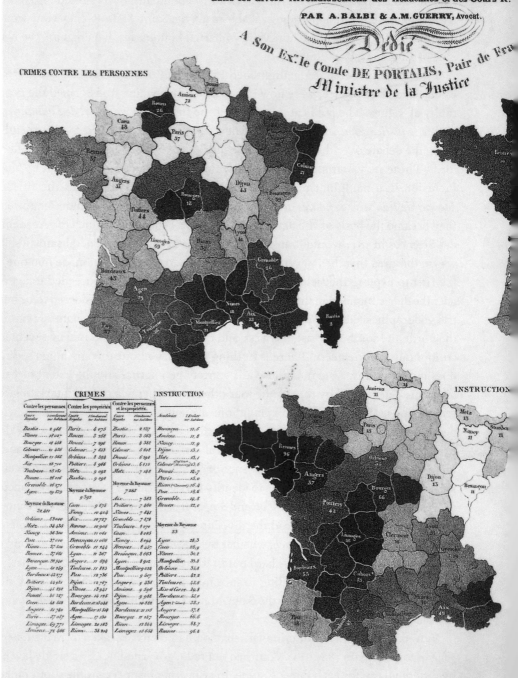

STATISTIQUE COMPAR[É]

DE L'ÉTAT DE L'INSTRUCTION ET DU NOMBRE

dans les divers Arrondissemens des Académies et des Cours R.

PAR A. BALBI & A. M. GUERRY, Avocat.

Dédié

A Son Ex. le Comte DE PORTALIS, Pair de Fra[nce]

Ministre de la Justice

CRIMES CONTRE LES PERSONNES

INSTRUCTION

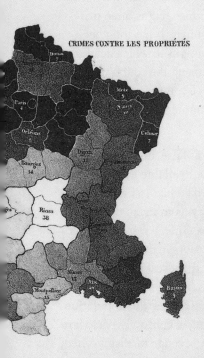

CRIMES CONTRE LES PROPRIÉTÉS

Les deux premières cartes présentent d'après le Compte général de l'Administration de la Justice criminelle pour les années 1825, 1826 et 1827, et d'après le dernier recensement, le rapport moyen du nombre des condamnés à la population dans les départemens qui forment l'arrondissement de chaque Cour Royale. Les diverses dégradations des teintes correspondent au nombre des crimes, mais on observera qu'elles ne sont comparables que dans la même carte. Les chiffres indiquent sur combien de mille habitans se rencontre un condamné. Ainsi, pour les crimes contre les personnes, l'arrondissement de la Cour royale de Bastia en compte 1 sur 2,000, celui de la Cour royale d'Amiens 1 sur 72,000.

La troisième carte, divisée par académies dent les arrondissemens sont les mêmes que ceux des Cours royales, (à l'exception de la Corse qui ressort de l'académie d'Aix,) offre d'après les derniers états officiels dressés au Ministère de l'Instruction publique et qui remontent à 1822, le rapport du nombre des étudians mâles à la population du royaume à cette époque. Ici l'obscurité des teintes correspond à l'ignorance, les chiffres indiquent sur quel nombre d'habitans il y a un écolier. On voit que, dans l'arrondissement de l'académie de Rennes, il se trouve 1 sur 96 et 1 sur 11 dans les académies de Besançon d'Amiens et de Nancy.

Prix 3 francs.

A Paris, chez Jules Renouard, Libraire, rue de Tournon, N°6.

first, the east second, the north third, the west and center last. But crimes against property yielded a different result, with the west and center still in last place, the east in second, but the order of south and north reversed, with the north most likely to provoke crimes of this type. There was reason for optimism in this pattern, since "the parts of the kingdom that produce the most attacks against persons produce very few crimes against property."[30] Nevertheless, the figures raised a crucial question, that of the relation between ignorance and crime. Guerry used new data on education to bolster his argument. The figures on school attendance on which Malte-Brun and Dupin had relied were inadequate; it was better to use information on the percentage of recruits able to read and write, figures that were available from 1827 on. These new statistics revealed a France divided into three parts: in the north and east nearly three-quarters of all youths were literate; illiteracy was highest in the center and west; and the south occupied a median position. Guerry thus rediscovered the tripartite division of French territory outlined by Dupin in 1826 and used it to refute the idea of a link between crime and ignorance. People in the north were better educated yet committed more crimes against property, and the south was violent but not the most illiterate of the country's regions. Guerry thus claimed to have proved that "the *départements* where there is the most ignorance are not, as people say every day, the ones where the greatest number of crimes against persons are committed. And there is no point in speaking of crimes against properties here, since they occur primarily in the *départements* where there is the most education."[31]

Guerry's argument offered no new ideas, yet it appears to have set a pattern for later theorizing

FIGURE 12.1   In 1832 in the *Revue encyclopédique,* and later in an *Essai sur la statistique morale de la France,* Guerry examined the link between crime and ignorance. The better-educated parts of the country were also the areas were crimes against property were most numerous, and the most ignorant parts of the country were not the most violent.

because of the very terms in which it was couched. In fact, Guerry was not the first to question the relation between better education and reduced crime rates. Similar objections were raised by other writers, among them Benoiston de Chateauneuf, who had this to say in 1827:

> If one observes the religious countries, one does not find that they are less fertile in crime than the others, while those in which ignorance reigns often produce fewer crimes than those in which enlightenment shines. It has long been accepted that in Berry, Poitou, Auvergne, and Savoy, regions to which academies and the sciences have not brought much enlightenment, the courts rarely had a criminal to punish, while robbery and murder were common among the Spaniards, an eminently religious people, as well as among the English, an eminently enlightened nation.[32]

This proposition by itself did not prove that its converse was false, however, nor did it put an end to the endless round of arguments that the available evidence was insufficient to settle. For Guerry, therefore, the observed data had to be reinforced by constructing the statistics and geography in such a way as to make the desired conclusion seem as incontrovertible as the facts themselves. Guerry resorted to geographical argument, and thus to a scheme of territorial division, in the context of his efforts to put widely held opinions and popular beliefs to the test. French territory became his experimental laboratory, and his researches led him to two conclusions: explicitly, that schools alone cannot prevent "demoralization" of the population, and, implicitly, that morality remained most robust in the most culturally backward parts of France. In his own quiet way he thus initiated the revenge of disinherited, illiterate France.

That revenge took a more blatant, as well as more polemical, form in research on pauperism. Bigot de Morogues[33] and Villeneuve-Bargemont[34] turned the argument about the two Frances into a political war machine aimed squarely at the views of Baron Dupin. They accepted the Saint-Malo–Geneva line, but only to place an entirely different construction on its significance. For Bigot de Morogues, the line marked the frontier of prosperity and morality in such away that the fifty-four *départements* of the south enjoyed all the advantages: a smaller number of convicted criminals, less frequent crimes against property, a lower suicide rate. He summed up his findings prettily: "Those who speculate and calculate with our great northern industrialists often drown themselves in the river, while those who laugh and dance with our southern peasants are careful not to fall in."[35] In addition to the statistics celebrating the sociability of the south, Villeneuve-Bargemont, in *Économie politique chrétienne*, cited another important indicator having to do with the distribution of poverty. According to his data and calculations, the north counted one pauper for every nine residents, whereas the south had only one in twenty. If, moreover, one looked carefully at the statistics of men invalided out of the military for infirmity or deformity, it became clear that "the physical state and condition of health of the working classes of the south is incomparably better than that of the same classes in the north."[36] The two Frances thus exchanged places on the scale of values because industrial development was equated with the physical, material, and moral squalor of the majority.

This lesson was true not only of France but also of Europe. An astonishing map showing the gradations of pauperism yielded the following ranking: one of every six Englishman was a pauper, compared with one in seven Dutchmen, one in ten Swiss, one in twenty Germans, one in twenty-five Austrians, Danes, French, Italians, Portuguese, and Swedes, one in thirty Prussians, one in forty Turks, and one in a hundred Russians. The logic of this distribution was simple: "Everywhere one finds that the number of paupers increases owing to the growth and crowding of the working-class population, the predominance of manufacturing industry over agricultural industry, the application of English doctrines of civilization and political economy, and the abandonment of the charitable and religious principle."[37] In locating hell in England and paradise in Russia Villeneuve-Bargemont gave away his ideology as Christian, aristocratic, and agrarian, and identified his enemy, broadly characterized as Protestantism, philosophy, and industry. France, which stood in the middle range of European pauperism, was divided by the "front" separating two political economies, the English and the Christian. Wherever English political economy had already prevailed, namely, in northern and eastern France, industry had ushered in its train of woes: "The system of industry and agriculture followed in this part of France tends constantly on the one hand to increase the manufacturing population and on the other hand to lower wages, concentrate industrial capital and profits, and introduce all the factors that promote pauperism."[38] This iron law could be reversed only by adopting the model set by southern France, where a proper balance had been struck between charity and agriculture, and by denouncing the views of those who, like Dupin, would force the entire country to accept the "bitter fruits of modern material civilization." The Saint-Malo—Geneva line must be erased, but only by rejecting innovations stemming from the north.

This text by Villeneuve-Bargemont, while in part naively reactionary, is worthy of attention in two respects. First, it shows how the two-France theme could become a staple of political struggle under the July Monarchy. The choice of statistical indices, the way in which they were related, and the value attached to a region or territory were by no means innocent but reflected radically opposed programs or platforms. References furnished by history were combined with or replaced by contradictory conclusions based on social data. Clashes over old issues hid behind battles over figures and maps. Politics thus took on a new guise, as the investigation of the spatial distribution of recently compiled statistical data for a time moderated the formative influence of history since the Revolution. Second, *L'Économie politique chrétienne* more than any other work set France in its European context. In the work of Dupin or, later, of Angeville, French territory remained hermetically sealed. No doubt there were administrative reasons for this, for the statistics used were difficult to correlate with data from foreign sources. But that may not be the key factor: if one wanted to think in terms of differences and their distribution, it was in fact essential to reason in terms of a closed totality. In order to analyze France in terms of regional subdivisions, the country already had to be isolated from its context. It took all of Villeneuve-Bargemont's ideological Manichaeanism to place France within a larger cultural space that explained much of what one observed domestically.

This early effort was followed by the better-known text of Adolphe d'Angeville, published in 1836.[39] In several respects this work can be regarded as definitive, not least owing to the unusual breadth of the statistical data it contained. Ninety-seven different indices were compiled in eight tables. Thirty-three of these had to do with "moral statistics," twenty-seven with data pertaining to physical and cultural anthropology, seventeen with economics, and sixteen with population. With such an abundance of data, d'Angeville was able to correlate his indices in many ways and try out "all sorts of combinations" for the purpose either of testing previously asserted relations among social facts, such as education and criminality (p. 69) and industry and poverty (pp. 102–103), or of proposing new ones, such as Catholic spirit and morality (p. 104) or education and diet (p. 116). The *Essai sur la statistique de la population française* is thus a summation of fifteen years of work and statistical controversies. It was not innovative in either its use of quantitative data or its reliance on correlations, but it pursued its goals with an amplitude unrivaled by earlier arithmeticians.

In his work one also finds a juxtaposition of perceptions of French space on several different scales. The basic grid was defined by a "study of departmental France," in the form of a series of individual reports, each presented in a similar fashion and arranged in alphabetical order, thus eschewing both Dupin's device of presenting his findings in the form of a fictional journey and the regional groupings occasionally found in works published during the Empire. Of the large number of indices examined, sixteen were displayed on maps in such a way as to exhibit legible "groupings" and thus an apparent segmentation of the national territory. Beyond that, the maps and statistics together revealed a single central division, thus harking back to Dupin and his dichotomy: "The more one studies human statistics, the more rational this division seems when viewed in terms of facts pertinent to the population. Indeed, one is almost tempted to think that two populations entered France and collided along the line that joins the port of Saint-Malo to the city of Geneva."[40] D'Angeville added only two minor corrections to Dupin's two Frances: he quietly included the Loiret département in northern France and the Ain in the south, and he used geographical terminology borrowed from Buache to express the fundamental division, with the Rhine, Seine, and Saône "basins" on one side, and the Rhône, Garonne, and Loire "basins" on the other. He thus combined all the various spatial approaches to French reality into one, and in this, too, he was simply accepting and systematizing the legacy of the age.

What got him into difficulty was the need to pronounce judgment on which France was the better of the two. For him, the comparison of north and south revealed no clear winner. The maps by *département* themselves showed discordances among the indices: size and diet were better in the north, but life expectancy was longer in the south, whose citizens were more robust; education was more widely available in the north, but crime was also more common there; the north was wealthier than the south but morally inferior. The final diagnosis merely summarized these contradictions in a discourse whose tone was factual rather than polemical.[41] With d'Angeville, spatial reflection lost its pedagogical and polemical force to the extent that it was no longer so completely defined by reference to a preexisting model, whether it be that of the English manufacturer or the traditional agrarian. An agricultural modernizer, d'Angeville was also a political conservative, yet he made a case for manufacturing: "If France were to join the industrial system, parts of the center, which are so backward and lifeless, might prosper; the country would become more homogeneous." Yet he also knew the cost and, after 1834, the risks of industrialization, and unlike Dupin he wanted to slow its pace: "It is to be hoped that no one will confuse the orderly development of industry, which is desirable for our rural areas and second-rank cities, with the kind of industrial centralization which accumulates masses of proletarians in the same cities and masses of capital in the hands of a few; we are far from being envious of England for its so-called advantage in this regard."[42] No doubt d'Angeville was a "developmental theorist," but, alerted by the complex lesson of the two Frances, the development he dreamed of was dispersed in nature.

Over the fifteen years between 1822 and 1836, a theme emerged, took hold, and became the focal point of a whole series of political and scientific debates. It makes sense to end with d'Angeville, our last and exemplary specimen from the period prior to the *Statistique générale de la France*, but it is nevertheless tempting to look back to the eighteenth century to see what spatial readings of France were proposed then. Though necessarily incomplete, my research led me first to the Physiocrats and the political arithmeticians, both of whom mapped out global perceptions of the kingdom's spatial organization, though in different ways. The Physiocrats' theory of space relied on distinctions set forth by Quesnay in two *Encyclopédie* articles. In "Farmers" he asserted that "land is commonly cultivated by farmers with horses or by sharecroppers with oxen."[43] And in "Grains" he had this to say: "We have already examined the state of agriculture in France and the two types of cultivation found there: large-scale cultivation *(la grande culture)*, which is done with horses, and small-scale cultivation *(la petite culture)*, which is done with oxen."[44] These two economic categories, defined in abstract terms within a theoretical framework combining technology with mode of cultivation, became the primary analytic tools of the Physiocratic school. As evidence for this statement, consider the following passage, in which de Butré is still more explicit about the contrast between *grande* and *petite culture*: "In France there are two types of cultivation, *la grande culture*, which is practiced by wealthy Farmers and carried out with horses; and *la petite culture*, which is practiced by Sharecroppers who use only oxen. These two types of cultivation differ markedly in their use of land, cost of production, and products."[45]

Although the Physiocrats used these two categories as central economic concepts, they could also be translated into spatial terms. With them it was possible to map the geographical contours of what was presented as a fundamental economic difference. Both Quesnay and de Butré sought to show how geographically limited *la grande culture* was in order to encourage rational imitation of what they considered to be superior agricultural practice. Listen to Quesnay: "*La grande culture* is at present confined to roughly six million acres of land, comprising primarily the provinces of Normandy, Beauce, Ile-de-France, Picardy, French Flanders, Hainault, and a few others."[46] De Butré mentioned these same provinces but added Artois and part of Champagne while excluding part of Normandy.[47] Six million acres out of a total of thirty million under cultivation left vast expanses to *la petite culture:* "Nearly all the provinces of the interior have succumbed to *la petite culture*."[48] Thus the Physiocrats' France was also divided in two, but its two parts were even more unequal than they would be for Dupin insofar as their geographical division invoked a past in which things were different, a history that could be read as a process of decay. To say that the regions of *la grande culture* were shrinking away to nothing was also to say that the agriculture of the kingdom had fallen into a degraded state.

With the help of further distinctions, both the economic analysis and its geographical correlates could be extended. De Butré actually argued that there were three types of *grande culture*, which could be ranked in terms of the ratio between capital advanced and net product: in the case of opulent properties, the ratio was 100 percent; in average properties it was no more than 70 percent; whereas weak properties produced little or no net product. Once again, theoretical economic categories could be translated into geographic regions on a map. As it turned out, what governed the distribution of the resulting regions was proximity to urban areas. Thus, *la grande culture opulente* "is rarely found outside provinces located close to the capital or some other large city, which offers outlets and ensures commodity prices high enough to defray the costs of cultivation."[49] Similarly, *la petite culture* could also be broken down into three groups and located geographically. Here, however, the groups were defined in terms of the amount of income on cultivable land. In the top-ranked *petite culture* group, that income was sufficient to pay "1. Costs; 2. Taxes; and 3. A very small income to the landowners." In the next group, "land yields no income in itself, the harvest being just sufficient to pay costs and taxes. What is called income is the product of pasturing, which yields slightly less than the interest on the money capital invested in the herd or flock." The third and final group comprised "land that does not even earn enough to pay costs and taxes, the bulk of which must be derived from the yield on pasturing."[50] The three groups of property formed concentric circles around urban centers. The first type of *petite culture* is found "only in the vicinity of capitals and other cities in the *petite culture* provinces." The second emerges "after one has passed through the capital suburbs and other large cities in the provinces of *petite culture* and as one moves away from the banks of rivers." The third is limited to "the interiors of provinces far removed from the capital."[51]

De Butré's text thus laid the foundations for a spatial economics, a forerunner in some respects of Thünen's.[52] It also yielded a simple principle for classifying space that owed nothing to either history or the picturesque. Interestingly, moreover, the geographic distribution was defined by urban centers, especially provincial capitals. Even the basic division between *grande* and *petite culture* depended on the location of the capital, the city of cities. So strong was the urban influence that it overwhelmed natural factors, so that the city itself became the primary force governing the development of the rural area around it: "Compared with the provinces of *la grande culture,* those less accessible to the capital are in many ways reminiscent of new-world countries and climates."[53] Whereas later schemes tended to obscure the role of cities, here we see their full importance as centers of the imbricated and overlapping spaces of which the kingdom was composed. Though the full complexity of de Butré's scheme was forgotten, the Physiocratic interpretation did not disappear without a trace. For example, in the work of Chaptal, who thought in terms of unities, the only global division of French space is precisely that proposed by Quesnay.[54]

For the demographers of the eighteenth century the situation is not as clear. Different writers relied on different principles of spatial interpretation, each invoking whatever factor he considered decisive for the study of population-related phenomena. For Moheau, the key to demographic behavior, as reflected in population density, lay in the nature of economic activity. He ranked agricultural sites in terms of their aptitude to support a dense population. Seacoasts ranked first, "because people living there can easily procure fish as a dietary staple and find steady wages in the jobs with which workers are provided by trade." Next came vine-growing regions, followed, "a long way back," by wheat-producing regions, pasture lands, and, last of all, forests and moorlands.[55] This scale of densities was purely theoretical, however; in reality, different types of production tended to overlap: vines never existed without other crops, wheat and other cereal grains were never totally absent, and therefore it was impossible to divide up the territory in a clear, legible manner on the basis of agricultural activity alone. Defeated by his own premises, Moheau never succeeded in developing a geographical interpretation capable of making sense of the demographic data. His example is interesting, however, because it shows how a theoretical distinction can lead to a quandary when it comes to taking in the facts of concrete geographical reality.

Nevertheless, other political arithmeticians did produce workable classifications that allowed them to gather statistical data and propose interpretations. Des Pommelles, for one, divided France into five strips delimited by parallels of latitude.[56] He was clearly influenced by atmosphericist (*aériste*) theories that saw the nature, heat, and humidity of the atmosphere as the key factors governing human behavior. Neo-Hippocratic medical theorists of the eighteenth century stressed the importance of geographical location and thus encouraged a theoretical division of French territory along purely geometric lines. Messance, for his part, divided France into three rather than five strips, one in the north, a second in the middle, and a third in the south. In spite of appearances, atmosphericism was not the only basis for this division, which its author claimed was justified by a complex combination of natural, demographic, and economic factors: "Since justice requires that all burdens be distributed proportionately among the provinces in accordance with their respective strengths in number of inhabitants, productive output, industry, commerce, and location, and since reason requires that one compare neighboring provinces as partaking more or less of the same things, analogy illuminates and continues the comparison in ever greater detail, until enlightenment extends from one extremity to the other."[57] This passage reflects the inescapable fact that the roots of political arithmetic lay in fiscal policy, while at the same time expressing the hope that with information and reflection it should be possible to define geographic regions that could serve as a basis for analytic investigation.

All eighteenth-century demographers agreed that population phenomena were governed by a simple logic, a steady, regular progression from south to north. Messance made the point in relation to density: "Why is the north of France more [densely] populated than the south, and why is the south less [densely] populated than the middle?"[58] So did des Pommelles: "It will be seen that population per square league diminishes steadily for every two degrees one moves from north to south."[59] In seeking the cause of this progression, des Pommelles found an opportunity to flesh out the atmosphericist view of the matter: in the north, he argued, "the landscape is less taken up with mountains, and the land, being more fertile, provides its inhabitants with more ample sustenance." Messance, however, gave a different reason: "It is because there are more cities in the north of France than in the two other parts, and until such time as it is proven that the greater population of the north is due to some other cause, the larger number of cities that exist there and form a larger base of consumers can be regarded as one of the main causes, if not the only cause. In that case, moreover, cities would populate the countryside, which is the reverse of what people have said."[60] Demographic differences thus served as an argument in one of the century's major debates, and the discovery of population-density differences between north and south offered an opportunity to refute the idea that cities were death-houses, parasites on rural areas, and a drain on their population.

If density decreased from north to south, fertility increased. Both Moheau and des Pommelles emphasized the point. The latter saw this as proof, if proof were needed, of atmosphericist theories: the ratio of births to marriages "increases steadily as one proceeds from north to south, with the exception of provinces in which the extent of wood and pasture land is great enough to make the air very moist (e.g., La Rochelle, Poitiers, etc.); it seems to me that one can conclude from this that when bad habits and other moral factors do not hinder the influence of nature, marriages are more fertile in warm regions, where the air is dry, and in elevated sites, than in low-lying, swampy areas where the air is thick."[61] Ten years later, Moheau accepted this analysis with a slight proviso having to do with diet: "The type of nourishment has no less influence and effect, and individuals who drink wine or spirit beverages and eat astringent foods possess greater prolific virtues than others."[62] Mortality was a more difficult matter to approach, owing to the lack of a statistical index as simple as the birth/marriage ratio. Investigators therefore tended to focus on life expectancy instead. Once again, air quality was found to be decisive: "In the north, where lack of heat leads to less active individual development, the periods of formation, perfection, and decay should be longer."[63] Topographical factors could intervene, however: "People appear to enjoy longer lives in hilly and mountainous regions. Life is shortest in marshlands. Plains and valleys can, depending on their orientation, either preserve or shorten the lives of their inhabitants."[64]

For the political arithmeticians of the eighteenth century, organizing French space into homogeneous entities was a source of tension. Nearly all of them worked within comprehensive systems of thought that influenced their views on every subject. Atmosphericist medicine revealed the primary cause because, as Moheau put it, "the imperious law of the climate acts on anything that vegetates or breathes." Their France was therefore above all a place of varying climates, in which the decisive factors were latitude and elevation, which, taken together, determined the properties of the air. The same principle held good at each stage. It explained regional differences and at the same time governed the division of the kingdom into its principal parts, whether three or five in number. Once that was done, however, the original certainty abated somewhat. Indeed, it was not easy to eradicate other factors capable of influencing demographic phenomena autonomously, even if they depended in some way on the climate. Thus it was conceded that economic activity, cultural habits, and moral attitudes could play a part. The primacy accorded to atmospheric qualities governed the perception of space, which involved not so much an opposition between north and south as a progressive gradation. On this broad canvas, however, other pictures began to emerge, pictures that owed nothing to the tyranny of climate: Messance, for instance, contrasted urbanized France with rural France and a wholly agricultural central France with a France of the peripheries, to the north, west, and south, where "large factories and major commercial enterprises" were concentrated.[65] In terms of the construction of space, these contradictory tendencies were a major embarrassment at the very heart of the old demographic epistemology.

What determined France's position on the map of Europe was thus not so much demographic facts as the data of physical anthropology, which until d'Angeville came along writers were likely to overlook. First Moheau and then Expilly focused on physical size, noting that the French were not as tall as the Swiss or Germans. One possible explanation for this was historical: "In France, whose ancient inhabitants were, according to the Romans themselves, notable for both their height and strength, I believe that the main reason why the race may have degenerated is that subsistence became more difficult for the bulk of the population."[66] But the relatively short stature of the French was due not so much to a shrinking process as to the north-south law that governed all such statistics. For one thing, stature was indicative of France's place in Europe: "In France, as well as in countries farther to the south, such as Spain, Portugal, the states of Morocco, Algiers, Tunis, Tripoli, and so on, one finds people among the wealthiest, tallest, and strongest of human beings, but their numbers are not as great in those places as in northern countries such as Switzerland and Germany."[67] Furthermore, the same principle could account for contrasts observed within France: "The provinces of France differ among themselves, and it has been observed that the northern ones generally exhibit a taller population than the southern ones. The case records of deserters from various provinces, which contain data on physical characteristics, reveal that deserters from Flanders and Picardy are markedly taller than deserters from Provence."[68]

Despite this monotone north-south decrease in height, it was still possible for the French to feel that, on the whole, they belonged to southern Europe. Expilly made the point almost in passing: "France cannot boast of the height of its inhabitants.... The same is true of the *other* southern countries." Similarly, Moheau, in discussing the high fertility rates of the southern provinces, mentions that the kingdom appears to enjoy the same advantage "vis-à-vis the north of Europe." The theme according to which France itself was divided because it was torn between northern and southern Europe had yet to be stated, no doubt because it depended on the prior recognition of a dividing line marking a sharp division within France itself. For the demographers of the eighteenth century, and perhaps for others (yet to be examined in detail), France belonged to the community of southern nations. This consciousness of belonging to the south remains to be explained in terms of political allegiances, economic relations, and cultural divisions.

Thus for the Physiocrats and the political arithmeticians a global organizational scheme for classifying French territory was conceivable. By using such a scheme, writers could identify those areas most propitious (as well as least propitious) to achieving the goal of their school, whether it be to extend the area of *grande culture* or to increase the population. No such interpretation of space occurred outside these two schools, however, and this absence is what I shall now try to explain by examining two parallel bodies of work. If one looks at the geographers of the second half of the eighteenth century, it is clear that their primary purpose was to produce regional monographs, more often than not with the words "natural history" in the title.[69] By far the larger proportion of such monographs was devoted to the provinces of the south, in part no doubt because learned institutions were more prevalent there but also perhaps because the pre-Romantic preference for mountainous landscapes was already exerting an influence. The internal organization of these "natural histories" reveals a tension between the administrative (with the facts being set forth in a framework determined by such administrative divisions as *bailliage, sénéchaussée, diocèse civil,* and *généralité*) and the geographical, as the more innovative writers based their descriptions on Buache's theory of river basins. This regionalist writing produced its own theoretical legitimations. Among the principles invoked was that local studies must necessarily take precedence over global ones: "Only after the provinces have been accurately described through direct observation by observers living in the area can we hope to see a general and complete description of France."[70] It was also argued that local studies, more than simply gratifying curiosity, were pragmatically useful: "If the purpose of the natural history of a province were simply to enumerate its fossils and describe its mountain ranges, climate, and production, it would be useful only for gratifying curiosity. It is perhaps a much more valuable exercise to relate these different areas to one another and attempt to draw conclusions relevant to the human race and, insofar as possible, the public welfare."[71] The most pressing and justifiable task was that of regional description of a fairly wide area; such wide-ranging natural histories made it easy to see how different phenomena were related and could be framed in ecological terms. To the extent that their geographical curiosities did not wander abroad, the Philosophes made such regional studies a major genre (and soon forged ties with firms specializing in provincial cartography); the more or less moribund tradition of Piganiol de La Force, with its comprehensive catalogues of France, went into relative eclipse. A corollary of this emphasis on regionalism was that it became impossible, at least initially, to conceptualize the kingdom as a whole and therefore to describe its large-scale spatial organization.

The same regionalist self-affirmation is evident in some of the collective ventures of the provincial academies.[72] Indeed, half of them set out to produce local histories, whether of a city or a province, and a few, such as the academies of Bordeaux, Clermont, and Auxerre, proposed to catalogue the wealth and resources of their regions. The limited horizons of the *petite patrie* were emphasized not only for obvious emotional reasons but also because the local setting was one suitable for observation. The Benedictines had had the same idea long before the provincial academicians: they had planned a series of regional histories to cover the entire kingdom. In the end, these remained in manuscript, except for the one on Languedoc.[73] For the purposes of "natural and literary history," space once again proved quite malleable: spatial limitations were defined in such a way as to permit exhaustive cataloguing and useful, logical categorization of the data. In their own way the provincial academies thus reflected the discovery of the provinces that marked the second half of the eighteenth century, another sign of which is to be found in the variety of literary forms (comedies, novels, essays) that drew a contrast between society in the capital and in the provinces.[74] Neglected by the cartographic statisticians of the July Monarchy, this tension occasionally resurfaced, as in Guerry's geography of suicide: "In general, no matter what place in France one is speaking about, the number of suicides increases as one proceeds toward the capital."[75] This reminder of the nefarious influence of big cities bears the imprint of another old idea: namely, that Paris and the provinces also represent two distinct Frances whose differences are worth exploring. It was no doubt this contrast with which people of the period were most familiar.[76] The provinces did not form a homogeneous unit, however, and in order to understand them it was necessary to compile inventories of individual provinces one at a time, given the way in which the territory of the nation had been fragmented by history and nature.

An excellent illustration of the method is provided by medical topographies of France. Their history is well known. It unfolded in three stages: to begin with, Lepecq de La Clôture organized a network of correspondents from Rouen in 1768. Then, in August 1776, the Conseil created the Société Royale de Médecine and undertook a national inquiry into the causes of epidemic disease. Finally, in October 1778, the Société Royale approved plans for compiling a series of regional monographs, which, taken together, would provide a physical-medical description of the kingdom.[77] Out of this grew a genre that developed in the local and provincial setting and reached its apogee in the nineteenth century. This vast resource has yet to be fully catalogued, but a look at Normandy gives an idea of the scale of investigation: some focused on individual cities (with or without their surrounding countryside), others on electoral districts (*arrondissements*), still others on the *département* as a whole.[78] In 1778 the Société Royale had recommended the "canton" or province. The medical topographies illustrate the consolidation of a regional consciousness that deliberately confined itself to relatively narrow areas; without a doubt it was the development of such regional consciousness in the eighteenth century that constituted the principal obstacle to seeing the kingdom in macroscopic terms. This representation of France persisted into the next century: it was a picture of a country divided not into two or three major sections but fragmented into a multiplicity of units, each with its own irreducible originality. Here, then, is proof that, while the "two-France" theme may have structured the major debates, it did not altogether eliminate persistent recognition of local roots.

The crucial question raised by this brief survey, limited both as to its source materials (a single corpus of documents) and its time frame (a single century), has to do with the relation between statistical and geographical thinking and the exercise of power. For a considerable time the political authorities seem to have accommodated themselves to the disparities that made French territory so checkered. They accepted— indeed, except for a few people of systematic cast of mind, they appreciated—the fact that France was an "aggregate of disunited peoples." Vis-à-vis the capital, *la province* existed as an entity, but an entity with many facets. Eagerly and earnestly the men of the late eighteenth century compiled careful catalogues of each province's past and future promise. In the last days of an absolutism that had always had to cope with this flourishing diversity, projects of reform were put together in a regionalist and provincial context, and projects of rebellion grew out regionalist and provincial consciousness. Revolutionary and imperial Jacobinism would attempt to alter the terms on which a self-styled centralizing government coexisted with a fragmented nation. The success or failure of these efforts is of little importance here. What is clear is that the attempt changed the relation between political power and the terrain on which it was exercised. Homogeneity of the national space became at once a desire and a goal, a condition and a token of successful policy. It should come as no surprise, therefore, that under the July Monarchy we find prominent political leaders writing as arithmeticians. Their awareness of continuing disparities, be they economic, cultural, or moral, was a clear indication of both a failure of policy and a risk to stability; the way to deal with the situation was to take differences that could and did seem arbitrary and reduce them to a set of simple laws. Ideally, any program for changing society wants a smooth surface to which it can apply itself, or at the very least a broad agreement as to what the primary inequalities are. The two-France theme, born of nostalgia for unity, embodied contradictory hopes. In its very ambiguity it expressed a new way of conceiving of the relation between society and power.

After the beginning of the nineteenth century, social statistics abandoned the region to the archaeological curiosities of local learned societies and used a different set of spatial categories as a basis for the scientific study of social facts. Early in the twentieth century, a bitter dispute between geographers and sociologists revived the old opposition between these two ways of apprehending space. Looking into the terms of this debate, from which the Saint-Malo–Geneva line seems to have vanished, is perhaps a way of shedding light on the reasons why, fifty years later, French historians began once again to focus on this primary dividing line, thereby to some extent disassociating themselves from the geographical tradition of their forebears. For Vidal de La Blache and other adepts of the "human geography" school, the region was in fact the only space within which it was legitimate to reason about the relation between the influence of the natural environment and the voluntary behavior of human social groups. This emphasis on regional monographs was also what distinguished the French school of geography from Ratzel's "anthropogeography," which worked with space on a broader scale and was therefore more likely to believe in some form of determinism based on natural conditions. Within the space of five years, several theses—Demangeon's on Picardy in 1905, Blanchard's on Flanders in 1906, Vallaux's on lower Brittany in 1907, and Sion's on eastern Normandy in 1909[79]—established a distinctive method of describing the geographical roots of social organizations. Basic to the method was a division of space into regions that were neither too large nor too small, whose coherence was in some sense clearly visible and capable of being treated as self-evident. What exactly did the word *region* mean to these Vidalian geographers? It was an expanse of territory that could be defined neither by history nor by the conscious designation of its residents but solely by its geographical individuality. It was a space to be constructed in such a way that it was homogeneous in its fundamental characteristics and clearly distinct from the regions surrounding it. The Vidalian geographers' natural regions were thus spaces inscribed on the surface of the earth itself, yet regions whose existence and boundaries had been neither sanctioned by political borders nor perceived by the societies that they had sustained and would continue to sustain. Designating such regions was an intellectual operation, a matter of geographical identification. This operation revealed the unity of the regions that it designated and thus established them as a legitimate setting for scientific description.

Even when a natural region bore the same name as a historical one, the two spatial entities did not necessarily coincide. For example, the Flanders defined by Blanchard contrasted with the surrounding regions in that it was low, flat, and moist: "The territory that is a natural region in view of these characteristic traits does not correspond exactly to the territory customarily regarded as the historical Flanders; its boundaries sometimes extend beyond political borders and sometimes remain inside them."[80] In other places the geographer is obliged not only to identify the natural unit in terms of purely geographical criteria but also to *name* it. Such is the case with the plain of Picardy:

This area belongs to three different provinces of Old France, Picardy, Artois, and Cabanel. Yet one passes from one of these provinces to the next without perceiving any difference. On either side [of the provincial border] one finds the same fields, the same rivers, the same villages. Yet the people who live here have apparently never noticed this unity. Never in history has the area borne a unique name. Neither the cultivated nor the uncultivated, the official nor the commonplace language possesses a word that encompasses and defines the whole territory. No province, no state, no human group owes its existence or individuality to the area.... While the region thus possesses no historical personality, its geographical personality is written all over it, based on the unity of its physical nature and consolidated by the works of its inhabitants."[81]

Similarly, eastern Normandy is a territory whose very designation stems from geographical observation alone. It is "an organic ensemble of natural regions": "Physical geography does not separate them.... Human geography is even less capable of distinguishing these territories, which have all had the same history and, but for a few exceptions, the same laws. It notes that the very variety of their products has involved them in continuous relations for a long time.... This unity also manifests itself in the social state."[82]

If, from one text to the next, the operation by which a natural region is identified and denoted as a purely geographic space is similar, the criteria on which that operation is based change somewhat. The unity of Blanchard's Flanders is based on the nature and impermeability of the soil and on the flatness and low elevation of the land. By the use of these criteria, it proves possible to isolate a homogeneous territory and draw the outlines of a Flanders that owes nothing to existing political or linguistic boundaries. Demangeon's initial definition is not purely natural, because the chalky subsoil extends beyond the limits of the Picardian Plain, which is taken to be a grain-growing region, distinct from the forests, pastures, and industrial areas that surround it: "The Picardian Plain thus fails to coincide exactly with either the natural extent of any particular terrain or the artificial compass of any administrative territory. In a country like France, civilized and populated since ancient times, it often happens that a geographic region is instead defined by a set of relations between man and the natural environment.... The distinctiveness of a geographic physiognomy is therefore the product of a synthesis of natural and human factors."[83] Hence it is the very concept of contingent as opposed to necessary relations between natural conditions and human social action that is invoked here to justify the designation of a geographical entity. Jules Sion places still greater stress on human factors in defining his area of study. Despite its (comparative) natural unity, eastern Normandy is in fact a composite of regions that are "diverse as to soil and crops." If it can nevertheless be treated as a homogeneous entity, it is basically for socioeconomic reasons having to do with the ownership and exploitation of the land, trade, and industrial history. It therefore follows—a key point—that the region's "geographical unity comes from man more than from nature."[84]

The foregoing survey of the Vidalian geographers suggests two things. First, all of them clearly set out to invent new ways of dividing up French territory. Regions as they defined them were based neither on historical patterns nor on their inhabitants' sense of belonging. They were objective data, more often than not forgotten by history and overlooked by man, so that only the geographical analyst stood in a position to restore their true contours by identifying certain distinctive factors. However—and this second point is sometimes forgotten—the nature of these dominant factors varied widely from writer to writer. Although the natural and the human were generally balanced in the school's rhetoric, different authors emphasized one or the other to varying degrees, from Blanchard, who identified a topographical unity, to Sion, who based his definition of the region essentially on economic criteria. This disparity led, moreover, to some symptomatic inversions. Blanchard's Flanders may have been unified in its physical definition, but that unity fell apart as his description proceeded: "Thus within this Flemish plain, apparently so uniform and unvarying in all its aspects, a variety of unexpected characteristics reveal themselves, defining *regions* whose crops, industry, customs, and interests are as different as their temperatures, soils, and streams. These differences are not subtle: they define distinct territories, known to inhabitants and named by them in view of their differences [my italics]."[85] On the other hand, the diversity of the "natural regions" that make up Sion's eastern Normandy (Caux, Bray, Vexin, the Seine valley, and so on) is gradually transformed into unity through analysis of their common structures. The vocabulary of the geographers, who used the word *région* to refer to territories of vastly different scale, reveals in its very ambiguity a fundamental uncertainty: how to relate one region to another, how to individualize territories whose internal diversity somehow left homogeneity—or at any rate, as Maximilien Sorre put it, "a certain homogeneity of the component parts"—intact.

Less assured and unanimous in the final analysis than they might at first seem, the Vidalian geographers had to endure the critical onslaught of Durkheimian sociology. Here, the fundamental text is a brief critical analysis by François Simiand of the four books by Blanchard, Demangeon, Vallaux, and Sion. Published in *L'Année sociologique*,[86] this text, along with a review of a book of Ratzel's by Maurice Halbwachs, constituted the first half of the section on "Social Morphology," which bore the title, "The Geographical Bases of Social Life." Simiand's critique of the geographers was threefold: 1. They unduly extended the notion of a geographical fact to include all material and mental facts, thus destroying what ought to have been the proper domain of geography (namely, the study of those facts for which physical localization was a constitutive or explanatory factor).[87] 2. They assumed the existence of an "essential action of the physical milieu" on economic facts and social institutions, whereas their own observations often contradicted the existence of such a relation; furthermore, "the true explanatory fact is [always] human and psychological, and the physical fact is at most a condition." 3. They condemn themselves to uncertainty by limiting their observations to the narrow framework of regional description. For Simiand, this was probably the major error. It little mattered how the region was defined. Whatever the criteria, the definition inevitably masked the true explanatory relations: "To limit oneself to so narrow a region is to close off the only path that permits distinguishing between accidental or noninfluential coincidences and true correlations, for it is to close off the path of comparison among a relatively large number of different entities; in a matter so complex, to limit oneself to a single observed case is to condemn oneself in advance to the impossibility of proving anything."

The procedures that a "science of social morphology" ought properly to adopt were contrasted one by one with the misguided approach of the geographers. What one ought to do, it was argued, was consider not how the territory should be divided up but how various interesting phenomena should be analyzed. The most conventional of territories (France or western Europe, say) could therefore serve as legitimate frameworks, for their very breadth increased the number of sites from which it was possible to observe relations between the relevant social facts and the various factors likely to account for them. The only spatial prerequisite of social morphology was extension, hence the region was totally disqualified as a pertinent analytic space. The social sciences were offered a research program in which the number one task was analysis of various social facts. Geographers had a role to play in this program provided they turned their methodology on its head and gave up on the misguided attempt to write regional monographs: "Suppose that, instead of devoting themselves to a problem that for the time being (and very likely for a long time to come) remains quite insoluble, the same men, conscientious, erudite, careful in their research and determined to be scientific in their approach, had applied themselves to studying, say, types of habitation or the localization of particular industries throughout France or even, if need be, throughout western Europe, in the present and also, as will no doubt prove necessary, in the past as well. Does anyone think that they would not have come up with more conclusive results or penetrated more quickly and more accurately to the heart of phenomena that a science of social morphology can legitimately set itself the task of explaining?"

Such an approach, which implicitly assumes that geographical conditions have only a minor influence on social phenomena, makes regional description the ultimate stage of knowledge, to be undertaken only after the general laws governing each of the elementary social facts have been ascertained: "If one assumes that the regions considered are in fact unified human and geographic entities (often, in fact, more human than geographic), and if one begins by studying the region as a whole, by attempting to grasp and explain all the relevant factors at once, one will make the mistake of beginning with what is most difficult, what can at best be conceived of as a goal of science. It is tantamount, in effect, to wanting to explain all the complex individuality of the individual rather than begin, as in all science, with the analysis of simple general relations." This criticism was aimed squarely at a credo that the geographers of the twentieth century had inherited from their eighteenth-century forebears: the necessary primacy of local studies, a sufficient number of which had to be amassed before any attempt was made to examine things at the national level. For Simiand, regional description was at best still premature. Only a comparative, analytical approach, conducted within a territory whose precise contours were of no importance provided it was sufficiently large, was capable of revealing the general laws governing the forms of social life.

After Simiand's radical critique, the notion of a natural region as used by Demangeon, Blanchard, and Sion also faced a challenge mounted within the Vidalian school itself. It is in this sense that one must understand Maximilien Sorre's thesis, *Les Pyrénées méditerranéennes* (published in 1913).[88] This was not a regional geography, and in any case it cannot be placed on the same footing as the earlier monographs (although this is what Lucien Febvre did in *La Terre et l'évolution humaine*[89]). Sorre in fact points out two ways in which his approach is original. In the first place, the territory he was studying was in no sense a natural region but rather a "collection of small, relatively individualized regions,"[90] lacking homogeneity within itself and not sharply distinguished from surrounding areas. Furthermore, his goal was not to set forth the totality of natural and human facts circumscribed by the area under examination but rather to state a problem: "To show how ways of life are transformed under the impact of transformation in the vegetal environment— and vice versa—upon contact with two societies and under the influence of climatic changes."[91] The terrain was chosen not for the unity but for the diversity of its sites, which were differentiated by elevation, distance from the sea, and climate. Sorre thus laid out a laboratory space that did not correspond to any natural region and gave it a somewhat paradoxical name: the Mediterranean Pyrenees.

Though ostensibly faithful to Vidal de La Blache, Sorre's book unavowedly and perhaps unwittingly placed the sociologists' concerns at the heart of his investigation. Among his themes, for instance, we find Simiand's contention that the way to identify universal laws is to increase the number of comparisons and observations of repetitions.

> We would not have deliberately dispensed with the notion of natural region if we had not believed that the loss was compensated by an appreciable gain. When one studies a region, one hopes to point out what is singular about the

combination of phenomena that occur there. One studies individualized geographical areas that are fundamentally distinct from neighboring areas. Finally, one presents the facts or groups of facts in light of their *opposition*. But it is just as essential, in doing science, to present the facts in light of their *repetition*.... The advantage of the viewpoint that we have adopted is precisely that it allows for comparisons.... In sum, the advantage of our method is to give prominence to the general character of the phenomena under study."[92]

For Sorre, the region is therefore an artifact constructed in such a way as to test the possible interactions among natural milieus and ways of life. Choosing a limited space enables him to make careful observations of differences (such as the interrelationship of four distinct ways of life in the "Mediterranean Pyrenees"), but the aim of his descriptions is to establish the principles by virtue of which equivalent natural conditions at different sites define comparable ways of life, which then in turn have a similar transformative effect on the milieu. Unlike the "natural regions," which were held to be distinctively individual, the regions identified by Sorre were supposed to exhibit a broad spectrum of combinations also visible elsewhere. The definition of a limited framework of study is in no way in contradiction with the generalization of results that it makes possible: on the contrary, it is a prerequisite of such generalization. On the terrain of biological geography we thus find morphological analysis combined with localized observation.

In the debate between "anthropogeographers" and sociologists, Lucien Febvre's position was quite clear, for two fundamental reasons. The first had to do with his very conception of scientific work. For him, the only way to amass a large body of data (whether in the field or in the archives) was through monographs tailored to the dimensions of individual research. Only by imposing spatial limits on research could one be sure of gathering reliable data. It was therefore illusory to try to establish "simple general relations" before compiling preliminary descriptions of territorial units. Conversely, it was only through the accumulation of local studies that one could hope to develop a pertinent set of questions for investigating the forms and distributions of the fundamental social facts: "Only when we have in hand a few good new regional monographs will we be able, by comparing and contrasting them in minute detail, to take up the fundamental question and take a new and decisive step toward our goal. To proceed in any other way would be to embark on a sort of rapid survey equipped with two or three simple, crude ideas. In most cases it would mean missing the particular, the individual, the irregular—which is to say, what on the whole is most interesting."[93] This text repeats an idea that Febvre had expressed earlier in the foreword to his thesis, namely, that any comparative approach would have to be based on gauging the disparities between regional situations described in the most thorough manner possible. In 1912, for example, he called for additional historical studies of the provinces that joined the French kingdom at a relatively late date, which he said were "in a sense like comparative, experimental laboratories placed and maintained on the borders by life and the centuries themselves."[94] Whether one focused on the natural regions of the geographers or the politically distinctive regions of the historians was of little importance: the methods were identical insofar as they relied on the monograph as the basis of all comparison. Beyond the primacy accorded to regional studies, moreover, was an underlying conception of social description more concerned with difference than with repetition. Choosing a limited framework was thus not simply a matter of convenience or feasibility but also a way of defining the object of study itself, for in this area variations and singularities were more common than stable and universal relations. The choice of the regional thus involved an unavowed investment in a particular representation of social facts, of their causes and relations, which was precisely the opposite of Simiand's.

Victor Karady's research suggests several hypotheses concerning, among other methodological differences, the contrasting conceptions of what constituted a legitimate and relevant space for social science at the beginning of the twentieth century.[95] When the Vidalian geographers and Durkheimian sociologists clashed, the position of the two disciplines was not identical. Geography, the first among the social sciences to break the monopoly of the classical disciplines in the faculties of letters, already enjoyed substantial institutional legitimacy, reinforced by the fact that the geographers had been able to tap into the legitimacy of history itself, having attracted the interest of *normalien* and *agrégé* historians (that is, graduates of the École Normale Supérieure and others who had passed the difficult *agrégation* required for admission to higher teaching posts in the *lycées*), who stood at the top of the academic hierarchy. It also enjoyed increasing scientific legitimacy, based on the definition of a specific object (the region) and a novel research methodology (involving landscape analysis, correlation of natural and human data, and other new methods), without having renounced that crucial warrant of respectability that comes from working in a historical dimension. In order to win recognition of this growing legitimacy, Vidalian geographers used various tactics common to all the new disciplines of the beginning of the century: somewhat circumspect references to German science, in this case Ratzel's inspirational yet criticized anthropogeography; the creation of a journal, the *Annales de géographie*, founded in 1891, which both presented an intelligible, unified image of the group and enabled it to discredit older or competing approaches; and a new manner of presenting its results, which were, to be sure, cast in a traditional form, the thesis for the *doctorat d'État*, but reinforced by new signs of scientificity, such as the use of maps, not as an aid to locating places but as a device for presenting observational data, of photographs, not as illustrations but as ways of defining objects for further study, of sketches and monographs borrowed from the natural sciences, and so on.

In this period, the Sociological School appeared to be overshadowed in two respects. To be sure, it too recruited from the cream of the academic system, attracting *normaliens* and *agrégés*, yet it still had a difficult time establishing itself within the university system and gaining universal recognition of its scientific legitimacy. It therefore resorted to a strategy on which Karady has shed a good deal of light:

> In order to guarantee the scientific legitimacy of sociology and win a place for it equivalent to that of the classical disciplines in the curriculum, links of interdependency had to be forged with those sciences of man already established in the universities (primarily history, geography, and philosophy but also psychology). This was done both by offering services and by initiating an effective and radical critique of their epistemological presuppositions. The strategy was thus one of alliance with the legitimate disciplines while at the same time attempting to supplant them and take their terrain away by occupying it.[96]

When applied specifically to relations between sociologists and geographers and to the question of the division of space, the foregoing description helps us to understand the twofold significance of sociology's rejection of the notion of region. On the one hand it justified a takeover of the subject matter of human geography while totally redefining the framework within which that subject matter was treated. The results of geography were incorporated even as they were rejected, pushed in the direction of "social morphology," which allowed a description of the basis of social life richer than that of a mere economic infrastructure. On the other hand the rejection of region enabled the sociologists to play one of the few trump cards they held against the historians and geographers, namely, their philosophical background, hence their status as an abstract theoretical science committed to concepts and generalizations, whereas geographical studies, more than any other social science and no doubt especially on account of regional description, remained confined to the concrete and the terrain, to local observations and a descriptive approach. To reject regional monographs in favor of comparative, analytical studies on the grounds that only the latter could reveal general laws was to translate into terms of disciplinary methodology one of sociology's most remunerative features: its proximity to philosophy, indeed its claim to be philosophy. Though peripheral to the academic chessboard, sociology attempted, in compensation, to define its subject matter in terms of universal method and national scope. It therefore denied all legitimacy to disciplines within the heart of the academic system that treated, or rather mistreated, the same subject matter in a fragmented fashion, dividing it up in accordance with a piecemeal empiricist method.

For historians, the debate over the region proved to be of decisive importance. In the wake of Febvre, and following a certain latency period—the major theses in "regional" history were undertaken in the 1950s—they devoted their efforts to achieving a global understanding of a carefully circumscribed territory. To be sure, the "region" as defined by Vidalian geographers was no longer the obligatory modulus, or spatial unit, and the spaces explored differed widely in nature, size, and definition: from a *pays* (the Beauvaisis) to a province (Languedoc) to a nation (albeit a stifled one, Catalonia), to mention only the three greatest successes, often imitated by subsequent researchers. Yet while the scale varied, the overall approach was similar: research focused on majority groups, took the long view (generally embracing a century or more), and sought to describe basic demographic, economic, and social structures.

Over the past twenty years, the rediscovery of the Saint-Malo–Geneva line as a key for organizing French disparities in some sense offered a counterpoint to this long-standing interest in regional peculiarities. The widely held but unsubstantiated perception of a divided France was developed into a scientific finding supported by a variety of data.[97] This helped French historians to move away from the catalogue approach inherited from their old association with human geography. In the past history had sought to map peculiarities whose explanation was thought to lie in the diversity of natural conditions and local histories. The discovery of sharp macroscopic differences on either side of a readily identifiable line opened the way to a different approach, a search for large-scale patterns and correlations, which harked back to the long-rejected tradition of social morphology as defined by Durkheimian sociology. Thus restored to a central place in our thinking about French history, a division first discovered by the political arithmeticians of the Restoration took on a twofold significance. First, by "de-regionalizing" historians' descriptions of the social world, it helped to give (or restore to) history the status of a general science. Meanwhile, outside the academic world, it established a way of looking at France's unequal development as well as an explanation for it. Today, of course, the gap between northern and southern France alone no longer seems sufficient to account for certain long-term internal disparities and imbalances. Nevertheless, the division remains as one of the fundamental ways in which the nation's consciousness and memory of internal division have found their expression.

FIGURE 13.0   Montage.

CHAPTER 13

Generation

Pierre Nora

It is difficult to think of a notion that has become more commonplace yet at the same time more opaque than that of "generation." Or of a notion more ancient, one that draws on biological roots that stretch all the way back to the Bible, Herodotus, and Plutarch, yet takes its meaning exclusively from the more recent universe of democratic individualism. Wholly "epidermic," it clings to the surface of the young and to their times, and to fashion, yet no other notion strikes more directly to the vital core of our historical perception of the present. How much of this idea of "generation" belongs particularly to France? In precisely what sense is it a *lieu de mémoire?* And what sorts of distinctions does it permit us to make in the present context?

For twenty years there has been a spate of sociological, economic, demographic, and historical investigations centered on the idea of "generation."[1] The theme, a favorite of pollsters everywhere, has been harped on to the point of exhaustion. Yet none of this might have come to pass without May '68. And of course the "events" that occurred in France at that time must themselves be understood in the context of the international youth rebellion that Margaret Mead was the first to interpret as a symptom of the worldwide generation gap.[2] Long viewed, by historians at least, with skeptical indifference, the elusive idea of a generation suddenly became a focal point of countless studies, all haunted in one way or another by the specter of '68. This sudden surge of interest is all the more curious in that, concerning the explosion of '68 itself, a number of excellent observers have found it impossible not to deplore the paucity of serious historical research, as distinct from the unstanchable flood of (spontaneous or commissioned) reminiscence and self-celebratory observance by those who took part,[3] as if one could somehow sum up a conflagration that no one saw coming and that no rational account could fully explain as nothing more or less than the affirmation of a "generation."

The fabrication of the sacrosanct generation of '68 did not begin with the "events" themselves. At intervals of a decade, anniversary celebrations in 1978 and 1988 set the pace, albeit in markedly different historical contexts.[4] The tenth anniversary of the "events" was an occasion for nostalgic stocktaking, for melancholy reassessment of the *gauchiste* adventure, of those doleful "orphan years"[5] at the end of which one journalist went in quest of a "lost generation" and its memories.[6] The twentieth anniversary came at the tense conclusion of a period of "cohabitation,"[7] a period caught in a pincers between, on the one hand, what Serge July, a central figure in the saga, did not shrink from calling the "premature ejaculation" of the December 1986 student movement[8] and, on the other, the already-launched campaigns for upcoming presidential and legislative elections and ongoing preparations for the Bicentennial of the French Revolution. What emerged, however, from those two anniversaries—crowned by the publication of Hervé Hamon and Patrick Rotman's *Génération*, the first work ever to bear that simple and majestic title—was more than anything else the capacity of a handful of ex-Trotskyite, ex-Maoist, ex–Gauche Prolétarienne activists and chroniclers, risen to positions of leadership, to set themselves up (or persuade others to set them up) as spokesmen for an entire generation, for whose commemoration they assumed sole responsibility.[9]

This mania for celebration is in itself significant. No historical event of substantive content has elicited anything of the kind: World War I, the Popular Front, the Resistance, the Liberation. It is profoundly revealing of the very nature of May '68: its capacity to serve as a looking glass, its symbolic malleability, its historical elasticity, and its characteristic tendency to ascribe greater importance to the subjective experience of the moment than to the objective substance of the facts. Memory was germinating even as the movement unfolded, for what was it, with its barricades as historical quotation and its theater of allusion, but an enactment of revolutionary memory without a revolutionary opportunity?

Generation, memory, symbol: May '68 was its own commemorative anniversary. The construction of a memory went hand in hand with the self-affirmation of a generation, two faces of a single phenomenon. The elimination of the historian as intermediary only highlighted the generational dynamic of 1968 and the uniquely symbolic content attached at the time to expression, culminating a vast historical cycle that began with nothing less than the French Revolution and ended in the events of May. The emergence of a "generation" in its pure, intransitive state revealed the sovereignty of the notion's retrospective explanatory power, thereby constituting it, from its inception and in a primary, purely temporal sense, as a *lieu de mémoire*.

A Retrospective Overview of the Notion

Whether in an international context or a more specific French one, the culmination of the idea of "generation" in '68 can only be understood by returning directly to the root of the phenomenon, the French Revolution. I am by no means unaware that to telescope '68 and '89 may strike some readers as indecent or incongruous,[9] as if the Event in its pure state, the advent of the modern event, were in any way commensurate with the later so-called events, about which it was immediately asked in what respect they could be said to constitute events at all. The short circuit is nevertheless enlightening. It reveals the existence of a sort of historical watershed and a gamut of definitions of generation from the properly historical to the essentially symbolic.

The event of '68 magnified the generational dimension, whereas '89 minimized it. Yet it was omnipresent. Restif de La Bretonne noted this at the time: "It was [Rousseau's] *Émile* that brought us this teasing, stubborn, insolent, impudent, headstrong generation, which speaks loudly, shuts the mouths of the elderly, and with equal audacity demonstrates now its innate folly, reinforced by education, now its immature wisdom, as raw and sharp as grapes pressed in mid-August."[10] It had already made its appearance in the twenty years that preceded the revolutionary explosion, in the form of youth movements and demonstrations, which recent research has shown to have existed in both Paris and the provinces.[11] It erupted in the Tennis Court Oath, the first triumph of the principle of fraternal solidarity over paternal judgment.[12] It might have remained more in evidence, moreover, had it not been quickly overshadowed by the idea of faction. The generational concept found clear expression in revolutionary explorations of the link between the end of hereditary rule and the legitimacy of representative government, as can be seen in a curious pamphlet, *The First Principles of Government* (5 Messidor, Year III) by Thomas Paine, in which the Anglo-American propagandist, steeped in the Jeffersonian tradition,[13] after some rather tricky calculations pertaining to the substitution of the young for the old delineated the precise rights of each:

> Since every generation has equal rights, it follows that none has the slightest right to establish a hereditary government.... Every age, every generation is and should be (with respect to rights) as free to act for itself in all cases as were previous ages and generations.... If we have another gospel on this point, we behave as slaves or as tyrants; as slaves if we believe that some first generation had any right whatsoever to fetter us; as tyrants if we arrogate to ourselves the authority to bind the generations that shall follow us.[14]

The concept of generation can also be found, in the most solemn of terms, in the founding texts of the French Republic. The Declaration of the Rights of Man of 1793—Condorcet's text—goes so far as to proclaim that "a generation has no right to subject any future generation to its laws" (Article 30).[15] The same concept was already implicit in the Constitution of 1791, which at one stroke abolished both hereditary rights and corporate regulations, thus laying the groundwork for a society of free and equal individuals. It was also implicit in revolutionary measures concerning the family and paternal authority, particularly those that responded to the demands of youth, such as abolishing primogeniture, setting the age of majority at twenty-one, allowing marriage without paternal consent, and denying fathers the right to disinherit their children. Saint-Just, typical of the rising generation, summed up these measures: "You have therefore decided that one generation cannot place another in chains."[16] The Revolution was intrinsically generational, nowhere more so than in its rhetoric, its ambition to be a historical, initiatory rite of passage from the night of despotism to the bright day of liberty. Generation-Regeneration: the two themes were closely associated in all their biological, psychological, moral, religious, and messianic connotations.[17] In a more profound sense, the Revolution was generational in its pedagogical obsession and reversal of time, in its eschatology of rupture, in its instantaneous transition from the Old to the New. The twilight of legitimacy, the dawn of the notion of generation. The past is no longer the law: this is the very essence of the phenomenon.

The Revolution thus marked the absolute but invisible advent of the notion of generation. It has often been noted that the careers which the revolutionary adventure and the abolition of privileges opened to talent progressed rapidly, as evidenced by that of Bonaparte. But people were more struck by individual youthfulness, such as Saint-Just's, than by a general rejuvenation of history's *personae*. The care that Chateaubriand, for one, took to postdate his birth by one year—1769 rather than 1768—has generally been attributed to a wish to hitch his star to Napoleon's rather than to a desire to count himself among those who were "twenty years old in 1789." Only recently, in the light of our retrospective interest in the generational theme, have scholars (most of them English-speaking, by the way) thought to calculate the average age of assembly members.[18] And so the sudden burst of youth onto the political scene stands revealed: if the average age of deputies in the Constituent Assembly was still forty, that of deputies in the Legislative Assembly was only twenty-six: a fantastic rejuvenation of the historical cast. This neglected aspect of the Revolution calls for a wholesale reinterpretation of the event. It emerges even more clearly when we look into the details of things: the Montagnards, for example, were far younger than their rivals, the Girondins. But the youthful dimension of the Revolution passed largely unnoticed, melted back into the Revolution itself. The dynamism of a particular group, youth, fused with the universality of the Revolution's principles to become not the extreme or radical form of revolutionary politics but its fundamental reality. From a historical point of view this is the deeper meaning of the Burke-Paine polemic, which without exaggeration can be described as having marked the historical baptism of the notion of generation. Against Burke's *Reflections* on the merits of tradition, so full of irony toward the "usurpers," those "political novices," those "summer flies" that had "given themselves *carte blanche* to set themselves in business without a stock in trade" and to "refuse the government of examples," Thomas Paine, invoking novel inaugural formulas against the "usurped authority of the dead," championed each generation's right to set its own course: "Man has no property in man; neither has any generation a property in the generations which are to follow."[19]

Thus the Revolution established the notion of a generation, not only because it gave birth to one (a proposition whose proof would itself be an effect of retrospective genealogy) but because it cleared the way for, made possible, and accelerated the advent of a world of change, an egalitarian world in which "generational consciousness" was born. The phenomenon was not limited to France, although there the longevity of monarchical succession and the Oedipal brutality of the king's murder lent particular intensity to the French case. It was intrinsic to the Atlantic revolution and the principle of representative democracy. In the United States, however, the problem was resolved at one stroke, and so successfully that the issue of generational replacement has never arisen there in the political sphere as such, whereas in France the Revolution inaugurated an enduring conflict and infused into politics a rhythm with a perceptible generational pulse. French political history could indeed be written in terms of generations and generational themes: from Louis XVIII to Thiers, from Pétain to de Gaulle, that history could be read as a story of youth's revolt against the authority of the fathers. This narrative is the ground bass, the warp and woof of French political life; it forms the political backbone of French memory, and, in a country where political change has been rapid as well as rocky, it has made the seizure of power a central feature of the generational concept. For that reason alone, the word *generation* in French is almost invariably associated with the word *dominant*.

The two dates—'89 and '68—thus mark the ends of a broad spectrum of social representations. In 1789 the Event completely subsumed the generational symbolism by allowing it full expression, thereby masking its presence. In 1968, by contrast, the event owed its existence to its generational dimension, so that one may ask Ranke's question: *Wie es eigentlich gewesen?* or, What, apart from the individual experiences and effects on the lives of those involved, actually happened? And the answer, in Hegelian terms and in the eyes of that History which is written in letters of blood, is Nothing.

Precisely this historical vacuum was necessary, however, in order for the truth to bubble up: what happened in '68 was a symbolic rupture, and it is just this kind of rupture that is the key to the generational concept. A generation is a category of representative comprehension; it is a violent affirmation of horizontal identity that suddenly dominates and transcends all forms of vertical solidarity. Sixty-eight revealed the essence of the generational phenomenon: a dynamic of belonging, simple in some ways and complex in others. The "youth movement" developed throughout the world, yet it had no crucial shared experience on which to find common ground, unless it was the experience of having missed such traumatic engagements as the World War II resistance against fascism or the opposition to the Algerian War. The revolutionary mime of 1968 ran against the tide of the moment: it occurred at the peak of a period of rapid economic growth and in a time of full employment, as orthodox revolutionary ideologies were crumbling. Even the participants were surprised by the rapidity with which strategic population centers erupted in flames. A "demand to be heard" was of course part of the event itself, and would-be authoritative analyses appeared immediately in its wake, yet this purely generational explosion was so disconcerting that some commentators tried hard to shift the blame to other generations and events.[20] Demographers, for example, argued that the force of the eruption reflected the accumulated explosive potential of three distinct generations: the demobilized generation of the Algerian War (people born between 1935 and 1941), followed by a relatively small generation untouched by ideology (people born during World War II), both of which were ostensibly energized by the first wave of the post–World War II baby boom.[21] For the cultural psychologists, attuned to the movement's romantic nostalgia and its analogies with the revolution of 1848, it was the very absence of historical events that served as the triggering trauma, a hypothesis confirmed by the utopian and narcissistic character of this adolescent and rather anarchical protest.[22] For one journalist of sociological bent, the generation of 1968 was merely the shadow cast by the Algerian War generation, much influenced by de Gaulle's return to power ten years earlier.[23] And for one former *gauchiste* lately repentant of his youthful commitments, the '68 generation was rather the midwife of the 70s generation, marked by fading memories of the Algerian episode and liberated from the fascination that the Communist Party still exerted on its predecessor.[24] The pendulum has not stopped swinging.

The difficulty of simply defining or even identifying the last and most visible of our generations mirrors the difficulty faced by a whole series of analysts since Auguste Comte the moment they try to move from the concrete, empirical description of a group of people of roughly the same age held together by some common set of experiences to a more theoretical definition.[25] It has been argued, in fact, that the notion has no operational or scientific interest unless clear and precise answers can be given to four key sets of questions: temporal, demographic, historical, and sociological. How long does a generation last? How quickly are generations replaced, given that sons are perpetually taking over from their fathers? What date defines a generation: the date of birth or the conventional benchmark of the twentieth year, which is assumed to mark the end of the adolescent's period of maximal receptivity? Exactly what role do events play in the determination of a generation, where the term *events*, broadly construed, encompasses both ordinary experience and *the* traumatic event? Is generation a conscious or unconscious phenomenon? Is it something imposed from without or freely chosen? Is it a statistical or a psychological phenomenon? Or, to put it another way, who does and who does not belong to a given generation, and how does that belonging manifest itself, given that one or more different age cohorts may identify with a generation without taking part in the vicissitudes of its existence?

Bringing all these questions together in one place makes it clear that the notion of generation inevitably leads to insoluble contradictions and uncertainties. These are too obvious to dwell on here, and much ink has already been spilled in discussing them. Even the most innovative of the thinkers who have found the notion of generation interesting enough to explore have encountered these dilemmas. Take, for example, the sociologist Karl Mannheim, who in his classic 1928 essay saw generations as "one of the fundamental factors in the unfolding dynamic of history" yet found it difficult to distill a clear concept from an impure composite.[26] Most writers who use the notion have moved from a flexible, concrete, almost neutral definition to a rigid mathematism, or vice versa. After World War I, for example, François Mentré saw a generation as embodying "a new way of feeling and understanding life, opposed to or at least different from what went before."[27] And after World War II, the literary historian Henri Peyre defined a generation as "united initially by shared hostilities and by having been subjected to the same influences between the ages of sixteen and twenty-five, if not earlier."[28] Yet neither writer had the slightest hesitation about drawing up endless, tedious tables demonstrating the march of generations from some arbitrarily chosen initial date: 1490 for one (Clouet, Du Bellay, Marguerite de Navarre, Rabelais, Marot), 1600 for the other (Descartes, Poussin, Mansart, Corneille, Claude Lorrain, Fermat). One of the most surprising examples of the kind can be found in the work of the Spanish writer Julián Marías, a disciple of Ortega y Gasset, who, in attempting to give a systematic demonstration of his teacher's ideas, came up with the following rather startling series of dates for the significant generations of the nineteenth and twentieth centuries: 1812, 1827, 1842, 1857, 1872, 1887, 1902, 1917, 1932, 1947.[29] In contrast, Yves Renouard, who in 1953 became one of the first historians to hail the idea of generation as "an illuminating beacon" which "alone could help to compose a dynamic portrait of a society," called for a more precise definition: "A collection of age cohorts, a group of men and women whose ideas, feelings, and lifestyles are the same, and who are shaped by the same physical, intellectual, and moral conditions as the major facts and events affecting the society of which they are a part." Yet he advocated caution and prudence in applying his narrow approach.[30]

The problem is that all the writers who have ventured to treat the subject in terms of rather vague categories and approximate definitions invariably become prisoners of what might be called the "dialectic of the hard and the soft." The generational instrument seems scientific to them only if it is precise, but if it is applied precisely one runs up against life's inconsistencies. The attempt to escape from the impressionistic ends up being impressionistic. After so many brave attempts one is reminded of the fellow who discovered that rubber had every imaginable quality, its only problem being its lamentable elasticity. The generational concept would make a wonderfully precise instrument if only its precision didn't make it impossible to apply to the unclassifiable disorder of reality. As for the duration of a generation, any number of equally plausible answers have been given, from Albert Thibaudet's ambling thirty years (in *Histoire de la littérature française depuis 1789*, a book based entirely on the idea of generation[31]), to Ortega y Gasset's and Yves Renouard's quicker-paced fifteen to Henri Peyre's and François Mentré's blistering ten. One is left with a situation in which some authorities confidently see a dozen literary generations from 1789 to the present where others see only five. As for birth dates, not even the authorities are above a certain amount of juggling and finagling. Thibaudet, for example, is quite unhappy with the idea of including in the generation that led the assault on 1789 not only men born in the period 1766–1769 (such as Chateaubriand, Napoleon, Senancour, Benjamin Constant, and Maine de Biran) but also writers such as Rivarol and Joubert, who were fifteen years older than Napoleon and Chateaubriand. Nor does he hesitate to place Montherlant alongside Proust in the generation of World War I, even though thirty years separated the two men. What if we make major events our sole criterion? We must then differentiate between events endured and events freely chosen, between formative events and determinative events. All events are multigenerational, moreover, and the greater their magnitude (like World War I), the less simple it is to identify the groups most affected by them. Yves Renouard proposes four types of generational reactions to events: the indifference of the elderly, the unconsciousness of children, and, between the two, the reactions of those who wield power over events and of those who challenge that power. And what, finally, if we choose to rely on statistical criteria? On the one hand there is the clear and simple demographic definition: a generation is nothing but a cohort, a group of people born in a given year. Economists and statisticians have found this objective definition quite useful. On the other hand there is the undecidable question of generational representativity. In other words, what entitles us to say that people who knew nothing of Victor Hugo's famous play belonged to the "generation of *Hernani*," or that people who took no part in World War II belonged to the "generation of the Resistance?" Can we identify a generation with those who speak in its name, availing ourselves of a natural confusion that has proved particularly fruitful and rewarding when applied to such articulate groups as artists, intellectuals, and men of letters?

Although each of these solutions offers its share of persuasive insights, in every attempt to hone a sharp analytic scalpel, the recalcitrance of the material has ended by blunting the instrument's cutting edge. Hence it will come as no surprise that the most careful historians, though by no means unaware of the unique light that the notion of generation can shed on the past, have generally rejected the concept as schematic, unworkable, crude, and in the end less enriching than reductive. In particular, the founders of the journal *Annales,* who in their desire to work with the most concrete social data inevitably encountered generational phenomena, were severe in their judgment, dismissing the idea of generation as an *artifact,* an illusion that people engaged in social action held about themselves. Marc Bloch somewhat grudgingly allowed it the virtue of "laying the preliminary groundwork."[32] Lucien Febvre, however, had no doubt about the verdict: "Better forget it!"[33] Despite some successful recent attempts to breathe historical life into the phenomenon, to identify, with subtlety and tact, generational constellations in the political[34] and intellectual[35] realms, the fundamental judgment has not wavered.[36]

The problem is that any attempt to give a precise definition of generation, or at any rate to provide as much precision as any definition requires, inevitably falls into a trap—or twin traps—inherent in the notion itself. First, a generation is by its very nature a purely individual phenomenon that only makes sense when seen collectively. And second, although the notion originated in a philosophical framework of continuity, it makes sense only in a framework of discontinuity and rupture.[37] Although the idea is based on a biological analogy, it thrives when time is chopped up into symbolic segments rather than treated as a continuous chronological quantity. We are all conscious of belonging to several generations, to which we feel connected in varying degrees. We do not necessarily feel that we belong to the generation to which the dates of our birth would consign us. What accounts for the special interest in this very distinctive type of periodization (the only type not somehow mathematically determined) is not the material and temporal determinism that it fatally entails but the dynamics of belonging that it authorizes. As for the notion of generation, there are two basic attitudes, not to say two radically contradictory philosophies. According to one view, a generation is essentially determined by a principle of inclusion, of assigned social membership and defined existential limits, hence it is a reinforcement of the notion of finitude that caused Heidegger, following the German romantic philosophers, to say that "the fact of living in and with one's generation concludes the drama of human existence."[38] The other view is that egalitarian democracy has unleashed an incredible potential for identification, which has been invested in identification with one's generation because such identification allows for freedom and self-amplification. Pure generational solidarity,

which is the whole essence of the phenomenon, is freedom, insofar as the horizontality that it assumes is in a sense the ideal and idealized image of egalitarian democracy. A generation embodies and epitomizes the principle of equality out of which
it was born. Surely this is what endows it with its potential for radical simplification.
At one stroke it abolishes all other differences. Or better still, the idea of generation
completes the squaring of the circle that is the problem of all democracy: it converts
the imposed into the willed, the simple fact of birth into an affirmation of existence.
This is perhaps the only way to feel free nowadays while being bound to something.

"The generation" is the daughter of democracy and of the acceleration of history.
Identification with events corresponded to an era of slow changes and clear tempi
that impressed themselves on the minds of participants. The absence of an unmistakable reference point for truly collective memory, together with an increasingly
rapid pace of change, has led to the opposite situation: the identification of temporal flow with the very notion of generation. Not that great events have vanished—
quite the contrary. But events too have changed in nature: they are banalized by
their very multiplicity, made unreal by the way in which they are received and experienced, and extended in their impact to a much broader population. The historical
milieu in which events unfold has exploded to include the entire world. France,
which long saw history as centered on itself, is increasingly bound to acknowledge
that the center is elsewhere. The social upheavals of the past twenty-five years have
reinforced this view, expanding the middle class and introducing a convergence of
lifestyles and consumer habits.[39] The accent of novelty now falls on microevents,
on technological or social innovation. Finally, demographic changes have accentuated the transformation of the phenomenon, with the aging of the population, a
result of increased life expectancy and decreased birth rate, coupled with a relative
increase in the number of the young owing to a delayed commencement of work
life and the emergence of the new stage of "post-adolescence."[40] This simultaneous
increase in the French population of the proportion of the young and of the old
makes for a situation of ever more stark confrontation, since whatever is not
"young" is immediately perceived as "old." History, society, and demography have
thus powerfully conspired to democratize an essentially democratic phenomenon.
The notion of generation has thus been subverted from within in much the same
way as the modern "mediatized" event.[41] There is no longer a "dominant generation" or total historical phenomenon; atomized, what the generational theme now
conveys is social everydayness in all its aspects. People used to reckon three generations per century. Nowadays we count a new generation almost daily. As I write
these lines in May of 1989, several of the month's periodicals have appeared with
articles on generational topics: the weekly magazine *Le Nouvel Observateur* has a
feature on "Thirty-Year-Olds: Portrait of a Generation"; a major daily newspaper,

Libération, has a literary supplement entitled "The Vernant Generation," after Jean-Pierre Vernant, a retired scholar; the magazine *Infini* has baptized a group of young writers "The '89 Generation"; a special issue of the journal *Vingtième Siècle* is devoted to "Generations"; and two graduates of the prestigious École Nationale d'Administration, members of the group "Generation 1992," have published a book entitled *Generation Europe*! For journalists and ad agency copywriters "generation" is a notion that floats as freely as the franc in the European monetary system, drifting from the key of technology—Moulinex generation, Pampers generation—to that of psychology— Generation X, the rap generation, the singles generation. The latest in political advertising—call it a bluff or a stroke of genius as you will—is a poster touting the "Mitterrand Generation," and it is hard to say whether the noted adman who thought it up was motivated more by a propitiatory reflex or ironic loyalty. This destructive, obsessive inflation of the idea—what the Situationists used to call a *détournement*—has been described, quite understandably, as the premature obsolescence of a notion well-suited to the explanation of a long and arduous nineteenth century but inappropriate to a momentarily more frivolous age.[42] The obsolescence of the notion is not obvious, however. Its atomization, not to say banalization, has done nothing to limit its sacralization, radicalization, and transgressive vocation—quite the contrary.

The real question raised by the contemporary transformation, use, and diffusion of the notion is this: As the pace of change increases, how and why has the horizontal identification of individuals of roughly the same age been able to supplant all forms of vertical identification? In the past, generations were identified by other categories, such as family, class (in both the social and scholastic senses), career, and nation, but nowadays the generational phenomenon is more powerful: the old categories have been blasted away to make room for the assertion of new identities. The generational idea took wing, as it were, even as it took on weight. It proved its strength by demonstrating its capacity to make and unmake social categories. This was possible only because the importance of traditional criteria of social classification diminished and traditional social identities proved inadequate. Earlier modes of filiation and affiliation did not disappear but did to some extent lose the power to create structures. The subsequent void strengthened the generational concept. As Paul Yonnet and other sociologists attuned to contemporary realities have shown,[43] the generational idea simultaneously simplified and complicated the network of social allegiances. Superimposed on older forms of solidarity, generational solidarities created a sturdy yet flexible new structure that defined new limits and new forms of transgression. It was the very plasticity of this new structure that made it so effective; the void that it filled ultimately became its content. Thus a vague, imprecise, supererogatory notion became an instrument with substantial, precise, and crucial consequences. In a curious reversal, the generation affirmed its classificatory hegemony to the precise extent that its original historical function weakened.

Such a reversal can be understood only in terms of an inversion of what one might call the age-prestige pyramid (by analogy with the "age pyramid" of the demographers). And that brings us to a thorny problem: the growing autonomy of that new continent, Youth, an autonomy that over the past twenty-five years has increased at a rapidly accelerating pace.[44] Youth has ceased to be a transitory stage of life; it has emancipated itself from the sociological reality of being a social minority and even freed itself from the symbolism of age to become an organizing principle for society as a whole, a mental image that guides the distribution of roles and positions, an end unto itself. Youth is not "merely a word."[45] A great deal of research suggests that its status has been transformed in three main stages. In the aftermath of the Revolution, which broke an age-old cycle and at the cost of deep upheaval opened up a new world, the young really did take on adult roles. They carried much of the burden of social and political transformation. A revealing detail is that the word *gérontocratie* first appeared in 1825 (was it Béranger who coined it or the pamphleteer J. J. Fazy?[46]). In other words, the word came into use at the very beginning of the liberal assault on the Restoration's attempt to consolidate a return to the habits of the Ancien Régime. All the revolutions of the nineteenth century began as youth insurrections. The second stage in the transformation of youth occurred as the structure of the family evolved and other social changes initiated by the Revolution gradually took hold: wealth was redistributed as a result of new laws of inheritance, intensifying conflict between fathers and sons; careers were opened to talent, and the brightest young men sought to enter the Grandes Écoles. In the process of generational renewal youths can assume adult social responsibilities earlier in life or later, violently or peacefully, calmly or frenetically. Much of the literature of the nineteenth and early twentieth centuries drew on this theme, from Balzac to Jules Romains, from Flaubert's *L'Éducation sentimentale* to Marcel Arland's *L'Ordre* and Jean-Paul Sartre's *Sursis*.[47] More recently the subject has been taken up for scientific study by economists and sociologists, in whose literature it appears under the head of "generational cycles."[48] In this long process of stabilization, during which the generational concept also first crystallized, youth movements and organizations from the Scouts to various Catholic and Communist youth groups were essentially just structures for preparing young people for or integrating them into the structures, ideologies, and parties of adult society.[49] Then, suddenly, came the secession and democratization of the phenomenon. When precisely did this occur? There can be no doubt that it was sometime between 1959, when polls and social images suggest that the youth myth for the first time began to take on negative connotations (associated with the "black leather jacket" of the "rebel without a cause"), and 1965, when statisticians first noted a decline in the birth rate, which within ten years fell below the level needed to sustain a stable population. In that same year Roger Daltrey with his blue-eyed Cockney look sang "My G-generation." Suddenly youth erupted into the public consciousness[50] as a world unto itself, with its own laws, clothing, vocabulary, recognition signs, idols—Jack Kerouac, Johnny Halliday—mythology (from *Planète* to *Salut les copains*), and its great celebratory occasions, the first of which, the memorable *Nuit des copains* (Buddies' Night), held in Paris on June 21, 1963, drew more than 150,000 young people and is still remembered as a revelation.[51]

The more important point to notice, however, is that the definition of youth now became exclusive and discriminatory: this fixation on age was precisely what enabled the generational idea to assert its hegemony over all ages and to explode in all directions. The triumph of the principal of horizontality, which offers no assurances and promises no future, may have established the independence of youth, but it did not guarantee young people any actual preeminence or promise them a monopoly of the generational idea. On the contrary, it merely laid the groundwork for all age groups to appropriate the notion and for society as a whole to internalize the phenomenon. The increase in life expectancy helped in this: as the spectrum of ages expanded, so did the number of possible generations, and it would not be difficult, for example, to demonstrate a subtle range of generational shadings from the young-old all the way to the old-old. This marks the end of the road and signals what the idea of generation has become: a purely psychological notion, private and individual, an identity for internal use only. In a world in the grip of democratic atomization, belonging to a generation is not simply a way to be free, it is also the only way not to be alone.

The Historical Construction of the Model

In every country, it seems, one generation has served as a model and pattern for all subsequent generations. In Russia it was the political and ideological generation of Chernyshevsky (early 1860s). In Spain it was the legendary generation of 1898, in which Unamuno spearheaded a literary reaction. In the United States it was not until after World War I that a secession from "the American way of life" gave rise to the "Lost Generation." But the truest parallel with France is to be found in Germany: the histories of the two countries have been closely intertwined since the Revolution, each influencing and reacting to the other.[52] One can therefore ask what generation in Germany had the same fundamental, archetypal significance as the "romantic generation" in France? By general agreement the answer is not the generation of the *Aufklärung* or of *Sturm und Drang* but the generation of Prussian youth that from 1815 to 1820 fought for intellectual freedom and national unity.[53] In any case, the romantics, who "gave the nineteenth century its principal formula"[54] and were hailed as "a sort of natural entelechy,"[55] left a blazing trail in history and myth.

In 1836, Musset belatedly gave the romantics a poetic name: *enfants du siècle*. This flight of lyricism, which wreathed its object in a *"je ne sais quoi* of fluctuation and drift,"[56] nevertheless points toward a very specific historical situation. First came the repression of student and *carbonari* demonstrations in 1819–20. Then, in 1823, the short-lived *Muse française,* the cradle of France's poetic revival, appeared for the first time. In 1825, the generation's flagship newspaper the *Globe* appeared. Finally, out of the eruption of 1830 came a generation that would reign for the next twenty years—brilliant enough to dazzle and all but overwhelm even the likes of Baudelaire and Flaubert. Call this the generation of 1820 or 1830, it makes no difference which. It had, according to the American historian Allan B. Spitzer, some 183 members, mostly born between 1795 and 1802: Thierry (1795), Vigny (1797), Thiers (1797), Michelet (1798), Comte (1798), Pierre Leroux (1797), Cournot (1801), Delacroix (1798), Balzac (1799), and Hugo (1802), to name a few. Spitzer was able to show what youthful connections existed among the members, what groups they formed, and what kinds of influence they exerted on one another. Taken as a whole, the generation formed a tactical alliance in which young royalist writers engaged in literary insurrection joined forces with militant republican students involved in conspiratorial sects. They were quick to proclaim themselves a generation, moreover, most notably in a celebrated text by Théodore Jouffroy (born in 1796). Jouffroy, a *carbonaro* who lost his position as a professor at the École Normale, wrote his piece in 1823 but did not publish it in *Le Globe* until 1825. Though mediocre, it attracted a great deal of attention, and Sainte-Beuve would later recognize it as "the most explicit manifesto of the persecuted young elite."[57]

> A new generation is rising, a generation born in a skeptical age when two parties shared the podium. It listened and it understood. These children have already sensed the emptiness of their fathers' teachings and gone beyond them.... Superior to all that surrounds them, they will not accept either a rebirth of fanaticism or a faithless selfishness such as that which envelops today's society.... They have a sense of their mission and an understanding of their age. They understand what their fathers did not understand, what corrupt tyrants will never understand. They know what a revolution is, and they know it because they came on the scene at the right moment.[58]

These gestational years left them with blessed, electrified memories of a kind of new dawn in the world. "What marvelous times!" Théophile Gautier put it later, describing the meetings of the first Cénacle in his *Histoire du romantisme*.[59] "How young it all was, how new, how full of strange colors and strong, intoxicating flavors! Our heads were turned. We seemed to be venturing into unknown worlds."

And a quarter of a century later, Alfred de Vigny, still under the charm of this early Eden, recalled how at *La Muse française* he found "a few very young men, strangers to one another, meditating on a new poetry. Each of them, in silence, had felt a mission in his heart."[60] What gave this group, or, as Thibaudet might call it, this "brood," this squadron of "recruits," its poetic or social or political mission was its historical situation: it was the revolutionary generation *deferred*. That is why it was immediately recognized and hailed by the very people whom it intended to replace: the baptism of the fathers is in fact the primary and crucial condition that a generation must meet if it is to be deemed legitimate. It was old Lafayette himself who, as early as 1820, spoke of "this new generation, enlightened and generous, above succumbing to the influence of Jacobinism and Bonapartism, which will, I'm sure, support the right to pure liberty."[61] And it was Benjamin Constant, speaking from the podium of the Chamber of Deputies in 1822, who hailed "today's youth, less frivolous than the youth of the Ancien Régime, less impassioned than the youth of the Revolution, which stands out by dint of its thirst for knowledge, its love of hard work, and its devotion to truth."[62] To these youths, born at the turn of the century, educated in the barracks-schools of the Empire, and familiar with Napoleon only through the saga of France's glory and humiliation, the Restoration entrusted the task of expressing in the form of generational consciousness the capital that the Revolution had invested in action. This was the source of its Herculean enthusiasm and of the juvenile belief that it constituted an army: "In the romantic army as in the Army of Italy," Gautier later wrote, "everyone was young."[63] It was also the source of its sense of responsibility, its cohesiveness, and its idea that an enemy front was there to be breached. If chronology laid the groundwork, the political and social situation consolidated it.[64] Although there were those among the bureaucratic and political personnel of the Restoration who were quick to climb or premature to reach the top of the ladder of success, those happy few were not numerous enough to counter the regime's reputation as a place for powdered old men, "screech owls afraid of the light and contemptuous of newcomers," as Balzac, indefatigable on the subject, once put it. The Restoration was the very image of political reaction, of a historical enfeeblement compounded by the partial failure of 1830, social retrenchment, provincial traditionalism, frenetic competition, and a career crisis, a shortage of opportunities, that gave rise to the Balzacian phrase, not to say myth, of "the vast graduating class of '89," whose way forward was blocked and barricaded, another crucial condition for the formation of a generational consciousness being precisely a sense of persecution.

The historical underpinning was not the whole story, however. What made the romantic generation a dominant model was not simply that it was a complete generation, by which I mean a cohort whose social, political, intellectual, and academic profile made it representative of *the* crucial moment in modern French history, a cohort, moreover, whose contours had been sharpened by social evolution and which had witnessed the brutal clash of July 1830. What turned this generational panoply into a creative, formative pattern was the linking of all these features to the two dimensions that have always been central to the idea of a generation in France, namely, politics and literature, power and words (here construed as an active magical force, poetry, upon which the romantics bestowed truly miraculous powers).[65] Therein lies the core of French generational identity. Other countries may construct their patterns around other key factors: Russia, for example, around the triangle of state power, civil society, and public education; or the United States around the breakdown of a consensus concerning prosperity. In France, generations are identified by their relation to power on the one hand and to expression—literary, intellectual, or musical—on the other. Together these two ingredients are the yeast that makes the bread rise. No doubt there have been generations, such as the symbolists and surrealists, that were confined mainly to literary circles, although Mallarmé's involvement in the Dreyfus Affair and Breton's in revolutionary politics might suggest otherwise. And no doubt there have been generations such as that of the Resistance or of Cold War Communism, whose sensibility was exclusively political, though here, too, Éluard and Aragon run counter to the main current. But these are a historian's quibbles, unimportant compared with the primary factor, the distinctive mixture of the political and the literary that gives each French generation its unique stamp. Could there have been a "Dreyfus generation" without Péguy's visceral lyricism? Could there have been an "existentialist generation" without Sartre and his concept of "existence"? Since generation implies conflict and self-conscious self-proclamation, what better arenas for self-expression could any generation find than politics and literature? It was the yoking together of the political-historical and the literary-symbolic that gave the concept explanatory amplitude and enabled it to survive for two centuries—the period during which politics and literature have been linked. We rarely think of political generations in isolation from literary generations. Indeed, the related spheres of literature and politics overlap the concept of generation; that is why the concept has been so useful in writing the political history of France since the Revolution, and why it has proved so profitable to study first literary generations, then ideological generations, and now finally intellectual generations. It all goes back to 1820, that key moment in the history of the parliamentary monarchy, when the two Frances, one aesthetic, the other political, confronted each other. The Restoration and the beginnings of the July Monarchy intensified generational conflict of a type that the Revolution had originated but had not resolved, and at the same time made it more visible. A basic binary opposition thus left its indelible trace on the nation's collective memory, and this encouraged a whole series of binary splits: father-son, young-old, old-new. In this light it can be seen that the question of generational representativity becomes a false problem.

There is another aspect of the construction of the 1820 generation that should not be neglected: the importance that the generation itself attached to its engagement in history as well as to the inscription of that engagement in the historical record. It is striking to note that the same "generation" discovered both history and the concept of generation. Marcel Gauchet had occasion to point this out in an essay[66] in which he meticulously reconstructs the intellectual climate surrounding the inception of Augustin Thierry's *Lettres sur l'histoire de France* in 1820. "Historical reform," he noted, "smacked of the sudden emergence of a generation." Thierry was twenty-five when he formulated his program for a total revision of historical memory and a completely new approach to the past. He was among the younger of the group of historians responsible for the conception of history as a constitutive element of collective identity. He was born in 1795, Mignet in 1796, Thiers in 1797, Michelet in 1798, Quinet in 1803. He did not experience the Revolution as a child, unlike Guizot, born in 1787, or the Genevan Sismondi, a precursor who always remained on the margins yet who clearly set forth a basic framework for historical reform in the introduction to his *Histoire des Français*: "The Revolution, by putting an end to rights and privileges, arranged it so that all the centuries of the past are at virtually the same distance from us.... None governs us any longer through its institutions." The coincidence bears emphasizing, for it is fundamental: the same cohort simultaneously discovered what Gauchet rightly calls "the past as past" and therefore what can only be called "the present as present," a formula that could, if one absolutely must have a formula, be taken as the best historical definition of a generation. The two moments are inseparable. The advent of generational consciousness presupposes an idea of history. It was the historical radicality of the Revolution that made of generation a phenomenon initially national and French; but the revolutionaries did not conceive of their action as historical or insert it into history. On the contrary, they were intent on breaking with the past, on subverting it, on beginning history anew, free of the laws of filiation and the requirements of continuity. It was not until the next stage, in the vacuum created by inaction and under the full scourge of reaction, that a group united by age and dominated by the revolutionary event discovered not just history as man's production of his own existence but also the power of collective action and social germination and the role of time in the unfolding historical process. This deep immersion in history is absolutely inseparable from the emergence of an active generational consciousness: no rupture without a hypothesis of continuity, no selection of memory without resurrection of another memory. The importance attached to the reform of history and the romantics' new attitude toward the past, the Middle Ages, and its ruins consummated their invention of the concept of generation. There could be no future history of generations had that particular generation not discovered a past history. Out of this came the whole dynamic of generational replacement.

The dynamic of generational replacement: this assumes to begin with the whole ponderous, stable framework of the great cycle that runs, as we have seen, from the Revolution to 1968, with an offshoot extending to the present day and an abrupt change of direction sometime during the period 1960–1965. No matter how one views the pace or form of generational replacement, its endless round would be difficult to interpret were it not for certain durable, constant elements, which form a fixed background against which a variety of patterns stand out. This stability is sometimes described in terms of the "solidity" of French society, only the barest outline of which can be attempted here. The exceptional continuity of French national unity is the source of that solidity, despite internal cleavages. The supreme symbol of that unity is still the simple phrase "Union Sacrée." France has enjoyed exceptional demographic stability: with a population that stood steady at forty million from the end of the Second Empire to the government of Vichy, France achieved the miracle in Europe of zero population growth. Social mobility in France was slower than in any other industrialized country; peasants remained tenaciously rooted to the soil, with 50 percent of the active population still on the land in 1914 (and that percentage did not fall below ten percent until 1970). And the fourth and final source of French solidity has been the deep stability of political traditions and voting habits. What is distinctive about generational replacement in France, then, is not so much the quick pace of political life, as might at first appear to be the case, but the enduring features of the national, social, demographic, familial, and political context. These factors are crucial for understanding the potential force, in France, of the simple expression "a succession of generations" as well as the omnipresence of the generational theme in the definition of identity, in which it constitutes both the surface froth and the underlying current. They are also essential for understanding the intimate association between the overthrow of the fathers by the sons and such seemingly alien and unrelated notions as the nation, intellectuals, the future, and politics.

It is within this framework that the important natural mechanisms of generational replacement were able to operate. First—at the end of the Restoration and during the July Monarchy—came the bizarre and disparate coalition that suddenly gave rise to the generational phenomenon: a generation, Delecluze remarked, "which prior to the revolution of 1830 was said to be so well-behaved and studious and which immediately thereafter turned out to be sneeringly merciless and ungrateful toward people of previous generations."[67] The generation that Balzac had called a "steam boiler" suddenly turned into a locomotive,[68] the force behind the sudden upsurge of violent political rioting in the aftermath of 1830 and its disappointments. Caught up in the new violence were what Guizot called "transplants," ambitious provincials drawn to the capital and suddenly liberated from family discipline; students from the first classes to attend the Grandes Écoles, "young scamps who," in Musset's words, "sow terror in the Faubourg Saint-Germain";[69] and, for shock troops, apprentice physicians and lawyers competing for social advantage, young workingmen impatient with the corporative traditions of their trades, young peasants tired of village *charivaris*—the whole menagerie of those whom Balzac in 1833 described as "condemned by the new legality," excluded from politics and the ballot box, and with whom we are so familiar from literature: the Marcases, Julien Sorel, the Deslauriers gang.

After this, and so long as the great institutions of Church, army, family, and above all school remained unshaken, came a second phase, during which generations were increasingly defined by the nineteenth century's mechanisms of democratic advancement, by systems of civic and meritocratic selection that sifted through the whole of society, set "barriers and criteria,"[70] organized generations into more or less annual platoons by "class" and "graduation date," and filled the yearbooks of the Grandes Écoles and the ranks of graduate organizations. Although these avenues of promotion have lost nothing of their operational efficacy even today, they have nevertheless begun to reek of obsolescence. Meanwhile, within the official institutions—obligatory stops on the road to advancement—associations of a more voluntary kind found room to flourish: youth groups and movements of various kinds in which age alone was sufficient to create networks, to establish hidden, informal, yet often powerful solidarities that could and did last a lifetime. These ranged from personal friendships to generational solidarity of the sort that young people derive from participation in demonstrations, music festivals, organizations, groups, clubs, or circles—the "concrete groups" that Karl Mannheim saw as the fountainhead of generational expression.

More recently, in the third phase of the evolution of the generational phenomenon, the regular succession of generation after generation has ceased to operate as in the past. This phase coincides with the advent of a civilization of the image, a growing consumer economy, advances in technology, the internationalization of youth ("We are all German Jews!" as the '68 wall slogan had it), the crisis of traditional education, and a lowering if not complete elimination of the barriers that once separated middle-class and working-class youth.

The heart of the generational dynamic is not to be found in this mechanism of replacement, however. It is crucial to understand the inversion of the time vector: by this I mean the process whereby society invests that mythical age during which access to power is supposed to be possible—the twenties—with certain values, with an idea of what society itself could and should be, and in the light of which it passes judgment on what it actually is. Earlier we saw this crucial mechanism at work under the Restoration, at the very inception of the generational split that bestowed upon the sons of the Revolution the task of making a still better revolution. This same mechanism reproduced itself at each stage. The older generation endlessly congratulates itself on (and through) the wonder of its progeny. Take, for example, the enthusiastic welcome that the nationalist and anti-Dreyfusard old guard accorded to the various youth surveys that preceded the outbreak of World War I, the best known of these being "The Young People of Today," published by Henri Massis and Alfred de Tarde under the pseudonym Agathon in *L'Opinion* (1912).[71] The elders had been obsessed with fears that the younger generation had been ruined by socialist schoolteachers: it turned out that young people were athletic, combative, patriotic, reasonable, and respectful toward tradition. "The new and rising generation promises to be one of the best our country has ever known," Maurice Barrès confided to his *Cahiers*. "Vive la jeunesse française!" And Paul Bourget had this to say in his response to Émile Boutroux's speech accepting a seat in the Académie Française:

> So we see generations rising for which the heavens are once again filled with stars, generations whose best spokesmen tell us that, because they, too, turn to experience for the verification of thought, they have begun again to believe without ever having ceased to understand, generations that remain resolutely, consciously attached to the religious and philosophical tradition of old France.

A half century later and at the other end of the political spectrum, one is equally astonished to read, say, Edgar Morin's instant analysis of May '68 in *La Brèche* or Laurent Joffrin's of the 1986 demonstrations by high school students.[72] Of all the problems that the notion of generation raises for historians, perhaps the most serious is to understand how and why adult society has gradually transformed youth into a repository, conservator, and projection screen for all that is best in itself. How did this occur? What malaise, what transference, made it possible? What secret acquiescence on the part of the older generation in its own failure, its own incompleteness, its members' own individual self-destruction, was required? What accounts for this drive for fulfillment by proxy? Without this initial investment of the fathers in the sons, without this summons to complete the fathers' work by killing them off, it would be impossible to understand how a phenomenon that is in essence one of rupture and negation could also incorporate aspects of continuity and revival of tradition.

Such is the model in basic outline, but historians have written the music of generations in many keys and endless variations. Often the political-historical and artistic-literary threads are intertwined.[73] But one can blend the basic elements in different proportions. Some like to contrast "strong" generations (1800, 1820, 1840, etc.) with "weak" ones (1810, 1830, 1850, etc.). Others set "complete" generations, which explode in every direction, against "those relatively pallid intermediate cohorts" in which, for example, writers like Paul Thibaud and Claude Nicolet modestly place themselves on the grounds that, since their generation came of age between the Resistance and the Algerian War, it had only the Cold War with which to identify itself.[74] I know that generation, for it is my own, and I do not recognize myself in that description. And then there are writers who, being concerned more with the actual experience of "concrete groups," strive for more subtle forms of analysis. If, for example, you are interested in the Jews of France, you might single out the generation of the Holocaust, that of the awakening of Jewish consciousness following the Six-Day War (1967), that of the arrival of the Sephardic Jews from North Africa, and that of the disenchantment with Israel in the wake of the Israeli invasion of Lebanon. If you are interested in the women's liberation movement, you might distinguish between the pioneer generation (women in France obtained the right to vote in 1945; Simone de Beauvoir wrote *Le Deuxième Sexe* in 1947; and Brigitte Bardot starred in *God Created Woman* in 1956, the year that also saw the institution of France's first official family-planning agency) and the assertive generation that culminated in the legalization of abortion (Veil Law, 1975)—in short, the Beauvoir generation and the generation of the women's movement. Along the way you can take your pick of milestones: Françoise Sagan's novel *Bonjour tristesse* or the birth-control pill, the washing machine,[75] painless childbirth, a female student finishing at the top of her class at Polytechnique. The choice makes no difference unless you are concerned with its degree of representativity. The range of possibilities is in fact infinite, and the interest of any particular choice stems not from the available spectrum or the history that it enables you to reconstruct but solely from the rules governing the model, with its implicit hierarchy and invariant features. Beating beneath the history of France from the Revolution to the present one can indeed make out the generational pulse. Why?

One question remains: If generation is truly a *lieu de mémoire*, why has France been its promised land? The question is in fact inescapable, and I see three possible answers. The first invokes a kind of historical predisposition: France has always been divided and pitted against itself. Indeed, the present volume of *Les Lieux de mémoire* is based entirely on such internal cleavages, which one does not find in other countries to the same degree or on the same scale. France's consciousness of itself is therefore also divided, and these divisions have become bound up with and reinforced the simple yet fundamental father-son split that is at the root of the problem of generations. In spatial terms, there is the relation of center to periphery, of Paris to the provinces. In terms of statecraft, there is the relation of the central government to local governments. In historical terms, there is the relation of unity to diversity. In social terms, there is the relation of the majority to minorities. In national terms, the alien is defined in relation to some norm. In France the problem of power is therefore consubstantial with the problem of generations. In the final analysis it is always a question of maintaining or losing control. The very long period during which monarchical authority and divine right held sway over the French mind, together with the slow and far-reaching process of building a centralized state, surely contains part of the explanation for the ubiquity of conflict at the heart of France's relation to itself. The Revolution forced open that internal structure, yet—as Tocqueville pointed out—without altering the symbolic concentration of power. The whole national dramaturgy could mold itself around, pattern itself after, and adapt itself to the spontaneous dramaturgy of generational replacement, which in some ways still constitutes one of its basic dimensions. Now we can see why Freud always saw France as the country that would be most allergic to psychoanalysis. There, the conflict that he delineated in anthropological, psychological, and individual terms was already genetically inscribed in national, political, and collective ones. Geography, history, politics, and society all are imbued with a latent, persistent generational brew. For a proof by contradiction, note that the recent progress toward consensus that has been so much remarked on coincides exactly with the obvious disappearance of conflict between fathers and sons over the issue of generational autonomy.

The second answer has to do with the conservatism, backwardness, and traditionalism that led Raymond Aron to say that France was a country that could achieve reform only by means of revolution. This inertia, apparent in every sphere, has given rise to a particularly striking contrast between the universalism of French principles and the immobility of French realities. It was therefore relatively easy to superimpose an oppositional, generational model on the persistence of features of the old regime within the very heart of the new. This contrast and this persistence at the heart of French existence leapt to the eye of foreign observers of France, especially the group of researchers from Harvard who, taking up Michel Crozier and Stanley Hoffmann's ideas of "stalled society" and "republican synthesis," set out "in search of France"[76] in the early 1960s, at precisely the moment when modernity gripped a country they knew well yet no longer recognized. Without the aid of such detached ethnographic scrutiny the French might have failed to appreciate the degree to which age-old monarchical, Christian, and agrarian traditions had been reinvested in a democratic, secular, and capitalist society. Themselves alien to those traditions, the Harvard researchers were the first to emphasize the continuity of aristocratic values within bourgeois values; the incorporation of the idea of salvation in that of success; the shift of sacrality from church to state; the preservation, in a society that began with their abolition, of privileges of all kinds associated with office and seniority;[77] passive resistance to the egalitarian procedures of democracy; and the preference for security over liberty. From Turgot to Mendès France, the lack of aptitude for reform and the tendency to cling to the past have made generational reaction central to the French collective identity.

The same sources feed into the third factor underlying the special importance of the generational phenomenon in France, which might be called "the rebelliousness of the French." Every country develops its own particular mode of contesting the established order. Russia forced its protesters into terrorism and, in the more recent past, into dissidence. The United States produced its California counterculture to follow up its Lost Generation. The English, thanks to their aristocratic tradition, have made eccentricity a natural right. France, owing to its history and its civilization, has developed a reflex of rebelliousness, a habit linked to the formalist, hierarchical style of authority inherited from the divine-right monarchy and perpetuated by governmental and bureaucratic centralization, and this style has insinuated itself into all French institutions from top to bottom, including the army, the school, and the factory, while at the same time affecting social relations down to the level of the couple and the family: *La France, terre de commandement* (France, land of command).[78] The upshot of this has been a latent anarchism, a dialectic of order and subversion that forms the background of intellectual as well as political history. This can be seen in men of genius as typically French as Paul Valéry, a paragon of conformism as well as the author of *Principes d'anarchie pure et appliquée*. It can also be seen in historical situations as typically French as the Dreyfus Affair, in which the writer Paul Léautaud could, with deep irony and disgust, send the Action Française a contribution toward a monument for Colonel Henry together with these words: "For order, against justice and truth." In what other country would such a gesture be conceivable? Indeed, the same reflex animates every crucial episode in French history (Pétain–de Gaulle, for example) to emerge as the crucial element in the students' May '68. It can also be felt at work setting the pace of all intellectual life, which is similarly imbued with an invisible hierarchy,[79] controlling the replacement of generations from the romantics to the surrealists to Michel Foucault. The "avant garde," a notion whose historical efficacy precisely parallels that of generation (to which it clings as shadow to object or, rather, as light to shadow), has long held out the promise of generational subversion in two associated spheres, the political and the intellectual.

The cult of authority gives rise to the culture of revolt and legitimates it in advance. Therein, perhaps, lies the final mystery surrounding the central role that the idea of generation has played in the historical cycle initiated by the French Revolution: in the reason why French society established and bestowed upon youth, its supreme hope and supreme thought, the mission of fulfilling a destiny with which it is prepared to identify itself fully. In its ultimate and sacred form, this mission requires individuals to sacrifice themselves in violence, whether of war, for which youth bears the brunt of the cost, or of revolution, in which youth serves as the spearhead. Ultimately, it is because youth bears this sacrificial responsibility that the legitimacy of its rebellion is secretly recognized. Thus the theme of a "sacrificed generation," which Barrès and Péguy successfully planted in the French collective consciousness around the beginning of the twentieth century, is intimately intertwined with the theme of generation itself. "People are always right to rebel," Sartre said,[80] but he proposed this formula for predestined radicalism at the very moment it was ceasing to be true, after two centuries during which the volume of blood shed in the Europe of nations and the France of revolutions was ultimately responsible for the density of memory in the national model of the generational phenomenon.

Immersed in Memory

Generations have always been mixtures of memory and history, but the amount and role of each in the mix appear to have shifted over time. The least abstract, most carnal, temporal, and biological historical notion—"from Abraham to David are fourteen generations; and from David until the carrying away into Babylon are fourteen generations; and from the carrying away into Babylon unto Christ are fourteen generations" (Matt. 1:17)—is also, from our standpoint, the least susceptible of historical explanation, a pure memory.

Yet it is also completely saturated in history, if only because it is concerned with a basically constructed phenomenon, a fabrication of hindsight. A generation is not something that emerges spontaneously from the heat of action: it is an observation, a summing up, a self-examination for the purpose of giving a firsthand historical account. However "generational" it may have been, the '68 generation defined itself as such only later, in the waning years of *gauchisme*. It was ten years after the Dreyfus Affair that Péguy looked back on *Notre jeunesse* (1910). By the time Musset baptized the *enfants du siècle*, they had become adults. The attempt at rejuvenation in fact added to their years. When a writer takes note of his date of birth, it is a sign of his years (in this case Victor Hugo's): "This century was two years old." A generation is a product of memory, an effect of remembering. It cannot conceive of itself except in terms of difference and opposition.

This very general phenomenon has never been more clear than it was in the crisis of the late nineteenth century, in which the generational theme was reshaped and took on new depth as its Dreyfusard and nationalist extremes came together through their representative spokesmen, Péguy and Barrès. Both men were able to express more clearly than anyone else the nature of their strong conviction of belonging to a generation, which was the same for both yet also different. For Péguy it was a generation that grew up together on the same schoolroom benches and in the *thurnes* (dormitory studies) of the École Normale, a generation compounded of suffering and *amitié* ("friendship," a word that in his hands took on a very broad connotation). For Barrès it was a generation of "princes of youth" and entirely aesthetic in its affiliations. For both men, the sacralization of generation was equally intense and destined to serve their own consecration, but in each case the meaning of that sacralization and that consecration was different. With Péguy it was a sense of belonging to the "last generation to share the republican mystique," of having been a witness to the last defeat ("we are a defeated generation"), of being a unique repository of a moral experience incarnate. Such was the tenor of his 1909 text, "Aux amis, à nos abonnés," a veritable epitaph for his generation in which Péguy spoke in particular of the visit of a fine young man who came to interview him about the Dreyfus Affair:

> He was quite docile. He held his hat in his hand. He listened to me, listened to me, and drank in my words. I have never understood as clearly as I did then, in a flash, an instant, what history was; and the unbridgeable gulf that exists, that opens up between the real event and the historical one; the absolute, total incompatibility; the total strangeness; the absence of communication; the incommensurability: literally, the absence of any possible common measure.... I narrated, I pronounced, I related, I passed on a certain Dreyfus Affair, the real Dreyfus Affair...in which we of this generation remain immersed.[81]

The Barrèsian and generally nationalist message of generation was quite different. Barrès of course attacked "the failure of our fathers," unable to shake off German intellectual hegemony or to understand the regenerative traditionalism of the Boulangist movement. He was highly conscious of his generation's distinctive qualities. But the traditionalism that he discovered and conquered immediately placed his generation in a long line of others (*La Marche montante d'une génération*) as a link in a chain that would continue to grow link by link from the Henri Massis of *Évocations* to Montherlant, Drieu La Rochelle, and even the Malraux of *D'une jeunesse européenne* (1927), to Thierry Maulnier and the Robert Brasillach of *Notre avant-guerre*, and on to the Roger Nimier of the postwar years, only to end up today with someone like Régis Debray. Here, then, we have two archetypal constructions of generations, two exemplary ways of inscribing them in history. Every generation is unique, but one is, as Péguy put it, "a front that rises and falls in the same instant," while the other, as for Barrès, is "a provisional link in the chain that is the Nation."

Generational memory is therefore historical, but not just by virtue of comparative hindsight or reflection on its own construction over time. It is historical above all because it is first imposed from without, then violently internalized. Generational self-proclamation is in fact the outcome of a solicitation from outside, a response to an appeal, a reflection of external scrutiny by parents, "teachers," journalists, or public opinion, which has a cumulative or snowball effect. The Agathon survey concretized the image of a "1912 generation" that had no demographic or social counterpart other than a rapid increase in the number of students, a factor that the authors did not take into account.[82] Nevertheless, the enormous response it received, the ten other surveys it spawned, the spate of books that seemed to confirm its findings, the fact that it appeared shortly before the outbreak of World War I—all these things helped to create out of whole cloth a mythical image that first captured the public imagination and then found its way into works of history and textbooks: the World War I era was indeed the period during which the generational idea reached its zenith. The phenomenon has repeated itself many times, although on a smaller scale: witness, for instance, the 1957 *Express* survey of the "New Wave" or the press campaign launched by the "Nouveaux Philosophes" in April 1978, both of which served to crystallize generational phenomena. Other attempts were less successful. On May 30, 1949, François Mauriac published an editorial in *Figaro* in which he called for a new survey similar to that of Agathon: "The other day, Gilbert Sigaux, a young writer and editor, suggested to me that perhaps the time had come for his generation to take stock of itself in much the same way as another generation did around 1910 with the publication of the Agathon survey." Two years later, Robert Kanters, an associate of Sigaux's, published the results of that survey under the title *Vingt ans en 1951* (Twenty Years Old in 1951). This was immediately emulated by *La Table ronde* and *Aspects de la France*, where Michel Braspart (alias Roland Laudenbach) for the first time linked the names of the writers Antoine Blondin, Jacques Laurent, and Roger Nimier for "their insolent attitude" toward "liberal idols."[83] But still not enough yeast had been added to make the dough rise. In those days the right wing was probably still too discredited and too isolated to focus the limelight on itself. It was not until three years later, when *Les Temps modernes* published a stinging attack from the left on the same group of writers, whom Bernard Frank referred to as "*hussards et grognards*," that this segment of a generation finally achieved public visibility.[84] Subsequent polling showed that the *hussard* attitude was not limited to a small circle of writers and gave the term a more sociological and scientific basis. Yet the principle of identifying a generation from outside remained the same. And since the product sells well, the principle has been abused. Contemporary society is as rife with generations that never really developed as the news is full of inconsequential events.

Last but not least, generational memory is also historical in another, infinitely more significant sense, in that it is imbued with history to its very core, not to say crushed by history's weight. The moments that loom largest in a generation's consciousness of itself are invariably moments of despair and helplessness in the face of history's overwhelming, inaccessible majesty, its penchant for denying those who aspire to its tragic grandeur. The Revolution for the romantics; the entire nine-teenth century for the "fin-de-siècle" generations; World War I for the generation that fought it as well as the Depression generation; World War II for postwar gen-erations;[85] the Revolution again, together with all the wars they did not fight, for the generations of '68 and afterwards. This obsession with a history that is over and done with and leaves nothing but a void haunts the imagination of all so-called strong generations and a fortiori of intermediate generations; it controls the way their memory works. At the inception of a generation there is a sense of lack, some-thing in the nature of a mourning. Generational memory is stocked with remem-brances not so much of what its members have experienced as of what they have not experienced. It is these memories of what stands behind them that the members of a generation share in common, a painful, never-ending fantasy that holds them together far more than what stands in front of and divides them. This permanent antecedence structures the whole economy of generational memory, which there-fore becomes an interminable discourse about origins, an endless saga. The whole literature of the 1920s and 1930s from Montherlant to Céline, from Aragon and Drieu to Malraux, transformed the memory of World War I veterans into halluci-natory images. May '68 immediately became its own commemoration: by October 1988, 124 books on the subject had been published. The history of romanticism began with romanticism itself. It is a sobering and striking thing to discover that Michelet, the greatest of romantic historians and a member of the very generation that invented the idea of generation so as to savor its experience under the sign of "genius," gave credit for that invention to the Revolution, for the simple reason that he was in the grip of a transference and consequently inclined to exalt his forebears' achievements. The passage is worth quoting:

> If one were to seek the cause of this astonishing eruption of genius, one might of course say that men found in the Revolution the most powerful of stimuli, a new freedom of spirit, etc. In my view, however, there was an even more fundamental cause: these admirable children were conceived and delivered even as the century, morally uplifted by the genius of Rousseau, was redis-covering hope and faith. With that dawn of a new religion, women awoke. What resulted was a generation more than human.[86]

It was this intrinsically mythological and commemorative historical celebration that moved the idea of generation out of history and into memory.

With the idea of generation one indeed enters into the realm of pure memory—and that is why, in particular, that idea interests us here. Pure memory is memory that thumbs its nose at history, that ignores lapses of time and chains of cause and effect, that forgets the prose of the quotidian and the obstacles to progress. It advances in "flashes," powerful images, jumping from one stalwart mooring to the next. It abolishes time's duration, leaving only an ahistorical present. In a national context, the most striking example of such an abolition of time is again to be found in the Revolution, whose sudden invention, in the late summer of 1789, of the dismissive expression *Ancien Régime* detemporalized six centuries of history in one fell swoop (see François Furet's essay in this volume). With each new stage the operation is repeated at every level from the most general to the most particular. One might even say that the generational rupture—at once a source of creative fecundity and of repetitive poverty—consists essentially in "immemorializing" the past the better to "memorialize" the present. In this sense generations are powerfully, perhaps even primarily, fabricators of *lieux de mémoire,* or mnemonic sites, which form the fabric of their provisional identities and stake out the boundaries of their generational memories. These mnemonic sites generate or become charged with unfathomable powers of symbolic evocation, passwords and mutual recognition signals, all endlessly revivified by narrative, documents, firsthand accounts, and the magic of photography. The exploration of a generational memory begins with an inventory of these sites. That, in the end, is precisely the purpose of these volumes, for France and measured against my own generation. Some will protest that I am here merely harking back to the old distinction that Bergsonian psychologists like Janet made between affective memory and intellectual memory or to the work of Durkheimian sociologists such as Halbwachs on the social contexts of collective memory. But I am talking about something very different, because generational memory is not a matter of individual psychology. The sites in which it condenses and finds expression are public places, centers of collective participation which are nevertheless susceptible of immediate personal appropriation. For political generations these include meetings, newspapers, demonstrations, conventions, organizations, and mass symbols. For intellectual generations they include publishing houses and journals, cafés and salons, colloquia, bookstores, and preparatory schools. They do not include the private recollections of individuals who link their personal memories to important public events, nor do they include shared individual emotions. Generational memory grows out of social interactions that are in the first place historical and collective and are later internalized in a deeply visceral and unconscious way so as to dictate vital choices and control reflexes of loyalty—matters in which "I" is simultaneously "we."

At this level of incarnation and decantation, memory no longer has much to do with time. It is at this point, no doubt, that we come closest to the truth of the idea of generation. Closed in on itself and fixed in its identity, impervious by definition to history and its "lessons," the generational monad is perhaps most closely related to what the historian of science Thomas Kuhn calls "paradigms," which according to Kuhn determine the structure of scientific revolutions.[87] It is surprisingly easy to take the behavior of Kuhn's communities of theorists and experimentalists, united as well as constrained by a shared explanatory model and held together by crucial reflexes born of intellectual consensus, a common educational background and working style, and a shared jargon, and to translate it into the terms used here to describe generations. And just as scientific communities define themselves by radical opposition even while sharing implicitly the bulk of the established scientific tradition, each generation shares with others at once almost nothing and almost everything. This comparison of generations with scientific communities, which Daniel Milo has pursued in detail,[88] is valuable for assigning a proper place, decisive yet marginal, to those historical markers of memory around which generations, those fleeting yet crucial phenomena, align themselves. The generational paradigm, which even though hermetically sealed is traversed by every conceivable temporal flow, persists without change until it is blotted out and replaced by subsequent generations, which nevertheless hold what they supplant in reserve for possible revival toward new ends. Thus, for example, what might be called the "paradigm of war and occupation," which is central to contemporary French consciousness and identity, has, after a long conspiracy of silence, lately become the object of a series of investments. The first wave came in the early 1960s and was limited to a small group of historians interested mainly in what went before, that is, the 1930s. It originated with men such as Jean Touchard and René Remond who had experienced that turbulent era as youths, and it raised, discreetly and scientifically, the central question of whether or not a French fascism existed.[89] But it was once again the '68 generation that made the war its touchstone. It began in 1968 with the publication of *La Place de l'Étoile,* the novel with which Patrick Modiano at age twenty began his hallucinatory reconstruction of the *lieux de mémoire* sites of the Occupation. It continued in 1971 with the release of the film *The Sorrow and the Pity,* a documentary that explored the Occupation years in the city of Clermont-Ferrand. What followed has been called *la mode rétro,* or "Forties Revival," a headlong plunge into the shadowy depths of those "four years to be expunged from our history," as Chief Prosecutor Mornet put it in 1949: those years of darkness were now lit from every possible angle, including works of history, fiction, social science, and film.[90] And no end is in sight.

We are now in a position to measure how far the idea of generation has come and how completely it has been transformed. We have in hand a fair sampling of empirical studies, covering the entire social sphere and based on a full spectrum of historical, demographic, and psychological theories. Clearly memory is today the linchpin of definitions of generation, and consequently a generation is now a purely symbolic unit of time, a favorite device for representing change whose acceptance reflects and consecrates the advent of the social actor. In any case, Tocqueville long ago called attention to the likelihood that age would become an increasingly important organizing and classifying principle in a democratic era in which "the notion of the *similar* is less obscure" than in aristocratic times; yet by "inducing people to forget their ancestors and by concealing their offspring" democracy would also "distend and loosen the bonds of human affection."[91] There is no better delineation of the place, central yet all in all modest, of this very special category of contemporary periodization. "Generation" lacks the anthropological amplitude of "age," the religiosity of "era," the historical dignity of "century," and the richness of color and dimension of "epoch" or "period." By instituting a mélange of the individual and the collective, the notion deprives the former of its psychological depth and the latter of its expressive potential. Yet surely it is an inexhaustible notion, like the unconscious, and just as fascinating, yet at the same time just as constricted, impoverished, and repetitious. In a world of constant change, in which every individual has occasion to become his or her own historian, the generation is the most instinctive way of converting memory into history. Ultimately that is what a generation is: the spontaneous horizon of individual historical objectification.

What makes the notion of generation so topical here and now and gives it its explanatory force, however, is the unique historical situation of France, which since World War II has suffered from a split historical personality. On the one hand it has invested too much in the heavy legacy of the past, in a history more burdensome than that of any other European country, while on the other hand it has gone through a profound process of disengagement from world history that has relegated it to memorial rumination on its own historical experience. The phenomenon is unique, complex, and so peculiar to France that we have no choice but to measure its extent and explore the various historical threads that find their point of intersection here.

Let us rapidly rehearse the major episodes of France's recent history. France was the only country to emerge from World War II half victor, half vanquished. England went united from mortal peril to ultimate victory. Germany of course went down to defeat, but complete catastrophe simplified the surgical removal of some of the complexities of its past, and it was not until precisely one generation had passed that it rediscovered, with the help of youthful Greens and a raucous *Historikerstreit* (historians' controversy) some of the dramas of conscience that have once again moved its history closer to that of France. Spain avoided the debacle altogether. The pain that followed the Liberation of France, by contrast, impelled the country, with help from the Resistance and de Gaulle, to seek solace among the victors while bearing the burden of the vanquished. Shattered, humiliated, and ravaged by internal division, France was all the more obsessed with recovering its "place" in the world because it no longer possessed the wherewithal of a world power. Just as it was beginning to get back on its feet, the Cold War broke out, compelling governments everywhere to choose sides. But once again France was different, because it had a powerful Communist Party and because it still had to contend with the thorny issue of decolonization, a problem it had been unable to resolve in 1945. Hence it was the only country in western Europe to internalize the clash between the Western and Soviet blocs, a dispute it was powerless to resolve; and the only country obliged to live with a divided conscience, politically impotent and institutionally paralyzed, to the point of ultimate collapse. This came with the Algerian War, comparable in its consequences to the American Civil War. The Algerian War became a means for settling old scores. It mired French history in a provincial struggle. More than that, the nation's conflict was complicated by a conflict within the left, which was the real reason for the war's interminable length and corrosive moral effects. And it revived Gaullism, which from the standpoint of historical escalation that concerns us here, was an ambiguous episode. On the one hand, de Gaulle, the champion of nationalism, was the man who disguised France's retreat into its metropolitan borders behind a partly rhetorical, partly real reinvigoration of foreign policy. On the other hand, he was instrumental in bringing about a new industrial revolution, an agent of the old Louis-Philippard dream of an industrialized France, who prosaically lived off the profits of growth.

In broad outline, then, this is the story of France's overzealous investment in history. That investment took place, however, at a time when France was withdrawing from history in a larger sense; having avoided the main thrust of twentieth-century history, France passively endured its side-effects. By degrees and with occasional hard knocks it declined from the status of a great power to that of a medium power. There were grinding adjustments in 1918, 1945, and 1962: each of these dates, which respectively mark the ends of World War I, World War II, and the Algerian War, brought its quota of mutilating reality and compensatory illusions. A country that previously prided itself on having been the first to know all the historical experiences that shaped the European identity from the Crusades to colonialism by way of the nation-state, absolute monarchy, dictatorship, and revolution, now knew only the consequences and aftershocks. France did not bear the full brunt of the socialist revolution or Nazi totalitarianism or the Depression or consumer society; it knew these things only by way of invasion, aftershock, or replay. We must grasp this overlapping of two different and contradictory registers of historical consciousness, this aptitude for becoming so bogged down in the past as to require painful disengagement, before we can understand why the past repeatedly and compulsively resurfaces in the present, why France is plagued with a tragic overinvestment in a national history that is nothing more than the local version of a neglected world history perceived by way of memory alone. What is more, France's historical memory is itself split and unbalanced: on one level the French celebrate their unanimity ("In lieu of a great present, we have a great past"), while on another they cannot keep themselves from sifting through the past, especially the recent past, to find out whether it was really as great or as shameful as it has been made out to be. Ultimately the Bicentennial of the French Revolution thrived on this divided memory, which is why it will always be remembered as ambiguous. The Revolution may be over, or it may not be. It may have been a *bloc* (a monolithic whole), or it may not. The Vendée may have been a genocide, or it may not. Robespierre may have been a great man or a mass murderer. The Terror may have been a product of circumstances, or it may have set a pattern for French political culture. The Declaration of the Rights of Man may have set forth universal or universalizable principles, or it may have served strictly internal purposes. No matter: yes or no, it all happened in France, and all eyes were once again on the country of the Revolution. This was the gist of President Mitterrand's message: "The world still has its eye on us, and I am at center stage."

We thus come back to the explosive potential of the problem of generations and their interrogative succession, particularly as the pace of succession picks up, as upheaval becomes constant, and individual life expectancies increase. The past never passes; those who took part in it linger on the scene, even as newcomers crowd their way in. Together these three factors have made the generational phenomenon more important than ever, turning it into a vast echo chamber for the century's tragedies. In theoretical and practical terms this raises, in our two-dimensional model, the question of where the dividing line falls between that which belongs *exclusively* under the head of generational memory and that which belongs *exclusively* to historical memory, or, if you will, to memory and history. Note that this division itself has two dimensions. *Temporally,* there is the moment when memory passes from the generations that are its bearers to the historians who reconstitute a past they have not experienced. *Intellectually,* there is the transition from first-hand account to critical reconstruction. Neither of these transitions is one-to-one in generational terms: there can be, and are, excellent critics of their own generation's memory who become its historians, and there are generations of historians, no less distinguished, whose work is essentially to reexamine their subject from the standpoint of their own generational memory. The Bicentennial made it possible to verify this general truth in the particular case of the French Revolution. France's withdrawal from world history and entry into the historically empty era of pregnant memory both called attention to generational agency and broadened the issue to the scale of national history in the two most dramatically intense moments of French history: the Revolution and World War II.

We can now give clear answers to the questions we raised at the outset. There are indeed "French" generations. If, moreover, a generation is a *lieu de mémoire,* it is not at all in the simple sense that shared experiences imply shared memories. It is rather as a result of the simple yet subtle interplay of memory and history, of the eternally reemerging dialectic of a past that remains present, of actors who become their own witnesses, and of new witnesses in turn transformed into actors. When all three of these elements are present, a mere spark can ignite a blaze. It is their presence in today's France, that tinderbox of memory, that fuels the "generational" blaze. In this time and this place. The play goes on, and it is up to each generation to rewrite its generational history. But how long will coming generations have to wait for such a combination of circumstances to reoccur and shed a comparably unsparing light?

NOTES TO FOREWORD

1   For a discussion of this concept see Benedict R. Anderson, *Imagined Communities* (London: Verson, 1983).
2   Frances Yates, *The Art of Memory* (Chicago: University of Chicago Press, 1966) and Maurice Halbwachs, *Les Cadres sociaux de la mémoire* (Paris: 1925); New York: Arno Press, 1975.

PREFACE TO THE ENGLISH-LANGUAGE EDITION

1   The term has no precise English equivalent. For this reason, I suggested that Arthur Goldhammer keep the French expression wherever possible, while substituting *place* or *site* only when these English words seem to capture the sense adequately. As for the title, Lawrence Kritzman and I long despaired of finding an adequate English equivalent and therefore thought of retaining the French title. I am grateful to my friend Robert Silvers for suggesting the best possible translation: *Realms of Memory*.
2   A selection of the remaining articles, which could not be fitted into the redesigned series, will be published later by The University of Chicago Press in a series of volumes covering the themes "State," "Space," and "Culture and Historiography."
3   Published in French in 1974 and partly translated into English in 1985 under the title *Constructing the Past* (published jointly by Cambridge University Press and the Editions de la Maisons des Sciences de l'Homme).
4   The sociologist Henri Mendras calls this period the Second French Revolution, whose appearance he dates from 1965, but I feel that its effects became perceptible only ten years later. See Henri Mendras, *La Second Révolution française, 1965–1984* (Paris: Gallimard, 1988).

CHAPTER 1   FRANKS AND GAULS

1   Alain Duval and Henry Rousso kindly shared their knowledge and counsel, the former in regard to recent developments in Gallic archaeology, the latter concerning the Gallic theme under Vichy. I wish to express my gratitude to both.

2   C. Éluère, *L'Or des Celtes* (Fribourg, 1987); *Trésors des princes celtes,* exhibition catalogue, Galeries Nationales du Grand Palais, October 20, 1987–February 15, 1988 (Paris, 1987).

3   See, for example, R. Amberlin, *Les Traditions celtiques: Doctrine initiatique de l'Occident* (1945; repr. Saint Jean-de-Braye, 1977), and, for the antecedents of occult Celtism, A. Mercier, *Édouard Schuré et le renouveau idéaliste en Europe* (Lille, 1980). One key sign of public interest is a new edition of a book that sums up our knowledge of the subject, F. Le Roux and C. J. Guyonvarc'h, *Les Druides* (1st ed., 1978; repr. Rennes, 1987).

4   See *Nos ancêtres les Gaulois* (Clermont-Ferrand, 1982), abbreviated hereafter as *N.A.G.*, and, on the colloquium itself, M. Ozouf, "Les Gaulois à Clermont," *Le Débat,* 6 (1980): 93–103; J.-P. Rioux, "Autopsie de nos ancêtres les Gaulois," *L'Histoire,* 27 (1980): 85.

5   See the 1980–1984 articles quoted by C. Amalvi, "De Vercingétorix à Astérix, de la Gaule à de Gaulle ou les métamorphoses idéologiques et culturelles de nos origines nationales," *Dialogues d'histoire ancienne,* 10 (1984): 310–312; P.-M. Duval, *Pourquoi "Nos ancêtres les Gaulois"* (Paris, 1982); P. Quentel, "Et nos ancêtres les Gaulois," *Le Monde* (October 10, 1987); M. Duverger, "Rendez-nous Clovis et Charlemagne," *Le Monde* (November 13, 1987), with this final appeal: "Do not cut the tree off from our roots. Give us back our ancestors the Gauls. Give us back Vercingetorix. Give us back Ausonius and Sidonius Apollinaris. Give us back Clovis and Charlemagne."

6   The Gallic cock has become so common a figure of speech that it appears in the definition of the word *Gaulois* in the *Petit Robert* dictionary. See also Michel Pastoureau, "Le Coq gaulois," in Pierre Nora, ed., *Les Lieux de mémoire,* part 3, *Les France,* vol. 3, *De l'archive à l'emblème* (Paris: Gallimard, 1992).

7   See *Paris-Soir* (August 24 and 25, 1942); *L'Oeuvre* (August 24, 1942); *La Renaissance nationale* (August 27, 1942); *L'Avenir du Plateau central* (August 27, 1942), with the program of the Gergovie ceremonies.

8   The document is quoted in *L'Avenir du Plateau central* (August 31, 1942). These are not the only references to the Gauls. The *Journal des débats politiques et littéraires,* for example, published an article on Vercingetorix, the "expression of the purest national mysticism," along with an article on Gergovie in its August 29–30, 1942, issue. Gergovie was also the subject of an article in the same paper on December 6, 1941.

9   See A. Ehrard, "Vercingétorix contre Gergovie?" in *N.A.G.,* 313–315.

10   *L'Avenir du Plateau central* (August 24, 1942).

11   Broadcast from Radio London, August 29, 1942, in J.-L. Crémieux-Brilhac, ed., *Les Voix de la liberté: Ici Londres 1940–1944* (Paris, 1975), 2: 200–201.

12   Quoted in F. Gaspard and G. Grunberg, "Les Titulaires de la francisque gallique," in J. Bourdin and R. Rémond, ed., *Le Gouvernement de Vichy et la Révolution nationale 1940–1942* (Paris, 1972), 72.

13   Speech by P. Gaziot, minister of agriculture under Vichy, January 19, 1941, quoted in C. Faure, "Folklore et révolution nationale: Doctrine et action sous Vichy (1940–1944)" (thesis, University of Lyons II, 1986), 1: 241 ff.

14   See C. Jullian, *Aimons la France, conférences: 1914–1919* (Paris, 1919), and *Au seuil de notre histoire*, vol. 2, *1914–1923* (Paris, 1931), 268.

15   See P. Birnbaum, *Un Mythe politique: "La République juive"* (Paris, 1988).

16   See A. Chante, "Les Gaulois dans l'hébdomadaire *Tintin*"; D. and P. Cogny, "La 'Rhétorix' d'Astérix le Gaulois"; and D.-H. Pageaux, "De l'imagerie culturelle au mythe politique: Astérix le Gaulois," all in *N.A.G.*, 421–426, 429–435, and 437–444; A. Simon, "Les Gaulois dans la B.D.," *Le Débat*, 16 (1981): 96–108.

17   See J. Ehrard and L.-L. Hollopeau, ed., *Nos ancêtres les Gaulois*, exhibition catalogue, Musée Bargoin, June 25–September 30, 1980 (Clermont-Ferrand, 1980).

18   See H. Martin, *Histoire de France depuis les temps les plus réculés jusqu'en juillet 1830* (Paris, 1834), 1: 52 and 107.

19   See, for example, H. Martin, *Les Origines de la France depuis les premières migrations jusqu'aux maires du Palais* (Paris, 1891), 8, 17, 49, 73.

20   See Ehrard and Hollopeau, *Nos ancêtres les Gaulois*, 6, and E. Delacroix, *Journal, 1822–1853* (Paris, 1980), 831.

21   See L. Dimier, *Histoire de la peinture française au XIXe siècle (1793–1903)* (Paris, 1914), 224–225; P. Vaisse, "Les Gaulois dans la peinture officielle (1870–1914)," in *N.A.G.*, 321–326.

22   See A. Pingeot, "Les Gaulois sculptés (1850–1914)," in *N.A.G.*, 255–275.

23   See the publicity poster from Éditions Furne announcing the fourth edition of Henri Martin's *Histoire de France*, which also features an advertisement for a *Collection de portraits et vignettes pour l'Histoire de France de Henri Martin*, Bibl. nat., 8° L 35.202 C; S. Reinach, *Album de moulages et modèles en vente au Musée des antiquités nationales à Saint-Germain-en-Laye*, vol. 1 (Paris, n.d. [after 1908]); for Gallic objects, see plate 18 ff. In August 1907 there were eight series on sale, and in August 1914 there were fourteen series of ten post cards on subjects related to Alesia. Various "Pro Alesia" casts were also sold. An advertisement appeared on the final cover page of the journal *Pro Alesia* every year; the journal's first series was published from 1906 to 1914.

24   See C. Amalvi, "Vercingétorix dans l'enseignement primaire: 1830–1940"; A. Gérard, "La Vision de la défaite gauloise dans l'enseignement secondaire (particulièrement entre 1870 et 1914)," and S. Citron, "De la cohérence historiographique au bric-à-brac: Les Gaulois dans quelques manuels récents," all in *N.A.G.*, 349–355, 357–365, and 403–409.

25   See A. Stoll, *Astérix, l'épopée burlesque de la France* (Paris, 1978).

26   See A. Grenier, *Manuel d'archéologie gallo-romaine* (Paris, 1931), 1: 20 ("chaussées Brunehaut").

27   See S. Reinach, "Esquisse d'une histoire de l'archéologie gauloise (préhistorique, celtique, gallo-romaine et franque)," *Revue celtique*, 19 (1898): 101–117 and 292–307.

28   See B. de Montfaucon, *L'Antiquité expliquée et représentée en figures* (Paris, 1719), vol. 5, part 2: 194–196.

29   See C.-C. Baudelot de Dairval, *Description des bas-reliefs anciens trouvés depuis peu dans l'église cathédrale de Paris* (Paris, 1711), and for the present state of interpretation, P.-

M. Duval, "Le Groupe des bas-reliefs des nautae Parisiaci," in *Monuments et mémoires de la fondation Eugène Piot*, 48, 2 (1956): 63–90, fig. 1–14.

30   See H. Omont, *Le Cabinet d'antiquités de Saint-Germain-des-Prés au XVIIIe siècle*, excerpted from *Recueil de mémoires publiés par la Société des antiquaires de France à l'occasion de son centenaire* (Paris, 1904), 2, 8 (no. 104), 11 (nos. 222–225); B. de Montfaucon, *L'Antiquité expliquée*, ibid. Montfaucon's errors in the publication of Gallic objects were pointed out and corrected by S. Reinach, "Esquisse d'une histoire de l'archéologie gauloise." See also A. Laming Emperaire, *Les Origines de l'archéologie préhistorique en France* (Paris, 1964), 77 ff., 91 ff.

31   See N.-J. Foucault, *Mémoires*, ed. F. Bauchy (Paris, 1862), xxxviii.

32   See Laming-Emperaire, *Les Origines*, 97; J.-Y. Veillard, *Catalogue des objets d'archéologie armoricaine (Préhistoire, protohistoire et époque gallo-romaine) de la collection du président de Robien* (Rennes, 1972). The Comte de Caylus, *Recueil d'Antiquités égyptiennes, étrusques, grecques et romaines* (Paris, 1752–1767), 7 vols., mentions the names of several *parlementaires* interested in archaeology.

33   See P.-J. Fournier, "Historique de fouilles sur l'emplacement de Gergovie (1755–1934)," *Revue d'Auvergne*, 49 (1935): 154–155.

34   See G. Testart, "Les Anciennes Fouilles du mont Auxois: II, Fouilles de 1784," *Pro Alesia*, 2 (1907): 230–236.

35   See S. Maffei, *Galliae antiquitates quaedam selectae atque in plures epistolas distributae* (Paris, 1733), and on Caylus's reaction to Maffei's interpretation of an ancient monument, K. Pomian, *Collectionneurs, amateurs et curieux: Paris, Venise: XVIe–XVIIIe siècle* (Paris, 1987), 193–211; trans. by Elizabeth Wiles-Porter as *Collectors and Curiosities: Paris and Venice, 1500–1800* (Cambridge, 1990), 169–182.

36   Caylus, *Recueil*, 3: 324.

37   Ibid., 6: 406

38   Ibid., 7: 238

39   "These figures seemed to me so clearly Gallic that I wanted to bring them back," ibid., 3: 375.

40   Ibid., 3: 323.

41   Ibid., 6: 75, 82–83.

42   Ibid., 5: pl. 101-103 and pp. 281–289.

43   Ibid., 6: 328 and pl. 104.

44   Ibid., 5: 325.

45   The oldest drawing depicting a raised stone dates from 1561. See *Poitiers: Archéologues d'hier, archéologie d'aujourd'hui*, exhibition catalogue, Musée Sainte-Croix, December 19, 1980–March 2, 1981 (Poitiers, 1980), 11; on megaliths, see Dubuisson Aubenay, *Itinéraire de Bretagne (1636)*, 2 vols. (Nantes, 1892–1895), quoted in P. Sébillot, *Le Folk-lore de France* (Paris, 1968), 4: 4.

46   See E.-T. Hamy, "Mémoire inédit de Montfaucon sur les armes des anciens Gaulois et des nations voisines," *Revue archéologique*, new ser., 7 and 8 (1906): 37–48.

47   Caylus, *Recueil*, 4: CXI, 370–373; here, 371.

48   Ibid., 6: pl. 115, 117, 118-121, and pp. 361–363, 367–369, 369–388.

49   Ibid., 6: 384–387.

50   See F. Le Royer d'Artezet de La Sauvagère, *Recueil d'antiquités dans les Gaules* (Paris, 1770); Grivaud de la Vincelle, *Recueil de monuments antiques la plupart inédits et découverts dans l'ancienne Gaule; ouvrage enrichi de cartes et planches en taille douce qui peut faire suite aux Recueils du Comte de Caylus et de La Sauvagère* (Paris, 1817), 2 vols.

51   See P.-J.-B. Legrand d'Aussy, *Mémoire sur les anciennes sépultures nationales et les ornemens extérieurs qui y furent employés, sur les embaumemens, sur les tombeaux des rois francs dans la ci-devant église de Saint-Germain-des-Prés et sur un projet de fouilles à faire dans nos départemens* (Paris, Year VII [1798]). I am quoting from an edition titled *Des Sépultures nationales et particulièrement de celles des Rois de France* (Paris, 1824). See also Laming-Emperaire, *Les Origines*, 99 ff.

52   Legrand d'Aussy, *Mémoire*, 181–182.

53   Ibid., 206–207, 208. "M. Coret" is La Tour d'Auvergne Corret. On him, see J. Balcou, "La Tour d'Auvergne, théoricien breton du mythe gaulois," in *N.A.G.*, 107–113, and below n. 146.

54   Ibid., 251.

55   Ibid., 225.

56   Ibid., 226.

57   Ibid., 227.

58   J. Cambry, *Monumens celtiques, ou Recherches sur le culte des pierres, précédées d'une notice sur les celtes et sur les druides, et suivies d'etymologies celtiques* (Paris, Year XIII [1805]), xxvii. On the Celtic Academy, see J.-Y. Guiomar, "Le *Barʒaʒ-Breiʒ*," in Nora, *Les Lieux de mémoire*, part 3, *Les France*, vol. 2, *Traditions* (Paris: Galli-mard, 1992).

59   In 1807, for example, Saint-Morys asked that the Celtic Academy be turned into "a society for national antiquities." See F. Arquié-Bruley, "Un Précurseur: Le comte de Saint-Morys (1782–1817), collectionneur d' 'Antiquités nationales,' " *Gazette des Beaux-Arts*, 96 (1980): 109–118, and 97 (1981): 61–77.

60   See F. Bercé, "Arcisse de Caumont et les sociétés savantes," in Nora, *Les Lieux de mémoire*, part 2, *La Nation* (Paris: Gallimard, 1986), 2: 533–557.

61   See M. Ozouf, "L'Invention de l'ethnographie française: Le questionnaire de l'Académie celtique," *Annales E.S.C.* (1981): 210–230.

62   Martin, *Histoire de France*, 1: 15.

63   Laming-Emperaire, *Les Origines*, 119–121. The distinction between Celts and Gauls seems to have been introduced by Alexandre Bertrand. See his paper "Les Galates ou Gaulois" (1875) in Bertrand, *Archéologie celtique et gauloise: Mémoires et documents relatifs aux premiers temps de notre histoire nationale* (Paris, 1876), 384–421, esp. 413–414.

64   See Cambry, *Monumens celtiques*, and A. De Laborde, *Les monumens de France classés chronologiquement et considérés sous le rapport des faits historiques et des études des arts* (Paris, 1816), 1: pl. 5 and 6, and commentary on 61–62.

65   See, for example, Arcisse de Caumont, *Cours d'antiquités monumentales*, vol. 1, part 1, *Ere celtique* (Paris, 1830).

66   For Boucher de Perthes the word "Celtic" already meant "prehistoric." See *Antiquités celtiques et antédiluviennes: Mémoire sur l'industrie primitive et les arts à leur origine* (Paris, 1864), 3:346–346 and 390 n.

67   Bertrand, "Les Monumens dits celtiques," in *Archéologie celtique et gauloise*, 82–131; here, 87–88.

68   See S. Reinach, "Terminologie régionale et scientifique des monuments méga-lithiques" (1903), in *Cultes, mythes et religions* (Paris, 1913), 3: 434–448.

69   See Alexandre Lenoir, *Description historique et chronologique des monumens de sculpture réunis au Musée des monumens français*, 7th ed. (Paris, Year V [1797]), 41–55. On Lenoir, see also D. Poulot, "Alexandre Lenoir et les musées des monuments français," in Nora, *Les Lieux de mémoire*, part 2, *La Nation*, 2: 497–531.

70   Legrand d'Aussy, *Mémoire*, 355–359.

71   Grivaud de la Vincelle, *Antiquités gauloises et romaines recueillies dans les jardins du Palais du Sénat pendant les travaux d'embellissement qui y ont été exécutés depuis l'An IX jusqu'à ce jour* (Paris, 1807), 239. Grivaud would renew his efforts ten years later. See *Recueil de monumens antiques*, 2: 1.

72   See Pomian, *Collectionneurs, amateurs et curieux*, 206–210 (Eng. trans., 179–184).

73   See R. Schneider, *Quatremère de Quincy et son intervention dans les arts (1788–1830)* (Paris, 1910), 85–90.

74   Albert Lenoir, *Projet d'un musée historique formé par la réunion du palais des Thermes et de l'hôtel de Cluny, exposé dans les salles du Louvre sous le n° 1546* (Paris, 1833), 4–6.

75   F. Arago, "Rapport sur le projet de loi relatif à un crédit extraordinaire de 590 000 francs pour l'acquisition de l'hôtel de Cluny et de la Collection Du Sommerard," in *Oeuvres complètes* (Paris-Leipzig, 1856), 3: 522.

76   See P. Marot, "Les Origines d'un Musée d'antiquités nationales: De la protection du 'Palais des Thermes' à l'institution du 'musée de Cluny,'" *Mémoires de la Société nationale des antiquaires de France*, 9th ser., vol. 4 (1968): 259–327.

77   See A. de Caumont, *Cours d'antiquités monumentales*, 1: 209, 211, 214–216, 225, 227, 229, 230, 234, 238, 252–254 (references to private collections, antique displays, and museums in western France). See also the letter from the minister of the interior to the Comte de Rambuteau, prefect of the Seine département, dated May 6, 1839, in Albert Lenoir, *Le Musée des Thermes et l'hôtel de Cluny: Documents sur la création du Musée d'antiquités nationales suivant le projet exposé au Louvre en 1833 sous le n° 1546* (Paris, 1862), 63–64; A. Lemaître, *Des Musées archéologiques et numismatiques en France* (Paris, 1867).

78   See J.-M. Gautier, "L'Épisode de Velléda dans *Les Martyrs* de Chateaubriand," and J. Joly, " 'Oltre ogni humana idea': Le mythe, la tragédie, l'opéra dans la *Norma* de Bellini," in *N.A.G.*, 153–161, esp. 156–157 and 165–176; on February 15, 1852, Delacroix listened to Gounod's Gallic choir, "which seems quite a good thing." The cantata *Gallia* dates from 1871. See Delacroix, *Journal*, 289.

79   See E. Desjardins, *Alesia (septième campagne de Jules César): Résumé du débat, réponse à l'article de la* Revue des Deux Mondes *du 1ᵉʳ mai 1858, conclusion suivie d'un appendice renfermant des notes inédités écrites de la main de Napoléon Iᵉʳ sur les Commentaires de Jules César* (Paris, 1859); A. Castan, "Jules Quicherat, défenseur d'Alaise," in J. Quicherat, *Mélanges d'archéologie et d'histoire: Antiquités celtiques, romaines et gallo-romaines*, ed. A. Giry and A. Castan (Paris, 1885), 468–474. See also J. Le Gall, *Alésia: Archéologie et histoire* (Paris, 1980), 38 ff.; and O. Buchsenschutz and

A. Schnapp, "Alésia," in Nora, *Les Lieux de mémoire*, part 3, *Les France*, vol. 3, *De l'archive à l'emblème* (Paris: Gallimard, 1992).

80 H. Martin, *Études d'archéologie celtique: Notes de voyage dans les pays celtiques et scandinaves* (Paris, 1872), 26–27.

81 See R. Lantier, "Aux origines du Musée des antiquités nationales," in *Hommages à Albert Grenier*, ed. M. Renard (Brussels-Berchem, 1962), 940–947.

82 See S. Reinach, *Antiquités nationales: Description raisonnée du musée de Saint-Germain-en-Laye* (Paris, [1899?]), 1: 16, 21 ff.

83 Cf. G. de Mortillet, *Promenades au musée de Saint-Germain* (Paris, 1869), 22.

84 Ibid., 40–56, and F. de Saulcy, "La Salle d'Alésia au musée de Saint-Germain-en-Laye," *Journal des savants* (1880): 558–565 and 622–630. See also S. Reinach, *Catalogue illustré du Musée des antiquités nationales au château de Saint-Germain-en-Laye*, 2 vols (Paris, 1917–1921), 2: 107–125.

85 G. Boissier, "Le musée de Saint-Germain," *Revue des deux mondes*, 46 (1881): 721–749; here, 723.

86 P.-M. Duval, *La Gaule jusqu'au milieu du Ve siècle*, 2 vols. (Paris, 1971), 1: 49.

87 See Julius Caesar, *Guerre des Gaules*, ed. L.-A. Constans (Paris: Collection des Universités de France, 1972), introduction, xx n.

88 Calculated using information from the *Catalogue de la Bibliothèque nationale*, 25: col. 873–916.

89 See L. F. Flutre and K. Sneyders de Vogel, ed., *Li Fet des Romains compilé ensemble de Saluste et de Suetoine et de Lucan*, 2 vols. (Paris and Groningen, 1938); L. F. Flutre, *Li Fait des Romains dans les littratures françaises et italiennes du XIIe au XVIe siècle* (Paris, 1932).

90 M. Schmidt-Chazan, "Les Traductions de la *Guerre des Gaules* et le sentiment national au Moyen Age," *Annales de Bretagne et des Pays de l'Ouest*, 87 (1980): 387–407.

91 Calculated using information from the *Catalogue de la Bibliothèque nationale*.

92 C.-E. Ruelle, *Bibliographie des Gaules*, 2 vols. (Paris, 1880), no. 412–483.

93 Sébillot, *Le Folk-lore en France*, 4: 319 ff.

94 M. Lugge, *"Gallia" und "Francia" im Mittelalter* (Bonn, 1960), esp. 180 ff.

95 See *Alésia*, 2nd ed. (Paris, 1980), 139–141 and 162–163. The ancient literary texts were ed. by J. Le Gall, E. de Saint-Denis, and R. Weil; the medieval texts by Canon J. Marilier.

96 See Aimoin de Fleury, preface to *Historia Francorum*, P.L., 139: col. 627, and C. Jullian, "En lisant la préface d'Aimoin," (Gallo-Roman notes, 67), *Revue des études anciennes*, 17 (1915): 186–192.

97 J. Viard, ed., *Les Grandes Chroniques de France* (Paris: Société de l'histoire de France, 1920), 1: 22, and Bernard Guenée, "Les *Grandes Chroniques de France*," in Nora, *Les Lieux de mémoire*, part 2, *La Nation*, 1: 189–214.

98 See A. Vincent, "Gallia et Gaule," *Revue belge de philologie et d'histoire*, 27 (1949): 712–726, here 721.

99 K. Pomian, *Przeszlosc jako przedmiot wiary: Historia i filozofia w mysli sredniowiecza* (The past, object of faith: History and philosophy in the thought of the Middle Ages)

(Warsaw, 1968), 13 ff., 239 ff. See also C. Beaune, "L'Utilisation politique du mythe des origines troyennes en France à la fin du Moyen Age," in *Lectures médiévales de Virgile: Actes du colloque organisé par l'École française de Rome (Rome, 25–28 octobre 1982)* (Rome, 1985), 331–355.

100   For example Polydore Virgil for English history or Paul Émile for French history. See T. D. Kendrick, *British Antiquity* (London, 1950), 78 ff.; C. Vivanti, "Paulus Aemilius Gallis condidit historias?" *Annales E.S.C.* 19 (1964): 1117–1124.

101   Strabo, *Geographie*, ed. G. Aujac (Collection des Universités de France), vol. 1, part 1 (Paris, 1969), 68 ff.

102   C. Beaune, "L'Image du fondateur: Vercingétorix et Brennus de 1450 à 1550," in *La Monarchie absolutiste et l'histoire en France* (Paris, 1986), 29–50.

103   C. Beaune, *Naissance de la nation France* (Paris, 1985), 19 ff.; here, 33.

104   G. Huppert, *L'Idée de l'histoire parfaite* (Paris, 1973), 77 ff.

105   Annius of Viterbo (Giovanni Nanni), *Commentarii fratris Joannis Annii Viterbiensis super opera diversorum auctorum de antiquitatibus loquentium* (Rome, 1498), with several later eds.

106   R. Weiss, "Traccia per una biografia di Annio da Viterbo," *Italia medievale e umanistica*, 5 (1962): 425–441; C. R. Ligota, "Annius of Viterbo and Historical Method," *Journal of the Warburg and Courtauld Institutes*, 50 (1987): 44–56.

107   C.-G. Dubois, *Celtes et Gaulois au XVIe siècle: Le développement littéraire d'un mythe nationaliste* (Paris, 1972), esp. 177–182.

108   See *Les Trésors des églises de France: Catalogue de l'exposition du Musée des arts décoratifs* (Paris, 1965), 39, no. 87.

109   H. Duranton, "Le Mythe de la continuité monarchique chez les historiens français du XVIIIe siècle," in *Modèles et moyens de réflexion politique au XVIIIe siècle* (Lille, 1979), 3: 203–226.

110   F. Hotman, *Franco-Gallia* (Geneva, 1573).

111   C. Fauchet, *Recueil des antiquitez gauloises et françoises* (Paris, 1579), book 2, ch. 2: 3.

112   On these historians, see C. Vivanti, *Lotta politica e pace religiosa in Francia fra cinque e seicento*, 2d ed. (Turin, 1974), and idem., "*Les Recherches de la France* d'Étienne Pasquier," in Nora, *Les Lieux de mémoire*, part 2, *La Nation*, 3: 215–245.

113   P. Pezron, *Antiquité de la religion et de la langue des Celtes, autrement appelés Gaulois* (Paris, 1703), and J. Solé, "Le Mythe gaulois sous Louis XIV: Paul Pezron et son *Antiquité des Celtes* de 1703," in *N.A.G.*, 37–40.

114   J. Martin, *La Religion des Gaulois, tirée des plus pures sources de l'Antiquité*, 2 vols. (Paris, 1727), and R. Mas, "Dom Jacques Martin, historien des Gaulois (1684–1751)," in *N.A.G.*, 41–50.

115   S. Pelloutier, *Histoire des Celtes, et particulièrement des Gaulois et des Germains*, 2 vols. (Paris, 3 successive eds., 1741–1750 and 1770–1771).

116   G. G. Leibniz, *De origine Francorum disquisitio* (Hanover, 1715), with a reply by Father Tournemine, *Journal de Trévoux*, 16 (1716): 10–22, and a response by Leibniz in idem., *Opera omnia*, ed. Dutens, vol. 4, part 2: 167–173. See also H. Duranton, " 'Nos ancêtres, les Gaulois': Genèse et avatars d'un cliché historique," *Cahiers d'histoire*, 4 (1969): 340–370, esp. 343–347.

117 A. de Valois, *Notitia Galliarum, ordine litterarum digesta* (Paris, 1675); d'Anville, *Eclaircissements géographiques sur l'ancienne Gaule, précédées d'un traité des mesures itinéraires des Romains et de la lieue gauloise* (Paris, 1741); idem, *Notice de l'ancienne Gaule, tirée des monuments romains* (Paris, 1760).

118 For an idea of all of this production, see J. Le Long, *Bibliothèque historique de la France*, ed. Fevret de Fontette (Paris, 1768), nos. 23 to 389 (ancient geography of the Gauls) and 3730 to 3952 (history of the ancient Gauls). See also H. Duranton, "La Recherche historique à l'académie des Inscriptions: L'exemple de l'histoire de France," in K. Hammer and J. Voss, ed., *Historische Forschung im 18. Jahrhundert* (Bonn, 1976), 207–235, and *N.A.G.*, 75–140.

119 E. Carcassonne, *Montesquieu et le problème de la constitution française au XVIIIe siècle* (1927; repr. Geneva, 1978).

120 On Boulainvilliers, see R. Simon, *Henry de Boulainviller* [sic]*: Historien, politique, philosophe, astrologue* (Gap, 1940), 46 ff., and on Le Laboureur, who anticipated certain ideas that Boulainvilliers would develop, see Carcassonne, *Montesquieu*, 11–14.

121 H. de Boulainvilliers, *Abrégé chronologique de l'histoire de France* (The Hague, 1733), 40–44; idem., *Histoire de l'ancien gouvernement de la France*, and *XIV lettres historiques sur les Parlemens ou États-Généraux* (The Hague–Amsterdam, 1727), 1: 29, 39 ff.

122 Idem., *Histoire de l'ancien gouvernement*, 1: 34–35.

123 Ibid., 1: 55.

124 Idem, *Lettres historiques*, second letter, 218.

125 Idem, *Histoire de l'ancien gouvernment*, 149–150, and *Lettres historiques*, third letter, 289.

126 *Lettres historiques*, second letter, 241–242.

127 Ibid., 325 ff. and 304. See also idem., *Essais sur la noblesse de France, contenans une dissertation sur son origine et abaissement* (Amsterdam, 1732), 230 ff.

128 Ibid., 66–67.

129 J.-B. Dubos, *Histoire critique de l'établissement de la monarchie françoise dans les Gaules* (Paris, 1734), 1: 14.

130 Ibid., 1: 204.

131 Ibid., 1: 12.

132 Ibid., 3: 210–211.

133 Ibid., 3: 375–376.

134 Ibid., 3: 260 ff., 264.

135 Ibid., 3: 504–505.

136 Ibid., 3: 533–534.

137 Ibid., 3: 294 ff.

138 Ibid., 3: 329 ff.

139 Ibid., 3: 340 ff., 370–371, 408 ff.

140 Ibid., 3: 442.

141 Ibid., 3: 543 ff.

142 Ibid., 3: 460.

143 Montesquieu, *De l'esprit des lois*, book 28, ch. 3; book 30, ch. 12, 15, 17.

144 "The Comte de Boulainvilliers and Abbé Dubos have both formulated systems, one of which appears to be a conspiracy against the third estate and the other a conspiracy

against the nobility," ibid., book 30, ch. 10; see also Augustin Thierry, *Considérations sur l'histoire de France*, in *Oeuvres complètes*, vol. 4 (Paris, 1879), and Carcassonne, *Montesquieu*, 87 ff. and 179 ff.

145 Sieyès, *Qu'est-ce que le tiers état?* ed. R. Zapperi (Geneva, 1970), 128.

146 Duranton, " 'Nos ancêtres les Gaulois,' " 361–363.

147 La Tour d'Auvergne Corret, *Nouvelles recherches sur la langue, l'origine et l'antiquité des Bretons pour servir à l'histoire de ce peuple* (Bayonne, 1792); idem., *Origines gauloises, celles des plus anciens peuples de l'Europe puisées dans leur vraie source; ou Recherches sur la langue, l'origine et les antiquités des Celto-Bretons de l'Armorique, pour servir à l'histoire de ce peuple et à celle des Français* (Paris, Year V [1796]), 211–213 n. *Le Moniteur* for 15 Germinal, Year 5 (April 4, 1797), published an article of praise by P.-L. David.

148 J. Picot, *Histoire des Gaulois depuis leur origine jusqu'à leur mélange avec les Francs et jusqu'aux commencements de la monarchie Française*, 3 vols. (Geneva, Year XI [1804]), 1: xviii and 9 ff.

149 The *Décade philosophique* for 20 Messidor, Year XII, 82–89, published an excerpt from Picot's book done by Ginguené. On the tenth of the same month it published an anonymous excerpt from Serieys, *Eléments de l'histoire des Gaules*. These were the only two books on the subject to which the *Décade* reacted. See M. Regaldo, *Un Milieu intellectuel: la* Décade philosophique *(1794–1807)* (Lille-Paris, 1976), 4: 173.

150 Picot, *Histoire des Gaulois*, 3: 187.

151 See F.-D. de Reynaud, Comte de Montlosier, *De la monarchie française, depuis son établissement jusqu'à nos jours, ou Recherches sur les anciennes institutions françaises et sur les causes qui ont amené la Révolution* (Paris, 1814), 3 vols.

152 Augustin Thierry, *Sur l'antipathie de race qui divise la nation française* (1820), in *Oeuvres complètes* (Paris, 1866), 3: 482–487; here, 486.

153 F. Guizot, *Du gouvernement de la France depuis la Restauration et du ministère actuel* (Paris, 1820), lii and 2.

154 M. Gauchet, "Les *Lettres sur l'histoire de France* d'Augustin Theirry," in Nora, *Les Lieux de mémoire*, part 2, *La Nation*, 1: 247–316.

155 In the case of Thierry, this is most apparent in his *Histoire de la conquête de l'Angleterre par les Normands* (1825). In Guizot it is in the *Histoire de la civilisation en Europe* (1828).

156 F. Guizot, *Cours d'histoire moderne: Histoire de la civilisation en France depuis la chute de l'Empire romain jusqu'en 1789* (Paris, 1829), 4 vols.

157 See, for example, A. Bertrand, *Nos origines: La Gaule avant les Gaulois d'après les monuments et les textes* (Paris, 1891), 5, 233, 254–255.

158 On the popularity of Henri Martin's works, see R. Mallet, "Henri Martin et les Gaulois: Histoire et mythe," in *N.A.G.*, 231–244. Martin's reputation apparently did not suffer much from the critique by H. d'Arbois de Jubainville, *Quelques observations sur les six premiers volumes (4ᵉ édition) de l'Histoire de France de M. Henri Martin* (Troyes-Paris, 1857). See also T. Lavalée, *Histoire des Français depuis le temps des Gaulois jusqu'en 1830* (Paris, 1838) in any of twenty editions, the last of which appeared in 1876.

159 Amédée Thierry, *Histoire des Gaulois depuis les temps les plus reculés jusqu'à l'entière soumission de la Gaule à la domination romaine*, 3d ed. (Paris, 1844), 2: 42.

160 Ibid., 1: xiv-xv.

161   Ibid., 2: 52–53.

162   Ibid., 2: 65.

163   Ibid., 2: 103–104.

164   Ibid., 2: 107.

165   Thierry applied the term "civilization" to the Gauls. See, for example, ibid., 1: xiv and xvii, and also C. Lacoste, "Les Gaulois d'Amédée Thierry," in *N.A.G.*, 203–209.

166   Thierry, *Histoire des Gaulois,* 1: x.

167   W. F. Edwards, *Des Caractères physiologiques des races humaines considérés dans leurs rapports avec l'histoire* (Paris, 1829).

168   Thierry, *Histoire des Gaulois,* 1: xii.

169   Ibid., 2: 155.

170   Ibid., 3: 88, 90, 99, 140, 141, 148, 167.

171   Ibid., 3: 161.

172   Ibid., 3: 174.

173   Guizot, *Cours d'histoire moderne,* 2: 61–62.

174   Thierry, *Histoire des Gaulois,* 3: 255.

175   Ibid., Thierry, *Histoire des Gaulois,* 2: 5.

176   R. de Lasteyrie, "Jules Quicherat, sa vie et ses travaux," in Quicherat, *Mélanges,* 15.

177   D. Bertin and J.-P. Guillaumet, *Bibracte (Saône-et-Loire): Une ville gauloise sur le mont Beuvray* (Paris, 1987), 33 ff., 45 ff.

178   Le Gall, *Alésia,* 53 ff., 118 ff.

179   J. Déchelette, *Manuel d'archéologie préhistorique, celtique et gallo-romaine,* vol. 1, *Archéologie préhistorique* (Paris, 1908 and after).

180   E. Desjardins, *Géographie historique et administrative de la Gaule romaine,* 4 vols. (Paris, 1876–1893).

181   A. Blanchet, *Traité des monnaies gauloises* (Paris, 1905).

182   E.-J. Espérandieu, *Recueil général des bas-reliefs de la Gaule romaine* (Paris, 1907 and after).

183   V. Tourneur, *Esquisse d'une histoire des études celtiques* (Liège, 1905), 212.

184   A. Bertrand, "Cours d'archéologie nationale," in *Nos origines,* 1 ff. J. Toutain, "A. Héron de Villefosse (1845–1919)," *Pro Alesia,* 5 (1919): 76 ff.; Tourner, *Esquisse,* 219.

185   C. Jullian, "La Vie et l'étude des monuments français," in *Au seuil de notre histoire* (Paris, 1930), 1: 30.

186   J. C. L. Simonde de Sismondi, *Histoire des Français* (Paris, 1821), 1: 1, 8, 129.

187   H. Martin, *Histoire de France depuis les temps les plus reculés jusqu'en 1789,* 4th ed. (Paris, 1855), 1: 1.

188   Ibid., 333.

189   Martin borrowed even his phrasing from Michelet. Compare the passage in ibid., 332–333, with the passage in J. Michelet, *Histoire de France,* 1 (I am quoting from a modern edition: Michelet, *Le Moyen Age* [Paris, 1981], 71). On the Gauls in Michelet, see C. Croisille, "Michelet et les Gaulois ou les séductions de la patrie celtique," in *N.A.G.,* 211–219.

190   R. de Lasteyrie, "Jules Quicherat, sa vie et ses travaux," in Quicherat, *Mélanges,* 2, 5–6; C. Jullian, *Notes sur l'histoire en France au 19ᵉ siècle* (1897; repr. Paris-Geneva, 1979),

esp. lxxxiii, cii, cxxi; idem, "L'ancienneté de l'idée de nation," in Jullian, *Au seuil de notre histoir* 1: 166 ff.

191 J. Michelet, preface of 1869 to *Histoire de France* (in ed. cited above, n 188), 17.

192 Ibid., 82.

193 Ibid., 79.

194 Ibid.

195 Ibid., 51.

196 Ibid., 35.

197 Ibid., 82.

198 Ibid., 72.

199 Ibid., 182.

200 Fustel de Coulanges, *Histoire des institutions politiques de l'ancienne France: La Gaule romaine* (Paris, 1891), 50.

201 Ibid., 12.

202 Ibid., 84.

203 P. Michel, *Un Mythe romantique: Les barbares (1789–1848)* (Lyons, 1981), and "Mythe barbare et mythe gaulois," in *N.A.G.*, 221–229.

204 Fustel de Coulanges, *La Gaule romaine*, 137.

205 Idem, *Histoire des institutions politiques de l'ancienne France: L'invasion germanique et la fin de l'Empire* (Paris, 1891), 225–226.

206 *Guizot, Cours d'histoire moderne*, 2: 288, 297.

207 Fustel de Coulanges, *L'Invasion germanique*, 558.

208 See, for example, the children's book by M. Moreau-Christophe, *Les Gaulois nos aïeux* (Tours, 1880, repr. 1881, 1885, 1887, and 1889).

209 Boissier, "Le Musée de Saint-Germain," 736–737.

210 C. Jullian, *Gallia: Tableau sommaire de la Gaule sous la domination romaine* (Paris, n.d.; preface dated July 1, 1892), 5.

211 The journal published poems (see *Pro Alesia*, 3 [1908–1909]: 405–408, and 5 [1910–1914]: 750–752, 772–776, 827–832) and reports of visits to excavation sites by officers and students (1 [1905–1907]: 190–192). During one visit by five hundred lycée students, a page of Camille Jullian's *Vercingétorix* was read, along with a poem by L. Matruchot: see 2 (1907–1908): 362–368. See also L. Matruchot, "Alise, lieu de pèlerinage patriotique," 3 (1908–1909): 424.

212 Unsigned editorial, "*Pro Alesia*, revue gallo-romaine," *Pro Alesia*, n.s., 2 (1915–1916): 18.

213 See letters of April 10, 1896, and October 26, 1898, in *Lettres de Camille Jullian à Henri d'Arbois de Jubainville*, ed. M. Toussaint (Nancy, 1951), 10–11 and 18; see also A. Grenier, *Camille Jullian: Un demi-siècle de science historique et de progrès français 1880–1930* (Paris, 1944).

214 See Grenier, *Camille Jullian*, 199 ff.; P.-M. Duval, introduction to *Histoire de la Gaule*, by C. Jullian, abridged ed. (Paris, 1971), xvii-xxxiii.

215 For the subjects treated in this course, see "Les Conditions géographiques de l'histoire de France," in C. Jullian, *Au seuil de notre histoire*, 1: 231–233; on Jullian and Vidal, see Grenier, *Camille Jullian*, 19 and passim.

216 C. Jullian, *Histoire de la Gaule*, 8 vols. (Paris, 1908–1926); here, 1: ch. 1–3, and vol. 5.

217 See, for example, 1: 159 ff.; 5: 174 ff., 216 ff.; 6: 166 ff.

218 C. Jullian, "Plaidoyer pour la préhistoire," in *Au seuil de notre histoire*, 1: 57–58. When Marc Bloch, in a famous passage, compared the historian to "the ogre of legend," he probably had this passage from Jullian in mind.

219 Jullian, *Histoire de la Gaule*, 2: 443–444.

220 Ibid., 2: 448.

221 Ibid., 2: 449 ff.

222 Ibid., 2: 547.

223 Ibid., 2: 550.

224 Ibid., 3: 29.

225 Ibid., 3: 32–33.

226 Ibid., 3: 30.

227 Ibid., 3: 421.

228 Ibid., 3: 487).

229 Ibid., 3: 535.

230 Ibid., 3: 539–540.

231 Ibid., 6: 528 ff., esp. 533.

232 See, for example, J.-L. Brunaux, *Les Gaulois, sanctuaires et rites* (Paris, 1986); P. Méniel, *Chasse et élevage chez les Gaulois* (Paris, 1987); J.-L. Brunaux and B. Lambot, *Guerre et armement chez les Gaulois* (Paris, 1988); A. Duval, "Autour de Vercingétorix: De l'archéologie à l'histoire économique et sociale," in *Le Deuxième Age du fer en Auvergne et en Forez* (Sheffield–Saint-Étienne, 1982), 298–335; idem, "Économies et sociétés en Gaule non méditrranéenne, IIIe–Ie siècle avant notre ère, d'après les données archéologiques," in *Archéologie et rapports sociaux en Gaule,* ed. A. Daubigney, Annales littéraires de l'université de Besançon (Besançon, 1984), 55–68; P.-M. Duval, *Travaux sur la Gaule (1946–1986)*, 2 vols. (Rome, 1990); C. Goudineau, *César et la Gaule* (Paris, 1990).

233 P. Vidal-Naquet, "Gaulois à tout faire," and M. Fischer, J.-L. Brunaux, and O. Buchen-schutz, "L'Éternel Retour des Gaulois," *L'Histoire*, 109 (March 1988): 7 and 28–37; see also *Revue historique des armées*, 167 (June 1986), which contains important information on Alesia.

234 M. Rambaud, *L'Art de la déformation historique dans les* Commentaires de César, 2d ed. (Paris, 1966), and M.-T. Moisset, "L'Iconographie de Vercingétorix à travers les manuels d'histoire," *Antiquités nationales*, 8 (1976): 84–90.

235 Fustel de Coulanges, *L'Invasion germanique*, 533.

CHAPTER 2   THE ANCIÉN REGIME AND THE REVOLUTION

1   *The Works of John Adams*, ed. Charles Francis Adams (Boston, 1850–1856; repr. Freeport, N.Y.: Books for Libraries, 1969); Thomas Paine, *The Complete Writings,* ed. Philip S. Foner (New York: Citadel, 1945).

2   John Adams, *Canon and Feudal Law*, part 1.

3   Ibid.

4   Among recent writers Louis Hartz is the most profound commentator on the exceptional character of the founding of the United States. See *The Liberal Tradition in America: An Interpretation of American Political Thought Since the Revolution* (New York: Harvest/H.B.J. Book, 1955) and *The Founding of New Societies* (New York: Harvest/H.B.J. Book, 1964).

5   On this subject, classic since Tocqueville and Taine, see Keith Baker, *Condorcet* (Chicago: University of Chicago Press, 1975), esp. ch. 4.

6   See my article on Tocqueville in François Furet and Mona Ozouf, ed., *Dictionnaire critique de la Révolution française* (Paris: Flammarion, 1988), trans. by Arthur Goldhammer as *A Critical Dictionary of the French Revolution* (Cambridge, Mass.: Harvard University Press, 1989).

7   On the appearance of the phrase "Ancien Régime" in 1789, I am here following the analysis given in the article "Ancien Régime" in the *Dictionnaire critique* (see n. 6). See also Diego Venturino, "La Formulation de l'idée d' 'Ancien Régime,' " in Colin Lucas, ed., *The French Revolution and the Creation of Modern Political Culture*, vol. 2, *The Political Culture of the French Revolution* (Oxford: Pergamon Press, 1988).

8   See *Le Moniteur*, 13 (July–September 1792): 441–442.

9   This is the central argument of my book *La Révolution, de Turgot à Jules Ferry* (Paris: Hachette, 1988).

10   On Guizot, see two recent works: Pierre Rosanvallon, *Le Moment Guizot* (Paris: Gallimard, 1985), and Marina Valenise, ed., *François Guizot et la culture politique de son temps,* colloquium of the Fondation Guizot–Val Richer (Paris: Gallimard—Éditions du Seuil, 1991).

CHAPTER 3   CATHOLICS AND SECULARS

1   In French, the word *laïc* (a noun or adjective), and its associated words *laïcité, laïciser, laïcisme,* and *laïcisation,* refer to a history, a set of practices, and a memory. There is even a certain ambiguity in the term, since *laïc* can be opposed to *prêtre* (layman versus priest) or to *catholique* (secular versus Catholic). In the English text, this family of words is translated by *secular, secularize, secularization,* etc., and where necessary to avoid ambiguity by *laymen, laity.* A conceptual difficulty remains, however, since sociologists have for some time now worked with a concept of "secularization," which has become part of the field's technical vocabulary. Nevertheless, most French historians and sociologists, including the author of these lines, distinguish fairly sharply between the two related phenomena of *sécularisation* and *laïcisation.*—TRANS.

2   *L'Assiette au beurre* (March 19, 1904), in Élisabeth Dixmier and Michel Dixmier, *L'Assiette au beurre* (Paris: Maspero, 1974). The present essay intersects with a number of others in this collection (*Les Lieux de mémoire* in its French form), this being one of the glories—or is it dangers?—of a series published over a considerable number of years. In particular, the first volume, *La République,* exhibits from a number of different angles the emergence of a "secularized" or secular memory. The reader is urged to

consult this volume for general background. Here I have availed myself of the excellent work done by others in tracing the more familiar pathways to explore some lesser-known byways; I also attempt to come full circle and begin an explanation rather than yet another exercise in remembering.

3 Compare the persistent representations of heaven and hell in the iconography of the Breton missions: Fanch Roudaut, Alain Croix, and Fanch Froudic, *Les Chemins du paradis, Taolennou ar Barradoẑ* (Douerarnenez: Éditions de l'Estran, 1988).

4 Antoine de Baecque, *La Caricature révolutionnaire* (Paris: Presses du CNRS, 1988).

5 See in particular Eugen Weber, *Satan franc-maçon: La mystification de Léo Taxil* (Paris: Julliard, 1964).

6 René Rémond, *L'Anticléricalisme en France de 1815 à nos jours*, 2d ed. (Brussels: Éditions Complexe, 1985).

7 Besse, OSB, *Veillons sur notre histoire* (1907), 10. Quoted in Georges Weill, *Histoire de l'idée laïque en France au XIXᵉ siècle* (Paris: Félix Alcan, 1925), 359.

8 Weill, *Histoire de l'idée laïque.*

9 Georges de Lagarde, The translated version is as you see it here, beginning with Lagarde's work *Naissance de l'esprit laïque au déclin du Moyen Age* (Paris: Desclée de Brouwer, 1934). The subsequent volumes were *L'Anticléricalisme et l'affaire Dreyfus* (Toulouse: Imprimerie Régionale, 1948) and *Histoire contemporaine de la laïcité républicaine*, 3 vols. (Librairie Marcel Rivière, 1957 and 1960; Nouvelles Éditions Latines, 1961).

10 Georges de Lagarde, *Naissance de l'esprit laïque au déclin du Moyen Age* (Levallois-Perret: Société Industrielle d'Imprimerie, 1934), vol. 1, in 2 parts (repr. Paris: Presses Universitaires de France, 1948).

11 Ibid., foreword to vol. 1.

12 Capéran, *Histoire contemporaine*, 1: 9.

13 Antoine Prost, *L'École et la famille dans une société en mutation* (Paris: G. V. Labat, 1982).

14 See, for example, the poll by the Institut Française d'Opinion Politique, February 10–12, 1973 (*La Vie catholique*). The vote by Catholic militants for the Socialist Party (24 percent) and the Communist Party (18 percent) was the same as for the population generally (24 and 19 percent respectively). By contrast, the vote by regular practicing Catholics dropped to 10 percent for the P.S. and 1 percent for the P.C.

15 For a longer-range perspective, see Émile Poulat, *Liberté, laïcité: La guerre des deux France et le principe de la modernité* (Paris: Cerf-Cujas, 1987).

16 For the 19th century this can be verifiedby using Second Empire demographic statistics that mention religious affiliation or by using the relative allocations to each sect in the official budget.

17 Claude Langlois, "Trente ans d'histoire religieuse: Suggestions pour une future enquête," *Archives de sciences sociales des religions*, 63 (1): 85–114.

18 See the significantly entitled work marking the three-hundredth anniversary of the revocation of the Edict of Nantes: Jean Baubérot, *Le Retour des Huguenots* (Paris: Cerf-Labor and Fides, 1985); see also, by the same author, *Le Protestantisme doit-il mourir?* (Paris: Éditions du Seuil, 1988).

19   Quoted in Marcel Launay, *L'Église et l'école en France, XIXe–XXe siècles* (Paris: Desclée), 156.

20   Doris Bensimon, *Les Juifs de France et leurs relations avec Israël (1945-1966)* (Paris: L'Harmattan, 1989), 25–40.

21   Gilles Kepel, *Les Banlieues de l'Islam: Naissance d'une religion en France* (Paris: Éditions du Seuil, 1987).

22   See Bruno Étienne, *La France et l'Islam* (Paris: Hachette, 1989).

23   Maurice Agulhon, *Marianne au pouvoir* (Paris: Flammarion, 1989).

24   Rémond, *L'Anticléricalisme en France*, 164–166. Sainte-Beuve is speaking only of the "clerical party."

25   Ibid., 175–186.

26   Eckmann-Chatrian, *Lettre d'un électeur à son député* (Paris, 1873), 11 ff.

27   François Lebrun, ed., *Histoire des catholiques en France* (Paris: Privat, 1985), 284–392.

28   Jean-Marie Mayeur, *Des Partis catholiques à la démocratie chrétienne* (Paris: Armand Colin, 1980). According to Mayeur, the obsession with clericalism, which both conservatives and republicans reject, makes it impossible to establish a Catholic party: "This attitude stems from a conception of Catholicism that distinguishes sharply between the spiritual and the temporal and is wary of confusing the two" (p. 89).

29   The title of a famous book by Daniel Halévy, reprinted in 1972.

30   Eugen Weber, *Peasants into Frenchmen* (Stanford: Stanford University Press, 1976), the French translation bears the title *La Fin des terroirs*.

31   See François Furet and Mona Ozouf, *Dictionnaire critique de la Révolution française* (Paris: Flammarion, 1988); trans. by Arthur Goldhammer as *A Critical Dictionary of the French Revolution* (Cambridge, Mass.: Harvard University Press, 1989).

32   The archetype is Albert de Mun. See Philippe Levillain, *Albert de Mun: Catholicisme français et catholicisme romain du Syllabus au ralliement* (Rome: École Française de Rome, 1983).

33   Claude Nicolet, *L'Idée républicaine en France (1789–1924): Essai d'histoire critique* (Paris: Gallimard, 1982), 273.

34   François Furet, ed., *Jules Ferry, fondateur de la République* (Paris: Éditions de l'École des Hautes Études en Sciences Sociales, 1985).

35   His letter to teachers of November 17, 1883, can be read in Launay, *L'Église et l'Éecole en France*, 81.

36   François Furet and Jacques Ozouf, *Lire et écrire: L'alphabétisation des Français de Calvin à Jules Ferry* (Paris: Éditions de Minuit, 1977).

37   Pierre Zind, *L'Enseignement religieux dans l'instruction publique en France (1850–1873)* (Lyons: Centre d'Histoire du Catholicisme, 1971). For example, Victor Duruy was the author of a *Histoire sainte d'après la Bible*, which begins with the opening lines of Genesis. The work was still being reprinted at the beginning of the twentieth century.

38   Mona Ozouf, *La Classe ininterrompue: Cahiers de la famille Sandre, enseignants, 1789–1960* (Paris: Hachette, 1979).

39   Jacques Gavoille, *L'École publique dans le département du Doubs, 1870–1960* (Paris: Les Belles Lettres, 1981).

40 Michel Leniaud, *L'Administration des cultes pendant la période concordataire* (Paris: Nouvelles Éditions Latines, 1988), 305–364.

41 Poulat, *Liberté, laïcité*, 294–304.

42 Claude Langlois, "L'Introduction des congrégations féminines dans le système pénitentiaire français, 1839–1880," in Jacques G. Petit, ed., *La Prison, le bagne et l'histoire* (Geneva: Médecine et Hygiène, 1984), 129–140.

43 The law of August 14, 1884, abrogated Paragraph 3 of Article 1 of the Constitutional Law of July 16, 1874: "On the Sunday following the opening of the term, public prayers will be addressed to God in the churches and temples asking for His assistance in the work of the Assemblies."

44 Charles Monsch, "La Naissance de *La Croix*," in René Rémond and Émile Poulat, ed., *Cent ans d'histoire de* La Croix (Paris: Le Centurion, 1988) 21–34.

45 François Laplanche, "La Notion de 'science catholique': Ses origines au début du XIXe siècle," *Revue d'histoire de l'Église de France*, 192 (January–June 1988): 63–90.

46 Jacqueline Lalouette, "Science et foi dans l'idéologie libre-penseuse (1866–1914)," in *Christianisme et science* (Paris: Vrin, 1989), 21–54.

47 Ibid., 32.

48 Danielle Delorme, Nicole Gault, and Josiane Gonthier, *Les Premières Institutrices laïques* (Paris: Mercure de France, 1980).

49 Françoise Mayeur, *L'Éducation des filles en France au XIXe siècle* (Paris: Hachette, 1979), 152.

50 *Paul Abadie, architecte, 1812-1884,* Musée d'Angoulême, 1984–85 exposition catalogue, p. 143. And see François Loyer, "Le Sacré-Coeur de Montmartre," in Pierre Nora, ed., *Les Lieux de mémoire*, part 3, *Les France*, vol. 3, *De l'archive à l'emblème* (Paris, Éditions Gallimard, 1992).

51 *Paul Abadie, architecte,* 134.

52 Michel Lagrée, "1889, premier centenaire de la Révolution en Bretagne," *Annales de Bretagne et des pays de l'Ouest*, 3 (1984): 255. And see Henri Loyrette, "La Tour Eiffel," in Nora, *Les Lieux de mémoire*, part 3, *Les France*, vol. 3, *De l'archive à l'emblème*.

53 Besides Ferdinand Buisson, one should mention Jules Steeg, Pauline Kergomard, *directrice des écoles maternelles*, as well as Félix Pécaut and Mme Jules Favre, who provided spiritual and moral guidance at the Écoles Normales Supérieures of Fontenay-aux-Roses and Sèvres, respectively.

54 Yves Marchasson, "*La Croix* et le ralliement," in Rémond and Poulat, *Cent Ans d'histoire*, 69–106.

55 Pierre Chevallier, *La Séparation de l'Église et de l'école* (Paris: Fayard, 1981).

56 For statistics, see Antoine Prost, *L'Enseignement en France, 1800–1967* (Paris: Armand Colin, 1968), 45.

57 Jean-Marie Mayeur, *La Séparation des églises et de l'état* (Paris: Julliard, 1966).

58 This was an allusion to revolutionary repression in the Vendée, where Carrier ordered mass executions using boats that could be towed into the middle of a river and then sunk—TRANS.

58 *Le Bonnet rouge*, December 23, 1915, in Rémond, *L'Anticléricalisme en France*, 233.

60 In addition to Father Doncoeur's famous letter, "We will not go," glued to walls everywhere, there were the posters of the Ligue des Droits du Religieux Ancien Combattant (or DRAC, as it soon came to be called). See, for example, Rémi Paillart, *Affiches 14–18* (Reims: published by the author, 1986), 297.

61 *L'École libératrice*, December 6, 1930, summary of the argument.

62 Jacqueline Freyssinet-Dominjon, *Les Manuels d'histoire de l'école libre, 1882–1959* (Paris: Armand Colin, 1969).

63 Yan Fauchois, *Religion et France révolutionnaire* (Paris: Herscher, 1989).

64 *Révolutions de France et de Brabant*, 2, no. 23: 454.

65 François Furet, *Penser la Révolution française* (Paris: Gallimard, 1978), 77 ff., on the aristocratic conspiracy; trans. by J. Mandelbaum as *Conceptualizing the French Revolution*.

66 Claude Langlois, "Religion, culte et opinion religieuse: La politique des révolutionnaires," *Revue française de sociologie* (1989), 3–4: 471–496.

67 See Henry Cros, *Claude Fauchet, 1744–1793: Ses idées politiques, économiques et sociales* (Paris: E. Larose, 1912), and Gary Kates, *The Cercle Social, the Girondins, and the French Revolution* (Princeton: Princeton University Press, 1985).

68 Bernard Cousin, Monique Cubells, and René Moulinas, *La Pique et la Croix: Histoire religieuse de la Révolution française* (Paris: Le Centurion, 1989).

69 Jean Jaurès, *Histoire socialiste de la Révolution* (Paris: Éditions Sociales, 1968), 1: 791: "The Civil Constitution of the Clergy in some respects secularized the Church itself."

70 Timothy Tackett, *Religion, Revolution, and Regional Culture in Eighteenth-Century France: The Ecclesiastical Oath of 1791* (Princeton: Princeton University Press, 1986); trans. into French as *La Révolution, l'Église, la France: Le serment de 1791* (Paris: Éditions du Seuil, 1986).

71 Claude Langlois, "Crise du serment et retour de l'antichristianisme des Lumières (1791)," in *Mélanges Gadille* (forthcoming). The crisis surrounding the oath occasioned a revival of criticisms of the Enlightenment and a new propensity to portray the clergy as a fundamental element of the Ancien Régime.

72 Albert Mathiez, *La Théophilanthropie et le culte décadaire* (Paris: Alcan, 1903), 707.

73 Dominique Julia, *Les Trois Couleurs du tableau noir: La Révolution* (Paris: Belin, 1981), 199. The formula is that of a deputy named Opoix, from Seine-et-Marne, to the Convention (1793).

74 Read the long argument for the superiority of Christianity by M.-E. Petit (October 1, 1793) in Julia, *Les Trois Couleurs*, 200–201.

75 Bronislaw Baczko, *Une Éducation pour la démocratie: Textes et projets de l'époque révolutionnaire* (Paris: Éditions Garnier, 1982), 297–298.

76 Report of 24 Germinal, Year II, in Baczko, *Une Éducation*, 297–298.

77 Notes of Condorcet, in Baczko, *Une Éducation*, 250.

78 Report of Condorcet, April 20 and 21, 1792, in Baczko, *Une Éducation*, 185.

79 Ibid., 259.

80 Nicolet, *L'Idée républicaine en France*, 76–80.

81 Étienne Fouilloux and Claude Langlois, "Les Parrainages civils à Ivry-sur-Seine au XXe siècle," in, *Libre Pensée et religion laïque en France* (Strasbourg: CERDIC, 1980), 193–210.

82 Jules Michelet, *Histoire de la Révolution française* (Paris: Gallimard, 1952), 1: 21.

83 Jean-Clément Martin, *La Vendée de la mémoire (1800–1980)* (Paris: Éditions du Seuil, 1989).

84 Tackett, *La Révolution*, 251–318.

85 Claude Langlois, "La Déchirure," afterword to the French ed. of Tackett, *La Révolution*, 319–337.

86 See Maurice Gontard, *L'Enseignement primaire en France, de la Révolution à la loi Guizot* (Paris: Les Belles Lettres, 1959), and Pierre Zind, *Les Nouvelles Congrégations de frères enseignants en France de 1800 à 1830* (Paris: Klincksieck, 1974), 405.

87 Prost, *L'Enseignement en France*, 13.

88 Claude Langlois, *Le Diocèse de Vannes au XIXe siècle: 1800–1830* (Paris: Klincksieck, 1974), 405.

89 Rémond, *L'Anticléricalisme en France*, 113–114.

90 Robert Casanova, *Montlosier et le parti prêtre* (Paris: Robert Laffont, 1970).

91 Philippe Boutry, *Prêtres et paroisses au pays du curé d'Ars* (Paris: Éditions du Cerf, 1986), 641; see also 644.

92 Ibid., 641. The quotation is from the highly official *Messager du dimanche* in 1875, in response to the declaration that the clergy must not engage in politics.

93 Odile Rudelle, *La République absolue, 1870–1889*, 2d ed. (Paris: Publications de la Sorbonne, 1986).

94 The thought is inspired by the title of an article by Christian Lahalle, "Émile Combes, réveille-toi!" in *Éléments*, September-October 1989, a publication of the "new right" organization GRECE. The issue is devoted to the "right of blasphemy."

CHAPTER 4 FRENCH AND FOREIGNERS

1 The slogan was chanted by young North African demonstrators in December 1983, and is quoted in Françoise Gaspard and Claude Servan-Schreiber, *La Fin des immigrés* (Paris: Éditions du Seuil, 1985), 184. Such statements are of course exaggerated and reveal a confusion about the definition of the term *immigration*. Various (official and unofficial) statistics make it appear plausible that one in three current residents of France may have immigrant "ancestors" (going back as far as the great-grandparents). See Gérard Noiriel, *Immigration, Citizenship, and National Identity in France (19th–20th Centuries)*, (Minneapolis: University of Minnesota Press, forthcoming). But this is more a symbolic figure, intended to underscore the historical importance of immigration, rather than a precise statistic. In keeping with republican political philosophy, French legal and administrative classifications have omitted any reference to ethnic or national origin since the nineteenth century. Results based on the few available opinion polls are not reliable for memories beyond the grandparents' generation. In an excellent illustration of the impoverishment of modern genealogical memory, one recent poll showed that 24 percent of French people were unable to name at least one of their eight great-grandparents, while only 13 percent knew the names of two. See François Decaris, "Les Français et leurs racines," *Gé-Magazine*, 1 (November 1982). A final rea-

son for caution in dealing with the statistics has to do with the complexity of defining the term *immigrant*. I shall come back to this subject in what follows. Note, however, that the word is not to be confused with *migrant* (for in that case everyone in France would indeed have immigrant ancestors) or with the legal term *foreigner* (the inhabitants of Savoy and Alsace-Lorraine were not "immigrants" even when their territory was not under French sovereignty).

2   Alexis de Tocqueville, *De la démocratie en Amérique* (1st ed., 1835–1840; repr. Paris: Flammarion, 1981), 1: 26.

3   The term *immigrant* is an American invention. It was first used in the year in which the Constitution was drafted. See Jeanine Brun, *America! America! Trois siècles d'émigration aux États-Unis* (Paris: Julliard-Gallimard, 1980).

4   Nathan Glazer, ed., *Clamor at the Gates: The New American Immigration* (San Francisco: I.C.S. Press, 1985), 3.

5   Gary Cross, *Immigrant Workers in Industrial France: The Making of a New Laboring Class* (Philadelphia: Temple University Press, 1983).

6   I elaborate on this question in Gérard Noiriel, *Workers in French Society in the Nineteenth and Twentieth Centuries* (Oxford: Berg, 1990).

7   The hypothesis of a close connection between peasant resistance to industrialization, political democracy, and immigration is explored by Don Digan in "Europe's Melting Pot: A Century of Large-Scale Immigration into France," *Ethnic and Racial Studies* (April 1981).

8   Jean Portemer, "L'Étranger dans le droit de la Révolution française," in *L'Étranger: Recueil de la Société Jean-Bodin* (Paris, 1959), 535 ff.

9   *Archives parlementaires,* 8: 479. Cited hereafter as *A.P.*

10   *A.P.,* 9: 478.

11   *A.P.,* 10: 756.

12   Adolphe Landry, who sponsored an immigration bill early in World War I, was the first to point out that the republican tradition of the rights of man prevented establishing a truly "scientific" policy for the recruitment of immigrants. See Archives Nationales, C 7725. Many subsequent works would take up this theme.

13   As shown by Jean-Pierre Hassoun and Yinh Phong Tan, "Les Réfugiés de l'Asie du Sud-Est de langue chinoise" (research report of the Mission du Patrimoine Ethnologique, 1986; typescript).

14   Émile Durkheim, *Le Suicide* (1897; repr. Paris: Presses Universitaires de France, 1983), 356.

15   Jean-Jacques Rousseau, *Émile,* in *Oeuvres complètes* (Paris: Gallimard, 1959–1969), 1: 248–249; quoted in Tzvetan Todorov, *Nous et les autres: La réflexion française sur la diversité humaine* (Paris: Éditions du Seuil, 1989), 207 and 209.

16   Albert Mathiez, *La Révolution et les étrangers: Cosmopolitisme et défense nationale* (Paris: La Renaissance du Livre, 1918).

17   *A.P.,* 17: 629, italics in the original. Note, however, the "modern" quality of the reservations expressed by one deputy, Andrieu, who asked for "limits to be set to the law" in order to avoid a massive influx of foreigners seeking "to acquire national properties in our country whose income they would consume in theirs."

18   A full legal survey with historical background can be found in the report of the Commission on Nationality chaired by Marceau Long, *Etre français aujourd'hui*, 2 vols. (Paris: UGE, 1988)

19   Mathiez, *La Révolution et les étrangers*, 1.

20   For this period see especially Pierre Milza, *Français et Italiens à la fin du XIX* siècle (Rome: Publications de l'École Française, 1981); Judy Reardon, "Belgian Workers in Roubaix, France, in the 19th Century" (thesis, University of Maryland, 1977); Nancy Green, *Les Travailleurs immigrés juifs à la Belle Epoque* (Paris: Fayard, 1985); and the overview edited by Yves Lequin, *La Mosaïque France: Histoire des étrangers et de l'immigration en France* (Paris: Larousse, 1988).

21   Quoted in Anne-Marie Faidutti-Rudolph, *L'Immigration italienne dans le sud-est de la France* (Gap: Louis Jean, 1964), 96.

22   Michelle Perrot, "Les Rapports entre ouvriers français et étrangers (1871–1893)," *Bulletin de la Société d'histoire moderne* (1960).

23   Alain Dantoing, "Une Manifestation de défense ouvrière contre le travail étranger dans les mines du Pas-de-Calais en 1892," *Revue d'histoire belge contemporaine* (1974).

24   *Le Petit Marseillais* (June 19, 1881).

25   For this episode, see Teodosio Vertone's article in Jean-Baptiste Duroselle and Emilio Serra, ed., *L'emigrazione italiana in Francia prima del 1914* (Milan: Franco Angeli, 1978).

26   The first Italian workers to be attacked were members of the Club Nazionale Italiano, who jeered at French soldiers from the Vincendon Brigade upon their return from Tunisia.

27   Over the past century large industrial and agricultural concerns with substantial demand for foreign manual labor have often defended foreign workers against outbreaks of xenophobia. In this respect they differ from smaller firms and businesses.

28   The unions fought for equal treatment of French and foreign workers all the more vigorously because any penalization of immigrants in terms of wages or working conditions ultimately cost French workers as well (employers will always hire the cheapest workers available). By contrast, the left's position on employment before 1914 was much more ambiguous. The Millerand laws of 1899 prohibited public works projects from employing more than ten percent foreign workers. About this time the unions also won the right to monitor the hiring of immigrant workers by participating in the operation of government hiring offices.

29   See Janine Ponty, *Polonais méconnus* (Paris: Publications de la Sorbonne, 1988).

30   Jean-Charles Bonnet, "Les Pouvoirs publics et l'immigration dans l'entre-deux-guerres" (thesis, Publications du Centre Pierre-Léon, University of Lyons, 1974), 206 ff.

31   See Ralph Schor, *L'Opinion française et les étrangers, 1919–1939* (Paris: Publications de la Sorbonne, 1985).

32   Jean-Marie Le Pen, *Les Français d'abord* (Paris: Carrère-Lafon, 1984), 167, quoted in Pierre Milza, *Fascisme français: Passé et présent* (Paris: Flammarion, 1987), 423.

33   Another reason for this constant hostility toward strangers is the number of bloody wars that France has fought over the centuries, wars that have created a mental climate receptive to arguments of this type. France has a "long memory" of repeated invasions, passed down from generation to generation, in some cases over many centuries.

Ernest Lavisse tells this anecdote about a dance in a village near his native Nouvion: "A boy, furious that I should have offered my arm to his mistress—I was then a young gentleman of fifteen—called me a Paulac. I write the word as he pronounced it. He had no idea, nor did I, for that matter, that he was referring to the Poles, who in the seventeenth century were called Pollaques, who fought in Picardy in the service of the emperor." Ernest Lavisse, *Souvenirs* (1912; repr. Paris: Calmann-Lévy, 1988), 40.

34   Dominique Schnapper, *La France de l'intégration* (Paris: Gallimard, 1991).

35   There is no space here to discuss the reasonableness of this judgment. It is not simply that recent research does not corroborate it. Various studies challenge the idea that there is anything special about the problem of North Africans (which many people confuse with the problem of Muslims). After analyzing a number of works on the educational issue, Michel Oriol observed (in "Bilan des études sur les aspects culturels et humains des migrations internationales (1918–1979)," [Strasbourg: Fondation Européennes des Sciences, 1981; typescript]): "Various studies of the matter agree that Portuguese students commonly do worse than Algerians." Similarly, concerning Muslims in France, Rémi Leveau and Dominique Schnapper argue that it is time to "question the common idea...that [Muslims] today are incapable of assimilating into French society." (Leveau and Schnapper, "Religion et politique: juifs et musulmans maghrébins en France," in Leveau and Gilles Keppel, ed., *Les Musulmans dans la société française* [Paris: Presses de la Fondation Nationale des Sciences Politiques, 1988], 137.)

36   Albin Chalandon, "La Nationalité française doit être un objet de fierté," *L'Evénement du jeudi* (November 20–26, 1986).

37   Jean-Yves Le Gallou, "Identité nationale et préférence nationale," in Le Club de l'Horloge, *L'Identité de la France* (Paris: Albin Michel, 1985), 246.

38   Jean Laumonier, *La Nationalité française,* vol. 2, *Les Hommes* (Paris: Chamuel, 1892), 350 ff.

39   Jules Rochard, *Bulletin de l'Académie de médecine* (1883), 281.

40   Georges Vacher de Lapouge, *Race et milieu social* (Paris: Marcel Rivière, 1909), 69.

41   Laumonier, *La Nationalité française,* 371.

42   Jules Soury, quoted in Zeev Sternhell, *Maurice Barrès et le nationalisme français* (1972; repr. Brussels: Éditions Complexe, 1985), 259.

43   Maurice Barrès, *L'Appel au soldat,* quoted in Sternhell, *Maurice Barrès,* 265.

44   Charles Seignobos, *Histoire sincère de la nation française* (1933; repr. Paris: Presses Universitaires de France, 1982), 337.

45   Georges Mauco, "Mémoire sur l'assimilation des étrangers en France" (Geneva: Institut International de Coopération Intellectuelle, 1937; typescript), 23.

46   René Martial, *Les Métis* (Paris: Flammarion, 1942), 26.

47   Jean Pluyette, *La Sélection de l'immigration en France et la doctrine des races* (Paris: Pierre Bosseret, 1930), 138.

48   After World War II but just before the spotlight turned to the North Africans, an INED study still maintained that "the resistance of Russians to assimilation is such that French women married to Russian men appear more likely to adapt to Russian ways than to serve as agents of assimilation." And this: "Russian children remain Russian in

spite of school." Through careful calculation the author is able to affirm that the proportion of assimilated Russian immigrants declined from 27.8 to 24.4 percent between 1930 and 1936. See Madeleine Doré, "Enquête sur l'immigration russe,"in INED, Louis Chevalier, ed., *Documents sur l'immigration* (Paris: Presses Universitaires de France, 1947), 154–158.

49 Mauco, "Mémoire," 42.

50 From *Républicain lorrain* (November 18, 1988); see Maria Liberatore-Lefebvre, *Le Passé simple* (Maxéville: Imprimerie Rubrecht, 1988).

51 For the Spanish see C. Azas, "Migrants espagnols dans le Biterrois (1886–1934)" (thesis, University of Paris-V, 1981; typescript); for the Italians, A. Sportiello, *Les Pêcheurs du Vieux Port: Fêtes et traditions* (Marseilles: Jeanne Laffite, 1981); for the Poles, Danielle Ducellier, "L'Immigration polonaise dans le bassin de Blanzy dans l'entre-deux-guerres," *Revue périodique de la "Physiophyle"* (Montceau-les-Mines: 1981 and 1982); for the Armenians, Martine Hovanessian, *Le Lien communautaire: Trois générations d'Arméniens* (Paris: Armand Colin, 1992).

52 *Le Monde* (April 13–14, 1986).

53 Hovanessian, *Le Lien communautaire.*

54 A second preface by the *proviseur* of the lycée, Jean-Paul Llinares, goes even further, stating that the city's inhabitants "have kept their unique customs and ways. This diversity is what makes the population so abundantly original." Office Départemental d'Action Culturelle de l'Hérault, *Paroles: Histoires d'une migration; des Espagnols racontent* (Montpellier, n. d.).

55 Maurizio Catani in Michel Oriol and Marie-Claire Hily, ed., "Les Réseaux associatifs des immigrés en Europe occidentale" (University of Nice, IDERIC, 1985; typescript); see also the article by G. Campani in the same work.

56 See Laurence Bertoïa and Gérard Noiriel, "Aperçu sur l'histoire du mouvement associatif chez les immigrés en France," in Maurizio Catani and Salvatore Palidda, ed., "Le Rôle du mouvement associatif dans l'évolution des communautés immigrées" (report for the Fonds d'Action Sociale and the Ministère des Affaires Sociales, February 1987; typescript) 66–81.

57 Ponty, *Polonais méconnus,* 167.

58 Arnam Turabian, *Trente ans en France: Ma vie* (Marseilles: L'Aiguillon, 1928), 20.

59 Alexandre de Kronowski, preface to *Almanach historique ou souvenir de l'émigration polonaise* (Paris: Bourgogne et Martinet, 1837–1838).

60 Khoren Margossian, *Odysée d'un enfant arménien* (Paris: La Pensée Universelle, 1975), 13. The question of writing as a trace or track of origin can even constitute a literary project, as in the case of Georges Perec, whose father, a Polish Jewish immigrant to France, died in combat in 1940 and whose mother died in a German concentration camp. See C. Burgelin, *Georges Perec* (Paris: Éditions du Seuil, 1988).

61 Mary Antin, *The Promised Land* (Boston: Houghton-Mifflin, 1912).

62 Simone Signoret, *Adieu Volodia* (Paris: Fayard, 1985).

63 See Robert Park and Herbert Miller, *Old World Traits Transplanted* (1921; repr. New York: Paterson-Smith, 1969).

64 Giorgio Amendola, *L'Ile* (1981) (Paris: Messinger, 1983), 225.

65 Robert Park, "The Immigrant Press and Its Control," quoted in Ralph Turner, *Robert Park: On Social Control and Collective Behavior* (Chicago: The University of Chicago Press, 1967), 119.

66 Alain Girard and Jean Stoetzel, *Français et immigrés*, 2 vols.; INED Travaux et Documents, cahiers 19 and 20 (Paris: Presses Universitaires de France, 1953 and 1954). Given the small size of the sample (slightly more than 500 people in all), the figures in this study are not conclusive but can serve as indications.

67 Park, quoted in Turner, *Robert Park*, 143.

68 Leveau and Schnapper, "Religion et politique," 137.

69 Geneviève Bardakdjian, "La Communauté arménienne de Décines (1925–1971)," *Bulletin du Centre d'histoire économique et sociale de l'Université de Lyon-II* (1973); see also Aznive Keuroghlian, "Les Arméniens dans la région Rhône-Alpes" (thesis, University of Lyons, 1975; typescript).

70 K. Partchevsky, "Statistique générale et situation légale des émigrés en France," *Russie et Chrétienté*, 1 (January–March 1937).

71 Benigno Cacérès, *La Solitude des autres* (Paris: Éditions du Seuil, 1970), 74.

72 Leveau and Schnapper, "Religion et politique," 132.

73 This problem is not limited to immigrants. Norbert Elias argues that assimilation through inculcation of dominant norms in ever-expanding circles of society was a central aspect of the civilizing process in Europe from the Renaissance on. See Norbert Elias, *La Civilisation des moeurs* (1939; repr. Paris: Calmann-Lévy, 1982).

74 Étienne Balibar, "La Forme nation: Histoire et idéologie," in Balibar and Immanuel Wallerstein, *Race, nation, classe: Les identités ambigües* (Paris: La Découverte, 1988), 135.

75 Bardakdjian, "La Communauté arménienne de Décines."

76 Jan Gruszynski, "La Communauté polonaise en France de 1919 à 1975: Problèmes d'intégration de trois générations" (thesis, University of Paris-V, 1977; typescript).

77 "In an urban environment children are more likely to stay in school," according to Girard and Stoetzel, *Français et immigrés*, 80.

78 Jean-Louis Borkowski, "L'Insertion sociale des immigrés et de leurs enfants," *Données sociales* (INSEE: 1990), 310–314. The figures for this study were taken from a survey of living conditions in France conducted in 1986–87.

79 See Schnapper, *La France de l'intégration*.

80 On language issues, see Simone Bonnafous, *L'Immigration prise aux mots* (Paris: Kimé, 1991).

81 Assimilation is defined here as the process whereby the child acquires the cultural codes of the dominant society, beginning with language. On this point see Stéphane Beaud and Gérard Noiriel, "L'Assimilation: Un concept en panne," in Pierre-André Taguieff, *Face au racisme* (Paris: La Découverte, 1991), 2: 261–282.

CHAPTER 5   VICHY

1   See especially Jean-Pierre Azéma, *De Munich à la Libération 1938–1944* (Paris: Éditions du Seuil, 1979); Robert O. Paxton, *Vichy France, 1940–1944* (New York: Norton,

1972); Stanley Hoffmann, *Decline or Renewal: France since the 1930s* (New York: Viking, 1974).

2   Message of July 11, 1940, in Philippe Pétain, *Discours aux Français,* ed. J.-C. Barbas (Paris: Albin Michel, 1989), 68; message of October 10, 1940, p. 88.

3   Charles Maurras, *La Seule France: Chronique des jours d'épreuve* (Lyons: Lardanchet, 1941), 32–34.

4   Free French legal scholars held that the National Assembly had exceeded its powers in delegating an authority that belonged to it exclusively, but here I am simply concerned with the facts about this vote.

5   Jean-Baptiste Duroselle, *L'Abîme, 1939–1945* (Paris: Imprimerie Nationale, 1982), 449.

6   See Denis Peschanski, "Gouvernants et gouvernés dans la France de Vichy: Juillet 1940–avril 1942," in *Vichy, 1940–1944: Archives de guerre d'Angelo Tasca* (Paris-Milan: CNRS Feltrinelli, 1986), 41 ff.; and idem, "Vichy au singulier, Vichy au pluriel: Une tentative avortée d'encadrement de la société (1941–1942)," *Annales ESC.* (May–June 1988): 639–661; see also Pierre Laborie, *L'Opinion française sous Vichy* (Paris: Éditions du Seuil, 1990).

7   Ian Kershaw, *The "Hitler Myth': ' Image and Reality in the Third Reich* (London: Oxford University Press, 1987).

8   Pétain, *Discours aux Français,* 172.

9   See, for example, ibid., 78 (appeal of August 13, 1940); 85 (appeal of October 9, 1940); 103 (message of December 24, 1940).

10   Ibid., 216.

11   Henry Rousso, *Le Syndrome de Vichy, 1944–198...* (Paris: Éditions du Seuil, 1987) 304; trans. by Arthur Goldhammer as *The Vichy Syndrome* (Cambridge, Mass.: Harvard University Press, 1992), based on rev. paperback ed. [Seuil's "Points" collection, 1990]).

12   Robert O. Paxton and Michael Marrus, *Vichy France and the Jews* (New York: Basic Books, 1981); Serge Klarsfeld, *Vichy-Auschwitz,* 2 vols. (Paris: Fayard, 1983–1985).

13   Article published in *La Revue des deux mondes* (September 15, 1940), reproduced in Jean Thouvenin, *D'ordre du Maréchal Pétain* (*La France Nouvelle, II*) (Paris: Sequana, 1940), 90.

14   Ibid., 89.

15   Philippe Pétain, "Individualisme et nation," *Revue universelle* (January 1, 1941), reproduced in idem, *Paroles aux Français* (Lyons: Lardanchet, 1941), 184.

16   *Discours aux Français,* 153 (speech of July 8, 1941).

17   Olivier Wormser, *Les Origines doctrinales de la "Révolution nationale"* (Paris, 1971).

18   Pétain, for example, made an approving reference to the Convention, which, like Henri IV and Richelieu, had respected "the sacred law of national unity" by crushing "without flinching any disturbances that tended to divide the nation against itself" (*Discours aux Français,* 120, speech of April 7, 1941).

19   See note 13, pp. 91–92.

20   *Discours aux Français,* 150–151 (speech of July 8, 1941).

21   *Paroles aux Français,* 14 and 16 (speech of 1938 to the congress of the Union Nationale des Anciens Combattants).

22 Ernest Renan, *La Réforme intellectuelle et morale de la France*, in *Oeuvres complètes* (Paris: Calmann-Lévy, 1947), 1: 369 and 401.

23 André Simon, *Vercingétorix et l'idéologie française* (Paris: Imago, 1989).

24 *Discours aux Français*, 66 (appeal of June 25, 1940).

25 See note 13, p. 10.

26 Thouvenin, *D'ordre du Maréchal Pétain*, 56 (Pétain's statement to a group of American journalists on August 24, 1940).

27 *Discours aux Français*, p. 62 (appeal of June 23, 1940).

28 Ibid., 78 (speech of August 13, 1940).

29 Benjamin Constant, *De l'esprit de conquête et de l'usurpation*, in *De la liberté chez les modernes*, ed. Marcel Gauchet (Paris: Pluriel, 1980), 252.

30 Christian Faure, *Le Projet culturel de Vichy: Folklore et Révolution nationale, 1940–1944* (Lyons: Presses Universitaires de Lyon, Éditions du CNRS, 1989).

31 Rousso, *Le Syndrome de Vichy*. For wartime memory as reflected in fiction, see the papers by Michael Kelly and Colin Nettlebeck in G. Hirschfeld and P. Marsch, ed., *Collaboration in France: Politics and Culture during the Nazi Occupation, 1940–1944* (Oxford, New York, and Munich: Berg, 1989).

32 See the discussion of the Rémy affair in Rousso, *Le Syndrome Vichy*, 43 ff.

33 It will suffice to recall a few sentences from the first page of de Gaulle's memoirs: "All my life I have held a certain idea of France.... Instinctively I had the impression that Providence created France for great successes or exemplary misfortunes." But "France cannot be France without grandeur." *Mémoires de guerre: L'Appel 1940–1942* (Paris: Plon, 1954), 1.

34 See Pascal Ory's 1981 overview, "Comme de l'an quarante: Dix années de 'retro satanas,' " *Le Débat*, 16 (November 1981): 109–117.

35 Bernard-Henri Lévy, *L'Idéologie française* (Paris: Grasset, 1981).

36 Zeev Sternhell, *La Droite révolutionnaire (1885–1914): Les origines françaises du fascisme* (Paris: Éditions du Seuil, 1978); and *Ni droite ni gauche: L'idéologie fasciste en France* (Paris: Éditions du Seuil, 1983).

CHAPTER 6 GAULLISTS AND COMMUNISTS

1 For data, see the poll "Les années de Gaulle" of June 14, 1990, conducted by the IFOP for *Libération*, TF1 (a French TV network), and France Inter, which dealt with the man, the president, and Gaullism. It emerges that for 57 percent of the French "little" or "nothing" of de Gaulle remains. Above all see the S.O.F.R.E.S. poll commisssioned by the Institut Charles-de-Gaulle for the Journées Internationales at UNESCO, November 19–24, 1990, on "De Gaulle en son siècle," which can be found in Olivier Duhamel and Jérôme Jaffre, ed., *S.O.F.R.E.S.: L'état de l'opinion 1991* (Paris: Éditions du Seuil, 1991).

   Three earlier polls were published in 1989: one, the IPSOS–*Le Monde* poll of January 4, portrayed de Gaulle as "the best at carrying on the traditions of the Revolution"; another, by Louis Harris–France for *L'Histoire* 124 (July-August), depicted him as the greatest builder of a united Europe; the third, again by Louis Harris–France, for *L'Express* of November 10, found de Gaulle's return to power in 1958 to be "the most fateful event since the beginning of the century." But these data are truly meaningful only when compared with the results of polls taken on the tenth anniversary of de Gaulle's death, in 1980. There were four such major polls: the IFOP-*VSD* of February 12–18, which found that 53 percent of those questioned stated that they would have responded to a new June 18 Appeal (61 percent of those 50–60 years old); S.O.F.R.E.S.–*Histoire* Magazine of August 22–28 (published in December), in which 81 percent of the French declared de Gaulle's action to be "very" or "fairly" positive; Louis Harris–France for *L'Histoire* on December 12–17 (published in April 1981, no. 33), in which de Gaulle is pictured as "the figure from French history with whom you'd most like to spend an hour talking," with the general receiving 19.5 percent to 13 for Napoleon; and finally, an IFOP-*Les Nouvelles Littéraires* poll on January 26–31, 1981 (published February 16, in the middle of an electoral campaign), in which de Gaulle, was seen as "the most right-wing" president of the Fifth Republic. For earlier polls, see Jean Charlot, *Les Français et de Gaulle* (Paris: IFOP, 1971).

2 In connection with the Journées Internationales of November 19–24, 1990, the Institut Charles-de-Gaulle asked a number of people where they stood on the subject of de Gaulle, among them François Bloch-Lainé, Claude Bourdet, Raymond Bourgine, Jean Cathala, Michel Crozier, Jean Daniel, Jacques Fauvet, Françoise Giroud, Alfred Grosser, André Jeanson, Alain Krivine, Jean Lacouture, Bertrand Renouvin, Jean-François Revel, Guy Sorman, and Michel Winock. Their answers can be found in *De Gaulle en son siècle*, vol. 1, *Dans la mémoire des hommes et des peuples* (Paris: La Documentation Française-Plon, 1991), 483–525.

3 For a journalistic overview, see Henri-Christian Giraud, *De Gaulle et les Communistes*, 2 vols. (Paris: Albin Michel, 1988–89).

4 See Stéphane Courtois and Marc Lazar, ed., *Cinquante ans d'une passion française: de Gaulle et les communistes* (Paris: Balland, 1991). I draw on this work frequently in what follows.

5 Marie-Claire Lavabre has studied the written and oral memories of Communist officials following a plan sketched out in "Mémoire et identité partisane: le cas du P.C.F.," (Salzburg: Consortium européen de recherche politique, April 13–18, 1984; mimeographed, 16 pp.), which I thank the author for making available, since it is not easy to find; see also Nicole Racine-Furlaud, "La Mémoire du 18 juin 1940," in *De Gaulle en son siècle*, 1: 549–563. The two views can also be contrasted, as the same authors do in Courtois and Lazar, *Cinquante ans d'une passion française,* where the first studies "Souvenirs et images de De Gaulle chez les militants communistes" and the second reviews the symbolic battle "18 June 1940 or 10 July 1940." Gérard Namer was the first to pursue this line of inquiry in his indispensable *La Commémoration en France 1944–1982* (Paris: Papyrus, 1983).

6 I outlined the problem in a lecture to the XXVIe Rencontres Internationales of Geneva on power (*Pouvoir* [Neuchâtel: Éditions de la Baconnière, 1978]), also published in revised form as "Quatre coins de la mémoire," *H histoire*, 2 (June 1979).

7   For an overview of the problem see Olivier Duhamel, *La Gauche et la V*e République (Paris: Presses Universitaires de France, 1980), and Olivier Duhamel and Jean-Luc Parodi, ed., *La Constitution de la V*e République, new ed. (Paris: Presses de la FNSP, 1988).

8   See Alain Duhamel, *De Gaulle–Mitterrand, la marque et la trace* (Paris: Flammarion, 1991).

9   On de Gaulle's relations with the left, their original connivance, their repeated engagements and eternally deferred wedding, there is no more perspicacious commentary than the article published by Jacques Ozouf at the time of the general's death, "Elle et lui," *Le Nouvel Observateur* (November 16, 1970).

10   Max Gallo in *L'Express* (November 8–14, 1980).

11   General de Gaulle himself set the theme to music, admittedly on rare occasions, as in an interview with Michel Droit on December 16, 1965, after he had failed to win an absolute majority in the first round of the presidential election: "France is not the left!... France is not the right!" He rarely used either word. See Jean-Marie Cotteret and René Moreau, *Le Vocabulaire du général de Gaulle* (Paris: Armand Colin, 1969).

12   See Jean Pierre Rioux, "Le Souverain en mémoire (1969–1990)," in *De Gaulle en son siècle*, 1: 303–315. The paper is based on Rioux's seminar at the Institut d'Études Politiques in 1988–89, and I am grateful to him for having kindly shared his notes with me. I lack both space and time to give them the full treatment they deserve.

13   André Malraux, *Le Miroir des limbes* (Paris: Gallimard, 1976), 729.

14   Bernard Rigaud, "Funérailles nationales, deuils internationaux, 1969–1970: Les obsèques de J. F. Kennedy, P. Tagliatti, W. Churchill, Ch. de Gaulle" (thesis, École des Hautes Études en Sciences Sociales, Paris, 1985; mimeographed). See also Jacques Dupuy, "Les Réactions internationales à la mort du général de Gaulle," in *De Gaulle en son siècle*, 1: 607–611.

15   Branko Lazitch, *Le Rapport Khrouchtchev et son histoire* (Paris: Éditions du Seuil, 1976).

16   After the broadcast of *L'Aveu*, in which Jean Kanapa stated that if the Communists had known, they would have reacted and that "the moment they did know, they voiced their disapproval," Jean Ellenstein wrote in *Le Monde* on December 29, 1976, that Communist parties outside the Soviet Union, including the P.C.F., were informed of the text only the morning before it was to be delivered and were required to promise not to talk about it. The next day *L'Humanité* categorically denied Ellenstein's statement, only to be forced to issue a denial of its own denial two weeks later. Kanapa's remarks can be compared with what he said twenty years earlier from the podium of the Fourteenth Congress of the P.C.F. after the release of the Khrushchev Report: "The revelation of certain of Comrade Stalin's acts and certain violations of socialist legality of course caused us deep pain...but regret? What have we to regret? Our tenacious and unconditional defense of the Soviet Union against its systematic detractors? Our having made use of our party spirit to maintain intact the solid front of our Communist Party and our past? No! Whatever trials, difficulties, faults, and hesitations we may have known in the past, no, we will never regret the beautiful, hard school of history which has instructed our party in the pastand to which we owe our combative spirit at the head of the revolutionary movement."

17 Roger Martelli, *1956, le choc du XX*[e] Congrès: Textes et documents (Paris: Messidor–Éditions Sociales, 1982).

18 See, in particular, two documents issued in early July 1977 by the Conseil Permanent de l'Episcopat Français, which inaugurated a wide debate: *Le Marxisme, l'Homme et la Foi chrétienne*. The Council affirmed that "we cannot link our Christian hope to the historical and dialectical materialism of the Communist Party." See also *Foi et Marxisme en monde ouvrier*, from the Commission Episcopale du Monde Ouvrier, which proposed "welcoming Marxist philosophy in order to question it" (Paris: Éditions du Centurion, 1977).

19 Implicit in the Socialist Project adopted by the Congress of the Parti Socialiste on December 13–15, 1991; see Congrès du Parti Socialiste, *Un Nouvel Horizon* (Paris: Gallimard, 1992).

20 Voline (pseudonym of V. M. Eichenbaum), *La Révolution inconnue, 1917–1921: Documentation inédite sur la révolution russe* (Paris: Belfond, 1969; new ed. 1986).

21 To say nothing of Louis Althusser's stubborn insistence on a return to Stalinism; see his *Réponse à John Lewis* (Paris: Maspero, 1973); *Éléments d'autocritique (1964–1975)* (Paris: Maspero, 1976); *Ce qui ne peut pas durer dans le Parti communiste* (Paris: Maspero, 1978).

22 Ferrat's lectures (Paris: Bureau du Mouvement Ouvrier, 1931; repr. Paris: Éditions Gît-le-Coeur, 1969). André Ferrat, member of the Politburo at 25, in 1927, delegate with Thorez to the the Sixth Congress of the International, and representative of the P.C.F. in Moscow from 1924 to 1931, would end by being expelled from the party in 1937 for leftist opposition.

23 Odile Rudelle, "Politique de la mémoire; politique de la postérité," in *De Gaulle en son siècle*, 1: 149 162.

24 Details in Rioux, "Le Souverain en mémoire."

25 André Guettard's analysis of polls in "La Légende gaulliste et le dixième anniversaire de la mort du général de Gaulle" (master's thesis directed by Raoul Girardet, Institut d'Études Politiques, 1981; mimeographed) shows that the crucial features of the legend were already in place.

26 Between the general's death in 1970 and 1974, 132 books and photo collections appeared, or an average of 26 works per year. Compare this with 17 per year for 1958–69 and 16 for 1975–90.

27 The importance of photographic selection is evident from the original work of Jacques Borgé and Nicolas Viasnof, *De Gaulle et les photographes* (Paris: EPA-Vilo, 1979).

28 Here again the pace of production is significant: "Mon Général" by Olivier Guichard and "Le Verbe et l'image" by Pierre Lefranc and Pierre-André Boutang appeared in 1980. "Français si vous saviez" by André Harris and Alain de Sédouy came as a counterattack in 1982. The important series "De Gaulle ou l'éternel défi" by Jean Lacouture, Roland Mehl, and Jean Labib was broadcast on TF1 in May–June 1988, while Seuil simultaneously brought out the book under the same title: these works dominated the period leading up to the centenary. From November 21 to December 11, 1990, the Vidéothèque de Paris held a major show of television productions concerning de Gaulle.

29   In Jean-Pierre Rioux's seminar at the Institut d'Études Politiques, Marie-Hélène Pradines catalogued 77 baccalaureate exam questions concerning de Gaulle from the period 1978–88. Her work showed that some academies were particularly "Gaullist," including Nice, Lille, and Montpellier, while others were more or less resistant, such as Limoges, Dijon, Poitiers, and Rennes.

30   The Institut Charles-de-Gaulle, located at 5 Rue de Solferino, in the building where the general had offices for eleven years, is a private association launched by the general when he left office and officially founded on February 20, 1971, with Pierre Lefrance as president. It has played an important role through its committees, meetings of "friends," lecture series, colloquia, and courses. It also organizes study groups and traveling shows and publishes the quarterly *Espoir* and a collection of books under the same name, and it maintains the bookstore Notre Siècle, which sells photo collections and scholarly reference books such as the *Index des thèmes de l'oeuvre du général de Gaulle* (Paris: Plon, 1978). Its mixture of hagiographic piety and scientific scruples, its organization, at once debonair and military, its vigilant activity and discreet efficiency, deserve careful study.

31   The selection and introduction to the *Lettres, notes et carnets* by Admiral Philippe de Gaulle immediately drew criticism from historians, particularly Jean-Noël Jeanneney in *Le Monde* (June 18, 1980).

32   Claude Mauriac's *Aimer de Gaulle* (Paris: Grasset, 1978) was immediately followed by a salvo of books from the big guns: Pierre Lefranc, *Avec qui vous savez* (Paris: Plon, 1979); Jacques Chaban-Delmas, *Charles de Gaulle* (Paris: Paris-Match/Éditions No. 1, 1980); Marcel Jullian, *L'Homme de 1940* (Paris: Robert Laffont, 1980); Maurice Schumann, *Un certain 18 juin* (Paris: Plon, 1980).

33   Régis Debray's *A demain de Gaulle* (Paris: Gallimard, 1990) was an immediate success, selling over 40,000 copies.

34   Two thirds of those books have appeared in the past ten years. An international bibliography for the period 1940–1981 has been published by the Institut Charles-de-Gaulle. Another is in preparation.

35   See especially Pierre Viansson-Ponté, *La République gaullienne* (Paris: Fayard, 1971).

36   I dealt with this topic in *De Gaulle en son siècle*, 1: 172–178, the main points of which I repeat here.

37   Goguel is paradoxically joined on this point by Jean-François Revel in his response to the question mentioned in note 2 above: see his "De la légende vivante au mythe posthume," introduction to the 1988 reprint (Éditions Complexe) of his *Style du Général* (Paris: Julliard, 1959)

38   Stanley and Inge Hoffmann, *De Gaulle artiste de la politique* (Paris: Éditions du Seuil, 1973).

39   Jean Lacouture, *De Gaulle*, vol. 1, *Le Rebelle;* vol. 2, *Le Politique;* vol. 3, *Le Souverain* (Paris: Éditions du Seuil, 1984–86), which received unanimous praise from the critics; an English translation by Patrick O'Brian has been published by Norton.

40   See Jean Serroy, ed., *De Gaulle et les écrivains* (Grenoble: Presses Universitaires de Grenoble, 1991).

41 See Nicole Racine, "État des travaux sur le communisme en France," in *Le Communisme en France* (Paris: Armand Colin, 1969), 305–346; Annie Kriegel, "L'Historiographie du communisme français: Premier bilan et orientations de recherches," in the appendix to the first edition of her classic work *Les Communistes français, essai d'ethnographie politique* (Paris: Éditions du Seuil, 1968), rev. and expanded with Guillaume Bourgeois in *Les Communistes français dans leur premier demi-siècle* (Paris: Éditions du Seuil, 1985), appendices 1 and 2. See also Roger Martelli, "Bref aperçu des publications consacrées au P.C.F. depuis 1969," *Étudier le P.C.F.*, nos. 29–30 of the *Cahiers d'histoire de l'Institut Maurice-Thorez* (1979): 128–170. Additional information can be found in Marie-Claire Lavabre and Denis Peschanski, "L'Histoire pour boussole? Note sur l'historiographie communiste, 1977–1981," *Communisme*, 4 (1983): 105–114, and Marie-Claire Lavabre, ibid., 7 (1985). For a survey of the question, see the discussion between Stéphane Courtois and Roger Martelli, "Où en est l'histoire du P.C.F.? Un échange," *Le Débat*, 31 (September 1984): 149–177.

42 See Georges Lavau, "L'Historiographie communiste: Une pratique politique," in Pierre Birnbaum and Jean-Marie Vincent, ed., *Critique des pratiques politiques* (Paris: Galilée, 1978), 121–163.

43 Jacques Duclos and François Billoux, *Histoire du Parti communiste français* (Paris: Éditions Sociales, 1964), 10.

44 For example, Florimond Bonte, *De l'ombre à la lumière* (Paris: Éditions Sociales, 1965).

45 See, for example, for the Cold War period alone (and taking no account of subsequently published works) the fifteen titles used by Francine Simon in her thesis, "La Mémoire communiste, les dissidents français et la guerre froide" (Institut d'Études Politiques, 1978; mimeographed). In chronological order these were André Marty, *L'Affaire Marty* (Paris: Les Deux Rives, 1955); Pierre Hervé, *Ce que je crois* (Paris: Grasset, 1958); Edgar Morin, *Autocritique* (Paris: Les Lettres Nouvelles, 1958); Auguste Lecoeur, *Le Partisan* (Paris: Flammarion, 1963); Claude Roy, *Moi, je, Nous, Somme toute* (Paris: Gallimard, 1969, 1972, 1976); Dominique Desanti, *Les Staliniens, 1944–1956* (Paris: Fayard, 1974); Simone Signoret, *La Nostalgie n'est plus ce qu'elle était* (Paris: Éditions du Seuil, 1976); Pierre Daix, *J'ai cru au matin* (Paris: Robert Laffont, 1976); Jean Duvignaud, *Le Ça perché* (Paris: Stock, 1976); Jean-Pierre Chabrol, *La Folie des miens* (Paris: Gallimard, 1977); Raymond Lévy, *Schartzenmurtz ou l'esprit de parti* (Paris: Albin Michel, 1977); Philipppe Robrieux, *Notre génération communiste* (Paris: Robert Laffont, 1977); Charles Tillon, *On chantait rouge* (Paris: Robert Laffont, 1977); Roger Pannequin, *Les Années sans suite*, 2 vols. (Paris: Le Sagittaire, 1977); and Jean Rony, *Trente ans de part, un communist s'interroge* (Paris: Christian Bourgois, 1978). This list does not include the memoirs of communist officials published during the same period, of which the principal were Virgile Barel, *Cinquante années de lutte* (Paris: Éditions Sociales, 1966); Jacques Duclos, *Mémoires*, 6 vols. (Paris: Fayard, 1968–1972), of which vol. 4, *Sur la brèche, 1945–1952*, and 5, *Dans la mêlée, 1952–1958*, deal with the period; Léo Figuières, *Jeunesse militante* (Paris: Éditions Sociales, 1971); Fernand Grenier, *Ce bonheur-là* (Paris: Éditions Sociales, 1974); Raoul Culas, *Souvenirs d'un condamné à mort* (Paris: Éditions Sociales, 1976); Étienne Fajon, *Ma vie s'appelle liberté* (Paris: Robert Laffont, 1976).

46   Edgar Morin, *Autocritique* (Paris: Les Lettres Nouvelles, 1958; repr. Paris: Éditions du Seuil, 1966); and Artur London, *L'Aveu* (Paris: Gallimard, 1968). These two book-events deserve a study of their reception. On the second, see Annie Kriegel, *Les Grands Procès dans les systèmes communistes: La pédagogie infernale* (Paris: Gallimard, 1972).

47   Annie Kriegel, *Aux origines du communisme français, 1914–1920*, 2 vols. (Paris: Mouton, 1964), initiated the academic study of French communism. See also her introduction to *Congrès de Tours* (Paris: Julliard, 1964).

48   Philippe Robrieux, *Maurice Thorez, vie secrète et vie publique* (Paris: Fayard, 1975), and idem, *L'Histoire intérieure du Parti communiste*, 4 vols. (Paris: Fayard, 1980–1984).

49   Stéphane Courtois, *Le P.C.F. dans la guerre, de Gaulle, la Résistance, Staline* (Paris: Ramsay, 1980). See also the proceedings of an important and tumultuous colloquium on the subject held at the École Normale Supérieure, Paris, October 1983: Jean-Pierre Azéma, Antoine Prost, and Jean-Pierre Rioux, ed., *Le Parti communiste des années sombres* (Paris: Éditions du Seuil, 1986), and *Les Communistes français de Munich à Châteaubriant, 1938–1941* (Paris: Presses de Fondation Nationale de Science Politique, 1987).

50   Yves Santamaria, "Le P.C.F. et son histoire: le pacte germano soviétique—Étude de l'historiographie communiste (1943–1968)" (master's thesis, University of Paris IV, 1983; mimeographed). The secret protocol provided for the partition of Poland after a joint victory.

51   The appeal of July 10, 1940, is a tract entitled *Peuple de France* and signed by Maurice Thorez and Jacques Duclos, of which 23 of 500 lines can be considered a call for a "Front of liberty, independence, and rebirth for France." A. Rossi, in *La Physiologie du Parti communiste français*, denounced this "patriotic forgery" and proved that the clandestine issue of *L'Humanité* dated July 10, 1940, and containing what in the meantime had become the official version of the "Appeal" (a facsimile of which was reproduced in *L'Humanité* of December 12, 1947) was also a forgery. On the political issues involved, see Nicole Racine-Furlaud, "18 juin 1940 ou 10 juillet 1940, bataille des mémoires," in Courtois and Lazar, *Cinquante ans d'une passion française.*

52   Jacques Fauvet, in collaboration with Alain Duhamel, examined this in his *Histoire du Parti communiste français*, 2 vols. (Paris: Fayard, 1964–1965).

53   Stéphane Courtois, "Luttes politiques et élaboration d'une histoire: le P.C.F. historien du P.C.F. dans la Deuxième Guerre mondiale," *Communisme*, 4 (1983): 5–26.

54   Lavabre and Peschanski, "L'histoire pour boussole?," point out that nearly a third of the historical articles published in *Cahiers du communisme* from 1977 to 1982 were devoted to the wartime years. As recently as 1990, Roger Bourderon of the Institut de Recherches Marxistes devoted an entire issue of *Cahiers d'histoire*, 42, to the year 1940, together with a special section of *La Pensée*, 275 (May-June 1990).

55   Marie-Claire Lavabre and Denis Peschanski, "Histoire militante: La formation historique dans quatre organisations de gauche," especially "Part communiste, la ligne générale," *Espaces-Temps*, 9 (1978): 50–69.

56   The distinction is borrowed from Danielle Taratowski's contribution to *Étudier le P.C.F.*, in which she writes: "History and Marxism enjoy a special status in Marxism and there-

fore in the P.C.F. Unlike philosophy, history has, I think, finally finished paying the price." See also her *Une Histoire du P.C.F.* (Paris: Presses Universitaires de France, 1982).

57 The Institut Maurice-Thorez, founded immediately after the death of the secretary general in October 1964, publishes the *Cahiers*, retitled *Cahiers d'histoire*, of which one of the most important was *Étudier le P.C.F.*, 29–30 (1979), which brought together a whole team of young Communist historians: Roger Bourderon, Jean Burles, Jacques Girault, Roger Martelli, Jean-Louis Robert, Jean-Paul Scot, Danielle Tartakowsky, Germaine Willard, and Serge Wolikow. The same team collaborated on *Le P.C.F.: Étapes et problèmes, 1920–1972* (Paris: Éditions Sociales, 1981).

58 J. Burles, in *Etudier le P.C.F.*, p. 21. The same point is made by S. Wolikow: "The communist historian cannot ignore the relationship between politics and the history of his party, but he must define these things as they are today...and conecptualize them in relation to the needs of his political strategy," ibid., 30.

59 Georges Marchais, January 25, 1977, statement to journalists.

60 See Henry Rousso, *Le Syndrome de Vichy* (Paris: Éditions du Seuil, 1987), which does not hesitate to define the Liberation as a "screen memory," 25 and 29; English trans. by Arthur Goldhammer, *The Vichy Syndrome* (Cambridge, Mass.: Harvard University Press, 1992).

61 See the polemic launched by the publication of the first two volumes of Daniel Cordier's monumental biography *Jean Moulin, l'inconnu du Panthéon* (Paris: Jean-Claude Lattès, 1989). Cordier, Moulin's former secretary, attacked Henri Frenay, leader of the Resistance group Combat, for having written in November 1940 a "manifesto" sympathetic to the National Revolution, and assigned blame for the betrayal and arrest of Moulin at Caluire, one of the great mysteries of the Resistance.

62 André Malraux's funeral oration for Jean Moulin is the ultimate example of de Gaulle's appropriative and identificatory version of resistantialism. For a good analysis see Rousso, *Le Syndrome de Vichy*, 95–111.

63 Pascal Ory, "Comme de l'an quarante: Dix années de 'retro satanas,' " *Le Débat*, 16 (November 1981): 109–117; and idem, *L'Entre-deux-Mai: Histoire culturelle de la France, mai 1958–mai 1968* (Paris: Éditions du Seuil, 1983), 118–127.

64 The best analysis of *The Sorrow and the Pity* is to my mind that of Stanley Hoffmann, *Decline or Renewal: Essays on France*.

65 Jacques Ozouf, "Un Vieux Ménage," *Le Nouvel Observateur*, (January 5, 1972), commenting on the IFOP poll results presented by Jean Charlot.

66 The enduring contrast between the terrifying appearance of the Communist Party and its actual weakness is apparent throughout Vincent Auriol's *Journal du septennat*, vol. 1, *L'année 1947*, complete version (Paris: Armand Colin, 1970), as when Thorez astonished the president at the height of the May crisis by telling him, "I'm at the end of my tether."

67 Annie Kriegel, "Le Parti communiste français, la Résistance, la Libération et l'établissement de la IVᵉ République (1944–1947)," paper given at the French-Italian colloquium in Naples, 1973, repr. in *Communismes au miroir français* (Paris: Gallimard, 1974), 160–176; and Maurice Agulhon, "Les Communistes et la Libération de la

France," paper given at the international colloquium on the Liberation of France, 1974, repr. in *Histoire vagabonde* (Paris: Gallimard, 1968), 2: 177–208.

68 Apart from memoirs, there is a good description of Communist sociabiity in Gérard Vincent, "Etre communiste? Une manière d'être," in Philippe Ariès and Georges Duby, ed., *Histoire de la vie privée* (Paris: Éditions du Seuil, 1987), 4: 427–458; trans. by Arthur Goldhammer as *A History of Private Life*, vol. 4 (Cambridge, Mass.: Harvard University Press, 1990). See also Jean-Pierre Bernard, *Paris rouge, 1944–1964: Les communistes français dans la capitale* (Paris: Champvallon, 1991). The journal *Autrement* devoted a special issue to "La Culture des camarades," 78 (1986), but the contributions are of uneven quality.

69 See the anthropological analysis in Jacqueline Mer, *Le Parti de Maurice Thorez ou le bonheur communiste français* (Paris: Payot, 1977).

70 I borrow this idea from Jean-Marie Goulemot, *Le Clairon de Staline* (Paris: Ly Sycomore, 1981), on Stalin's seventieth birthday. See also Serge Collet, "La Manifestation de rue comme production culturelle militante," *Ethnologie française*, 12, no. 2 (April–June 1982): 167–176.

71 Gabor T. Rittersporn, "Qui lit la *Pravda*, comment et pourquoi?" *Le Débat*, 2 (June 1980): 82–92.

72 See Noëlle Gérôme and Danielle Tartakowsky, *La Fête de* L'Humanité (Paris: Éditions Sociales, 1988).

73 Jean-Pierre A. Bernard, "La Liturgie funèbre des communistes (1924–1983)," *Vingtième Siècle, revue d'histoire*, 9 (January–March 1986): 37–53, offers a rich analysis.

74 Françoise Thom, *La Langue de bois* (Paris: Jullaird, 1987), as well as the special issue of *Mots*, 21 (December 1989), "Langues de bois?," which indicates the origins of various expressions.

75 Goulemot, *Le Clairon de Staline*, makes the comparison. On the *Tour de la France par deux enfants*, see Jacques and Mona Ozouf, "Le Tour de la France par deux enfants," in Pierre Nora, ed., *Les Lieux de mémoire*, part 1, *La République* (Paris: Gallimard, 1984).

76 Annie Kriegel outlined the themes in my seminar at the École des Hautes Études en Sciences Sociales, 1979. She has gone into greater detail since then. See for example Marie-Claire Lavabre and Marc Lazar, "Se ressembler à sa ressemblance: Lecture de quelques récits autobiographiques, 1981–1983," *Communisme*, 4 (1983): 114–119.

77 Claude Roy, *Nous* (Paris: Gallimard, 1972), 396.

78 Annie Kriegel, *Ce que j'ai cru comprendre* (Paris: Robert Laffont, 1991).

79 The television series was broadcast on FR3 in 1990.

80 Compare with work in political science such as Jean Charlot, *Le Phénomène gaulliste* (Paris: Fayard, 1970).

81 The expression should be read in context: "As the irreovocable words went out into the air, I felt one life ending, the life that I had led in a solid France and an indivisible army. At age forty-nine I was embarking on an adventure, as a man whom fate had pushed off all known paths." *Mémoires de guerre*, 1, *L'Appel* (Paris: Plon, 1954), 71.

82 Well described by Jean-Pierre Rioux, "Les Paysages du général de Gaulle," *L'Histoire*, 134 (June 1990): 24–29, with many excellent quotations.

83   Alain Peyrefitte, "De Gaulle et les grands personnages de l'histoire de France," in *De Gaulle en son siècle*, 1: 107–115.

84   Jean Lacouture was kind enough to sketch the layers of this memory for me as we looked through his library. From the tide of the "revelation" (Philippe Barrès, Lucien Nachin, Madeleine Bainville, Georges Cattaui, Jean Gaulmier, Maurice Schumann, Colonel Rémy, Jacques Soustelle, the François Mauriac of *Bâillon dénoué*) to the ebb after the return to power (Jacques Soustelle new version, Robert Mengin, Alfred Fabre-Luce, Jean-François Revel, Colonel Argoud, Colonel Trinquier, François Mitterrand) by way of the first wave of criticism of the war, the memoirs, etc. These indications suggest what might be added to our knowledge of the construction of the personage by a careful examination of the bibliography with proper attention to periods, genres, themes, and authors.

85   Nicholas Wahl sketched a typology at my seminar at the École des Hautes Études en Sciences Sociales (1979).

86   André Malraux, speech to Assises Nationales of the R.P.F., February 12, 1949. See Jeanine Mossuz-Lavau, *Malraux et le Gaullisme* (Paris: Presses de la Fondation Nationale des Sciences Politiques, 1982).

87   Stéphane Courtois, "De Gaulle et les communistes: confrontation de deux légitimités" (paper read to the Journées Internationales at UNESCO, November 1990).

88   Maurice Thorez, "Rapport à la conférence internationale du P.C.F., 17–18 juillet 1958," *L'Humanité* (July 18, 1958), quoted in Marc Lazar, "Le P.C.F. et le gaullisme, 1958–1969" (paper read to the Journées Internationales at UNESCO, November 1990). For further information, see Marie Claire Lavabre, "Les Communistes et de Gaulle: Une mémoire polémique," in *De Gaulle en son siècle*, 1: 564–573.

89   See Pierre Daix, *Les Hérétiques du P.C.F.* (Paris: Robert Laffont, 1980).

90   Pierre Pucheu, a pugnacious boss, member of the P.P.F. (Parti Populaire Français), and minister of the interior under Vichy before the arrival of Laval, whom he found too pro-German, went to Morocco in the spring of 1942 with encouragement from Giraud, who stated his willingness to "give him a place in a combat unit." Arrested, jailed, and hastily judged in Algiers, he was, under pressure from the Communists, who charged him with having drawn up the list of 47 hostages to be executed at Châteaubriant on October 21, 1941, sentenced to death and shot. General de Gaulle refused to pardon him for "reasons of state," although he did inform Pucheu of his "esteem" and pledge to oversee personally the education of Pucheu's children. This was the first, and painful, barrier of blood between de Gaulle and Vichy.

91   A personal experience: in 1963, when I was working on the "Archives" collection for Julliard, and being aware of the existence of notebooks of Marcel Cachin, I did all I could to persuade his daughter, Marie-Louise Jacquier, who had possession of them, to make them available for examination and to permit the publication of excerpts, along with Jules Humbert-Droz's *L'Oeil de Moscou à Paris*. My request was of course refused as though state secrets were at stake. Now that they have been delivered to the Archives Nationales by Marcelle Hertzog for publication, it is the publisher who needs to be persuaded to bring out these huge volumes.

92   Admiral de Gaulle (the general's son), however, has blocked access even to those papers no longer protected by archive rules on the dubious ground that these are private archives.

93   See the analysis by Stanley Hoffmann in *Decline or Renewal*.

94   The portrait of Léon Blum in vol. 5 was vituperative and anti-Semitic: "His real name was Lévy-Coeur. He had a caressing voice, elegant manners, and fine, soft hands that seemed to melt at the touch. He attacked all that was virile, pure, healthy, or popular, and that had any faith in ideas, in feelings, in great men, or in human beings.... A worm's instinct...a cunning politician...filthy Tartuffe, repugnant reptile.... The jackal Blum, a recidivist in treason, a police stooge, stool-pigeon Blum...like Lady Macbeth he must look with terror upon the innocent blood that forever stains his long, crooked fingers," and so on.

95   An exception typical of the left-wing anti-Gaullism of the period is found in Arthur Delcroix (pseudonym of François Furet), "Vingt ans de légitimité," *Les Temps modernes*, 167–169 (February-March 1960): "It's the 'it is legal because I wish it' of Louis XVI in 1788, it is the fiction of the '19th year of the reign' in 1814, it is the Maurrassian appeal to the 'real country' against the 'legal country.' This is the 'divine right' side of Gaullism, which combines monarchical tradition with a political practice much closer to Bonapartism. Bourgeois France wants it that way."

96   On this episode see Hervé Hamon and Patrick Rotman, *Génération* (Paris: Éditions du Seuil, 1987), vol. 1, ch. 9.

97   Henri Mendras, *La Seconde Révolution française* (Paris: Gallimard, 1989).

98   François Mauriac, *De Gaulle* (Paris: Grasset, 1964), 339.

99   Stéphane Courtois, "Gaullisme et communisme: La double réponse à la crise de l'identité française," in Courtois and Lazar, *Cinquantes ans d'une passion française*, 305–332.

100   To relieve him of this reputation took Jean Lacouture's very original chapter on de Gaulle's relations in the 1920s with the very republican Colonel Émile Mayer, to whom Henri Lerner had called attention in "Le Général de Gaulle et le cercle du colonel Mayer," *Revue historique* (January-March 1983).

101   See Jean-Paul Cointet, "De Gaulle et la République ou la double reconaissance (1940–1944)"; Jean-Pierre Rioux, "De Gaulle en République de Courseulles à Bayeux (1944–1946)"; Jean Lacouture, "De Gaulle, une certaine idée de la République," all in Paul Isoart and Christian Bidegaray, *Des Républiques françaises* (Paris: Economica, 1988), 683–729. See also Maurice Agulhon, "La Tradition républicaine et le général de Gaulle," and Dominique Colas, "Portrait de la République selon Charles de Gaulle," in *De Gaulle en son siècle*, 1: 188–202. Also worth consulting are Odile Rudelle, *Mai 1958, De Gaulle et la République* (Paris: Plon, 1988), and "Le Gaullisme et la crise de l'identité républicaine," in Jean-Pierre Rioux, ed., *La Guerre d'Algérie et les Français* (Paris: Fayard, 1990), 180–202. For an overview, see Maurice Agulhon, *La République, de Jules Ferry à François Mitterrand, 1880 à nos jours* (Paris: Hachette, 1990).

102   After careful consideration, René Rémond ended by classifying him as a Bonapartist, however, in *Les Droites en France* (Paris: Aubier-Montaigne, 1982), 313–350.

103   See especially the letter to his son dated April 30, 1969, which caused a considerable stir when it was published in the twelfth volume of *Lettres, notes et carnets:* "My dear

Philippe, If in the near future I should pass away without revealing who, under the present circumstances, I would like the French people to elect as my immediate successor as President of the Republic, I ask you to publish the attached statement. I say: my immediate successor, because I hope that after him you yourself might wish and be in a position to assume the burden of leading France."

104 See the extensive analysis of Lucien Jaume, "L'Etat républicain selon de Gaulle," *Commentaire*, 51 and 52 (autumn and winter 1990): 523–532 and 749–757.

105 Yet the episode was significant and had numerous consequences. See Jean Charlot, *Le Gaullisme d'opposition, 1946–1958* (Paris: Fayard, 1983).

106 *Mémoires d'espoir* (Paris: Plon, 1970), 1: 23. For de Gaulle's reference to the Revolution, see Odile Rudelle, "Lieux de mémoire révolutionnaire et communion républicaine," *Vingtième Siècle, revue d'histoire*, 24 (October-December 1989).

107 In particular in *Penser la Révolution française* (Paris: Gallimard, 1978), ch. "Le Catéchisme révolutionnaire."

108 See "Communisme et Révolution française," *Communisme*, 20–21: 1988–1989.

109 See Tamara Kondratieva, *Bolcheviks et Jacobins, itinéraire des analogies* (Paris: Payot, 1989).

110 L.-O. Frossard, *De Jaurès à Lénine* (Paris, 1930), 155. This dogma was consistently reaffirmed. For example, André Fréville: "Its [i.e., the Communist Party's] creation was due neither to chance nor to arbitrary will but was the result of the evolution of the entire French workers' movement," *La Nuit finit à Tours* (Paris: Éditions Sociales, 1950), 160. Or Georges Cogniot at a colloquium marking the anniversary of the October Revolution: "The event of December 1920 is the very type of the necessary historical event," *Cahiers de l'I.M.T.*, 78 (November-December 1967).

111 See Frédéric Bon, *Les Discours de la politique* (Paris: Economica, 1991), ch. 3.

112 Maurice Thorez, "Union et action de tous les Républicains pour le *non* au référendum plébiscité," *Cahiers du communisme*, 34, 8 (August 1958): 1128.

113 See, in particular, concerning Waldeck-Rochet's attempt at de-Sovietization, the analysis of Philippe Robrieux, *Histoire intérieure du Parti communiste,* ˇ ¿≤ 2: ch. 8.

114 Pierre Viansson-Ponté, *Les Gaullistes, rituel et annuaire* (Paris: Éditions du Seuil, 1963).

115 See Jacques Revel, "La Cour," in Pierre Nora, ed., *Les Lieux de mémoire*, part 3, *La France*, vol 2, *Traditions* (Paris, Gallimard, 1986).

116 See Alain Boureau, "Le Roi," in Pierre Nora, ed., *Les Lieux de mémoire*, part 3, *La France*, vol 3, *De l'archive à l'emblème* (Paris, Gallimard, 1992).

117 See the eloquent sentence with which René Rémond begins the chapter on the Fourth Republic in *Les Droites en France*, p. 238: "In 1945, it truly appeared that the time had come to finish off the history of the right with the phrase 'The End.' "

118 Although this would be essential to take into account in a political analysis, it was not necessary for the purposes of this essay.

119 See Michel Verret, "Mémoire ouvrière, mémoire communiste," *Revue française de science politique*, 34, 3 (June 1984).

120 Gérard Noiriel, *Les Ouvriers dans la société française, XIXᵉ–XXᵉ siècle* (Paris: Éditions du Seuil), ch. 6. See also Marc Lazar, "Le Mineur de fond: Un exemple de l'identité du P.C.F.," *Revue française de science politique* (April 1985): 190–205.

121 The historical importance of the May 28, 1952, demonstration against General Ridgway, Eisenhower's successor as commander of SHAPE, has always been emphasized. See Michel Pigenet, "De la démonstration 'dure' à l'affrontement physique," in Pierre Favre, ed., *La Manifestation* (Paris: Presses de la Fondation Nationale des Sciences Politiques, 1990), 245–268.

122 François Furet, Jacques Julliard, and Pierre Rosanvallon, *La République du centre* (Paris: Calmann-Lévy, 1989).

123 Paul Vaillaneix, "Michelet et la Révélation de 1789," *Romantisme*, 50: 61–74.

124 Chateaubriand, *Mémoires d'outre-tome* (Paris: Gallimard, 1951), 2: 4.

CHAPTER 7   RIGHT AND LEFT

1 Edward Chamberlayne, *L'Estat présent de l'Angleterre* (Amsterdam, 1672), 2: 59. Quoted by Fraser Mackensie, *Les Relations de la France et de l'Angleterre d'après le vocabulaire*, vol. 1 (Paris, 1939).

2 According to Étienne Dumont, *Souvenirs sur Mirabeau et sur les deux premières assemblées législatives* (Paris: Presses Universitaires de France, 1951), 107–108. For another version see his "Discours préliminaire" to the translation of Jeremy Bentham, *Tactique des assemblées législatives* (Paris, 1822), 1: x. In general see the introduction to François Furet and Ran Halevi, *Orateurs de la Révolution française* (Paris: Gallimard, 1989), and Patrick Brasart, *Paroles de la Révolution: Les assemblées parlementaires, 1789–1791* (Paris: Minerve, 1988), as well as the older work of Gaston Dodu, *Le Parlementarisme et les parlementaires sous la Révolution (1789–1799)* (Paris, 1911).

3 Brasart, *Paroles*, 32.

4 Pierre-Paul Nairac, *Journal*, quoted in Edna Hindie Lemay, *La Vie quotidienne des députés aux États généraux* (Paris: Hachette, 1988), 189.

5 *Réimpression de l'ancien Moniteur* (Paris, 1850), 1: 393. This occurs in one of the stories that those who reprinted the *Moniteur* in Year IV put together to re-create the missing issues from May 5 to November 24, 1789, when the *Moniteur* actually first appeared, in order to have it cover the entire Revolution from the opening of the Estates General. The accounts are taken from firsthand narratives and from the first histories of the events, which began to appear toward the end of 1789.

6 Brasart's suggestion, based on an analysis of Helmann's celebrated engraving of the Night of August Fourth: *Paroles*, 241. On the basis of other evidence I am inclined to believe that the process of clarification was much more gradual.

7 *Journal d'Adrien Duquesnoy, député du tiers état de Bar-le-Duc, sur l'Assemblée constituante (3 mai 1789–avril 1790)*, ed. Robert de Crèvecoeur (Paris, 1894), 1: 311. For an analysis of the August 23 session, see my *La Révolution des droits de l'homme* (Paris: Gallimard, 1989), esp. 167–174.

8 *Journal du baron de Gauville, député de la noblesse aux États généraux*, ed. E. Barthélemy (Paris, 1864), 20.

9 Pierre Rétat, "Partis et factions en 1789: Emergence des désignants politiques," *Mots*, 16 (1988): 68–89.

10   *Révolutions de France et de Brabant,* no. 5 (December 26, 1789): 194–195.

11   *L'Ami des patriotes,* no. 13, vol. 1: 371 n, and no. 21, vol. 2: 142: "The members of the right of the assembly have long since been reduced to such insignificance that it is hard to count them for much in any political speculation; but the left is divided into two very distinct, very opposed parties." See also no. 26 (May 21, 1791): 285–286 n: when Cazalès asked for the floor, "the whole right rose to refuse his request, while the whole left granted it to him." Also in early 1791, a time of agitated debate over the Civil Constitution of the Clergy, the *Moniteur* refers to interventions by "several members of the right" (8: 44). During the session of January 14, we read that "applause on the left smothered murmurs and shouts on the right" (8: 135). On February 25, "the right shouts No! No! while the left murmurs" (ibid., 184). There are references to "voices on the left" and "members of the right." Such instances are relatively rare, I repeat, compared with the large number of geographical references to "sides" or "parts" of the chamber; in keeping with the rules for professional argot, these shortened forms appear to be merely elliptical variants.

12   Alphonse Aulard, *La Société des Jacobins: Recueil de documents* (Paris, 1889), 4: 276 (session of September 10, 1792).

13   Mme Roland, *Lettres* (Paris, 1902), 2: 252 (letter of March 29, 1791), quoted in Ferdinand Brunot, *Histoire de la langue française,* vol. 9, *La Révolution et l'Empire* (Paris, 1967), 769. (An exception: Mme Roland generally speaks of the right side as "blacks.") See also Max Frey, *Les Transformations du vocabulaire français à l'époque de la Révolution* (Paris, 1925), which gives other examples.

14   The account of this trajectory is somewhat idealized. In reality, simple and complex denominations overlapped and were superimposed until "left extremity" finally caught on. To concentrate on the *Moniteur* alone, "the extremity of the left side" appeared in a report of the session of February 20, 1791, (7: 439), whereas "loud cries from the left extremity" appeared on March 24 (8: 343). "The extremity of the right part" is mentioned along with "right extremity" in a report of the session of March 26, 1791 (8: 726). One even finds "extreme right" on February 14, but only to note the sudden alacrity of a deputy who broke several minutes of silence: "M. Foucault, on the extreme right, strode hastily to the podium" (ibid., 390).

15   Mathieu Dumas, *Souvenirs* (Paris, 1839), 2: 4–5.

16   *Journal de Duquesnoy,* 1: 312.

17   A. C. Thibaudeau, *Mémoires sur la Convention et le Directoire* (Paris, 1824), 47–48.

18   *Moniteur,* 17: 382. Other examples in Brasart, *Paroles* 149–150.

19   *Moniteur,* 24: 115. The report of the session points out that when the petitioners entered, "the members seated on the left extremity, as well as the people in the gallery above them, applauded vigorously" (ibid., 111). There are a great many illustrations from the period in which the left extremity is particularly prominent, and many parliamentary accounts bear this out.

20   Account by L.-M. La Revellière-Lepeaux, *Moniteur,* 25: 748.

21   Ibid.

22   Ibid., 749.

23   *Moniteur,* vol. 25: 296. In a similar vein, Lezay-Marnesia distinguished between "the constitutional or *conservative* side, commonly called the right side, and its opposition on the revolutionary or *destructive* side, also known as the left side." The left sides, he notes, "begin revolutions, the right sides finish them, and the middle parties pull them along." (*De la faiblesse d'un gouvernment qui commence* [Paris, 1796], 58–59).

24   *Annales historiques des sessions du corps législatif,* by X and Gautier du Var (Paris, 1817), covering the years 1814, 1815, 1816; 2: 392–393. In 1815 the president of the chamber urged a deputy to refrain from expressions suggesting that the assembly contained "not only the formation but the consolidation of a party," *Archives parlementaires,* 2d series, vol. 16: 594.

25   Prosper Duvergier de Hauranne, *Histoire du gouvernement parlementaire en France* (Paris, 1857), 3: 293.

26   Ibid., 348.

27   Vitrolles, "Aperçu de la situation de la France au 15 août 1816," in *Mémoires* (Paris: Gallimard, 1951), 2: 450. Ministers complained "about party passions and spirits," according to Vitrolles, "so that they are unaware that the government adopted is nothing other than the regular constitution of the parties," where "the balance of Whigs and Tories over the past 140 years" provides the right model to follow.

28   Letter to Decazes, October 10, 1820, quoted in Ernest Daudet, *Louis XVIII et le duc Decazes* (Paris, 1899), 74.

29   Duvergier de Hauranne, *Histoire,* 4: 535.

30   Ibid., 5: 315.

31   These documents apparently began to appear during the 1818 session. They are collected in Series Le 55 at the Bibliothèque Nationale (abbreviated hereafter as B.N.).

32   *Statistique de la Chambre des députés,* May 6, 1819 (B.N. Le 55 13).

33   Eugène Duclerc and Laurent Paguerre, ed., *Dictionnaire politique* (1842; repr. Paris, 1868), 207.

34   Letter to his wife dated December 18, 1819, in. J., Comte de Villèle, *Mémoires et correspondance* (Paris, 1888), 2: 248.

35   *Le Censeur européen,* October 30, 1819. On January 15, 1820, the same newspaper referred to "all the deputies of the extreme left." On February 16, 1820, it mentioned "four other members of the extreme right." Abundant documentation in Bernhard Monch, "Der Politische Wortschatz der französischen Restauration in Parlament und Presse" (thesis, Bonn, 1960).

36   Quoted in Duvergier de Hauranne, *Histoire,* 5: 287.

37   Ibid., 306.

38   Quoted in Paul Thureau-Dangin, *Le Parti libéral sous la Restauration* (Paris, 1888), 211.

39   Alphonse Bérenger, "Le Ventru, ou compte rendu de la session de 1818," in *Oeuvres complètes* (Paris, 1839), 2: 2. Villèle alludes to a possible "fissure between the right and center right" in 1821 (quoted in Thureau-Dangin, *Le Parti libéral,* 233). In 1819, Rémusat wanted to "reinforce the center left" (*Correspondance de M. de Rémusat pendant les premières années de la Restauration* [Paris, 1833], 6: 96). In 1818 he also proposed a humorous political classification that was particularly ferocious toward the *ventres*

(ibid., 4: 157). Finally, a critical brochure of 1820, *Les Hommes du centre*, observed that "it is remarkable that the center is itself divided in three parts: it has its right side, its left side, and its central point" (p. 26).

40 Paul-Louis Courier, *Lettres particulières*, in *Oeuvres complètes* (Paris: Gallimard, 1951), 63.

41 Stendhal, *Mélanges d'art* (Paris, 1932), 6, quoted by Francis Haskell, "L'Art et le langage de la politique," in *De l'art et du goût* (Paris: Gallimard, 1989), 152.

42 Augustin Thierry, *Considérations sur l'histoire de France*, in *Oeuvres complètes* (Paris, 1858), 4: 117.

43 According to the Vicomte de Saint-Chamans, *De l'état des partis dans les chambres* (Paris, 1828), 43.

44 Quoted in Thureau-Dangin, *Le Parti libéral*, 408.

45 Ibid., 408.

46 Ibid., 409.

47 Saint-Chamans, *De l'état des partis*, 41.

48 Ibid., 177.

49 Ibid., 173.

50 Quoted in Thureau-Dangin, *Le Parti libéral*, 408.

51 Duclerc and Paguerre, *Dictionnaire politique*, 425. Good evidence for this state of affairs can be found in Joseph Tanski, *Voyage autour de la Chambre des députés* (Paris, 1845), who remarks on the difference between this and the first Restoration, noting the "scattering" of parliamentary personnel and the "little overall coherence in its action," as well as the confusion of topographical markers: for example, Lamartine, "who voted alternately with the centers, the left, and the extreme left, is seated in the first seat of the third bench on the extreme right" (277).

52 P.-J. Proudhon, *Oeuvres complètes* (Paris, 1929), 8: 77.

53 Edgar Morin, *Commune en France: La métamorphose de Plodémet* (Paris: Fayard, 1967).

54 Quoted in Michel Soulié, *Le Cartel des gauches* (Paris: Dullis, 1975), 83.

55 The socialist H. Boulay in Mâcon, for example. See the *Recueil des textes authentiques des programmes et professions de foi et engagements électoraux des députés proclamés élus* (cited hereafter as *Recueil Barodet*, with the year of the election) for the elections of 1936 (Paris, 1937), 1251. These volumes were published under the auspices of the Assembly, generally in the year following the elections. Another socialist, R. Muager, in Blois: "Red against whites: this, once again, is characteristic of this battle" (ibid., 662). Recall the slogan of the Croix de Feu: "Neither white nor red but blue, white, and red."

56 L. Ulbach, *La Cloche* for June 12, 1869, quoted in Jean Dubois, *Le Vocabulaire politique et social de la France de 1869 à 1872* (Paris: Larousse, 1962), 311.

57 *Discours et plaidoyers politiques de M. Gambetta* (Paris, 1881), 1: 432.

58 Ibid. We find the word used in a broader sense, but one noted by the writer as unusual, in a text by Eugène Aubry-Vitet from the following year: "A remarkable thing is the *left*, the advanced party, that is, the portion of voters who should be most satisfied by the mere universality of the right to vote" ("Le Suffrage universel dans l'avenir," *La Revue des Deux Mondes* [May 15, 1870]: 387).

59   The formation of these groups has been minutely reconstructed by Rainer Hüdemann, *Fraktionsbildung im französischen Parlament: Zur Entwicklung des Parteiensystems in der frühen Dritten Republik (1871–1875)* (Munich: Artemis Verlag, 1979). For later developments, see M. Tournier, "Vers une grammaire des désignations socio-politiques au début de la III⁵ République, 1879–1905," *Mots*, 2 (1981): 51–71.

60   Manifesto of February 28, 1885, quoted by Jacques Kayser, *Les Grandes Batailles du radicalisme, des origines aux portes du pouvoir* (Paris: Rivière, 1962), 125.

61   *Le Temps*, April 27, 1873, after the Barodet election, quoted in Kayser, *Les Grandes Batailles*, 70.

62   *Le Temps*, March 11, 1874, quoted in François Caron, *La France des patriotes de 1851 à 1918* (Paris: Fayard, 1985), 256.

63   Quoted in Kayser, *Les Grandes Batailles*, 105. Another point of crystallization might be "the union of the left" that Gambetta failed to achieve in March 1876.

64   A Bonapartist newspaper quoted in *L'Année politique* (Paris, 1877), 5–6.

65   Speech at Épinal, June 19, 1881, in *Discours et opinions* (Paris, 1897), 6: 60.

66   Speech at Le Havre, October 14, 1883, ibid., 172.

67   *Recueil Barodet* (Paris, 1886), 79.

68   The debate has been analyzed by Odile Rudelle, *La République absolue: Aux origines de l'instabilité constiutionnelle de la France républicaine* (Paris: Publications de la Sorbonne, 1982), 177.

69   Dubois, *Le Vocabulaire politique et social*, 121–122 and 411–412, provides abundant evidence of this effervescence.

70   *Recueil Barodet*. Antoine Prost has systematically analyzed samples of these statements from a limited period in *Le Vocabulaire des proclamations électorales de 1881, 1885 et 1889* (Paris: Presses Universitaires de France, 1974).

71   *Recueil Barodet*, 1889, 587 and 59.

72   André Siegfried, *Tableau politique de la France de l'Ouest sous la III⁵ République* (Paris: Armand Colin, 1913), 496–497.

73   Charles Seignobos in the multiauthor work *Politique républicaine* (Paris, 1924), 60.

74   Cazeneuve, 4th district of Lyons, *Recueil Barodet*, 688. In Joigny, Loup spoke similarly of "true republicans" and joked about "monarchist republicans": "There must be some, otherwise the series would not be complete" (ibid., 1001).

75   Renoult in Lure, *Recueil Barodet*, 713.

76   Which corresponds, by the way, to the identity that Siegfried rationalized and hypostasized in his theory of "political temperaments," in a book that is as valuable a document concerning the establishment of right and left as it is an analysis. Platforms, parties, and labels change, while temperaments remain the same, so that if Lamartine, Thiers, or Gambetta were to return to the political scene, they would not sit in the place marked by their former *ideas* but would instinctively align themselves with "people of the same *temperament* as themselves, whether on the left, in the center, or on the ceiling." See Siegfried, *Tableau*, 497, for more in this vein.

77   On the history of the Comité Central d'Action Républicaine, which merged with the Association pour les Réformes Républicaines in 1895 to become the Comité d'Action

pour les Réformes Républicaines, see Kayser, *Les Grandes Batailles;* Jean-Thomas Nordmann, *La France radicale* (Paris: Gallimard-Julliard, 1977); Serge Berstein, *Histoire du parti radical,* vol. 1 (Paris: Presses de la Fondation Nationale des Sciences Politiques, 1980).

78 René Renoult, February 24, 1895, quoted in Kayser, *Les Grandes Batailles,* 226.

79 Acts of the *Premier Congrès du Parti républicain, radical et radical socialiste* (1901), 4. Repeated in Mesureur's speech, 10.

80 François Goguel, *La Politique des partis sous la IIIe République* (Paris: Éditions du Seuil, 1958), 19.

81 It is striking to discover that Combes, for example, never used other expressions in the campaign speeches collected in *Une campagne laïque (1902–1903)* (Paris, 1904).

82 This assertion calls for lengthy substantiation. A purely quantitative analysis would be insufficient, though the number of mentions clearly rose sharply. What is needed is a careful analysis of significant occurrences, those for example that reveal a substitution of terms, as in this speech by Empereur at Moutiers: "Its army constitutes the right bloc or the reactionary bloc. On the other side is the left bloc, the republican bloc." *Recueil Barodet,* 808. Every conceivable permutation is represented.

83 The examples are taken, respectively, from Isoard at Forcalquier (*Recueil Barodet,* 46), Chenavaz at Grenoble (437), Dehove at Avesnes (619).

84 Moisei Ostrogorski, *La Démocratie et l'organisation des partis politiques,* 2 vols. (Paris, 1903); Robert Michels, *Zur Soziologie des Parteiwesens in der modernen Demokratie: Untersuchungen über oligarchischen Tendenzen des Gruppenlebens* (Leipzig, 1911).

85 In response to a survey conducted by Emmanuel Beau de Loménie, *Qu'appelez-vous droite et gauche?* (Paris, 1931), 77.

86 Renaud Jean, June 15, 1923, quoted by Georges Bourgin, *Manuel des partis politiques en France* (Paris, 1931), 77.

87 Statement of the Bloc Ouvrier et Paysan of Charente-Inférieure, *Recueil Barodet,* 169. The manifesto of the Bloc Ouvrier et Paysan of Seine-et-Oise is also worth quoting, for it inaugurated a use of the word "left" in quotes that would have a bright future: "Against the National Bloc you will be pitiless. Against the candidates of the 'left' you will be ruthless" (ibid., 846).

88 The formula was proposed by the Ligue de la République, which was created in October 1921, whose manifesto states: "The essential aim of the league is to pave the way for the union of the left." Quoted in Bourgin, *Manuel,* 207.

89 Meurthe-et-Moselle, *Recueil Barodet,* 538.

90 Ardennes, ibid., 71.

91 Allier, ibid., 34.

92 Minutes of the Congress of Tours, quoted in Annie Kriegel, *Le Congrès de Tours (1920): Naissance du P.C.F.* (Paris: Julliard, 1964), 241. This language was taken up by the orators themselves: Frossard, for example, whose arrival on the podium was greeted "with applause on the left," spoke of "our friends of the right and center" (ibid., 159).

93 *Cahiers du bolchevisme,* December 12, 1924, text in Louis Bodin and Nicole Racine, *Le Parti communiste français pendant l'entre-deux-guerres* (Paris: Armand Colin, 1972), 135.

94 Central Committee, *Lettre ouverte aux membres du parti,* in Bodin and Racine, *Le Parti communist français,* 96.

95 Ibid.

96 *Oeuvres de Maurice Thorez* (Paris, 1950), book 2, vol. 5: 20, in Bodin and Racine, *Le Parti communist français,* 228.

97 *Marianne,* March 28, 1934, quoted in Claude Estier, *La Gauche hebdomadaire (1914–1962)* (Paris: Armand Colin, 1962), 102.

98 *Oeuvres de Maurice Thorez,* book 3, vol. 11: 104, in Bodin and Racine, *Le Parti communist français,* 243.

99 *Lettre du Comité central à Édouard Daladier,* October 17, 1936, in Bodin and Racine, *Le Parti communist français,* 257.

100 The unsurpassed source in this genre is *Les Temps modernes,* special issue on "The Left," no. 112–113 (1955). See especially the articles by Jean Pouillon, Dionys Mascolo, and Jean-Toussaint Dessanti, brilliant illustrations of the ambiguity whose principle we are trying to discern here. Sacralization and suspicion go hand in hand.

101 The expression, among dozens of possible sources, is taken from Blaisot at Caen in 1936 (*Recueil Barodet,* 222). For the ultimate in this vein, see the proclamation of the republican and national union list in the 1924 elections: "[To put] the parties of the left in power is tantamount to making foreigners masters in our home" (*Recueil Barodet,* 31). Abel Bonnard provides a very interesting example in *Les Modérés,* where he speaks abundantly of the left but not of the right, which he explains thus: "Since there is only one party in France, the party that encompasses the left and the extreme left, and the moderates are not a separate party, what are they then?" ([1936; repr. Paris: Livre-club du Labyrinthe, 1986], 75). "There is but one excess in French politics," Bonnard went on, "that of the left: it exists without counterweight, it reigns, it governs, and the moderates, in their ideas, feelings, and actions, are directly dependent on it" (ibid., 122).

102 "Lettre aux cocus de la droite," *Combat,* March 1936. Quoted in Louis Bodin and Jean Touchard, *Front populaire, 1936* (Paris: Armand Colin), 35.

103 Quoted in Zeev Sternhell, *Ni droite, ni gauche: L'idéologie fasciste en France* (Brussels: Complexe, 1987), 40. Sternhell's book is full of examples.

104 Jean-Pierre Maxence, *Histoire de dix ans* (Paris, 1939), 328–329.

105 Sternhell, *Ni droite, ni gauche,* 145; Georges Valois, *Le Fascisme* (Paris, 1927), 67 and 139.

106 We saw this with Maxence's quotation marks. An eloquent title in the press of the time: *La Droite, celle qui n'abdique pas (1930–1937).* In the other camp there were "leftist" variations such as *opposition de gauche, gauche révolutionnaire,* and *ultra-gauche,* as well as the significant emergence of Communist irony toward "intellectuals of the 'left.' "

107 In Barrès's *Cahiers* one finds a self-confidence that is quite revealing of the choice that this division of labor implied for individuals engaged in politics: "I would prefer Mun, I would prefer Jaurès, but we must resign ourselves to order. Resign ourselves to the center, humiliate ourselves in the center along with the average man, who wants only to sleep, eat, and multiply." Quoted in Michel Toda, *Henri Massis: Un témoin intellectuelle* (Paris: La Table Ronde, 1987), 180. In Alain we also find a remarkable exam-

ple of this dialectic of the center and extremes: "It's anarchy, this extreme left, on which the whole left lives. And it is the monastic spirit, dumbstruck with obedience, on which the whole right lives" (*Propos* [Paris: Gallimard, 1956], 1: 1285–1286, a comment dating from 1935). This does not, however, prevent him from noting elsewhere that "man is average, man is mixed, man is of the center, and all come back to it, like those radicals among whom I'm not sure I don't belong who beat a more or less dignified retreat when they saw the francs in their pockets melt away. Men of the right also have these natural movements" (ibid., 984, comment of 1930).

108 Rebatet makes a penetrating remark on this point in the midst of the abrupt rhetoric of *Décombres*: "The entire left had received the same party education, which created, according to individual temperaments, Communists, hard-core socialists, soft-core socialists, or more or less Marxified Radicals.... The right, apart from a few dyed-in-the-wool Maurrassians and independents of our sort, were raised on liberal principles...which admirably prepared families of moderates steeped in cheap individualism, while the most intelligent minds turned to jelly in interminable, anarchic, and sterile debates." *Les Mémoires d'un fasciste*, vol. 1, *Les Décombres, 1938–1940*, (repr. Paris: J.-J. Pauvert, 1976), 52.

109 *La Droite en France de 1815 à nos jours: Continuité et diversité d'une tradition politique* (Paris: Aubier-Montaigne, 1954). The title was changed to *Les Droites en France* with the 1982 edition.

110 Albert Thibaudet, *Les Idées politiques de la France* (Paris, 1932).

111 My position here is similar to that of Jacques Julliard in André Burguière and Jacques Revel, *Histoire de la France: L'état et les conflits*, vol. 3 (Paris: Éditions du Seuil, 1990), 343–347. Julliard distinguishes three enduring systems within French party culture: an ideological system, an electoral system, and a governmental system. I would add that there is also a system of systems, which coordinates all three.

112 Data in J. A. Laponce, *Left and Right: The Topography of Political Perceptions* (Toronto: University of Toronto Press, 1981), and in R. Inghehart and H. D. Klingemann, "Party Identification, Ideological Preference and the Left-Right Dimension among Western Mass Publics," in I. Budge, I. Crewe, and D. Farlie, ed., *Party Identification and Beyond: Representations of Voting and Party Competition* (London–New York: Wiley, 1976), 243–273.

113 Pierre Proudhon, *Confessions d'un révolutionnaire*, vol. 8 in *Oeuvres complètes*, 71. The whole text is remarkable for its effort to construct a rational typology of parties. Particularly worthy of attention is the way in which Proudhon shows the rise of two middle parties between two extreme parties (77).

114 François Goguel, *La Politique des partis sous la IIIe République* (Paris: Éditions du Seuil, 1958).

115 Krzysztof Pomian, "La Crise de l'avenir," *Le Débat*, no. 7 (1980).

116 Paul Valéry, *Cahiers* (Paris: Gallimard, 1974), 2: 1494.

117 Ibid., 1491–1492.

118 Louis Dumont, "Sur l'idéologie politique française: Une perspective comparative," *Le Débat*, no. 58 (1990).

119 See especially the afterword to the new edition of idem, *Homo hierarchicus: Le système des castes et ses implications* (Paris: Gallimard, 1979), and "La Valeur chez les modernes et chez les autres," in *Essais sur l'individualisme* (Paris: Éditions du Seuil, 1983).

120 Élie Halévy, *L'ère des tyrannies: Études sur le socialisme et la guerre* (Paris: Gallimard, 1938;, new ed. 1990), 213 ff. Jean Labasse emphasizes the "respective splits on the right and left stemming from the economic realm, where class interests clash" in *Hommes de droite, hommes de gauche* (Paris, 1947), 51.

121 See the powerful passages by Raymond Aron in *Espoir et peur du siècle: Essais non partisans* (Paris: Calmann-Lévy, 1957), esp. "De la droite," 13–21. See also the remarkable studies by Aurel Kornai, "Konservatives und revolutionäres Ethos," in *Rekonstruktion des Konservatismus,* ed. G.-K. Kaltenbrunner (Freiburg-im-Brisgau: Verlag Rombach, 1973), 95–136, and "The Moral Theme in Political Division," *Philosophy* (July 1960): 234–254. Kornai goes so far as to suggest in an unpublished note, "La Dialectique de l'extrémisme et la dialectique de la modération," that the division and reversal of positions is part of the nature of things. It is impossible not to choose and impossible to master the dialectic of historical reality: "Utopia, by coming to pass, refutes itself," and "every success of moderation has the character of a lucky accident" which leaves it at the mercy of a resurgence of extremist forces.

122 This is the argument of Guy Rossi-Landi, *Le Chassé-croisé: La droite et la gauche en France de 1789 à nos jours* (Paris: Éditions Jean-Claude Lattès, 1978). For the roots of division in cultural "temperaments," see Alain-Gérard Slama, *Les Chasseurs d'absolu: Genèse de la gauche et de la droite* (Paris: Grasset, 1980).

CHAPTER 8   PORT-ROYAL: THE JANSENIST SCHISM

1 Cécile Gazier, *Histoire de la société et de la bibliothèque de Port-Royal* (Paris, 1966).

2 *Le Recueil de factum sur plusieurs questions importantes de droit civil* (Lyons, 1710; B.N.F. 14 305) and *Recueil de pièces et de mémoires concernant le testament de M. Rouillé des Filletières attaqué par ses héritiers et confirmé par arrêt de la Grande Chambre du Parlement de Paris le 5 avril 1781 après 8 audiences et sur les conclusions de M. Seguier, avocat général* (B.N., factum 28 446) make it possible to trace how the Nicole collection was passed on through the end of the eighteenth century.

3 Being judicial, rather than legislative, bodies, the French *parlements* were quite different from the English Parliament, and it is therefore misleading to use the adjective *parliamentary* to refer to them. In this article, therefore, the term *parlementary,* formed by adapting the French adjective *parlementaire* to English spelling, has been used with the meaning "of or relating to the *parlements* or their members or supporters."—TRANS.

4 Louis Cognet, *Le Jansénisme* (Paris: Presses Universitaires de France, 1975), 124–125.

5 See the brief bibliographical essay in appendix 1 to this article.

6 The *Nouveau Testament en français avec des réflexions morales,* the first complete version of which appeared in four volumes in 1692, originated in Quesnel's commentaries on the evangelists, which were printed in 1672 under the title *Abrégé de la morale de l'Évangile ou pensées chrétiennes.*

7   Geneviève Reynes, *Couvents de femmes: La vie des religieuses cloîtrées dans la France des XVIIᵉ et XVIIIᵉ siècles* (Paris: Fayard, 1987).

8   *Les Constitutions du monastère de Port-Royal du Saint-Sacrament* (Mons, 1665; Brussels, 1674; Paris, 1721), and *L'Image d'une religieuse parfaite et d'une imparfaite: Avec les occupations intérieures pour toute la journée* (Mons, 1665), by Jeanne Catherine Arnauld (Mère Agnès de Saint-Paul), were circulated as works of piety.

9   Louis Cognet, *La Réforme de Port-Royal* (Paris, 1950), 263.

10 *Mémoires et relations sur ce qui s'est passé à Port-Royal des Champs* (1716), 6.

11 F. Ellen Weaver, *The Evolution of the Reform of Port-Royal: From the Rule of Cîteaux to Jansenism* (Paris, 1970); idem, "Angélique de Saint-Jean, abbesse et mythographe de Port-Royal," *Chronique de Port-Royal* (1985) 93–108.

12 She tells her story in the foreword to the *Mémoires pour servir à l'histoire de Port-Royal et à la vie de la Révérende Mère Angélique* (Utrecht, 1742).

13 Bibliothèque de Port-Royal (hereafter cited as BPR), PR 6, f° 129. Thanks to Mlle Odette Barenne, the director of the library and the editor of an inventory of the library of Louis-Isaac Le Maître de Sacy, *Une grande bibliothèque de Port-Royal* (Paris: Études Augustiniennes, 1985), for calling this unpublished text to my attention.

14 See the obituary by Abbé de Sartre, published as a *Mémoire* in 1784, and the study by Cécile Gazier, "Une Amie des derniers jours de Port-Royal: Françoise-Marguerite de Joncoux (1668–1715)," *Revue de Paris,* no. 36 (April 1929).

15 The Saint-Germain collection was moved to the Bibliothèque Nationale during the Revolution.

16 According to the "Mémoire pour servir à la vie de M. Collard," which prefaces her *Lettres spirituelles* (Avignon, 1734), 19, and *La Vie de Monsieur de Pâris, diacre* (1731), 76, it appears that a small community that formed around Deacon François de Pâris, the Abbé Collard, and the brothers Desessarts in the parish of Saint-Médard on the Rue de Bourgogne between 1724 and 1727 was responsible for many of these copies, especially the memoirs of Lancelot and Fontaine.

17 François Ravaisson, *Archives de la Bastille,* 19 vols. (Paris, 1866–1904), 15: 55.

18 There are also copies in the Bibliothèque Nationale, the Arsenal, Sainte-Geneviève, the municipal library of Troyes, which was a Jansenist refuge in the eighteenth century, and the Utrecht library.

19 Among the most important: Jean-Baptiste Le Sesne des Ménilles d'Étemare and Pierre Boyer, *Gémissements d'une âme vivement touchée de la destruction du Saint-Monastère de Port-Royal des Champs,* 3 vols. (1710–1713). This was followed by a *Quatrième gémissement d'une âme vivement touchée de la Constitution de N.S.P. le pape Clément XI* (1714); Michel Tronchay, *Histoire abrégée de l'abbaye de Port-Royal, depuis sa fondation en 1204 jusqu'à l'enlèvement des religieuses en 1709* (1710); Jacques Fouillou, *Mémoires sur la destruction de Port-Royal des Champs* (1711); Pasquier Quesnel, *Relation de captivité de la Mère Angélique de Saint-Jean* (1711); idem, *Mémoires et relations sur ce qui s'est passé à Port-Royal des Champs depuis le commencement de la réforme de cette abbaye* (1714; repr. 1716).

20 See appendix 2.

21   Abbé Pinault, *Histoire abrégée de la dernière persécution de Port-Royal*, 3 vols. (1750). The abbé, who died in 1737, produced a history that is more an anthology of documents than a continuous narrative.

22   Françoise-Marguerite de Joncoux, Jacques Fouillou, Jean-Baptiste Louail, *Histoire abrégée du jansénisme avec des remarques sur l'ordonnance de M. l'Archevêque de Paris* (Cologne, 1698), in response to the condemnation of the publication of Barcos's *Exposition de la foi* in 1697. Gerberon, *Histoire générale du jansénisme*, 3 vols. (Amsterdam, 1700), an attack on the manuscript "Histoire générale du jansénisme" by the Jesuit Father Rapin.

23   Pinault, *Histoire abrégée*, 2: 178.

24   Henri Schmitz du Moulin, "L'Édition de la *Relation de Captivité* de la mère Angélique de Saint-Jean (1711)," *Chroniques de Port-Royal* (1985): 40.

25   Tronchay, *Histoire abrégée*, 58.

26   Catherine L. Maire, *Les Convulsionnaires de Saint-Médard* (Paris: Gallimard, 1985).

27   Jacques-Joseph Duguet, *Règles pour l'intelligence des Saintes Écritures* (Paris, 1716). On d'Étemare, see Bruno Neveu, "Port-Royal à l'âge des lumières," *Lias*, vol. 4 (1977): 115–153, n 1.

28   D'Étemare, *Quatrième Gémissement*.

29   Concerning the percentage of signatures in support of the various Jansenist interventions against the papal bull, see Marie-José Michel, "Clergé et pastorale janséniste à Paris (1665–1730," *Revue d'histoire moderne et contemporaine*, 27 (April-June 1979): 182, and Dominique Minet and Marie-Claude Dinet-Leconte, "Les Appelants contre la bulle *Unigenitus* d'après Gabriel-Nicolas Nivelle," *Histoire, économie et société*, 3 (1990): 365–385.

30   In particular, Jean-Baptiste Le Sesne des Ménilles d'Étemare, *La Quatrième Colonne des Hexaples*, 2 vols. (1723); Jean-Baptiste Raymond de Pavie de Fourquevaux, *Catéchisme historique et dogmatique sur les contestations qui divisent maintenant l'Église*, 2 vols. (1729–1730); L.-F. Boursier, *L'Explication abrégée des principales questions qui ont rapport aux affaires présentes* (1732); Nicolas Legros, *Abrégée des principales questions qui ont rapport aux affaires présentes* (1732); idem, *Abrégé chronologique des principaux événements qui ont précédé la Constitution Unigenitus* (Utrecht, 1730), with several subsequent versions extending to 1762; idem., *Abrégé historique et chronologique dans lequel on démontre par les faits* (1733); idem., *Étrennes jansénistes* (1733); Louis Adrien Le Paige, *Annales pour servir d'étrennes aux amis de la vérité* (no place or date of publication given, probably 1734); the three works titled *Vie du diacre Pâris* published in 1731 belong to this corpus.

31   Françoise Bontoux, "Paris janséniste au XVIIIe siècle: Les *Nouvelles ecclésiastiques*," *Mémoires de la Fédération des sociétés historiques et archéologiques de Paris et de l'Ile-de-France*, 7 (1955): 205–220.

32   The most complete bibliography of Jansenist figurist prophecies is in Alfred-Félix Vaucher, *Lacunziana: Essais sur les prophéties bibliques*, 2d ser. (Collonges-sous-Salèves, 1952).

33   J. Dedieu, "L'Agonie du jansénisme," *Revue d'histoire de l'Église de France*, 14 (1928): 101–214.

34 René Cerveau, "Grillot" entry, *Nécrologe des plus célèbres défenseurs et confesseurs de la vérité au XVIIIe siècle* (1760–1778), 6: 406.

35 Jean Mesnard, "Le Maistre de Sacy et son secrétaire Fontaine,"in *Chroniques de Port-Royal* (1984).

36 Sainte-Beuve, *Port-Royal* (Paris: Gallimard, 1953), 1: 804; 2: 104.

37 See the "Journal de Le Maître," the "Récit de la conduite et des exercices des illustres solitaires," and the "Mémoire des écoles de Port-Royal."

38 *Mémoires pour servir à l'histoire de Port-Royal et à la vie de la Révérende Mère Angélique de Sainte-Magdeleine Arnauld, réformatrice du monastère,* 3 vols. (Utrecht, 1742).

39 Jérôme Besoigne, *Histoire de l'abbaye de Port-Royal— Première partie: histoire des religieuses; Deuxième partie: histoire des Messieurs,* 6 vols. (Cologne, 1752); idem, *Vie des quatre évêques engagés dans la cause de Port Royal, M. d'Aleth, M. d'Angers, M. de Beauvais, M. de Pamiers,* 2 vols. (1756); Charles Clémencet, *Histoire générale de Port-Royal, depuis la réforme de l'abbaye jusqu'à son entière destruction,* 10 vols. (Amsterdam: Jean Vanduren, 1755–1757); idem., "Histoire littéraire de Port-Royal" and "Histoire de la vie et des ouvrages de Claude Lancelot" (MS, B.S.H.P.F.); Pierre Guilbert, *Mémoires historiques et chronologiques sur l'abbaye de Port-Royal des Champs,* 7 vols. (Utrecht, 1755–1756); idem, *Mémoires historiques et chronologiques sur l'abbaye de Port-Royal des Champs depuis sa fondation en 1204 jusqu'à la mort des dernières religieuses et amis de ce monastère, partie première,* 2 vols. (Utrecht, 1758–1759)

40 *Les Très Humbles Remontrances au Roi* (1753), 135.

41 *Nouvelles ecclésiastiques* (1751): 94.

42 L.-A. Le Paige and Abbé Coudrette, *Histoire générale de la naissance et des progrès de la Compagnie de Jésus et analyse de leurs constitutions et privilèges,* 5 vols. (Amsterdam, 1760; repr. 1784, 5 vols.).

43 Author of five quarto volumes of *Annales des soi-disant Jésuites* (1764).

44 Dale Van Kley, *The Jansenists and the Expulsion of the Jesuits from France* (New Haven: Yale University Press, 1975).

45 Pierre Barral (author of the *Manuel des Souverains* [1754]), *Appelans célèbres* (1754); Pierre-François Labelle (an Oratorian priest), *Nécrologe des appelans et des opposans à la bulle Unigenitus* (1755); René Cerveau (a priest in the Jansenist parish of Saint-Étienne du Mont), *Nécrologe des défenseurs de la Vérité,* 7 vols. (1760–1778).

46 J.-B.-M. de Pavie de Fourquevaux and Louis Troya d'Assigny, *Catéchisme historique et dogmatique,* 5 vols. (Nancy, 1750–1768).

47 Louis-Adrien Le Paige, *Lettre à un curé de Paris par les fidèles de sa paroisse au sujet du mandement de Mgr l'Archevêque de Paris contre les Nouvelles ecclésiastiques* (1732).

48 Idem, *Lettres pacifiques ou lettres adressées à MM. les Commissaires nommés par le Roi pour délibérer sur l'affaire présente du Parlement au sujet du refus des Sacrements* (1752; rev. and repr. 1753).

49 Among the major works of Le Paige are *Lettres historiques sur les fonctions essentielles du Parlement,* 2 vols. (1753); *Mémoire au sujet d'un nouvel écrit contre le Parlement* (1754); *La Légitimité et la nécessité de la loi du silence contre les réflexions d'un prétendu docteur en théologie sur la déclaration qui impose le silence* (1759); *Observations sur les actes de*

l'assemblée du clergé de 1765 (1765); *Le Philosophe redressé* (Au Bois Valon, 1765); *Principles de la législation française provués par les monuments de cette nation relatifs aux affaires du temps* (1771).

50   Term used by certain parlementary correspondents on letters to Le Paige, B.P.R., LP 541.

51   B.P.R., LP 480.

52   Jules Flammermont, *Remontrances du Parlement de Paris* (Paris, 1888); idem., *Le Chancelier Maupeou et les parlements* (Paris, 1883).

53   Mlle Poulain, *Nouvelle Histoire abrégée de l'abbaye de Port-Royal:* [. . .] *On y trouvera tout à la fois de l'amusement, de l'édification et une grandeur d'âme qui frappe et qui ravit,* 4 vols. (Paris, 1786); Mother Angélique de Saint-Jean, *Exercices de piété à l'usage des religieuses de Port-Royal du Saint-Sacrement,* (1787), a book of edification; Dupac de Bellegarde, *La Vie de Messire Antoine Arnauld Dr. de la Maison et Société de Sorbonne,* 43 vols. (Paris-Lausanne, 1775–1783); Noël Castera de Larrière, *La Vie de Messire Antoine Arnauld* (Paris and Lausanne, 1783).

54   Jacob-Nicolas Moreau, *Mes souvenirs,* 2 vols. (Paris, 1898–1901), 1: 44 and 50.

55   Louis Adrien Le Paige, Letter to de Murard, March 20, 1772, B.P.R., 541.

56   Maultrot, Mey et al., *Maximes du droit public français,* 2 vols. (Amsterdam, 1775); Maultrot, *Origine et étendue de la puissance royale suivant les livres saints et la tradition,* 3 vols. (1789–1790).

57   Yann Fauchois, "Jansénisme et politique au XVIIIe siècle," *Revue d'histoire moderne et contemporaine,* 34 (July-September 1987): 473–491.

58   In his *Mémoires pour servir à l'histoire du jacobinisme,* composed after a wave of dechristianization, Barruel no longer included the Jansenists in his list of conspirators.

59   Emmanuel, Comte d'Antraigues, *Dénonciation aux français catholiques des moyens employés par l'Assemblée nationale, pour détruire en France la religion catholique* (London, 1791).

60   Henri-Baptiste Grégoire, Jean-Baptiste Royer, Éléonore Marie Desbois de Rochefort, Jean-Pierre Saurine, Augustin Jean Charles Clément, Charles Saillant.

61   *Mémoires secrets sur la vie de M. Clément, Évêque de Versailles, pour servir à l'éclaircissement de l'histoire ecclésiastique du XVIIIe siècle* (1812) 53–54.

62   The group included former Jansenists, some of whom had belonged to the constitutional clergy (Baillet, Girard, Cady, Varlet, Rondeau, Constantin), and published a periodical, the *Annales de la Religion.*

63   *Les Ruines* was published in May 1801 in the *Annales de la Religion* and later as a separate brochure.

64   Antoine Arnauld, *Le Véritable Portrait de Guillaume Henry de Nassau, nouvel Absalom, nouvel Hérode, nouveau Cromwel, nouveau Néron* (no place or date).

65   Maurice Vaussard, *Jansénisme et gallicanisme, aux origines religieuses du Risorgimento* (Paris, 1959); Edmond Préclin, "L'influence du jansénisme français à l'étranger," *Revue historique,* 182 (1982).

66   Ruth Clark, *Strangers and Sojourners at Port-Royal* (Cambridge, 1932), mentions Mary Anne Schimmelpennick, a friend of Hannah More's, who wrote *Select Memoirs of Port-Royal* (London, 1835); Frances Martin, *Angelique Arnauld, Abbess of Port-Royal*

(London, 1876); Ethel Romanes, *The Story of Port-Royal* (London, 1907); M. E. Lowndes, *The Nuns of Port-Royal as Seen in Their Own Narratives* (Oxford, 1909).

67 From 1818 to 1821 *La Chronique religieuse;* from 1838 to 1848 *La Revue ecclésiastique;* from 1855 to 1863 *L'Observateur catholique*. On this subject see René Taveneaux, "Permanences jansénistes au XIXe siècle," *Dix-huitième siècle*, no. 129, 32nd year (1980): 394–414.

68 René Rémond, *L'Anticléricalisme en France de 1615 à nos jours* (Paris, 1985).

69 Published in *Les Nouveaux Mélanges historiques et littéraires* (Paris, 1827).

70 Joseph de Maistre, *De l'Église gallicane* (Paris, 1821).

71 Félicité de Lamennais, *De la religion dans ses rapports avec l'ordre politique et civil* (Paris, 1826), 188.

72 Austin Gough, *Paris and Rome, the Gallican Church and the Ultramontane Campaign, 1848–1853* (Oxford, 1986), 225.

73 Raphaël Molho, *L'Ordre et les ténèbres ou la naissance d'un mythe du XVIIe siècle chez Sainte-Beuve* (Paris: Armand Colin, 1972), the work on which I rely for my account of Sainte-Beuve.

74 *Revue de Paris,* January–February 1834.

75 Quoted in Molho, *L'Ordre;* original in Collection Spooelberch de Lovenjoul, D 581, fol. 57.

76 His Jansenist library of 678 volumes was acquired by the Société d'Histoire du Protestantisme Français in 1872. On this question, see the article by Cécile Gazier, "Les Sources de Sainte-Beuve," *Revue bleue,* 17 (July 1926), and "Une Heure avec M. Royer-Collard," in Jean Pommier, *Dialogues avec le passé* (Paris, 1967).

77 Along with two insignificant articles by Lerminier in the *Revue des deux mondes* of June 1, 1840, and Frédéric Chavannes in the *Revue suisse* of July 1840, and the overtly hostile, not to say vicious, article by Balzac in the *Revue parisienne* of August 25, 1840, only the Protestant pastor Vinet, in two articles that appeared in *Semeur* of December 2 and 30, 1840, expressed sincere admiration for the study's "Christian spirit," "understanding of true Christianity," and "moral method."

78 Hippolyte Taine, *Histoire de la littérature anglaise,* 1: xii-xiv.

79 Brunetière, *Livre d'or de Sainte-Beuve* (Paris, 1904).

80 Victor Cousin, *Blaise Pascal* (Paris, 1842). Cousin also sought to give due credit to those women of letters, the *"belles amies de Port-Royal,"* in *Jacqueline Pascal* (Paris, 1842); *Madame de Longueville* (Paris, 1853); *Madame de Sablé* (Paris, 1854). See also Cécile Gazier, *Les Belles Amies de Port-Royal* (Paris, 1930).

81 *Port-Royal des Champs* (1874; rev. and expanded 1893 and 1913), a historical note for visitors.

82 Augustin Gazier, "Les Écoles de charité du faubourg Saint-Antoine, école normale et groupes scolaires, 1713–1887," *Revue internationale de l'enseignement,* 51 (1906): 217–237, 314–326. Cécile Gazier, *Après Port-Royal, l'ordre hospitalier des soeurs de Sainte-Marthe* (Paris, 1923).

83 Among his major works: *Études sur l'histoire religieuse de la Révolution française* (Paris, 1887); *Histoire générale du mouvement janséniste, depuis ses origines jusqu'à nos jours*

(Paris, 1922); *Une Suite à l'histoire de Port-Royal d'après des documents inédits: Jeanne de Boisignorel et Christophe de Beaumont (1750–1782)* (Paris, 1906).

84   Félix Cadet, *L'Éducation à Port-Royal* (Paris, 1887), 79.

85   Irénée Carré, *Les Pédagogues de Port-Royal—Histoire des petites écoles* (Paris, 1887).

86   Carré, article "Port-Royal (Petites Écoles)," in Buisson, *Nouveau Dictionnaire de pédagogie* (1911), 1663.

87   Speech by Ferdinand Buisson at the grave of Jules Steeg, quoted by Jean-Marie Mayeur, *Les Débuts de la IIIe République, 1871–1898* (Paris: Éditions du Seuil, 1973), 114.

88   Fact reported in brochure of *L'Union pour l'action morale*, no. 19 (August 1, 1903): 899.

89   Ibid., 884.

90   Philippe Sellier, "Port-Royal ou le 'génie' du christianisme," *Destin et enjeux du XVIIe siècle* (Paris: Presses Universitaires de France, 1985).

91   *Grammaire générale et raisonnée*, with an introduction by Michel Foucault (Paris, 1969); Noam Chomsky, *Cartesian Linguistics: A Chapter in the History of Rationalist Thought* (Lanham, Md.: University Press of America, 1983); Arnauld and Nicole, *La Logique ou l'art de penser* (Lille, 1974; Paris: Presses Universitaires de France, 1965; Geneva, 1972; Paris, Flammarion "Champs," 1970; Paris, Gallimard "Tel," 1992).

92   Leszek Kolakowski, "Georges Sorel, Jansenist Marxist," *Dissent*, 22 (1975).

93   Paul Valéry, *Degas* (Paris, 1936), 179.

94   Blaise Cendrars, *L'Homme foudroyé* (Paris, 1945), 135.

95   André Bazin, "William Wyler ou le jansénisme de la mise en scène," *Qu'est-ce que le cinéma?* (Paris, 1958), 1: 149–173.

96   Colloquium on "Jansénisme et révolution," *Chroniques de Port-Royal* (Paris: Vrin, 1990); Catherine Maire, "L'Église et la Nation: Du dépôt de la vérité au dépôt des lois—La trajectoire janséniste au XVIIIe siècle," *Annales E.S.C.*, 5 (September–October 1991): 177–205.

CHAPTER 9   THE MUSEUM OF THE DESERT: THE PROTESTANT MINORITY

1   Jean Bastide, *Histoire abrégée des protestants de France, textes et récits à l'usage des cours d'instruction religieuse* (Dieulefit, 1910; 2d ed. 1933), v. For another example, see Charles Bost, *Histoire des protestants de France en trente-cinq leçons pour les écoles*, which met with great success and went through three editions (1924, 1926, and 1931).

2   Respectively, 1927 and 1925.

3   Charles Bost completely abandons the hagiographic perspective and does not hesitate to show Camisard violence. See Philippe Joutard, *La Légende des camisards* (Paris: Gallimard, 1977), 252–258. Besides *Histoire pour les écoles*, Bost wrote four historically inspired plays.

4   Insert to *National Geographic Magazine* (October 1978): 8.

5   Robert Louis Stevenson, *Travels with a Donkey in the Cevennes* (London: Macmillan, 1962), 96.

6   *Protestantisme français*, collective work (1945), 23.

7   Marc Bloch, *Apologie pour l'histoire ou métier d'historien*, 4th ed. (Paris: Armand Colin, 1961), 10.

8   Pierre Gaudin and Claire Reverchon, "Le Légendaire historique drômois" (thesis, University of Provence, 1982; mimeograph).

9   Oral inquiry in Cévennes from 1967 to 1973.

10 *Bulletin de la Société de l'histoire du protestantisme français*, 1 (1853): 499; hereafter abbreviated *B.S.H.P.F.*

11 Memo to the pastor reproduced in *Notice sur la Société de l'histoire du protestantisme français*, 1852–1872 (Paris, 1874), 80.

12 *B.S.H.P.F.*, 16 (1867): 571, and 18 (1869): 170.

13 *B.S.H.P.F.*, 32 (1883): 435 ff.

14 *B.S.H.P.F.*, 34 (1885): 547 and 558.

15 See *La Cévenole*, 1 (1885): 1 and 2; the ceremony is described in the September 1885 issue.

16 After Mont Lozère, the three highest peaks in the Cévennes.

17 *Le Foyer protestant* (August 1887).

18 *La Cévenole* (September 1885): 1, and *Le Foyer protestant* (August 14, 1887): 8.

19 Musée du Désert, 1685–1787, Fondation Frank Puaux et Edmond Hugues, *Guide du visiteur, notice historique et régionale*, in Cévennes (Le Mas-Soubeyran, Mialet, Gard, 1964), 5.

20 Ibid., 71–73: list of invited speakers and themes from 1911 to 1962. See Florence Morillère, "Essai sur les assemblées commémoratives du musée du Désert" (thesis, École Pratique des Hautes Études, 1981; mimeograph).

21 Ibid.

22 *Guide du visiteur*, 73–75.

23 *Quatre dernières assemblées, 1924–1925*, in Cévennes, 1924–1925), 41 and 74, and *Deuxième centenaire de la libération des dernières prisonnières huguenotes de la tour de Constance, 1768–1968*, supplement to *Bulletin de la Société de l'histoire du protestantisme français*, 115 (January–March 1969).

24 "Rapport de Jacques Bompaire présenté à l'Assemblée générale de la S.H.P.F. du 19 juin 1989," *B.S.H.P.F.*, 135 (October–December 1989): 477.

25 The general outline of the program and Charles Read's intervention are reproduced in *Notice sur la Société*, 20–27 and 43.

26 Based on the number of pages and fractions thereof referring to each subject. As crude as this index is, it yields a clear measure of the relative importance of each area of interest.

27 Jacques Pannier, *Catalogue du Musée de la Société de l'histoire du protestantisme français: Une heure de promenade historique à travers quatre siècles, livret-guide du visiteur* (Paris: S.H.P.F., 1927).

28 Statistics based on tables compiled by Morillère, "Essai sur les assemblées," 258–267, which I completed for the present period on the basis of reviews in *B.S.H.P.F.*

29 Quoted in "Protestantisme et liberté, rencontre des 12 et 13 octobre 1985 à la Mutualité, Paris," *Bulletin du C.P.E.D.*, 313 (June-July 1986): 209. On the history of this com-

memoration, in addition to pp. 11–17 of this issue of the *C.P.E.D.*, see Jean Beaubérot, *Le Protestantisme doit-il mourir?* (Paris: Éditions du Seuil, 1988), 142–145.

30   See the critical notice by Remy Scheurer, "La Révocation de l'édit de Nantes et le refuge huguenot," *Revue suisse d'histoire* (1986), 3: 346–367.

31   I have studied this reversal of perspective in my *Légende des camisards*, 188–212.

32   *B.S.H.P.F.*, 35 (1885): 552.

33   Morillère, "Essai sur les assemblées," 234–235.

34   *Allocutions prononcées le dimanche 1ᵉʳ septembre 1935*, (Musée du Désert, n. d.), 16.

35   *Réforme* (August 31, 1985): 5.

36   Morillère, "Essai sur les assemblées," 234–235.

37   Élisabeth Labrousse, *Pierre Bayle et l'instrument critique* (Paris: Seghers, 1965), 46.

38   Gaston de Félice, *Histoire des protestants de France* (1850; quoted from the 6th ed., Toulouse: Société des Livres Religieux, 1874), 9.

39   Quoted in E. Labrousse, *Pierre Bayle*, vol. 1, *Du pays de Foix à la cité d'Erasme* (The Hague–Paris: Mouton, 1963), 53.

40   Nicole Thévenet, "Sensibilité protestante dans la vallée d'Aigues" (master's thesis in history, University of Provence, 1978; typescript), 32.

41   *Quatre Dernières Assemblées*, v.

42   Joutard, *La Légende des camisards*, 304.

43   *Prédication et allocutions de l'Assemblée du dimanche 4 septembre 1949* (Anduze, n. d.), 15–16. François Puaux published his *Histoire de la Réformation française* in 1863, *Vie de Jean Cavalier* in 1868, and *Histoire des camisards* in 1872, which met with great success and was reprinted in 1878 and 1898. His son Frank published the first edition of Cavalier's *Mémoires* in 1919.

44   *Vingt complaintes sur les prédicants des Cévennes martyrisés au XVIIIᵉ siècle*, in *Cévennes*, (1932) 152. The title is somewhat misleading, since the *complaintes* (laments) concern not just lay preachers, and many of the victims were not from the Cévennes. Désubas himself was a native of the Vivarais.

45   Pastor Manen and I have shown an example from the parish of La Pervenche in the Vivarais: *Une foi enracinée: La Pervenche* (Valence, 1972).

46   *Réforme* (August 31, 1985).

47   Quoted in Joutard, *La Légende des camisards*, 206–207.

48   François Furet, *La Gauche et la Révolution française au milieu du XIXᵉ siècle: Edgar Quinet et la question du jacobinisme (1865–1870)* (Paris: Hachette, 1986).

49   Beaubérot, *Le Protestantisme*, 53–61.

50   Joutard, *La Légende des camisards*, 230. Additional examples in subsequent pages.

51   Ibid., 262–263.

52   Quoted in "Évangile et liberté, pour la commémoration du tricentenaire de l'édit de Nantes," *Unité des chrétiens* (July 1985): 8.

53   Ibid., 22.

54   Philippe Joutard, "La Révocation de l'édit de Nantes et le protestantisme français en 1685,"in *Actes du colloque de Paris (15–19 octobre 1985)*, collected by Roger Zuber and Laurent Theis (Paris, 1986), 299–311.

55 See the press review in *Réforme* (October 19, 1985): 7. The quotation is taken from *L'Express.*

56 *Quatre Dernières Assemblées,* 27.

57 Ibid., 24–25.

58 Philippe Joutard, Jacques Poujol, and Patrick Cabanel, *Cévennes, Terre de Refuge, 1940–1944* (Montpellier: Presses du Languedoc, 1987), 250–253.

59 Quoted in Robert Poujol, *Aigoual 44* (Ganges, 1951), 52.

60 *Réforme* (October 19, 1985): 11.

CHAPTER 10   GRÉGOIRE, DREYFUS, DRANCY, AND RUE COPERNIC:
JEWS AT THE HEART OF FRENCH HISTORY

1 In June 1991 the statue of Léon Blum finally found its natural place on Place Léon-Blum in the Eleventh Arrondissement of Paris.

2 Jacques Durin, *Drancy, 1941–1944* (Paris: Le Bourget, 1982).

3 Anne Grynberg, *Les Camps de la honte: Les internés juifs des camps français, 1939–1944* (Paris: La Découverte, 1991), 10.

4 Robert Weyl, *Le Cimetière juif de Rosenwiller* (Strasbourg: Éditions Salde, 1988). More generally, see Vicki Caron, *Between France and Germany: The Jews of Alsace-Lorraine, 1871–1918* (Stanford: Stanford University Press, 1988).

5 Colette Beaune, *Naissance de la nation France* (Paris: Gallimard, 1985), 213. On the place of the Jews in the French nation, see Frances Malino and Bernard Wasserstein, *The Jews in Modern France* (Hanover: Brandeis University Press, 1985).

6 Annette Wieviorka, "Un Lieu de mémoire: Le Mémorial du martyr juif inconnu," *Pardès,* 1982.

7 Georges Passerat, "L'Émeute des Pastoureaux et le massacre de Verdun (1320)," in *Juifs et sources juives en Occitanie* (Albi: Vent Tarral, 1988).

8 René Moulinas, *Les Juifs du pape en France: Les communautés d'Avignon et du Comtat Venaissin aux XVIIe et XVIIIe siècles* (Toulouse: Privat, 1981).

9 Yosef Yerushalmi, *Zakhor* (Washington: University of Washington, 1982).

10 Roland Auguet, *Le Juif errant* (Paris: Payot, 1977), 35, 117, and 139.

11 Émile Zola, *L'Argent* (Paris: Le Livre de Poche, n. d.), 438.

12 Georges Dairnwaell, *Histoire édifiante et curieuse de Rothschild Ier, Roi des Juifs* (Paris, 1846); Jacques de Biez, *Les Rothschild et le péril juif* (Paris, 1891); Jules Guesde, "A mort, Rothschild," in *État, politique et morale de classe* (Paris: Giard, 1901), 446. On this legend and its influence in France, see Jean Bouvier, *Les Rothschild* (Paris: Fayard, 1967).

13 Norman Cohn, *Warrant for Genocide: The Myth of the Jewish World Conspiracy and the Protocols of the Elders of Zion* (New York: Harper & Row, 1967); Pierre Nora, "1898: Le Thème du complot et la définition de l'identité juive," in *Le Racisme, Mythes et sciences: Pour Léon Poliakov* (Brussels: Éditions Complexe, 1981); Pierre Birnbaum, "Les Protocoles dans l'imaginaire politique français," in Pierre-André Taguieff, *Les Protocoles des sages de Sion* (Berg, 1992).

14   On the image of Jews in French Catholic thought, Pierre Sorlin, *La Croix et les Juifs* (Paris: Grasset, 1967); Pierre Pierrard, *Juifs et Catholiques français* (Paris: Fayard, 1970); Jacques Petit, *Bernanos, Bloy, Claudel, Péguy: Quatre écrivains catholiques face à Israël* (Paris: Calmann-Lévy, 1972); Charlotte Wardi, *Le Juif dans le roman français, 1933–1948* (Paris: Nizet, 1973); Béatrice Philippe, *Etre juif dans la société française* (Paris: Pluriel, 1979); Lazare Landau, *De l'aversion à l'estime: Juifs et Catholiques en France* (Paris: Le Centurion, 1980); Jeffrey Mehlman, *Legs de l'anitsémitisme en France* (Paris: Denoël, 1984); Pierre Birnbaum, *La France aux Français* (Paris: Éditions du Seuil, 1993).

15   Frances Malino, *The Sephardic Jews of Bordeaux: Assimilation and Emancipation in Revolutionary and Napoleonic France* (Birmingham: University of Alabama Press, 1978).

16   Abbé Grégoire, *Essai sur la Régénération physique, morale et politique des Juifs* (Paris: Flammarion, 1989). See Paul Catrice, "L'Abbé Grégoire, 'Amie de tous les hommes,' et la régénération des Juifs," *Mélanges de science religieuse*, 36 (1979); Pierre Birnbaum, "Sur l'étatisation révolutionnaire: L'abbé Grégoire et le destin de l'identité juive," *Le Débat*, 53 (January–February 1989).

17   David Feuerwerker, *L'Émancipation des juifs en France, de l'Ancien Régime à la fin du second Empire* (Paris: Albin Michel, 1976); Bernhard Blumenkranz and Albert Soboul, ed., *Les Juifs et la Révolution française* (Toulouse: Privat, 1976); Shmuel Trigano, *La République et les Juifs* (Paris: Les Presses d'Aujourd'hui, 1982).

18   Quoted in S. Posener, *Adolphe Crémieux* (Paris: Félix Alcan, 1943), 2: 149 and 220; see also Daniel Amson, *Adolphe Crémieux, l'oublié de la gloire* (Paris: Éditions du Seuil, 1988).

19   *La Nation* (May 6, 1889).

20   Théodore Reinach, *Histoire des Israélites depuis l'époque de leur dispersion jusqu'à nos jours* (Paris: Hachette, 1885), 325.

21   Michael Marrus, *The Politics of Assimilation: The Jewish Community in France at the Time of the Dreyfus Affair* (Oxford: Oxford University Press, 1980); Laurent Bensaïd, "Cent ans de fidélité à la République," *H Histoire*, 3 (1979); Jean-Marc Chouraqui, "De l'émancipation des juifs à l'émancipation du judaïsme: Le regard des rabbins français du XIXe siècle," in Pierre Birnbaum, ed., *Histoire politique des juifs de France* (Paris: Presses de la Fondation Nationale des Sciences Politiques, 1990).

22   Phyllis Albert Cohen, *The Modernization of French Jewry: Consistory and Community in the Nineteenth Century* (Hanover: Brandeis University Press, 1977); Eric Smilevitch, "Halakha et Code civil, questions sur le Grand Sanhédrin," *Pardès*, 3 (1986).

23   Reinach, *Histoire des Israélites*, 384. See also, by the same author, the article "Juif" in the *Grande Encyclpédie* (Paris, 1894), and his speech, "Ce que nous sommes" (Paris: Union Libérale Israélite, n.d.).

24   Quoted in Christine Piette, *Les Juifs de Paris (1808–1840): La marche vers l'assimilation* (Quebec: Presses de l'Université du Québec, 1983), 137.

25   Doris Bensimon-Donath, *Socio-démographie des juifs de France et d'Algérie* (Paris: A.L.C., 1976).

26   Yosef Yerushalmi, "Un Champ à Anathoth: Vers une histoire de l'espoir juif," in
     Mémoire et histoire (Paris: Denoël, 1986), 106.

27   The foregoing draws heavily on Michael Graetz, *Les Juifs en France au XIX*[e] siècle: De
     la Révolution française à l'Alliance israélite universelle (Paris: Éditions du Seuil, 1989),
     and the doctoral thesis of Perrine Simon-Nahum, "Contribution à l'étude de la bour-
     geoisie intellectuelle juive, 1830–1914" (Paris, École des Hautes Études en Sciences
     Sociales, 1989).

28   Aron Rodrigue, *De l'instruction à l'émancipation: Les enseignants de l'Alliance israélite
     universelle et les juifs d'Orient. 1860–1939* (Paris: Calmann-Lévy, 1989); idem, *French
     Jews, Turkish Jews: The Alliance Israélite Universelle and the Politics of Jewish Schooling
     in Turkey, 1860–1925* (Bloomington: Indiana University Press, 1990).

29   Alexis de Tocqueville, *Souvenirs* (Paris: Gallimard, 1964), 163–165.

30   Pierre Birnbaum, *Un Mythe politique: "La République juive," de Léon Blum à Pierre
     Mendès France* (Paris: Fayard, 1988).

31   Marrus, *The Politics of Assimilation;* Paula Hyman, *From Dreyfus to Vichy* (Oxford:
     Blackwell, 1992).

32   *Archives israélites,* successively June 11, 1908; May 14, 1914; April 24, 1902.

33   On Drumont see Robert Byrnes, *Antisemitism in Modern France* (New Brunswick,
     1950); Stephen Wilson, *Ideology and Experience: Antisemitism in France at the Time of
     the Dreyfus Affair* (London: Associated Press, 1982); Michel Winock, *Édouard Drumont
     et C*[ie]: Antisémitisme et fascisme en France (Paris: Éditions du Seuil, 1982); Frederik
     Busi, *The Pope of Antisemitism: The Career and Legacy of Édouard Drumont* (New
     York: University Press of America, 1986).

34   Zeev Sternhell, *Maurice Barrès et le nationalisme français* (Paris: Armand Colin, 1972).

35   Anatole France, *L'Orme du mail* (Paris: Calmann-Lévy, 1986), 31, 67, 80, and 183.

36   *La Dépêche* (February 5, 1890).

37   *La Croix,* (January 28, 1882). See Pierre Sorlin, La Croix *et les Juifs,* and Jeanne
     Verdès-Leroux, *Scandale financier et antisémitisme catholique: Le krach de l'Union
     nationale* (Paris: Le Centurion, 1969).

38   Jean-Yves Mollier, *Le Scandale de Panama* (Paris: Fayard, 1991).

39   See, for example, Robert Nye, *The Origins of Crowd Psychology: Gustave Le Bon and the
     Crisis of Mass Democracy in the Third Republic* (London: Sage, 1976); Suzanna
     Barrows, *Miroirs déformants: Réflexions sur la foule en France à la fin du XIX*[e] siècle
     (Paris: Aubier, 1990).

40   Michel Winock, "Les affaires Dreyfus," *Vingtième Siècle* (January–March 1985).

41   Pierre Quillard, *Le Monument Henry* (Paris, 1889); Wilson, *Ideology and Experience;*
     Marcel Thomas, "Le Cas Valéry," in *Les Écrivains et l'affaire Dreyfus* (Paris: Presses
     Universitaires de France, 1983); Nelly Wilson, *Bernard-Lazare: Antisemitism and the
     Emblem of Jewish Identity* (Cambridge, England: Cambridge University Press, 1975);
     Pascal Ory and Jean-François Sirinelli, *Les Intellectuels en France: De l'affaire Dreyfus
     à nos jours* (Paris: Armand Colin, 1986); Norman Kleeblatt, ed., *The Dreyfus Affair:
     Art, Truth and Justice* (Berkeley: University of California Press, 1987); Michael Burns,
     Dreyfus: A Family Affair (New York: Harper's, 1991).

42 Michael Marrus, "Vichy before Vichy: Antisemitic Currents in France during the 1930s," *Bulletin of the Wiener Library*, vol. 3 (1980); Michael Marrus and Robert Paxton, *Vichy France and the Jews* (New York: Basic Books, 1981); Georges Wellers, André Kaspi, and Serge Klarsfeld, *La France et la question juive, 1940–1944* (Paris: Sylvie Messinger, 1981); Serge Klarsfeld, *Vichy-Auschwitz* (Paris: Fayard, 1985); Denis Peschanski, "La France, terre de camps?" in Karel Bartosek, René Gallisot, and Denis Peschanski, *De l'exil à la résistance: Réfugiés et immigrés d'Europe centrale en France, 1933–1945* (Saint-Denis: Presses Universitaires de Vincennes, 1989).

43 *Le Statut des juifs de Vichy: Documentation* (Paris: Centre de Documentation Juive Contemporaine, 1990).

44 See Joseph-Barthélemy, *Ministre de la Justice: Vichy 1941–1943* (Paris: Pygmalion, 1989). The notes are a gold mine of information concerning the role of high Vichy officials.

45 Roderick Kedward and Roger Austin, ed., *Vichy, France and the Resistance: Culture and Ideology* (London: Croom Helm, 1985); Christian Faure, *Le Projet culturel de Vichy* (Lyons: Presses Universitaires de Lyon, 1989).

46 Georges Wormser, *Français israélites* (Paris: Éditions de Minuit, 1963), 11–14.

47 Archives du Consistoire Central, boxes 9 and 32.

48 Quoted in Brigitte Bergmann, "Paul Grunebaum-Ballin, un siècle au service de la République, 1871–1969" (thesis, D.E.A., Institut d'Études Politiques, Paris, 1988).

49 Marc Ferro, *Pétain* (Paris: Fayard, 1987).

50 Bernard Leguerre, "Les Dénaturalisés de Vichy, 1940–1944," *Vingtième Siècle* (October–December 1988).

51 Pierre Pierrard, *Juifs et Catholiques français* (Paris: Fayard, 1970).

52 Gérard Loiseux, *La Littérature française de la défaite et de la collaboration* (Paris: Publications de la Sorbonne, 1984); see also François Garçon, *De Blum à Pétain* (Paris: Éditions du Cerf, 1984).

53 Pascal Fouché, *L'Édition française sous l'occupation, 1940–1944* (Paris: Bibliothèque de Littérature Française Contemporaine de l'Université Paris-VII, 1987).

54 Stéphane Courtois, Denis Peschanski, and Adam Rayski, *Le Sang des étrangers* (Paris: Fayard, 1989).

55 Jacques Derville and Simon Wichné, *Drancy la Juive ou la deuxième Inquisition* (Cachan: Breger Frères, 1945); Georges Wellers, *L'Étoile jaune à l'heure de Vichy ou de Drancy à Auschwitz* (Paris: Fayard, 1973).

56 Pierre Laborie, *L'Opinion française sous Vichy* (Paris: Éditions du Seuil, 1990).

57 Henri de Lubac, *Résistance chrétienne à l'antisémitisme* (Paris: Fayard, 1988).

58 Georges Friedmann, *Fin du peuple juif?* (Paris: Gallimard, 1965), 8–11.

59 Catherine Nicault, "La France et le sionisme" (doctoral thesis, University of Paris-I, 1985); Michel Abitbol, *Les Deux Terres promises: Les Juifs de France et le sionisme* (Paris: Olivier Orban, 1989). And, more generally, Annie Kriegel, *Les Juifs et le monde moderne, essai sur les logiques d'émancipation* (Paris: Éditions du Seuil, 1977).

60 Dominique Schnapper, *Juifs et Israélites* (Paris: Gallimard, 1980), trans. by Arthur Goldhammer as *Jewish Identities in France: An Analysis of Contemporary French Jewry*

(Chicago: The University of Chicago Press, 1983); Chantal Benayoun, *Les Juifs et la politique* (Paris: Éditions du Centre National de Recherche Scientifique, 1984).

61 Marc Agi, *René Cassin, fantassin des droits de l'homme* (Paris: Plon, 1979), ch. 11.

62 Raymond Aron, *Essais sur la condition juive contemporaine* (Paris: Éditions de Fallois, 1989), 51. On this period, see Henry Weinberg, *The Myth of the Jew in France, 1967–1982* (Oakville: Mosaic Press, 1987).

63 Judith Friedlander, *Vilna on the Seine: Jewish Intellectuals in France since 1968* (New Haven: Yale University Press, 1990).

64 Henry Rousso, *Le Syndrome de Vichy: 1944–198...* (Paris: Éditions du Seuil, 1987), trans. by Arthur Goldhammer as *The Vichy Syndrome* (Cambridge, Mass.: Harvard University Press, 1992).

65 For example, the "revisionist" campaign associated with the name of Robert Faurisson, which erupted into public view in 1980 with the publication of his *Mémoire en défense*, and a devastating critique by Pierre Vidal-Naquet, "Un Eichmann de papier," *Esprit* (September 1980), repr. in *Les Juifs, la mémoire et le présent* (Paris: Maspero, 1981); and idem, *Les Assassins de la mémoire* (Paris: La Découverte, 1987), trans. by Jeffrey Mehlman as *The Assassins of Memory: Essays on the Denial of the Holocaust* (New York: Columbia University Press, 1993).

CHAPTER 11 PARIS-PROVINCE

1 Alexandre Pineu Duval, *Les Héritiers ou le naufrage* (Paris: J. N. Barba, 1820).

2 "*La province* does not exist by itself," Balzac wrote in 1841. See "La Femme de province," in "Province," in *Les Français peints par eux-mêmes* (Paris: L. Curmer, 1841), 1: 8.

3 Jean Émelina, "Comique et géographie au XVIIe siècle," in *Les Provinciaux sous Louis XIV,* 5th Marseilles Colloquium, *Revue de Marseille,* no. 101 (2d quarter 1975): 198, cited hereafter as *Les Provinciaux.*

4 Quoted in Isabelle Landy-Houillon, "Bussy-Rabutin et Mme de Sévigné, provinciaux malgré eux," in *Les Provinciaux,* 16. I have drawn on this fine article for material concerning the two exiles as well as for several remarks on the emergence of the notion of *province.*

5 Jean Serroy, "*Le Roman comique* et *Le Roman bourgeois,* romans provinciaux ou romans parisiens?" in *Les Provinciaux,* 164.

6 Quoted in Landy-Houillon, "Bussy-Rabutin et Mme de Sévigné," 11.

7 See Jean-Pierre Collinet, "René le Pays, précieux de province," in *Les Provinciaux,* 23.

8 "*Province*—said also of regions remote from the Court or the capital city. *Il est allé demeurer en Province. C'est un homme de Province, qui n'a pas l'air du beau monde.*" Antoine Furetière, *Dictionnaire universel,* 1690. Bear in mind that the notion of "province" also refers implicitly to ancient Rome, especially in the age of Cicero and Augustus.

9 See Émelina, "Comique," 198.

10 See Jacques Bailbé, "Quelques écrivains provinciaux de l'Académie de Caen," in *Les Provinciaux,* 30.

11   On the foregoing, see Fausta Garavini, "Les Gascons contre eux-mêmes?" in *Les Provinciaux*, 189 ff.

12   In 1654, Quinault mocked the provincial in *L'Amant indiscret*. *Les Précieuses ridicules* appeared in 1659. In 1662, Raymond Poisson coarsened the parody in *Le Baron de la Crasse*. A few years later Molière depicted *Monsieur de Pourceaugnac* and *La Comtesse d'Escarbagnas*.

13   See Émelina, "Comique," 198.

14   Balzac, deploring the absence of a word to define the Parisian nature, proposed *parisiénisme*. See "La Femme de province," 5.

15   Jean-Louis Vissière, "Le Provincial chez Dancourt, 1661–1725," in *Les Provinciaux*, 153.

16   For what follows, see ibid., 153, and Robert Mac Bride, "Le Provincial dans la comédie de Molière," in *Les Provinciaux*, 149–152.

17   See Vissière, "Le Provincial," 155.

18   Daniel Roche, "La Fondation des premières académies provinciales," in *Les Provinciaux*, 134; and the introduction by Robert Mandrou, ibid., 98.

19   Interpretation of Jean-Marie Goulemot, "Pouvoirs et savoirs provinciaux au XVIIIe siècle," *Critique*, 397–398 (June–July 1980): 603–613.

20   See Garavini, "Les Gascons contre eux-mêmes?" followed by a comment by Philippe Joutard on p. 195.

21   Serroy, "*Le Roman Comique*," 167.

22   Marivaux, *La Provinciale* (1761).

23   Hélène Himelfarb, "Versailles, fonctions et légendes," in Pierre Nora, ed., *Les Lieux de mémoire*, part 2,: *La Nation*, 2: 235 ff. Concerning the establishment of the court at Versailles, she writes that there was "no wrenching break—rich with future significance and implication—between Versailles and Paris."

24   Mandrou, comment, quoted in *Les Provinciaux*, 33.

25   Marc Fumaroli, "La Coupole," in Nora, *Les Lieux de mémoire*, part 2, *La Nation*, 3: 321–388, and "La Conversation," part 3, *Les Frances*, vol. 2, *Traditions* (Paris: Gallimard, 1992).

26   For a more extensive treatment see my *Le Miasme et la jonquille: L'odorat et l'imaginaire social, XVIIIe-XIXe siècles* (Paris: Aubier, 1982), 60–65, trans. as *The Foul and the Fragrant: Odor and the French Social Imagination* (Cambridge, Mass., Harvard University Press: 1986).

27   In 1943, Édouard Estaunié emphasized, in this connection, the importance of the publication of *La Nouvelle Héloïse*, the fundamental work in a series of provincial novels whose history he sought to trace in *Roman et province* (Paris: Robert Laffont, 1943), 55.

28   Even more revealing in this regard is the English case. The vogue for spas and the new yearning for gardens, seasides, lakes, and mountains are familiar features of England under the early Hanoverian monarchs, but these cannot be taken as signs of an exaltation of provincial life.

29   Daniel Roche, *Le Siècle des lumières en province: Académies et académiciens provinciaux* (Paris–The Hague: Mouton, 1979).

30 Goulemot, "Pouvoirs et savoirs provinciaux," 604.

31 Here I am relying primarily on the very detailed study by Marie-Vic Ozouf-Marignier, *La Formation des départements: La représentation du territoire français à la fin du XVIIIe siècle* (Paris: Éditions de l'École des Hautes Études en Sciences Sociales, 1989). See also the article "Département" by Mona Ozouf in *Dictionnaire critique de la Révolution française,* ed. François Furet and Mona Ozouf (Paris: Flammarion, 1988), trans. by Arthur Goldhammer as *A Critical Dictionary of the French Revolution* (Cambridge, Mass.: Harvard University Press, 1989).

32 Ozouf-Marignier, *La Formation,* 302.

33 Ted Margadant, "Urban Crisis, Bourgeois Ambition and Revolutionary Ideology in Provincial France, 1789–1790" (paper given at the 28th Annual Congress of the Society for French Historical Studies, 1982).

34 Quoted in Ozouf-Marignier, *La Formation,* 112.

35 On the evolution of the image of Paris during the Revolution, see the well-documented article by Raymonde Monnier, on which I have relied heavily: "L'Image de Paris de 1789 à 1794: Paris capitale de la Révolution," in *L'Image de la Révolution française,* ed. Michel Vovelle (Paris: Pergamon Press, 1989), 1: 73–82.

36 *Le Moniteur* (13 October 1789), 2: 50; quoted in Monnier, "L'Image," 74.

37 Mona Ozouf, "La Révolution française et la perception de l'espace national: fédérations, fédéralisme et stéréotypes régionaux," in *L'École de la France* (Paris: Gallimard, 1984), 37–38.

38 Ibid., 38.

39 See the well-documented article by Alan Forrest, "Le Fédéralisme et l'image de la Révolution parisienne," in Vovelle, *L'Image,* 1: 65–72; as well as Ozouf, "La Révolution," and the article "Fédéralisme" in Furet and Ozouf, ed., *Dictionnaire critique,* 85 ff.

40 Quoted in Ozouf, "La Révolution," 44.

41 Forrest, "Le Fédéralisme," 70.

42 On the role of Paris and its relations with the rest of revolutionary France, see Michel Vovelle, ed., *Paris et la Révolution* (Paris: Publications de la Sorbonne, 1989).

43 Which did not disappear, however. In 1801, Picard presented *La Petite Ville,* which enjoyed success for more than a century.

44 On the contrary; in 1817 *Le Nouveau Pourceaugnac* by Scribe portrayed the Limousin Rouffignac. Pineu Duval, however, took his inspiration from Molière when he created the character of Vernissac, a landowner with property near Pézeanas, in *La Vieille Tante ou les Collatéraux* (1811).

45 Pierre Durand (Eugène Guinot), *Physiologie du provincial à Paris* (Paris, 1842), illustrated by Gavarni.

46 Vicomte de Launay (pseudonym of Delphine Gay, Mme de Girardin), letter 9, May 18, 1844, in *Lettres parisiennes* (Paris: Mercure de France, 1986), 2: 259 and 264.

47 Especially the "sneak thieves" who robbed "simple-looking" provincials: see *Mémoires de Canler* (Paris: Mercure de France, 1968), 121.

48 Honoré de Balzac, *La Muse du département* (Paris: Le Club Français du Livre, 1963), 9: 50.

49 Vicomte de Launay (Delphine Gay), ibid., 265; subsequent quotations are from the same source.

50 Durand, *Physiologie du provincial*, 7.

51 Marcel Roncayolo, "Le Paysage du savant," in Nora, *Les Lieux de mémoire*, part 2, *La Nation*, 1: 487–529; Jean-Yves Guiomar, "Le *Tableau de la géographie de la France* de Vidal de La Blache," ibid., 569–599.

52 Jules Michelet, *Tableau de la France*, 156–157, quoted in Guiomar, "Le *Tableau*," 575.

53 See Marie-Noëlle Bourguet, "Race et folklore: L'image officielle de la France en 1800," *Annales E.S.C.* (July–August 1976): 802–824.

54 Mona Ozouf, "L'Invention de l'ethnographie française: Le questionnaire de l'Académie celtique," *Annales E.S.C.* (March–April 1981): 210–230.

55 See Catherine Bertho, "L'Invention de la Bretagne: Genèse sociale d'un stéréotype," "L'Identité," *Actes de la recherche en sciences sociales*, 35 (November 1980) and Denise Delouche, "Les Peintres de la Bretagne avant Gauguin" (thesis, University of Rennes II, 1978).

56 Jules Janin, "La Ville de Saint-Étienne," *Revue de Paris* (August 1829): 319–331, esp. 320–321; on this fabrication of imagery, see Jean Lorcin, "La Région de Saint-Étienne de la grande dépression à la second Guerre mondiale" (doctoral thesis, University of Paris I, 1987).

57 Jean-François Soulet, *Les Pyrénées au XIXe siècle* (Toulouse: Eché, 1986), 1: 13–46.

58 Nicole Mozet, *La Ville de province dans l'Oeuvre de Balzac* (CDU-SEDES, 1982). What follows is greatly indebted to this important work.

59 This, too, occurred in the capital: see the excellent book by Jeannine Guichardet, *Balzac "archéologue" de Paris* (Paris: SEDES, 1986), which contains some important observations on Balzac as "moral archaeologist."

60 A plan set forth in the introduction to *Béatrix*, the foreword to the *Comédie humaine*, and the first few pages of *La Recherche de l'Absolu*. In *Béatrix*, for example, Balzac wrote: "Anyone who wishes to travel as a moral archaeologist and observe men rather than rocks can find an image of the century of Louis XV in a village of Provence, one of the century of Louis XIV in the depths of Poitou, and of even earlier centuries in the wilds of Brittany." In effect, the provinces contained "a number of cities that have been wholly insulated from the social changes that have given the nineteenth century its physiognomy." Honoré de Balzac, *Béatrix*, in *La Comédie humaine* (Paris: Gallimard, 1976), 2: 637–638.

61 Mozet, *La Ville de province*, 23.

62 Balzac, *La Muse du département*, 46.

63 Mozet, *La Ville de province*, 145.

64 Stressed by Balzac, "La Femme de province," 8.

65 Mozet, *La Ville de province*, 15.

66 Balzac, *La Muse du département*, 48.

67 Theme developed by Michel Butor, "Les Parisiens en Province," *Répertoires III* (Paris: Éditions de Minuit, 1968), 169 ff.

68 See the definition of the "provincial woman" in *La Muse de département*, 50.

69 Mozet, *La Ville de province*, 37.

70   For example, Eugénie de Guérin or Fanny Odoard. See Rambert George, *Chronique intime d'une famille de notables au XIXe siècle*: Les Odoard de Mercurol (Lyons: Presse Universitaires de Lyon, 1981).

71   Gabrille Houbre, "Frères et soeurs dans la première moitié du XIXe siècle" (master's thesis, University of Tours, 1985).

72   Mozet, *La Ville de province*, 10.

73   Ibid., 34, n 1.

74   Anne Martin-Fugier has shown the importance of these in "La Formation des élites: Les 'conférences' sous la Restauration et la Monarchie de juillet," *Revue d'histoire moderne et contemporaine*, 36 (April–June 1989): 211–244.

75   On the important influx of young scholars, see Philippe Ariès, *Communications*, no. 35, and especially the thesis of Jean-Claude Caron, "La Jeunesse des écoles à Paris, 1815–1851" (University of Paris I, 1989), from which I take the following statistics: Between 1815 and 1848, Parisian faculties and schools conferred 66 percent of all doctorates in letters, 51.72 percent of all bachelor of science degrees, and 70 percent of pharmacy degrees. Paris was just as dominant in the realm of law. Under the July Monarchy, nearly two thirds of all law students studied in Paris; 55.4 percent of licentiates were conferred there, along with 58 percent of doctorates. Between 1815 and 1848, Paris trained two thirds of all French doctors. During the July Monarchy, 92 percent of Parisian students were born in the provinces.

76   These feelings were described by Victor Hugo in *Les Misérables*.

77   On the importance of such connections in the first half of the century, see Christophe Charle, *Les Hauts Fonctionnaires en France au XIXe siècle* (Paris: Gallimard, 1980).

78   In Jules Janin, *Le Chemin de traverse*, which relates the tribulations of the hero, who has come to Paris to seek his fortune.

79   As Balzac showed in *La Muse du département*.

80   Balzac, "La Femme de province," 1.

81   Guinot, *Physiologie du provincial*, 9.

82   Entry "Provincial," in *Grand dictionnaire universel du XIXe* siècle. Following Pascal Ory ("Le *Grand Dictionnaire* de Pierre Larousse, alphabet de la République," in Nora, *Les Lieux de mémoire*, part 1, *La République*, 245), I shall treat the several authors as one "collective writer."

83   Balzac places great stress on the provincial's reluctance to own up to boredom. The "provincial woman," he contends, is obsessed with a need to justify her condition: "She boasts about her rancid nuts and lard and extols her economical mousehole and her gray life with its monastic odor." See "La Femme de province," 4.

84   *La Muse du département*, 46.

85   Durand, *Physiologie du provincial*, 38.

86   *Grand dictionnaire*.

87   "Here," notes Balzac, "jokes, like the past six months' rent under the Empire, are almost always late." See "La Femme de province," 2.

88   Vicomte de Launay (Delphine Gay), letter of December 11, 1842, ibid., 2: 157–158, 163, and of October 12, 1844, 2: 316. My italics.

89   See Pierre Rosanvallon, *Le Moment Guizot* (Paris: Gallimard, 1985).

90   On this theme, see the excellent book by André-Jean Tudesq, *Les Grands Notables en France (1840–1849), étude historique d'une psychologie sociale,* 2 vols. (Paris: Presses Universitaires de France, 1964).

91   Taken from Alain Corbin, *Archaïsme et modernité en Limousin au XIXe siècle* (Paris: Marcel Rivière, 1975).

92   Worth noting are his wife's efforts not to disparage one of the most provincial small towns in the kingdom, which became, during the summer when Mme de Girardin came to visit, "a strange mélange of boulders and bankers, lawyers and waterfalls, wolves and plumed hats, wild boar and lace, flounces and snakes." See Vicomte de Launay (Delphine Gay), letter 5, November 24, 1838, ibid., 1: 345–346.

93   See Alexis de Tocqueville, *Souvenirs,* vol. 11 of *Oeuvres complètes* (Paris: Gallimard, 1964), 106 ff.

94   Historians have not sufficiently emphasized the importance of Parisian mockery of provincial "reds" in the aftermath of the June Days of 1848. Countless satirical poems, tales, and plays attacked the *saucialistes* and *clubistes* of the provinces. See, for example, those quoted in Francis Ronsin, "Du divorce et de la séparation de corps en France au XIXe siècle" (thesis, University of Paris VII, 1988), 2: 442 ff. (especially the one-act play *Un socialiste en province* by Louis Dubrel and *Le Club champenois* by Lefranc and Labiche); and Jean-Yves Mollier, *Michel et Calmann Lévy ou la naissance de l'édition moderne* (Paris: Calmann-Lévy, 1984), 143 ff.

95   A leitmotif in the letters of Delphine Gay, who nevertheless supported the July Monarchy. See Anne Martin-Fugier, "La Cour et la ville sous la Monarchie de juillet d'après les feuilletons mondains," *Revue historique,* 563 (July–September 1987): 107–133.

96   Tocqueville, *Oeuvres complètes,* 108.

97   These words of Jules Janin were widely reported by annoyed Limousin journalists.

98   Mme Lafarge, née Marie Cappelle, *Mémoires* (1841; 2d ed. Paris: Michel Lévy, 1867), 215.

99   Ibid., p. 220; subsequent quotations may be found on pp. 214, 219, and 222.

100   Louis Blanc, *Histoire de la Révolution de 1848* (Paris: Michel Lévy, 1870), 304–306.

101   To be sure, "peasantry" and "province" were not the same thing.

102   Ted Margadant, *French Peasants in Revolt* (Princeton: Princeton University Press, 1979).

103   From June 1848 to October 1877 the attitude of *la province* was shaped by a desire to defend universal suffrage and the legitimacy of governments based on it. As a result, *la province* was frequently wary of, and at times hostile to, the Paris populace.

104   Well described in Howard C. Payne, *The Police State of Louis Napoléon* (Seattle, 1966).

105   For example, Jean-Pierre Chaline, *Les Bourgeois de Rouen* (Paris: Presses de la Fondation Nationale des Sciences Politiques, 1982), 161–190.

106   Jeanne Gaillard, *Paris, la Ville, 1852–1870: L'urbanisme parisien à l'heure d'Haussmann— Des provinciaux aux Parisiens* (Paris: Champion, 1977), 246. The author investigates how provincials were integrated into Parisian society, emphasizing the importance of schools, restaurants, and hospitals.

107   See Pascal Ory, *Les Expositions universelles de Paris: Panorama raisonné* (Paris: Ramsay, 1982).

108 See Timothy J. Clark, *The Painting of Modern Life: Paris in the Art of Manet and His Followers* (New York: Knopf, 1984).

109 Hippolyte Taine, *Carnets de voyage: Notes sur la Province, 1863–1865* (Paris: Hachette, 1897), 169–170 and 231.

110 Late nineteenth century anthropology noted the superiority of the capital. Gustave Le Bon, for example, began a summary of various observations with the following: "In the most intelligent races, such as the Parisians.... " See Le Bon, "Recherches anatomiques sur les lois des variations du volume du cerveau et sur les relations avec l'intelligence," *Revue d'anthropologie*, 2d series, vol. 2 (1897), 27–104.

111 François Mauriac, *La Province* (Paris: Hachette, 1964), 8 and 95.

112 Ibid., 39. In 1943, Édouard Estaunié wrote that *la province* yields the "leisure of passion": "*En province,* unlike Paris, one has time to love and hate."

113 Michel Denis, *Les Royalistes de la Mayenne et le monde moderne—XIX–XXe siècles* (Paris: Klincksieck, 1977).

114 René Bazin, *En province* (Paris: Calmann-Lévy, 1896), 153.

115 This and subsequent quotations are from the article "Provincial," *Grand Dictionnaire*.

116 Ibid. Note the allusion to Carpentras, one of the comical provincial towns of an earlier period.

117 Alain Corbin, *Les Filles de noce* (Paris: Aubier, 1978), trans. by Alan Sheridan as *Women for Hire: Prostitution and Sexuality in France after 1850* (Cambridge, Mass: Harvard University Press, 1990).

118 Dominique Amrouche-Antoine, "Espéraza, 1870–1940: Une ville ouvrière chante," *Ethnologie française*, 14, no. 3 (July–September 1984): 234–249.

119 This and subsequent quotations are from the *Grand Dictionnaire*.

120. See Jean Dubois, *Le Vocabulaire politique et social en France de 1869 à 1872* (Paris: Larousse, 1962).

121 There was a rebirth of provincial consciousness in French literature in this period, as scholars have noted for some time now. See, for example, Pierre Moreau, "La Littérature et le retour à la province," *Actes du IVe Congrès international d'histoire littéraire moderne (1948)* (Paris: Boivin, 1950), 83–93. The author dates the beginning of this new consciousness as 1841, when the series *Les Français peints par eux-mêmes* began to appear. The pace accelerated in 1852, when Fortoul and Jean-Jacques Ampère detailed their plans for studying regional folklore. According to Moreau, the phenomenon culminated in 1902, when Gustave Lanson proposed a vast program for the study of provincial literary life in France and inaugurated a series of literary geographies.

122 J. F. Daniel, *Historique de la ville de Landerneau et du Léonais* (Brest, 1874), 20 and 21.

123 Ibid., 17.

124 The origins of "stir in Landerneau" phrase were explored in a number of articles. See Jehan Bazin, *Landerneau, ancienne capitale de la province de Léon* (Brest: Presse Libérale du Finistère, 1962), esp.130–131, "Du bruit à Landerneau," which contain a brief bibliography of the subject.

125 Bazin, *Landerneau*, 131 and 132.

126 S.v. "Landerneau," *Grand Dictionnaire,*

127 See Pierre Barral, *Les Agrariens français de Méline à Pisani* (Paris: Armand Colin, 1968).

128 On the fictional village of the 1950s and 1960s, see Rose-Marie Lagrave, *Le Village romanesque* (Le Paradou: Actes-Sud, 1980).

129 A pair of books by Msgr. Edmond Loutil (Pierre L'Ermite), *La Fille aux yeux ouverts* (Paris: Bonne Presse, 1946) and *La Fille aux yeux fermés* (Paris: Bonne Presse, 1946), is quite revealing in this regard. The eponymous heroine of the first book understands Paris to be a place of perdition, whereas maintaining one's roots in the provinces is seen as the way to salvation, happiness, and a moral life; the title character of the second book naturally confirms the thesis by going to Paris and losing her soul.

130 In the literary realm as well, twentieth-century Paris continued to transcend the regions and regional styles exemplified by Ernest Perochon, Eugène Le Roy, Louis Pergaud, Jean de La Varende, Alphonse de Chateaubriant, André Chamson, and Maurice Genevoix; it was Paris that distinguished Jean Giono from this cohort of lesser writers. Among the authors of the first half of the nineteenth century, Émile Souvestre deserves further study from this point of view. In 1870 the town library of Landerneau owned thirty-three of his works, making him by far the best represented author. (The Landerneau library catalogues are preserved at the Bibliothèque Nationale.)

131 Joris-Karl Huysmans, *En rade*.

132 According to Jocelyne George, "Les Maires dans le département du Var de 1800 à 1940" (thesis, University of Paris I, 1987), 601, it was during the 1880s, and thus shortly after the publication of *Tartarin de Tarascon*, that "a negative, satirical image of the southern rural mayor began to spread."

133 See Hubert Lussier, "Associations volontaires en milieu populaire: Les compagnies de sapeurs-pompiers français au XIXe siècle" (thesis, University of Paris I, 1985).

134 Odile Roynette, "Les Images du troupier dans la littérature du début de la IIIe République" (master's thesis, University of Paris I, 1988).

135 Anne Martin-Fugier, *La Place des bonnes: La domesticité féminine à Paris en 1900* (Paris: Grasset, 1979), 149–156.

136 See Jules Renard's *Journal*.

137 Daniel Halévy, *La Fin des notables* (Paris: Grasset, 1930), and Jean Lhomme, *La Grande Bourgeoisie au pouvoir, 1830–1880* (Paris: Presses Universitaires de France, 1960). More recently, Arno Mayer, *The Persistence of the Old Regime* (????), has strongly challenged the notion of an early collapse of the old elite.

138 Jean Estèbe, *Les Ministres de la République, 1871–1914* (Paris: Presses de la Fondation Nationale des Sciences Politiques, 1982), 51–78. The author notes, moreover, that many of the southern deputies were "humble folks," which allowed the old mockery to continue. On this, see Alphonse Daudet, *Numa Roumestan*.

139 See Gilles Le Béguec, "L'Entrée au Palais-Bourbon" (doctoral thesis, University of Paris X–Nanterre, June 1989). In *L'Opinion* (18 and 25 March 1911) Maurice Colrat published an article entitled "La prépondérance du Midi: Souillac, capitale de la France," in *L'Opinion* (March 18 and 25, 1911) to which Henri Poincaré and Henry Joly responded.

140 Christophe Charle, *Les Élites de la République, 1880–1900* (Paris: Fayard, 1987), 58–59.

141 See *La Vie politique et le personnel parlementaire dans les régions du Centre-Ouest sous la IIIᵉ République* (Limoges: Souny, 1987). This work was the proceedings of the preliminary session of the colloquium on the deputies of the Third Republic held by the Centre d'Histoire du XIXᵉ Siècle of the Universities of Paris I and IV, whose still preliminary findings inspire what follows.

142 Le Béguec, "L'Entrée," 475.

143 Charle, *Les Élites,* 58.

144 From the abundant literature on this subject, see especially Françoise Raison-Jourde, *La Colonie auvergnate de Paris au XIXᵉ siècle* (Paris: Bibliothèque Historique de la Ville de Paris, 1976), and the special issue of *Ethnologie française,* "Provinciaux et province à Paris," 10, no. 2 (April–June 1980). See my article, "Les Paysans de Paris," pp. 169–178 in this issue, for more on Limousins in Paris.

145 Gilles Le Béguec, "Caractères généraux du recrutement parlementaire dans les régions du Centre-Ouest durant la seconde moitié de la IIIᵉ République, Groupements de jeunesse et sociétés d'originaires," in *La Vie politique et le personnel parlementaire,* 43–50.

146 Mauriac, *La Province,* 86: "Paris is *la province* become aware of itself."

147 Jacques Fourcade, *La République de la province: Origine des partis, fresques et silhouettes* (Paris: Grasset, 1936), 123 and 128.

148 Jean Planchais, *Les Provinciaux ou la France sans Paris* (Paris: Éditions du Seuil, 1970), 9.

CHAPTER 12   THE SAINT-MALO——GENEVA LINE

1 This essay combines revised versions of two previous articles, "Les Deux France: Histoire d'une géographie," *Cahiers d'histoire,* 22 (1978): 393–415, and "Science sociale et découpage régional: Note sur deux débats 1820–1920," *Actes de la recherche en sciences sociales,* 35 (1980): 27–36.

2 On the correlation of demographic, economic, and anthropological data, see Emmanuel Le Roy Ladurie, "Un Théoricien du développement: Adolphe d'Angeville," introduction to a new edition of *Essai sur la statistique de la population française, considérée sous quelques-uns de ses rapports physiques et moraux,* by Adolphe d'Angeville (The Hague: Mouton, 1969), repr. in *Le Territoire de l'historien* (Paris: Gallimard, 1973), 349–392, and idem, "Nord-Sud," in Pierre Nora, ed., *Les Lieux de mémoire,* part 2, *La Nation* (Paris: Gallimard, 1986), 2: 117–140.

3 For two recent discussions of the pertinence of the Saint-Malo—Geneva line to an explanation of developmental inequalities within France, see Bernard Lepetit, "Sur les dénivellations de l'espace économique en France, dans les années 1830," *Annales E.S.C.* (1986), 1243–1272, and Marcel Roncayolo, "L'Aménagement du territoire XVIIIᵉ–XXᵉ siècle," in *Histoire de la France: L'espace français,* ed. André Burguière and Jacques Revel (Paris: Éditions du Seuil, 1989), 539–551, "Découvertes des inégalités géographiques."

4 Adrien Balbi, *Essai statistique sur le royaume de Portugal et d'Algarve comparé aux autres états de l'Europe* (Paris, 1822), 2: 134–149 (the table listing numbers of students in each

of the twenty-six academies is on p. 146). I wish to thank Catherine Duprat for pointing out the existence of this text and for answering my questions with patience and knowledge.

5   Dominique Julia and Paul Pressly, "La Population scolaire en 1789: Les extravagances statistiques du ministre Villemain," *Annales E.S.C.* (1975): 1516–1561.

6   A. M. Guerry, "Statistique comparée de l'état de l'instruction et du nombre des crimes," *Revue encyclopédique* (August 1832).

7   Konrad Malte-Brun, review of a book by A. Balbi, in *Journal des débats* (June 17, July 4, and July 21, 1823); the quoted passage occurs in the third part of the review.

8   Charles Dupin, *Effets de l'enseignement populaire de la lecture, de l'écriture et de l'arithmétique, de la géométrie et de la mécanique appliquées aux arts, sur les propriétés de la France,* initial lecture in the regular course in applied geometry and mechanics, delivered on November 30, 1826, at the Conservatoire des Arts et Métiers (Paris, 1826), 27. The map used to illustrate this lecture was reproduced in *Force productives et commerciales de la France* (Paris, 1827), plate 1, repr. by Marie-Madeleine Compère in Roger Chartier, Marie-Madeleine Compère, and Dominique Julia, *L'Éducation en France du XVIe au XVIIIe siècle* (Paris: SEDES, 1976), 17.

9   Dupin, *Effets de l'enseignement populaire,* 28.

10   Ibid., 34–35.

11   Edward W. Fox, *L'Autre France* (Paris: Flammarion, 1973).

12   Stendhal, *Vie de Henri Brulard,* published in its entirety for the first time by Henry Debraye (Paris: Champion, 1913), 1:. 240–241; text quoted and commented on by François Furet and Jacques Ozouf, "Trois siècles de métissage culturel," *Annales E.S.C.* (1977): 500–501.

13   Dupin, *Forces,* 2: 249–280.

14   See Jean-Claude Perrot, "L'Age d'or de la statistique régionale (an IV-1804)," *Annales historiques de la Révolution française* (April–June 1976): 215–276, and Marie-Noëlle Bourguet, *Déchiffrer la France: La statistique départementale à l'époque napoléonienne* (Paris: Éditions des Archives Contemporaines, 1988).

15   J. Peuchet, *Statistique élémentaire de la France* (Paris, 1805), and, with P. Chanlaire, *Description topographique et statistique de la France* (Paris, 1810).

16   Jean-Antoine Chaptal, *De l'industrie française* (Paris, 1819). Here are two examples of the mode of description used: "Everything was returned to cultivation, and harvests multiplied tenfold. Examples of this kind can be found in *all* parts of France" (p. 153); and "the number of livestock is insufficient *everywhere,* except for two or three provinces" (p. 154; my italics).

17   On the tension between the particular and the uniform in prefectural statistics, see Bourguet, "Passion taxinomique," in *Déchiffrer la France,* 238–253.

18   Dupin, *Forces,* 2: 252.

19   Ibid., 263.

20   Ibid., 273–274.

21   Ibid., 1: 1.

22   Ibid., 2: 267.

23 Ibid., 1: 1.

24 On this essential document, see Michelle Perrot, "Délinquance et système pénitentiaire en France au XIXe siècle," *Annales E.S.C.* (1975): 67–91.

25 The full title of this "broadsheet" (in the strict typographic sense), which sold for six francs (or eight if glued to canvas), tells us a great deal about both the elements of statistics and its audience: *La Monarchie Française comparée aux principaux États du Monde ou Essai sur la statistique de la France considérée sous les rapports géographiques, moral et politique, offrant, dans un seul Tableau, le maximum, le minimum et le terme moyen de sa population, de la richesse, de l'industrie, du commerce, de l'instruction et de la moralité de ses habitants, comparés à leurs corrélatifs dans plusieurs pays de l'Ancien et du Nouveau Monde; à l'usage des hommes d'état, des administrateurs, des banquiers, des négociants, des voyageurs, et spécialement de MM. les pairs de France et de MM. les députés* (Paris, 1828).

26 A. M. Guerry, *Essai sur la statistique morale de la France* (Paris, 1833); an excerpt from this work had been published in the *Revue encyclopédique* in August 1832.

27 Ibid., 9.

28 Dupin, *Forces*, 1: 1.

29 Marie-Vic Ozouf-Marignier, *La Formation des départements: La représentation du territoire français à la fin du XVIIIe siècle* (Paris: Éditions de l'École des Hautes Études en Sciences Sociales, 1989).

30 Guerry, *Essai sur la statistique morale*, 42.

31 Ibid., 47.

32 Benoiston de Chateauneuf, *De la colonisation des condamnés* (Paris, 1827), 3–4.

33 P. Bigot de Morogues, *De la misère des ouvriers et de la marche à suivre pour y remédier* (Paris, 1832).

34 Villeneuve-Bargemont, *Économie politique chrétienne ou recherches sur la nature et les causes du paupérisme en France et en Europe* (Paris, 1834).

35 Bigot de Morogues, *De la misère*, 120.

36 Villeneuve-Bargemont, *Économie politique*, 2: 46.

37 Ibid., 10.

38 Ibid., 23.

39 Adolphe d'Angeville, *Essai sur la statistique de la population française, considérée sous quelques-uns de ses rapports physiques et moraux* (Bourg-en-Bresse, 1836).

40 Ibid., 15–16.

41 Ibid., 125–126.

42 Ibid., 124.

43 François Quesnay, article "Fermiers (Econ. polit.)," January 1756, in *François Quesnay et la physiocratie* (Paris, 1958), 2: 428.

44 Ibid., article "Grains," November 1757, 2: 461.

45 De Butré, "Apologie pour la Science Économique sur la distinction entre la grande et la petite culture contre les critiques de M. de F.," *Ephémérides du Citoyen* (1769), vols. 9, 10, 11 (here, 10: 8–9). I wish to thank Jean-Claude Perrot for pointing this reference out to me.

46 Quesnay, "Grains," 2: 461.

47   De Butré, "Apologie," 9: 21.

48   Le Trosne, *La Liberté du commerce des grains toujours utile et jamais nuisible* (1765), 28–29.

49   De Butré, "Apologie," 9: 21.

50   Ibid., 10: 133–134.

51   Ibid., 10: 78, 88, and 119.

52   Jean-Claude Perrot, *Genèse d'une ville moderne: Caen au XVIIIᵉ siècle* (Paris–The Hague: Mouton, 1975), 1: 237–240.

53   De Butré, "Apologie," 10: 80–81.

54   Chaptal, *De l'industrie française*, 140.

55   Moheau, *Recherches et considérations sur la population de la France* (Paris, 1778), 67–69.

56   Des Pommelles, *Tableau de la population de toutes les provinces de France* (Paris, 1789), 55.

57   Messance, *Nouvelles recherches sur la population de la France* (Lyons, 1788), 43.

58   Ibid., 48.

59   Des Pommelles, *Tableau de la population*, 56.

60   Messance, *Nouvelles recherches*, 87.

61   Des Pommelles, *Tableau de la population*, 63.

62   Moheau, *Recherches*, 139.

63   Ibid., 191.

64   Ibid., 202.

65   Messance, *Nouvelles recherches*, 87.

66   J.-J. Expilly, *Tableau de la population de la France* (Paris, 1780), 28.

67   Ibid.

68   Moheau, *Recherches*, 118.

69   Numa Broc, *La Géographie des Philosophes: Géographes et voyageurs français au XVIIIᵉ siècle* (Paris, 1975), 406–419.

70   E. Beguillet and C. Courtepée, introduction to *Description générale particulière du duché de Bourgogne* (Dijon, 1774–1785), quoted in Broc, *La Géographie*, 415.

71   M. Darluc, *Histoire naturelle de la Provence* (Avignon, 1782–1786), vii, quoted in Broc, *La Géographie*, 407.

72   Daniel Roche, *Le Siècle des Lumières en Province: Académies et académiciens provinciaux (1680–1789)* (Paris–The Hague: Mouton, 1978), ch. 6.

73   Blandine Barret-Kriegel, *Les Académies de l'histoire* (Paris, 1988), 82–94, which extends the work of M. Lecomte, "Les Bénédictins et l'histoire des provinces," *Revue Mabillon* (1927–1928).

74   J.-C. Perrot, *Genèse d'une ville moderne*, vol. 2, appendix 28, p. 1028, provides a partial catalog of the literature on the Paris-*province* pair, with 21 titles published between 1737 and 1793. See Roger Chartier, *Les Origines culturelles de la Révolution française* (Paris: Éditions du Seuil, 1990), 220–225, trans. by Lydia Cochrane as *The Cultural Origins of the French Revolution* (Durham: Duke University Press, 1991).

75   Guerry, *Essai*, 65.

76 The following text, one among many, is taken from Roche, *Le Siècle des Lumières en Province*. It is from a letter by the perpetual secretary of the Académie of Marseilles to the members of the Académie Française dated January 12, 1726: "You, Sirs, have already secured good taste within the heart of the kingdom, and all that remains is to provide for it on the frontier."

77 Jean-Pierre Peter, "Une Enquête de la Société royale de médecine (1774–1794): Malades et maladies à la fin du XVIIIe siècle," *Annales E.S.C.* (1967): 711–751, and J. C. Perrot, "L'Age d'or de la statistique régionale," 222.

78 J.-C. Perrot, *Genèse d'une ville moderne*, 2: 892, n 168.

79 Albert Demangeon, *La Picardie et les régions voisines, Artois-Cambrésis-Beauvaisis* (Paris, 1905); Raoul Blanchard, *La Flandre: Étude géographique de la plaine flamande en France, Belgique et Hollande* (Lille, 1906); Camille Vallaux, *La Basse Bretagne: Étude de géographie humaine* (Paris, 1907); Jules Sion, *Les Paysans de la Normandie orientale: Pays de Caux, Bray, Vexin normand, vallée de la Seine* (Paris, 1909).

80 Blanchard, *La Flandre*, 17.

81 Demangeon, 2–3.

82 Sion, *Les Paysans de la Normandie orientale*, 12.

83 Demangeon, *La Picardie*, 455–456.

84 Sion, *Les Paysans de la Normandie orientale*, 12.

85 Blanchard, *La Flandre*, 117.

86 François Simiand in *L'Année sociologique*, vol. 11 (1906–1909): 723–732.

87 Which explains Simiand's praise for Vacher's *Le Berry*, published in 1908, which stays within the legitimate domain of geography by confining its attention to "truly" geographical facts such as the soil model, hydrography, and climate.

88 Maximilien Sorre, *Les Pyrénées méditerranéennes: Étude de géographie biologique* (Paris, 1913).

89 Lucien Febvre, *La Terre et l'évolution humaine: Introduction géographique à l'histoire* (Paris, 1922; repr. Paris: Albin Michel, 1970), 29.

90 Sorre, *Les Pyrénées méditerranéennes*, 2.

91 Ibid., 17.

92 Ibid., 12–13.

93 Febvre, *La Terre et l'évolution humaine*, 92–93.

94 Lucien Febvre, *Philippe II et la Franche-Comté: Étude d'histoire politique, religieuse et sociale* (Paris, 1912; repr. Paris: Flammarion, 1970), 11.

95 Victor Karady, "Durkheim, les sciences sociales et l'Université: Bilan d'un semi-échec," *Revue française de sociologie*, 15 (1976): 267–311, and idem, "Stratégies de réussite et modes de faire-valoir de la sociologie chez les durkheimiens," *Revue française de sociologie*, 20 (1979): 49–82.

96 Karady, "Durkheim," 305.

97 On the relation between the preconstruction of a prejudice and a scientific formulation, see Pierre Bourdieu, "Le Nord et le Midi: Contribution à une analyse de l'effet Montesquieu," *Actes de la recherche en sciences sociales*, 35 (1980): 21–25.

CHAPTER 13   GENERATION

1   Here it will suffice to mention only a few key works with extensive bibliographical notes, starting with the article "Génération" in the *Encyclopoedia Universalis* by Philippe Parrot and S. N. Eisenstadt, the latter being the author of the classic *From Generation to Generation* (Glencoe, Il.: The Free Press, 1956), and Hans Jaeger, "Generations in History: Reflections on a Controversial Concept," *History and Theory*, 2 (1978): 273–292, which sheds light on the historiography of the notion. See also Alan B. Spitzer, "The Historical Problem of Generations," *American Historical Review*, 78 (December 1973): 1353–1385, which investigates some implications of the notion and surveys the abundant American sociological bibliography. Also Claudine Attias-Donfut, *Sociologie des générations* (Paris: Presses Universitaires de France, 1988), and Pierre Favre, "De la question sociologique des générations et de la difficulté à la résoudre dans le cas de la France," ch. 8 of *Générations et politique*, ed. Jean Crète and Pierre Favre (Paris: Economica, 1989), a revised version of a paper read to the colloquium "Générations et changements politiques" at the Université Laval in Quebec, June 1984, and his introduction, "Génération: Un concept pour les sciences sociales?," to the round table organized by Annick Percheron at the Paris convention of the Association Française de Science Politique, Génération et Politique, October 22–24, 1981. A bibliography of 277 books and articles was assembled for the occasion. Current interest in the topic in connection with the history of contemporary France is evident from the special issue "Les Générations" of *Vingtième siècle, revue d'histoire*, 22 (April–June 1989). The use of the notion in psychology, ethnology, economics, and demographics will be apparent from succeeding notes.

2   Margaret Mead, *Culture and Commitment: A Study of the Generation Gap* (London, 1970).

3   In particular, Antoine Prost, "Quoi de neuf sur le mai français?" *Le Mouvement social*, 143 (April–June 1988): 81–89, devoted to "memoirs and histories of 1968," surveys the topic.

4   Jean-Pierre Rioux, "A propos des célébrations décennales du Mai français," *Vingtième siècle, revue d'histoire*, 23 (July–September 1989): 49–58, a rich analysis that I follow closely here.

5   Jean-Claude Guillebaud, *Les Années orphelines (1968–1978)* (Paris: Éditions du Seuil, 1978).

6   Jacques Paugam, *Génération perdue* (Paris: Robert Laffont, 1977), which contains interviews with F. Lévy, J.-P. Dollé, C. Jambet, J.-M. Benoist, M. Lebris, J.-E. Hallier, M. Butel, J.-P. Faye, B. Kouchner, B.-H. Lévy, M. Halter, P. Sollers, A. de Gaudemar.

7   During which France was ruled by a rightist coalition government under a Socialist president—TRANS.

8   Serge July, "La Révolution en creux," *Libération* (May 27, 1988).

9   Hervé Hamon and Patrick Rotman, *Génération*, 2 vols. (Paris: Éditions du Seuil, 1987–1988).

10   The comparison is sketched out in *Espaces-Temps*, no. 38–39, 1988: "Concevoir la Révolution, 89, 68, confrontations."

10 Nicolas Restif de la Bretonne, *Les Nuits de Paris (1789–1794)*, ed. Patrice Boussel (Paris: Union Générale de l'Édition, 1963), 193.

11 As a result, in fact, of renewed interest in the subject of generations: see Jean Nicolas, "Génération 1789," *L'Histoire*, 123 (June 1989): 28–34.

12 See Mona Ozouf, article "Fraternité," in *Dictionnaire critique de la Révolution française*, ed. François Furet and Mona Ozouf (Paris: Flammarion, 1988), 731–740; trans. by Arthur Goldhammer as *A Critical Dictionary of the French Revolution* (Cambridge, Mass.: Harvard University Press, 1989); and, subsequent to this, Antoine de Baecque, "La Révolution française et les âges de la vie," in *Age et politique*, by Annick Percheron and René Rémond (Paris: Economica, 1991), ch. 2, 39–59.

13 Jefferson gave the clearest formulation of the right of generations to determine their own fate: "The dead have no rights. They are nothing; and nothing cannot own something." Letter to Samuel Kerchevol, July 1816, *Writings* (New York: Literary Classics, 1984), 1402. And this: "We may consider each generation as a distinct nation, with a right, by the will of its majority, to bind themselves, but none to bind the succeeding generation more than the inhabitants of another country." Letter to John Wayles Eppes, June 24, 1813, ibid., 1280. See Patrick Thierry, "De la Révolution américaine à la Révolution française," *Critique* (June–July 1987). Jefferson came to the conclusion that all laws should be submitted to a fresh vote every nineteen years.

14 What is interesting about this little-known text, taken from a French edition, whose existence was pointed out to me by Marcel Gauchet, is its awareness of the practical consequences of the transition from a natural definition of generation to a social and political one, which "includes all individuals who are more than twenty years old at the time in question" and which will remain in power for fourteen to twenty-one years, "that is, until the number of minors coming of age is greater than the number of survivors of the first class."

15 Text in Marcel Gauchet, *La Révolution des droits de l'homme* (Paris: Gallimard, 1989), 328. On p. 193 he also cites a letter written by Condorcet on August 30, 1789, congratulating Comte Mathieu de Montmorency on having this idea. Montmorency was one of those political newcomers in whom Condorcet was amazed to discover "a young man bred for war giving the peaceful rights of man an extent that would have astonished philosophers twenty years ago." Condorcet, *Oeuvres*, vol. 9.

16 *Le Moniteur*, 16: 215.

17 See Mona Ozouf, article "Régénération," *Dictionnaire critique de la Révolution française*, 821–831, and idem, *L'Homme régénéré* (Paris: Gallimard, 1989). See also Antoine de Baecque, "Le Peuple briseur de chaînes, fracture historique et mutations de l'homme dans l'imaginaire politique au début de la Révolution française," *Révolte et société*, Actes du IVe colloque d'histoire au présent, Paris, May 1988 (Paris: Publications de la Sorbonne, February 1989), 1: 211–217; and idem, "L'Homme nouveau est arrivé: L'image de la régénération des Français dans la presse patriotique des débuts de la Révolution," *Dix-huitième Siècle* (1988).

18 Marie-Hélène Parinaud, "Membres des assemblées et volontaires nationaux (1789–1792): Contribution à l'étude de l'effet de génération dans la Révolution

française" 2 vols. (thesis, École des Hautes Etudes en Sciences Sociales, 1985; mimeograph).

19   Edmund Burke, *Reflections on the Revolution in France* (1790; repr. New York: Bobbs-Merril, 1955); Thomas Paine, *The Rights of Man* (2 parts, 1791, 1792; repr. in *Common Sense, the Rights of Man, and Other Essential Writings of Thomas Paine* [N.Y.: New American Library, 1984]). On the controversy, see Robert B. Dishman, *Burke and Paine, on Revolution and the Rights of Man* (New York, 1971), and, more recently, Marilyn Butler, *Burke, Paine, Godwin and the Revolution Controversy* (Cambridge, England: Cambridge University Press, 1984; 2d ed., 1988). See also Judith Schlanger, "Les Débats sur la signification du passé à la fin du XVIIIᵉ siècle," in *Le Préromantisme, hypothèque ou hypothèse?*, Colloquium at Clermont-Ferrand, June 29–30, 1972 (Paris: Klincksieck, 1975).

20   See in particular "Le Mystère 68," proceedings of a round table organized by *Le Débat*, 50 and 51 (May–August and September–October 1988).

21   As Herve Le Bras maintains, for example. See ibid.

22   For example, Didier Anzieu, *Les Idées de mai* (Paris: Fayard, 1969); André Stéphane, *L'Univers contestationnaire* (Paris: Payot, 1969); Gérard Mendel, *La Crise de générations* (Paris: Payot, 1969).

23   Pierre Viansson-Ponté, "La Nouvelle Génération perdue," *Le Monde* (September 6, 1967; repr. in *Couleur du temps qui passe*, vol. 2 [Paris: Stock, 1979]), 247. This chronicle inspired the November–December 1976 television programs of Jacques Paugam, and Viansson-Ponté contributed the preface to Paugam's *Génération perdue*, a book with the subtitle "Ceux qui avaient vingt ans en 1968? Ceux qui avaient vingt ans à la fin de la guerre d'Algérie? Ou ni les uns ni les autres? [Twenty years old in 1968? Twenty years old at the end of the Algerian War? Or neither?]: "Let's not quibble about whether or not you form a generation. That is secondary. But lost you are! Lost with keys in your pockets: your identity, your credentials, your assurance."

24   Eric Vigne, "Des Générations 68?" *Le Débat*, 51 (September–October 1988): 157–161.

25   Auguste Comte was the first to reflect on the importance of the rhythm of generational replacement for the evolution of society and the progress of the human spirit. See his *Cours de philosophie positive* (Paris, 1839), vol. 4, 51st lesson.

26   Karl Mannheim, "The Problem of Generations," in *Essays in the Sociology of Knowledge* (London: Routledge and Kegan Paul, 1959), 278–322, trans. of "Das Problem der Generationen" in *Kölner Viertel Jahrshefte für Soziologie, 1928*.

27   François Mentré, *Les Générations sociales* (Paris: Bossard, 1920).

28   Henri Peyre, *Les Générations littéraires* (Paris: Goivin et Cie, 1948).

29   Julián Marías, *El método histórico de las generaciones* (Madrid: Revista de Occidente, 1949).

30   Yves Renouard, "La Notion de génération en histoire," *Revue historique* (1953): 1–23, repr. in *Études d'histoire médiévale*, 2 vols. (Paris: Sevpen, 1968).

31   Albert Thibaudet, *Histoire de la littérature française de 1789 à nos jours* (Paris: Stock, 1936). Thibaudet devoted one of his columns to the criticism of François Mentré: see *La Nouvelle Revue française* (May 1, 1921), repr. in *Réflexions sur la littérature* (Paris: Gallimard, 1938).

32   Marc Bloch, *Apologie pour l'histoire ou métier d'historien* (Paris: Armand Colin, 1961), 94.

33   Lucien Febvre, "Générations," *Revue de synthèse historique* (June 1920).

34   See in particular Annie Kriegel's analyses of generations of Communists in *Les Communistes français, essai d'ethnographie politique* (Paris: Éditions du Seuil, 1968). And, most recently, Jean-Pierre Rioux and Jean-François Sirinelli, ed., *La Guerre d'Algérie et les intellectuels français*, Cahiers de l'IHTP, no. 10 (November 1988).

35   See especially Jean-François Sirinelli, *Génération intellectuelle: Khâgneux et normaliens dans l'entre-deux-guerres* (Paris: Fayard, 1988), and idem, ed., *Générations intellectuelles*, Cahiers de l'IHTP, no. 6 (November 1987).

36   See, for example, Raoul Girardet, "Remarques perplexes sur le concept de génération et les virtualités de son bon usage," paper read to the First Congress of the Association Française de Science Politique, October 22–24, 1981, exp. and repr. in "Du concept de génération à la notion de contemporanéité," *Revue d'histoire moderne et contemporaine*, 30 (April–June 1983): 257–270; and Jacques Le Goff: "I remain wary of the use of the notion of generation in history, for what is a generation and when can we speak of one?" in Pierre Nora, ed., *Essais d'ego-histoire* (Paris: Gallimard, 1987), 238.

37   See the views of the semiotician Eric Landowski, "Continuité et discontinuité: Vivre la génération," paper read to First Congress of the Association Française de Science Politique, October 22–24, 1981, pr. in *La Société réfléchie* (Paris: Éditions du Seuil, 1989), 57–73.

38   Martin Heidegger, *Sein und Zeit*, (1927); the quotation is from the French trans. by Jean-François Vezin, *Etre et temps* (Paris: Gallimard, 1986), 449. The passage is interesting in part because it refers to Wilhelm Dilthey, the first thinker to exploit the idea historically.

39   See Henri Mendras, *La Seconde Révolution française* (Paris: Gallimard, 1988).

40   See Hervé Le Bras, "L'Interminable Adolescence ou les ruses de la famille," and André Béjin, "De l'adolescence à la post-adolescence, les années indécises" both part of "Entrer dans la vie aujourd'hui," *Le Débat*, 25 (May 1983).

41   See Pierre Nora, "Le Retour de l'événement," in vol. 1 of *Faire de l'histoire*, ed. Jacques Le Goff and Pierre Nora (Paris: Gallimard, 1974).

42   This is the thesis of the important article by Annie Kriegel, "Le Concept politique de génération: Apogée et déclin," *Commentaire*, 7 (autumn 1979).

43   Paul Yonnet, "Faits de génération, effets de génération," unpublished.

44   Michel Philibert, *L'Échelle des âges* (Paris: Éditions du Seuil, 1968); Philippe Ariès, "Les Ages de la vie," *Contrepoint*, 1 (May 1970): 23–30, and idem, article "Generazioni" in the *Encyclopedia Einaudi;* John Gillis, *Youth and History* (New York, 1974); Kenneth Keniston, "Youth: A 'New' Stage of Life," *American Scholar*, 39 (autumn 1970); *Rapport au temps et fossé des générations*, proceedings of a colloquium, CNRS/Association des FED'ages, Gif-sur-Yvette, November 29–30, 1979. Nothing essential will be left out thanks to the Proceedings of the International Colloquium on the History of Childhood and Youth, Athens, October 1–5, 1984, *Archives historiques de la jeunesse grecque*, no. 6 (Athens, 1986), with a substantial bibliography. See also Olivier Galland, *Les Jeunes*

(Paris: La Découverte, 1985), and the results of two colloquia held in 1985, the International Year of Youth: Classes d'âge et sociétés de jeunesse, Le Creusot, May 30–June 1, 1985, synopsis in *Bulletin de la Société française d'ethnologie,* 12 (1986), and *Proceedings* of the Colloquium Les Jeunes et les autres, contribution des sciences de l'homme à la question des jeunes, Ministère de la Recherche et de la Technologie, December 9–10, 1985, introduction by Michelle Perrot and Annick Percheron, 2 vols. (Vaucresson: CRIV, 1986), See also Gérard Mauger, *Tableau des recherches sur les jeunes en France* (report PIRTTEM-CNRS, 1988).

45 See Pierre Bourdieu, "La 'jeunesse' n'est qu'un mot," in *Questions de sociologie* (Paris: Éditions de Minuit, 1980), 143–154.

46 Robert's dictionary attributes the word to Béranger in 1825, but Fazy, *De la géronto-cratie ou abus de la sagesse des vieillards dans le gouvernement de la France* (Paris, 1928), writes of "this new word, which I have put together out of the language of the Greeks."

47 Jean-Yves Tadié, "Le Roman de génération," in *Le Roman au XXe siècle* (Paris: Belfond, 1990), 99–102.

48 See Dominique Strauss-Kahn, *Économie de la famille et accumulation patrimoniale* (Paris: Éditions Cujas, 1977); *Accumulation et répartition des patrimoines,* Proceedings of the International Colloquium of the CNRS, July 5–7, 1978 (Paris: Economica, 1982); Claude Thelot, *Tel père, tel fils? Position sociale et origine familiale* (Paris: Dunod, 1982); and Denis Kessler and André Masson, ed., *Cycles de vie et générations* (Paris: Economica, 1985). See also Xavier Gaullier, "La Mutation des âges," *Le Débat,* 61 (September–October 1990).

49 See in particular Antoine Prost, "Jeunesse et société dans l'entre-deux-guerres," *Vingtième Siècle, revue d'histoire,* 13 (January–March 1987): 35–43.

50 The phenomenon was immediately reflected in the work of economists and demographers: Alfred Sauvy, *La Montée des jeunes* (Paris: Calmann-Lévy, 1959); historians: Philippe Ariès, *L'Enfant et la vie familiale sous l'Ancien Régime* (Paris: Plon, 1960); sociologists: Edgar Morin, *L'Esprit du temps* (Paris: Plon, 1962); "Salut les copains," *Le Monde* (July 6–8, 1963); Georges Lapassade, *L'Entrée dans la vie* (Paris: Éditions de Minuit, 1963). A chronology of "the adventure of ideas" prepared for *Le Débat,* 50 (May–August 1988), by Anne Simonin and published in expanded book form as *Les Idées en France, 1945–1988, une chronologie* (Paris: Folio-Histoire, 1989), offers a rich series of convergent landmarks for this period.

51 See Paul Yonnet, "Rock, pop, punk, masques et vertiges du peuple adolescent," and "L'Esthétique rock," *Le Débat,* 25 and 40, repr. in *Jeux, modes et masses* (Paris: Gallimard, 1986).

52 Witness this note by a historian of the period, Capefigue, in *Le Gouvernement de juillet, les partis et les hommes politiques, 1830–1835* (Paris, 1835), 1: 22: "It was in 1818 that the effect of Germany was first felt in France: bold thoughts of German unity resounded, and the youth of our schools fraternized with the ardent generation that Schiller had favored with so many of his plays and which had been organized as a military government by mass conscription in 1812 and 1813."

53 On the romantic generation the most important recent book is Alan B. Spitzer, *The French Generation of 1820* (Princeton: Princeton University Press, 1987). The conclusion contains a comparison with contemporary German student movements, in particular the Burschenschaften, and there is a bibliography (p. 267). Spitzer's judgment indirectly corroborates the temperate views of Henri Brunschwig, *La Crise de l'état prussien à la fin du XVIIIe siècle et la genèse de la mentalité romantique* (Paris: Presses Universitaires de France, 1947), 104 and 270.

Certain aspects of the generational comparison of the two countries that deserve systematic treatment can be found in Claude Digeon, *La Crise allemande de la pensée française, 1870–1914* (Paris: Presses Universitaires de France, 1959), which is based on a generational analysis, and Robert Wohl, *The Generation of 1914* (Cambridge, Mass.: Harvard University Press, 1980), with successive chapters on France and Germany. Published after this article was written is Jean-Claude Caron, *Générations romantiques: Les étudiants de Paris et le quartier Latin (1814–1851)* (Paris: Armand Colin, 1991).

54 Augustin Challamel, *Souvenirs d'un hugolâtre, portrait d'une génération* (Paris, 1885): "For the past twenty years or more orators have been likely to utter these words over the grave of this or that illustrious personage: 'He belonged to the vibrant, valiant generation of 1830..'.. No one will deny it: in politics, in literature, in science, in art, the generation of 1830, including all or nearly all the French alive at that time, has done splendid work from the beginning of this century and into its second half."

55 Sébastien Charléty, *La Monarchie de juillet*, vol. 5 of *L'Histoire de France contemporaine*, ed. Ernest Lavisse (1921), 47.

56 The formula deserves to be put back in its context: "Three ingredients went to make up the life that was open to young people at the time: behind them, a past forever destroyed, still squirming on its ruins, with all the fossils of centuries of absolutism; before them, the dawn along a vast horizon, the first glimmers of the future; and between those two worlds...something like the ocean that separates the old continent from the young America, a *je ne sais quoi* of fluctuation and drift, a stormy sea in which many a ship went down and across which, in the distance, passed from time to time a white sail or a ship spewing thick clouds of steam; in a word, the present century, standing between the past and the future, neither the one nor the other yet resembling both, so that with every step you never knew whether you were walking on new growth or old debris." Alfred de Musset, *La Confession d'un enfant du siècle*. Remember that Musset, who was born in 1810, was ten years younger than most of the romantic generation.

57 Sainte-Beuve, born in 1804, made several attempts to arrange his portraits by generation. Severe toward his contemporaries, he noted everything that linked him to them by their twentieth year: "Every literary generation dates from itself.... For the generation that is twenty today, the melancholy of Olympio will produce the effect of Lamartine's 'lake.' It takes a good deal of firmness and breadth of mind for judgment to triumph over such impressions" (*Notes et pensées*, no. 187). For additional references, see the short chapter on Sainte-Beuve in Peyre, *Les Générations littéraires*, 53–58.

58 Théodore Jouffroy, *Comment les dogmes finissent*, quoted in S. Charléty, *La Restauration*, vol. 4 of *L'Histoire de France contemporaine*, ed. Ernest Lavisse, ch. 3, p. 197.

59 Théophile Gautier, *Histoire du romantisme* (Paris, 1872), 11. Recall that Gautier, born in 1811, represents, like Musset, the disillusionment of the post-romantics. See Paul Bénichou, *Le Sacre de l'écrivain* (Paris: José Corti, 1973), 452–462, and *Les Mages romantiques* (Paris: Gallimard, 1988).

60 Alfred de Vigny, *Discours de réception à l'Académie française,* January 26, 1864, in *Oeuvres* (Paris: Gallimard, 1948), 1: 968. See Bénichou, *Le Sacre,* 288 ff.

61 Letter from Lafayette to James Monroe, July 20, 1820, in Gilbert de La Fayette, *Mémoires, correspondance et manuscrits du général La Fayette* (Paris, 1837–1838), 1: 93, quoted in Spitzer, *The French Generation of 1820,* 4.

62 *Archives parlementaires,* 2d series, 35: 466.

63 Gautier, *Histoire du romantisme,* 9.

64 See the enlightening article by Louis Mazoyer, "Catégories d'âge et groupes sociaux, les jeunes générations françaises de 1830," *Annales d'histoire économique et sociale,* 53 (September 1938): 385–419.

65 Yves Vadé, *L'Enchantement littéraire: Écriture et magie de Chateaubriand à Rimbaud* (Paris: Gallimard, 1990).

66 Marcel Gauchet, "Les *Lettres sur l'histoire de France* d'Augustin Thierry," in Pierre Nora, ed., *Les Lieux de mémoire,* part 2, *La Nation,* 1: 266.

67 Delecluze, "De la politesse en 1832," in *Le Livre des Cent-un* (Paris, no date), 13: 107.

68 Honoré de Balzac: "Youth will explode like the boiler of a steam engine," *Z. Marcas,* in *La Comédie humaine* (Paris: Gallimard, 1978), 8: 847.

69 Alfred de Musset, *Mélanges de littérature et de critique* (May 23, 1831).

70 See Edmond Goblot, *La Barrière et le niveau, étude sociale sur la bourgeoisie française moderne* (Paris: Alcan, 1925).

71 See the extensive analysis of the Agathon survey in Philippe Bénéton, "La Génération de 1912–1914: Image, mythe et réalité?" *Revue française de science politique,* 21 (1971): 981–1009.

72 Edgar Morin, Claude Lefort, Jean-Marc Coudray, *Mai 1968: La brèche* (Paris: Fayard, 1968); Laurent Joffrin, *Un Coup de jeune, portrait d'une génération morale* (Paris: Grasset, 1987).

73 Michel Winock did just this in a subtle reconstitution of the eight intellectual generations which, in his view, succeeded one another from the Dreyfus Affair to 1968. See *Vingtième Siècle, revue d'histoire,* 22 (April–June 1989): 17–39.

74 Paul Thibaud: "This generation was conformist. It followed the model of the elder generation and—what is rarer—of the younger." See "Les Décrocheurs," *Esprit* (July 1985). Claude Nicolet: "We were, in short, a generation abandoned by history." See *Pierre Mendès France ou le métier de Cassandre* (Paris: Julliard, 1959), 37. Quoted in Jean-Pierre Azéma, "La Clef générationnelle," *Vingtième Siècle, revue d'histoire,* 22 (April–June 1989).

75 Yves Stourdzé, in "Autopsie d'une machine à laver, la société française face à l'innovation grand public," *Le Débat,* 17 (December 1981): 15–35, pointed out how reluctant women were from 1965 to 1970 to buy a machine that would free them from a difficult but traditional household chore.

76 S. Hoffmann, ed., *In Search of France* (pub data???). See in particular the article by Jesse Pitts.

77 François de Closets, *Toujours plus!* (Paris: Grasset, 1982), and Alain Minc, *La Machine égalitaire* (Paris: Grasset, 1987).

78 "La France, terre de commandement," was the title of an article by Michel Crozier in a special issue of *Esprit* (December 1957): 779–797.

79 See Marc Fumaroli, "La Coupole," in Nora, *Les Lieux de mémoire,* part 2, *La Nation,* vol. 3.

80 Jean-Paul Sartre, *On a toujours raison de se révolter* (Paris: Mercure de France, 1974).

81 Charles Péguy, *Oeuvres en prose* (Paris: Gallimard, 1988), 2: 1309. It is significant of the process of generational remembrance that this—striking—passage should have reemerged in the work of a Jewish essayist of the 1968 generation, Alain Finkielkraut, who uses it to begin his reflection on the trial of Lyons Gestapo chief Klaus Barbie: *La Mémoire vaine* (Paris: Gallimard, 1989).

82 Bénéton, "La Génération de 1912–1914," also shows how the survey results were biased either by the choice of questions or by the elimination of inconsistent answers such as that of Emmanuel Berl, *A contretemps* (Paris: Gallimard, 1969), 155. He lists other surveys, the best known of which, after the Agathon, is Émile Henriot's in *Le Temps* (April–June 1912), published in 1913 under the title *A quoi revient les jeunes gens?* Also published at the same time were Étienne Rey, *La Renaissance de l'orgueil français,* Gaston Riou, *Aux écoutes de la France,* and Ernest Psichari, *L'Appel des armes.* The chapter on France in Robert Wohl's *The Generation of 1914* relies entirely on such expressions of opinion, which it takes for coin of the realm.

83 See Marc Dambre, *Roger Nimier, hussard du demi-siècle* (Paris: Flammarion, 1989), 253.

84 Bernard Frank, "Hussards et grognards," *Les Temps modernes,* repr. in bound edition (Paris, 1988).

85 A curious illustration can be found in an editorial in the journal *Courrier* which Armand Petitjean addressed to the "mobilizable" youths of 1939, reprinted in *Combats prélimi-naires* (Paris: Gallimard, 1941). Two examples related to Communist commitments in the Cold War period: Emmanuel Le Roy Ladurie, *Paris-Montpellier P.C.–P.S.U. 1945–1963* (Paris: Gallimard, 1982), and Maurice Agulhon, "Vu des coulisses," in Nora, *Essais d'ego-histoire,* 20 ff. And, from a slightly later period, Philippe Robrieux, *Notre génération communiste, 1953–1968* (Paris: Robert Laffont, 1977).

86 Jules Michelet, *Histoire de la Révolution française* (Paris: Gallimard, 1952), book 4, ch. 1.

87 Thomas S. Kuhn, *The Structure of Scientific Revolutions* (Chicago: University of Chicago Press, 1962).

88 See Daniel Milo, "Neutraliser la chronologie: 'Génération' comme paradigme scientifique," ch. 9 of *Trahir le temps (Histoire)* (Paris: Les Belles Lettres, 1990).

89 The essay by Jean Touchard, "L'Esprit des années 1930," published in *Tendances politiques dans la vie française depuis 1789,* ed. Guy Michaud (Paris: Hachette, 1960), directly inspired the classic by Jean-Louis Loubet del Bayle, *Les Non-conformistes des années 30* (Paris: Éditions du Seuil, 1969). The question had been broached as early as 1954 with the publication of René Rémond's *La Droite en France* (Paris: Aubier-

Montaigne, 1954), which, with the publication of the 4th ed. in 1982, became *Les Droites en France*, of which ch. 10 begins with the question "Is there a French fascism?" The question has engendered a good deal of commentary since then, including the work of Zeev Sternhell and the polemic surrounding it.

90   See in particular Pascal Ory, "Comme de l'an quarante: Dix années de retro-satanas," *Le Débat*, 16 (November 1981): 109–117, which includes a useful chronology for the period 1968–1981.

91   Alexis de Tocqueville, "De l'individualisme dans les pays démocratiques," ch. 2 of vol. 2, part 2 of *De la démocratie en Amérique* (Paris: Gallimard, 1961), 106.

Note: Illustrations are indicated by an "i" after the page number.

Index compiled by Fred Leise

Note: Unless otherwise noted, headings refer to things French, e.g., Revolution refers to the French Revolution. Headings to general topics are indicated by "(gen.)." Illustrations are designated by "i" following the page number.

Index compiled by Fred Leise

Text: Fournier
Compositor: Columbia University Press
Printer: Edward Brothers
Binder: Edward Brothers